Internet:
The Complete Reference,
Millennium Edition

About the Authors

Margaret Levine Young is the best-selling author of over two dozen books with various coauthors, including John Levine on *The Internet for Dummies* and *Windows 98: The Complete Reference*. In addition to teaching, writing, and lecturing about the Internet, Margaret writes a regular column called "Webwise" with her husband Jordan Young for *Seven Days* in Burlington, Vermont. She holds a B.A. in computer science from Yale University and has two children.

Doug Muder is a semi-retired mathematician who has contributed to a number of books about computers and the Internet, including *Windows 98: The Complete Reference* and *VRML for Dummies*. He is also the author of numerous research papers in geometry and information theory. Doug lives with his wife, Deborah Bodeau, in Nashua, New Hampshire, and amuses himself by playing with other people's children, writing fiction, and dabbling in all forms of mysticism. He holds a Ph.D. in mathematics from the University of Chicago.

Dave Kay is a writer, former engineer, and aspiring artist, naturalist, and wildlife tracker. His business, BrightLeaf Communications, provides marketing communications services for high-technology companies. His books, authored singly or with friends, include McGraw-Hill's *Graphics File Formats*, plus several titles in IDG Books Worldwide's *...for Dummies* series, most recently *Microsoft Works Suite for Dummies*.

Kathy Warfel is a technical writer who has been teaching people how to use computers and writing about computers for the past 15 years. She was hooked on the Internet from the first time she logged on and saw a six-second news video of a politician giving a speech. She holds a B.S. in journalism from the University of Colorado, and hopes one day to own a small-town online newspaper.

Alison Barrows is the author of several computer books, including IDG Books Worldwide's *Dummies 101: 1-2-3 97*, *Dummies 101: WordPerfect 8*, and *Access 97 for Dummies Quick Reference*. She teaches and consults about the Internet in the Boston area.

Internet:
The Complete Reference,
Millennium Edition

Margaret Levine Young
Doug Muder
Dave Kay
Kathy Warfel
Alison Barrows

Osborne/**McGraw-Hill**

Berkeley   New York   St. Louis   San Francisco
Auckland   Bogotá   Hamburg   London   Madrid
Mexico City   Milan   Montreal   New Delhi   Panama City
Paris   São Paulo   Singapore   Sydney
Tokyo   Toronto

Osborne/**McGraw-Hill**
2600 Tenth Street
Berkeley, California 94710
U.S.A.

For information on translations or book distributors outside the U.S.A., or to arrange bulk purchase discounts for sales promotions, premiums, or fund-raisers, please contact Osborne/**McGraw-Hill** at the above address.

Internet: The Complete Reference, Millennium Edition

34567890 AGM AGM 90198765432109

ISBN 0-07-211942-X

Publisher	**Copy Editor**
Brandon A. Nordin	Bill McManus
Associate Publisher and Editor-in-Chief	**Proofreader**
Scott Rogers	Karen Mead
Acquisitions Editor	**Indexer**
Megg Bonar	Rebecca Plunkett
Project Editor	**Computer Designers**
Emily Rader Perez	Ann Sellers
	Gary Corrigan
Editorial Assistant	**Illustrators**
Stephane Thomas	Beth Young
	Brian Wells
Technical Editor	
Terrie Solomon	**Series Design**
	Peter Hancik

I dedicate this book to my children's grandparents,
Robert J. Levine, Virginia Arnold Levine,
Diane Sherman Levine, Dionir Young,
and Jordan M. Young.

Contents

Part 1

Connecting to the Internet

Part II

Exchanging E-mail

Part III

Chatting and Conferencing on the Internet

Part IV

Viewing the World Wide Web

Part V

Creating and Maintaining Web Sites

Part VI

File Transfer and Downloading

Part VII

Other Internet Topics

Acknowledgments

The authors would like to thank Megg Bonar, Scott Rogers, Stephane Thomas, Emily Rader, Heidi Poulin, and many others at Osborne/McGraw-Hill for making this book happen. We also thank John Daly for information about Macintosh Internet connections, David Guertin for information about Windows NT Dial-Up Networking, Ellen Francik for writing the chapter on high-speed Internet connections, Rebecca Tapley for information about secure e-mail, Kathryn Toyer for writing chapters on IRC and Usenet newsreaders, Donald Griggs for writing the chapter on creating audio files for the Web, Cliff Allen for writing chapters on building and analyzing Web traffic, Curtis Frye for writing the chapter on Web commerce, and Zigurd Mednieks for writing the chapter on Internet telephony.

Margy would also like to thank Shoreham Internet of Shoreham, Vermont, and SoVerNet of Bellows Falls, Vermont, for providing Internet access, Jordan for making all of our computers work, and John Levine for hosting the Web site for this book.

Introduction

The Internet has grown a lot over the last five years, with explosive growth in the number of users, the amount of information that it makes available, and the number of different programs you can use. If you've gotten started on the Internet, and can send and read e-mail and browse the World Wide Web, you've probably run into snags, such as handling e-mail attachments, accepting cookies, and downloading and installing software. This book can help you with the complexity of the Internet and help you solve these problems. It covers the most important aspects of the Internet, with clear instructions for how to use the major Internet services.

Who Is This Book For?

This book is for anyone who uses the Internet and wants to know more. You might have one of the following questions, for example:

- How do I reconfigure my Internet connection and e-mail program if I change Internet service providers?
- Is it safe to buy products over the World Wide Web?
- What are cookies, anyway?
- How can I deal with the increasing number of e-mail messages I get each day?
- How do I send a file by e-mail?
- Can I run my own e-mail discussion list?
- Is voice conferencing possible over the Internet, and is it hard to set up?

This book answers all of these questions and thousands more. It describes programs for Windows 98, Windows 95, Windows 3.1, Windows NT 4, Macintoshes, and UNIX, and covers how to connect to the Internet over the phone, choose an e-mail program, configure your Web browser, get an encryption program so you can send and receive secure e-mail, set up an intranet, and much more.

While writing this book, the authors assume that you know how to use your computer—whether it's Windows, a Mac, or UNIX. We assume that you know how to run programs, give commands, and use the mouse.

What's in This Book?

The major parts of the book are as follows.

Part I: Connecting to the Internet

Part I describes the components of the Internet—hosts, domains, and Internet services, as well as how to connect to the Internet.

Chapter 1 covers Internet concepts, including the kinds of software you use to connect to the Internet. If you use a dial-up Internet account, Chapter 2 contains the instructions you need to configure your computer to connect to your account. Chapter 3 describes fast Internet connections, including ISDN and ADSL telephone connections, as well as how to connect by cable modem. If you want to connect an entire local area network (LAN) to the Internet as an "intranet," read Chapter 4.

Part II: Exchanging E-mail

The most widely used Internet service is e-mail, and a variety of e-mail programs are popular. This part of the book describes how to send and receive e-mail, as well as how to take advantage of the more advanced features your program may offer.

Chapter 5 covers basic e-mail concepts, like addresses, headers, and attachments. The basics of the most popular e-mail programs—Outlook, Netscape Messenger, Eudora, and others—are described in Chapter 6. If you want to send or receive files by e-mail, read Chapter 7 to learn about file attachments. Chapter 8 has instructions for handling the increasing amount of e-mail many people receive, including how to configure your e-mail program to presort your incoming messages like a competent secretary. In Chapter 9, you learn how to encrypt your e-mail if you need to make sure that unauthorized people can't read it, and how to sign messages so that you can prove that only you could have sent them. Chapter 10 describes how to send form letters using e-mail stationery, how to format your e-mail messages, and how to set up your e-mail program to send and receive messages from multiple Internet accounts.

Part III: Chatting and Conferencing on the Internet

Online chat and conferencing are ways for people to communicate over the Internet in real time, and they occur in many forms. This part of the book describes the various Internet services that allow groups of people to communicate over the Internet.

Chapter 11 describes the basic concepts of Internet conferencing and chatting, including *netiquette* (Internet etiquette) and safety considerations. In Chapter 12, you learn how to participate in e-mail mailing lists (free e-mail–based online conferences) and set up your own mailing lists. If you want to use Usenet newsgroups, another form of public conferencing, read Chapter 13 for the basic concepts and Chapter 14 for how to use the most popular Usenet newsreading programs. Chapter 15 is an introduction to the world of Internet Relay Chat (IRC), the real-time, fast-moving chat network. Chapter 16 describes other ways to communicate over the Internet: direct chat systems that let you "page" your friends online, Web sites that let you participate in online chats by using your browser, and MUDs (multiuser dimensions), which are multiuser role-playing games over the Internet. For voice and videoconferencing, look at Chapter 17.

Part IV: Viewing the World Wide Web

The World Wide Web has emerged as a new public medium that may rival the printing press in importance. This part of the book describes how to take advantage of the possibilities of the Web.

Chapter 18 gives you an overview of how the Web works, and defines the terms you will run into, and Chapters 19 and 20 describe the two most popular browsers, Netscape Navigator and Internet Explorer. If you'd like to try a lesser-known browser, or if you use a UNIX or DOS system that can't run Navigator or Internet Explorer, read Chapter 21 for some alternatives. In Chapter 22, you can learn how to use Web pages that include more than just text and pictures: this chapter describes how to install plug-ins and ActiveX controls to enable your browser to run Web-based programs. Chapter 23 contains hints for finding information and people on the Web. If you want Web-based information to arrive on your computer screen without you having to request it, read Chapter 24 about channels and subscriptions. Chapter 25 has a huge listing of interesting Web sites, including the best sources of news, weather, sports, entertainment, shopping, investing, travel, family, health, and reference information.

Part V: Creating and Maintaining Web Sites

If you or your organization wants to provide information over the Web, you need to plan, design, create, test, and maintain a Web site. This part of the book tells you how.

Chapter 26 covers the concepts of Web site creation, including HTML, Web site design, and programs for creating pages. In Chapter 27, you learn how to create Web pages using a text editor, inserting the necessary HTML codes yourself. Chapter 28 describes a variety of Web page editing programs, including programs that come with Windows 98 and Netscape Communicator. To create or edit graphics files to enliven your Web pages, read Chapter 29, and if you want your Web site to include audio clips, take a look at Chapter 30.

Once you have created and tested your Web site on your own computer, Chapter 31 describes how to upload it to a Web server so that the rest of the world can see it, too. Chapter 32 tells you how to find out how many people are visiting your site, where they come from, and how they move from page to page. To increase the number of visitors your Web site receives, see the tips in Chapter 33. Chapter 34 describes how to make your Web site interactive by using CGI scripts and other methods. In Chapter 35, you can find out how to turn your Web site into a retail store.

Part VI: File Transfer and Downloading

Whether you have created a Web page and need to upload it to your Web server, or you've heard about a program that you can get from a Web-based shareware library, sooner or later you'll need to upload or download files. Chapter 36 has an overview of FTP (File Transfer Protocol) concepts, and Chapter 37 contains step-by-step instructions for using FTP programs. In Chapter 38, you learn what to do with the files you have downloaded (or received by e-mail), including how to install programs.

Part VII: Other Internet Topics

Chapter 39 describes how the Internet can supplement the telephone system, possibly replacing costly long-distance phone calls. If you use a UNIX shell account or ever need to connect to and use a UNIX system, Chapter 40 describes the basics of UNIX commands, as well as how to connect to a UNIX system over the Internet.

Conventions Used in This Book

This book uses several icons to highlight special advice:

A handy way to make the Internet work for you.

An observation that gives you insight into the way the Internet works.

Something to watch out for, so you don't have to learn the hard way.

When you see a reference to related material elsewhere in the book, you see the name of the section that contains the information you might want to read. If the section is in a different chapter, you see the chapter number, too.

When you see instructions to choose commands from a menu, the parts of the command are separated by vertical bars (|). For example, "choose View | Internet Options" means to choose View from the menu bar, and then choose Internet Options from the View menu that appears. If the command begins with "Start | ", then click the Start button on the Windows Taskbar as the first step. Unless otherwise noted, all the instructions in this book are for Windows 98 and 95. If you need more information about using Windows 98, refer to *Windows 98: The Complete Reference* (Berkeley, CA: Osborne/McGraw-Hill, 1998).

To find out which button is which on the toolbar of most programs, move the mouse pointer to the button and wait a few seconds without clicking. Most programs display a little box with the name of the button.

Contacting the Authors

This book isn't just a book—it's a Web site, too. For updated information about the Internet, including all the Internet addresses listed in Chapter 25, use your browser to see our Web site at **http://net.gurus.com/nettcr**. While you're there, you can tell us what you thought of the book, or you can let us know by writing to us at **nettcr@gurus.com**. Please don't ask us a lot of questions about the Internet, though— we're so busy updating this book and writing new ones that we don't have time to provide e-mail consulting. With luck, you'll find some answers at the book's Web site.

The Complete Reference

Internet

Part 1

Connecting to the Internet

Chapter 1

Internet Connection Concepts

To connect to the Internet, you need an Internet provider, a method of connecting your computer to the Internet, and connection software. This chapter contains an introduction to the Internet and what you need to get connected, including the services that the Internet provides (such as e-mail, the Web, Usenet newsgroups, online chat, and file transfer), the components that make up the Internet (such as computers, domains, and servers), and the kinds of accounts that you can get. The rest of the chapters in this part describe the steps to follow to set up an Internet connection: Chapter 2 describes dial-up accounts, Chapter 3 covers high-speed connections, and Chapter 4 describes connecting local area networks to the Internet.

Tip *If your computer is already connected to the Internet, you can skip Part I of this book.*

What Is the Internet?

The Internet is a network of networks that connects computers all over the world. The Internet has its roots in the U.S. military, which funded a network in 1969, called the ARPANET, to connect the computers at some of the colleges and universities where military research took place. As more and more computers connected, the ARPANET was replaced by the NSFNET, which was run by the National Science Foundation. By the late 1980s, the Internet had shed its military and research heritage and was available for use by the general public. *Internet service providers* (ISPs) began offering dial-up Internet accounts for a monthly fee, giving users access to e-mail, discussion groups, and file transfer. In 1989, the World Wide Web (an Internet-based system of interlinked pages of information) was born, and in the early 1990s, the combination of e-mail, the Web, and online chat propelled the Internet into national and international prominence.

Computers connected to the Internet communicate by using the *Internet Protocol (IP)*, which slices information into *packets* (chunks of data to be transmitted separately) and routes them to their destination. One definition of the Internet is all the computers that pass packets to each other by using IP. Because the Internet was designed to operate even during a war, it uses *dynamic routing*, so that even if one part of the network is knocked out, packets can be rerouted around the problem. Warfare hasn't been a problem for Internet communications (yet), but dynamic rerouting helps the Internet deal with other types of equipment failures. Along with IP, most computers on the Internet communicate with *Transmission Control Protocol (TCP)*, and the combination is called *TCP/IP*.

Computers on the Internet

Each computer on the Internet is called a *host computer* or *host*. The computers on the Internet—and there are now millions of Internet hosts—are connected by cables, phone lines, and satellite connections. They include large mainframe computers, smaller minicomputers, and personal computers. When your PC or Mac dials in to an Internet account, your computer is an Internet host, too.

CONNECTING TO THE INTERNET

Numeric Computer (IP) Addresses

Each host computer on the Internet has a unique number, called its *IP address*. IP addresses are in the format *xxx.xxx.xxx.xxx*, where each *xxx* is a number from 0 to 255. IP addresses identify the host computers, so that packets of information reach the correct computer. You may have to type IP addresses when you configure your computer for connection to the Internet.

If you connect to the Internet by using a dial-up account, your ISP (Internet Service Provider; see "Internet PPP and SLIP Accounts" later in this chapter) assigns your computer an IP address each time that you connect. This system enables your ISP to get along with fewer IP addresses, because it needs only enough IP addresses for the number of users who are connected simultaneously (as opposed to assigning a permanent IP address to each customer of the ISP).

Domain and Host Names

So that people don't have to remember strings of numbers, host computers also have names. The name of each host computer consists of a series of words separated by dots. The last part of the domain name is called the *top-level domain* (*TLD*), or *zone*, and is either two or three letters long. The three-letter zones are used mainly in the U.S., and indicate the type of organization that owns the domain. The six three-letter zones are listed in Table 1-1.

The two-letter zones indicate the country in which the organization that owns the computer is located. U.S. organizations can register domains that end with **us**. Canadian organizations, for instance, usually have the zone **ca**. You can find the full list of geographic domain extensions on the Web at **http://net.gurus.com/countries**.

The last two parts of a host computer name constitute the *domain*. The second-to-last part of the name (the *second-level domain*) is chosen by the organization that owns the computer, and is usually some variant of the organization's name. For example, computers at the U.S. President's offices at the White House have the domain **whitehouse.gov**. Computers at Yale University have names that end with **yale.edu**,

Domain	Example	Description
com	ibm.com	Commercial organizations, as well as individuals
net	att.net	Internet service providers and other network-related companies
org	npr.org	Noncommercial (often nonprofit) organizations
gov	senate.gov	U.S. government agencies
mil	army.mil	U.S. military
edu	yale.edu	Educational domains

Table 1-1. *Three-letter top-level domains*

since Yale is an educational institution. Computers at the McGraw-Hill publishing company are named with the domain **mcgraw-hill.com**.

Because most organizations own more than one computer on the Internet, most host computer names have at least one more part, preceding the domain name. This additional part (or parts) is assigned by the organization itself. For example, the **gurus.com** domain (which is owned by one of the authors of this book) has several host names, including **www.gurus.com** (the main Web site), **net.gurus.com** (the Internet Gurus Web site), and **wine.gurus.com** (the Web site of the Society of Wine Educators). By far, the most widely used computer name is *www*, because it is frequently used for an organization's Web server (the computer that stores Web pages). Some organizations name their computers using stars, planets, animals, or other themes, so don't be surprised if e-mail from Middlebury College comes from **panther.middlebury.edu**.

Capitalization doesn't matter in host names. **Gurus.Com** and **gurus.com** are both valid forms of the same name. Host names usually appear in lowercase.

One host computer can have many different names. For example, many ISPs also offer *domain hosting*, which means that they allow your domain name to be applied to one of their host computers. Domain hosting enables you to have your own domain name, even if you don't have a host computer. See the sidebars "Registering com, edu, net, and org Domain Names" and "Registering Domain Names in Country Zones" for information on how to register a domain name.

Registering com, edu, net, and org Domain Names

Where do domain names come from? Who controls which organization owns easy-to-remember domain names, such as **books.com** and **internet.com**? Currently, domains in the **com**, **edu**, **net**, and **org** zones are assigned by Network Solutions' InterNIC Registration Services, at **http://www.internic.net**.

To register a domain name, you need a computer on the Internet to assign the name to, and two Internet host computers that promise to provide domain name service for your domain (described in the section "The Domain Name System and DNS Servers," later in this chapter). To begin the process, go to the InterNIC Registration Services Web site and follow these steps:

1. Use the WHOIS search box on the InterNIC home page to check whether or not the domain name that you want to use has already been taken. If the name you want is taken, choose another one. If you own the trademark to the name, you may be able to get InterNIC to reassign the domain to you instead, but you'll have to go through a formal dispute process.

2. Click the link on the InterNIC home page to read the instructions for registering.

3. Ask your ISP, Web hosting service, or another organization that runs Internet host computers to provide domain name service for your domain. Most ISPs do this for a modest fee. Ask your ISP for the IP addresses of the two domain name servers that will list your new domain.

4. Fill out an application, located online at the InterNIC Web site, which asks for the name, address, phone number, fax number, and e-mail address of the administrative contact, technical contact, and billing contact for the organization that will use the new domain. It also asks for the IP addresses of two domain name servers. You can use the Web-based application form, or you can copy the application into your e-mail program and e-mail the completed application to **hostmaster@internic.net**. You have to use the exact template that InterNIC provides. No printed or faxed applications are accepted.

5. InterNIC confirms that it has received your application. If the application had no errors, InterNIC sends you a confirmation that the domain has been assigned to you. Information about your domain is added to the tables of domain names that InterNIC sends throughout the Internet daily, so it may take a day or two for your domain name to work.

6. Check that your domain name works by using the Ping program in Windows 98 (see the section "Pinging Another Computer" in Chapter 2). Talk to your ISP or Web hosting service about how to upload pages to your new Web site. Test e-mail to your new domain, too.

7. When you receive an invoice for your domain registration, pay it. As of the end of 1998, registering a domain costs $70, which includes the first two years of use. After the two years is over, you have to pay $35 per year to retain use of the domain name.

Registering Domain Names in Country Zones

Domains in the two-letter zones (top-level domains) are assigned by the country where the organization that owns the host computer is located. In general, each two-letter country zone is administered by a separate agency. Any organization can usually apply for a domain in its country's zone.

The **us** (United States) zone is administered by the U.S. Domain Registry at the Information Sciences Institute of the University of Southern California (ISI), under the Internet Assigned Numbers Authority (IANA). Domains in the **us** zone must follow a set of naming rules, which require that the second-to-last (second-level) domain name be the two-letter state abbreviation, except for some special second-level names such as **fed** (for the Federal Government) or **nsn** (for Native American Nations). Preceding the second-level name is a county or town name, or special names such as **k12** (for schools), **ci** (for city governments), **co** (for country governments), and **state** (for state governments). An organization name can precede that. For example, the domain name for an organization named IECC in Trumansburg, New York might have the domain name **iecc.trumansburg.ny.us**. To register a domain in the **us** zone, go to the **http://www.isi.edu/in-notes/usdnr** Web site.

For information about how to register with other countries, see the IANA Web page at **http://www.iana.org/cctld.html**.

Servers, Clients, and Ports

Many of the host computers on the Internet offer services to other computers on the Internet. For example, your ISP probably has a host computer that handles your incoming and outgoing mail. Computers that provide services for other computers to use are called *servers*. The software run by server computers to provide services is called *server software*.

Conversely, many of the computers on the Internet use servers to get information. For example, when your computer dials into an Internet account, your e-mail program downloads your incoming messages from your ISP's mail server. Programs that ask servers for services are called *clients*. Your e-mail program is more properly called an *e-mail client*.

Here are some types of servers and clients that you may encounter (for more information about what each of these services is used for, see the section "Internet Services," later in this chapter):

- ■ **Mail servers**   Handle incoming and outgoing mail. Specifically, *Post Office Protocol (POP) servers* (or *POP3 servers*) store incoming mail, while *Simple Mail Transfer Protocol (SMTP) servers* relay outgoing mail. *Mail clients* get incoming messages from, and send outgoing messages to, a mail server, and enable you to read, write, save, and print messages.

- ■ **Web servers**   Store Web pages and transmit them in response to requests from *Web clients*, which are usually called *browsers*.

- ■ **FTP servers**   Store files that you can transfer to or from your computer if you have an *FTP client*.

- ■ **New servers**   Store Usenet newsgroup articles that you can read and send if you have a *news client* or *newsreader*.
- ■ **IRC servers**   Act as a switchboard for Internet-based online chats. To participate, you use an *IRC client*.

One host computer can run more than one server program. For example, a small ISP might have one computer running a POP server, SMTP server, Web server, and news server. To keep requests for information straight, each type of server responds to packets sent to specific *ports* (input for a specific Internet service). Ports are numbered, and standard port numbers are used throughout the Internet. You almost never need to type port numbers, but here are some widely used port numbers in case you do:

Port Number	Internet Service
21	FTP (file transfer)
23	Telnet (remote login)
25	SMTP (mail relaying)
80	World Wide Web
110	POP3 (storage of incoming mail)
194 (as well as 6667 and many others)	IRC (online chat)
532	Usenet newsgroups (discussion groups)

The Domain Name System and DNS Servers

You use one other type of Internet server almost every time that you request information from an Internet host. A *Domain Name System server* (*DNS server*) translates between the numeric IP addresses that identify each host computer on the Internet and the corresponding domain names. People prefer to use host names, because they are easier to type and remember, but actual Internet communications use the numeric addresses. For example, if your browser requests a Web page from the Yahoo! Web site, which has the host name **www.yahoo.com**, a DNS server translates that name to 204.71.200.69, one of Yahoo!'s Web servers, and then sends the request to that IP address.

Your ISP provides a DNS server to handle domain name translations. If the DNS server isn't working properly or you have configured your computer with the wrong IP address for the DNS server, your computer can't find any of the computers on the Internet that you specify by host name, because it has no way to translate host names to IP addresses. You may see error messages such as "Unable to locate host" or "Server does not have a DNS entry." (Contact your ISP to fix the problem, or consult the section "Changing the Settings for a Dial-Up Networking Connection" in Chapter 2.)

Internet Services

The Internet provides a mechanism for millions of computers to communicate, but what kind of information is transmitted? Many services are available over the Internet, and the following are the most popular ones:

- **E-mail** Enables people to send private messages, as well as files, to one or more other people (see Chapter 5).

- **Mailing lists** Enable groups of people to conduct group conversations by e-mail, and provide a way of distributing newsletters by e-mail (see Chapter 12).

- **Usenet newsgroups** Enable ongoing group discussions to occur, using a system of news servers to store messages to any of over 10,000 newsgroups that are identified by topic (see Chapter 13).

- **Online chat** Provides a way for real-time online chatting to occur, whereby participants read each other's messages within seconds of when they are sent. (See Chapter 15 for details on how to use Internet Relay Chat, and Chapter 16 for information on other types of chat.)

- **Voice and video conferencing** Enable two or more people to hear and see each other, share a whiteboard, and share other applications (see Chapter 17). Chapter 39 describes the state of *VoIP* (voice over IP, or Internet telephony).

- **The World Wide Web** A distributed system of interlinked pages that include text, pictures, sound, and other information. See Part IV for instructions on how to use the Web, and Part V for information on how to create your own Web pages.

- **File transfer** Lets people download files from public file servers, including a wide variety of programs (see Chapter 36).

Types of Accounts

To connect to the Internet, you can use one of several types of accounts: PPP and SLIP accounts, UNIX shell accounts, or online services.

Internet PPP and SLIP Accounts

A *Point-to-Point Protocol (PPP)* or *Serial Line Internet Protocol (SLIP)* account is an Internet account that uses the PPP or SLIP communications protocol, respectively. These are the most popular accounts, because the most popular software—Internet Explorer, Netscape Navigator, Eudora, and other programs—are designed to work with PPP and SLIP accounts. PPP is a more modern communications protocol than SLIP, so choose PPP if you have a choice when opening an account (almost all Internet providers offer PPP). Occasionally, you may run into a *compressed SLIP (CSLIP)* account, which is a more efficient version of SLIP, but still isn't as good as PPP. This book refers to PPP, CSLIP, and SLIP accounts as *PPP accounts* or *Internet accounts*.

An *Internet service provider* (*ISP*) is an organization that provides dial-in Internet accounts, usually PPP, CSLIP, or SLIP accounts, but sometimes UNIX shell accounts. Thousands of ISPs exist in the U.S., including dozens of ISPs with access phone numbers throughout the country, and many with phone numbers in limited regions. For example, AT&T WorldNet has access phone numbers in all major U.S. cities, whereas SoVerNet has phone numbers only in Vermont and surrounding states, but provides local access from many towns that AT&T WorldNet doesn't cover.

To use a PPP account, you need a PPP-compatible communications program, such as Windows 98's Dial-Up Networking program (described in the section "TCP/IP and Connection Software," later in this chapter). This program dials the phone by using your modem (or connects using a higher-speed equivalent, as described in Chapter 3), connects to your ISP, logs in to your account by using your user name and password, and then establishes a PPP connection, thus connecting your computer to the Internet. While connected, you can use a variety of programs to read your e-mail, browse the Web, and access other information from the Internet. When you are done, you use Dial-Up Networking to disconnect from your Internet account. (See Chapter 2 for more information on how to set up a connection to a PPP Internet account.)

UNIX Shell Accounts

Before the advent of PPP and SLIP accounts, most Internet accounts were text-only *UNIX shell accounts*, and these accounts are still available from some ISPs. You run a *terminal-emulation program* (a program that pretends that your PC is a computer terminal) on your PC to connect to an Internet host computer. Most Internet hosts run UNIX, a powerful but frequently confusing operating system, and you have to type UNIX commands to use a UNIX shell account. To send and receive e-mail or browse the Web, you run text-only programs, such as Pine (the most popular UNIX e-mail program) and Lynx (the most widely used UNIX Web browser). When you use a UNIX shell account, you don't see graphics or use a mouse, and you can't easily store information on your own computer.

Some providers give you both a PPP account and a UNIX shell account; you use the PPP account for your regular Internet work, and the UNIX shell account only when you need to change your account's password. For information about using UNIX shell accounts, see Chapter 40.

Online Services

An *online service* is a commercial service that enables you to connect to and access its proprietary information system. Most online services also provide an Internet connection, e-mail, the World Wide Web, and, sometimes, other Internet services. Online services usually require special programs to connect to and use your account.

The three most popular online services are the following:

- **America Online (AOL)**   The world's most popular online service, with a wide range of AOL-only features. To connect to AOL, read AOL e-mail, browse the Web, and access other AOL services, you use AOL's proprietary program: the latest version is AOL 4.

- **CompuServe (CIS)**   One of the oldest online services, with an excellent selection of proprietary technical- and business-oriented discussion groups. CompuServe was purchased by America Online, so the two services may merge. CompuServe has access phone numbers in dozens of countries. To connect to CompuServe and access its services, you use CompuServe's proprietary program: the latest version is CompuServe 4.

- **Microsoft Network (MSN)**   Microsoft's online service. You connect to MSN by using Dial-Up Networking, send and receive e-mail by using Outlook or Outlook Express, and browse the Web by using Internet Explorer.

Other online services (such as Prodigy Classic and Delphi) exist, but they aren't nearly as popular as these three. Some computers (including those with Windows 98) come equipped with sign-up software for some online services. You can also call these online services for a free sign-up kit: in the U.S., call AOL at 800-827-6364, CompuServe at 800-336-6823, or MSN at 800-386-5550.

Connecting Through AOL or CompuServe

America Online and CompuServe aren't ISPs: they are commercial online services that give you information that's not available on the Internet. Both host online conferences, provide libraries or downloadable files, and run other proprietary services. Internet users who don't have an AOL or CompuServe account can't use these proprietary services.

Originally, these services had no connection to the Internet. But as the Internet became popular, AOL and CompuServe created Internet connections, which initially were limited to exchanging e-mail with the Internet. Then they added more Internet services, such as access to the Web and Usenet newsgroups. Now, AOL and CompuServe let you run almost any Winsock-compatible Internet client (described in "TCP/IP and Connection Software," later in this chapter) to access Internet services. An exception is that AOL doesn't provide a POP server, so you must read your AOL mail either by using the AOL software or by accessing AOL's Web site.

Telephone, Cable, and Satellite Connections

Your computer is connected to the Internet if it is connected to another computer or network that is connect to the Internet. Several methods of connection are possible, requiring different kinds of hardware.

Dial-Up Internet Accounts

Most people connect to the Internet by using a modem and phone line to dial in to a PPP account on an Internet provider's computer. Most ISPs support modems at speeds of 14.4Kbps, 28.8Kbps, and 56Kbps. You connect only when you want to use Internet services, and disconnect (hang up) when you are done. Setting up your computer to connect to a dial-up Internet account is described in Chapter 2.

ISDN, ADSL, and Leased Line Connections

Some ISPs allow you to connect at higher speeds than a regular phone line allows. *Integrated Services Digital Network (ISDN)* and *Asymmetric Digital Subscriber Line (ADSL)* are two all-digital, high-speed types of phone lines that provide a faster way to connect to the Internet. Your phone company sells you the special ISDN or ADSL line (not all phone companies offer them) and you get the hardware that connects the computer to the special phone line (see Chapter 3 for details).

If your computer needs to be connected to the Internet all the time, contact your telephone company for a *leased line*, the same type of line that large organizations use. Leased lines come in various speeds, including *T1* (1.5Mbps, or enough for 24 voice channels) and *T3* (44Mbps, or enough for 672 voice channels). If you don't need quite that much speed, you can ask for a *fractional-T1* (half or a quarter of a T1 line). You also need to contact your ISP for a leased-line account, which costs more than a dial-up account.

Cable and DSS Internet Accounts

Some television cable companies also offer Internet access over the same cable that brings you TV programs. You need a cable connection box and an account with a local cable company. (See Chapter 3 for more information.)

Digital Satellite Systems (DSS), or direct broadcast satellite, lets you get Internet information by satellite. Hughes DirecPC is the only company to offer this service, which includes a 24-inch antenna, a coaxial cable, a PC adapter card, and Windows-based software. You *receive* data from the Internet at a high speed via the satellite, but to *send* data to the Internet, you need a dial-up connection and an ISP. Setup can be difficult and pricing has been controversial (how much you pay used to depend on how much data you downloaded). More information is available at **http://www.direcpc.com**, or call 800-DIRECPC (in the U.S.).

WebTV

If you have a television but no computer, you can access the Internet by using your TV. WebTV (which is partly owned by Microsoft) is the most popular TV-based Internet connection. To use WebTV, you need a WebTV receiver that connects both to your TV and to a phone line: you can buy these receivers at many consumer electronics stores. You use your TV screen as the monitor and your remote control to browse the Web. With the optional keyboard, you can send and receive e-mail. For more information, see the Web site **http://www.webtv.net** or call 800-GO-WEBTV (in the U.S.).

Intranets

Organizations that have many PCs can connect the computers in a network, and then connect that network to the Internet. This method is more efficient than connecting each PC to the Internet by using its own modem and phone line. (See Chapter 4 for more information.)

Choosing an ISP

To connect to the Internet by using a dial-up phone line, high-speed phone line, or leased line, you first need to choose an ISP. (If you connect via cable, your cable company serves as your ISP. If you use WebTV, you can use WebTV as your ISP or choose a different ISP.)

ISP Features

To choose an ISP, consider the following factors:

- **Local phone number**   Most ISPs have many phone numbers that your computer can call to connect to the Internet. If the ISP doesn't have an access phone number that is a local phone call for you, you can spend more on long-distance charges that on your Internet account.

- **Price**   In the U.S., the standard price for unlimited usage of a dial-up (PPP) Internet account for modem speeds up to 56Kbps is $20 per month. Some ISPs offer lower prices for fewer hours (for example, $7.95 per month for up to five hours of Internet usage). Some ISPs charge a one-time setup fee.

- **Software**   Many ISPs provide a CD-ROM or diskette with software that you can use to connect to and use the Internet. If you have Windows 98, 95, or NT, or a Mac with System 7.6.1 or later, your computer already has the software that you need. But if you run Windows 3.1 or an older version of the Mac system, you need connection software.

- **Support**   You never know when you're going to have a problem, so your ISP's technical support phone number (and e-mail help desk) should be open 24 hours a day, 7 days a week.

- **Speed**   Most ISPs have local access numbers that work with 28.8Kbps, 33.6Kbps, and 56Kbps modems. Some also support high-speed connections such as ISDN and ADSL (described in Chapter 3) at extra cost.

- **Accessibility**   If the ISP's access numbers are frequently busy, you can waste a lot of time redialing until you connect. Ask Internet users in your area whether they have trouble getting connected to the ISP.

In addition to connecting you to the Internet, here are some other features that your Internet account may provide:

- **POP mailboxes**   Your account almost certainly comes with an e-mail mailbox on a POP server. Some ISPs allow you to have more than one mailbox, so that each member of your family can read his or her mail separately, either as part of the cost of the account or for an extra fee.

- **Web server space**   Most Internet accounts include a modest amount of disk space on a Web server, so that you can make your own Web pages accessible to the Internet. If you need more space, you can usually buy more for a small monthly fee.

- **Domain hosting**   If you want your own domain name (refer to "Domain and Host Names," earlier in this chapter), most ISPs can host your domain, so that e-mail to the domain lands in your mailbox, and Web addresses in your domain refer to Web pages that you store on your ISP's Web server.

If you plan to create a large Web site or one that requires a secure server, shopping cart application, CGI scripts, or other advanced Web server options, consider using a Web hosting server rather than your ISP (see Chapter 26).

Finding ISPs

To find ISPs that have local phone numbers in your area, try these sources of information:

- **Look at The List**   Use someone else's Internet connection to display The List, at **http://thelist.internet.com**. This Web site lists over 5,000 ISPs by state or province, country, or area code. For each ISP, you see the area code(s) that it serves, the modem speeds that it supports, the address of the ISP's Web site, its fees, and its sales telephone number.

- **Ask friends**   Find out which ISPs your friends have had good luck with, including getting help configuring their computer to connect, and getting through to the access numbers without encountering busy signals.

- **Look for ads**   Look in the business section of the local paper or in your local Yellow Pages.

See our Web site at **http://net.gurus.com/isp** for other pointers about choosing an ISP.

 Always check that the access number that you plan to use is really local. Just because an ISP says that it's a local phone call for you doesn't necessarily mean it is. Check the front of your phone book for a list of telephone exchanges that are a local call from your line, or check with your local phone company.

Choosing User Names and Passwords

Unless you are signing up with a small ISP or have an unusual last name, most of the good user names are already taken. You can ask for your user name to be any combination of your name or initials. Or you can choose a fanciful name or one that relates to a hobby, but consider that you will probably use your e-mail address for a wide variety of purposes for years to come, so don't choose something that might eventually be embarrassing.

What kind of password should you choose? A good password is easy to remember and hard to guess. It's hard to find a password that has both properties. A very simple, easy-to-remember password (such as the name of the street that you live on, for example) is also easy for someone else to figure out. A really difficult password (a random collection of letters and numbers, such as *ER3k76tB*) will probably keep out almost anyone—including you.

Writing down your password solves some problems, but creates others. If you travel with a laptop and keep a file named Passwd.txt, then anyone who steals your laptop can get into your accounts. Using the same password for all of your accounts saves wear-and-tear on your memory, but it's dangerous. If you tell someone how to use your *Wall Street Journal* account to read the news, the same password lets them get into your brokerage account and make trades. In a nightmare scenario, someone could establish an attractive Web site and ask people to register, simply to collect their favorite passwords and break into other accounts that they have.

You shouldn't let security issues keep you from using the Internet, but you should remain just paranoid enough to take a few precautions, such as the following:

- *Have a different password for each kind of account.* If you're the kind of person who likes to sign up for free things, you could easily wind up registering at dozens of Web sites. Don't try to create and remember a different password for each one. Choose three or four passwords at different levels of difficulty, and use the same password for all accounts of the same type.

- *Vary the difficulty of the passwords depending on what you're trying to protect.* Some passwords are more for the Web site's protection than for yours. For example, if someone could guess your ESPN SportZone password, they could pretend to be you and read the members-only parts of ESPN SportZone, without paying the subscription fee. That would annoy ESPN a lot more than it would annoy you. So a password such as *LetMeIn* might be sufficient.

On the other hand, if you have an account with a retailer, and the retailer keeps your credit card number on file, someone who guesses your password can buy products with your credit card. Someone who guesses your online banking password may be able to write checks. Someone who guesses your online brokerage account password can buy and sell stocks for you. These accounts need very strong passwords.

Some passwords protect your private information. The password on an e-mail account, for example, prevents someone else from reading your e-mail and sending out messages that appear to be from you. Would that be a huge disaster, or merely a nuisance? Choose your password accordingly.

- *If you're protecting anything important, don't use any English word or common name.* Passwords are stored in an encrypted form that is very difficult to decrypt. But password-cracking programs work by running through a large number of guesses, encrypting the guesses, and checking to see whether the encryption matches the encrypted password. Such a program can run through all the words in a dictionary very quickly.

- *Use your brain sludge.* If you can't use words or names, where are you going to get all of these passwords, especially the difficult ones? And how are you going to remember them? The best passwords take advantage of what humorist Dave Barry calls "brain sludge"—all those useless odds and ends that stick in your memory for no good reason. Maybe you still remember the phone number of a high school girlfriend. She doesn't live there anymore and maybe you wouldn't call her if she did, but that number is taking up space in your head. Use it in a password. Let the guy who steals your laptop try to figure that one out.

- *Use acronyms.* You can make up a lot of easy-to-remember but hard-to-guess passwords by taking the first letter from each word of a memorable phrase. Nathan Hale's famous "I regret that I have but one life to give for my country" produces "IRTIHB1LTGFMC." Can you guess where the password "t42&24t" comes from? It's the first line of the song *Tea For Two*. The famous Richard M. Nixon quote "I am not a crook" could give you the password "rmnimnac." They look like random strings of characters, but they aren't. Best of all is an acronym based on a quote that isn't even famous; maybe it's just something that your Aunt Betty used to say all the time.

- *Stick a number in, or spell it wrong (or backwards).* For example, to use friends' names spelled backwards, with a digit in the middle (like *nas3uS*).

- *Don't write down passwords, write down hints.* If you need to write something down, all you need is a hint that will activate the appropriate brain sludge. The notation "AOL-Tracy" might be enough to remind you that your American Online password has something to do with that high school girlfriend. Jotting down "Watergate" or "Hale" might be all you need to remember the Nixon or Hale passwords.

Changing Your Password

Some ISPs give you a UNIX shell account along with your Internet PPP account. If so, you can use the shell account when you want to change your password. See Chapter 40 for directions on how to dial into a UNIX shell account and change your password.

If your ISP doesn't provide you with a UNIX shell account, check its Web site or call its support phone line to find out how to change your password.

TCP/IP and Connection Software

After you sign up for an Internet account, install your communications hardware (usually a modem), and connect it to your phone line or other communications line, you need a program that allows your PC to communicate over the Internet via TCP/IP (the Internet protocols described in the earlier section "What Is the Internet?"). A TCP/IP connection program is called (for historical reasons) a *TCP/IP stack*. Windows 98, 95, and NT come with a TCP/IP stack called Dial-Up Networking (you can also get TCP/IP stacks for Windows 3.1).

As the Internet was first becoming popular, the producers of Windows-based Internet software got together and created a standard way for Internet client programs to work with TCP/IP stacks. This standard is called *Winsock* (short for *Windows sockets*). Windows 98, 95, and NT Dial-Up Networking are all Winsock-compatible, so you can run almost any Internet client program.

A similar standard exists for the Macintosh: MacTCP. MacOS 7.6.1 or later come with a MacTCP-compatible TCP/IP stack. In 7.6.1 through 8.1, it's called *Open Transport/PPP*, while in MacOS 8.5, the TCP/IP stack is part of *Apple Remote Access*.

The next chapter describes how to install and configure a TCP/IP stack to connect your Windows 98, 95, NT, 3.1, or Mac system to the Internet. The chapters in Parts II through VII describe the wide variety of Winsock-compatible programs that you can use to access Internet services after you connect to the Internet.

Chapter 2

Connecting to Dial-Up Internet Accounts

Chapter 1 described the TCP/IP networking concepts that you'll run into when you connect your computer to the Internet. This chapter contains the steps for connecting your computer to a dial-up Internet account. Most of the sections describe Windows 98, but sections at the end of the chapter contain instructions for connecting Windows 3.1, Windows 95, Windows NT, and Macintosh systems to dial-up accounts.

For information about using faster Internet connections, such as cable modems, ISDN, and ADSL accounts, see Chapter 3. If you are setting up an intranet (connecting a local area network to the Internet), see Chapter 4.

Elements of Windows 98 Dial-Up Networking

To connect to a dial-up Internet account with Windows 98, you use Dial-Up Networking and the Dial-Up Adapter, which are both built into Windows 98. The Internet Connection Wizard can step you through most of the configuration process. This section describes each of the Windows components that you use when setting up an Internet connection.

Dial-Up Networking

Dial-Up Networking programs come with Windows 98, 95, and NT. You use Dial-Up Networking to connect to an Internet PPP, CSLIP, or SLIP account (see Chapter 1 for details on these accounts). Dial-Up Networking uses the Dial-Up Adapter to communicate with Internet accounts via TCP/IP, the communications protocol used on the Internet. You don't have to use Dial-Up Networking to connect to your Internet account—you can use another compatible communications program, such as Trumpet Winsock, instead—but Dial-Up Networking works well, and comes with the Internet Connection Wizard to set it up.

Note *Dial-Up Networking provides only the communication link needed by Internet services; you use Winsock-compatible applications to read e-mail, browse the Web, and transmit and receive other information on the Internet.*

To use Dial-Up Networking, you create a *Dial-Up Networking connection*, a file with all the settings required to connect to an Internet account. You can have several Dial-Up Networking connections on one computer. For example, your laptop might have one connection for the local Internet service provider (ISP) that you use every day, and another connection for the national Internet provider you use when you travel.

To work with Dial-Up Networking—either to create a new connection, connect to the Internet, edit the settings for an existing connection, or get rid of a connection—choose Start | Programs | Accessories | Communications | Dial-Up Networking. You see the Dial-Up Networking window, shown in Figure 2-1 (your window may be configured to

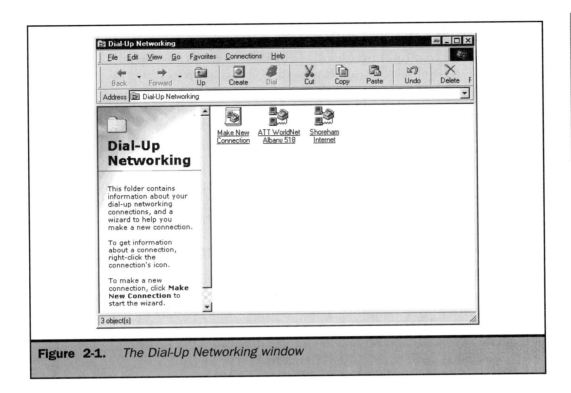

Figure 2-1.   *The Dial-Up Networking window*

look different). You can also see the contents of the Dial-Up Networking window by using Windows Explorer. At the bottom of the folder tree, Dial-Up Networking is listed as a subfolder of My Computer.

The section "Setting Up a Dial-Up Networking Connection Manually," later in this chapter, describes how to create and use Dial-Up Networking connections.

The Dial-Up Adapter

The Dial-Up Adapter is a Windows 98 *network driver* (a program that controls the way Windows 98 communicates over a network) that Dial-Up Networking uses to connect to the Internet with a modem or ISDN line. When you use the Dial-Up Adapter with an Internet account, you configure the Dial-Up Adapter to communicate via TCP/IP.

To check whether the Dial-Up Adapter is already installed on your computer and configured to communicate using TCP/IP, see the section "Installing and Configuring the Dial-Up Adapter and TCP/IP," later in this chapter.

Internet and Modem Properties

The Windows 98 Control Panel (displayed by choosing Start | Settings | Control Panel) includes two icons that you may need to use when connecting your system to the Internet:

- **Internet** Displays the Internet Properties dialog box. Most of the tabs in this dialog box contain settings for Internet Explorer (Microsoft's Web browser), but you can use the Connection tab to tell Windows 98 to connect to the Internet automatically.

- **Modems** Displays the Modems Properties dialog box, which you use when configuring your modem for a dial-up connection. With luck, Windows 98 configured your modem automatically when it detected the modem.

The Internet Connection Wizard and the Make New Connection Wizard

The Internet Connection Wizard comes with Windows 98 (you can also download it from the Microsoft Web site). This Wizard can help you to sign up for a new Internet account or configure your computer to work with an existing account. The Wizard doesn't always do all the configuration needed to get your Windows 98 system on the Internet; you may need to do further configuration yourself.

Another Wizard, the Make New Connection Wizard, creates a new Dial-Up Networking connection, without handling the rest of the configuration that the Internet Connection Wizard does.

Later in this chapter, "Creating a Dial-Up Networking Connection Using the Internet Connection Wizard" describes how to use the Internet Connection Wizard, and the section "Making a New Dial-Up Networking Connection" explains how to use the Make New Connection Wizard.

Setting Up a Connection with Windows 98

There are at least three ways to sign-up for an Internet account and configure Windows 98 to connect to it:

- *Run an automated sign-up program.* Windows 98 comes with automated sign-up programs that you can use to sign up with one of several large Internet providers (U.S. versions include programs for AT&T WorldNet and Prodigy Internet). These programs may also let you configure your computer for an existing account with the ISP. (See "Signing Up with Microsoft's Selected ISPs," later in this chapter.)

- *Run the Internet Connection Wizard.* The Wizard can sign you up for a new account with one of dozens of Internet providers who have arranged with Microsoft to be included in the Wizard's list of ISPs. (See "Creating a Dial-Up Networking Connection Using the Internet Connection Wizard," later in this chapter.)

- *Contact the ISP of your choice and sign up for an account.* The ISP may send you a CD-ROM with a configuration program, or you can create your own Dial-Up Networking connection manually. (See "Setting Up a Dial-Up Networking Connection Manually," later in this chapter.)

Each of the preceding three methods leaves you with the same result: an Internet account and a Dial-Up Networking connection configured to dial in to that account. All three ways require that your modem work and that Windows 98 be configured to use it.

Configuring Windows 98 to Use Your Modem

When you install a modem, Windows either determines what kind of modem it is or asks you what kind it is. Windows installs a modem driver that includes information about the commands that the modem understands. To view or change your modem configuration settings, choose Start | Settings | Control Panel, and then run the Modems program. Click or double-click the Modems icon, depending on whether your desktop is configured as Web style or Classic style.

If Windows doesn't know that you have a modem, the Install New Modem Wizard runs; make sure that your modem is on (if it is external) and follow the Wizard's instructions to set up the modem. Then, you see the Modems Properties dialog box, shown in Figure 2-2.

Select the modem from the list of installed modems on the Modems Properties dialog box, and then click the Properties button to see another Properties dialog box. (The exact appearance of this dialog box depends on the modem driver.)

If you have trouble getting your modem to connect, here are some things to check:

- *Determine whether the right modem driver is installed.* Look on the General tab of the Modems Properties dialog box to make sure that the right modem is listed. Remove any drivers for modems that you don't have installed. If the wrong modem is listed, click Add to run the Install New Modem Wizard. If your modem doesn't appear on the Wizard's list of models, choose Standard Modem Types for the manufacturer and choose the modem speed from the list of models.

- *Check whether the modem driver is enabled.* Windows 98 has two versions of the properties dialog box about your modem, and one is more complete. To see a larger array of settings, from the Control Panel, run the System program to

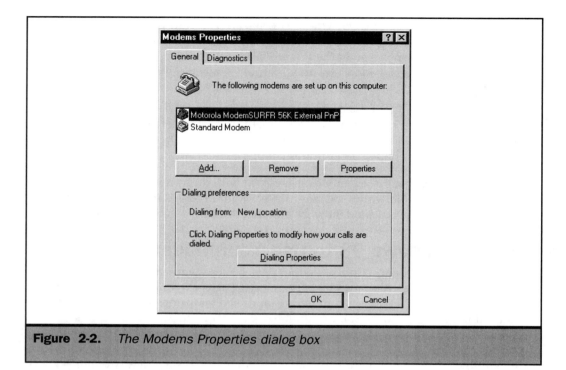

Figure 2-2. *The Modems Properties dialog box*

display the System Properties dialog box. Click the Device Manager tab. Click View Devices by Type and then click the plus box next to the Modems entry on the list of devices. Your modem should appear. Click it and then click the Properties button. (The Properties dialog box that appears contains many more settings than the one you see if you run the Modems program in Control Panel and click the Properties button.) On the General tab, make sure that the modem isn't disabled.

- *Determine whether the modem is connected to the right port.* Display the properties dialog box for the modem, as described in the preceding paragraph. On the Modem tab, check the port to which Windows says that the modem is connected.

- *Check the modem speed.* On the Modem tab of the properties dialog box for the modem, check the Maximum Speed setting. Choosing a lower speed solves some connection problems.

You can also use the Windows 98 Modem Troubleshooter to pinpoint the problem. From the Control Panel, run the Modems program, click the Diagnostics tab on the Modems Properties dialog box, and then click Help. Follow the instructions in the Internet Explorer window that appears, answering the questions that the Troubleshooter poses.

If you have an external modem, make sure that the modem is turned on and that the serial cable isn't loose.

Signing Up with Microsoft's Selected ISPs

U.S. versions of Windows 98 come with automated sign-up programs for three online services (America Online, CompuServe, and The Microsoft Network) and two Internet service providers (AT&T WorldNet and Prodigy Internet). Non-U.S. versions may come with sign-up programs for other ISPs and online services, varying country by country.

AT&T WorldNet is one of the largest ISPs in the U.S. and is also available in Canada and some other countries. Prodigy Internet is the new incarnation of Prodigy, one of the older online services. (The old version of Prodigy, renamed Prodigy Classic, still exists, but the sign-up software for it doesn't come with Windows 98.) AT&T WorldNet and Prodigy Internet both give you a standard PPP account to which you can connect by using Dial-Up Networking.

You'll need a credit card so that the online service or ISP can bill you. If you don't use credit cards, contact your smaller local ISPs and ask if you can open an account and prepay by check.

Running the Automated Sign-Up Programs

To sign up for one of these ISPs, or to set up your computer to use an existing account with one of these providers, follow these steps:

1. Choose Start | Programs | Online Services, and then choose a provider. Or, open the Online Services folder on your desktop and open the icon for the provider. Click or double-click the icon, depending on whether your Windows desktop is configured to use Web style or Classic style.

2. Follow the instructions that the sign-up program displays. During the sign-up process, the provider may display information about your account, including your account name, password, e-mail password, support phone numbers, and other information. Write down all the information that you see! You may need it.

3. The process may involve restarting Windows, so save any files that you are editing and exit all other programs. When you are done installing AT&T WorldNet or Prodigy, a new command appears under Start | Programs.

Caution

Before you use your account, find out whether the number that your modem will be dialing to connect to the account is a local call for you. Check your telephone book or call your local phone company to ask. If the access number is long distance from where you are, you should probably cancel the account, because the long-distance charges for using the account will be many times the cost of the account itself. Instead, find a local ISP with a local phone number.

Notes for AT&T WorldNet Users

If you sign up for AT&T WorldNet, the installation program can create a file named *Account.txt* that records all the information about your Internet account. If you lose your settings, or if you want to connect to WorldNet from a different computer, you can use this file. The WorldNet setup program suggests that you have a blank, formatted diskette on which to store this file.

To connect to an existing WorldNet account, you need your account name, password, e-mail password, and the last eight digits of the credit card number with which you are paying for your account. (Note that capitalization *does* matter when you type your e-mail password.) Or, you need the Account.txt file that WorldNet created when you set up the account.

AT&T WorldNet uses its own AT&T WorldNet Connection Manager to connect to WorldNet, although you can manually configure Dial-Up Networking to do the same thing, if you prefer.

Creating a Dial-Up Networking Connection Using the Internet Connection Wizard

To create a new Dial-Up Networking connection to an Internet provider, you can use the Internet Connection Wizard to create a Dial-Up Networking connection. The Wizard can help you to sign up for a new Internet account or configure your computer to work with an existing account.

You can start the Wizard by choosing Start | Programs | Internet Explorer | Connection Wizard. The Internet Connection Wizard gives you three choices:

- Sign up for a new Internet account and configure Dial-Up Networking to connect to it.
- Configure Dial-Up Networking to connect to an existing account.
- Do nothing, and don't run this Wizard in the future.

| Note | *If you want to create a new Dial-Up Networking connection without any help from a Wizard, run the Make New Connection Wizard instead (see "Setting Up a Dial-Up Networking Connection Manually," later in this chapter, for directions).* |

Creating a New Account Using the Wizard

If you choose to set up a new account by using the Internet Connection Wizard, the Wizard asks you for your phone number and then (if you are in the U.S.) connects to the Microsoft Internet Referral server, using a toll-free number. After a delay, you see a window that lists its suggested ISPs. You can read about each ISP by clicking the document icon to the right of its name, or you can decide to sign up with a provider by clicking the check mark to the right of its name. The sign-up procedure varies by provider.

Microsoft's list of providers doesn't include local providers, only a few of the large national ones. In fact, Microsoft may choose to make a deal with one or two big ISPs and recommend only those ISPs to everyone. The providers listed don't necessarily have local numbers in your area, even though you told Microsoft your area code and exchange. Before you choose an ISP, look for ads in the business section of your local newspaper to see what local providers are available. A small local ISP may give you better service and support than a large ISP, and probably has a better selection of local numbers.

If you choose to create a new account by using one of the providers that Microsoft lists, the Wizard asks you to provide information about yourself, including a credit card to which you want to charge your account. During the sign-up, be sure to write down all the information that the sign-up program displays, including technical support phone numbers, account numbers, and passwords.

Creating a Connection to an Existing Account Using the Wizard

If you choose to create a connection to an existing account, the Internet Connection Wizard asks you to enter the following information about your Internet account:

- Whether your connection is via a local area network or a phone line.
- Whether to use an existing Dial-Up Networking connection or create a new one.
- The phone number that you dial to connect to the account.
- The user name and password for the account.
- The name that you want to use for the connection (this name appears under the Dial-Up Networking icon that the Wizard creates).
- Whether you want to set up Microsoft Outlook Express to handle e-mail for this account. The Wizard can create a new mail account on your computer, into which mail from your Internet account is downloaded. (Outlook Express can handle mail from multiple accounts.) If you choose to configure Outlook Express to get your mail, you need to provide your e-mail address, your account name (if it is different from your e-mail address), which type of mail server your account provides (usually either a POP3 or IMAP server), the name of your ISP's POP server (which handles incoming mail), the name of your ISP's SMTP server (which handles outgoing mail), and your e-mail password (usually the same as your account password). See Chapters 5 and 6 for information about e-mail and Outlook Express.

■ Whether you want to set up Outlook Express to enable you to read Usenet newsgroups. If you do, you must provide the e-mail address that you want included in your newsgroup postings, and the name of your ISP's NNTP server (which handles newsgroup postings). See Chapter 13 for information about Usenet newsgroups.

■ Whether you want to set up a "white pages" directory service (*LDAP*, or *Lightweight Directory Assistance Protocol*) for this account. Some accounts include an LDAP server that acts as a centralized directory of names and e-mail addresses. If your account provider hasn't told you about an LDAP server, answer No to this question.

When the Wizard is done running, it creates a Dial-Up Networking connection (with an icon in the Dial-Up Networking window) and configures Outlook Express for the account.

   When you installed Windows 98, you may not have installed all the program files that the Internet Connection Wizard needs. If not, the Wizard prompts you to insert your Windows 98 CD-ROM or diskettes so that it can load the program files that it needs. It may also require that you restart Windows before it can proceed.

Setting Up a Dial-Up Networking Connection Manually

You don't have to use the Internet Connection Wizard to create a Dial-Up Networking connection and configure your Windows 98 system to use it. You can install and configure a Dial-Up Networking connection yourself. Knowing how to do this is helpful, because the Internet Connection Wizard can't create every connection that you might need, and occasionally you'll want to change the details of an account that the Wizard set up. The Wizard doesn't know how to create a connection for most small ISPs, for example.

Before you make a new Dial-Up Networking connection, you need to make sure that the Dial-Up Adapter is installed and configured to work with TCP/IP.

Installing and Configuring the Dial-Up Adapter and TCP/IP

The Dial-Up Adapter and TCP/IP may not have been installed when you installed Windows 98. If you know that they have been installed on your computer, skip ahead to "Making a New Dial-Up Networking Connection."

DISPLAYING YOUR NETWORK ADAPTERS AND PROTOCOLS   To check whether the Dial-Up Adapter and TCP/IP are installed, choose Start | Settings | Control Panel and then run the Network program to display the Network dialog box, shown in Figure 2-3. Click the Configuration tab, if it is not already selected. If networking has been installed, you can also right-click the Network Neighborhood icon on the desktop and select Properties from the shortcut menu that appears.

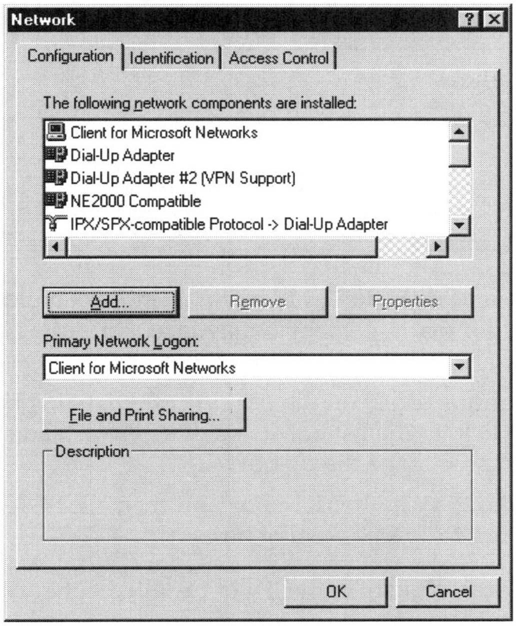

Figure 2-3.   *The Network dialog box*

Check whether the list of network components includes the following items (you may need to scroll down to see them):

■ Dial-Up Adapter

■ TCP/IP -> Dial-Up Adapter

This second item indicates that the Dial-Up Adapter is configured to communicate using TCP/IP. (The Dial-Up Adapter can also work with other network protocols, such as NetBEUI and IPX/SPX, if your computer connects by phone to a local area network, or *LAN*.)

INSTALLING THE DIAL-UP ADAPTER   If the Dial-Up Adapter doesn't appear on your list, follow these steps:

1. In the Network dialog box, click the Add button. You see the Select Network Component Type dialog box, shown next, which lists the types of network software that you might need to install.

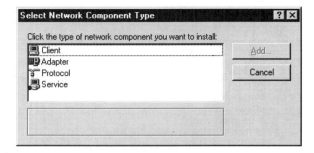

2. Select Adapter, and then click Add again. Windows builds a database of the network drivers of that type, which may take a minute. Next, you see the Select Network Adapters dialog box, shown in Figure 2-4.

3. In the list of manufacturers on the left side of the dialog box, scroll down to find Microsoft and click it. The list of Microsoft's network adapters appears in the box on the right side of the dialog box.

4. Click Dial-Up Adapter in the right box and then click OK. Click OK again to close the Network Properties dialog box.

Now the Dial-Up Adapter appears in the list of installed network components in the Network dialog box.

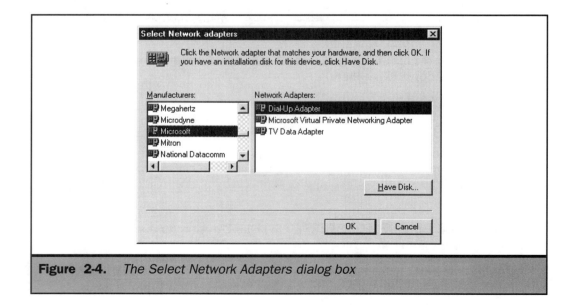

Figure 2-4.   *The Select Network Adapters dialog box*

If the TCP/IP -> Dial-Up Adapter entry doesn't appear on your list, follow these steps:

1. In the Network dialog box, click the Add button. You see the Select Network Component Type dialog box (shown in the previous section).

2. Select Protocol and then click Add again. You see the Select Network Protocol dialog box, shown in Figure 2-5.

3. In the list of manufacturers on the left side of the dialog box, scroll down to find Microsoft and click it. The list of Microsoft's network protocols appears in the box on the right side of the dialog box.

4. Click TCP/IP in the right box and then click OK to install the protocol and return to the Network dialog box.

TCP/IP -> Dial-Up Adapter now appears on the list of installed network components, enabling you to use the Dial-Up Adapter with TCP/IP to communicate with the Internet. Click OK to close the Network dialog box. Windows prompts you to restart Windows so that the new network settings take effect.

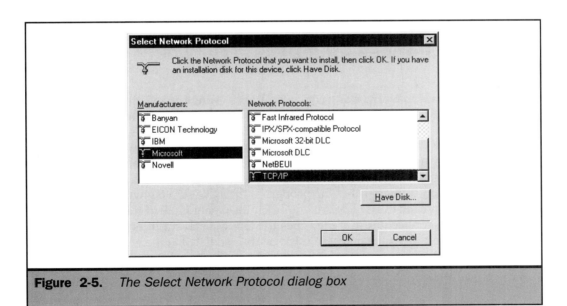

Figure 2-5. *The Select Network Protocol dialog box*

Don't Configure Your Dial-Up Adapter

The Dial-Up Adapter has many settings that control how it connects to other computers. You can configure these TCP/IP settings by using the Properties button on the Network dialog box, but it's better not to. Instead, configure each of your Dial-Up Networking connections with the appropriate settings for the account to which it connects.

 If you are not connected to any network other than an Internet account, you can delete all the protocols except TCP/IP. To delete NetBEUI and IPX/SPX, select the entries for them from the list of components in the Network dialog box and click Remove.

Making a New Dial-Up Networking Connection

To make a new Dial-Up Networking connection, choose Start | Programs | Accessories | Communications | Dial-Up Networking to see the Dial-Up Networking window (refer to Figure 2-1). Run the Make New Connection icon.

The Make New Connection Wizard asks what you want to call the connection and what phone number to dial to connect to the account. Next, the Wizard creates a new icon in your Dial-Up Networking window. Unless you are dialing in to an ISP with the very latest autoconfiguration systems, you probably still need to configure some settings; see the next section for how to enter the rest of the settings yourself.

Changing the Settings for a Dial-Up Networking Connection

To configure a Dial-Up Networking connection or to change an existing connection's configuration, right-click the icon for the connection in the Dial-Up Networking window and then choose Properties from the menu that appears. Alternatively, select the connection icon and choose File | Properties from the Dial-Up Networking menu bar. Either way, you see the Properties dialog box for the Dial-Up Networking connection (see Figure 2-6); the name of the dialog box depends on the name that you gave the connection. Table 2-1 lists the properties for a Dial-Up Networking connection. (If you click the Configure button on the General tab of the Properties dialog box for the connection, and then click the Options tab, additional Internet-related settings appear. These settings are also listed at the end of Table 2-1.)

CONNECTING TO THE
INTERNET

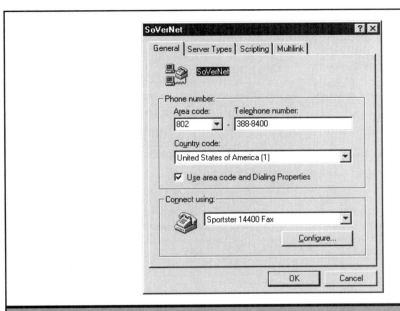

Figure 2-6.   *The Properties dialog box for a Dial-Up Networking connection*

Tab in Properties Window	Setting	Description
General	Phone Number	Specifies the phone number that your computer dials to connect to the account. Composed of the area code, telephone number, and country code (you choose from a list of countries).
General	Connect Using	Specifies which modem to use to connect. Click the Configure button by this setting to check or change the configuration of the modem.

Table 2-1.   *Settings for a Dial-Up Networking Connection*

Tab in Properties Window	Setting	Description
Server Types	Type of Dial-Up Server	Specifies the type of account; all ISPs provide PPP. Choice of SLIP, CSLIP, PPP (three standard types of accounts available from ISPs), NRN (NetWare Connect for NetWare-based LANs), or Windows for Workgroups and Windows NT 3.1 (for Windows-based LANs).
Server Types	Log On to Network	Tells Dial-Up Networking to log on to the account by using your Windows 98 user name and password. Usually not selected for Internet accounts.
Server Types	Enable Software Compression	Compresses information sent between this computer and the account; your Internet account must also support compression (PPP and CSLIP accounts do).
Server Types	Require Encrypted Password	Encrypts your password before sending it to your Internet account when logging on. Your Internet account must support password encryption (most don't).
Server Types	Require Data Encryption	Encrypts all data to and from this connection. Your Internet account must support encryption (most don't).
Server Types	Record a Log File for This Connection	Saves all the information sent to and from this connection in a file.
Server Types	Allowed Network Protocols	Specifies how to communicate over the network. You can select any of these: NetBEUI, IPX/SPX, and TCP/IP. Select TCP/IP for Internet accounts and deselect NetBEUI and IPX/SPX unless your computer is connected to a LAN. To set options for TCP/IP accounts, click the TCP/IP Settings button (see Table 2-2).

Table 2-1.   *Settings for a Dial-Up Networking Connection* (continued)

Tab in Properties Window	Setting	Description
Scripting	File Name	Specifies the name of the file containing the logon script for this connection. Click Edit to edit a script file, or click Browse to select an existing file. See "Creating and Using Logon Scripts," later in this chapter.
Scripting	Step Through Script	Runs the logon script for this connection.
Scripting	Start Terminal Screen Minimized	Minimizes the terminal window that shows the interaction between the Dial-Up Networking connection and the account while the logon script is running. During debugging, deselect this setting so that you can see the terminal window.
Multilink	Do Not Use Additional Devices	Specifies that this connection uses only one device (usually a modem) to connect.
Multilink	Use Additional Devices	Specifies that this connection uses more than one device to connect (for example, two modems). The large box below this setting lists the additional devices used by this connection, and the Add, Remove, and Edit buttons, respectively, let you add, delete, or change devices on the list. See "Creating a Multilink Connection with Windows 98," later in this chapter.
Options	Bring Up Terminal Window Before Dialing	Displays a terminal window, before dialing, that you can use to type modem commands and see the results. (Refer to your modem's manual for the commands that it understands.)
Options	Bring Up Terminal Window After Dialing	Displays a terminal window, after dialing, that you can use to type commands and see the results.

Table 2-1. *Settings for a Dial-Up Networking Connection* (continued)

Tab in Properties Window	Setting	Description
Options	Operator Assisted or Manual Dial	Prompts you to dial the phone manually, for situations in which you need to speak to an operator. When you are connected, click the Connect button and hang up your phone.
Options	Wait for Credit Card Tone: ___ Seconds	Specifies the number of seconds to wait for a tone when you are using a telephone credit card.
Options	Display Modem Status	Displays a status window indicating the progress of your phone connection.

Table 2-1. *Settings for a Dial-Up Networking Connection* (continued)

For most dial-up Internet accounts, you can leave alone almost all of these settings. Just check the phone number and modem on the General tab, and the type of connection and network protocols on the Server Types tab.

If you don't expect to connect to a particular account in the future, delete its connection from the Dial-Up Networking window by selecting the icon for the connection and pressing the DEL key. Be sure to delete any shortcuts to the connection, too.

Configuring TCP/IP Settings for an Internet Account

For an Internet account, you may also need to configure the TCP/IP protocol. On the Properties dialog box for the connection, click the Server Types tab, select TCP/IP as an allowed network protocol, and then click the TCP/IP Settings button. You see the TCP/IP Settings dialog box, shown in Figure 2-7. Table 2-2 shows the settings on this dialog box. Contact your ISP for the settings and addresses to enter.

Most ISPs now use *server-assigned IP addresses*, which means that when you connect, the ISP assigns your computer an IP address for that session (see Chapter 1 for an explanation of IP addresses and the DNS system). When you disconnect, the ISP is free to assign that IP address to the next user who connects. Few ISPs have enough IP addresses assigned to them to permanently assign one to each user. As a result, you can probably leave the Server Assigned IP Address setting selected on the TCP/IP Settings dialog box.

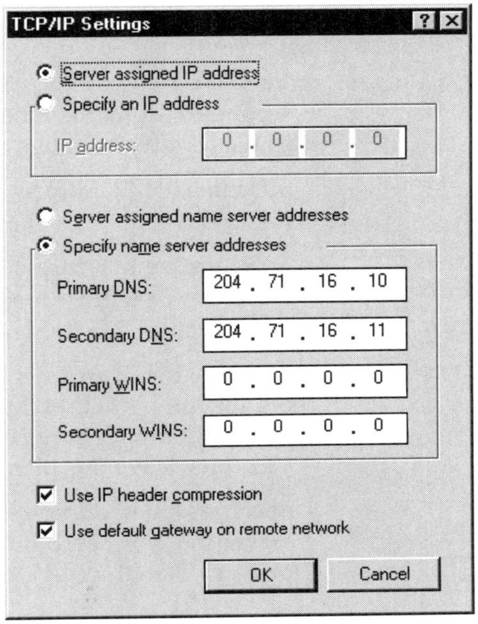

Figure 2-7. *The TCP/IP Settings dialog box*

Setting	Description
Server Assigned IP Address	Specifies that your ISP assigns an IP address to your computer when you log on (most ISP accounts do this).
Specify an IP Address	Indicates that your computer has a permanently assigned IP address, which you specify in the IP Address setting.
IP Address	Specifies your permanently assigned IP address.
Server Assigned Name Server Addresses	Specifies that your ISP assigns domain name servers to your computer when you log on (most ISP accounts do this).

Table 2-2. *TCP/IP Settings*

Setting	Description
Specify Name Server Addresses	Indicates that you have entered primary and secondary domain name server IP addresses in the next two settings.
Primary DNS	Specifies the IP address of your ISP's domain name server.
Secondary DNS	Specifies the IP address of another domain name server that your account can use when the primary DNS does not respond.
Primary WINS	Specifies the IP address of your organization's WINS (Microsoft's Windows Internet Naming Service) server. For dial-up accounts, leave this blank.
Secondary WINS	Specifies the IP address of another WINS server that your account can use when the primary WINS server does not respond.
Use IP Header Compression	Specifies that packet headers should be compressed for faster transmission (the default is on).
Use Default Gateway on Remote Network	Specifies how IP packets to the rest of the Internet are routed (leave on, unless your ISP tells you to change it).

Table 2-2. *TCP/IP Settings* (continued)

Most ISPs also now use *server-assigned name server addresses,* so that when you connect, the ISP informs Dial-Up Networking of the IP addresses to use for your DNS server (described in Chapter 1). If your ISP uses such addresses, you can leave the Server Assigned Name Server Addresses setting selected, too. But if your ISP gave you the IP address of its domain name servers, you need to enter them on the TCP/IP Settings dialog box. Select Specify Name Server Addresses and enter the IP addresses in the Primary DNS and Secondary DNS settings.

Some ISPs (not many) also provide WINS (Microsoft's *Windows Internet Naming Service*) servers, which provide other name lookups. If your computer is connected to a large corporate system via a LAN or by dialing in, your connection may use WINS to manage network parameters automatically. Your computer contacts the WINS server, either at boot time (if you connect via a LAN) or when you dial up, to get its own configuration information.

Setting Additional Dial-Up Networking Options

You might think that all the properties of a Dial-Up Networking connection appear on the connection's Properties dialog box (refer to Figure 2-6), but they don't. A few additional settings appear on the Internet Properties and Dial-Up Settings dialog boxes. The Internet Properties dialog box has miscellaneous settings, including those that control the default mail, e-mail, and other Internet application programs. The Dial-Up Settings dialog box controls how often Dial-Up Networking redials if the line is busy, and how long a connection can remain inactive before Dial-Up Networking hangs up. (See "Dialing the Internet Automatically," later in this chapter, for directions on how to use the Dial-Up Settings dialog box.)

To display the Internet Properties dialog box, choose Start | Settings | Control Panel and run the Internet program. Figure 2-8 shows the Connection tab of the Internet Properties dialog box. Most of the settings on the various tabs of this dialog box apply to using the Microsoft Internet Explorer Web browser, and are covered in Chapter 20 (another way to display a version of this dialog box is to choose View | Internet Options from the Internet Explorer Web browser). However, most of the settings on the Connection tab control your Internet connection; the settings that do are listed in Table 2-3.

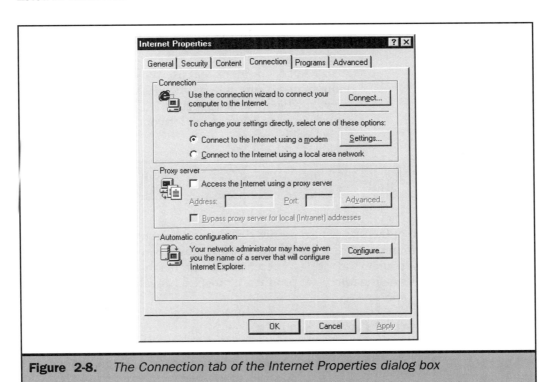

Figure 2-8.   *The Connection tab of the Internet Properties dialog box*

Setting	Description
Connect to the Internet Using a Modem/Connect to the Internet Using a Local Area Network	Specifies whether you connect to the Internet via a modem or via a local area network.
Settings	Displays the Dial-Up Settings dialog box (see Table 2-4 for details).
Access the Internet Using a Proxy Server	For connections via a LAN or intranet, specifies whether you connect via a *proxy server* (a server that acts as a gatekeeper between your LAN and the rest of the Internet). See Chapter 4 for details.
Address	For connections via a proxy server, specifies the address of the proxy server.
Port	For connections via a proxy server, specifies the port number of the proxy server.
Advanced	Displays the Proxy Settings dialog box, in which you specify addresses for use with your proxy server.
Configure	For LAN connections that use WINS or some other automated configuration system, displays a dialog box in which you can specify the URL of the configuration information for your Internet Explorer program.

Table 2-3. *Connection-Related Settings on the Internet Properties Dialog Box*

The Programs tab of the Internet Properties dialog box also contains settings about your Internet account. In the Messaging section of the dialog box, you can select the e-mail program, newsreader, and video conferencing programs that you use. Unfortunately, Windows lists Microsoft products almost exclusively, so the programs that you use may not appear.

Creating and Using Logon Scripts

Dial-Up Networking tries to log on to your account automatically. Most accounts follow a standard series of steps: they transmit your user name and your account's password, and then receive confirmation that you are logged in and that communications can begin.

If your account uses a nonstandard series of commands for logging in, Dial-Up Networking can't log in automatically. You can automate logging in by creating a *logon script*, a text file that contains a small program that tells Dial-Up Networking what prompts to wait for and what to type in response. For example, if your ISP's computer uses a nonstandard prompt to ask for your password, or requires you to type a command to begin a PPP session, you can write a script to log on for you.

To use a logon script, follow these steps:

1. Log on manually, making notes about which prompts you see and what you must type in response to those prompts. To log in manually, you can use your Dial-Up Networking connection with a *terminal window*, which allows you to see the session and type commands to your ISP. To tell Windows to open a terminal window while connecting, click the Configure button on the General tab of the Properties dialog box for the connection, which displays the Properties dialog box for your modem. Then, click the Options tab and select the Bring Up Terminal Window After Dialing check box. Or, you can use HyperTerminal to connect to your Internet provider.

2. Create a logon script by using a text editor, such as Notepad. Windows 98 comes with a short manual about writing logon scripts, located in the file C:\Windows\Script.doc.

3. Tell Windows 98 about the logon script by typing the filename in the Script File Name box on the Scripting tab of the Properties dialog box for the Dial-Up Networking connection (refer to Table 2-1.)

4. Test the script, editing it with your text editor and viewing the results in a terminal window.

Dial-Up Networking comes with a set of well-commented sample scripts. Usually, customizing one of the sample scripts is easier than writing your own from scratch.

Creating a Multilink Connection with Windows 98

Multilink enables you to use multiple modems and phone lines (usually two modems and two phone lines) for a single Internet connection, to increase the effective connection speed (*throughput*). For example, you could use two 56Kbps modems together to simulate a 108Kbps connection to the Internet. Data flows through both modems and both phone lines for a single connection.

Your ISP must support multilink connections for you to use such a connection, because the ISP's hardware and software must be able to combine the packets of information from the two phone lines into one Internet connection. Multilink connections, where they're available, usually cost more than a regular dial-up Internet account; contact your ISP for details.

When you create a multilink connection, you specify one device—usually a modem—on the General tab of the connection's Properties dialog box. Then, you list the other device(s)—usually one other modem—on the Multilink tab. Click the Use Additional Devices setting to tell Windows that this is a multilink connection, and then add the additional devices. To add a device, click the Add button, and then in the window that appears, select the name of the device to use (usually a second modem) and the phone number to dial. (The Add button doesn't work unless you have two modems installed on your PC.) When you are done, the device name appears in the large box in the Multilink tab of the Properties dialog box for the connection.

To change the configuration of a device, select it and click the Edit button. To remove a device from the list, select it and click Remove.

After you set up a multilink connection, it works just like a regular Internet connection, but faster.

Connecting and Disconnecting with Windows 98

After you set up your Dial-Up Networking connection, connecting and disconnecting is easy.

Connecting to Your Internet Account

To connect to an Internet account by using Dial-Up Networking, follow these steps:

1. Choose Start | Programs | Accessories | Communications | Dial-Up Networking to display the Dial-Up Networking window. Then, run the connection icon. If a connection icon appears on your desktop, you can run it instead. You see the Connect To dialog box, shown in Figure 2-9.

2. Unless you are worried about someone else using your computer to connect to your account, select the Save Password check box so that you don't have to type your password each time that you connect. (If you use a terminal window or a script to log on, leave this box blank.)

3. Click the Connect button. Dial-Up Networking dials your account, logs in, and starts the type of connection that you set in the Type of Dial-Up Server setting in the Properties dialog box for the connection. You see a window telling you that you are connected to the account (Figure 2-10). In addition, the Dial-Up Networking icon appears in the system tray on the Taskbar.

Tip *Click the Do Not Show This Dialog Box in the Future check box, so that you don't have to see this confirmation dialog box each time that you connect to the Internet.*

4. Click the Close button.

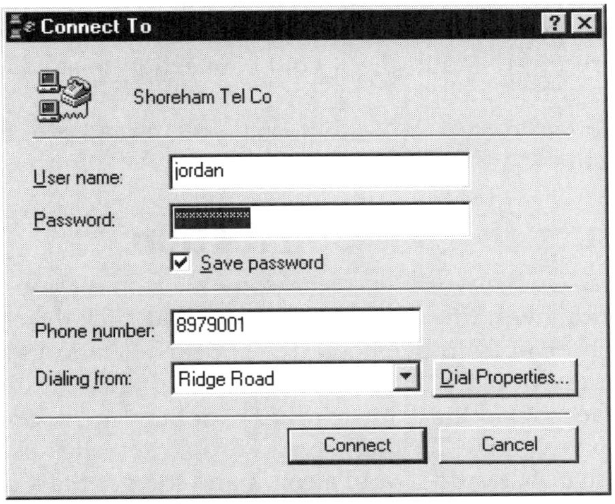

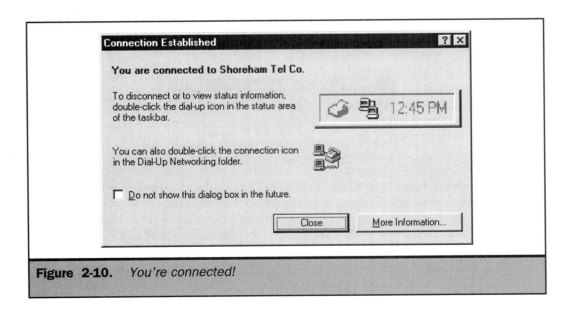

Figure 2-9. *Connecting using Dial-Up Networking*

Figure 2-10. *You're connected!*

While you are connected, the Dial-Up Networking icon appears in the system tray on the Taskbar. Move the mouse pointer to it (without clicking) to see how many bytes have been sent and received and to check your connection speed. Double-click the icon to see more details.

Once you are connected, you are ready to run your e-mail program, Web browser, or other Internet client programs.

Creating Shortcuts to Your Connection

To make starting Dial-Up Networking easier, copy the icon for your connection from the Dial-Up Networking window to your desktop. Right-click the connection's icon and choose Create Shortcut from the menu that appears. Windows asks whether to put the shortcut on your desktop. Click Yes.

You may also want to add the connection to your Start menu or Programs menu (right-click a blank place on the Taskbar, choose Properties, click the Start Menu Programs tab, and then click Add to add a command to your Start menu).

If you create a desktop shortcut to your Dial-Up Networking connection, you can also assign it a shortcut key. For example, you can assign the key combination CTRL+ALT+I to connect to the Internet. Right-click the desktop shortcut and choose Properties from the menu that appears. On the properties dialog box for the shortcut, click in the Shortcut Key box and type a letter (for example, I). CTRL+ALT+*letter* appears in the Shortcut Key box (for example, CTRL+ALT+I). Click OK. Now whenever you press CTRL+ALT+I, Windows displays your Dial-Up Networking connection dialog box.

Disconnecting from Your Account

To disconnect your Internet connection, double-click the Dial-Up Networking icon in the system tray. You see the Connected dialog box, shown here. Click Disconnect.

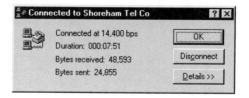

Another way to hang up is to right-click the Dial-Up Networking icon on the system tray and choose Disconnect from the menu that appears.

If you are connected to your Internet account and don't use it for a while (usually 20 minutes), Windows or your ISP may disconnect you automatically. You may see this dialog box asking whether you'd like to disconnect:

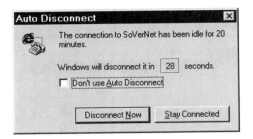

Or, you may see a dialog box saying that you have been disconnected and asking whether you'd like to reconnect. See the next section for instructions on how to configure Windows to connect and disconnect automatically.

Dialing the Internet Automatically

What happens if you are not connected to the Internet and you tell your e-mail program to fetch your mail, or ask your Web browser to display a Web page? Dial-Up Networking can dial up and connect to your Internet account automatically when you request Internet-based information.

To set Windows to connect automatically, follow these steps:

1. Choose Start | Settings | Control Panel and run the Internet program. Click the Connection tab on the Internet Properties dialog box and make sure that the Connect to the Internet Using a Modem setting is selected.

2. Click the Settings button to display the Dial-Up Settings dialog box, shown in Figure 2-11.

3. In the first box, choose the Dial-Up Networking connection that you want to use when connecting automatically to the Internet.

4. Set the other options to tell Windows how many times to try to make a connection and how long to wait between attempts (if your ISP's line is busy, for example). Also, type your user name and password. If you want Windows to disconnect automatically after a period of inactivity, choose the Disconnect If Idle for __ Minutes check box and type the number of minutes.

5. Click OK to dismiss the Dial-Up Settings dialog box and then click OK again to dismiss the Internet Properties dialog box.

Tip   *The first time that you run an Internet client program—such as a browser or e-mail program—and you aren't connected to the Internet, Windows may display the Internet Autodial window, which asks a series of questions to configure the same options that appear in the Dial-Up Settings dialog box.*

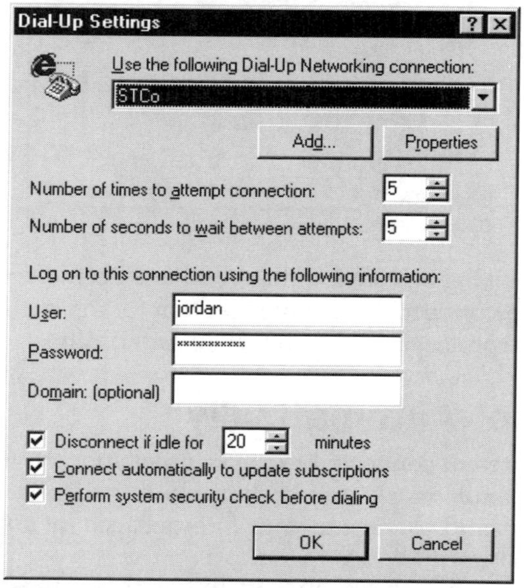

Figure 2-11. *The Dial-Up Settings dialog box*

Table 2-4 lists the settings and buttons on the Dial-Up Settings dialog box.

Setting or Button	Description
Add	Runs the Make New Connection Wizard.
Properties	Displays the properties of the Dial-Up Networking connection.
Number of Times to Attempt Connection	Specifies how many times Dial-Up Networking dials the connection. The default is five times.
Number of Seconds to Wait Between Attempts	Specifies how long to wait before trying again after one attempt to connect fails. The default is five seconds.
User	Specifies the user name to use when logging in.

Table 2-4. *Settings and Buttons on the Dial-Up Settings Dialog Box*

Setting or Button	Description
Password	Specifies the password to use when logging in.
Domain	Specifies the domain name for your account, if your ISP requires one. The default is blank.
Disconnect if Idle for __ Minutes	Specifies whether to disconnect automatically after a period of inactivity. The blank contains the number of minutes after which to disconnect. The default is 20 minutes.
Connect Automatically to Update Subscriptions	Specifies whether to connect automatically to update the information from Web sites to which you have subscribed.
Perform System Security Check Before Dialing	Specifies whether to require a password each time the system dials out.

Table 2-4. *Settings and Buttons on the Dial-Up Settings Dialog Box* (continued)

When you use an Internet program and Windows detects that you are asking for information from the Internet, you see the Dial-up Connection dialog box, shown in the left side of Figure 2-12. Type your Internet user name and password. If you aren't worried about anyone else using your computer to connect to your Internet account, select the Save Password setting. If you want Windows to connect automatically (without requiring you to click anything) whenever you request information from the Internet, select the Connect Automatically setting. Then click Connect.

While Windows is dialing the phone, you see the Dialing Progress dialog box, shown in the right side of Figure 2-12. The dialog box displays messages as it dials, connects, and logs in to your Internet account.

Testing Connections with Windows 98

After dialing a Dial-Up Networking connection, you can use Windows 98's Ping program to test whether packets of information can make the round trip from your computer, out over the Internet to another computer, and back to your computer. You can use the Tracert program to check which route packets take to get from your computer to another computer. And you can use the Netstat program to find out which computers your computer is talking to.

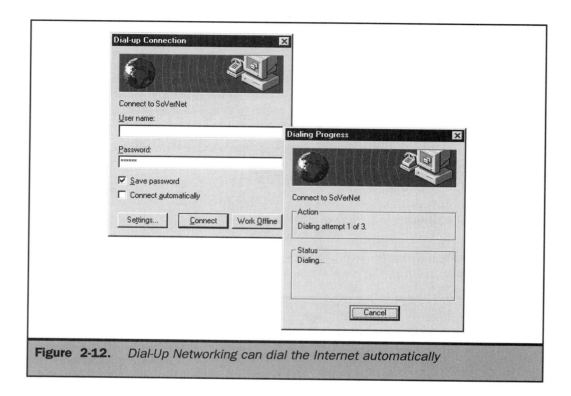

Figure 2-12. *Dial-Up Networking can dial the Internet automatically*

Pinging Another Computer

Sending a small text packet on a round trip is called *pinging*, and you can use Windows 98's built-in Ping program to send one.

To run Ping, open a DOS window by choosing Start | Programs | MS-DOS Prompt. Then, type the Ping command:

    ping *system*

Replace *system* with either the numeric IP address or the host name of the computer that you want to ping. Choose any Internet host computer that you are sure is up and running, such as your ISP's mail server, and then press ENTER.

For example, you can ping the Web server at InterNIC (the Internet Information Center), which has the IP address 204.159.111.101, by typing

    ping 204.159.111.101

Ping sends out four test packets (pings) and reports how long the packets take to get to InterNIC's computer and back to yours (see Figure 2-13). For each packet, you see how

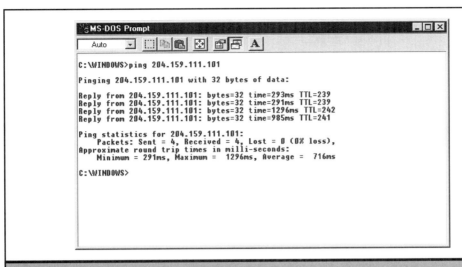

Figure 2-13.   *Ping tests your Internet connection*

long the roundtrip takes in milliseconds, as well as summary information about all four packets' trips. Ping has several options that are listed in Table 2-5, as well as other options, not listed here, that are useful only to network managers.

> **Tip**   *First try Ping with a numeric IP address, to see whether packets get out to the Internet and back. Then try Ping with a host name, such as www.internic.net, to see whether you successfully contact your DNS to convert the name into an IP address. If the first test works and the second doesn't, your connection isn't set up properly to contact a DNS server.*

Option	Description
-a	Reports numeric addresses rather than host names.
-f	Specifies that packets contain a Do Not Fragment flag, so that packets are not fragmented on route. (Useful to test very slow dial-up connections.)

Table 2-5.   *Options for the Ping Program*

Option	Description
-i *ttl*	Specifies the *Time To Live* for the packets (how many times the packet can be passed from one computer to another while in transit on the network).
-l *length*	Specifies the length of the packets to send. The default length is 64 bytes. The maximum length is 8192 (8K).
-n *n*	Specifies to send *n* pings. (The default is four.)
-r *n*	Specifies that the outgoing and returning packets should record the first *n* hosts on the route that they take, using the Return Route field. *n* is a number from one to nine.
-t	Specifies to continue pinging until you interrupt it. (Otherwise, it pings four times.)
-w *n*	Specifies a timeout of *n* milliseconds for each packet.

Table 2-5. *Options for the Ping Program* (continued)

Tracing Packets over the Internet

Packets of information don't usually go directly from one computer to another computer over the Internet. Instead, they are involved in a huge game of "whisper-down-the-lane," in which packets are passed from computer to computer until they reach their destination. If your data seems to be moving slowly, you can use the Tracert (short for *trace route*) program to follow your packets across the Internet, from your computer to an Internet host that you frequently use. The technique that Tracert uses doesn't always work, so it's quite possible that running Tracert to a remote computer can fail even though the computer is working and accessible.

To run Tracert, open a DOS window by choosing Start | Programs | MS-DOS Prompt. Then, type the Tracert command:

tracert *system*

Replace *system* with either the numeric IP address or the Internet name of the computer to which you want to trace the route, and then press ENTER.

For example, you can trace the route of packets from your computer to the Yahoo! Web directory at **www.yahoo.com** by typing:

tracert www.yahoo.com

You see a listing like the one in Figure 2-14, showing the route that the packets took from your computer to the specified host (sometimes, Tracert reports a different host

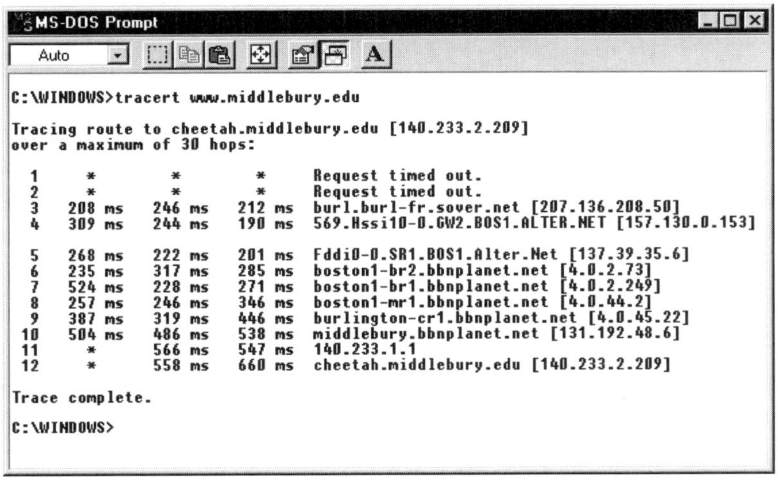

```
MS-DOS Prompt                                              _ □ ×
 Auto     ▼  ☐ ▣ ▣  ▣  ▣ ▣  A

C:\WINDOWS>tracert www.middlebury.edu

Tracing route to cheetah.middlebury.edu [140.233.2.209]
over a maximum of 30 hops:

  1     *        *        *      Request timed out.
  2     *        *        *      Request timed out.
  3   208 ms   246 ms   212 ms   burl.burl-fr.sover.net [207.136.208.50]
  4   309 ms   244 ms   190 ms   569.Hssi10-0.GW2.BOS1.ALTER.NET [157.130.0.153]
  5   268 ms   222 ms   201 ms   Fddi0-0.SR1.BOS1.Alter.Net [137.39.35.6]
  6   235 ms   317 ms   285 ms   boston1-br2.bbnplanet.net [4.0.2.73]
  7   524 ms   228 ms   271 ms   boston1-br1.bbnplanet.net [4.0.2.249]
  8   257 ms   246 ms   346 ms   boston1-mr1.bbnplanet.net [4.0.44.2]
  9   387 ms   319 ms   446 ms   burlington-cr1.bbnplanet.net [4.0.45.22]
 10   504 ms   486 ms   538 ms   middlebury.bbnplanet.net [131.192.48.6]
 11     *      566 ms   547 ms   140.233.1.1
 12     *      558 ms   660 ms   cheetah.middlebury.edu [140.233.2.209]

Trace complete.

C:\WINDOWS>
```

Figure 2-14.   *Tracert shows the route that packets take from your computer to an Internet host*

name from the one that you specified, which means that the host has more than one name). For each *hop* (stage of the route), Tracert sends out three packets and reports the time that each packet takes to reach that far. It also reports the name and numeric IP address of the host.

Table 2-6 shows the options that you can use with the Tracert program. A few other options, not listed here, are useful only to network managers.

Option	Description
-d	Specifies not to resolve addresses to host names, so that the resulting list of hosts consists only of numeric IP addresses.
-h *n*	Specifies a maximum number of *n* hops to trace before giving up.
-w *n*	Specifies that the program wait *n* milliseconds for each reply before giving up.

Table 2-6.   *Options for the Tracert Program*

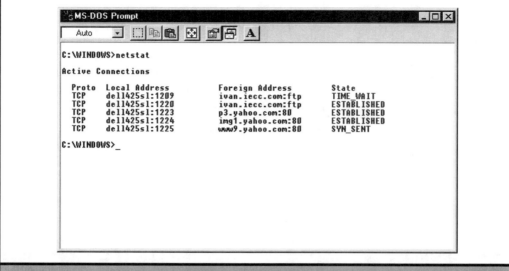

Figure 2-15. *The Netstat program lists Internet hosts that you are using*

Displaying Internet Connections Using Netstat

Netstat is a network diagnostic program that you can use for any TCP/IP connection—Internet connections or LANs. You can run Netstat to see which computers your computer is connected to over the Internet—not the ISP to which you dial in, but other Internet hosts to or from which you are transferring information.

To run Netstat, open a DOS window by choosing Start | Programs | MS-DOS Prompt. Then, type **netstat** and press ENTER. You see a listing of the Internet connections that are currently running. Figure 2-15 shows that the computer is connected to the host **ivan.iecc.com** for FTP file transfer. The computer is also connected to several computers at the Yahoo! Web directory, probably to receive Web pages (the 80 at the end of the address signifies the port commonly used for Web page retrieval).

Connecting from Other Systems

If you have Windows NT, Windows 95, Windows 3.1, or a Macintosh, read the following sections for information about how to connect to the Internet.

Connecting from Windows NT

Windows NT 4 comes with Dial-Up Networking, but its version works differently from Windows 98's. You need to set up your modem if its drivers aren't already installed, install TCP/IP networking, install Remote Access Service (RAS), and create a phonebook entry for your ISP (this is the Windows NT equivalent of making a Windows 98 Dial-Up Networking connection).

Configuring Windows NT to Use Your Modem

If your modem is already installed, skip to the next section. To tell Windows NT what kind of modem you have and to install the modem drivers, follow these steps:

1. Choose Start I Settings I Control Panel.

2. Select the Modems program, which displays the Install New Modem window (Figure 2-16).

3. To let Windows NT detect your modem automatically, select Next.

4. Windows NT searches for a modem on one of the serial ports of the computer (usually COM1, COM2, COM3, or COM4). When it finds a modem, you see a window with the type of modem, usually Standard Modem.

5. If you know the manufacturer and model of your modem, you can specify it to Windows NT. (Specifying the exact model of the modem is more likely to ensure a correct configuration than using the default Standard Modem setting.) Otherwise, skip to step 8. Click Change. Windows NT displays a list of manufacturers and models (Figure 2-17).

6. Select the appropriate manufacture of the modem and then choose the model by that modem.

7. Click OK, click Next, click OK again, and then click Finish. You see the Modems Properties dialog box (Figure 2-18), containing the modem that you just added.

8. Select the modem (if more than one appears) and then click Properties. You see the properties dialog box for the modem (Figure 2-19).

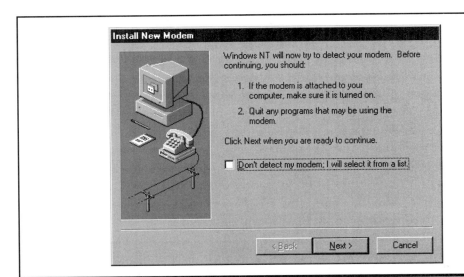

Figure 2-16. *The Install New Modem window in Windows NT*

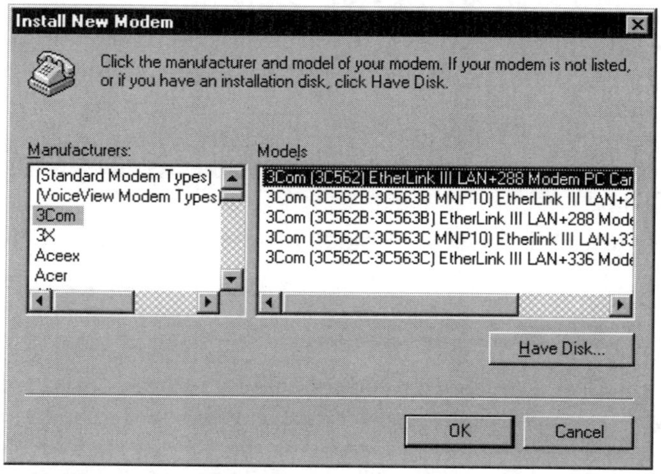

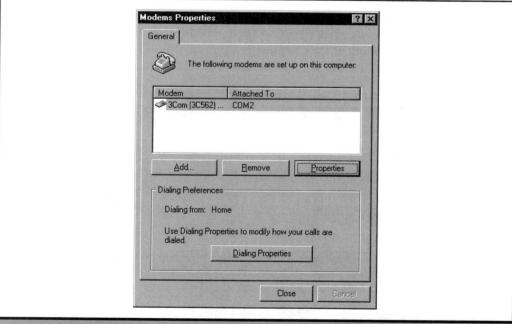

Figure 2-17.   *Specifying a modem model (in this example, a 3Com 3C562)*

Figure 2-18.   *The Modems Properties dialog box in Windows NT*

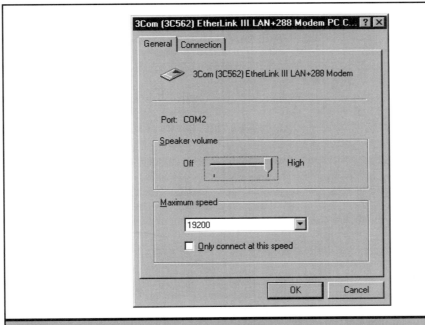

Figure 2-19. *Setting the properties of a modem in Windows NT*

9. On the General tab, set the maximum speed to match the maximum speed to use between your PC and your modem. Don't worry about setting it too high; the modem automatically adjusts to communicate at the highest speed possible (as long as you don't select the Only Connect at This Speed check box). If you set this option too low, however, the modem will only communicate at the speed that you set. Settings under the Connection tab can usually be left alone.

10. Click OK to close the properties dialog box for the modem. You need to reboot the computer for the new modem settings to take effect.

Configuring Windows NT Networking

After you configure your modem, you can tell Windows NT what kind of networking to use it for—TCP/IP—along with some configuration information about your ISP, as follows:

1. Select Start | Settings | Control Panel.

2. Select the Network program, which displays the Network dialog box (Figure 2-20). The most important tabs to consider are the Protocols and Adapters tabs.

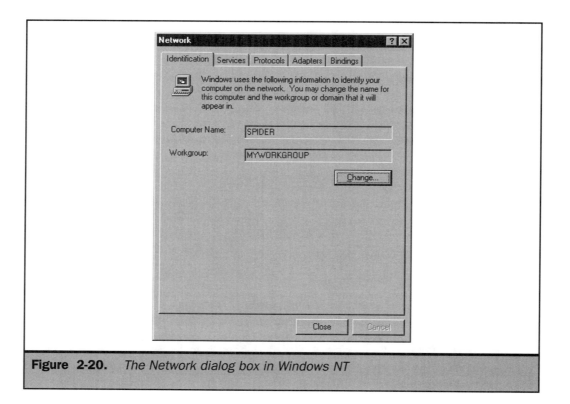

Figure 2-20.   *The Network dialog box in Windows NT*

3. Click the Adapters tab and then click Add. A list of modems appears.

4. Select the modem that matches the one in your computer. A setup window pops up.

5. For most modems, you can probably leave these settings alone. Don't change them unless you really know that they should be changed! Depending on your computer and modem type, you may see another window with items specific to the system. Look them over, select the appropriate values for your system, and click OK. You return to the Network dialog box.

6. Click the Protocols tab and then click Add. A list of network protocol types appears (see Figure 2-21). Select TCP/IP (the protocol used on the Internet). If you need other protocols for a local area network, leave them unchanged. Click OK.

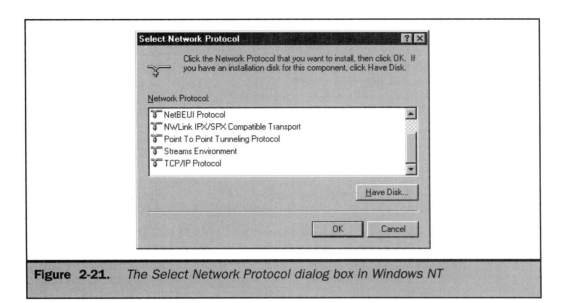

Figure 2-21.   *The Select Network Protocol dialog box in Windows NT*

7. Windows asks whether you want to use DHCP. Your ISP will tell you the answer to this question. In some cases, your ISP may provide you with a fixed IP address (a four-part number that looks something like 192.168.0.1, for example). Most people, though, should use DHCP, so click Yes unless your ISP says not to.

8. You return to the Network dialog box. Click Close to end your network setup.

9. Windows displays the Microsoft TCP/IP Properties dialog box (Figure 2-22).

10. Unless your ISP has provided you with a fixed IP address, click the Obtain an IP Address from a DHCP Server on the IP Address tab.

11. Click the DNS tab. For the Host Name, enter a name for your computer. (The name doesn't matter; this is the only place in this entire process where any creativity is allowed.) For Domain, type the domain name of your ISP, which is usually the last two parts of the ISP's e-mail address, such as *sover.net* or *earthlink.net*. In the DNS Service Search Order section, click Add and then type the IP address of your ISP's *domain name server (DNS)*, which your ISP should provide you with.

12. Leave the rest of the settings unchanged, and click OK at the bottom of the Microsoft TCP/IP Properties dialog box.

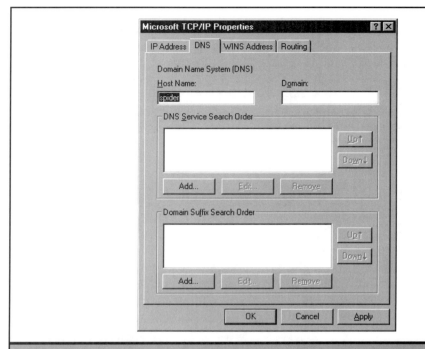

Figure 2-22. *The Microsoft TCP/IP Properties dialog box in Windows NT*

Setting Up Remote Access Service (RAS) and Dial-Up Networking

Now that Windows NT is configured to use your modem, and TCP/IP is installed, you can create a connection for your ISP:

1. Choose Start | Programs | Accessories | Dial-Up Networking and click the Install button.

2. Remote Access Service (RAS) Setup starts and prompts you regarding which modem to use. Click OK to use the modem that you already installed.

3. Click Configure and then select whether Dial-Up Networking should dial out only, receive calls only, or both dial out and receive calls. (If you are planning to call an ISP, choose to dial out only.)

4. Click Continue. Windows NT sets up RAS and prompts you to restart your computer.

5. After restarting your computer, select Start | Programs | Accessories | Dial-Up Networking again. The New Phonebook Entry Wizard appears, to step you through the process of creating a *phonebook entry* for your ISP.

6. Type a name for the connection that you are setting up.

7. Check the boxes that indicate you are calling the Internet, that you want to send a plain-text password (unless your ISP supports sending encrypted passwords), and that the server expects login information after connecting.

8. Type the phone number of your ISP.

9. Choose PPP (unless your ISP says to use SLIP instead).

10. For the login script, leave None selected.

11. Enter your IP address, or leave it as 0.0.0.0 if your ISP didn't assign you a fixed IP address (most don't).

12. Enter the IP address for the DNS of your ISP (the same IP address that you entered in Step 11 of the preceding section).

13. Click Dial, enter your user name and password, and click OK. If you check the Save Password box, you will not have to enter a password each time that you dial. (This is easier, but it almost guarantees that you will forget your password. Even worse, if someone gets access to your computer, they could log on to your Internet account without needing the password.)

You connect to the Internet.

Connecting and Disconnecting

After you follow the procedures to create a phonebook entry for your Internet account, connecting to the Internet is easy. Choose Start | Programs | Accessories | Dial-Up Networking, select the phonebook entry, and click Dial. Now you can run other programs that communicate over the Internet, such as e-mail programs and Web browsers.

When you are done using the Internet, right-click the connection icon on the Taskbar (if it appears) and choose Hang Up or Close, or click the Dial-Up Networking button on the Taskbar and click the Hang Up or Close button.

Connecting from Windows 95

Over the three years during which Windows 95 was sold, it came with slightly different Dial-Up Networking and Internet Connection Wizard software, depending on when you purchased the software. If you purchased Windows 95 during 1998 and received Internet Explorer 4 along with it, you probably also got OSR2, the second revision of Windows 95, which works very similarly to Windows 98.

Running the Internet Connection Wizard

Windows 95, like Windows 98, came with an Internet Connection Wizard to help you set up a Dial-Up Networking connection. To confuse matters, different versions of Windows 95 came with two different Internet Connection Wizards:

- **Inetwiz.exe**   Earlier versions of Windows 95 come with an Internet Connection Wizard that asks lots of questions about your Internet account and helps you to create a Dial-Up Networking connection for that account, which is perfect if you already have an Internet account. This Wizard is stored in Inetwiz.exe.

- **Icwconn1.exe**   Other versions of Windows 95 come with an Internet Connection Wizard that asks you where you live and presents you with a list of ISPs in your area (a list limited to those who have paid or otherwise arranged with Microsoft to be included, so the list is far from complete). This Wizard is stored in Iwconn1.exe.

Regardless of which version you have, try running the Internet Connection Wizard on your system by choosing either Start | Programs | Accessories | Internet Tools | Get On The Internet, or Start | Programs | Internet Explorer | Connection Wizard. You can also search for Inetwiz.exe or Icwconn1.exe by choosing Start | Find | Files Or Folders.

Configuring Your Own Dial-Up Networking Connection

Alternatively, you can create your own Dial-Up Networking connection either by choosing Start | Programs | Accessories | Dial-Up Networking or by opening the Dial-Up Networking folder that appears at the bottom-left of the window in Windows Explorer. Double-click the Make New Connection icon and start the Make New Connection Wizard (refer to "Making a New Dial-Up Networking Connection," earlier in this chapter).

Connecting and Disconnecting

After you create a Dial-Up Networking connection, connect by choosing Start | Programs | Accessories | Dial-Up Networking and double-clicking the icon for your connection. When you see the Connect To dialog box, make sure that the user name and phone number are right, type your password, and then click Connect. After your computer gets connected, a Connected dialog box appears.

Now you can run other programs that you want to use with the Internet. When you are ready to disconnect, click the Disconnect button on the Connected dialog box.

Connecting from Windows 3.1

Unlike newer operating systems, Windows 3.1 did not come with Internet connection software. Specifically, it did not come with a TCP/IP stack, the program that you use to dial-up an Internet account and connect to the Internet. You need to get a Windows 3.1-compatible TCP/IP stack and configure it for your Internet account.

Getting a TCP/IP Stack

You can get TCP/IP connection software from several sources:

- **Your ISP**   The best source of a Windows 3.1 TCP/IP stack is your ISP. Most ISPs provide Internet connection software—along with an e-mail program and a Web browser—free of charge, mainly because it doesn't cost them anything. If you get connection software from your ISP, follow the instructions that your ISP gives you. If you run into trouble, you can call them for help.

- **With a browser or another Internet program**   If you buy the Windows 3.1 retail version of Netscape Navigator, it comes with the Shiva PPP TCP/IP connection program built in. Follow the instructions in the package. You might be able to get a friend to download Microsoft Internet Explorer 3 with a built-in dialer (available from TUCOWS, at **http://www.tucows.com**, by choosing its Windows 3.*x* software, Networking category), but since the file is over 3MB, you may have trouble getting it from your friend's computer to yours.

- **Freeware**   Several freeware or shareware TCP/IP stacks are available. The best known is called Trumpet Winsock. Get a friend with an Internet connection to download a copy of Trumpet Winsock for you. It's so small that it fits on a diskette. You can get it from TUCOWS, at **http://www.tucows.com**, by choosing its Windows 3.*x* software, Networking category. It's also available from its Web site at **http://www.trumpet.com** or **http://www.trumpet.com.au**. Some older introductory Internet books came with Trumpet Winsock on a diskette in the back of the book. Installation instructions are in the next section.

Installing Trumpet Winsock

The latest version of Trumpet Winsock is version 3, and the program comes in a single file named Twsk30d.exe. (Version 4 is in the works.) Follow these steps to install the program:

1. In Windows File Manager, move the Twsk30d.exe file into the directory where you put temporary files (such as C:\Temp).

2. Still in File Manager, double-click the Twsk30d.exe filename to run the program that it contains. It self-extracts a bunch of programs into the same directory, including the installation program. Close the window that shows the results of the self-extracting program.

3. Press F5 to update the list of files in File Manager. You see a long list of new files, including one called Install.exe.

4. Double-click the Install.exe file in File Manager to run the installation program.

5. Follow the instructions that the installation program displays. It asks whether it can rename any existing files named Winsock.dll (answer yes, because you probably don't have any), it asks for the directory in which to store the Trumpet Winsock program (C:\Trumpet or C:\Internet are good names), and it tells you that it needs to modify your Autoexec.bat file (this is OK, so click Save to save its changes to the file).

6. When the installation program tells you that it needs to restart the computer, click OK, and then Restart.

7. If your computer doesn't restart and rerun Windows, exit Windows and restart the computer and Windows. A new program group named Trumpet Winsock appears in Program Manager, with icons for Trumpet Winsock and the utilities that come with it.

Now you have the Trumpet Winsock program on your Windows 3.1 system. The next step is to configure Trumpet Winsock for your Internet account.

Configuring Trumpet Winsock

Follow these steps to configure Trumpet Winsock:

1. Double-click the Trumpet Winsock icon to run the program. After a message reminding you to register (and pay for) the program if you decide to continue using it, you see the Trumpet Winsock Setup dialog box.

2. If your ISP gave you a permanent IP address (which is unlikely), type it in the IP Address box. Otherwise, leave this box containing 0.0.0.0.

3. In the DNS Server(s) box, type the IP address of your ISP's DNS server. (Ask your ISP if you don't know.)

4. In the Domain Suffix box, type your ISP's domain name (for example, sover.net or mindspring.com).

5. In the Driver Section, click the type of account you have (usually PPP).

6. Click the Dialler Settings button to display the Trumpet Winsock Dialler Settings dialog box, and choose the settings for your modem port and speed. Leave the rest of the settings alone, unless instructed by your ISP to change them. Click OK, and then click OK again.

7. Choose File | Exit to leave Trumpet Winsock and save all of your settings. Then, double-click its icon again to rerun it. You see the Trumpet Winsock window, which contains nothing but a menu bar and many lines of text.

You can change the configuration at any time by choosing File | Setup.

Connecting and Disconnecting

To connect to your Internet account, double-click the Trumpet Winsock icon to run the program. Choose Dialler | Login to display the Login Profile dialog box. Type your user name, password, and your ISP's phone number, and then click OK.

Trumpet Winsock dials and logs in to your Internet account by following a built-in script. The program's standard script works with most, but not all, ISPs. If the connection works, you see the message SCRIPT COMPLETED. If not, you see SCRIPT ABORTED, which means that you need to work with your ISP to change the script to match your ISP's login procedure. Once you are connected, you are ready to run your e-mail program, your Web browser, or other Internet client programs.

To disconnect from your Internet account, choose Dialler | Bye from the menu. If you don't plan to reconnect, choose File | Exit to leave the Trumpet Winsock program.

 *If you use the program, you should register it (it costs only $25 as of 1998). To register, use your Web browser to go to **http://www.trumpet.com/wsock3_price.html**.*

Connecting from Macintoshes

Connecting a Macintosh is easy as long as you have a recent version of the Macintosh operating system (Mac OS).

If You Use System 7.5.5

If you have a 68040 or better Mac with 24MB of RAM and a 500MB or greater hard drive, you should seriously consider upgrading to System 8.1. The upgrade is cheap and well worth it. If you have any "32-bit clean" Mac, but not a 68040, consider upgrading to System 7.6.1. If you don't have a "32-bit clean" Mac, consider that $799 will get you a full-fledged PowerMac system, with monitor and keyboard, and fully upgradable to a PowerPC G3.

System 7.5.5 doesn't come with Internet connection software. Instead, ask your ISP for an installer program that installs a third-party application. Most ISPs distribute a program called FreePPP, which comes with installation instructions. An alternative is to install Open Transport 1.2.1 (available at **http://www.apple.com**), install OT/PPP 1.0 on top of that, and follow the instructions for Systems 7.6 through 8.1.

If You Use System 7.6.1 Through 8.1

With the advent of System 7.6.1, Apple included Open Transport/PPP with every system, making Internet setup and connection a snap. If you have a modem that was made after the introduction of your version of System, you need to install the software for the modem.

If you are using Open Transport/PPP and you don't intend to use the fax or other special capabilities of your modem, you can save disk space by doing a custom install, installing only the OT/PPP/ARA 2.1 modem script. That's the only piece of software you need if all you want to do is connect to the Internet by using Open Transport/PPP.

Follow these steps:

1. Choose Apple | Control Panels | PPP.
2. Choose PPP | Modem to display the Modem control panel, shown in Figure 2-23.
3. In the Connect Via pull-down menu, select the modem port that your modem is plugged into.
4. In the Modem pull-down menu, select the script for your modem.
5. Select to have the sound turned on or off.
6. Unless your phone system accepts only pulse dialing, leave Dialing set to Tone.
7. Ignore Dial Tone is helpful if your phone uses an unusual beeping or dial tone to indicate that you have a message waiting. The modem will not dial if it doesn't detect a dial tone on your phone line, unless you check Ignore Dial Tone.
8. Close the Modem control panel and save your changes.
9. Choose PPP | TCP/IP to display the TCP/IP (Default) control panel, shown in Figure 2-24.

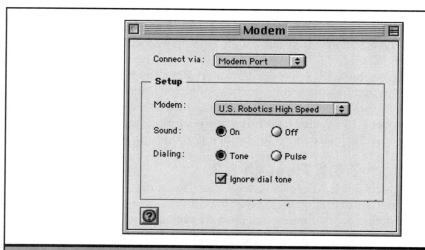

Figure 2-23.   *Configuring a modem on the Mac*

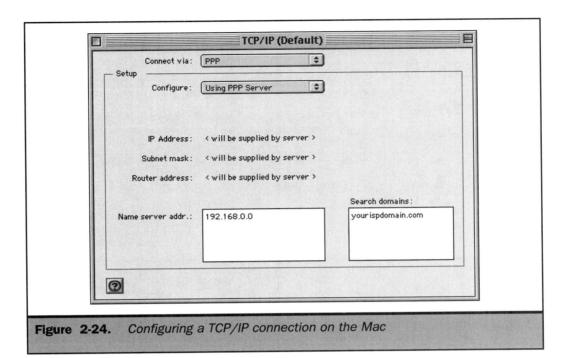

Figure 2-24.   *Configuring a TCP/IP connection on the Mac*

10. On the Connect Via pull-down menu, choose PPP.

11. On the Configure pull-down menu, choose PPP server.

12. In the Name Server Addr field, type the IP address of your ISP's DNS (domain name server; for example, 192.168.0.1). Ask your ISP for this information.

13. In the Search Domains field, type your ISP's domain name (for example, for EarthLink, this is earthlink.net).

14. Close the TCP/IP control panel and save your changes.

15. Click the Options button and click the Connection tab in the Options control panel (shown in Figure 2-25). Turn off the Prompt Every 5 Minutes to Maintain Connection setting and the Disconnect if Idle for 10 Minutes setting, so that your Mac doesn't nag you constantly to hang up.

16. Choose OK to return to the PPP control panel.

17. In the Name field, type your user name.

18. In the Password field, type your password. You can click the Save Password box, but if you do, anyone who has physical access to your machine will be able to log on to your Internet account.

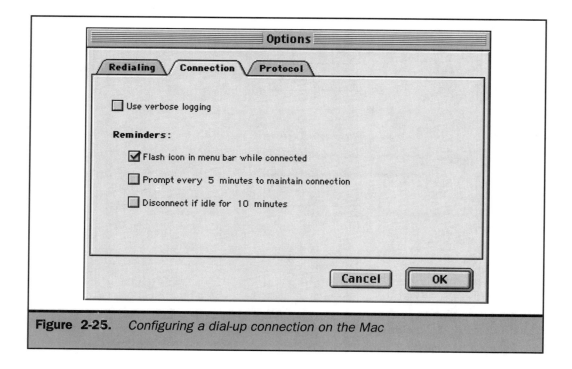

Figure 2-25. *Configuring a dial-up connection on the Mac*

19. In the Number field, type the phone number of your ISP. Include any extra digits that you need to dial, such as *70 to disable call waiting.

20. Click the Connect button.

Your Mac is connected to the Internet. You are ready to run your e-mail program, Web browser, or other Internet client program.

To connect the next time, just choose Apple | Control Panels | PPP and click Connect.

If You Have System 8.5

System 8.5 works exactly like 7.6 through 8.1, except that PPP is now included as part of Apple Remote Access 3.0.1. Instead of using the PPP control panel, you use the Remote Access control panel. When you install Mac OS 8.5, make sure to install Remote Access.

To get your Mac connected to the Internet, follow the instructions in the preceding section, except replace PPP with Remote Access throughout. Figure 2-26 shows the Remote Access control panel that you see in step 16.

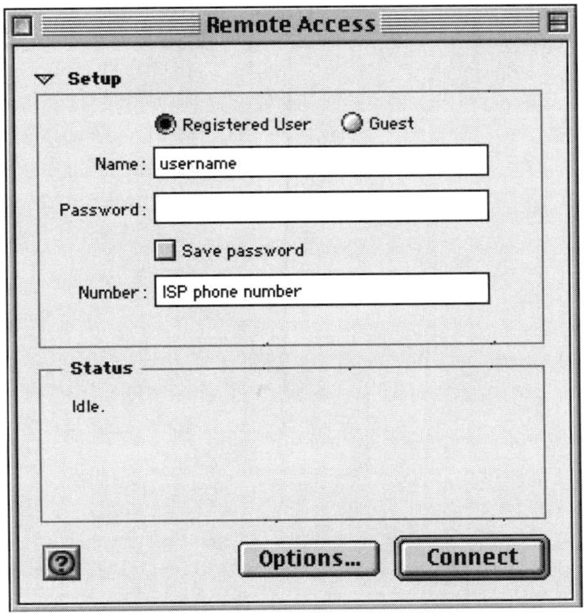

Figure 2-26.   *Configuring an Internet account in Mac OS 8.5*

To connect again, choose Apple | Control Panels | Remote Access and click Connect. Alternatively, click the icon that looks like a Mac and a telephone pole in the control strip, and click Connect.

The
Complete
Reference

Internet

Chapter 3

High-Speed Connections: ISDN, ADSL, and Cable Modems

If you're used to connecting to the Internet through an office network, then dialing from home can be disappointing. At the office, you're always connected to the Internet. You don't have to remember to dial up. Messages come in and news headlines are updated. File downloads are relatively quick. You might even take advantage of videoconferencing, streaming video news (such as CNN's Web site at **http://www.cnn.com/videoselect**), or Internet radio.

Now you can have that availability and speed in your small office or home. Until recently, you had to pay big-business prices for fast data services, but now serious bandwidth has become relatively affordable. These services differ in price and capabilities, and this chapter looks at each in depth. For more information about sharing a high-speed Internet connection among several computers on a local area network, see the next chapter.

The Contenders

The three services that you're most likely to find available to you are ISDN, ADSL, and cable modem service. Two wireless services might be useful in the future, but currently have limitations.

ISDN

Integrated Services Digital Network (ISDN) is available from nearly all local telephone companies. ISDN is an upgraded phone line that can be used for faster Internet access and for regular voice calls. Using one line, you can talk on the phone while you're surfing the Web. ISDN is all digital, which means that data doesn't have to be converted to an *analog signal* (that funny noise you hear modems make) for transmission.

The ISDN service intended for residential use is *Basic Rate Interface (BRI). On one ISDN line, BRI provides two 64Kbps channels, or B channels,* and one 16Kbps channel, or *D channel.* The D channel is mostly used for signaling—for instance, to indicate that the line is busy. The B channels are where the action is. When the B channels are combined, you have a 128Kbps line to the Internet. That's over twice the speed of the fastest analog modem, 56Kbps. If you want to talk on the phone or send a fax, your Internet access drops down to one 64Kbps B channel while the other B channel is used for voice.

For more technical details about ISDN, see Chapter 39.

ADSL

Asymmetric Digital Subscriber Line (ADSL), like ISDN, uses an upgraded phone line, all-digital technology, and supports simultaneous Internet browsing and phone use. ADSL is a much newer technology, so it's not as widely available or as clearly standardized. ADSL is optimized for the way many people use the Internet: more downloads than uploads. The line is *asymmetric,* because it has more capacity for data received by your computer (such as graphics, video, audio, and software upgrades) than for data that you send (such as e-mail and browser commands).

Configurations and prices vary. The *downstream* bandwidth from the Internet to your computer can range from 384Kbps to 8Mbps. The *upstream* bandwidth from your computer to the Internet can range from 90Kbps to 640Kbps. Moreover, ADSL is just one of a family of DSL products on the drawing board. See the ADSL Forum (**http://www.adsl.com**) and TeleChoice's xDSL site (**http://www.xdsl.com**) for more background.

Expect providers to support a simpler, entry-level solution: the emerging *G.Lite* standard. G.Lite streamlines installation—if you have a phone line in place, you won't need to have an installer come to your house to hook up the modem. G.Lite is anticipated to provide 1.544Mbps downstream and 512Kbps upstream. That downstream speed brings you a Web page 25 times faster than a 56Kbps analog modem.

Cable Modem Service

Cable modem service is the competitive threat that's caused phone companies to accelerate their ADSL efforts. The same network that brings you dozens of TV channels can now bring you millions of Web sites. The problem is that the cable network was designed to move information in one direction, from the broadcaster to you. Downstream speeds are impressive—the line can theoretically bring you data as fast as 30Mbps, much faster than your computer can handle it—but upstream speed depends on line quality. Large cable companies are spending money to upgrade their networks to *hybrid fiber-coax* (*HFC*) to better handle two-way traffic. Smaller providers can't afford the upgrade, so you use a phone line at 28.8Kbps for upstream data.

From a large company with an HFC network, expect downstream speeds of 1 to 2Mbps or more, and upstream speeds between 500Kbps and 1Mbps. These numbers aren't exact, because you share digital cable capacity with your neighbors. If more of them are online, you compete with them for bandwidth. See **http://www.cablemodeminfo.com** for in-depth coverage of cable modem issues, as well as DSL resources.

Wireless Alternatives

In a few urban areas, you can test *wireless* Internet access. To set it up, you attach a radio modem, about the size of a deck of cards, to your laptop. Wireless service made its debut at analog speeds (28.8Kbps), but it is being upgraded to 128Kbps, comparable to ISDN.

If you're outside an urban area, you're probably out of range for ISDN, ADSL, or cable modem service. If so, you might be tempted to acquire *satellite* access. All you need is an 18- or 21-inch satellite dish and a service provider contract. There are some drawbacks. Satellite access can be frustrating to set up. Also, although the dish receives data at up to 400Kbps, it can't send anything. That means you need a phone line for upstream data, and you are limited to analog modem speeds.

Choosing a High-Speed Connection

The first question when choosing a high-speed connection is: What's actually available in your location? ISDN and ADSL work over phone lines, but not over *all* phone lines. Your local phone company's *central office*, the facility serving your area, has to be set up to offer the service. Your distance from the central office also matters, as does the condition of the network. For example, to receive 1.544Mbps ADSL, you need to be within approximately three miles of the central office. Check with your local phone company to make sure that your phone line qualifies for ISDN or ADSL and ask your ISP if they provide ISDN and ADSL connections.

Cable modem service requires cable TV wiring. That leaves out remote areas and even some office parks. Even if you have cable TV, your provider may wait to offer cable modem service until it has upgraded the network for two-way data.

If ISDN, ADSL, and cable modem service are all available, you can make your choice based on cost and performance considerations.

Cost

Prepare for sticker shock. High-speed Internet access is not the world of cheap modems, flat-rate local calls to your Internet service provider, and $20-per-month Internet access. Even so, many providers are working to reduce the cost of equipment, to simplify installation, and to make monthly charges more predictable. Providers also package equipment, lines, and Internet service together, which makes it easier for them to get you online, and may give you a price break, too.

ISDN and ADSL prices vary greatly from region to region in the United States, due to the different pricing policies of the regional phone companies.

Equipment

You need a new modem (or in the case of ISDN, an *adapter*). ISDN adapters and ADSL modems currently cost $200 to $300. Cable modems generally are rented, not purchased. ADSL and cable modems usually connect through an *Ethernet* or other network card in your computer. If you don't have one, add another $50.

Installation

Installation charges are frequently waived. Some providers bundle a deeply discounted modem with installation. Your provider may even discount the modem *and* installation if you commit to buy its service for a year. Check for these installation fees:

- **Line upgrades**   In phone company lingo, upgrading your phone line is called *provisioning* your line with ISDN or ADSL. Even if you're using an existing phone line, converting it to ISDN or ADSL could cost over $100. This cost really depends on who your provider is.

■ **New lines** If you want a second (or third, or fourth) phone line to dedicate to ISDN or ADSL, someone needs to install it, typically either your local phone company or an independent firm.

■ **Internet service provider fees** Some ISPs charge for setting up your account for high-speed access. For ISDN and ADSL, this charge is about $30.

Cable modem service providers currently charge $100 to $150 for a complete installation, including adding a new cable line for your computer.

Monthly Charges

After you're over the startup costs, how much do you have to pay every month for Internet access? Your monthly cost depends on what kind of high-speed connection you have:

■ *ISDN rates depend on use.* The cost of an ISDN line usually depends on the number of minutes of use. It may also depend on time of day, with higher rates for business hours. The cost of Internet service accessed through ISDN also goes up with use. A typical ISDN package gives you a certain number of minutes per month "free," included in a base rate. Additional use is charged per minute. If you can stay within the base rate guidelines, you can get an ISDN line plus ISP access for about $60 per month. Look at your past usage patterns to see whether that's a realistic figure for you (for most heavy Internet users, it's not).

■ *ADSL rates depend on bandwidth.* Both line costs and ISP costs increase with the speed of your ADSL connection. Access at 1.544Mbps combined with ISP service costs approximately $100 to $270 per month, depending on the provider. Most providers offer slower rates with lower prices. A few offer faster rates.

■ *Cable modem rates are flat.* Both line use and ISP costs are combined in one monthly rate, about $40. That rate also includes modem rental. This could change, but for now, it's a great deal.

Clearly, ISDN is not intended to be left on all day. ADSL and cable modem service are. But with a new type of ISDN service, you'll never have to dial up again: *Always Cn/Dynamic ISDN (AO/DI)* uses the D channel to provide a constant 9.6Kbps connection to the Internet. E-mail is delivered, chat pals can find you, and your stock ticker stays up-to-date. When you need more capacity, AO/DI switches over to one or two of the B channels. If you are considering ISDN, ask whether AO/DI is available for your line—and compare its price.

Speed

Sure, everybody wants more speed. And the moment that you get it, all the Internet content providers clog up the pipes with video and audio, applets and animation. So it's hard to generalize about how much speed is enough. It's a moving target. It's also a matter of individual preference and the size of your pocketbook. But if you regularly do large downloads—such as software upgrades—you may be interested in the following comparison:

Modem Speed	Time to Download a 10MB File
28.8Kbps	46 minutes
56Kbps	24 minutes
128Kbps	10 minutes
1.544Mbps	52 seconds
4Mbps	20 seconds

Don't neglect your need for *upstream* speed, either. When you e-mail files, publish a Web page, or have a videoconference, you're sending data. If you set up a computer as a server and make information on it available to others, upstream speed *really* matters.

Phone Line Issues

Are you setting up or improving a home office? Are you hoping to consolidate your phone, fax, and Internet connection onto one line? ISDN and ADSL both provide that capability, but here are some caveats:

- **Cost of phone calls** ISDN pricing is typically usage-sensitive. If you currently make a lot of local phone calls and pay a flat fee every month for them, your bill might go up when you make calls over the ISDN line. You may be better off with flat-rate cable modem service plus a regular phone line. ADSL service is flat-rate for an Internet connection, but check with your provider about rates for voice calls.

- **Noise on the line** If you are using ADSL for a modem connection while talking on the phone, the ADSL signal may create noise interference. A *telephone filter* reduces this noise. Some modems have a filter built in, so that if you plug in your phone or fax machine directly to the modem, you won't have a problem. You can also buy telephone filters that attach to the line or mount on the wall jack. These filters are especially useful for extension phones that share the ADSL line with your computer.

- **Slower speeds for data**   With ADSL, the speed of your Internet connection may drop while you are talking on the phone. This information comes from an early field trial of G.Lite ADSL. It's not clear how large or consistent this effect is.

- **Emergency phone calls**   An ISDN line shouldn't be the only phone line in your house. Your regular analog phone will work only if it's connected through the ISDN terminal adapter. In an emergency, if the power goes out, the adapter can't power the phone and you can't make or receive any calls. Be sure to keep a regular analog line. The phone system can power a phone even if the rest of the power in your house is out. (ADSL lines don't have this problem. Phones can be plugged in directly to the line and draw their power from it.)

Remote Access

Do you use the Internet when you travel? If your laptop has a high-speed connection at home, what happens when you take it elsewhere? You're unlikely to find ISDN, ADSL, or cable modem access, so you need to keep your analog modem or buy a dual-purpose modem.

The big issue is having an ISP that supports both your dial-up access and high-speed access. Getting dial-up access usually isn't a problem if you buy an ISDN or ADSL package. An ISP who provides ISDN and ADSL accounts is frequently either a branch of the local phone company or an independent ISP that has provided dial-up access for years. But if you have a cable modem package, dial-up access to the cable company ISP is expensive—if it's provided at all.

One solution is to keep your current ISP for dial-up access. This may not be as expensive as you think, given the low prices for cable modem service and basic Internet dial-up. Keep your e-mail account with your dial-up ISP, use the same e-mail program that you use now, and make sure the program is configured to use your ISP's mail servers. When you're at home, your computer is plugged in to the cable modem, which gives you a fast connection to your ISP. When you're travelling, you can dial in as usual. See Chapter 2 for information on how to configure a dial-up connection, and Chapter 5 for how to configure e-mail programs.

Choice of Provider

Who do you want to do business with? You might expect to order ISDN or ADSL from your local phone company, and cable modem service from your cable TV company. You can also order ISDN or ADSL through some ISPs, who can take care of ordering the phone line for you. Modem manufacturers often help you order ISDN. In rare cases, an ISP resells cable modem service. In short, companies are vying for your attention. And because they want to get you up and running as quickly as possible, they provide one-stop shopping: high-speed connection, equipment, and Internet service in one package.

Summary of High-Speed Connection Choices

The widespread availability of ISDN may make it your only choice for a high-speed connection to the Internet. However, cable modem and ADSL are designed for "always-on," flat-rate access, and both offer speeds that are *many* times higher than ISDN. ADSL tends to be slower and more expensive than cable modem service, but ADSL's speed is yours alone—cable modem speed depends on usage patterns in your neighborhood. The following are some other points to consider:

- ISDN and ADSL allow you to consolidate phone and Internet service, though not without some problems.

- The big drawback of cable modem service is its current lack of affordable dial-up access, which is important to travelers.

All three methods of high-speed connection require you to buy or rent new equipment. You may have to pay for a visit by an installer, and you may have to change ISPs. Shop carefully and look for good package deals in this increasingly competitive market.

Connecting via ISDN

ISDN is more complicated to set up than ADSL or cable modem service. Although you can buy all the pieces separately—equipment, phone line, Internet access—the money that you save may not be worth the frustration. Many variables need to be set up for the line and for the equipment. If one of them is wrong, your connection won't work. Find a provider that offers a good package with excellent support, and you'll be online much more quickly.

If, after that warning, you still want to put together your own ISDN package, here's what to look for.

Choosing an ISDN "Modem"

An ISDN "modem" is more properly called a *terminal adapter* (*TA*). Modems convert analog signals to digital ones, and vice versa, so that your (digital) computer can exchange information over the (analog) phone line. With ISDN service, the line is already digital, so conversion isn't necessary.

Before you go adapter shopping, call your ISDN line provider. Find out what kind of switch is used to provide you with phone service. A *switch* is a device in the local phone company's central office; its hardware and software determine the capabilities that the phone company can provide to you. You need to make sure that your adapter works with the provider's switch type.

Next, decide whether you want an internal or external terminal adapter. If you have an older desktop computer, there's a tradeoff. External adapters plug in to the serial port, which, until recently, was limited to a top speed of 115.2Kbps. (Newer serial interfaces have faster chips.) Internal adapter cards bypass any serial port bottleneck, so you can get a full 128Kbps out of your ISDN line. However, external adapters are more likely to be flash-ROM upgradable.

For a laptop computer, get a credit-card-size PC Card terminal adapter. You can buy a card that supports both ISDN and 56Kbps analog modem connections, so that you can use the same card when you travel.

Next, ensure that your adapter provides a standard *U interface* instead of an *S/T* interface. The U interface is common in the U.S. and enables you to plug in the adapter directly to the ISDN wall jack. Otherwise, you need yet another piece of equipment called a *network terminator*, or *NT-1*.

If you're going to use a phone or fax machine on your ISDN line, make sure that your adapter has at least one analog phone jack on it. You plug in your existing equipment to the adapter. Also, check to see whether the adapter has full *ringing support*. That is, when a phone call comes in, does the phone actually ring or do you just get some flashing lights on the front of the adapter? Flashing lights are easy to miss when you're busy poring over your computer screen.

Make sure that your adapter allows you to link together both B channels for high-speed connections. The preferred method is *Multilink PPP*. Your ISP also needs to support Multilink.

Pay attention to how flexible and efficient the adapter is in its use of the two B channels. For example, if you are using both channels for a 128Kbps Internet connection when a phone call comes in, does the adapter dynamically allocate one of those channels to the call, and then shift it back to Internet use when the call is over?

Also take a close look at cost-saving features. ISDN providers typically charge more for using two B channels than for using one. Some of the best adapters try to balance performance with cost. They connect at the highest rate by using two channels, but drop back to one if your activity doesn't require that bandwidth. But beware: if the adapter throws you off and on the second B channel too frequently, you could end up spending *more* money. Some ISDN providers charge more for the first minute of connection than for subsequent minutes of use. If you're constantly reconnecting, you could spend more than if you just stay on the line.

In some cases, you can get more performance out of an ISDN line by using data compression. See which compression method(s) your adapter provides. Most ISPs don't support compression at their end, so 128Kbps is the best that you can do. However, if you are dialing in to a corporate network that *does* support compression, you will get better performance.

If you want to make sure that your ISDN adapter works even during power outages—so that you can make phone calls—look for one with a backup battery pack.

Ordering an ISDN Line

Ordering your ISDN phone line is the trickiest part. ISDN is flexible, which means that many ways exist to configure it. Only some of those ways will actually work for you. The exact configuration that you order depends on your adapter and your switch type.

Your ISDN line provider may also allow flexibility in choosing ISDN features, especially phone features such as Caller ID and three-way conferencing. If you have custom calling features on your phone now, you need to check with your ISDN provider about whether they're available on your ISDN line.

For basic line configuration, consult the manuals and box inserts that come with your adapter. You are likely to find switch-specific configuration instructions. Each set of instructions lists 10 to 20 parameters that must be set correctly for your adapter to work with that switch. You may want to fax the relevant instructions to your ISDN line provider.

Manufacturers and phone companies are working to simplify the process by using *ordering codes*. Each code is a shorthand way to refer to all the parameter settings in a configuration.

If you're interested in using a phone and a fax machine on the ISDN line, ask the provider whether you will have one or two phone numbers assigned to the line. If you get two numbers, you can have one number ring the phone and the other call the fax. You can also use both devices at the same time. If you get one phone number, then incoming calls ring both devices, and you can use only one at a time.

If you are adding a new phone line instead of converting an existing one, you definitely need a qualified installer to add it.

Before you sign up, ask your line provider about B channel speed. Ideally, it should be 64Kbps, which gives you the potential of 128Kbps when you link both channels. In some locations, it is 56Kbps instead. Also, shop carefully for an ISP. Some that nominally support Multilink (combining two channels into one Internet connection) can't provide a stable 128Kbps connection, so in practice, you're limited to one 64Kbps B channel.

Configuring Your Computer for ISDN

Physical installation of an ISDN adapter is like that of any other modem. An external adapter connects to the computer's serial port (or modem port) with a serial cable. External adapters also have a power supply. If you have an internal adapter, it's installed in one of the computer's empty slots. In either case, a phone cable provided with the adapter connects it to the ISDN wall jack. If desired, phones or fax machines are plugged in to the adapter's analog (telephone) ports.

Follow the manufacturer's directions for installing the hardware driver, so that your computer can access the new adapter. Depending on what type of computer and adapter you have, the computer may automatically detect the adapter and choose the appropriate driver.

To configure the adapter, however, you need additional information. Ask your phone company or other ISDN provider about the following:

- **Switch type**   If you researched and bought your own adapter, you already know this.
- **Phone number(s)**   Assigned to your ISDN line.
- **Service profile identifiers (SPIDs)**   *SPIDs* are codes that identify your ISDN line to the phone company equipment. Typically, you have two SPIDs, one for each B channel. They look like phone numbers plus extra digits that are specific to the switch type. For example, one of your B channels may have the phone number (925) 555-3434 and SPID 92555534340101. If your area code changes, then so does your ISDN phone number and the associated SPID.
- **B channel rate**   Ask the line provider whether it's 64 or 56Kbps.

Now, run the configuration software provided by the adapter manufacturer. Enter the switch type, phone number(s), and SPID(s). If your ISP supports Multilink PPP, then make sure Multilink is enabled here. If your B channel rate is a full 64Kbps, make sure that option is selected. If you have phones or fax machines connected, follow the adapter manufacturer's instructions to assign phone numbers to the devices.

| Tip | *If you have a PC running Windows 98, and your adapter is an internal card, you may run the Windows 98 ISDN Wizard instead. Choose Start / Programs / Accessories / Communications / ISDN Configuation Wizard.* |

The next task is to set up a network connection, as you would for any other modem. Contact your ISP and find one or more local numbers that are reserved for ISDN access. Create network connections that dial in to those numbers using your ISDN adapter. See the section "Setting Up a Connection with Windows 98" in Chapter 2 for more details.

Your ISDN provider or adapter manufacturer can tell you how to make sure that the TCP/IP network protocol is loaded. If you're getting a new ISP, you also need to enter its IP address, host name, domain name, mail server, and news server information. See Chapter 1 for more details.

If you are buying a complete ISDN package from one company, you usually get shrink-wrapped software for its ISP service. The software takes you through the installation of a customized browser, e-mail program, and other components. Check with the ISP if you prefer to use the software that you have now. You need to configure your software to work with the ISP's service.

Using ISDN

The ISDN setup discussed thus far meets the needs of many home users and telecommuters. With the B channels configured to handle both data and voice, and Multilink enabled, you have the flexibility to add a phone and a fax machine without sacrificing high-speed access to the Internet.

But ISDN can be set up more elaborately. You can have up to eight devices on an ISDN line, such as extension phones or a computer in another room. Depending on the capabilities of your switch, the devices could even have different phone numbers. Small office, anyone? You can't use all the devices at once, but any two of them could each take an available B channel. To connect multiple computers, you may want to buy a *router*. Check with your ISDN provider for more details and review **http://www.zdnet.com/ pcmag/features/pisdn/index.html**.

We also haven't talked much about the 16Kbps D channel. It's for data only, not voice. Some businesses use it for low-bandwidth transactions, such as to verify credit card charges. That keeps the B channels open for voice calls or larger data transactions. The D channel may also be used to provide Always On/Dynamic ISDN.

Finally, there's videoconferencing. With ISDN, you're not limited to calling your ISP. You can place a direct, high-speed call to a friend or colleague who also has ISDN, turn on your desktop video cameras, and talk face to face. Well, almost.

Connecting via ADSL

The telecommunications industry learned hard lessons from its struggle to sell ISDN. As a result, ADSL not only is faster than ISDN, but it also is simpler to install. New standards should further improve ADSL's ease of use.

Choosing an ADSL Modem

The market for ADSL equipment hasn't been as open as that for ISDN. The service is relatively new and implementation has varied from provider to provider. A modem that works with one provider's ADSL service isn't guaranteed to work with another's. As a result, ordering ADSL has meant buying the modem and the ADSL line from the same provider. (It has sometimes meant changing ISPs, as well, since only some of them provide ADSL access.)

The new G.Lite standard should improve the situation. Expect modem vendors to begin producing G.Lite equipment and selling it directly to consumers. But until the standard is widely adopted, play it safe. Before buying any modem, talk to your ADSL service provider to make sure the modem will work with its service.

G.Lite should also improve installation. One of the costs that providers *and* consumers want to eliminate is the need to have an installer come to your house. With most ADSL modems, the installer has to put in a *splitter*, a small device that separates the voice signal from the data signal on the line. G.Lite's "splitterless" design makes that visit unnecessary. As soon as your phone line has ADSL service, you can connect the modem to the wall jack, plug in a phone to the back of the modem, and finish the setup yourself.

Some computer manufacturers are starting to install splitterless ADSL modems as an option. These modems aren't necessarily G.Lite-compliant, although you may be able to upgrade them to G.Lite.

ADSL modems are available as external and internal models for desktop computers. The G.Lite standard should help to make PC Cards available for laptops.

If you get an external modem, it may need to connect to an Ethernet card or other network card in your computer. Many computers come with a built-in Ethernet adapter. Some ADSL modems take advantage of the new *Universal Serial Bus* (*USB*) ports and connect there instead. That means you don't have to open your computer to install an Ethernet card.

If you plan to use a phone or fax machine on your ADSL line, make sure the modem has a phone jack. If possible, choose a model with a built-in telephone filter.

Finally, if you want to tap in to ADSL speeds that are higher than G.Lite's 1.544Mbps—and some providers do support that, for a price—make sure that your modem can handle those speeds. Hybrid G.Lite/ADSL modems should be available.

Ordering an ADSL Line

The hardest part of ordering an ADSL line is having a phone line that qualifies for the service. Like ISDN, ADSL is sensitive to distance from the phone company's central office, and to the condition of the network. Depending on those factors, you might be limited to lower ADSL speeds (1.544Mbps or less), or you might not be able to get the service at all.

Many ADSL providers give you a choice of different speeds for different prices. You may need to schedule an installation visit if your modem requires a splitter. If you are adding a new phone line instead of converting an existing one, you definitely need an installer's assistance.

 With ADSL (unlike ISDN), you don't have to worry about ordering phone features such as Caller ID or three-way conferencing. If you have those features now, they'll still be there after your phone line is converted to ADSL.

Configuring Your Computer for ADSL

Physical installation of an ADSL modem is straightforward. The modem, internal or external, is connected to the ADSL line wall jack. An external modem also plugs in to a power source. A phone or fax machine may connect directly to a splitterless modem, or may instead need to be connected to a splitter on the phone line.

Follow the manufacturer's directions for installing the hardware driver, so that your computer can access the new modem. Depending on what type of computer and modem you have, the computer may automatically detect the modem and choose the appropriate driver.

The rest of the configuration is simpler than for ISDN: no SPIDs, no switch types, and no dial-up connections. Your ADSL provider or modem manufacturer can tell you how to make sure that the TCP/IP network protocol is loaded. If you're getting a new ISP, you also enter its IP address, host name, domain name, mail server, and news server information. See Chapter 1 for more details.

If you are buying a complete ADSL package from one company, you usually get shrink-wrapped software for its ISP service. The software takes you through the installation of a customized browser, e-mail program, and other components. Check with the ISP if you prefer to use the software that you have now. You need to configure it to work with the ISP's service.

Using ADSL

ADSL provides a high-speed data channel for Internet access, and a voice line for phone or fax calls. Both can be shared. Extension phones can simply be plugged in to wall jacks in other rooms (although you may want to add filters for them). To connect multiple computers, you need to buy a *hub* or perhaps a router. An inexpensive Ethernet hub works well for a two-computer household. Connect the modem to the hub and then connect each computer's Ethernet card to a port on the hub. You may need to purchase from your ISP separate IP addresses for each computer. For more information on this solution (and alternative configurations), see the Web site **http://www.tuketu.com/dsl/xdsl.htm** or **http://www.timhiggins.com/ppd/sharing.htm**. The latter site is about sharing cable modem access, but the principles are the same.

The main use of ADSL is as a high-speed connection, either to the Internet or to your office network for telecommuting. ADSL is appealing because:

- ■ *It's always on.* You don't have to connect and disconnect, you don't have to watch your time online, and the information on your desktop is always up-to-date.

- ■ *It's fast.* Audio and video presentations become much more enjoyable, multimegabyte software downloads take minutes instead of hours, and interactive games are more responsive.

ADSL boosters tout its use for videoconferencing. ADSL *is* many times faster than ISDN, even upstream. But most people will be using ADSL to go through the Internet, rather than to call another person directly. That means the speed and quality of your videoconference still depend on all the components between you and the other person.

Connecting via Cable Modem

Setting up cable modem service is more straightforward than for ISDN or even for ADSL, because you don't have to make very many choices. If you can get cable modem service in your neighborhood, it's typically through your cable TV company. It rents you a modem that works with its equipment, and arranges for installation of the line, the modem, and (to some extent) the software.

You don't have to make any decisions about phones or fax machines, because they can't be attached to a cable. If you want a phone in your home office, you need to keep your existing phone line.

Modem manufacturers and cable companies are converging on a standard called *data-over-cable service interface specification (DOCSIS)*. Eventually, DOCSIS will give you more choices in selecting a modem. But before you buy any modem, talk to your cable modem provider to make sure that the modem will work with the provider's service.

Hopefully, DOCSIS will streamline installation. Cable modem service providers, like ADSL providers, want to connect you to their service without having to send an installer to your house.

Ordering Cable Modem Service

Today, when you order cable modem service, an installer visits your house. He or she adds a splitter to your cable line and runs a new cable to the room where your computer is—unless you're ready to sacrifice the cable running to your TV.

If your cable modem service uses telephone return for the upstream channel—that is, if the data that you send has to go over a phone line—then you need a phone line in the room where your computer is. That phone line can't be used for voice calls or faxing while you're online.

Currently, cable modem service includes ISP service. In fact, some cable modem providers have very elaborate *portals*—home pages rich with news and information. (See Chapter 18 for more on portals.) ISP costs are included in the price of cable modem service, although you may want to keep an additional account with your current ISP for remote access. There is pressure for this to change, especially from competitors, who are calling for the "unbundling" of cable modem service. If this happens, you will be able to choose the cable line, the equipment, and the ISP separately. Cable companies may, in the meantime, strike deals with individual ISPs.

Configuring Your Computer for Cable Modem Service

Once the splitter and new cable are in place, cable modem installation is similar to ADSL modem installation. The cable line connects to the modem, and the modem connects to a power source and to either an Ethernet card or USB port on your computer. Follow the provider's or modem manufacturer's instructions for installing hardware drivers.

Your cable modem provider or modem manufacturer can tell you how to make sure that the TCP/IP network protocol is loaded. You also enter the IP address, host name, domain name, mail server, and news server information for the cable company's ISP. (See Chapter 1 for more details.)

You usually receive shrink-wrapped software for the cable company's ISP service. The software leads you through the installation of a customized browser, e-mail program, and other components. If you prefer to use the software that you already have, you need to configure it to work with the ISP's service. And if you're keeping a separate dial-up ISP for remote access, you need to configure your programs to point to that ISP's mail and news servers.

In most cases, the installer who puts in the splitter and new cable can also install your modem and software, too. Bear in mind that the installer may know more about cables than computers. He or she is probably following a checklist for standard software installation. Make sure that you understand any changes the installer makes to your computer. If you have questions about customizing your installation, contact your provider's technical support help line.

At this point, you may be eager to go online. Before you do, *turn off file sharing*. When it's on, other cable modem users may have access through the network to your files and printers. If you're determined to keep file sharing turned on, at least assign a password to any shared disks, devices, folders, or files. (In Windows 98, choose Start | Settings | Control Panel and run the Network program to display the Network dialog box. On the Configuration tab, click the File and Print Sharing button.)

Using Cable Modem Service

Cable modem speed can certainly be shared among computers in a household. As with ADSL, a hub or router gives your computers access to the modem. You may need to purchase from your ISP separate IP addresses for each computer. For more details on this solution (and alternative configurations), see **http://www.timhiggins.com/ ppd/sharing.htm**.

Cable modem service, like ADSL, is always on and is fast, and its list of benefits is the same: up-to-date information, fast access to audio and video, rapid downloads, and more responsive games.

Once you have cable modem service or ADSL, it's hard to go back to anything slower. Industry pundits like to talk about computers becoming convenient information "appliances." With an always-on, high-speed Internet connection, your computer comes much closer to being that kind of device.

The Complete Reference

Internet

Chapter 4

Intranets: Connecting LANs to the Internet

T he Internet isn't the only computer network: private computer networks have existed for years. Most large organizations have *local area networks* (*LANs*), networks of computers connected by cables, usually in one building or campus, that allow their computers to share files, printers, e-mail, and other resources. But the amazing growth of the Internet has changed the way users look at LANs. A new kind of LAN has emerged—the intranet—that allows people to access information within the organization by using Web browsers and other Internet programs. This chapter defines intranets, explains what components make up an intranet, and lists the general steps for creating an intranet. This chapter also describes programs that you can use to connect a small LAN (for example, a few networked computers at home or in a small office) to the Internet.

 Because intranets are so new, some of the terminology (and all the technology) is changing fast. After getting the basics from this chapter, be sure to visit some of the Web sites listed at the end of the chapter.

What Is an Intranet?

An *intranet* is a private network (usually a LAN, but may be larger) that uses TCP/IP and other Internet standard protocols. Because it uses TCP/IP (which is described in Chapter 1), the standard Internet communications protocol, an intranet can support TCP/IP-based protocols, such as HTTP (the protocol that Web browsers use to talk to Web servers), and SMTP and POP (the protocols that e-mail client programs use to send and receive mail). In other words, an intranet can run Web servers, Web clients, mail servers, and mail clients—it can work like a small, private Internet.

As the Web has become the most talked-about Internet service, intranets are also known as *internal webs*, because they allow an organization to have its own private Web sites for use only by users on the intranet. However, like the Internet, most intranets also carry lots of e-mail traffic: all those paper memos that used to float around large organizations have largely been replaced by e-mail messages.

Intranets vs. LANs

An intranet starts with a LAN and adds Internet protocols services. What's the advantage of running Internet protocols on your private network? Some LANs have their own transport protocols: NetBEUI (from Microsoft) and IPX/SPX (from Novell) are both commonly used LAN communications protocols. These protocols do a good job for file sharing and printer sharing on a LAN, but they aren't Internet-compatible and they don't support Web browsers and Web servers. Luckily, you don't have to choose between a LAN communication protocol and TCP/IP. In most cases, you can run both simultaneously—the computers on your network use a LAN protocol, such as NetBEUI or IPX/SPX, to share files or send information to a shared printer, and use TCP/IP to request Web pages. Most LANs of any size are converting to TCP/IP.

An intranet can run on a network larger than a LAN, too, such as *wide area networks* (*WANs*), the networks that large organizations use to connect geographically separate locations. An intranet can be three networked computers, a LAN of two hundred computers in a building, or six large LANs interconnected as a WAN. You can also create an *extranet*, an intranet that allows people to connect into the network over the Internet. For example, if your organization sends salespeople out into the field, they could connect to the Internet, and then use extranet features to connect to your organization's intranet.

On the other hand, if all you need is for everyone on your LAN to be able to view a private set of Web pages, you don't need an intranet nor a Web server. By using the File | Open command of almost any browser, you can view Web pages stored on any hard disk that is accessible over the network. Instead of using Web server URLs that start with **http://**, you can specify the hard disk and path name of the Web page to display by using file URLs that start with **file:///** (yes, that's three slashes). For example, you can make an internal home page for your small organization, store it on a hard disk that is accessible from all the computers on the LAN, and set it as the home page of your users' browsers.

Advantages and Disadvantages of an Intranet

LANs and intranets both let you share hardware, software, and information by connecting computers together. You don't need an intranet to share files and printers, or to send e-mail among the people on your network: a LAN can do those jobs. The following are some reasons to convert a LAN to an intranet, or to connect your computers together into an intranet:

- *Intranets use standard protocols.* Internet protocols such as TCP/IP are used on a huge number of diverse computers. More development is happening for Internet-based communication than other types of communication. For example, intranet users can choose from a wide variety of e-mail programs, because so many have been written for the Internet.

- *Intranets are scalable.* TCP/IP works fine on the Internet, which has millions of host computers. So you don't have to worry about your network outgrowing its communications protocol.

- *Intranet components are relatively cheap—and some are free.* Because the Internet started as an academic and military network (rather than a commercial one), there's a long tradition of free, cheap, and cooperative software development. Some of the best Internet software is free, including Apache (the most widely used Web server), Pegasus, and Eudora Lite (two excellent e-mail client programs).

- *Intranets enable you to set up Internet-style information services.* You can have your own private Web, using Web servers on your intranet to serve Web pages to members of your organization only (see the next section). You can also support chat, Usenet, telnet, FTP, or other Internet services privately on your network. Push technology (Web channels) can deliver assignments, job status, and group schedules to the user's desktop via his or her browser.

■ *Intranets let people share their information.* Everyone in your organization can make their information available to other employees by creating Web pages for the intranet. Because many word processing programs can now save documents as Web pages, creating pages for an intranet doesn't require a lot of training. Rather than printing and distributing reports, people can put them on the intranet and send e-mail to tell everyone where the report is stored.

Of course, intranets have some disadvantages, too, including these:

■ *Intranets cost money.* You may need to upgrade computers, buy new software, run new cabling, and teach people to use the new systems.

■ *People in your organization may waste time.* If you connect your intranet to the Internet, people may spend hours a week watching sports results or checking their stock options. Even if you don't connect to the Internet, people can use the intranet to build Web sites about the company softball team and send e-mail about upcoming baby showers. You'll need policies in place to determine how the intranet may be used.

What Can You Do with an Intranet?

Many organizations, especially those with large existing computer systems, have lots of information that is hard to get at. The intranet can change all that, by using Internet tools. Here are some ideas for ways that your organization—large or small—can use an intranet.

■ **E-mail within the organization and to and from the Internet**   People can use one e-mail program to exchange mail both with other intranet users and with the Internet.

■ **Private discussion groups**   Using a mailing list manager (described in Chapter 12) or a news server (described in Chapter 13) accessible only to people in your organization, you can set up mailing lists or newsgroups to encourage people to share information within departments or across the organization.

■ **Private Web sites**   Each department in your organization can create a Web site that is accessible only to people on the intranet. Instead of circulating memos and handbooks, information can go on these Web sites. For example, the human resources department can post all employee policies, job postings, and upcoming training opportunities. The marketing department can post information about products, including upcoming release dates, how products are targeted, and other information that isn't appropriate for a public site on the Internet-based Web. Every department can post Web pages to share its information with the other departments in the organization. By using the intranet instead of printing on paper, it's economical to publish large documents and documents that change frequently.

- **Access to legacy databases**   If your organization has information that's locked away in an inaccessible database, you can convert the information to Web pages so that everyone on the intranet can see it. (*Legacy* systems are those considered outdated by whoever is describing the system.) For example, a nonprofit organization might have a proprietary database containing all of its fundraising and membership information. By using a program that can display database information as Web pages and enter information from Web page forms into the database, all the people at the nonprofit organization can see, and even update, selected information from the database by using only a Web browser. Naturally, the program would need to limit who could see and change particular information in the database.

- **Teleconferencing**   Rather than spend big bucks on video teleconferencing systems, think about using your intranet (and the Internet), instead. If your organization has offices in several locations, you can use the Internet for online chats with text, voice, shared whiteboards, and even limited video. (See Chapter 17 for a description of Internet-based conferencing.)

Components of an Intranet

This section presents the components that make up an intranet, including computers (workstations and servers), cabling, and software.

Workstations and Client Software

Most of the computers that are connected together by an intranet are *workstations*—computers that are used directly by people. Workstations are the PCs that users probably already have sitting on their desks. A workstation can be almost any computer—a PC running Windows (98, 95, NT, or 3.1), a Macintosh, or a computer running UNIX. One intranet can combine different types of workstations: Windows, Macs, and UNIX computers. Each workstation's operating system must be able to support networking: Windows 98, Windows 95, Macs, and UNIX have networking built in. You'll probably find that older computers (PCs running Windows 3.1 or DOS, and older Macs) need hardware and operating system upgrades. (You can install TCP/IP software on Windows 3.1 and DOS computers, but it's a lot of extra work!)

In addition to other application programs, workstations run *client programs*, software that provides the user with access to network servers. On an intranet, workstations might run e-mail clients (such as Eudora, Outlook Express, or Netscape Messenger), Web browsers (such as Netscape Navigator or Internet Explorer), newsreaders (such as Outlook Express, Netscape Collabra, or Free Agent), or chat programs (such as mIRC or Ircle). In fact, intranet workstations can run any standard Internet client programs. These Internet client programs can give users access to both intranet and Internet services, if your intranet is connected to the Internet.

Servers and Network Operating Systems

Most intranets—all except the smallest networks—include computers that are not used directly by people. Instead, these servers provide services to the intranet. For example, a *file server* stores files to be shared by users on the network, a *print server* controls a printer that network users can print on, a *Web server* provides Web pages, and a *mail server* controls incoming and/or outgoing mail messages.

Like a workstation, a server can be almost any computer. Except on the tiniest intranets, server computers run a *network operating system* (*NOS*). Windows 98 and 95 come with some networking capabilities built in, but for larger networks, servers usually run Windows NT or a NOS such as Novell NetWare, Banyan VINES, Apple Open Transport (for Macs only), or UNIX (or Linux, a freeware version of UNIX).

Servers also run *server software*, such as Web server software, mail server software, or a mailing list manager. Many intranet server programs run on UNIX, some on Windows 98 and NT, and a few on Macs. If you have a UNIX server, you can run lots of freeware and shareware server programs that are used on Internet host computers (for example, the Apache Web server, and standard UNIX mail programs, such as sendmail). Windows NT servers come with a Web server (Microsoft Internet Information Server).

For lists of server software that runs on UNIX, Windows NT, and other platforms, visit the ServerWatch Web site at **http://serverwatch.internet.com**. This site includes listings of Web servers, e-mail servers, chat servers, mailing list servers, and other types of servers.

An intranet can have one or many servers, and they can either all run the same NOS or run different ones. For example, a medium-sized intranet might have two Novell NetWare servers—one to handle file and printer sharing and one to handle routing e-mail within the intranet—and a UNIX server to route e-mail to and from the Internet and to run Web server and mailing-list server software. On large networks, each server computer runs only one server program, which occupies it full-time.

Your intranet may also run *middleware*, software that translates between application programs and the intranet. Middleware can provide access to a database from a Web browser, for example, by using calls to the database program to read and write records, and by creating Web pages on-the-fly as the user requests database information.

Network Cards, Cabling, and Hubs

A critical component of any intranet is the cabling and other hardware that connect the computers together. (Wireless LANs exist, but they require boxes to allow the computers to communicate without cabling.) The most widely used method for connecting computers to a LAN is called *Ethernet*. (Its main competitor, token ring, is declining in popularity.)

Several different Ethernet cabling schemes (or *topologies*) exist, and the two most popular are the star and bus topologies, shown in Figure 4-1. There are two commonly used types of cable, too: most bus networks use thin coaxial cable, while most star networks use unshielded twisted-pair (UTP) cable. (Star networks can also use coax.)

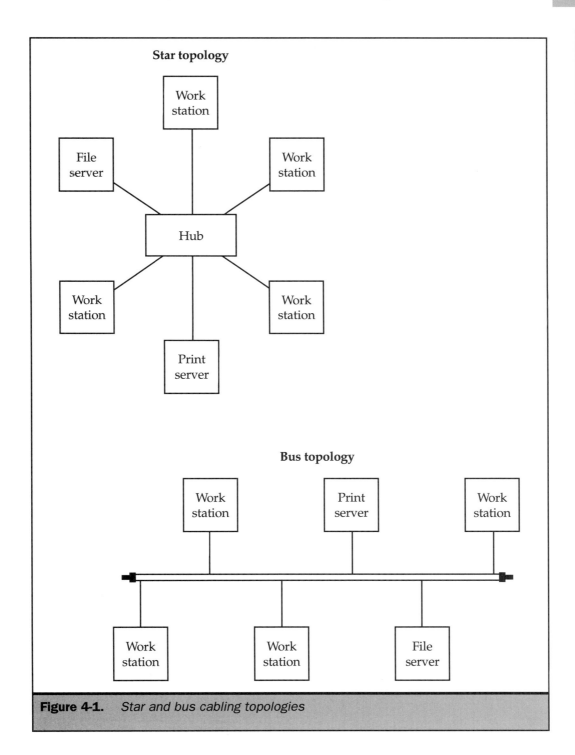

Figure 4-1. *Star and bus cabling topologies*

To connect the cable to the computers, each workstation and server needs an Ethernet *network adapter*, which is either an adapter card that installs inside a desktop computer or laptop base station, or a PC Card that installs in a laptop. Star topology networks also need a *hub*—a box to which cables from all the workstations connect—to serve as the center of the star.

For information on choosing and designing the cabling system for an intranet, see *Intranet Resource Kit*, edited by Prakash Ambegaonkar (Berkeley, CA: Osborne/McGraw-Hill, 1997). If you are setting up a small Windows 98-based intranet, see *Windows 98: The Complete Reference*, Part V, "Networking with Windows 98" (Berkeley, CA: Osborne/McGraw-Hill, 1998).

The Internet Connection

You can set up an intranet that has no connection to the Internet: the intranet can provide e-mail, a private Web, and other Internet-like services to your users, with no access to the Internet itself. However, many intranets connect to the Internet, so that users can send and receive e-mail from the Internet, browse pages on the Web, and use other public Internet services. If you connect your intranet to the Internet, you need to control what Internet services your intranet users can access, as well as what intranet resources the public Internet can access.

To connect your intranet to the Internet, you need an Internet service provider (ISP), described in Chapter 1. Contact ISPs in your area to discuss what kind of connection you need, depending on the size of your intranet, the types of services that you plan to provide to the intranet and the Internet, and the amount of data that you expect to transfer between the intranet and Internet. Your options include:

- A *dial-up line* with a 56K modem, for occasional connections to the Internet and small amounts of data transfer.

- An *ISDN line, ADSL line, or cable modem service* with a modem or adapter, for a faster connection to the Internet that still is not full-time. (See Chapter 3 for information about ISDN and ADSL connections.)

- A *dedicated line*, to connect your intranet to the Internet full-time, with a *router* (a box that connects the dedicated line to a computer). Dedicated lines come in various speeds, including T1 (1.5Mbps) or fractional T1s (one-half or one-quarter of a T1). A router can be a dedicated box (the most popular ones are from Cisco Systems) or a UNIX, Windows NT, or Windows 2000 Server system. (Linux comes with software to do Internet routing.)

The ISP can tell you what kind of hardware you need to connect the line that you choose to your intranet. If you use a modem or ISDN "modem," you make the connection to one computer on the intranet. If you use a router, it connects directly to the intranet. All the computers on the intranet connect to the Internet via this connection, so that each computer doesn't need its own modem, phone line, and account.

For large intranets, you usually can't get enough IP addresses for each computer on your network. Instead, you use *network address translation (NAT),* which translates addresses inside of your network to the network addresses that your ISP assigns to you. Your router handles network address translation for your intranet.

For the smallest intranet, you can use a program such as WinGate or WinProxy, described in the section "Connecting a Small LAN to the Internet" at the end of this chapter, to let all the users on the intranet share one fast modem and Internet connection. WinGate and WinProxy handle network address translation, too.

Security Systems

If your intranet connects to the Internet, you need to control the kinds of information that can pass between the Internet and your intranet. The hardware, software, and procedures that provide access control make up a *firewall* (named after the barrier that stops a fire from spreading from a car engine into the passenger compartment). A firewall can serve the following functions:

- Limit Internet access to e-mail only, so that no other types of information can pass between the intranet and the Internet
- Control who can *telnet* into your intranet (a method of logging in remotely, described in Chapter 40)
- Limit what other kinds of traffic can pass between your intranet and the Internet

A firewall can be simple or complex, depending on how specifically you want to control your Internet traffic. A simple firewall might require only that you configure the software in the router that connects your intranet to your ISP. A more complex firewall might be a computer running UNIX and specialized software. Firewall systems fall into two categories, network-level and application-level.

Network-Level Firewalls

These firewalls examine only the headers of each packet of information passing to or from the Internet. The firewall accepts or rejects packets based on the packet's sender, receiver, and port. (Each Internet service, such as e-mail or the Web, has a different port number.) For example, the firewall might allow e-mail and Web packets to and from any computer on the intranet, but allow telnet (remote login) packets to and from only selected computers.

Application-Level Firewalls

These firewalls handle packets for each Internet service separately, usually by running a program called a *proxy server,* which accepts e-mail, Web, chat, newsgroup, and other packets from computers on the intranet, strips off the information that identifies the source of the packet, and passes it along to the Internet (or vice versa). When the replies return, the proxy server passes the replies back to the computer that sent the original message. To the rest of the Internet, all packets appear to be from the proxy server, so no information leaks out about the individual computers on your intranet. You can configure your proxy server to limit access to Internet services; for example, you can permit outbound telnet packets, so that your users can use telnet to log in to other computers, but refuse inbound telnet packets, so that no one on the Internet can log in to your intranet's computers. A proxy server can also log all the packets that pass by, so that you have a record of who has access to your intranet from the Internet, and vice versa.

Security Policies

In addition to a firewall, you need to take steps to make sure that the intranet is used appropriately in your organization:

- *Establish acceptable-use policies.* Post rules for using the intranet, including the use of e-mail, the Web, and discussion groups both within the intranet and on the Internet.

- *Monitor usage.* We don't mean to suggest that you look over everyone's shoulders while they use the intranet, but make sure that someone monitors the content of the intranet's Web sites and discussion groups. Look for copyright infringements, personnel issues, and security lapses.

- *Close the door behind departing employees.* When someone leaves the organization, make sure that a system is devised to close the person's accounts, change passwords, and deny other access to the intranet.

- *Be vigilant about data in general, not just about the intranet.* The intranet's connection to the Internet can certainly be a security hazard, but important data can also walk out your organization's door on a diskette in someone's pocket, in a fax, or many other ways.

Caution *Firewalls don't protect your intranet against viruses: you need intranet-wide virus-protection software, too.*

For more information about firewalls, see the section "Finding Out More," at the end of this chapter.

Steps for Creating an Intranet

This section provides the general steps to create an intranet. Your exact steps depend on whether you are converting an existing LAN to an intranet or creating a new network, on the size of your intranet, and on whether you plan to connect your intranet to the Internet.

1. Decide on the key applications for your intranet and look at software to perform the application. If you are looking for e-mail, Web pages, and other general Internet services, almost any intranet system will do, but if you need specialized services, your choice of software may dictate the hardware and network operating system for at least one of the servers on your intranet. For example, if an important application for your intranet is to give users access to information in your corporate directory, which runs on a UNIX-based database, your intranet might need at least one UNIX server.

2. Decide whether and how the intranet will connect to the Internet. Shop for an ISP, choose the speed of your Internet connection (56Kbps dial-up, ISDN, ADSL, cable modem service, or dedicated line), and determine what hardware you need. While you are talking to your ISP, get a block of IP addresses for the computers on your intranet and register your domain name (if you don't already have one). (See Chapter 1 for an explanation of IP addresses.)

3. Configure the servers for your intranet. Choose the server programs (such as Web servers and e-mail servers), NOS, and hardware (CPU, RAM, disk drives, modem, and printer). Be sure to include some form of backup media, such as a tape drive.

4. Choose the client software, operating system, and hardware for the workstations on your intranet. You probably already own most of the computers that you want to connect to the intranet. If the computers are old (DOS, Windows 3.1, or older Mac computers), you need to upgrade or replace them. Client software usually includes an e-mail program (such as Pegasus or Eudora) and a browser, as well as other standard Internet programs.

5. Determine your cabling topology, if you are creating a new network. Draw a layout of the network, by working off building blueprints.

6. Configure your Internet connection and firewall, including the router, proxy server software, and other components.

7. If you are adapting a LAN as an intranet, you should already have a security system that is based on the capabilities of your NOSs. If you are creating a new network, you need to learn about your NOS's security system, assign users to groups, make an access profile for each group, and make an access profile for each user.

8. Consider adding an uninterruptible power supply (UPS) for all of your servers. Also, design a procedure for making regular backups of all the servers and workstations on the intranet. Choose a virus protection system.

9. Purchase the hardware, software, cabling, and other items.

10. Back up everything!

11. For each new or upgraded server and workstation, install the new hardware (including network adapters) and operating system, and test that the system runs correctly.

12. If you are running new cable, run the cable and connect each computer according to the layout that you drew. If you are running cable within or through walls, consult an electrician about building codes.

13. If you are creating a new network, configure the servers to communicate over the network. Configure the workstations to communicate over the network. Install and test file and printer sharing services. You now have a working LAN—but it's not an intranet until it runs Internet-like services, too.

14. If you plan an Internet connection, install the router, cabling, or other equipment to connect to the Internet, with help from your ISP. Test communications between the intranet and the Internet.

15. Install and test your mail server, the SMTP gateway for your existing e-mail system, or whatever system will route mail within the intranet and/or to and from the Internet. Install and test e-mail client programs on the workstations.

16. If you plan to have a Web server, install and test the Web server, then install Web browsers on the workstations and test that they can access Web pages stored on the Web server. Now it's an intranet!

17. If you plan to provide other intranet services, such as Usenet newsgroups, mailing lists, or intranet chat, install and test the server software on the servers, and then install and test the client software on the workstations.

18. Configure and test the firewall.

19. Make backups of all the servers and workstations, so that you have a copy of a "clean install" of all the software necessary for the intranet. Institute procedures for regular backups.

20. Teach the users how to use the new facilities of the intranet.

 Make a log book for each server, workstation, router, and other component of your intranet, and log each change that you make. Your logs will make troubleshooting much easier later!

Ongoing Maintenance

After your intranet is up and running, it requires ongoing work to keep it running, including the following tasks:

- Maintain logs for all the intranet servers. If you can maintain logs for all the workstations, too, do so, although users may install their own software.

- Keep up with news about new versions of the software that you use, and decide when to upgrade. You usually don't need to install each new version of every program, but if you get too many versions behind, you'll have trouble getting support if you have a problem.

- Teach the users of the intranet how to use e-mail, Web browsers, and other intranet facilities. Also, teach the acceptable use policy for your organization, as well as other standard procedures. Teach users to create Web pages, manage mailing lists, and create and maintain other intranet resources.

- Make regular backups of all the servers and workstations on the intranet.

Connecting a Small LAN to the Internet

If you have a tiny Windows-based LAN—two or three computers in a home office or small business—you can turn it into an intranet by using a product such as WinGate (or WinProxy, which works similarly to WinGate). WinGate allows all the users on a LAN to share a modem on one computer, and on one Internet account. When any user on the intranet tries to communicate with the Internet—for example, by running a Web browser or clicking the Check Mail button in an e-mail program—the request is routed to WinGate. WinGate connects to the Internet (if it is not already connected) and sends the request out to the Internet. When information comes from the Internet, WinGate routes the information to the computer that requested it. WinGate also serves as a proxy server, providing a firewall between your intranet and the Internet (refer to the section "Security Systems," earlier in this chapter).

WinGate requires you to assign an IP address (defined in Chapter 1) to each of the computers on your intranet. If your ISP gives you an IP address for each of your computers, go ahead and use them, but this situation is highly unlikely. (Most ISPs don't assign permanent IP addresses; instead, they assign you a temporary IP address each time that you connect to the Internet.) Luckily, you don't need to get IP addresses from your ISP. You can use a set of special addresses that are never used on the Internet: the IP addresses in the range from 192.168.0.1 through 192.168.0.255 (or one of several other unused ranges). These "private" IP addresses are never visible to the rest of the Internet, because WinGate translates all IP addresses before releasing them to the Internet. These IP addresses are used only for communication within your intranet.

WinGate (**http://www.wingate.com**) and WinProxy (**http://www.winproxy.com**) both run on Windows 98, Windows 95, and Windows NT, and both are available for download and purchase at their respective Web sites. To use WinGate or WinProxy, follow these general steps (see the instructions that come with the program for details):

1. Get the program from its Web site. The cost of the license depends on the number of computers on your intranet.

2. Install the program on one computer (the one with the fastest modem).

3. Configure the program to connect to the Internet by using an existing Dial-Up Networking connection (see Chapter 2).

4. Configure the various Internet services—e-mail, Web browsing, and any other services that you intend to use.

5. Assign a private IP address to each of the computers on your intranet, starting with 192.168.0.1 for the computer on which WinGate or WinProxy runs.

6. Configure each of the computers on the intranet to use WinGate or WinProxy for communication with the Internet, by configuring each e-mail program, Web browser, or other client program to communicate through the proxy server at IP address 192.168.0.1.

Once your mini-intranet is up and running, you can run a mail server, a Web server, or other servers just as you would on a larger intranet. For example, Windows 98 comes with Personal Web Server, which can serve as a Web server for a small intranet.

Finding Out More

Here are other places that you can learn about intranets:

- Read the Intranet FAQ, at **http://www.innergy.com/ifaq.html**.

- For information about firewalls, see the Internet Firewalls Frequently Asked Questions Web site, at **http://www.interhack.net/pubs/fwfaq**, or the Rotherwick Firewall Resource, at **http://www.zeuros.co.uk/firewall**.

- The Usenet newsgroup **comp.infosystems.intranet** discusses general intranet issues. You might also want to read the newsgroups in the **comp.infosystems.www.servers** hierarchy for information about Web servers, and the **comp.security.misc** newsgroup for intranet security. You can also read the **com.security.firewalls** Usenet newsgroup for information on connecting your intranet to the Internet through a firewall. (See Chapter 13 for directions on how to read Usenet newsgroups.)

- One mailing list discusses intranets, at **intranet@egroups.com**. To subscribe, go to the eGroups Web site at **http://www.egroups.com** or send a blank message to **intranet-subscribe@egroups.com**. There is also a mailing list about firewalls, **firewalls@greatcircle.com**. Send the command **subscribe firewalls** to **majordomo@greatcircle.com**.

- The following books all provide good information about intranets:

  The Intranet Bible, by Ed Tittel (Foster City, CA: IDG Books Worldwide, 1997)
  Introducing Intranets, by Gordon Benett (Indianapolis, IN: Que Education & Training, 1996)
  Intranet Web Development, by John Desborough (Indianapolis, IN: New Riders, 1996)

- Here is a good book to read to learn about firewalls:

  Building Internet Firewalls, by D. Brent Chapman and Elizabeth D. Zwicky (Sebastopol, CA: O'Reilly & Associates, 1995)

The Complete Reference

Internet

Part II

Exchanging E-mail

The
Complete
Reference

Internet

Chapter 5

E-mail Concepts

E-mail provides a wonderful means of communication. It's nonintrusive—your correspondents can read and answer your e-mail when they have the time to do it. But it's also very quick, far quicker than the U.S. Postal Service's "snail mail." For people who are logged on at work all day, e-mail can be an almost instantaneous way to communicate. E-mail has its drawbacks too: because e-mail is more casual than a letter or a memo, some people find they write things in an e-mail that they would never write in a regular letter. And because e-mail lacks the nuances of face-to-face or phone conversation, an e-mail message can be more easily misunderstood than verbal communication.

If you're not into e-mail already, you should be—e-mail is often the beginning of a foray into the Internet. The technical stuff can be complicated, but it doesn't have to be. This chapter explains e-mail concepts, and the rest of the chapters in this part of the book can help you with the technical side, so that you can get on with communicating.

How Do You Get Your E-mail?

How does e-mail work, anyway? In this book, discussions about e-mail refer to Internet e-mail. You may also get mail on an internal network, such as within your office or online service, but that isn't Internet e-mail. However, the majority of what you learn about e-mail in this section of the book also applies to local mail within your office or online service.

You receive Internet e-mail when it's sent to your unique e-mail address. E-mail messages are passed through the Internet by using a protocol called *Simple Mail Transfer Protocol (SMTP)*. SMTP is understood by all e-mail applications that package your Internet e-mail message for sending, and by all the computers (servers) that pass the message along its route.

Receiving Incoming Messages

How you collect and read your e-mail depends on how you're attached to the Internet. Most people don't have a computer that is permanently attached to the Internet— instead, they dial in when they want to do Internet stuff (including picking up and sending e-mail), and then disconnect when they're done. But since e-mail can arrive at any time, you need an e-mail *mailbox* that resides on a *mail server*, a computer that is permanently attached to the Internet (barring unforeseen problems) and is set up to handle your incoming e-mail. Like your postal service mailbox, the mail server is able to accept e-mail at any time and store it until you delete it. Depending on the type of connection that you have, you may download e-mail from the mail server to your computer, or you may read your e-mail while it sits on the mail server.

Mail servers receive and store e-mail messages in mailboxes by using a protocol called *Post Office Protocol (POP)* or *POP3* (since the current version of POP is version 3). Mail servers are sometimes also called *POP servers*.

To read your e-mail, you need an e-mail application (also called a *mail client* or *POP client*), such as Outlook or Eudora. A *client* application works in concert with a *server*—in the case of e-mail, a mail server collects your e-mail, and your mail client enables you to read it.

Sending Outgoing Messages

Sending e-mail requires a similar process. You write messages on your own computer by using your e-mail application. Then, you (or the e-mail application) transfer the messages to an *SMTP server*—a mail server that accepts outgoing e-mail. Your Internet service provider (ISP) probably runs both an SMTP server and a POP server for its customers: the SMTP server that takes care of sending your e-mail messages may be a different server than the POP server that collects your e-mail.

Ways of Accessing E-mail

There are a variety of ways to access your e-mail:

■ You may use a mail client, such as Eudora, Outlook, or any one of the other popular packages that downloads your incoming messages from the POP server to your computer and uploads your outgoing messages to the SMTP server. This may occur through a *local area network (LAN)* or through a dial-up connection. Mail clients are described in Chapter 6, including how to send, receive, reply to, forward, save, and print messages.

■ You may use a Web-based e-mail service. These Web sites are described in the section "Web-Based E-mail," later in this chapter.

■ You may use a commercial provider, such as CompuServe or America Online, which have their own e-mail programs.

■ You may get your e-mail through a LAN, a common system at large organizations. If your organization has some sort of Internet connection, e-mail arrives in the company's POP server. You then read your e-mail either on the server, using an e-mail application, or on your own computer, by downloading your e-mail from the server through the LAN by using an e-mail application. Your company may use a POP server or some kind of proprietary protocol (for instance, Lotus's cc:Mail, which is not a POP mail client). See Chapter 4 for more information about accessing the Internet over a LAN.

■ You may have a UNIX shell account (described in Chapter 40) and use a UNIX e-mail program (such as Pine, Elm, or Mutt) that reads your POP mailbox directly. Pine is described in Chapter 6.

E-mail Addressing

To send e-mail to someone, you must know his or her Internet e-mail address. Unlike the postal service, which can often deliver imprecisely addressed letters, the mechanics of the Internet require an exact e-mail address.

Internet e-mail addresses look like this:

sneezy@grimm.com

The e-mail address has two main parts, joined by @ (the at sign):

- **Username** In the preceding example, the username is *sneezy*. Usernames are usually pretty straightforward; often, companies give employees usernames that use one initial and one full name, like *jsmith*. However, usernames can also contain characters other than letters—they can contain numbers, underscores, periods, and some other special characters. They can't contain commas, spaces, or parentheses.

- **Host or domain name** In the prior example, *grimm.com* is the host name. The host name provides the Internet location of the mailbox, usually the name of a computer owned by a company or Internet service. For more about host names, see Chapter 1.

When people pronounce an e-mail address they call the @ symbol "at" and the period "dot;" for example "sneezy at grimm dot com."

Tip	*The e-mail address to write to with comments about this book is **nettcr@gurus.com**.*

Here are some other points about addresses:

- Capitalization usually isn't important in e-mail addresses (sometimes referred to as *case insensitive*). For example, **NetTCR@Gurus.Com** works just the same as **nettcr@gurus.com**. Of course, if you're sure that you have the right address, but you're getting error messages, you may want to try different capitalization.

- E-mail addresses do not have punctuation marks (such as square brackets or quotes) around them. You may see e-mail addresses displayed with extra punctuation, but when you send a message to the e-mail address, make sure to remove the extra characters. In addition, e-mail addresses never end with punctuation—so if you see one that does, it's almost definitely incorrect. Don't be confused when an e-mail address appears at the end of a sentence—the period is not part of the address!

- Most e-mail programs allow you to type angle brackets (<>) around e-mail addresses. You can also precede an e-mail address with the person's name in quotes. For example, the address for this book might appear like this:

"Internet Complete Reference book" <nettcr@gurus.com>

Local vs. Internet Addresses

The standard e-mail addresses just explained may not apply when you send e-mail within an organization. Your "in house" (and that may mean within your company or within your Internet service provider) addresses may not look at all like the ones explained here—you may be able to send mail to Jane Smith—with no @ sign and no periods. This all depends on the e-mail system that you are using—but if you are sending e-mail through the Internet, you *do* need to use an address that follows the naming conventions outlined here.

AOL Addresses

AOL addresses consist of the AOL *screen name* (the account name, or an additional name that the user has set up) followed by *@aol.com*. Screen names can contain spaces, and when one AOL user writes to another, spaces can be included in the address. But when sending mail over the Internet to an AOL account, omit the spaces in the screen name.

More About Host Names

All host names consist of at least two parts: the second-level domain (*grimm* in the preceding example given in the section, "E-mail Addressing") and the top-level domain or zone (*com* in the preceding example). Chapter 1 contains details about host names.

Host names can consist of more than two parts: computer names can appear at the beginning. For instance, in the host name **tigger.mediqual.com**, *tigger* is a computer in the domain *mediqual.com*.

You may see e-mail addresses with computer names. You usually do not need to include the computer name when you send e-mail: the main domain name usually gets the message to its recipient. For instance, if you receive e-mail from **alison@tigger.mediqual.com**, you can try replying to **alison@mediqual.com**—in most cases, the shortened e-mail address works fine.

Special Addresses

Many domains have special e-mail addresses that you can use to get information. If you're looking for a particular person and you know the domain name but not the username, you might try writing a very nice e-mail to **postmaster@*domainname.com*** (replacing *domainname.com* with the actual domain name). Other frequently used usernames include *info*, *webmaster*, and *sysadmin*.

Remember that the recipients of e-mail sent to these special addresses are just regular, probably overworked, folks—so be considerate when you make requests.

Message Headers

Every e-mail message sent starts with *headers*—lines of text that tell you about the message. The headers are like the envelope for the message, and include the addresses of the recipient and the sender. If you want to know more about where an e-mail came from, looking at headers can be useful.

Your e-mail package may not automatically show you all message headers—headers make the message look messy. If you check the help system for your e-mail application, under "headers," you should be able to find out how to display them. (See Chapter 6 for how to display the complete headers in several popular e-mail applications.)

Each header consists of the type of header, a colon, and the content of the header. For example, the header that shows who the message is addressed to consists of *To:* followed by one or more e-mail addresses. Headers that start with *X* are always optional headers, and many e-mail applications ignore them.

Table 5-1 lists the standard headers that almost every e-mail message includes, along with some common additional headers. Here is a sample of the complete headers for a message:

```
Delivered-To: nettcr@gurus.com
Received: (qmail 24114 invoked from network); 10 Sep 1998 03:41:55 -0000
Received: from smtp.america.net (199.170.121.14) by ivan.iecc.com with SMTP;
10 Sep 1998 03:41:55 -0000
Received: from PentiumPro (max1-40.shoreham.net [208.144.253.42]) by
smtp.america.net (8.9.1/8.8.7) with SMTP id XAA23871; Wed, 9 Sep 1998
23:41:20 -0400 (EDT)
Message-Id: <3.0.32.19980909223739.008be480@mail.gurus.com>
X-Sender: nettcr@mail.gurus.com
X-Mailer: Windows Eudora Pro Version 3.0 (32)
Date: Wed, 09 Sep 1998 23:41:47 -0400
To: santa@northpole.com
From: Internet Complete Reference Authors <nettcr@gurus.com>
Subject: Re: Low hits on Web site
Cc: info@mcgraw-hill.com
Mime-Version: 1.0
Content-Type: text/plain; charset="us-ascii"
X-UIDL: 68193b0f0132f554cd78c0ae2372eac0
```

Header Type	Description
Date	The date and time the message was sent, according to the sender's computer.
To	The e-mail address(es) of the primary recipient(s) of the message. The To line may also contain names.
From	Who the message is from.
Subject	What the message is about—according to the sender.
Cc	Additional recipient(s) of the message. (Cc is an abbreviation for "carbon copy," a term that is outdated but still in use.)
Date	When the message was sent.
Reply-To or Return-Path	Your e-mail application automatically uses this address when you reply to the message.
Received	Contains information from each host service that relayed the message.
Message-ID	The unique ID that identifies this message (generally not useful).
X-Sender	Adds a layer of authentication to the message by identifying the sender.
X-Mailer	The application used to compose the message (not all e-mail applications add this header to messages).
Mime-Version	The version of MIME used (the Multipurpose Internet Mail Extension is used for attachments and for HTML-formatted messages). (See the section "Formatted E-mail," later in this chapter, for more about MIME.)
Content-Type	The MIME data format used. Frequently, the data format is text/plain with some further information to identify the text type.
Lines	Number of lines of text in the message.
X-UIDL	A unique identifier added by some POP e-mail applications to identify messages that have been downloaded.

Table 5-1. *E-mail Message Headers*

Downloading E-mail

Several technical issues surround reading e-mail, and you may or may not ever have to know about them. However, the topics discussed in this section are not particularly technical, and may even save you money.

This section assumes that you have a dial-up connection to the Internet. These types of connections are now very common for home users, but less so for people who access their e-mail through a corporate system. If you have a dial-up connection, your e-mail is collected on a POP server and your e-mail application downloads the messages to your computer, so that you can read them.

When you use a dial-up connection and e-mail software that downloads your messages, you have the following options:

- You can usually work either offline or online.

- You can choose to either leave downloaded messages on the server or delete them from the server.

Working Offline

Most POP e-mail clients allow you to work offline, which can be a real money saver if your Internet provider charges by the minute or is a long-distance call. Working *offline* means that you read your e-mail by doing the following:

1. Connect to the Internet.

2. Download your e-mail.

3. Disconnect from the Internet.

4. Read your e-mail and write new messages. This is considered working offline—you're doing Internet-related tasks while you're not actually connected to the Internet.

5. Connect to the Internet.

6. Send your new messages and download any new messages that may have arrived.

7. Disconnect from the Internet.

Most of the time that you spend "doing" e-mail consists of reading and writing messages—you don't actually need to be connected to the Internet to do those tasks. Working offline may be as simple as following the preceding steps, or you may have to give your e-mail application a command to let it know when you're online and offline. Try disconnecting from the Internet and working in your e-mail application. (See Chapter 6 for the commands for working offline with several popular e-mail applications).

Deleting Messages from the Server

If a POP server stores your messages until you download them, your e-mail program usually deletes them from the POP server after downloading. Your e-mail application may have a setting that enables you to choose whether to delete the e-mail from the server and, if so, when to delete it. The people who maintain your POP server would greatly appreciate it if you delete your e-mail—in fact, they have every right to insist on it. Otherwise, your mailbox will balloon to an enormous size after a while. However, if your e-mail application supports it, you may want to leave your e-mail on the server for a day or two after you pick it up, so that if anything goes wrong, you can get the message again. See Chapter 6 for details on how to tell several popular e-mail applications when to delete your messages from the POP server.

E-mail Netiquette

E-mail provides a medium to send casual messages quickly. This makes e-mail tremendously useful—but it can also make it annoying, or even worse. For instance, while sending off a short request is easy, it is also easy for that request to sound brusque or even rude. It is usually worthwhile to spend an extra minute or so to write your message in a way that softens the request and doesn't raise the bristles of the recipient.

Netiquette is the term used for etiquette on the Internet—it is a set of suggestions intended to make the Internet community a more pleasant place to be. This section includes some netiquette guidelines for e-mail—you may see other guidelines that agree or disagree with these. Use your own judgment in deciding how to comport yourself online. Although it's a cliché, you should consider how you would feel being on the receiving end of any e-mail that you send, and remember that you are usually writing to a human being, not to a machine.

If you have some e-mail habits that don't gel with the following suggestions, you should reconsider your e-mail habits. While these rules are not enforceable, hanging out on the Internet is much more pleasant for everyone if e-mail doesn't make anyone angry or annoyed for one reason or another.

Netizens (Internet users) should follow these guidelines, to practice good netiquette:

- *Think twice before sending an emotional message.* The speed and ease of e-mail enable you to jot off a quick emotional reply to a message. Once you click send, it's gone—not like a letter that sits in the mailbox for a while—and you may regret it. So, consider letting emotional messages sit for a while before you send them—at least overnight, and sometimes longer.

- *Use the subject line well.* It's a help to both you and your recipient if the subject line tells you both what the message is about. If you store messages, you'll appreciate them having a useful subject line when you go looking for them again.

- *Don't flame. Flaming* is the Internet term for sending messages that contain little information and much vitriol and abuse. Flaming is all too rampant on the Internet, especially in some newsgroups. Messages that are abusive or defamatory are not fun to read or receive.

- *Check spelling and punctuation.* These don't need to be perfect, but don't annoy your friends and colleagues with funny punctuation (one particularly well-educated friend sends e-mail messages that are only punctuated with hyphens and ellipses—yuck!). And certainly make sure that no word is spelled so badly that the recipient has to guess what you mean. E-mail is certainly a casual form of communication, but it shouldn't be a sloppy one!

- *Watch the sarcasm.* Sarcasm isn't always easy to identify without seeing the facial expressions. Using smileys (described in the next section) may help to let people know that you're only kidding, but when in doubt, leave it out.

- *Don't send e-mail to people who don't want it.* Lots of people break this rule—including the people that send messages that advertise software that can be used to send e-mail to millions of people. But doing so is rude, and it costs money to the people who provide Internet resources at minimal cost. Even if you regularly forward jokes or information to a small list of friends, you should check in with your list recipients every now and then to offer them the chance to be removed from your list. See the section "Sending Spam" in Chapter 10.

- *Don't overquote, especially on mailing lists.* Most e-mail applications include the text of the message you're replying to. You should edit that original message to contain only the necessary information. This is especially important if you are sending a message to a newsgroup or mailing list, so that people don't have to see the same text over and over again in every response to a post. Deleting unrelated text is vital if you receive mailing lists in digests (daily collections of many messages), so that you don't send the entire digest in your response.

- *Don't use all capitals or any other weird formatting.* A message in all caps looks like shouting and is much more difficult to read than using mixed case (upper- and lowercase) text. You can use caps to highlight certain words, but you can also enclose words with asterisks or underscores to emphasize them.

- *Send e-mail that everyone can read.* If you're not sure whether your recipients can read formatted text, just send plain text. It's annoying not to be able to read a message, or to have to ignore all the HTML codes to read the text of the message. Don't send attached files unless you have asked the recipient whether they want and can deal with the file. Don't send attached files to mailing lists at all (unless the list has a policy that welcomes attachments).

- *Don't plagiarize.* Most people don't quote text without attribution to the author in a regular letter: don't do it with e-mail either. The author of an e-mail message retains the copyright to the e-mail message. Just because something is posted on the Internet does not mean that the text is in the public domain.

- *Don't pretend you're someone else.* Using a pen name is okay if you don't want people to know who you are, but don't misrepresent yourself and pretend to be someone you aren't. Misleading people is at best impolite, and at worst illegal.

- *Don't send frivolous messages.* If you don't have anything to say, don't say it! This rule applies threefold on mailing lists.

■ *Remember the law.* Laws about defamation, copyright, obscenity, fraudulent misrepresentation, freedom of information, and wrongful discrimination in written communication apply to e-mail messages also. If you have a concern about an unsolicited commercial e-mail message, forward it to the U.S. Federal Trade Commission at **uce@ftc.gov**.

■ *Don't forward chain letters and other junk e-mail.* These schemes are almost always illegal, and they annoy people, because they fill up e-mail mailboxes. Included in this category are bogus virus warnings—if you see a virus warning that looks authentic, *check it out before you send it on to all of your friends!* Most virus warnings are hoaxes. See the following sidebar entitled "Messages Never To Forward," for more information.

Messages Never to Forward

Many e-mail messages that are forwarded around the Internet in good faith are actually hoaxes. Sending these messages is unnecessary and fills people's e-mail boxes. Often, well-connected *Internauts* (Internet users) receive these messages over and over, necessitating many clicks of the Delete button. Many computer hoaxes tell you not to open an e-mail with a certain name. In general, you cannot infect your computer with a virus just by opening an e-mail—in any case, if you use the Internet much, you should install a good virus protection program and update it regularly with the latest virus definitions. You should also check the Web site of the manufacturer of your e-mail client and browser, to see whether any security issues have been found and whether an update of the software has been released to fix them. E-mail clients that handle Java are at special risk.

You can check out a virus warning at **http://ciac.llnl.gov/ciac/CIACHoaxes.html**, a U.S. government site that has a good list of virus and other e-mail hoaxes. Another good place to check to see whether a forwarded message is real is **http://www.snopes.com**, the Urban Legends Reference Pages. For information on real viruses, check out **http://www.search.mcafee.com/villib/query.asp**.

The following are some examples of e-mail hoaxes. Please don't forward any of these, and verify any others before forwarding them:

■ **Chain letters that ask you to send money to make money**   These are always pyramid schemes, and almost always illegal.

■ **Good Times virus**   This is an old hoax—there is no Good Times virus.

■ **Disney giveaway**   Disney is not tracking e-mail and giving away vacations or money. Ditto for Bill Gates.

■ **Modem tax**   The modem tax plan was squelched back in '87.

Using Smileys, Emoticons, and Abbreviations

For better or worse, some users of e-mail tend to enjoy shortcuts, including what have become known as *emoticons* (including smileys) and abbreviations of frequently used terms.

Smileys and Emoticons

Smileys are punctuation used to portray faces or other pictures. For instance, :-) is the standard smiley face—tip your head to the left to see the face. The standard use of a smiley is to indicate a joke when the text might not be clear that the author is kidding. People use a whole range of smileys and other *emoticons* (icons used to indicate emotion, which is usually lacking in written communication). Some of the most common emoticons are listed here:

:-)	Standard smiley face
:)	Alternate smiley face
:-(	Sad face
;-)	Winking face
:-o	Surprised face
&:-)	Smiley with curly hair
<g> or <grin>	Grin or smile
<sigh>	Sigh

For a good list, see **http://net.gurus.com/smileys.html**.

Abbreviations Used in E-mail

Like any group of people, e-mail users have made up abbreviations to save themselves time and to confuse newbies. Frequently used abbreviations in e-mail, as well as in newsgroups, mailing lists, and online chat sessions, include the following:

AKA	Also known as
BFN	Bye for now
BTW	By the way

FAQ	Frequently asked questions (many lists and topics have a list of frequently asked questions—and answers—that they refer you to)
FWIW	For what it's worth
FYI	For your information
IMHO	In my humble opinion
IMNSHO	In my not so humble opinion
IMO	In my opinion
NRN	No response necessary
LOL	Laughing out loud
OTOH	On the other hand
ROTFL	Rolling on the floor, laughing
ROTFLOL	Rolling on the floor, laughing out loud
RTFM	Read the (fine) manual
SNAFU	Situation normal all fouled up
TIA	Thanks in advance
TLA	Three-letter acronym
TTFN	Ta ta for now

You can find a far-too-complete list of abbreviations at BABEL: A Glossary of Computer Oriented Abbreviations and Acronyms, located at **http://www.access.digex.net/~ikind/babel.html**. You might also like the list of acronyms at **http://www.tiac.net/users/scg/jargpge.htm#Jargon**.

A Note About Confidentiality

You may think e-mail is by far the best way to communicate—and you won't find much disagreement from the authors of this book (although other methods sometimes are better). However, as good as e-mail is, you should never consider it to be confidential. Although e-mail is rarely hijacked through technical means, it is extremely easy and often tempting to forward a message—even (and maybe especially) one that the sender has asked you to keep confidential. So, never assume that only the people you send a message to will read it.

Formatted E-mail

E-mail that supports formatting (such as boldface and underlining) is a recent development. In the past, e-mail consisted only of text characters, and the only way to send someone a formatted document was to send it as an attachment (as described in Chapter 7). Now, if both you and your recipient's e-mail support it, you can send formatted e-mail. However, that's a pretty big *if*. Older e-mail packages don't support formatted e-mail. At best, your recipient will see the text of the message without the fancy formatting. At worst, they'll see all the codes that your e-mail package inserts to format the text, and they'll have to struggle to read the actual text. Many readers just press the DELETE key when they receive e-mail with formatting tags.

Formatted e-mail is likely to become more and more common, so you might as well know something about it. Currently, formatted e-mail comes in the following flavors:

- **HTML**   Formatted with HTML tags, just like Web pages. HTML formatting can include text formatting, numbering, bullets, alignment, horizontal lines, backgrounds, hyperlinks, and HTML styles. HTML-formatted e-mail is actually sent using the MIME protocol.

- **Rich text**   This is an older format that can be read by most word processing applications. Rich text formatting can include text formatting, bullets, and alignment.

- **MIME (Multipurpose Internet Mail Extension)**   Formatting created just for e-mail. MIME is also used for attachments (described in Chapter 7). Formatting can include text formatting, pictures, video, sound, and probably more. MIME looks (to a computer) like plain text—to you, it looks like a lot of funny characters. A single MIME message can contain plain text as well as all the fancy formatting and extra stuff.

- **Microsoft Word format**   Outlook enables you to use Microsoft Word and all of its features as your e-mail editor. Formatting can include any formatting that Word is capable of performing.

All of these formats require that the recipient's e-mail application be capable of handling them. Chapter 10 describes how to send formatted e-mail by using some popular e-mail programs.

Signatures and Stationery

Many e-mail programs include two features that save typing when you compose e-mail messages: signatures and stationery.

Signatures

Your name, e-mail address, and other identifying information should appear at the end of each e-mail message you send. To save having to type this information at the end of each message, many e-mail programs allow you to create a *signature*, that is, a file containing the list to be appended to each outgoing message. Chapter 6 describes how to create a signature in some popular e-mail programs.

Signatures generally should be limited to about four lines, so that your regular correspondents don't have to see a long signature each time they receive a message from you. Do include your name, e-mail address, and the organization (if any) you represent. You don't have to include your postal mailing address or phone number, since people who see your signature are more likely to contact you by e-mail. You can include a cute or informative tag line, but keep it short. Long poems, pictures created using lines of punctuation, and other fancy signatures wear thin after multiple viewings.

Stationery

If you send certain messages over and over with minor variations, check to see if your e-mail program lets you define *stationery*—e-mail form letters. Some e-mail programs let you save *stationery files* with the headers and text you want to include in your frequently-sent messages. To compose a message using stationery, you choose the name of the stationery file. You can then edit the message to insert information tailored to the recipient.

Eudora and Pegasus support text-based stationery. Outlook and Outlook Express use formatted stationery, so that the recipients can see the formatting only if their e-mail programs can handle formatted messages. See Chapter 10 for how to use stationery in some popular e-mail programs.

E-mail Attachments

The ability to send attachments was a great stride forward in the development of e-mail—it made collaboration on work over the Internet possible. By attaching files to e-mail, you can exchange documents for revision, pass on spreadsheets for data entry, or send a presentation for review. Of course, you can also attach electronic pictures, sounds, movies—whatever can be put in file form.

Because e-mail was originally designed to convey only text, your e-mail program must convert other types of files to a text-like format that can pass through the Internet mail system. The receiving e-mail program converts the message back to its original format. The following are the three most-common formats for e-mail attachments:

- **MIME**   MIME is the newest and best standard method for sending attachments.
- **Uuencoding**   Uuencoding is the old standard and is the only method supported by some older e-mail applications, especially UNIX e-mail programs.
- **BinHex**   BinHex, the least common format, is used primarily by Mac e-mail programs.

Attaching files to e-mail messages is described in detail in Chapter 7.

Web-Based E-mail

Web-based e-mail is a relatively new entry to the e-mail race, and provides some advantages and disadvantages. The main advantage is that if you can access the Web, you can read your e-mail—you don't have to be at your own computer to access your e-mail application. Also, most Web-based e-mail is free. On the downside, because it's free, you have to look at a lot of ads (someone has to pay for the service), and when you sign up, you are usually asked for personal information, so that specific ads can be selected for you. Also, security is not as good as with regular e-mail. However, for many people, the advantages outweigh the disadvantages. Even if you don't use Web-based e-mail all the time, you may find it useful when you're out of the office. Some people who have a business e-mail address at work use Web-based e-mail for their personal e-mail.

You can read two kinds of messages on the Web:

■ **Messages sent to a Web-only account**   For example, the Hotmail Web site at **http://www.hotmail.com** lets you sign up for a free e-mail mailbox, with a username that you pick. Your address is *username*@**hotmail.com**. You can read messages sent to your Hotmail address only at the Hotmail Web site.

■ **Messages stored in your POP mailbox**   Some Web sites allow you to enter the name of your POP server (the Internet host computer on which your mailbox is stored), your username, and your password. The site then retrieves the messages from your POP mailbox and displays them on a Web page, enabling you to read and respond to them. This service means that you can check your e-mail anytime that you have access to the Web—you don't need access to your regular e-mail application.

If you're choosing a Web-based e-mail service, look at the possibilities (use your favorite search engine to search for "Web-based e-mail" or "free e-mail"). Consider the following when looking for a package that meets your needs:

■ *Does it handle attachments?* If it doesn't handle both MIME and uuencoded attachments, find out which format you need by asking the people that you exchange attachments with which format their e-mail application supports.

■ *Is it free?* If so, can you handle the ads? If not, is the cost reasonable?

■ *Has it been in business long?* E-mail services do go out of business, so select one in the same way that you select any other service. If your e-mail service disappears, it takes your e-mail address (and possibly any messages waiting for you) with it.

- *Does it provide the features you need?* For instance, do you want to be able to forward your e-mail to another e-mail address, or check the spelling in your messages? Can you file messages in folders to keep them organized? Can you filter messages as they arrive?

- *How much space does it give you?* Most Web-based e-mail accounts limit the size of your folders.

- *Does it support formatted messages?* Some Web-based e-mail sites support HTML or other types of formatted messages.

- *Is it easy to use?* For instance, can you easily find your address book and figure out how to do all the common e-mail tasks?

- *How fast is it?* How long does it take the page to load on your system? How long does it take for a message to be delivered or received?

You can find a list of free e-mail services at **http://www.onecom.net/lamiya/email.html**. You may want to look at the following:

- **RocketMail (http://www.rocketmail.com)**   Provides both free e-mail accounts and access to your POP mailbox.

- **Microsoft's HotMail (http://www.hotmail.com)**   Ditto.

- **Yahoo! Mail (http://mail.yahoo.com)**   Comes from a well-respected Web portal company, provides free e-mail accounts, and also lets you read your POP mailbox.

- **Lycosmail (http://www.lycosemail.com)**   Offers both free e-mail and forwarding. It also owns 300 domain names, so you may be able to get an e-mail address such as *yourname@engineer.com*.

Caution   *Web e-mail is less secure than using a POP e-mail client, mainly because someone can click the Back button on your browser to read your e-mail. Someone even more clever can read any e-mail that the browser has stored in its cache. To prevent this, you should, at the very least, log out of the e-mail page and close your browser. For a greater degree of security, also empty the browser cache.*

Truly Free E-mail

Juno (**http://www.juno.com**) provides free e-mail even if you don't have an Internet connection—all you need is a modem. In the U.S., you can call 1-800-654-JUNO for free software.

Mail Away from Home

When you're away from your computer, you may still be able to read your e-mail, even if you don't regularly use a Web-based e-mail service (described in the preceding section). You may be able to dial in to your e-mail provider, or use a Web-based service.

If you use e-mail as part of your job and you travel on business, your e-mail administrator may have a created a way for you to get your e-mail when you're out of the office. You should check with him or her before you try to figure out the methods described here. One method that isn't explained here is to use a product such as Reach Out Remote to dial in to your office LAN, to access its resources—including e-mail.

Dialing In

Even if you usually download e-mail to your own computer, you may also be able to dial in or telnet in to the mail server to read your e-mail when you're not at your computer, but do have access to someone else's computer.

If you use a UNIX shell to access the Internet, you probably use Pine or Elm to read your e-mail. Not too many people use this kind of connection all the time (anymore), although quite a few people can access their e-mail by using Pine or Elm through telnet or a dial-up connection when they are traveling. Check out Chapter 40 for more information on UNIX shell accounts, and Chapter 6 for the basic commands for using Pine.

Reading Your E-mail on the Web

You may be able to use Web-based e-mail on occasion even if you don't use it regularly. RocktMail (**http://www.rocketmail.com**), Yahoo! Mail (**http://mail.yahoo.com**), MailStart (**http://www.mailstart.com**), and HotMail (**http://www.hotmail.com**) all allow you to pick up e-mail that is on a POP mail server.

If your office uses Microsoft's Exchange server for e-mail, you may be able to access your e-mail on the company server through the Web. This service, which converts e-mail into Web pages, is built into Microsoft Exchange Server 5.5, but some additional installation is necessary (the server must be running Microsoft's Web server). Check with your e-mail administrator to see if this service is available.

Common E-mail Error Messages

If you send a message that cannot be delivered, you usually receive an error message, called a *bounce*. Common bounce messages contain a lot of technical verbiage at the top, but if you scroll down, you eventually come to an explanation of the problem. Following the error messages is usually a complete copy of the e-mail that you sent. Here are the most common reasons for e-mail to bounce:

- **Bad address** If you misspell the address, or if the person has closed the account, your message is likely to bounce. Alternatively, your message may be delivered to the wrong person. (Jokes abound about this kind of thing.) The only remedy is to check the address and try again. If you are sure that you have the right e-mail address, you can write to **postmaster@***domain* (where *domain* is the person's mail server) to ask what's wrong.

- **Recipient's mailbox is full** Some Internet accounts (America Online in particular) have a limit on the number of message that can be stored in your mailbox. If you don't check your mail for a long time, the mailbox may fill up. Messages to a full mailbox bounce back to the sender. The only remedy is to wait and send the message later, or to call the recipient and tell the person to check his or her e-mail.

- **ISP trouble** If the recipient's ISP is temporarily offline, you may get a variety of error messages. Some messages may report that there is a temporary "non-fatal" delay and that you don't need to resend the message. Instead, your ISP's mail server keeps retrying your recipient's mail server. Eventually, your ISP's mail server gives up, and you receive a "fatal error" message. You may want to wait a day or two and try sending the message again.

Mail Forwarding

If you have found that your e-mail address changes frequently, you may benefit from an e-mail forwarding service. These services enable you to give out one e-mail address, and then forward your e-mail from that address to whatever e-mail address is most convenient for you to access. To find an e-mail forwarding service, use your favorite search engine to search for "e-mail forwarding." Some of the best known are Pobox (**http://www.pobox.com**), Bigfoot (**http://www.bigfoot.com**), and iFORWARD (**http://www.iforward.com**). Some free Web-based e-mail providers also provide this service.

You may want to pay a fee for this service if you really want it to be permanent—of course, there are no guarantees, but a paid provider is probably less likely to go out of business than a free one.

To forward your e-mail temporarily, you may be able to create a .forward file for your account. If you can log in to your account by using a UNIX shell (described in Chapter 40), you can create a special file named .forward that redirects your e-mail to another e-mail address. When you want to stop forwarding your e-mail, delete the .forward file. Chapter 40 describes how to create a .forward file.

Chapter 6

Basic E-mail Commands

To receive e-mail, you need an e-mail provider, a connection to your provider, and an e-mail client application, such as Eudora or Outlook. (These components are described in Chapter 5.) If your ISP has a Post Office Protocol (POP) server, you have a wide choice of e-mail applications. This chapter lists commands for the most widely used e-mail clients: Eudora, Outlook Express, Outlook 98, Pegasus, and Netscape Messenger, which are available in Mac and Windows versions. CompuServe, an online service, has a POP server, but AOL does not. You can't use most e-mail programs to get your e-mail if you use AOL; instead, you use AOL's own program or its Web site.

Before you can receive e-mail, your ISP must know who you are, your client application must be set up, and someone needs to send you e-mail. This chapter covers how to configure your e-mail program and how to do basic e-mail tasks, such as sending a message, replying to a message, and reading an incoming message. The first section covers some general definitions and should help you no matter which e-mail program you're using. The subsequent sections cover how to do the basic e-mail tasks with three types of e-mail applications: POP clients (Outlook Express, Eudora, Pegasus, Outlook 98, and Netscape), online services (AOL and CompuServe), and one UNIX mail program (Pine).

Common E-mail Tasks

E-mail programs tend to work alike, even down to the keystrokes required to execute a command. Whichever e-mail application you use, you do the same basic tasks—read and send e-mail.

Configuring an E-mail Application

When you install and configure a POP e-mail application, it always asks you for some basic information. The terms may change slightly, but the program needs to know the following:

- Your name (the name that will appear in the From line in messages that you send).
- Your e-mail address.
- Your login name (the name you use to log in to your e-mail provider).
- The incoming mail server on which your e-mail sits until you collect it. (Check with your ISP, but if your e-mail address is **alison@tiac.net**, for example, the server is probably tiac.net.)
- The type of incoming mail server (usually POP or POP3).
- The outgoing mail server (SMTP server) to which you send your outgoing e-mail. (Some e-mail applications assume that your outgoing e-mail goes through the same server as your incoming e-mail, so they don't ask this question.)

The setup process may ask you whether you want to store your password on your computer (so you don't have to type it each time the e-mail program logs in to the mail server). Choose to save your password only if your computer is relatively secure— otherwise, anyone can sit down at your computer and send e-mail using your name.

The setup process may also ask whether you want this e-mail program to be your default e-mail program. The default e-mail program is the one that springs into action when you click a mailto link on a Web page (that is, a link that contains an e-mail address), or otherwise initiate an e-mail message without first opening the e-mail program. If this is the only e-mail program that you are using, then by all means go ahead and make it the default program. If you are just trying it out, you probably want to continue using your other program as the default e-mail application.

If you are switching e-mail programs, several useful options may be available in the programs that you're switching from and to, such as the following:

- If you're just trying out an e-mail program or using a computer that you don't normally use to check e-mail, look for the option that allows you *not* to delete e-mail on your incoming mail server. By not deleting your e-mail, when you go back to your regular computer or regular e-mail program, you can get all of your messages.

- Changing e-mail programs can be a pain if you have lots of saved messages in different folders. Some e-mail programs can convert folders and messages from other programs—an option that you should explore.

- Some e-mail programs offer a redirect command, which allows you to forward a message while retaining the original sender. For example, if you receive a message that should really have gone to someone else, you can redirect the message to the appropriate recipient. If the e-mail program from which you are switching has the redirect feature, you can redirect the messages in your inbox or other folders to yourself, send them, and then receive them again with your new e-mail program.

If you will use the e-mail program to receive e-mail sent to more than one e-mail address, you will have to configure it to do so. More information is available in Chapter 10.

 If you have an Internet account (not AOL or CompuServe), changing which e-mail program you use has no effect on your e-mail address.

Receiving and Sending E-mail

Unless you're using a UNIX system or a computer on a LAN or intranet, it's unlikely that you're always logged on to your Internet provider, which means that you need to take an extra step to send and receive e-mail; otherwise, your outgoing e-mail sits on your computer and your incoming e-mail sits on the mail server. When you create an e-mail message and click the Send button, the message is queued to be sent, but it may not actually be sent until you connect to your ISP and give the command to send (and receive) messages. Most e-mail programs have one command for both sending and receiving e-mail, but some have two separate commands. If your program has one command, it probably has an option that allows you to either send or receive.

Most e-mail programs can be configured to pick up your e-mail automatically every so often, so that you don't have to click a button to see your new messages. You can also configure your operating system to dial the ISP when your e-mail program is ready to pick up your e-mail (see the section "Dialing the Internet Automatically" in Chapter 2). While this ability can be useful, you probably don't want your computer to dial your ISP every ten minutes all night long to check your e-mail. Close the e-mail program to prevent it from making your computer connect to your ISP to check your mail.

Reading E-mail

In most programs, to read an e-mail message, you display your list of incoming messages and then double-click the message information to display the text of the message. Most e-mail programs have an *Inbox*, one of several *folders* that display message summaries. Normally, a message summary appears on one line with the name of the sender, the subject of the message, and a date stamp. Some programs allow you to add different columns to the folder list—for instance, if you belong to mailing lists, it is useful to know who the message was sent to—you may want to add a column for the sender.

Most programs enable you to sort messages—often, you can sort messages by clicking the header that you want to sort by. For instance, if you want to sort by sender, click the header for the From or Sender column. If that doesn't work, look for a menu command that allows you to sort messages.

You may also want to change column widths from their default values. For instance, if you can see only the first names of the people who send you e-mail, you may want to make the From column wider. In most programs, to change column widths, you move the mouse pointer to the right side of the column header and then click and drag the divider to the left or right to make the column narrower or wider.

For a list of the headers that e-mail messages can contain, see the section "Message Headers" in Chapter 5. Most e-mail programs display only the most important headers, hiding the rest. Some programs have a command that lets you see all the headers when you are curious about the sender of a message or how the message got to you. This type of command can be useful when tracing the source of spam (unsolicited commercial e-mail).

Creating Messages

To create a new e-mail message in most e-mail programs, you click a New Message button on the toolbar to display a message composition window. That window contains boxes for several standard headers and a large box in which to type the message (of course, programs may have additional options). To create the message, fill in the headers, type the message, and then click the Send button (or give the send command). You'll see these common headers on e-mail messages:

- **To**   The alias or address of the person or people to whom you are sending the message.

- **Cc**   Additional people to whom you are sending the message. These are usually people for whom the message is informational only, and does not require any action or response by them.

- **Bcc**   Yet more people who will receive the message. Bcc stands for Blind Carbon Copy—that means that the other recipients of the message will not know that the message has been sent to the people who you put in this header.

- **Subject**   The subject of the message. Accuracy here makes it easier for both you and the recipient(s) to find the message later.

- **Attached**   The names of any attached files.

When you send a message, you should be sure to use these headers correctly. Inspect the list or recipients carefully to make sure you actually want to send the message to those people. It is useful to the recipient if you make good use of the Subject line by typing something that identifies the message. For instance, if you're working on the Sunshine project, you might use the subject line "Sunshine project" if you are writing a note to marketing, but if you are writing to someone who also is working on the project, a more specific Subject line differentiates this message from many others about the same project.

Rather than create messages from scratch, you may choose to reply to or forward messages:

- **Replying**   When you reply to a message, the sender's address is automatically put in the To header and the Subject of the original message is reused, preceded by Re, for the reply.

- **Forwarding**   When you forward a message, the subject of the original message is reused, with the prefix Fw (or something similar). You must specify the e-mail address of the recipient of a forwarded message.

- **Redirecting**   Some e-mail programs allow you to redirect messages. Redirecting a message is similar to forwarding a message, except that the message retains the original sender in the From header and adds a notation that the message came through you.

Filing Messages

Nearly all programs in wide use allow you to file messages in multiple folders, so that you can find them later. Some programs let you create folder structures very similar to the folder structure on your hard disk. Others are more limited and require that you designate that a folder hold messages, or only hold other folders.

When you create your folder structure, consider how you might look for messages in the future. Two ways to organize messages are by topic or by sender. Most people find that filing by topic works well. You may want to create subtopics for a topic about which you receive a lot of e-mail.

Most programs allow you to move messages by dragging them from one folder to another, while others require that you select the messages and then use a Move button or command.

If you find that folders aren't enough to help you find the message that you need, look for a Find command. Most programs let you search for a sender or a subject in all of your folders, and some let you search for specific text in the headers or body of the messages.

Addressing E-mail

Sometimes, the most difficult part of sending e-mail is finding the address of the person to whom you want to send the e-mail. After you find it, you should store it so that you don't have to look for it again. Most e-mail programs have some sort of address book—at the least, these address books store names and e-mail addresses, and frequently they store more. Address books often give you the option of calling someone by a nickname or alias. These are short names that are easy to type in the message headers. For instance, you may give your spouse the nickname "honey" so that you don't have to go looking for him in your long list of Matthew's.

The quickest way to use an address from the address book is usually to type the nickname or alias in one of the recipient headers of the new message. Alternatively, you can usually display the address book from the message and select addresses to add to the message.

For ways to find someone's e-mail address, see the section "Finding People" in Chapter 23.

Eudora Pro and Eudora Light

Eudora Pro and Eudora Lite are e-mail programs from QUALCOMM. Eudora has been one of the most popular e-mail programs for years, although recent competitors have reduced its market share. Eudora Lite is the free version of Eudora—it has fewer features, but is still a good e-mail program—especially for the price! A Web-based version of Eudora is also available from QUALCOMM.

This chapter describes the current versions of Eudora Pro (version 4.1) and Eudora Lite (version 3.0.5). You can get Eudora from QUALCOMM'S Web site at **http://eudora. qualcomm.com**. As of this writing, QUALCOMM offers a demo version of Eudora Pro that can be used for 30 days. Eudora Pro and Light are available for Windows 98/95, Windows 3.1, and the Mac. Many Eudora commands work the same way in earlier versions.

 *A great source for information about Eudora is **http://www.cs.nwu.edu/~beim/ eudora,** an unofficial page containing links to Eudora FAQs and other sources of Eudora information.*

Eudora Light and Eudora Pro Highlights

Here are the basic Eudora commands (first select a message in a folder or display it by double-clicking):

Print	Click the Print button on the toolbar, choose File | Print, or click CTRL+P.
Delete	Click the Delete Message(s) button on the toolbar (the first button) or the DELETE key.
Forward	Click the Forward button. You can also choose Message | Forward from the menu.
Reply	Click the Reply or Reply All button on the toolbar, or choose Message | Reply or Message | Reply to All.
Check Spelling	Press CTRL+6 or choose Edit | Check Spelling.

Configuring Eudora

The first time that you open Eudora, it guides you through setting up your account. You can use the Import Settings option if you currently have an e-mail application set up on your computer that uses the same e-mail account that you want to use with Eudora. Eudora can import settings from Outlook 98, Outlook Express, and Netscape Messenger. If you haven't used your e-mail account from the computer that you're working on, you need to use the Create a Brand New E-mail Account setting.

During the setup process, Eudora asks for the information listed in the section "Configuring an E-mail Application," earlier in this chapter. If you ever need to change these settings in Eudora, choose Tools | Options from the menu: the settings that the wizard took you through are all available by clicking the Getting Started icon on the Options dialog box.

Collecting and Reading Messages

To check e-mail manually, either press CTRL+M, click the Check Mail icon on the toolbar (the fourth button on the default toolbar), or choose File | Check Mail. Unless you already checked your e-mail and told Eudora to save your password, Eudora asks for your password now. If you have new e-mail, the letter icon appears on the taskbar. New e-mail appears in the In folder, as shown in Figure 6-1. You can display the In folder by double-clicking In under Eudora Mail in the folder list, or by clicking the Open in Mailbox button on the toolbar (the second button on the default toolbar).

To set Eudora to check your e-mail automatically, choose Tools | Options, click Checking Mail in the Category list, and then change the Check for Mail Every ____

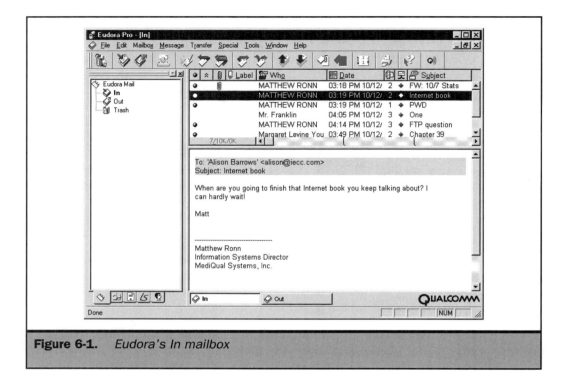

Figure 6-1.   *Eudora's In mailbox*

Minutes setting. If this setting is set to 0, Eudora checks for e-mail only when you give the check mail command by using one of the methods in the previous paragraph. If you want to leave the mail on the mail server even after you download it, click Incoming Mail in the Category list in the Options dialog box, and select the Leave Mail on Server option.

The left side of Figure 6-1 contains a list of folders (notice the five tabs at the bottom of this pane: the Mailboxes tab is selected to display mail folders). The right side of Figure 6-1 includes the contents of the selected folder in the top pane, and the text of the selected message in the bottom pane.

You can read a message by selecting it in the top pane, which displays the text of the message in the bottom pane. Alternatively, you can double-click the message to display it in its own window.

    If you want to see all the headers for a message you received, click the Show All Headers button (labeled Blah Blah Blah) on the toolbar. Click it again to see only the headers that Eudora normally displays.

Sending Messages

Follow these steps to send a message:

1. To create a new message, click the New Message button on the toolbar. You see a message composition window with headers at the top and an area for the message text at the bottom.

2. Fill in the headers. Press TAB to move between lines.

3. TAB down to the message area and type the text of your message.

4. Click the Queue or Send button on the toolbar of the message composition window to send the message. The message will be sent the next time that Eudora checks and sends e-mail.

Filing Messages

Eudora enables you to file messages in hierarchical folders. In Eudora terminology, you can create mailboxes and folders: mailboxes hold mail messages and folders hold mailboxes (and no messages). You can create a folder with several mailboxes, to organize your messages. To create a new mailbox or folder:

1. Choose Mailbox | New from the menu to see the New Mailbox dialog box:

2. Name the folder or mailbox in the space provided.

3. To create a folder, select the Make It a Folder check box.

4. Click OK to create the mailbox or folder.

To create mailboxes in a folder, select the folder before you choose Mailbox | New. Notice that the New Mailbox dialog box tells you where it is creating the new mailbox—in the Top Level, or in a particular folder.

To move e-mail to a folder, drag the message information to the folder, or select the message and use the Transfer menu to choose the folder to which you want to transfer it.

Turning On Automatic Spell Checking

Eudora can automatically check the spelling of each message when you click the Send button: to turn on the option, choose Tools | Options from the menu, click the Spell Checking icon, and then select the Check When Message Queued/Sent. You may also find the additional spelling options useful.

Storing Addresses

Eudora enables you to store e-mail addresses in its Address Book. Display the Address Book by clicking the Address Book icon on the toolbar. To create new entries, click the New button on the Address Book window, provide a nickname, and click OK. Then, type the address in the Addresses tab of the Address Book. You may want to add additional information about the person on the Notes and Info tabs.

To add an address from a message to the Address Book, select the message and click CTRL+K, or choose Special | Make Address Book Entry. You see the Make Address Book Entry dialog box, in which you can type the name that you want to use to store the address. The name that you use is known as the nickname, because it is a shortcut to the e-mail address. Eudora will make a guess about the name—you may choose to use a shorter name.

To use an address from the Address Book in an outgoing message, type the nickname in the To, Cc, or Bcc header. Alternatively, display the Address Book, select the address that you want to use, and then click the To, Cc, or Bcc button to add an address to the message.

Creating and Adding Signatures

Eudora enables you to append a signature to your outgoing e-mail messages. To create a signature, choose Tools | Signatures from the menu or click the Signatures tab if it appears. Figure 6-2 shows the Signatures tab. The Signatures tab contains at least one signature, your standard signature. However, the standard signature is blank until you type some text for it.

To create your standard signature, follow these steps:

1. Choose Tools | Signatures or click the Signatures tab if it appears.

2. Double-click Standard or right-click it and choose Edit. You see the Standard window.

3. Type the text of your signature in the Standard window.

4. Click the Standard window's close button. Eudora asks if you want to save changes to Standard.

5. Click Yes to save changes to your standard signature.

Figure 6-2. *The Signatures tab*

EXCHANGING E-MAIL

You can create an additional signature by right-clicking in the Signatures tab and choosing New. Eudora asks you to name your signature. Then, create and save the signature in the same way that you created and saved the Standard signature.

To append your signature to outgoing e-mail messages automatically, choose Tools | Options from the menu, click the Sending Mail icon, and choose a signature from the Default Signature drop-down list. To append a signature to a message manually, choose the signature name from the Signature drop-down list on the message toolbar (usually the second option on the message toolbar).

Outlook 98 and Outlook Express

Outlook 97, Outlook 98, and Outlook Express are Microsoft's major entries into the e-mail market. In fact, Outlook 97 and Outlook 98 do much more than e-mail—they also have calendars, track contacts, and more. All these versions of Outlook replace the Microsoft Internet Mail program that came with Internet Explorer 3.

Outlook 98 comes with Microsoft Office 97 and is available for downloading at **http://officeupdate.microsoft.com/Articles/outlook98fact.htm** or **http://www.microsoft.com/outlook**. (For instructions on downloading and installing programs from the Web, see Chapter 38.) Outlook 98 is more than an e-mail program: it includes an address book, calendar, To Do list, and other features. The program is free for registered users of Microsoft Office, and others can buy it in stores or from the Microsoft Web site. As Microsoft improves Outlook 98, the features have changed, so your version may not match the descriptions in this chapter exactly: check Microsoft's Web site for information about the latest version. Outlook 97 came with early versions of Office 97.

If you prefer an e-mail program that has fewer features and uses fewer computer resources, you may want to consider Outlook Express, which comes with Windows 98 and Internet Explorer 4. If you have Windows 98 but an Outlook Express icon doesn't appear in the Quick Launch section of your Taskbar (the small icons next to the Start button), choose Start | Settings | Control Panel, run Add/Remove Programs, click the Windows Setup tab, and select Microsoft Outlook Express from the list of Windows components.

This section describes Outlook 98, but most of the instructions also work for Outlook Express, although often you'll find that you can skip a step or two.

Outlook 98 and Outlook Express Highlights

Here are the basic Outlook commands (first select a message in a folder, or display it by double-clicking):

Print	Click the Print button on the toolbar, choose File | Print, or press CTRL+P.
Delete	Click the Delete button on the toolbar or press the DELETE key.
Forward	Click the Forward button. You can also either choose Action | Forward from the menu (Compose | Forward in Outlook Express) or press CTRL+F.
Reply	Click the Reply or Reply to All button on the toolbar, or choose Action | Reply or Action | Reply to All (Compose | Reply to Author and Compose | Reply to All in Outlook Express). The shortcut keys are CTRL+R and CTRL+SHIFT+R, respectively.
Check Spelling	Press F7 or choose Tools | Spelling. Outlook automatically checks the spelling of each message when you click the Send button, if you choose Tools | Options from the main menu, click the Spelling tab, and then select the Always Check Spelling Before Sending option.

Configuring Outlook 98 and Outlook Express

The first time that you open Outlook, it guides you through setting up your account. You can import Internet e-mail account settings from Eudora or Netscape. If you go through the complete setup process, Outlook asks you for the following:

- Your name
- Your e-mail address
- The type of server (usually POP)
- Your incoming e-mail server
- The server your outgoing e-mail goes through
- Your login name (the name you use to log in to your e-mail provider) and password
- A name for this e-mail account (so that you can give different e-mail accounts different names). You may want to name accounts by using the user's name or the e-mail provider's name. If you have many accounts, using the e-mail address as the account name may reduce confusion.
- How you connect to the Internet. If you connect from home, you probably connect using your phone line.

If you ever need to change these settings in Outlook 98, choose Tools | Services from the menu, select Internet Mail, and click the Properties button. In Outlook Express, choose Tools | Accounts, click the Mail tab, click the e-mail account you want to change, and click Properties.

Collecting and Reading Messages

To check e-mail manually, either click the Send and Receive button on the toolbar, choose Tools | Send and Receive | Internet E-mail, or press CTRL+M. When new e-mail arrives, you see a letter icon on your taskbar. To read e-mail, view the Inbox by clicking Inbox in the list on the left side of the window. Figure 6-3 shows the Outlook 98 window, and Figure 6-4 shows Outlook Express. Double-click a message to open it. Outlook opens a new window, with its own button on the taskbar for each open message. After you finish reading a message, you can close the message window, or use the Previous Item or Next Item button to view another message.

To tell Outlook to check for new e-mail automatically, choose Tools | Options, click the Internet E-mail tab (the General tab in Outlook Express), and then type a number in the setting named Check My Local Network Connection(s) for New Mail Every ___ Minute(s). In Outlook Express, the setting is called Check for New Messages Every ___ Minute(s).

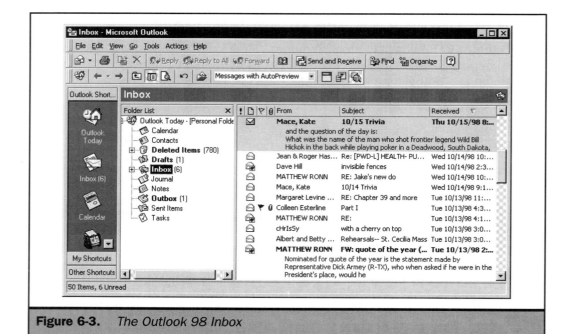

Figure 6-3. The Outlook 98 Inbox

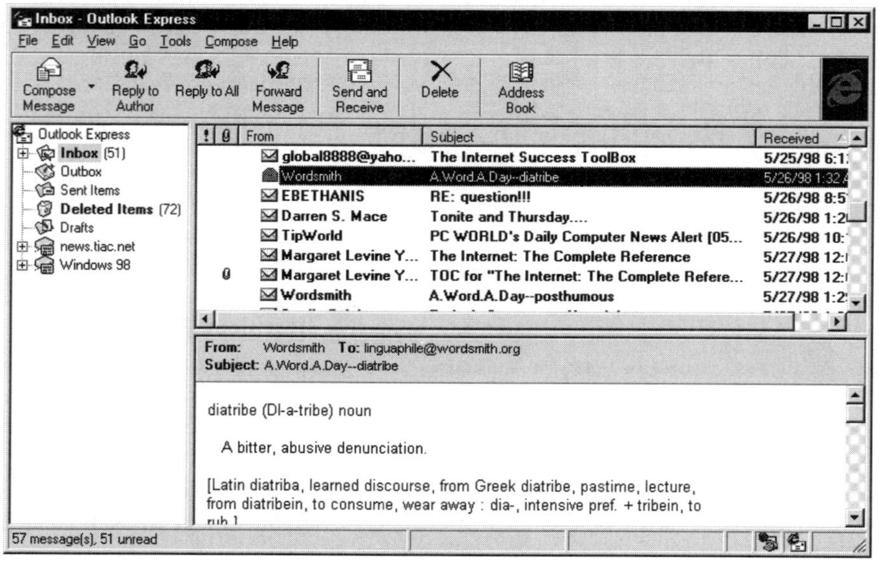

Figure 6-4. The Outlook Express Inbox

You can tell Outlook to leave the messages on your mail server even after you download them, so that you can download them again later. Choose Tools | Accounts, click the Mail tab, choose your e-mail account, click the Properties button, click the Advanced tab, and select the Leave a Copy of Messages on Server option.

You can display the contents of other folders by clicking the names of the folders in the folder list on the left side of the window. If you don't see the folder list (Outlook may display the Outlook bar and not the folder list), click the name of the folder to drop-down the folder list, or display the folder list more permanently by clicking the Folder List button or choosing View | Folder List from the menu. If a folder appears with a + next to it, it has subfolders—click the + to see the list of subfolders.

Tip   *To display all the headers for a message you receive in Outlook Express, display the message and choose File | Properties from the menu, then click the Details tab in the properties dialog box for the message. In Outlook 98, choose View | Options to display the Message Options dialog box: the complete headers appear at the bottom.*

Sending Messages

Create a new e-mail message by clicking the Create New Message button on the toolbar. You can also press CTRL+N to create a new e-mail message. Fill the To and Subject boxes, and write the message. Send the message by clicking the Send button, which appears to the right of the header information.

You can use Microsoft Word as your e-mail editor when you use Outlook 98 (not Outlook Express). Using Word enables you to take advantage of Word's automatic spell-checking and formatting features (although a recipient must have Outlook or another e-mail program that reads rich text e-mail messages to see the formatting). If you have Word and you're not already using it as your editor, choose Tools | Options from the menu, click the E-Mail tab, and then click the Use Microsoft Word as the E-Mail Editor option so that a check mark appears in the check box.

Filing Messages

Outlook allows you to file messages in hierarchical folders. All folders in Outlook can contain both messages and other folders. You may want to create all mail folders under the Inbox folder. To create a new mailbox or folder, follow these steps:

1. If the folder list is not displayed, display it by choosing View | Folder List from the menu.

2. Select the folder in which you want the new folder to be stored. For instance, if you want the new folder to appear indented under the Inbox, select Inbox in the folder list. If you want the new folder to be a top-level folder, select the folder that appears at the top of the folder list.

3. Select File | New | Folder from the menu or press CTRL+SHIFT+E. The Create New Folder dialog box is displayed.

4. Name the folder or mailbox in the space provided. You can change the location of the folder at this point if you need to.

5. Click OK or press ENTER to create the mailbox or folder.

To move mail to a folder, either drag the message information to the folder, or right-click the message, choose Move to Folder, and then select the folder from the folder list. (You can open folders in this dialog box by clicking the + next to a folder name.)

Turning On Automatic Spell Checking

Outlook automatically checks the spelling of each message when you click the Send button, if you turn on the option: choose Tools | Options from the menu, click the Spelling tab, and then select the Always Check Spelling Before Sending option.

Storing Addresses

Outlook allows you to store e-mail addresses in its Address Book. The easiest way to add an address is to use a message from the person whose address you want to add to the Address Book. Open the message, right-click the address, and choose Add To Personal Address Book from the shortcut menu.

To work with the Address Book and add addresses manually, display the Address Book by clicking the Address Book button on the toolbar. You can create new entries by clicking the New Entry button on the Address Book toolbar (the first button). Normally, you'll want to choose Other Address, put the address in the Personal Address book, and then click OK. Next, you see the window in which you can type information about the person. Type the display name (the person's real name or a nickname that you want to use) and e-mail address. You must provide an e-mail type—Internet or SMTP is usually appropriate. You may want to add additional information about the person on the other tabs before you click OK to close the entry.

To use an address from the Address Book in an outgoing message, type the nickname in the To, Cc, or Bcc header. If you don't remember the name that you used, click the To or Cc button to display the Address Book. Select the name(s) that you want to use and then click the To, Cc, or Bcc button on the Select Names dialog box to add the name and address to the e-mail message (you see only the name, although Outlook knows to send the message to the address).

Creating and Adding Signatures

Outlook allows you to append a signature to your outgoing e-mail messages. Create a signature in Outlook 98 by following these steps:

1. Choose Tools | Options from the menu and click the Mail Format tab.

2. Click the Signature Picker button near the bottom of the dialog box. You see the Signature Picker dialog box.

3. Click the New button, name the signature, and click Next.

4. Type the text of your signature in the Edit Signature dialog box and click Finish.

5. Click OK on the Signature Picker dialog box to return to the Options dialog box.

6. To add this signature to every message, select the signature name in the Use This Signature By Default setting. If you don't want to add this signature to every message that you create, Use This Signature By Default usually should be set to None. We suggest selecting the Don't Use When Replying or Forwarding option to keep replies and forwarded messages uncluttered. Click OK to close the window.

In Outlook Express, choose Tools | Stationery from the toolbar, click the Mail tab, and click the Signature button to display the Signature dialog box. Select the Add This Signature to All Outgoing Messages check box and type your signature in the Text box. Click OK twice.

If you choose not to append the signature automatically to each message that you create, you may still want to append the signature to certain messages. To do so, click the Signature button on the message toolbar.

Netscape Messenger

Netscape Messenger is the e-mail client packaged with Netscape Communicator 4 and 4.5. If you use Netscape Navigator (the browser that comes with the Netscape Communicator suite) to access the Web, you may want to use Messenger to send and receive e-mail. The program is available free from Netscape at **http://www.netscape.com/computing/download**, as well as from TUCOWS (**http://www.tucows.com**) and other sites. This section describes version 4.5, which is also available for the Mac.

To open Messenger, choose Start | Netscape Communicator | Netscape Messenger (in Windows 98/95), or choose Communicator | Messager from the menu of Netscape Navigator, or click the Inbox icon located on the Netscape Component Bar or at the bottom of the Navigator window. Messenger and the Netscape Component bar are shown in Figure 6-5.

Configuring Netscape Messenger

The first time that you open Netscape Messenger, it asks whether you want to make Messenger your default e-mail application. If you're just trying it out, answer No; otherwise, answer Yes.

EXCHANGING E-MAIL

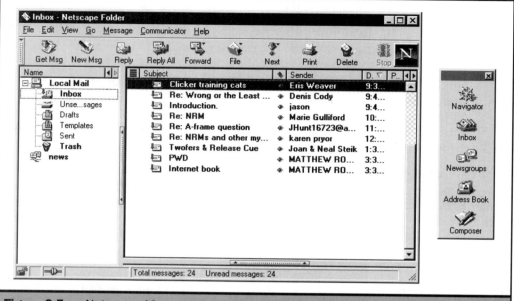

Figure 6-5. *Netscape Messenger window*

Netscape Messenger Highlights

Here are the basic Netscape Messenger commands (first select a message in a folder, or display it by double-clicking):

Print	Click the Print button on the toolbar, choose File	Print, or press CTRL+P.
Delete	Click the Delete button on the toolbar or press the DELETE key.
Forward	Click the Forward button. You can also choose Message	Forward from the menu or press CTRL+L.
Reply	Click the Reply or Reply All button on the toolbar, or choose Message	Reply or Message	Reply to All. The shortcut keys are CTRL+R and CTRL+SHIFT+R.
Check Spelling	Click the Spelling button on the message toolbar. Messenger automatically checks the spelling of each message when you click the Send button, if you choose Edit	Preferences from the main menu, click the Messages option, and select the Spell Check Messages Before Sending option.

Messenger does not immediately open a configuration wizard when you first run it, unlike many other e-mail applications. To configure Messenger to pick up and send e-mail, follow these steps:

1. Choose Edit | Preferences from the menu.

2. Select Mail Servers as the category on the left.

3. You may see the default mail server. Select that server and click the Edit button in the Incoming Mail Servers panel. You see the Mail Server Property dialog box.

4. Enter the name of the server on which your e-mail is stored.

5. Select the server type—POP3 (POP) or IMAP. Currently, most e-mail accounts are POP3.

6. Type your user name (the name you use to log in when you access your mail server).

7. Use the following two settings, according to your preferences. You may want Messenger to remember your password, and you may want it to pick up e-mail automatically every few minutes.

8. Type the name of your outgoing mail server in the Outgoing Mail (SMTP) Server text box.

9. Click the Identity category.

10. Fill in Your Name and E-mail Address. You may want to fill the other options on this page also.

11. Click OK to close the Preferences dialog box.

Note *Messenger allows you to have one POP3 server or multiple IMAP servers.*

If you ever need to change these settings, choose Edit | Preferences from the menu and select Mail Servers as the category.

Collecting and Reading Messages

To check e-mail manually, either click the Get Msg button on the toolbar or select File | Get New Messages. You can tell Messenger to check your mail automatically by following these steps:

1. Choose Edit | Preferences to display the Preferences dialog box.

2. Click the Mail & Newsgroups plus box in the Category list to display the types of e-mail settings available.

3. Click the Mail Servers category.

4. In the right side of the Preferences dialog box, choose the mail server from the Incoming Mail Servers list and click Edit to display the Mail Servers Properties dialog box.

5. On the General tab, select the Check for Mail Every ___ Minutes check box, and type the frequency (in minutes) to check the mail.

6. If you want to leave a copy of your messages on the mail server even after you download the messages, click the POP tab in the Mail Server Properties dialog box and choose the Leave Messages on Server setting.

7. Close all the windows by clicking OK on each.

To read e-mail, view the Inbox by clicking Inbox on the left side of the window. Double-click a message to open it. Messenger opens a new window with its own button on the taskbar for each open message. After you finish reading a message, you can close the message window, or use the Next button to view the next unread message.

You can display the contents of other folders by clicking the names of the folders in the folder list on the left side of the Messenger window. If a folder appears with a + next to it, it has hidden subfolders—click the + to see the list of subfolders.

 To see the complete headers for a message, display the message and choose View | Page Source or press CTRL+U.

Sending Messages

Create a new message by clicking the New Msg button, the first button on the toolbar. You can also press CTRL+M to create a new e-mail message. Messenger opens a separate message window that gets its own button on the Windows taskbar. Fill the To and Subject headers, and write the message. Send the message by clicking the Send button, the first button on the message window toolbar.

Filing Messages

Messenger enables you to file messages in hierarchical folders. All folders in Messenger can contain both messages and other folders. You may want to create all mail folders under the Inbox folder. To create a new mailbox or folder, follow these steps:

1. Choose File | New Folder from the menu.

2. Type a name for the folder in the Name text box.

3. Select a folder from the Create as a Subfolder Of option. This is the folder in which the new folder will be stored. For instance, if you want the new folder to appear indented under the Inbox, select Inbox in the folder list. If you want the new folder to be a top-level folder, select the Local Mail folder that appears at the top of the folder list.

4. Click OK or press ENTER to create the mailbox or folder.

To move e-mail to a folder, either drag the message information to the folder, or right-click the message, choose Move Message, and select the folder from the folder list.

Storing Addresses

Messenger allows you to store e-mail addresses in its Address Book.

The easiest way to add an address is to use a message that already contains the address. Right-click the message and choose Add Sender to Address Book from the shortcut menu. Alternatively, right-click the message and choose Add All to Address Book to add the address of the sender and all the recipients. Messenger displays the New Card dialog box for each address that it adds to the Address Book. You can accept all the entries by clicking OK, or correct or add to the information before clicking OK.

To work with the Address Book and add addresses manually, display the Address Book either by choosing Communicator | Address Book or by pressing CTRL+SHIFT+2. You can create new entries by clicking the New Card button on the Address Book toolbar (the first button). Type in the appropriate headers the name and e-mail address that you want to add to the Address Book. You may want to add additional information about the person on the other tabs before you click OK to close the entry.

To use an address from the Address Book in an outgoing message, type the nickname in the To header. If you don't remember the name that you used, position the cursor in the To header and click the Address button on the message toolbar. Select the name(s) of the person who you want to receive the e-mail and click To, Cc, or Bcc. Click OK after you select all the recipients.

Creating and Adding Signatures

Messenger allows you to append a signature to your outgoing e-mail messages. Create a signature by following these steps:

1. Open Notepad or another text editor. Type your signature and save it in a text file. You can store it anywhere on your hard disk, but you might want to put it where Netscape stores your bookmarks and other settings (which is usually C:\Program Files\Netscape\Users\default or C:\Program Files\Netscape\Users*username* if you have a Netscape user profile).

2. Choose Edit | Preferences from the menu and click the Identity category.

3. Type the name and path of your signature file in the Signature File text box at the bottom of the dialog box. You can browse to the file by clicking the Choose button.

After you set up a signature file, Messenger appends the signature to every message that you create. If you prefer not to include it in a particular message, delete it in the message window.

Pegasus

Pegasus is a full-featured, widely used e-mail program that has been around for years. It was written in 1990 by a New Zealander named David Harris, who continues to upgrade and support it. Unlike many other e-mail programs, Pegasus sends and retrieves e-mail in the background—in other words, you can continue to read and create e-mail messages at the same time Pegasus is sending or retrieving messages. Pegasus supports signatures, stationery, has extensive filtering features, and is available for Windows 98/95, Windows 3.1, DOS, and the Mac.

You can download Pegasus at **http://www.pegasus.usa.com**. Pegasus is free but the developer requests that you pay for the manuals if you want to support the

---

Pegasus Highlights

Here are the basic Pegasus commands (first select a message in a folder, or display it by double-clicking):

Print	Click the Print button on the toolbar, choose File | Print, or press CTRL+P.
Delete	Press the DELETE key. Pegasus asks you to confirm that you really want to delete the message.
Forward	Click the Forward button.
Reply	Click the Reply button on the toolbar, choose your reply options, and click OK. One of the reply options is to send the reply to all recipients.
Check Spelling	Click the Spelling button on the message window (the one with abc and a check mark). Pegasus automatically checks the spelling of each message when you click the Send button, if you choose Tools | Options from the main menu, click the Message Settings option, and select the Automatically Check Spelling Before Sending Document option.

continuing development of the program. You can find out more by clicking the second-to-last button on the toolbar—the one with the dollar sign. This section describes Pegasus version 3.

Configuring Pegasus

The first time that you run Pegasus, it asks some questions to correctly configure the application:

- **Number of users**   Either one person and one e-mail address, multiple people or e-mail addresses on one computer, or multiple people on a LAN.
- **User name**   The short name you use to log in to Pegasus when multiple users are selected.
- **Personal name**   The name that appears on messages from you.
- **E-mail address**   Your e-mail address.
- **POP3 server**   The name of the server your incoming e-mail goes to.
- **User name and password**   Your user name and password for your POP server.
- **SMTP server**   The name of the server that handles your outgoing e-mail.
- **Type of connection**   How you connect to the Internet (through a dialup or network connection).

To change any of these settings, choose Tools | Options and display the Network tab.

Collecting and Reading Messages

To check e-mail manually, click the Check Your POP3 Host for New Mail button or the Both Check and Send Mail in One Operation button (both buttons have globes on them). You can also choose File | Check Host for New Mail or File | Check and Send Mail. New e-mail appears in the New Mail folder (see Figure 6-6).

To display the New Mail folder, click the Open or Re-Scan Your New Mail Folder button (the second) on the toolbar. Double-click a message to open it. You see the message in a new window within the Pegasus window. After you finish reading a message, you can close the message window, or use the Previous or Next button to view another message.

The New Mail Folder window displays information about messages that have been received. Messages that have been read display a check mark next to them. Messages that you have composed a reply to appear with a blue dot to their left.

Tip   *To see all the headers for a displayed message, press* CTRL + H *or choose Reader | Show All Headers.*

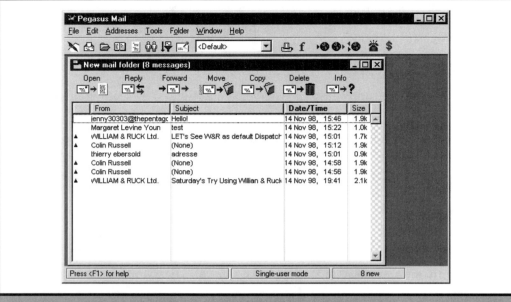

Figure 6-6.   *The New Mail folder in the Pegasus window*

To set up Pegasus to check e-mail automatically, follow these steps:

1. Choose Tools | Options from the menu to display the Pegasus Mail Options dialog box.

2. Click the Network tab.

3. Click the Advanced Network Configuration Options button to see the Advanced Configuration for Built-in Mailer dialog box.

4. In the third panel (Incoming (POP3) Mail), change the Check for New POP3 Mail Every ___ Seconds to an appropriate value. When this setting is 0, Pegasus collects e-mail only when you give the command.

5. If you want to leave copies of your messages on the mail server even after you have downloaded the messages, click the Delete Mail from Host Once Successfully Retrieved check box so it does not contain a check mark.

6. Click OK to close both dialog boxes.

Note   *You can work offline with Pegasus. Choose File | Enter Offline Mode to work offline. When you're done, choose File | Leave Offline Mode.*

If you want to see all the headers for the message you are reading, right-click the text of the message and choose Show Raw Message Data from the menu that appears.

Sending Messages

Create a new message by clicking the Start a New Mail Message button, the first button on the main toolbar. Provide the address or alias for the person to whom to send the message, type a subject, and the write your message. Send it by clicking the Send button on the message window.

Filing Messages

Pegasus enables you to file messages in hierarchical folders. Pegasus has two types of folders—message folders and filing trays. *Message folders* can contain messages, but not other folders or filing trays. *Filing trays* can contain message folders, but cannot store messages.

To create a new folder, first display the Folders window either by clicking the Work With Your Mail Folders button (the third on the toolbar) or by choosing File | Mail Folders. To create a new message folder or filing tray, click the New button on the Folders window toolbar. Name the new folder, choose Message Folder or Filing Tray, and then click OK. If you want to move the folder after you create it, click-and-drag it to its new location. For instance, if the new folder appears at the top level and you want it to be a subfolder of a filing tray that you created, simply drag-and-drop the new folder on the filing tray.

You can move a message to a folder by dragging the message to the Folder window. Alternatively, you can select the message and click the Move button. The Select a folder dialog box appears, in which you select the folder that you want to move the message to (you can open folders in this dialog box by clicking the + next to a folder name).

To view other folders, choose File | Mail Folders or press CTRL+L. When you see the Folders dialog box, double-click a folder name to open the folder.

Storing Addresses

The easiest way to add an address to the Address Book is to use a message from the person whose address you want to add to the Address Book. Drag the message from the folder window to the Address Book window to add the address.

Display the Address Book by clicking the Open or Manage Address Books button (the fourth on the toolbar). You see the Select an Address Book dialog box. To begin, you must create an Address Book (Pegasus allows you to have multiple Address Books)—click the New button, name the Address Book, and click OK. When you want to add entries to the Address Book, you first have to open the Address Book by double-clicking the Address Book name in the Select an Address Book dialog box.

To add entries to the Address Book, click the Add button and type information about the person—you may decide to enter only the name and e-mail address. After you enter the information, click OK.

To use an address from an Address Book, you can type the alias of the person to whom you want to send the message in the To, Cc, or Bcc header. If you don't remember the alias, you can open the Address Book and double-click the name that you want to use or click the Paste button.

Creating and Adding Signatures

Pegasus allows you to have up to nine separate signatures. To work with your signatures, choose Tools | Options from the menu and click the Signatures tab. To create a signature, click the Edit button for the signature that you want to create. Give the signature a name and type text for it. If you are using Pegasus for Internet mail (as opposed to intra-office mail), it is sufficient to type the signature text in the box labeled Use This Signature if the Message Is Sent via the Internet. Click Save to close the dialog box. Use the radio buttons on the Signatures tab to choose the default signature: the very last radio button is Default to No Signature.

When you create a message, the default signature is automatically appended to the message. If you want to change the signature to one of the others that you created, choose it from the Sig drop-down list on the message (the drop-down list appears to the right of the check boxes, near the Check Spelling button).

America Online (AOL)

America Online is a popular online service, because many people find that the easiest way to get online is to use one of the armload of free AOL CD-ROMs that they have received by mail or inserted into magazines. Using AOL saves you the hassle of choosing an ISP, it makes information relatively easy to find, and it has a well-attended array of chat rooms. AOL includes e-mail as part of its service: you can exchange e-mail with other AOL users or anyone with an Internet address.

Your Internet address is your screen name (without the spaces) with @aol.com tacked on to the end. If you create additional screen names (each AOL account can have up to five), each screen name has its own mailbox and its own Internet address.

After you install the AOL software, you don't have to configure it to get your e-mail. Because AOL doesn't offer a POP mail server, you can't use Outlook, Pegasus, or other e-mail programs to read your AOL mail. You can use the new NetMail, which enables you to get your AOL mail by using a Web browser, at **http://www.aol.com**. NetMail requires the Netscape Navigator browser (version 3 or later) or Internet Explorer (version 3 or later), and prompts you to download a plug-in or ActiveX control. NetMail displays a Web page that looks and works just like AOL's Online Mailbox window, as described in the next few sections. This section describes version 4 of AOL's software.

AOL 4 Highlights

Here are the basic AOL mail commands (first select a message in your Online Mailbox window, or display it by double-clicking):

Print	Click the Print button on the toolbar.
Delete	Click the Delete button or press the DELETE key.
Forward	Open the message and click the Forward button.
Reply	Open the message and click the Reply or Reply All button.
Check Spelling	When composing a message, choose Edit	Spell Check or press CTRL+=. To check spelling automatically, choose My AOL	Preferences, click Mail, select the Perform a Spell Check Before Sending Mail check box, and then click OK. (To disable automatic spell checking for one message, hold down CTRL while you click the Send button.)

Collecting and Reading Messages

When you log in to AOL, a message on the left side of the Welcome window tells you either "You Have Mail" or "No New Mail." To open the mailbox, either click the You Have Mail button in the Welcome window, click the Read button on the toolbar, press CTRL+R, or choose Mail Center | Read Mail. You then see your Online Mailbox window, with three tabs: New Mail, Old Mail, and Sent Mail.

Click the tab in the Online Mailbox window for the type of mail that you want to see. AOL lists all the messages of the type you chose (new, old, or sent). Double-click a message to see its text. If you want to see the complete headers for the messages, scroll down to the end of the message.

You can set up AOL to connect, go online, collect your e-mail, send any messages that you've composed, and sign off, so that you can read and write your e-mail offline. This system, which is called *Automatic AOL* or *Flashsessions*, is useful if you have to make a long-distance call to connect to AOL, or if you have chosen an AOL billing plan for which you pay by the hour to connect. To set up Automatic AOL (whether you are online or offline), choose Mail Center | Set Up Automatic AOL (Flashsessions), which displays the Automatic AOL Walk-Through window. Answer the questions that you see, and then choose the screen names for which you want to collect e-mail messages. If you want Automatic AOL to collect your messages automatically (for example, at 2:30 A.M. each morning), it asks what days and what time you want it to run. You can change your Automatic AOL configuration any time by choosing Mail Center | Set Up Automatic AOL (Flashsessions) again: click Schedule Automatic AOL on the window that appears, if you want to change its schedule.

After you configure Automatic AOL, you can tell AOL to connect and send/receive messages by choosing Mail Center | Run Automatic AOL (Flashsessions) Now.

 You can change your AOL mail settings by choosing Mail Center | Mail Center when you are online.

Sending Messages

To send a new message, click the Write button on the main toolbar or in the Mail Center window. In the Write Mail window, fill in the headers and type the message. Send the message by clicking the Send Now button. If you are offline, click Send Later to store the message to be sent the next time Automatic AOL goes online.

Filing Messages

AOL enables you to file messages in hierarchical folders. To add a folder, choose My Files | Personal Filing Cabinet. Click the location for the new folder, click Add Folder, and then name the new folder.

To move e-mail to a folder, drag the message information to the folder.

Storing Addresses

The easiest way to add an address is to use a message from the person whose address you want to add to the Address Book. To do so, open the message and click the Add Address button. You see the New Person dialog box. AOL fills in the address for you, and you can choose whether to fill in the other headers on the dialog box before you click OK.

To work with the Address Book, choose Address Book from the Mail Center. Click the New Person button to add a new address. Click OK when the information is complete.

To use an address from the Address Book in an outgoing message, either choose Mail Center | Address Book or click the Address Book button in the Write Mail window, and then double-click the name in the Address Book.

CompuServe

CompuServe is another popular online service that may suit you if want a hassle-free way to get online. Your CompuServe e-mail address is your Personal Address (a name that you choose during the setup process) with @compuserve.com on the end. After you install the CompuServe software, you don't have to configure the e-mail software. This section describes version 4 of the CompuServe software.

 CompuServe now offers POP mail, which gives you the option of using a POP e-mail client such as Eudora or Outlook.

CompuServe Highlights

Here are the basic CompuServe mail commands (first select a message in a folder, or display it by double-clicking):

Print	Open the message and click the Print menu.
Delete	Select or open the message and click the Delete button on the toolbar.
Forward	Open the message and click the Forward button.
Reply	Open the message and click the Reply or Reply to All button on the toolbar.

Collecting and Reading Messages

To view new e-mail, click the Get Mail button on the toolbar, to display the Online Mail window. To open a message, double-click it.

Sending Messages

Click the Create button on the main CompuServe toolbar. Fill in the headers and write the message. Send the message by clicking the Send button.

Filing Messages

File a message in a folder by clicking the File It button on the Online Mail window. Then, select a folder in which to file the message or create a new folder by clicking the New Folder button.

To see the contents of another folder, choose File | Filing Cabinet from the CompuServe main menu. Select the folder that you want to view and click Open.

Storing Addresses

The easiest way to store an address is to open a message from that address and click the Add Address button.

To work with the Address Book, choose Mail | Address Book from the main menu. Add an entry by clicking the New Entry button. To use an Address Book entry to address a message, open the Address Book, select the address, and then click Create Mail Message. You can also click the Recipients button on the new mail message's window and then click the Address Book button to see the Address Book. Double-click an address to send the message to that person.

Pine

If for some reason you're stuck using a UNIX shell account, you probably use Pine as your e-mail client. See Chapter 40 for a description of UNIX shell accounts and information about how to log in and give commands.

When you use a UNIX account, be sure to type commands exactly as we show them. Capitalization matters in UNIX, so if you see a command in lowercase, type it using lowercase. If you make a mistake, try BACKSPACE, DELETE or CTRL+H to delete one character, or press CTRL+U or CTRL+K to delete the whole command. CTRL+C cancels many commands.

Some users with POP accounts may use Pine to read their mail when they're away from their desks: if that describes you, you should look into the new Web-based free e-mail services that enable you to read mail on your POP server—they are far easier to use. See the section "Web-Based E-mail" in Chapter 5.

Collecting and Reading Messages

To open Pine, type **pine** (all lowercase) at the UNIX shell prompt and press ENTER. Pine lists all of its commands (See Figure 6-7). To execute a command, press the one letter that you see to the left of the command name. To see new e-mail, type **i** (for message index) and press ENTER. Press UP ARROW and DOWN ARROW to highlight a message, and press **v** to read the highlighted message. Press **m** to return to the main menu. You can look at the messages in other folders by pressing l (the lowercase letter *l*, for folder list) and choosing a folder from the list. When you're ready to leave Pine, press **q** to quit.

The one good thing about a UNIX shell account is that you don't have to collect your e-mail—you're already logged in to the computer where the e-mail is delivered, so as it arrives, it appears in Pine.

Pine Highlights

Create a new message	Press **c**.
Delete	Display the message and press **d**. The message is marked for deletion—it is deleted when you exit Pine.
Forward	Display the message and press **f**.
Reply	Display the message and press **r**.

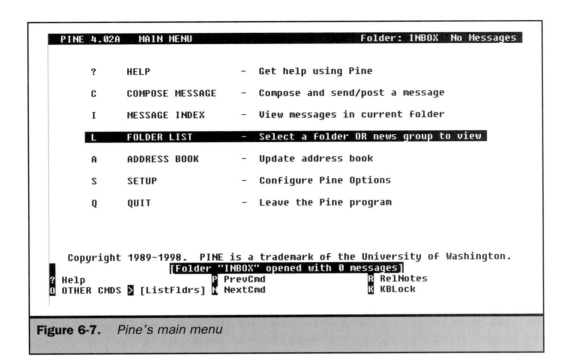

```
PINE 4.02A    MAIN MENU                    Folder: INBOX   No Messages


        ?    HELP              -  Get help using Pine

        C    COMPOSE MESSAGE   -  Compose and send/post a message

        I    MESSAGE INDEX     -  View messages in current folder

        L    FOLDER LIST       -  Select a folder OR news group to view

        A    ADDRESS BOOK      -  Update address book

        S    SETUP             -  Configure Pine Options

        Q    QUIT              -  Leave the Pine program



   Copyright 1989-1998.  PINE is a trademark of the University of Washington.
                    [Folder "INBOX" opened with 0 messages]
 ? Help                     P PrevCmd                  R RelNotes
 O OTHER CMDS > [ListFldrs] N NextCmd                  K KBLock
```

Figure 6-7. *Pine's main menu*

Sending Messages

The way that you edit your messages depends on the text editor that you use. You may use Vi, Emacs, Pico, or another editor. Pico is the easiest to use. Ask your system administrator how to edit a message that you type—alternatively, just type it right the first time.

To create a new e-mail message, type **c** (for compose). Fill in the headers and press the TAB or UP ARROW and DOWN ARROW keys to move between the headers. Type the text of the message under the Message Text Heading. Press CTRL+X to send the message. When Pine asks you whether you really want to send the message, press **y** to send it or CTRL+C to cancel. You can return to the main menu by pressing **m**.

Filing Messages

To save a message, press **s** (for save) when the message is selected or open. Name the folder in which you want to save the message. If you name a folder that doesn't exist, Pine creates a new folder.

To see the contents of a folder, press **l** (that is, the lowercase letter *l*, for folder list) to see a list of folders. Highlight the folder that you want to open and press ENTER.

Storing Addresses

To add an address to the Address Book from a message that you received, press **t**. Pine asks for additional information that you may choose to include and then adds the address to the Address Book.

You can see the Address Book by pressing **a** from the main menu. Add an entry to the Address Book by following these steps:

1. Press **a**.

2. Type the person's last name, a comma, and their first name. Press ENTER.

3. Type a nickname and press ENTER.

4. Type the e-mail address and press ENTER.

To use an address from the Address Book, you can type the nickname on one of the header lines of a new message.

Creating and Adding Signatures

To make a signature to add to the end of all your outgoing mail, press **s** (for setup) at the main menu, and then press **s** again (for signature). Pine runs a text editor so you can type the text of your signature. When you have done so, press CTRL+X. Pine asks you to confirm: press **y**.

Alternatively, you can create a signature file to append to all outgoing messages by creating a text file with the text of the signature and naming the file **signature**. You have to use a text editor to create the file—if you use Pico, you can type **pico.signature** to create the signature file. After you create the file, Pine automatically appends it to your outgoing messages. If you don't want to include it in a particular message, delete it from the message.

The
Complete
Reference

Internet

Chapter 7

Sending and Receiving Files by E-mail

Attaching files to an e-mail message is the easiest way to exchange files with someone—assuming that you don't both have access to the same hard drive over a local area network (LAN). Sending files via e-mail is quicker and cheaper than shipping diskettes, and it enables you to send files that might not fit on one diskette. By attaching files to an e-mail message, you can do such things as exchange documents for revision, pass on spreadsheets for data entry, or send a presentation for review. Of course, you can also attach electronic pictures, sounds, movies, or anything else that can be stored in a file.

This chapter contains general information about e-mail attachments, followed by specific instructions for the most popular e-mail programs. For the basic commands to use with these e-mail programs (including commands for sending and receiving e-mail), see Chapter 6. For information about what to do with files that you receive, including how to uncompress ZIP files and how to protect your computer from viruses, see Chapter 38.

Tip	*If the file that you want to send contains only text, you can avoid attaching the file entirely. Instead, you can use cut-and-paste to copy the text into the body of your message. Depending on which word processing program you are copying from and which e-mail program you use, the text may arrive in your message with formatting intact: see "Formatting E-mail" in Chapter 10.*

General Information About Attachments

The Internet e-mail system was designed to transmit only text, and thus can't handle *binary* (non-text) files such as graphics, audio, and programs. An *attachment* is a file that has been encoded as text, so that it can be included in an e-mail message. The following are the three common ways to encode e-mail attachments:

- **MIME**   *Multipurpose Internet Mail Extensions* is the standard method.
- **Uuencoding**   The old standard, and the only method supported by some older e-mail applications.
- **BinHex**   Used by some Mac e-mail programs.

You usually don't need to know what type of encoding you're using, because your e-mail application takes care of encoding and decoding messages. However, if you have trouble exchanging attachments with someone else, you may want to find out what type of encoding their e-mail application supports and make sure that you are using the same method. Try MIME first—it's the most commonly used encoding method.

Sending Attachments

To send a file by e-mail, you create a message to which you can attach the file. Address the message as usual and type a subject. You can also type text in the body of the message. Then, attach the file by choosing a menu command or by clicking a toolbar button (depending on which e-mail program you use). Some e-mail applications support dragging and dropping the file that you want to attach—drag it from Windows Explorer or a folder window to the open message.

Before you send an attachment with an e-mail message, consider these guidelines:

- Determine whether the person receiving the attachment has an e-mail program that can receive the file, and whether the person has the correct application needed to open or view the file. If necessary, send a message first (without the attachment) to ask.

- When you send a file, type an explanation in the body of the message to tell the recipient why you are sending them the attachment and what it is.

- Only send solicited attachments. This advice applies to mail in general, but it certainly goes for attachments, which can fill up a hard drive and take time to download.

- Don't send attachments to newsgroups and mailing lists unless the newsgroup or mailing list explicitly encourages attachments (for example, in a newsgroup for people exchanging pictures of fractals).

Some mail systems choke on large files, so you may need to compress them (using a program such as ZipMagic or WinZip, as described in Chapter 38) before sending them as an attachment. Sending and downloading large attachments can take some time, so you'll save both yourself and the recipient time if you make the file smaller by compressing it. Before you "zip" a file, make sure that your recipient has the software and the know-how to unzip it.

Tip   *If you have trouble sending or receiving attachments (which may happen with a particular recipient), you may want to use File Transfer Protocol (FTP) instead. Find an FTP site that you can both access, and upload your file to the FTP site, so that your recipient can then download it. FTP is covered in detail in Chapter 37.*

Receiving Attachments

Different e-mail applications handle attachments differently. Most store the attachment in the mail message. You need to open the message and then open or save the attachment before you can do anything else with it. When you delete a message with an attachment stored with it, you also may delete the attachment. To be able to use the attachment later, you need to save the attachment.

Other applications (notably Eudora) automatically save the attachment to a folder that you specify. If you are using one of these applications, you don't even need to open the message to use the attachment—you can open the attachment right from the folder where it is saved. You can choose whether deleting a message also deletes the files that were attached to that message.

Save attachments that you need rather than saving them with the message. Most people delete e-mail messages with abandon, and may accidentally delete a message with a needed attachment. If you are done with an attachment, delete it to save disk space.

Eudora and Eudora Light 4

Eudora Pro handles all three kinds of attachments. Eudora Light, however, can't deal with uuencoded files.

Sending an Attached File

To send a file attached to a Eudora message, follow these steps:

1. Create a new message by pressing CTRL+N or clicking the New Message button on the toolbar.

2. Drag a file from Windows Explorer or a folder window to the Eudora message window. You see the name and path of the file on the Attached line of the message. If you prefer, you can click the Attach File button on the toolbar or press CTRL+H. When you see the Attach File dialog box, select the file and click OK.

3. Choose the type of encoding on the toolbar (the third drop-down list).

4. Send the message.

If you click the Attach File button or press CTRL+H, Eudora creates a blank e-mail message and opens the Attach File dialog box in one step.

Receiving an Attached File

Eudora lets you know when a message has an attachment by including the paperclip icon in the message information. Figure 7-1 shows the Inbox: the highlighted message that is shown in the lower-right part of the Eudora Pro window contains an attachment.

When Eudora downloads messages, it puts any attachments in the folder that you specify in the Options dialog box (see the next section). To find out where the file is, open the message and position the cursor over the attachment icon (see Figure 7-1). Eudora displays the path and filename on the status line and in a pop-up box.

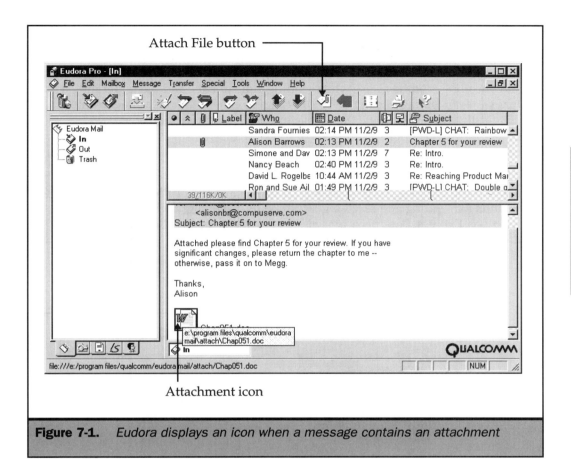

Attach File button

Attachment icon

Figure 7-1.   *Eudora displays an icon when a message contains an attachment*

The easiest way to open an attachment is to click the file icon in the message. You can open the file even if you see a message telling you that the attachment may have executable content; this message gives you a chance to not open a file that may be infected with a virus. Once you know where the file is located, you may prefer to open it another way, such as from Windows Explorer or from the application that you'll use to read the file.

Tip   *When you decide to keep an attachment, move the file out of your attachments folder into a more appropriate folder. Periodically delete files from the attachments directory so that you don't fill up your hard drive.*

Attachment Options

Choose Tools | Options and then click Attachments in the Category list to see options for sending and receiving attachments (see Figure 7-2). These options include the default encoding method to use when sending attachments, and the folder in which Eudora stores incoming attachments. You can also choose to delete attachments automatically when you delete the message to which they were attached.

Outlook 98 and Outlook Express

Outlook 98 and Outlook Express can handle MIME and uuencoded attachments. The commands for sending and receiving attachments differ slightly between Outlook 98 and Outlook Express. Both programs also have a mechanism called *linking files*, for sending files to other people on your local area network.

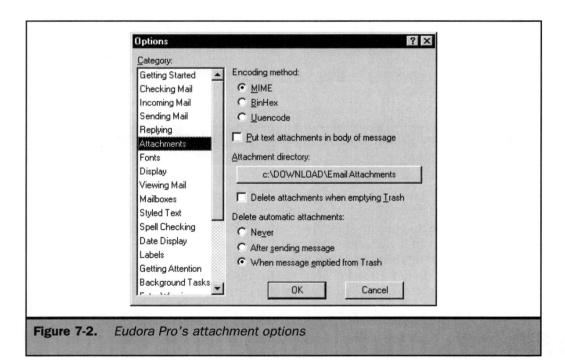

Figure 7-2.   *Eudora Pro's attachment options*

Sending an Attached File

The easiest way to attach a file to a message is to open a new message and drag the file to the message window. If you prefer to use a dialog box, open a new message and follow these steps:

1. Create a message and type the text that you want to include.

2. Put the cursor where you want the icon for the attached file to appear, and click the Insert File button on the message window toolbar (it looks like a paperclip) to display the Insert File dialog box. Alternatively, choose Insert | File (in Outlook 98) or Insert | File Attachment (in Outlook Express) to display the Insert File dialog box.

3. Double-click the file that you want to attach to the message.

4. Send the message as usual.

Linking a File (for LAN Users Only)

An alternative to sending a file with a message is to *link* the file to the message. A linked message is not included in the message, so it doesn't take up hard disk space. Instead, double-clicking the icon for a linked file opens a file in a specified location. Linking works only when you are sending a large file to a number of people, and all the recipients have access to a network drive or some other shared resource where you can store the file that you want them to have. In this case, linking a file is more efficient than attaching a file. However, linking doesn't work for sending files over the Internet.

To link a file, follow the steps for attaching a file. On the Insert File dialog box, click the Shortcut option (in Outlook 98) or Make a Shortcut to This File (in Outlook Express).

Receiving an Attached File

When you receive a message with an attachment, the message information appears with a paperclip icon. To access the attachment, open the message. In Outlook 98, attachments appear in messages as icons. In Outlook Express, a large paperclip icon appears at the top-right corner of the message.

Open the attachment by double-clicking the icon for the attached file in the message. To save the attachment without opening it, right-click the icon and choose Save As from the shortcut menu. Edit the file and folder names, if necessary, and click OK. Alternatively, you can save the file after you open it, by using the program that opened the file.

EXCHANGING E-MAIL

Because Outlook 98 and Outlook Express store attachments with the messages to which they are attached, deleting the message also deletes the attachment, unless you have saved it in a separate file.

Attachment Options

By default, Outlook 98 and Outlook Express use MIME when sending attachments. If you need to send a uuencoded attachment, or need to be sure which kind of attachment you're sending, you can check the program's attachment options.

In Outlook 98, follow these steps:

1. Choose Tools | Options to display the Options dialog box.
2. Click the Internet Mail tab.
3. The Internet E-mail Sending Format section contains MIME and uuencode options. The one that is selected is the method Outlook uses to send attachments. You can change this selection if you need to use the other format to send your attachment.

In Outlook Express, follow these steps:

1. Choose Tools | Options to display the Options dialog box.
2. Click the Send tab. Your Mail Sending Format should normally be set to Plain Text, so that recipients whose e-mail applications do not support HTML can easily read your message.
3. Click the Settings button next to the Plain Text option to see the Plain Text Options dialog box. The encoding method is set in the Message Format section of the dialog box.

Netscape Messenger

Netscape Messenger (which comes with the Netscape Communicator suite of programs) uses MIME encoding for attachments.

Sending an Attached File

When you compose a message in Netscape Messenger, you can see and specify information about attached files on the Attach Files & Documents tab in the headers section of the message window, as shown in Figure 7-3. (The headers section has three small tabs on the left side of the window: move your mouse pointer to a tab for a moment to display the name of that tab.)

Address Message tab

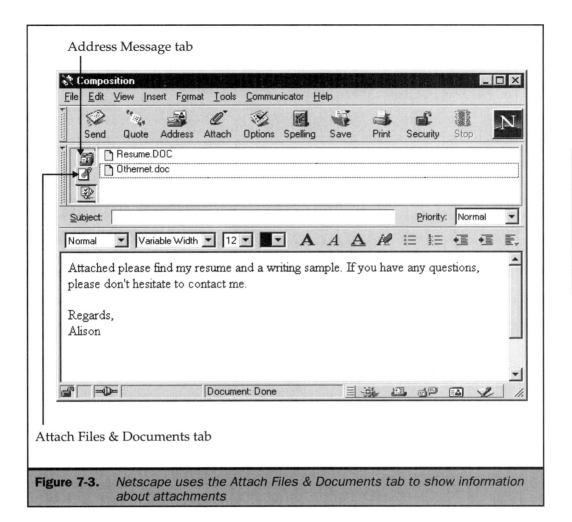

Attach Files & Documents tab

Figure 7-3. *Netscape uses the Attach Files & Documents tab to show information about attachments*

To send an attached file, follow these steps:

1. Open a new message.

2. Click the Attach button on the message window toolbar and choose File. Messenger displays the Enter File to Attach dialog box.

3. Select the file to attach and click Open. The Attach Files & Documents tab in the headers section of the message window is selected automatically, and you see

the name of the attached file. To view the more familiar header information, click the Address Message tab (the upper tab) in the top half of the window.

4. Send the message.

You can drag and drop a file to be attached, but it's a bit tricky. You must first click the Attach Files & Documents tab and then drag the files from Windows Explorer or a folder window to that section of the message window.

Receiving an Attached File

Messenger shows which messages have attachments, but the indicator is hard to see: The message icon, which usually looks like an envelope, has a small paperclip icon on it. To view the attachment, first open the message. Attachment information appears as shown in Figure 7-4: You may see either the information shown or simply an icon for

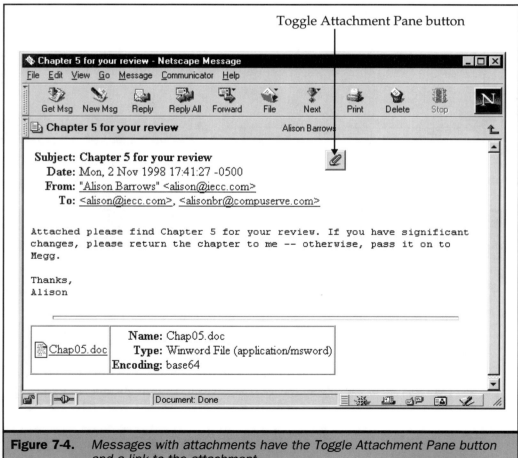

Figure 7-4. *Messages with attachments have the Toggle Attachment Pane button and a link to the attachment*

the attachment. You can toggle the display by clicking the Toggle Attachment Pane button (a paperclip icon) in the message headers.

To open or save an attached file, double-click the icon or the link to the file (depending on how the attachment information is displayed). You see a dialog box asking whether you want to open or save the file. If you open the file, consider whether you need to save it using the application that opens the file.

Pegasus

Pegasus can send and receive all three kinds of attachments: MIME, uuencoded, and BinHex. In fact, Pegasus offers you myriad options when you are sending attachments—more options than any of the other applications covered in this chapter.

Sending an Attached File

To send an attachment with an e-mail message, open a new message and then either click the Attachments tab on the message window or press F7. After the Attachments tab is displayed (shown in Figure 7-5), you can drag files that you want to attach to the message. If you prefer, you can use the bottom half of the Attachments tab to specify the path and filename. The full path names of attached files are displayed in the top half of the tab.

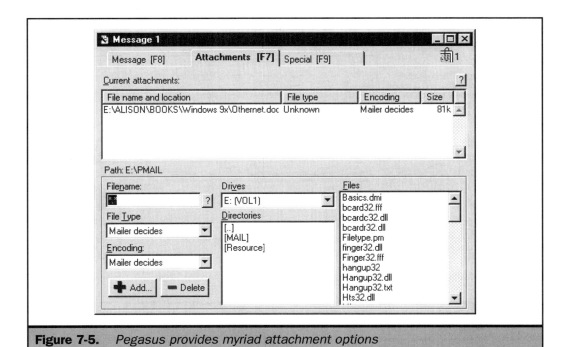

Figure 7-5.   *Pegasus provides myriad attachment options*

After you finish attaching files, click the Message tab to address the message and add some text to explain what the attached file is. Then, send the message as usual.

Pegasus gives you more options for attachments than many e-mail applications. These may be useful if your recipient has difficulty detaching and reading your attachments. However, the default settings usually work well, so try leaving the Mail Type and Encoding settings at Mailer Decides.

Receiving an Attached File

When you receive a message with an attachment, the message appears in the folder window with a small black box to the left of the message information. When you open the message, information about the attachment appears at the bottom of the message window. Figure 7-6 shows how Pegasus indicates attachments: You can see the black

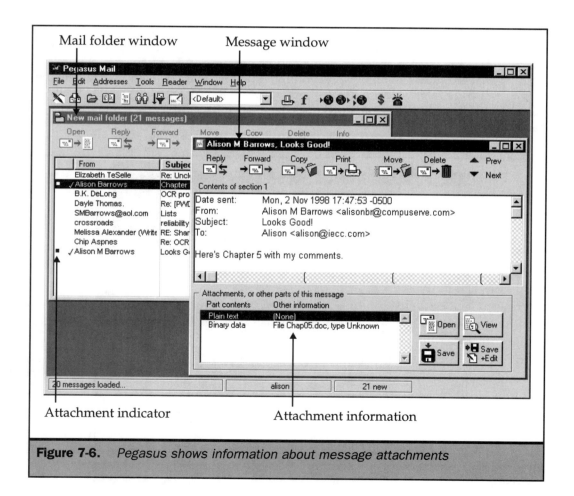

Figure 7-6. *Pegasus shows information about message attachments*

box in the mailbox window on the left, and the attachment information at the bottom of the message window on the right.

You can choose to open the attachment or save to disk by clicking the Open or Save button, respectively, in the message window. If you open the attachment, you may want to save it by using the application that was used to open it.

America Online (AOL)

AOL sends and receives MIME attachments.

Sending an Attached File

To attach a file to a message, follow these steps:

1. Create a new message, address it, and type explanatory text to go along with the file.

2. Click the Attachments button at the bottom of the Write Mail window. AOL displays the Attachments dialog box.

3. Click the Attach button to choose a file. Select the file and click Open.

4. Click OK to return to the Write Mail window.

5. Send the message. AOL displays a window showing the progress of the transfer of the file to AOL, and says "File's done!" when transfer is complete.

Receiving an Attached File

AOL gives you a very subtle indication that a message has an attachment: the message icon appears as an envelope with a disk behind it rather than as a simple envelope. When you open the message, you see the Download Now and Download Later buttons at the bottom of the message window (shown in Figure 7-7). Click the Download Now button to save the file to the folder that you select: the Download Manager window lets you choose where to save the file. Click Save to begin downloading, and then click OK when AOL informs you that the file has arrived.

If you are working offline or you'd rather not download the attached file now, click the Download Later button to add the file to the Download Manager. When you close AOL, you will be prompted to download files in the Download Manager.

CompuServe

CompuServe supports MIME attachments.

EXCHANGING E-MAIL

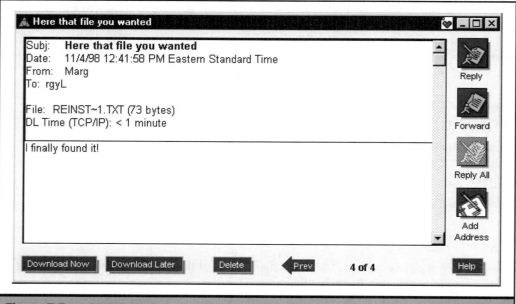

Figure 7-7. *Click Download Now in AOL's message window to download an attached file*

Sending an Attached File

To send an attached file, follow these steps:

1. Create a new message.
2. Click the Attach Mail button on the Create Mail window.
3. Select the file in the Enter File to Attach dialog box. You may need to navigate to a different folder to find the file.
4. Click the Open button.
5. You see the Attach Files dialog box, where all attached files are listed (shown in Figure 7-8). Choose the type of file that you are sending: text, GIF, or JPEG. If the file doesn't fall into any of those categories, select Binary. If you want to attach only one file, click the OK button. If you want to attach additional files, click the Add to List button to see the Enter File to Attach dialog box again. To remove a file from the list of attachments, click the Remove button.
6. Send the message.

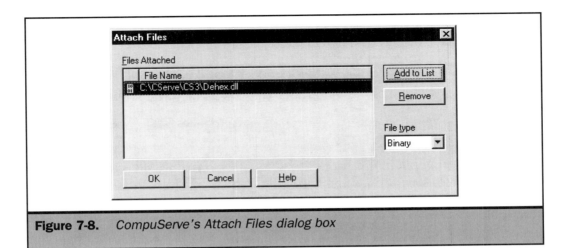

Figure 7-8.   *CompuServe's Attach Files dialog box*

Receiving an Attached File

CompuServe doesn't give you any indication that a message has an attachment until you open the message. Then, you see that the message has multiple parts with arrows to display the different parts, as shown in Figure 7-9. To view information about the attachment, click the right-arrow button to move to the next part of the message. The message area contains information about the file: in Figure 7-9, the file is named Chap05.doc. Click the Open File and Save File buttons, respectively, to open the file using the application that reads that file type or to save the file in the location that you specify on your computer.

Pine

Working with attachments using a UNIX shell account is made more difficult by the fact that you have to transfer files to and from the UNIX system. Normally, the files that you want to send are located on your PC, and when you receive files, you want to save them on your PC. However, Pine doesn't know how to access files on your PC, so attaching and detaching files is a two-step process. The section "Working with Files on Your Shell Account" in Chapter 40 explains how to transfer files to and from a UNIX account. The present section explains how to deal with attachments in Pine.

Pine can handle MIME attachments.

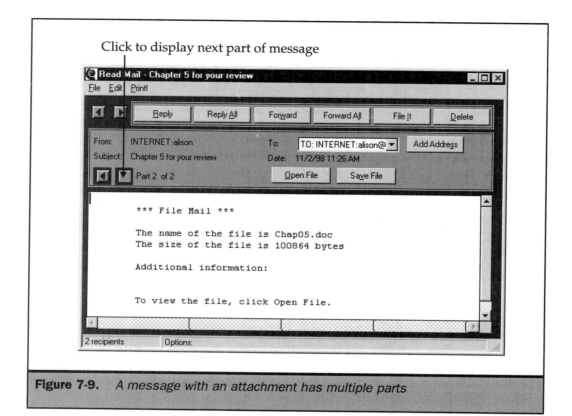

Figure 7-9. *A message with an attachment has multiple parts*

Sending an Attached File

Before you can attach a file to a message, the file must be on the UNIX machine. After you transfer the file from your PC or Mac, create a new message in Pine. Then, use one of the following two methods to attach or include the file in the message:

■ If you want to send the contents of a text file (that is, a file that contains only text: if you can open the file using Notepad, then it is a text file), press CTRL+R and type the path and name of the file. The text appears in the message, which you can then send as usual.

■ To attach a file to a message by using Pine, press CTRL+J, type the path and name of the file, and then enter a short description when prompted. You see the filename in the Attachmnt header for the message. You can attach additional files by repeating those steps. Then, send the file as usual.

Receiving an Attached File

In Pine, you can't tell that a message has an attachment until you open the message to read it. When you open a message with a file attached, you see a list of the attachments at the top of the message. At the end of the message, you see instructions for viewing each attachment: Pine usually says to press V to view or save the attachment.

When you press V, you see a list of the attached files, such as the list shown in Figure 7-10. If the attachment is text, Pine can show you the message—select the attachment and press ENTER. If you want to save the file, select the attachment (in Figure 7-10, the second file listed is the one that is being saved) and press S to save it. Pine saves the file in your default directory on the UNIX machine. If you need the file on your PC, download the file to your PC by using the instructions in Chapter 40.

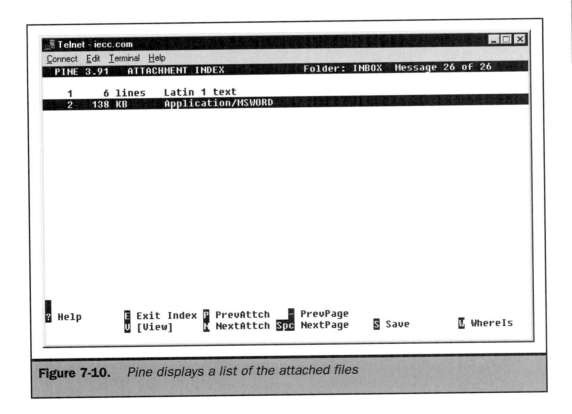

Figure 7-10.   *Pine displays a list of the attached files*

The
Complete
Reference

Internet

Chapter 8

Controlling Your E-mail Volume

While e-mail has provided a wonderful new means of communication for many people, it has also provided an additional distraction in already-busy lives. E-mail may be an integral part of your day, but you may also find that you spend far too much time sorting through your messages. Some of that e-mail overload may be from mailing lists that you've signed up for, some may be humor forwarded by friends, and some may be unsolicited offers from people you've never heard of. *Filtering*—sorting your mail in various mailboxes or folders as it arrives—can alleviate all of these problems, including throwing away unwanted e-mail ads (*spam*). *Autoreplying* is another useful e-mail feature that allows your e-mail program to reply to some messages with a standard response—without you lifting a finger.

This chapter explains filtering and autoreplying, and then describes the steps that are required to set up filtering and autoreplying in Eudora, Outlook 98, Outlook Express, Netscape Messenger, Pegasus, America Online, and Pine. (CompuServe does not support filters or autoreplies.) For more information about these programs, see Chapter 6.

The Advantages of Filtering E-mail

Filtering is not always a sure-fire way to get rid of unwanted mail, but it can help. All the major e-mail packages allow you to filter incoming messages—if yours doesn't, you might want to find one that does, especially if you have a high volume of e-mail.

How Filtering Works

When you set up a filter in your e-mail program, the program moves messages from your inbox to a designated folder as soon they are received. This process enables you to focus on the mail in your inbox when time is tight, and leave the filtered mail in other folders for when you have more time. Or, you may choose to target high-priority e-mail and filter it into another folder, which you attend to first.

Filtering works by looking at the contents of the message. Normally, you tell your e-mail application to look at the contents of the message and do something with the message based on what it finds. You may choose to look at the headers, such as who the message is to or from or what the subject line is. Or, you may want to look at specific words in the message. For instance, you may want to filter all messages written to a particular mailing list, and have them stored in a folder that you've created for that mailing list. And you may want to create another filter that moves to a Humor folder all mail from friends who pass along jokes that they've heard. You could even ask your friends to put the word "humor" on the subject line, so that you can easily filter the messages and not miss any personal notes.

To filter mail, you need to choose some criterion or rule—if the message matches the criterion or rule, then the e-mail application does whatever you specify with the message. It may put it in a folder, flag it in some way, or delete it. What a filter can do with a message depends on the application, but all applications that support filters can at least put the message in a folder that you specify.

Devising a rule to sort messages that always come from the same place or that are always addressed to the same address usually is easy. For instance, you can easily sort messages from a mailing list or from a small group of people (say, the eight colleagues working with you on a particular project). However, sorting junk mail (unsolicited marketing messages) out of your inbox is considerably more difficult, because you have to devise a rule that sorts only junk mail and not the mail that you actually want to read.

Filtering Mailing List Messages

The usual way to sort messages sent from a mailing list is to use the "To" address. Because messages sent to a mailing list are always sent to the same e-mail address, you can use that address to define your criteria. For instance, if the address for the mailing list is **click-L@ListService.net**, you can specify that all mail you receive that has **click-L@ListService.net** in the To line should be moved to a folder that you've created to hold mail from that mailing list.

Controlling E-mail Volume and Reducing Spam

Spam is the term that Internet users apply to unsolicited commercial e-mail (also called UCE). You receive spam because the sender has obtained your e-mail address, either from a mailing list or newsgroup, or directly from you on a Web site. Your address may be in one or more of the lists of e-mail addresses that are available for sale.

What Can You Do About Spam?

The following are a few ways to reduce the amount of spam that you receive:

- Be careful about who you give your address to.

- Set up several e-mail accounts and use them selectively (AOL lets you do this easily).

- Don't bother "unsubscribing" from any service that sends you messages unless you originally subscribed to the service. Rather than taking your name off the list, the sender may keep you on the list. In fact, your e-mail address becomes more valuable to spammers when they receive a removal request from you, because you've just confirmed that your e-mail address is valid. Exceptions are messages from mailing lists to which you actually subscribed, or messages from organizations from which you specifically requested information.

- Control the time that you spend on your own e-mail. Don't spend time on messages that you're not interested in—this takes some self-control. You don't actually have to open every e-mail that lands in your inbox.

- Don't contribute to the spam problem by forwarding unwanted messages or by sending your own messages to many recipients. If you pass along messages regularly, you should periodically check whether the recipients on your list still want to receive your messages.

- Create filters that automatically delete spam messages. (Make sure that your filter matches only spam, since you'll never see these messages!) Look at the headers of the spam you receive to identify domains used only by spammers.

Unless your friends or colleagues use the Bcc (blind carbon copy) header, you may want to automatically delete messages that contain your address on the Bcc line, since this technique is frequently used by spammers.

- If you post messages to Usenet newsgroups or web-based chat pages, don't include your e-mail address. E-mail addresses in newsgroups and web pages are "harvested" by spammers.

Stopping Spammers

You can do several things to reduce spam, but none of them is completely effective. If you feel strongly about spam, you may want to spend a little more time researching where it comes from and sending messages to the appropriate system administrators. If you complain to the sender's system administrator or postmaster, he or she may close the spammer's account. Be aware, though, that not all system administrators care that their domain is being used to send spam.

If you want to get more involved, many Web sites are available that discuss spam and what to do about it. You could start with these sites:

- **http://www.cauce.org**   The Coalition Against Unsolicited Commercial E-Mail (CAUCE)
- **http://www.abuse.net**   Network Abuse Clearinghouse
- **http://www.nags.org**   Netizens Against Gratuitous Spamming (NAGS)

Reporting Egregious Scams

If you are the victim of an e-mail scam and you are in the United States, you should file a complaint with the Federal Trade Commission (FTC). The FTC is a government agency whose purpose includes the following:

The Commission works to enhance the smooth operation of the marketplace by eliminating acts or practices that are unfair or deceptive. In general, the Commission's efforts are directed toward stopping actions that threaten consumers' opportunities to exercise informed choice.

Report scams that appear illegal (such as pyramid schemes, not just annoying e-mail) by using the complaint form that you can find at **http://www.ftc.gov**. Or forward the messages to **uce@ftc.gov**.

Sending Spam

If you have a business, you may want to advertise your wares on the Internet. Bulk e-mail packages are available that make it very easy to send an e-mail to hundreds or thousands of people. You may find the ability to so easily access so many people very tempting. But sending mail of this type, which is unsolicited bulk e-mail, has its problems. The most important issues relating to unsolicited bulk e-mail are that it is not very well received, and it may result in your ISP fining you or closing your account.

Renting a mailing list and sending unsolicited e-mail to thousands of unsuspecting users doesn't work, ruins the reputation of your company, and may cost you in fines, a lost Internet account, or legal problems. Don't do it!

Defining E-mail Abuse

Most people on the Internet believe that sending bulk unsolicited e-mail messages, even those that are basically advertisements similar to those that are delivered to you through the U.S. Postal Service, is abuse of the e-mail system. While bulk e-mail seems to be identical to bulk postal mail, there is one important difference—when you send postal mail, you pay for the service; when you send bulk e-mail, the people who own the servers that handle the mail you send pay for the service.

Although much e-mail is unsolicited, unsolicited e-mail is not in itself abuse of the system. However, sending unsolicited mail to numerous people or sending numerous unsolicited mail messages to one address is considered to be abuse.

People may solicit e-mail, either knowingly or unknowingly, if they do any of the following:

- Subscribe to a mailing list

- Request information or opinions from a mailing list or newsgroup

- Send e-mail to an address to get more information

- Provide an e-mail address on a Web site that explicitly states that the address will be used to send you information

You are not necessarily soliciting e-mail simply by providing your e-mail address to someone else, whether it is via a personal note, IRC (chat), newsgroup, mailing list, or purchase of a product.

What Are the Legal Issues?

Currently, no Federal law bans unsolicited e-mail. In fact, many people are concerned that laws prohibiting "junk" e-mail could negatively affect free speech and the free flow of information on the Internet. However, other laws may apply and other factors may dampen your enthusiasm about sending bulk mail:

■ Your ISP may limit or prohibit bulk e-mail. Because ISPs receive complaints about unsolicited e-mail sent through them, they often look for the account from which the messages originated, and may censure the sender in some way.

■ Some laws already apply to e-mail. For instance, if you send e-mail that meets the legal definition of harassment, you could be sued under harassment laws. Some states have a "truth in headers" law that makes it illegal to forge header information in an e-mail, such as who the message is from. Fraudulent e-mail offers are within the jurisdiction of the Federal Trade Commission.

■ Many spammers don't include their real return address, so that they don't receive bounced messages from bad e-mail addresses to which they send spam. As a result, the holder of the return address that the spammer inserted (or the postmaster of that domain) ends up receiving hundreds or thousands of bounced messages—along with messages of complaint—for messages sent by someone else. Legislation has been proposed that prohibits sending spam using a fraudulent return address.

Replying to Messages Automatically

An *autoreply* or *mailbot* is an automatic response to an e-mail. An autoreply may save you the time of sending a personal e-mail, or it may let the sender know why you aren't responding, and thus save you from receiving additional messages from that sender. Depending on the package that you use, you may be able to send autoreply messages that meet certain criteria, or you may have to send an autoreply to all received messages. If you can't chose which messages to autoreply to, then the feature is useful only if you are going to be out of the office or in some other situation in which you want to reply with the same message to everyone who sends you an e-mail.

Filters and Autoreplies in Eudora

Eudora Pro has easy-to-use filter and autoreply features. Eudora Light can filter messages, but does not have the autoreply feature. This section describes Eudora Pro and Eudora Light 4.

Filtering Messages

Eudora provides both ease and complexity in its filter features—making a simple filter is easily done on the Make Filter dialog box. To make a more complex filter, select Tools | Filters to see the Filters dialog box.

Creating Filters in Eudora Pro

The easiest way to create a filter is to select a message that meets your filtering criteria and then follow these steps:

1. Select Special | Make Filter, or right-click the message and choose Make Filter, to see the Make Filter dialog box, shown in Figure 8-1. The Make Filter dialog box copies information from the selected message for your filter. You can take the settings that you need and delete the others to create your filter.

2. Change the Match Conditions settings, as needed: choose the type of mail that you're filtering (that is, when Eudora should run the filter). Your choices are Incoming, Outgoing, and Manual. Select the header contents that you want to use to filter the message and use the accompanying text box to type the text you want the filter to find.

3. Choose the Action settings—choose whether to transfer the message to a new or existing folder, or delete the message. If you're moving the message, be sure to name the folder or select the existing folder that you want to use.

4. Click Create Filter to make the filter. If you want more control over the filter, click Add Details to see the filter in the Filters dialog box.

Creating Filters in Eudora Light

Eudora Light does not have the Special | Make Filters command. Instead, in both Eudora Light and Eudora Pro, you can create filters by choosing Tools | Filters from the menu, which displays the Filters dialog box (shown in Figure 8-2). Click the New button to create a new filter. Define the criteria in the top half of the dialog box, and, in the bottom half of the dialog box, define the action to take for the messages that match the defined criteria.

Making Filters That You Can Run Any Time

Eudora Pro has a neat feature that allows you to filter messages after they arrive on your computer—*manual filters*. If you get a bunch of messages that you want to filter, you can create a filter for them and set the filter type to Manual. To run the filter (and all the other manual filters that you have set up), choose Special | Filter Messages from the menu. (Eudora Light does not have this feature.)

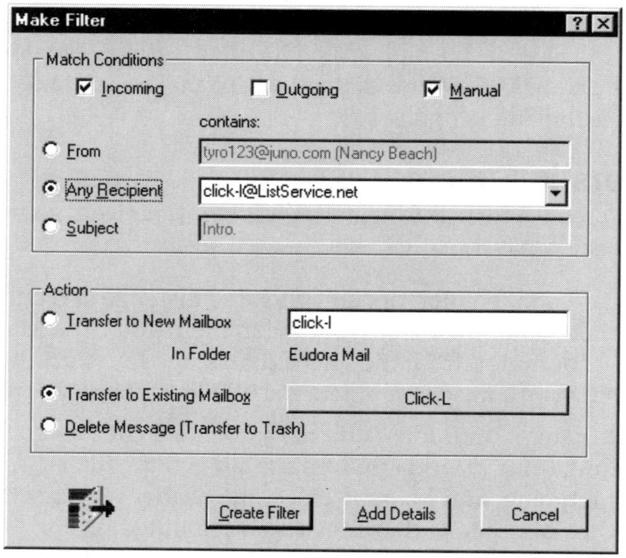

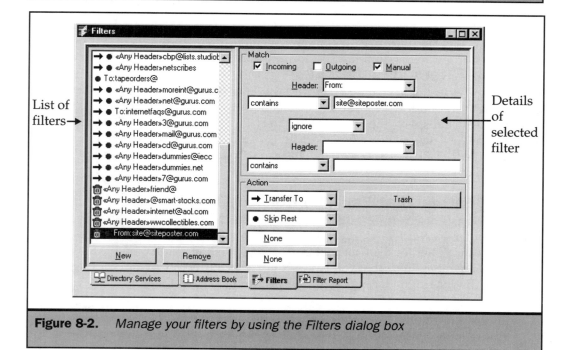

Figure 8-1. *The Make Filter dialog box uses information from the selected message*

Figure 8-2. *Manage your filters by using the Filters dialog box*

Editing and Deleting Filters

You can use the Filters dialog box to edit exiting filters, change the order in which Eudora executes the filters, or get rid of filters that you no longer want. Choose Tools | Filters from the menu to display the Filters dialog box. When you select a filter from the list on the left side of the window, the information about that filter appears in the boxes on the right side.

Sending Autoreplies

Eudora Pro lets you use filters to select messages for the autoreply feature, so you can autoreply to selected messages even when you're in the office.

Before you turn on the autoreply feature, you need to create the message that you want autoreply to send. Create stationery (form letters, described in the next chapter) by following these steps:

1. Choose Tools | Stationery from the menu.

2. Right-click in the Stationery window and choose New to display the Stationery form, which looks like a new message.

3. Create the message, leaving the To line blank. Type the subject and the text of the message.

4. Save the file by choosing File | Save As Stationery. Give the stationery a descriptive name that indicates what the message states.

To create an autoreply, follow these steps:

1. Open the Filters dialog box (choose Tools | Filters).

2. Create a new filter with the criteria for the messages to which you want to autoreply. If you want to send an autoreply in response to every message that you receive, you might create the criteria to find messages with any header containing your e-mail address.

3. In the action section, choose Reply With as the action, and choose as the message to automatically send the name of the stationery that you created.

Filters and Autoreplies in Outlook 98

To use Outlook 98's sophisticated filtering capabilities, you create a filter by using the Rules Wizard. In addition to regular filters, Outlook also has a feature to find and filter junk e-mail. (See the following section for information about Outlook Express.)

Filtering Messages

To create a filter, use Outlook's Rules Wizard. Start it by displaying any mail folder and choosing Tools | Rules Wizard from the menu. The Rules Wizard lists all the rules that you currently have defined. You can turn off a rule by clicking it to remove the check mark.

The easiest way to create a new rule is to find a message that meets your criteria and create a new rule based on that message. Here's how to do it:

1. Open the message.

2. Choose Actions | Create Rule from the message window menu to see the Rules Wizard. Answer its questions and click Next to move from screen to screen.

3. Select the aspect(s) of the message that you want to use to create the rule. For instance, you may want to filter all messages from this person or to this distribution list. Click the box next to your selection(s) so that a check mark appears. The selection(s) appears in the Rule Description box at the bottom of the dialog box.

4. You can edit the underlined text of any rules that you selected in the last step by clicking the text.

5. Next, the Rules Wizard asks you what you want to do with the messages that the rule finds. Frequently, you'll want to move the message to a specific folder—to do so, select the first option, Move It to the Inbox Folder, and then edit the folder name. You can select more than one option.

6. Edit any underlined text, as necessary. For instance, you may want to edit the name of the folder to which the message is sent or copied. When you click a folder name to edit it, Outlook displays a list of existing folders—you can pick from the list or create a new folder.

7. Next, the Wizard allows you to select exceptions to the rule.

8. The last step asks you to name the rule and gives you a last chance to make changes to the rule that you've defined (see Figure 8-3). You can change any of the underlined items by clicking them.

9. Click finish when you are done.

After you create a rule, you can turn it off or edit it from the Rules Wizard dialog box.

To create a new rule from scratch, display the Rules Wizard by choosing Tools | Rules Wizard and then click the New button on the Rules Wizard dialog box. The Rules Wizard guides you through the process of defining the following aspects of a filter:

- The type of rule that you want to create. Most of these choices have to do with the type of message that the filter is examining and what the filter does with the message. Move New Messages From Someone is useful for sorting mailing-list mail or mail from a particular person. Move Messages Based on Content is useful if you are looking at the content of the message rather than the message header.

- The conditions that the message has to meet to be filtered. For instance, you may want to filter all messages that list you on the Bcc line, or all messages sent to a particular distribution list.

- What you want to do with the message (for example, move it to a specified folder or delete it).

- Any exceptions to the filtering rule.

- A name for the filter.

You can click any underlined text—names and folders, for instance—in the filter to edit it.

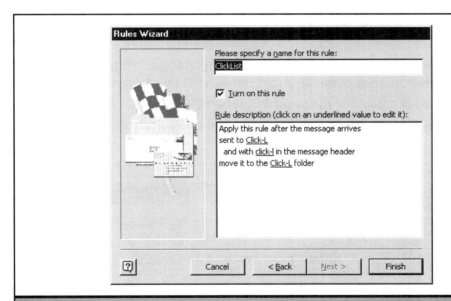

Figure 8-3. *Outlook's Rules Wizard asks you to name the new filter*

Deleting Junk E-mail

Outlook has a special "junk mail" feature that you can turn on. This feature looks for messages with words and phrases that are commonly used in junk mail, and messages from domains that are known for sending junk mail. A description of the filters included in the junk mail feature can be found in a file called Filters.txt, which is usually stored in the C:\Program Files\Microsoft Office\Office folder.

To turn on the Junk E-mail feature, click the Organize button that is on the toolbar when a mail folder is active. You see the Ways to Organize Inbox pane. Click the Junk E-mail tab to see the options shown in Figure 8-4.

The Junk E-Mail tab contains two options, one for junk messages and one for adult content messages. You can turn on or off these features by clicking the button next to the text describing the option. When these options are selected, messages identified as junk or adult content appear in your Inbox in a different color, enabling you to delete them quickly.

Remember that filters like this are never foolproof, so you should at least scan the message information before deleting it, to make sure that it is indeed a message that you want to delete. You can access more options related to junk e-mail by clicking the **click here** link at the bottom of the panel.

You can add to the addresses identified as junk or adult content mail by following these steps:

1. When you receive a message that you wish Outlook had identified as junk or adult content, right-click the message information in the folder.

2. Choose Junk E-Mail from the menu that appears.

3. Choose either Add to Junk Senders List or Add to Adult Content Senders List.

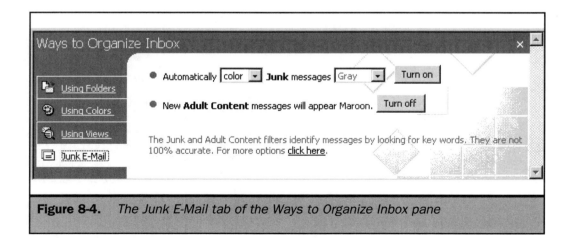

Figure 8-4. *The Junk E-Mail tab of the Ways to Organize Inbox pane*

Sending Autoreplies

If your version of Outlook has this feature, you can use the Out of Office Assistant to create a message to be sent to every person who sends you e-mail. Open the Out of Office Assistant by choosing Tools | Out of Office Assistant from the menu. Outlook must be running and picking up mail for this feature to work, unless your e-mail system uses Microsoft Exchange Server, in which case Outlook doesn't need to be running for rules to be applied.

The Rules Wizard allows you to select Reply Using a Specific Template as one of the options under What Do You Want to Do with This Message. You can store in the template a whole message that is automatically sent to people who send you a message that passes the rules for a particular filter.

Note   *Some versions of Outlook 98 don't have the Tools | Out of Office Assistant.*

Filters in Outlook Express

Like Outlook 98, Outlook Express also has filtering, although it doesn't support the complex criteria that Outlook supports. Outlook Express can't send autoreplies. (If you need autoreplies and you own Microsoft Office, consider downloading Outlook 98 from the Microsoft Web site at **http://www.microsoft.com/outlook**.) To set up a filter in Outlook Express, follow these steps:

1. Select a message with the criteria that you want to use for a filter, and make a note of the e-mail address or other information that identifies this type of message. Outlook Express doesn't allow you to base a filter on an existing message—when you create a filter, you do it from scratch. You may want to copy an e-mail address to the Clipboard so that you can copy it into the filter definition.

2. Select Tools | Inbox Assistant. The Inbox Assistant dialog box displays the filters that have already been defined. You can turn on and off a filter by clicking the check box next to the filter description.

3. Create a new filter by clicking the Add button on the Inbox Assistant dialog box. You see the Properties dialog box, shown in Figure 8-5.

4. Set the criteria in the top part of the window by entering information that identified the headers of the messages you want to filter. For instance, the filter shown in Figure 8-5 looks for messages that are written to the **list@studiobb.com** address. To be filtered, a message must meet all the criteria that you set.

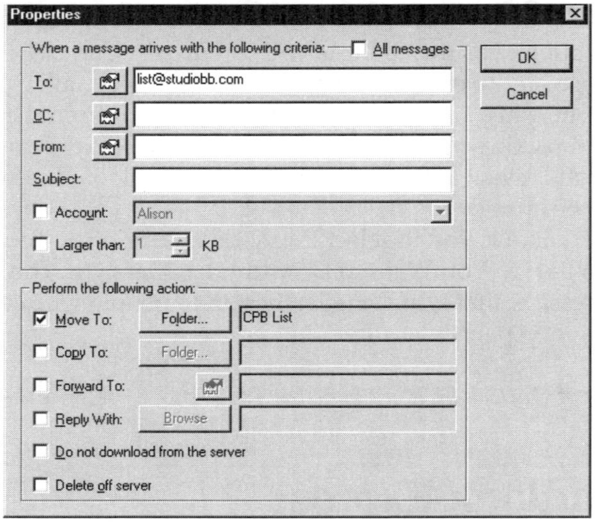

Figure 8-5.   *In Outlook Express, you define a filter by using the Properties dialog box*

5. In the bottom part of the window, define the action that Outlook Express should take when a message matches the filter. In Figure 8-5, messages meeting the criteria are moved to the CPB List folder.

6. After you define the filter, click OK.

Filters in Netscape Messenger

Netscape Navigator offers a straightforward method to create a simple or complex filter, but doesn't include a feature to do autoreplies. To create a filter, choose Edit | Message Filters from the main menu, which displays the Message Filters dialog box. Existing filters are listed in this dialog box. Filters with a check mark to their right are turned on.

To create a new filter, click the New button to display the Filter Rules dialog box, shown in Figure 8-6. To define a new filter, name the filter and then use the drop-down lists and the text box to define the details of the rule. If you want to add additional rules, click the More button to display another row. If you use multiple rules, you need to choose how the rules work together—either they all must be met or only one must be met—use the radio buttons to choose the appropriate setting. The description for the filter is optional, but it gives you a place to describe how the filter works.

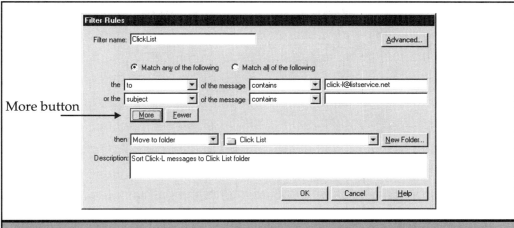

More button

Figure 8-6.   *The Filter Rules dialog box gives you a straightforward way to create filtering rules in Netscape Messenger*

Filters and Autoreplies in Pegasus

Pegasus provides both filtering and autoreplies. However, to send autoreplies, you must be on a local area network (or intranet) that uses the Mercury mail server (ask your system administrator). At-home dial-in users can't send autoreplies.

Filtering Messages

Pegasus allows you to create complex filters, but you may find them a little difficult to figure out. For instance, you not only can filter mail as it arrives, but you can also filter mail in a particular folder by using a filter that you can invoke at any time. To create a filter with Pegasus, follow these steps:

1. Choose Tools | Mail Filtering Rules | Rules Applied When Folder Is Opened or Rules Applied When Folder Is Closed. Which command you choose depends on when you want the messages in the folder to be filtered—when you open the folder (or when the folder is open), or when you close it. If you want mail to be filtered as it arrives and moved to different folders if it meets certain criteria, choose to filter when the folder is opened—this will filter messages as they arrive in the Inbox. Note that only unread mail is affected by a filter.

2. You see the New Mail Filtering Rules dialog box. To create a new rule, click the Add rule button to display a blank Edit Rule dialog box (Figure 8-7).

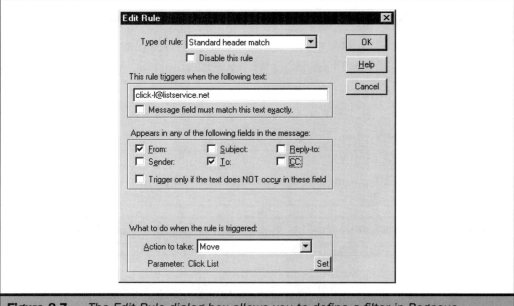

Figure 8-7. *The Edit Rule dialog box allows you to define a filter in Pegasus*

3. Define the Type of Rule by using the drop-down list at the top of the dialog box. The options on the dialog box change depending on the type of rule that you select. If you want to create a rule based on who the message is to or from, choose Standard Header Match. If you want the rule to scan the contents of messages, select Regular Expression Match.

4. Use the options on the dialog box to define the rule.

5. Define what to do with messages that meet the criteria. The setting that you use to define what to do with messages that meet the criteria always appears at the bottom of the dialog box (except when the Type of Rule is Comment or Label). Use the drop-down list to choose what to do with the message. Many of the options trigger a dialog box—for instance, if you choose to move or copy the message, you need to tell Pegasus the folder name. If you choose to forward the message, a dialog box appears in which you specify the e-mail address that you want the message forwarded to.

Sending Autoreplies

If you are using Pegasus's companion server product, Mercury, you can automatically reply to messages. The menu command to set up automatic replies is Tools | Automatic Reply.

Blocking Junk Mail in AOL

AOL doesn't have a "filter feature" as it has been defined in this chapter. However, it does have a feature that allows you to block certain mail. Unlike a filter, which allows you to choose what to do with mail that meets your criteria (for example, file it in a particular folder or delete it), AOL's mail controls only allow you to block mail entirely.

 Since you never see the messages that you block, you can never check that you're blocking only the mail that you don't want to read. Use AOL's mail controls conservatively, or you'll end up blocking incoming mail from friends and colleagues.

To access AOL's mail controls, choose Mail Center | Mail Controls from the toolbar, which displays the Mail Controls dialog box. This dialog box has three clickable areas:

- **Junk Mail**   You can choose to report junk mail to AOL, go to the Mail Controls screen, or see AOL's tips on how to recognize and avoid junk mail.

- **Parental Controls**   You can limit the content available to a particular screen name in your account. AOL has created the content screen so you can select the age of the child (who should have his/her own screen name) to block access to areas deemed inappropriate for that age group. You may prefer to use the set of Custom Controls, which gives you additional options.

- **Set Up Mail Controls**   You can block e-mail to a particular screen name. Seven blocking levels are available, from allowing all mail, to allowing only AOL mail, to allowing no mail at all. Most options enable you to specify domains and/or AOL members who you don't want to receive mail from.

Filters and Autoreplies in Pine

Pine allows you to filter incoming messages into folders and automatically reply to messages. However, Pine is a text-based UNIX application, and the lack of a graphical interface makes these tasks somewhat complicated.

EXCHANGING E-MAIL

Filtering Messages

To sort incoming mail, your UNIX mail system must have the *procmail* mail sorting system installed as the mail delivery program. Check with your system administrator to see whether procmail is used on your system. (If your system uses a different mail system, ask your system administrator how to create filters.)

Like any filtering system, Pine has two steps to filter incoming mail:

1. Create folders in which to put the mail.

2. Define criteria for sorting the mail into different folders. Before you begin this step, look at the messages that you want to sort, and consider what they have in common.

To create filtering criteria, edit or create a file called **.procmailrc** in your home directory. This file contains *recipes*, directions for how to identify mail that you want to filter and instructions on what to do with the mail. Each recipe has three lines, similar to the following:

:0
* *criteria*
Mail/*folder name*

The :0 marks the beginning of a recipe: the procmailrc file can contain multiple recipes. Replace *criteria* with the header information that identifies the messages to be filtered. Replace *folder name* with the name of the folder into which you want to move the messages. Here's an example:

```
:0
* From: click-l@ListService.net
Mail/clicklist
```

This example looks for mail from the click-l list and tells Pine to move messages that meet the criteria to the folder called clicklist.

The easiest criteria to write contain the exact header line that the messages contain, like To, From, Cc, and Subject. You also can use the asterisk as a wildcard in the pattern. For instance, you may want to filter mail with *make money* anywhere in the title. You can code that pattern as ***make money***. You may also want to add comments, to remind you what each recipe does: to do so, precede your comments with **#**.

Note   *Pine alerts you only when you have new mail in your Inbox. You have to check other folders to see whether you have new mail that has been filtered into them.*

Sending Autoreplies

UNIX has a program called *vacation* that enables you to send an automated reply to each person who sends you mail. The vacation program sends the message to a particular recipient only once a week. Here's how it works:

1. Use a text editor to type the text of the message that you want sent out as a reply to messages that you receive while you're away. The first line must have **From:** followed by a space and your e-mail address. The next line should be a **Subject:** line with a one-line reason explaining why you are sending this message. Leave the next line blank and then type the text that you want to send. Save the message in your home directory and call it **.vacation.msg**.

2. Type **vacation -i** at the prompt. This turns on the vacation program.

3. Create another text file in your home directory and call it **.forward**. Include the following text in this file: *****username*, **" | /usr/bin/vacation"**. Use your user name in place of *username*. This tells the mail system to store each message in your mailbox and to call the vacation program to respond to the message.

Note *Most UNIX systems run a program called* sendmail *to handle the mail. If your system uses a competing program called* qmail, *instead of creating a .forward file, create a file named .qmail containing two lines: a line that says* **./Mailbox** *to save incoming messages in your mailbox, and a second line that says* | **vacation** *to pass messages to the vacation program.*

When you come back from vacation, delete the .forward (or .qmail) file to turn off the vacation program. Then read the messages that you received while you were gone.

Chapter 9

Sending and Receiving Secure E-mail

More people use e-mail than any other Internet service, and e-mail is used increasingly to exchange sensitive information such as passwords and credit card numbers. Secure e-mail is an increasing concern for many Internet users. This chapter introduces the concepts of secure e-mail and describes the steps to follow to use encryption with some of the most popular e-mail programs that offer good security protection: Eudora, Outlook and Outlook Express, Netscape Messenger, and Pegasus. For a general discussion of Internet security, encryption, public key cryptography, and PGP, see "Secure Communications and Transactions" in Chapter 18.

What Is E-mail Security?

E-mail security deals with two issues: the safety of the information that you send and the reliability of the information that you receive. The main question on most people's minds, however, is *why* e-mail security is necessary. Is the vast majority of regular e-mail in that much jeopardy?

Reasons to Secure Your Messages

All information sent out over the Internet is distributed in *packets*, or small blocks, that are directed by your ISP's server, sent across the Internet, and reassembled by your recipient's server. These packets pass through many servers as they travel to their destination, and along the way, they may be detected by a *packet sniffer*, a program designed to identify certain groups of numbers or letters, such as credit card numbers or passwords.

Your e-mail can also be intercepted if you send or receive e-mail through a Web-based setup, because someone can attempt to guess your password and tamper with your account. And if you send e-mail by using your employer's e-mail programs and mail servers, all of your e-mail—sent and received—may be backed up and stored in the company's archives, without your knowledge or approval.

Most people don't send messages that would cause a security issue. But imagine that your organization used e-mail from salespeople in the field to place, confirm, and check the status of sales orders? You wouldn't want these messages to be read or tampered with by outsiders. If you or your organization is concerned about protecting your privacy, your credit, or other vulnerable e-mail information, consider using secure e-mail.

Public Key Cryptography

To send e-mail that unauthorized people can't read, you use *encryption*, which protects your information by *encoding* it—substituting letters and numbers with different characters, based on a code. Your e-mail is still sent over the Internet in packets, but the small strings of information that they contain appear scrambled, so that packet sniffers or casual hackers can't read what you've sent. With the right password, the recipient of your e-mail can decode the message and read it.

The best and most widely used type of encryption uses a pair of mathematically related numbers (or *keys*) rather than a single password. One number—your *private key*—is stored on the hard drive of your computer and is imprinted on every encrypted e-mail that you send. The public number—your *public key*—can be freely distributed, because only the two halves working together can decrypt your e-mail. In fact, many people who use secure e-mail routinely include the public part of their key pair in their signature files. This system of paired keys is called *public key cryptography*. (See "Public Key Cryptography" in Chapter 18 for more information.)

You can also use public key cryptography to *digitally sign* your messages, to prove that no one else could have sent them. By encrypting the message with your private key (which only you can do, because only you have the private key), anyone can decrypt it by using your public key. If the recipient's e-mail program can handle public key cryptography, it can inform the recipient that the sender definitely is you; otherwise, the digital signature just appears as an attachment.

Two standard systems of public key cryptography have emerged for use on the Internet: digital certificates and PGP. Both can be used to send and receive secure e-mail.

Digital Certificates

One system of public key cryptography uses a *digital certificate* to protect the information that you send, by attaching a secure signature. A digital certificate (also called a *digital ID*) acts like a passport or a driver's license; it authenticates your identity uniquely so that people who receive your e-mail know for sure that you're the sender. You keep the private part of your digital certificate on your hard disk, and the public part is available in several ways: if someone sends you a signed message, you can save the public part of that person's digital certificate, or you can search for a person's digital ID on one of several Web sites. You keep the public parts of your correspondents' digital certificates in your e-mail program's address book, so that you can decrypt encrypted messages from those people.

Like passwords or driver's licenses, digital certificates (also called digital IDs) are issued by a trusted agency—a *certificate authority*. VeriSign is the most popular and recognizable vendor of digital certificates. VeriSign offers several types of digital certificates: *Server IDs* for secure Web servers, *Developer IDs* for software developers, and *Personal Digital IDs* for individuals and organizations who want to use secure e-mail. For information about VeriSign, see its Web site at **http://www.verisign.com**. Another widely respected vendor of digital certificates is Thawte Consulting, at **http://www.thawte.com**.

Secure e-mail that uses digital certificates is called *S/MIME*. Digital certificates are used by the Outlook, Outlook Express, and Netscape Messenger e-mail programs. See the section "Getting and Using Digital Certificates," later in this chapter, for information on how to get your own Personal Digital ID from VeriSign and use it to send and receive secure e-mail. If you are interested in setting up a secure Web site, see "Digital Certificates" in Chapter 35.

PGP

PGP (which stands for *Pretty Good Privacy*) is another type of public key cryptography. PGP programs are available on the Internet that enable you to create your own key pairs (one public, one private). Many e-mail programs work with PGP, including Eudora and Outlook 97. Later in the chapter, the section "Getting and Using PGP" explains how to get and install a PGP program, create your own key pairs, and use PGP to send and receive secure e-mail.

*See the Web site at **http://www.well.com/user/abacard/pgp.html** for a good non-technical explanation of PGP. To learn more, read the Usenet newsgroup **alt.security.pgp** (see Chapter 13 for information about Usenet newsgroups).*

Using Cryptography with E-mail

Both digital certificates and PGP can be used with Internet e-mail. When you send a message, you can choose to encrypt it (encode it with the recipient's public key, so that only the recipient has the key to decrypt it) or sign it (add a signature encoded with your private key, which anyone can decrypt with your public key).

Before you send an encrypted message, you need to have the public key for the recipient. E-mail programs that can handle security usually also let you store the public keys of your correspondents in an address book. If the person to whom you want to send an encrypted file has a digital ID (either a digital certificate or a PGP key pair), you can assume that he or she also has an e-mail program that can handle the same type of security that your program uses.

Before you can send a signed message, you need to have your own private key installed in your e-mail program. You can send a signed message to anyone, because the signature doesn't affect the text of the message. If the recipient's e-mail program can't handle the type of security that you used, the signature just appears as an attachment at the end of the message.

*If you use Pegasus, another encryption system is available. The Pegasus Web site at **http://www.pegasus.usa.com** recommends a Pegasus add-on called RPK Invisimail, which uses neither PGP nor digital certificates.*

Getting and Using Digital Certificates

To get a digital certificate, you request one from a certificate authority, such as VeriSign or Thawte Consulting. You can use your digital certificate to send secure e-mail. Here's how to get your own certificate from VeriSign and use it with Netscape Messenger, Outlook, and Outlook Express.

*You can use digital certificates with Eudora if you buy the WorldSecure Client plug-in for Eudora: see **http://www.worldtalk.com.***

Getting Your Own Digital Certificate

To apply for a VeriSign Personal Digital ID, follow these steps:

1. If you use Outlook 98, choose Tools | Options, click the Security tab, and click the Get a Digital ID button. (If you are not online, your system connects to the Internet.) When you see the Microsoft Web page about digital IDs, click the VeriSign enrollment button. Skip to step 3.

2. If you use any other e-mail program (or if you'd rather get your certificate without help from Microsoft), go to VeriSign's Web site located at **http://www.verisign.com**. If you use Netscape Messenger as your e-mail program, it will be easier if you use Netscape Navigator to download the certificate, so that you don't have to reinstall the certificate in Netscape later. Similarly, if you use Outlook or Outlook Express as your e-mail program, use Internet Explorer to download the certificate.

3. Click the Individual Certificates button on the opening Web page to see VeriSign's Digital ID Center, where you can choose between buying it and trying it.

4. Follow the instructions on the Web page to identify yourself, choose which type of digital certificate to get, and (unless you choose the free trial) indicate how you plan to pay. Be sure to make a (mental) note of the password that you specify: you'll need it later. Then, a program generates your digital certificate and mails it to you at the e-mail address that you provided.

5. Check your e-mail program's inbox. When you receive a message from VeriSign, follow the instructions in the message to get your certificate. The instructions include the URL of the Web page to display and a password to type, so that no one else can get your certificate.

6. Use copy-and-paste to copy the URL and the password from the e-mail address to your Web browser. Follow the instructions on the Web page to generate your certificate. Figure 9-1 shows the window that Netscape Navigator displays when it downloads and installs your certificate. Be sure to follow the instructions to save the certificate in a separate file. You need to type the password that you specified in step 4 to save your certificate.

7. Test your certificate by following the instructions on the Web page.

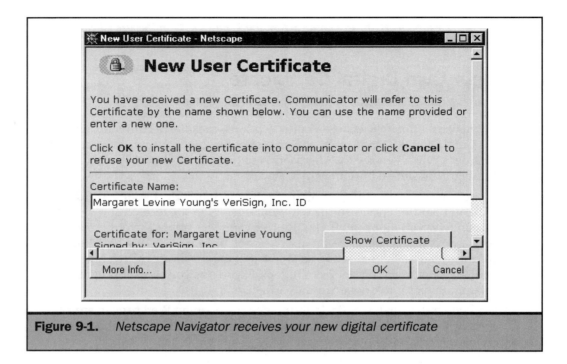

Figure 9-1.   *Netscape Navigator receives your new digital certificate*

When you are done, your digital certificate is stored in a small (5K) file on your hard disk in the location that you specified in Step 6. The file has the extension .P12 or .PFX. Copy the file to a diskette and store it somewhere safe. If you want to use your certificate on another computer or with other e-mail software than the one that comes with your browser, you'll need the file. In addition to the place that you specified to store a copy of your certificate, the certificate is stored in the files of the browser that you used to download the certificate. If you plan to use Netscape Messenger to send and receive secure e-mail, and you downloaded the certificate with Netscape Navigator, Messenger already knows about the certificate, too.

   If you run into trouble with your digital certificate, consult VeriSign's FAQ at **http://digitalid.verisign.com/client/help/faq.htm**.

The process for getting a digital certificate from Thawte Consulting (**http://www.thawte.com**) or another issuing organization is similar.

Backing Up Your Digital Certificate

If you want to use your certificate with an e-mail program other than the one that comes with the browser that you used to download your certificate, you need a copy of the certificate. If you made a copy when you downloaded the certificate, you can use that copy. Otherwise, the steps to export your digital certificate from Internet Explorer and Netscape Navigator are provided in the next two sections, respectively.

Exporting Your Digital Certificate from Internet Explorer

Follow these steps to save your certificate in a separate file:

1. In Internet Explorer, choose View | Internet Options from the menu. You see the Internet Options dialog box.

2. Click the Content tab and then click the Personal button to display the Client Authentication dialog box, shown in Figure 9-2.

3. Click the Export button to see the Export Personal Certificates dialog box.

4. In the first two boxes, type the password that you used to create the digital certificate. In the third box, type the filename in which to save the certificate. Unless you specify a complete pathname, the certificate will be stored in your C:\My Documents folder.

5. Click OK. Internet Explorer exports the certificate, adding the file extension .PFX. Click OK, Close, and then OK to exit from the remaining dialog boxes.

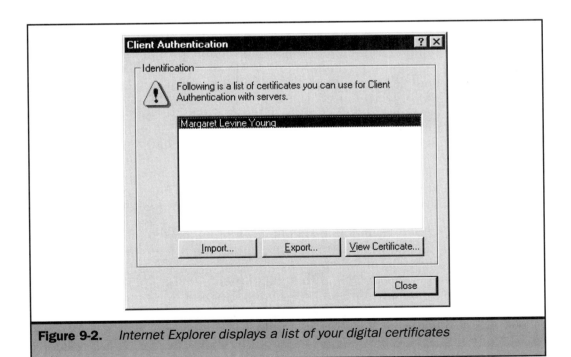

Figure 9-2.   *Internet Explorer displays a list of your digital certificates*

Exporting Your Digital Certificate from Netscape Navigator

Follow these steps to save your certificate in a separate file:

1. In Netscape Navigator, click the Security (padlock) icon on the toolbar. You see the Netscape Security Info window, with information about the Web page that you are currently viewing.

2. Click the Yours link under Certificates in the list at the left side of the window. Netscape displays a list of your certificates (as shown in Figure 9-3). These are certificates that belong to and identify you, not certificates of people with whom you correspond, so most people have only one.

3. Click the certificate name that you want to save, and click Export. Netscape displays the Password Entry dialog box.

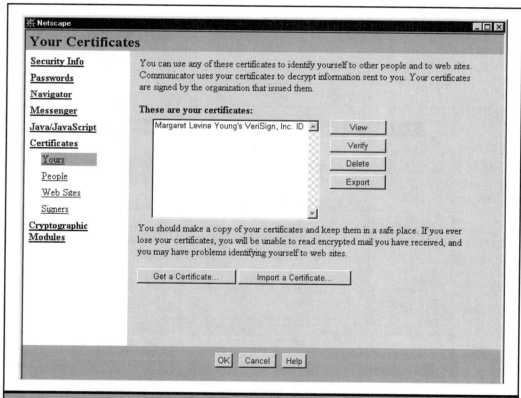

Figure 9-3.   *Netscape Navigator displays a list of your digital certificates*

4. Type the password that you used when you created the certificate. Then, type the same password for use when installing this copy of the certificate. Whenever you import this certificate, you need to type this password. Then click OK.

5. Choose the location and filename in which to save the certificate (for example, on a diskette in A:\ with the filename Certificate). Netscape adds the extension .P12 and saves the certificate.

Getting Other People's Digital Certificates

If you want to send an encrypted message so that only the recipient can read it, you need the public part of that person's digital certificate (or digital ID). The following are several ways to get the public part of other people's digital IDs:

- When someone sends you a signed message, it includes the public part of the sender's digital certificate, and you may be able to save it in your e-mail program's address book. See the sections pertaining to your e-mail program in the rest of the chapter for the steps to take.

- You can use a Web-based certificate repository to find someone's certificate. The easiest one to use is VeriSign, at **http://digitalid.verisign.com/query.htm**. Follow the instructions at this Web site to find and download the person's digital ID. (Naturally, you receive only the public part of the digital ID.)

- If you use Outlook, Outlook Express, or Netscape Messenger, you can use the built-in search features of these e-mail programs. (See the following sections in which each of these programs is discussed.)

Secure E-mail with Outlook 98 and Outlook Express

Outlook 98 and Outlook Express, which are described in Chapter 6, can send and receive e-mail using digital certificates. They share their list of certificates with Internet Explorer. This section describes how to send and receive e-mail in Outlook 98 and Outlook Express.

Importing Your Digital Certificate into Outlook 98

When you install Outlook 98, the two buttons labeled Digitally Sign Message and Encrypt Message Contents and Attachments may not appear on the toolbar in Outlook 98's message composition window. These two buttons are the most convenient way to indicate that you want to encrypt or sign a message. You can add them to the toolbar by following these steps:

1. Create an e-mail message by clicking the New Mail Message button on the toolbar. You see the message composition window.

2. Choose View | Toolbars | Customize from the message composition window's menu. You see the Customize dialog box.

3. Click the Commands tab and click Standard in the Categories list.

4. Scroll down to the bottom of the list in the Commands box to find the Digitally Sign Message and Encrypt Message Contents and Attachments commands. Drag each of these icons to the message composition window's toolbar.

5. Click Close. Now the two icons appear on the window composition's toolbar in the positions where you dragged them.

6. Close the window composition window.

Next, to determine whether Outlook 98 knows about your digital certificate, create a new e-mail message and look at the Digitally Sign Message and Encrypt Message Contents and Attachments icons on the toolbar. If they appear "grayed out," these commands are unavailable because Outlook hasn't imported your certificate. Close the message composition window and then follow these steps to import your certificate into Outlook:

1. In Outlook 98, choose Tools | Options from the menu and then click the Security tab.

2. In the Digital IDs part of the dialog box, click the Import/Export Digital ID button. (Don't click the Get a Digital ID button, which runs Internet Explorer to help you sign up for a new digital certificate, which you don't need because you already have a certificate.) You see the Import/Export Security Information and Digital ID dialog box, shown in Figure 9-4.

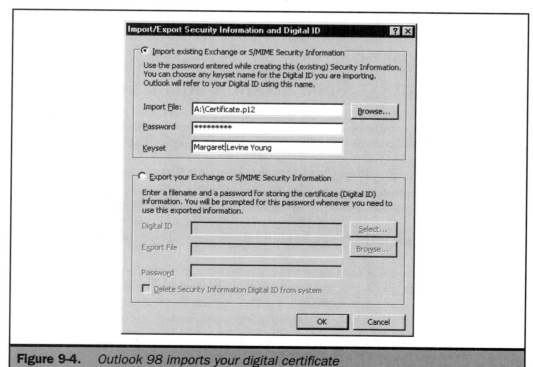

Figure 9-4. *Outlook 98 imports your digital certificate*

3. Make sure that the Import Existing Exchange or S/MIME Security Information setting is selected and then click the Browse button in the upper part of the dialog box.

4. Find the certificate file (which usually has the extension .PFX or .P12) and click Open. The pathname for the file appears in the Import File box.

5. In the Password box, type the password that you specified when you saved the certificate.

6. In the Keyset box, type the name that you want to use for this certificate—usually, your own name.

7. Click OK. Outlook imports the digital certificate and adds it to the list of certificates that it has on file for you. You return to the Options dialog box.

8. Click the Change Settings button in the Secure E-Mail part of the dialog box. You see the Change Security Settings dialog box, shown in Figure 9-5.

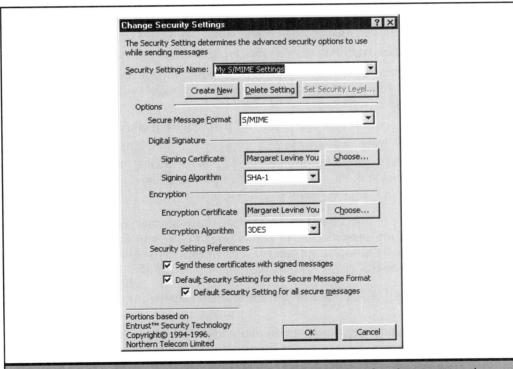

Figure 9-5. *Choosing which digital certificate Outlook uses for signatures and encryption*

9. Check that your digital certificate's name appears in the Signing Certificate and Encryption Certificate boxes. If not, or if you just want to take a look, click the Choose button next to either box to see a list of the certificates that you have on file for yourself.

10. Click OK to return to the Options dialog box. You can see that your certificates are now fully installed, because the Secure E-Mail settings at the top of the dialog box are now available. Click Close.

Importing Your Digital Certificate into Outlook Express

If you downloaded your digital certificate by using Internet Explorer, the copy of Outlook Express running on the same computer already knows about the certificate. If not, or if you downloaded the certificate on a different computer from the one that you are using now, you need to configure Internet Explorer to recognize your digital certificate by following these steps (once Internet Explorer has your certificate, Outlook Express can use it, too):

1. In Internet Explorer, choose View | Internet Options from the menu, click the Content tab, and then click the Personal button in the Certificates section of the dialog box. You see the Client Authentication dialog box (refer to Figure 9-2).

2. Click the Import button to display the Import Personal Certificates dialog box.

3. Click the Browse button and specify the location of your digital certificate file (the one that you saved when you downloaded the file), which has the extension .P12 or .PFX.

4. In the Password box, type the password that you used when you created the personal certificate.

5. Click OK. Internet Explorer imports the digital certificate, and your name appears in the list in the Client Authentication dialog box. Click Close and then OK to exit from the remaining dialog boxes.

You may have more than one digital certificate (for example, you might have one from VeriSign and another from Thawte Consulting). Before you can send signed e-mail, you have to tell Outlook Express which certificate to use (even if you only have one). Follow these steps:

1. Choose Tools | Accounts from the menu to display the Internet Accounts dialog box.

2. Choose the e-mail account that you plan to use with secure e-mail, and click the Properties button. You see the properties dialog box for your e-mail account.

3. Click the Security tab.

4. Click the Use a Digital ID When Sending Secure Messages From check box and then click the Digital ID button. You see a list of the digital certificates that Outlook or Outlook Express have stored to identify you.

5. Click the digital certificate that you want to use, and then click OK, OK again, and Close to close the dialog boxes.

Sending Signed or Encrypted Messages

You can tell Outlook 98 or Outlook Express to sign and encrypt all the messages that you send, or you can sign and encrypt only specific messages. To tell Outlook to sign and encrypt all your messages (at least all of those to recipients for whom you have a digital ID), follow these steps:

1. Choose Tools | Options from the menu. You see the Options dialog box.

2. Click the Security tab, shown in Figure 9-6. (Outlook 98's dialog box looks a little different.)

3. In the Secure Mail section, click the Digitally Sign All Outgoing Messages (or Add Digital Signature to Outgoing Messages) check box and the Encrypt Contents and Attachments for All Outgoing Messages check box. Then click OK.

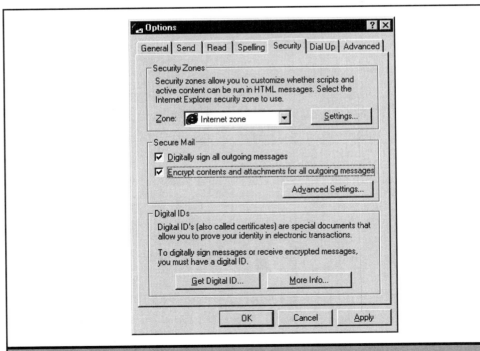

Figure 9-6.   *Configuring Outlook Express to sign all messages*

Regardless of whether you have configured Outlook to sign or encrypt all of your messages, you can sign or encrypt specific messages. Follow these steps to send one message that is signed, encrypted, or both:

1. Create a new e-mail message, as usual.

2. To digitally sign the message, click the Digitally Sign Message button on the message composition window's toolbar (an envelope with a ribbon) or choose Tools | Encrypt from the message composition window's menu. In Outlook Express, an icon appears, showing that the message will be signed (shown in Figure 9-7). In Outlook 98, the Digitally Sign Message icon on the toolbar appears depressed (pushed in).

3. To encrypt the message, click the Encrypt Message button (an envelope with a padlock) on the toolbar or choose Tools | Digitally Sign from the menu. In Outlook Express, an icon appears, showing that the message will be encrypted (refer to Figure 9-5). In Outlook 98, the icon on the toolbar appears depressed.

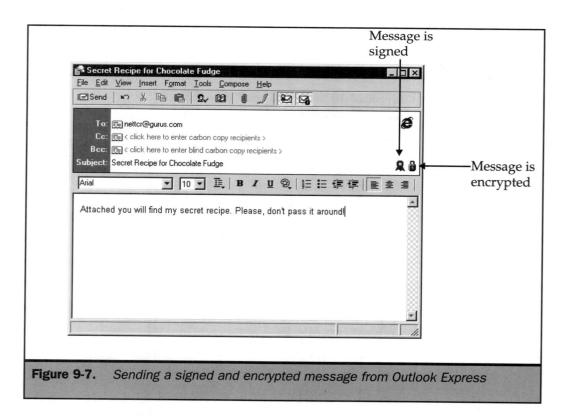

Figure 9-7. *Sending a signed and encrypted message from Outlook Express*

4. Click Send. If you chose to sign the message but haven't specified your default digital certificate, follow the steps in "Getting Your Own Digital Certificate," earlier in this section. If you chose to encrypt the message but you don't have the public part of the recipient's digital certificate, Outlook can't send the message until you get the public part, and thus displays a message asking whether to send the message unencrypted.

5. Outlook may ask for your certificate's password. If it does, type your password, verify it, and click OK.

It's a good idea to send the public part of your digital certificate along with any signed messages that you send, so that people can store the digital ID in their address books. To configure Outlook to include your public digital ID with signed messages, choose Tools | Options, click the Security tab, and then click the Advanced Settings button (in Outlook Express) or the Change Settings button (in Outlook 98). In Outlook Express, click the Include My Digital ID When Sending Signed Messages check box. In Outlook 98, click Send These Certificates with Signed Messages.

Receiving Signed or Encrypted Messages

To receive an encrypted or signed e-mail message in Outlook 98 or Outlook Express, follow these steps:

1. Open the message by double-clicking it. Outlook can't display an encrypted message in the preview pane: the message needs to appear in a separate window.

2. Outlook may ask for your certificate's password. The first time that you receive a signed or encrypted message, you may see a message from Outlook explaining how digital signatures and encryption work. Then, Outlook decrypts the message and any attachments. Icons in the message window indicate whether the message was signed (red ribbon icon), encrypted (blue padlock icon), or both (refer to Figure 9-7 to see what these icons look like).

Storing Other People's Digital IDs

When you receive a signed message, it may contain the public part of the sender's digital certificate. It's a good idea to save this public digital ID in your address book, for use when you want to send an encrypted message to the person.

In Outlook Express, follow these steps:

1. Open the message.

2. Choose File | Properties from the menu to display the properties dialog box for the message.

3. Click the Security tab (see Figure 9-8).

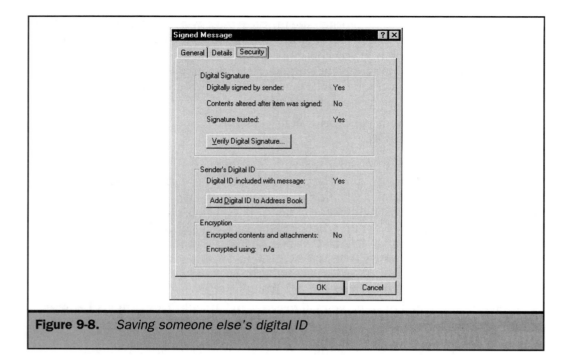

Figure 9-8. *Saving someone else's digital ID*

4. Click the Add Digital ID to Address Book button. Outlook saves the digital ID to the address book.

In Outlook 98, right-click the sender's name and choose Add to Contacts from the menu that appears. Outlook adds the sender to your address book, including the sender's digital ID. You can edit the address book entry and then click Save and Close.

If you get someone's digital ID from a Web-based certificate repository, or someone sends you a digital ID as an e-mail attachment, you can still store it in your address book. Follow these steps:

1. Create a new entry in your address book or edit the existing entry for the person (see the "Storing Addresses" section in the "Outlook 98" section of Chapter 6).

2. Click the Certificates or Digital IDs tab on the properties dialog box for the address book entry.

3. Click Import, specify the filename of the person's digital certificate, and then click Open.

4. Click Save and Close to save the digital ID in your address book.

On the Certificates or Digital IDs tab of the properties dialog box for an address book entry, you can view and delete digital IDs for your correspondents.

Secure E-mail with Netscape Messenger

Netscape Messenger, the e-mail program that comes with Netscape Communicator, is described in Chapter 6. You can send and receive secure e-mail with Messenger by using digital certificates. This section describes Netscape Messenger 4.5.

Importing Your Digital Certificate by Using Netscape Navigator

If you used Netscape Navigator to download your digital certificate, Messenger already knows about the certificate. If you used a different browser, or if you downloaded the certificate on another computer, follow these steps to configure Netscape Navigator and Messenger to use your digital certificate:

1. In Netscape Navigator, click the Security (padlock) icon on the toolbar. You see the Netscape Security Info window, with information about the Web page that you are currently viewing.

2. Click the Yours link under Certificates in the list at the left side of the window. Netscape displays a list of your certificates (refer to Figure 9-3).

3. Click the Import a Certificate button and specify the file that contains the certificate.

4. Click Open. Netscape asks for the password.

5. Type the password that you used when you saved the certificate in this file, and click OK.

6. Netscape imports the certificate, and it appears in the list. Click OK.

Sending Signed or Encrypted Messages

You can configure Messenger to sign all of your outgoing messages and encrypt all of those addressed to recipients for whom you have digital IDs. Follow these steps:

1. Choose Communicator | Tools | Security Info from the menu, or press CTRL+SHIFT+I, or click the padlock icon in the lower corner of the Messenger window. You see the Security Info window.

2. In the list of topics along the left side of the window, click Messenger. You see the security settings for Netscape Messenger (see Figure 9-9).

3. If you want to encrypt messages whenever you have the digital ID of the recipient, click the Encrypt Mail Messages When It Is Possible check box.

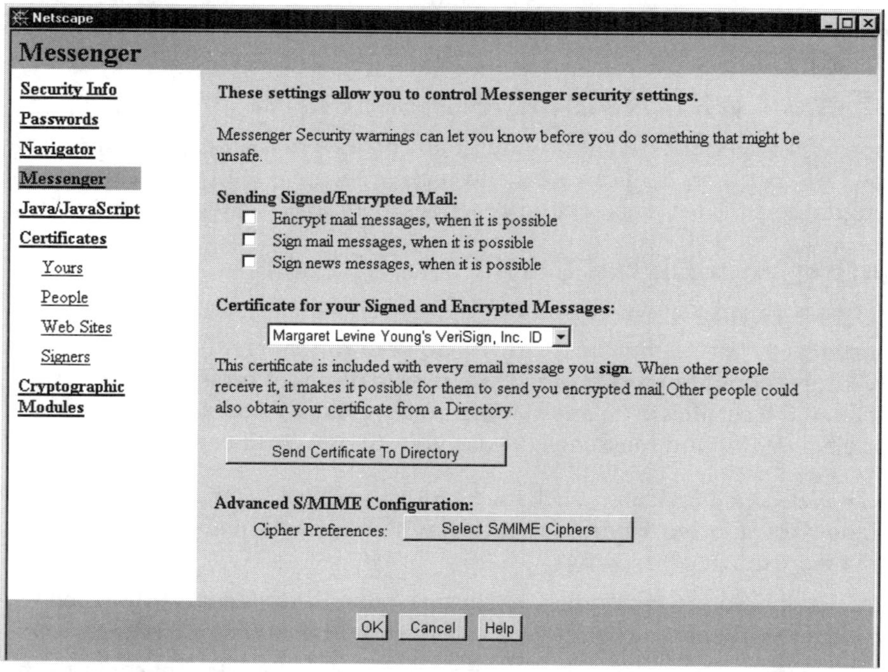

Figure 9-9. *Configuring Netscape Messenger to sign and encrypt all messages*

4. If you want to sign your messages, click the Sign Mail Messages When It Is Possible check box.

5. Make sure that your own digital certificate's name appears in the Certificate for Your Signed and Encrypted Messages box. If you have more than one certificate, set this box to display the certificate that you want Messenger to use.

6. Click OK.

Regardless of whether you configure Messenger to sign and encrypt all of your messages, when you send a message, you can choose to sign it, encrypt it, or both. Follow these steps:

1. Click the New Message button on the Messenger toolbar. Address and type your message as usual.

2. Click the Message Sending Options tab in the header section of the message composition window (see Figure 9-10).

Security settings ——→
Message Sending Options tab ——→

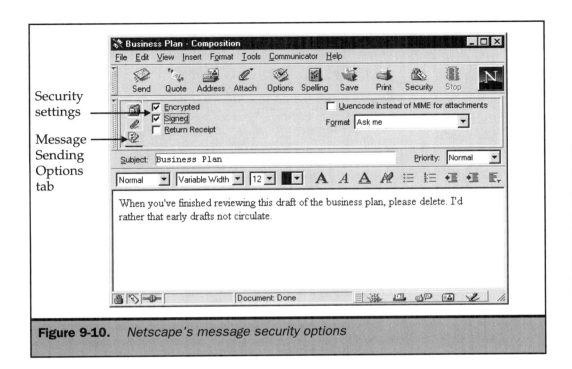

Figure 9-10. *Netscape's message security options*

3. If you want to sign the message, click the Signed check box on the Message Sending Options tab. The Security icon on the message composition window's toolbar changes: a little white tag appears attached to the padlock.

4. If you want to encrypt the message, click the Encrypted check box on the Message Sending Options tab. The Security icon changes from an open padlock to a locked one.

5. If you want to know the details of how Messenger plans to sign and encrypt the message, you can click the Security icon. You see the Security Info window, shown in Figure 9-11, displaying the security status of the message.

6. The top part of the window indicates whether Messenger will encrypt the message: if you requested encryption, but you don't have a digital ID for a recipient, Messenger lets you know. (If you want to encrypt your message but need to get a digital ID for a recipient, see "Storing Other People's Digital IDs," later in this section.) If Messenger indicates that you can encrypt the message, and you want to encrypt it, click the check box in the Encrypting Message part of the window (if not already checked).

EXCHANGING E-MAIL

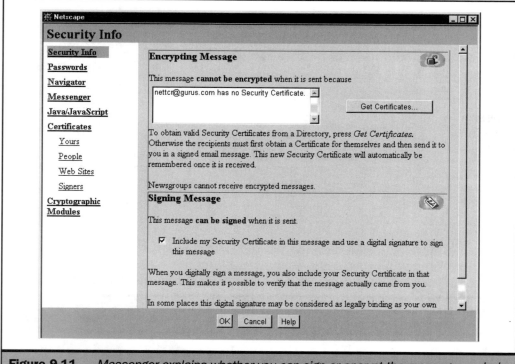

Figure 9-11.   *Messenger explains whether you can sign or encrypt the message, and why*

7. The bottom part of the window shows whether Messenger will sign the message. If you want to sign the message, click the check box in the Signing Message part of the window (if not already checked).

8. Click OK to dismiss the Security Info window and return to the message composition window.

9. Click Send. If you don't have the digital certificates that you need to sign or encrypt the message, Messenger asks whether to turn off encryption and send the message anyway.

Receiving Signed or Encrypted Messages

To receive and decrypt a secure e-mail message in Messenger, just display the message. Messenger displays the message in its own window, as shown in Figure 9-12.

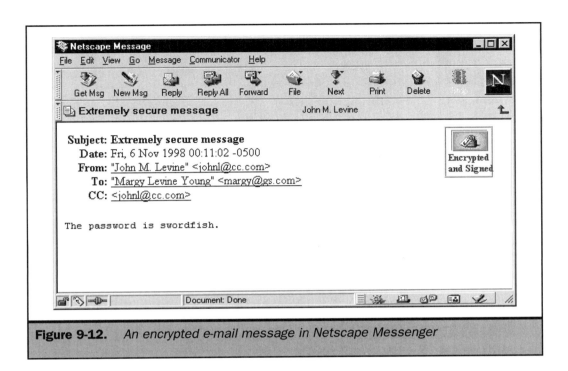

Figure 9-12.   *An encrypted e-mail message in Netscape Messenger*

Messenger automatically decrypts the message if you have a digital ID for the sender, and it automatically detects digital signatures. If a message is signed, encrypted, or both, then an icon appears on the right side of the message window.

If you want to know more about the encryption or digital signature, double-click the icon. You see a Security Info window with details about the message, including the name of the owner of the digital ID attached to the message.

Storing Other People's Digital IDs

To see whose digital IDs you have downloaded, either choose Communicator | Tools | Security Info from the menu, press CTRL+SHIFT+I, or click the padlock icon in the lower corner of the Messenger window. Click the People link in the Certificates section of the list that is located down the left side of the Security Info window (see Figure 9-13). You see a list of the certificates that you have on file (that is, the public parts of the digital certificates, which you use when encrypting messages that can be decrypted only by the certificate holder).

EXCHANGING E-MAIL

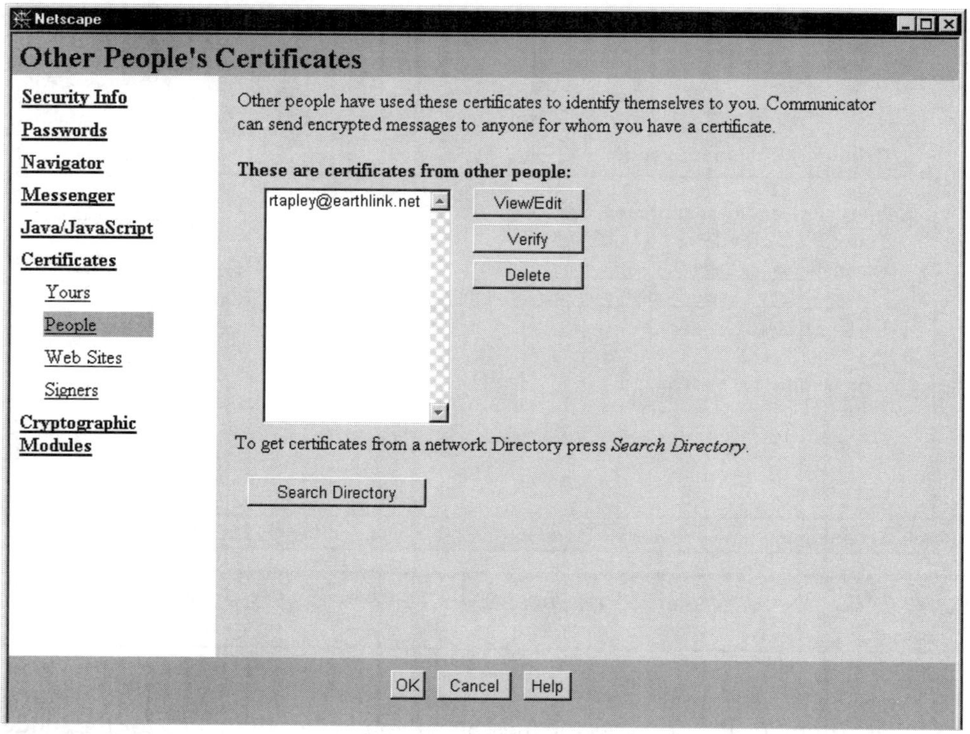

Figure 9-13. *Netscape Messenger displays your correspondents' digital IDs*

You can see details about a digital ID by clicking a name on the list and then clicking View. To check that the digital ID is valid and that it has not expired, click Verify.

If you want to send encrypted e-mail to someone, but you don't have the person's digital ID, you can search for it by starting from the People section of the Security Info window. Follow these steps:

1. Click the Search Directory button. You see the Search Directory for Certificates window, shown in Figure 9-14.

2. In the Directory box, choose the certificate directory that you want to search. Try one, and if you can't find the person, try another.

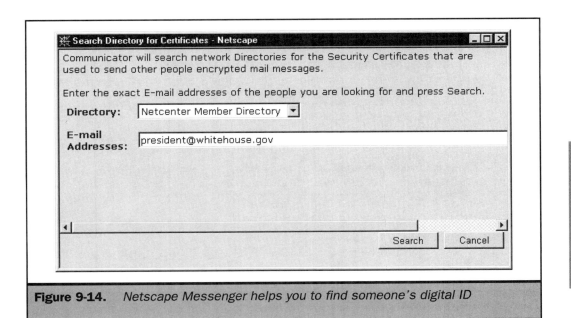

Figure 9-14. *Netscape Messenger helps you to find someone's digital ID*

3. In the E-mail Addresses box, type the e-mail address of the person whose digital ID you want to find. You can enter several e-mail addresses, separated by spaces.

4. Click the Search button. Netscape searches the certificate database and displays a message about what it finds. If it finds a certificate, click OK to download it and install it in Netscape.

Alternatively, you can use Netscape Navigator to use the Web site of a certificate database and perform the search yourself. For example, go to **http://digitalid.verisign.com/ query.htm** and follow the instructions on the Web page. When you find a digital ID that you want to download, choose to download it in the format for someone else's digital ID (not yours) for use with Navigator. When the download is complete, Navigator displays the window shown in Figure 9-15.

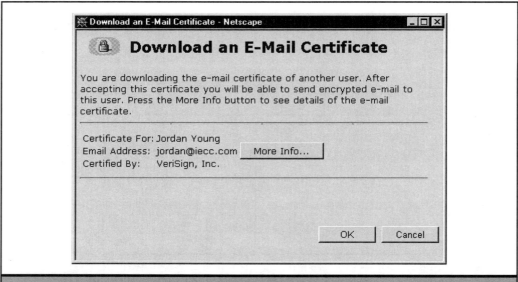

Figure 9-15. *Netscape accepts a downloaded digital ID for someone else*

Getting and Using PGP

Unlike digital certificates, PGP allows you to issue your own certificates. Rather than your certificates being guaranteed by a trusted certificate authority, PGP relies on a *web of trust*, whereby people sign each other's certificates. You download a PGP program to generate PGP key pairs. Once you have the program, you can create a key pair for yourself and start using it with your e-mail program. This section describes how to use PGP version 5.0.

The PGP program comes with plug-ins for use with Eudora and Outlook. If you use another e-mail program, you can still encrypt and sign messages by using the Windows Clipboard to transfer information between the e-mail program and the PGP program. Some e-mail programs (including Eudora with the PGP plug-in) can handle PGP/MIME, which enables you to encrypt and sign e-mail attachments, as long as the recipient's e-mail program also supports PGP/MIME.

The standard PGP program doesn't come with a plug-in for Pegasus, but you might want to try the PGP-compatible Invincible Mail program, which does support Pegasus, available from **http://www.incrypt.com/imail01.html**.

Getting a PGP Program

Business versions of the PGP program are available on the Web from Network Associates at **http://www.nai.com/products/security/personal.asp**. (Network Associates succeeded PGP, Inc., which was founded by the creator of PGP, Phil Zimmermann.) You can find beta versions and trial versions of security software here, though you have to pay for the full versions. For personal use, you can download a free PGP program from **http://web.mit.edu/network/pgp.html** in the U.S. or Canada. If you are outside the U.S. and Canada, go to the Where to Get PGP FAQ at **http://cryptography.org/getpgp.htm** and click the link labeled Where Can I FTP PGP Outside of North America. Note that exporting PGP programs from the U.S. is illegal. (See Chapter 38 for directions on how to download and install software from the Internet.)

The Windows version of the PGP program requires 8MB of RAM and 15MB of space on your hard disk, and comes with the following:

- **PGPkeys program** Makes pairs of keys, manages your keys, and encrypts, decrypts, and signs messages
- **PGPtray program** Displays a lock-and-key icon on the Windows system tray on the Taskbar
- **Eudora plug-in** Lets Eudora send and receive secure e-mail messages using PGP
- **Microsoft Outlook/Exchange plug-in** Lets Outlook and Exchange send and receive secure e-mail using PGP
- **User's manual** In Adobe Acrobat format (if you don't have the free Adobe Acrobat reader, you can download it from **http://www.adobe.com/prodindex/acrobat/readstep.html**).

When you install PGP, be sure to select the Eudora or Outlook/Exchange plug-in, if you use one of these e-mail programs.

After you install the PGP program, you should do two things: create a key pair for yourself and customize the PGP program to reflect your preferences. Then, you can begin using PGP as a stand-alone utility, or in combination with other e-mail programs, to send and receive secure e-mail.

Tip *To read the user manual that comes with the PGP program, Windows users can download the Adobe Acrobat program by choosing Start | Programs | Pretty Good Privacy | Download Adobe Acrobat, install the downloaded program, and then display the manual by choosing Start | Programs | Pretty Good Privacy | PGP50 Manual.*

Creating a Key Pair

To create a key pair for yourself:

1. Run the PGPKeys program that you installed (for example, choose Start | Programs | Pretty Good Privacy | PGPKeys). Windows users can also click the PGPtray icon on the system tray of the Taskbar and then choose Launch PGPkeys from the window that appears.

2. If the Key Generation Wizard doesn't run, choose Keys | New Key from the menu. The Key Generation Wizard steps you through the process of creating a key pair (Figure 9-16). Click Next.

3. The Wizard prompts you for the information that it needs to create your keys. Answer its questions and click Next to move to the next screen. When asked, type your full name and a valid e-mail address. It may ask which type of PGP keys you'd like; if it does, choose DSS/Hellman-Diffie keys. Choose a key pair size according to the degree of security that you need and the amount of time that you're willing to wait for encryption and decryption. The larger your key pair, the more difficulty troublemakers will have cracking your code—but computers will take longer to encode and decode secured messages. Most people choose 1536-bit or 2048-bit keys.

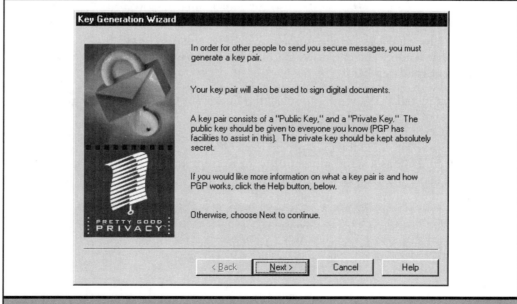

Figure 9-16.   *The PGP Key Generation Wizard*

4. When you see a question about key expiration, decide whether you want a time-limited key pair or a key pair that never expires. After you choose an expiration date for a key pair, you can't change your mind and can't use an expired key pair to encrypt mail that you send (it will still decode mail, though). On the other hand, you can run PGPkeys again to make a new pair of keys. Most people choose a key that never expires.

5. Type a *passphrase* (password), a combination of letters, numbers, and other symbols to protect the private half of your key pair. Choose a passphrase that is longer than eight characters and that contains numbers, punctuation marks, and/or both upper- and lowercase letters. Type the same passphrase in both boxes (see Figure 9-17). Vary the capitalization in your passphrase to throw off *dictionary attacks,* a type of packet sniffer that compares passphrases against every word in the dictionary. The catch is that dictionary attacks are case-specific, so you can sneak your passphrase past them just by including a few extra capital letters.

6. When you click Next, PGPkeys generates your key pair, but if you have a slow processor, it may take several minutes. Click Next when PGPkeys displays the Complete message.

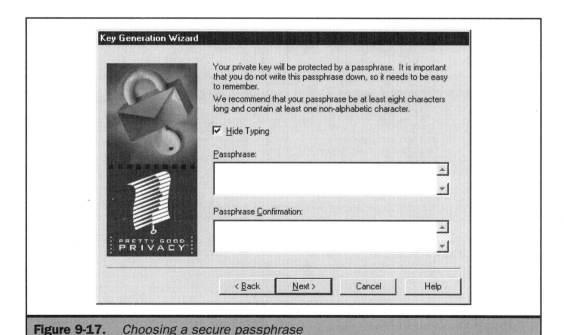

Figure 9-17.   *Choosing a secure passphrase*

7. PGPkeys asks whether you want to send the public key of your key pair to a *PGP keyserver* (public, Internet-based database of public keys), so that other people can find it. Registering with a keyserver is completely safe and makes it easier for recipients of signed e-mail to decode it, and for people to send you encrypted messages. Click the Send My Key to the Keyserver Now box and click Next.

8. PGP posts the public half of your key pair and tells you when it's finished. (If PGPkeys can't connect to the keyserver, you can register it later.) Click Next and then click Finish. You see the results in the PGPKeys window (Figure 9-18).

9. Close the PGPkeys window, so that the program prompts you to make a backup copy of your new key pair on diskettes. Click the Save Backup Now button to save the two files in which PGPkeys stores your keys.

If you want to run the Key Generation Wizard again to create another set of keys, run PGPkeys and choose Keys | New Key from the menu or press CTRL+N.

Managing Your Key Ring

PGPkeys stores your public keys (yours and those of people with whom you exchange secure e-mail) in a file called Pubring.pkr. It stores your private keys (you usually have only one) in a file called Secring.skr. Both files are usually stored in the same folder in which the PGPkeys program is installed. The collection of keys is called your *key ring*.

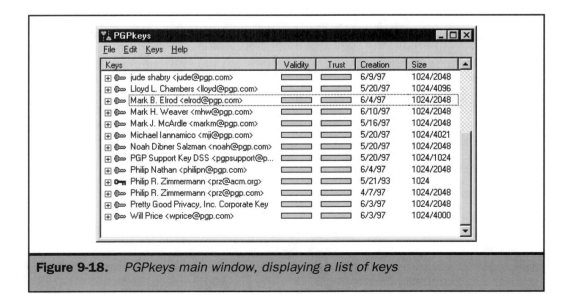

Figure 9-18. *PGPkeys main window, displaying a list of keys*

Your key ring contains the collection of public and private keys that you use for encrypting, decrypting, and signing e-mail. You can use PGPkeys to manage the keys on your key ring.

In the PGPkeys window (refer to Figure 9-18), the key icon to the left of the key names shows what type of key it is. A double-key icon means that you have both the public and private key—it's your key. A single key means that you have only the public key—it's someone else's key. Old-style RSA-format keys are blue, and new-style DSS/Diffie-Hellman keys are yellow.

The Validity column in the PGPkeys window shows an icon to indicate the *validity*, or trustworthiness, assigned to the keys. The validity is based on who has signed (vouched for) the key and how well you trust those signers. The four levels of validity are the following:

- **Striped bar**   Your own key.
- **Empty bar**   Untrustworthy user, or someone from whom you've received an invalid key in the past.
- **Half-shaded bar**   Someone who's marginally or partly trustworthy. Maybe you don't know this person very well, or you've received both valid and invalid keys from them in the past.
- **Shaded bar**   Completely trusted user.

The Trust column indicates how much you trust the holder of that key to sign (vouch for) the keys of others. You can change the Validity, Trust, and other properties of a key by double-clicking the entry in the PGPkeys window. To copy, delete, or perform other actions on a key, right-click the key's entry and choose a command from the menu that appears.

Distributing Your PGP Public Key

For other people to send encrypted e-mail to you or read e-mail messages that you have signed, they need your public key. You can include your public key whenever you send a signed message, so that everyone with whom you correspond has your public key on their key rings.

Registering with PGP Keyservers

Another convenient way for people to get your public key is for you to upload it to a PGP keyserver. If you're going to use PGP, registration of your public key is a very good idea, and you have nothing to lose by doing it. When you created your key, the Key Generation Wizard may have uploaded your public key to a keyserver for you.

The company that maintains the PGP program, Network Associates (NAI), maintains a PGP keyserver, at **http://www.nai.com/products/security/public_keys/ pub_key_default.asp**. Several other organizations around the world also run keyservers: for a list, see **http://www.pgpi.com/products/keyservers.shtml**. You can look for someone's public key (if they registered it to be placed on the public key directory) by searching for the person's name, or you can register your own public key.

You can also add your public key to a keyserver from the PGPkeys program. Right-click the entry for your keys and choose Keyserver | Send Selected Keys from the menu that appears.

Sending Your Public Key to Others

You can save your public key in a file and give or e-mail that file to other people, so that they can read your signed mail or send you encrypted mail. To save your public key in a file, right-click the entry for your key in the PGPkeys window and choose Export from the menu that appears. PGPkeys stores your key as a block of text in a file that has the extension .ASC.

Establishing PGP Preferences

Before you use your PGP key, configure the PGPkeys program's e-mail settings, as follows:

1. Run PGPkeys, if it's not already running.
2. Choose Edit | Preferences. You see the PGP Preferences dialog box with the General tab selected.
3. Click the Email tab, as shown in Figure 9-19. The Email Preferences specify whether encrypting and signing e-mail messages should be done automatically.

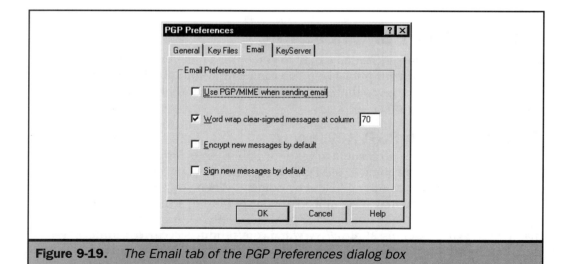

Figure 9-19.   *The Email tab of the PGP Preferences dialog box*

4. If you want all of your messages encrypted and signed by default, and your e-mail program supports the PGP/MIME standard (as Eudora does), select the Use PGP/MIME when Sending Email check box. Otherwise, choose the Encrypt New Messages by Default setting or the Sign New Messages by Default setting, respectively, if you want to encrypt or sign all messages by default.

5. Click OK.

Now you are ready to use your new PGP key pair to send and receive e-mail. The easiest way to send secure e-mail with PGP is to use an e-mail program that can handle PGP, or for which there is a plug-in that adds PGP capability to the program.

Secure E-mail with Eudora and Outlook 97

Eudora Light, Eudora Pro, and Outlook are described in Chapter 6. The PGP program comes with plug-ins that give Eudora and Outlook 97 (but not Outlook Express or Outlook 98) the ability to encrypt and sign messages with PGP. When you install the PGP program, be sure to select the plug-in for the e-mail program that you use.

> **Tip** *In Eudora, to see and change your PGP preferences (the same ones that you set in the PGPkeys program), choose Special | Message Plug-ins Settings from the menu, choose PGP from the dialog box that appears, and then click Settings. In Outlook, choose Tools | Option, click the PGP tab, and then click Preferences.*

Sending Encrypted or Signed Messages

To send a signed or encrypted message with your e-mail program and the PGP plug-in, you have two choices: send either with or without using PGP/MIME. Use PGP/MIME only if the recipient also uses PGP/MIME. The basic steps are the same either way:

1. Write a new message (see Chapter 6 for instructions).

2. To sign the message with your private key, click the Sign Message Before Sending button on the composition window's toolbar. The button stays depressed to show that the message will be signed when you send it (see Figure 9-20). If you decide not to sign the message, click the button again.

3. To encrypt the message, you must already have the recipient's public key. Click the Encrypt Message Before Sending icon, which stays depressed. If you decide not to encrypt the message, click the button again.

4. If the PGP/MIME button appears on the toolbar, the recipient's e-mail program also handles PGP/MIME, and you are sending attachments, click the PGP/MIME button on the toolbar.

EXCHANGING E-MAIL

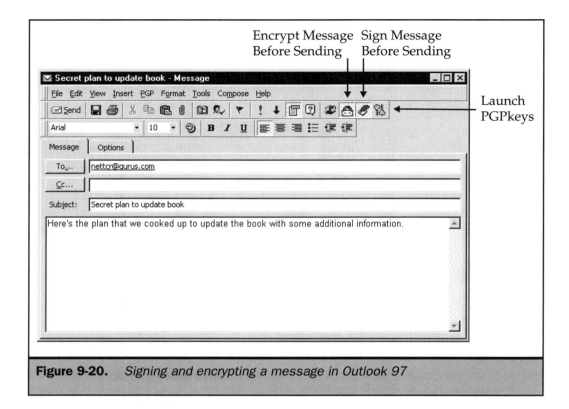

Figure 9-20. *Signing and encrypting a message in Outlook 97*

5. Click the Send or Queue button to send the message. Your e-mail program runs the PGP program to encrypt or sign your message. If the PGP program can't figure out which public key to use to encrypt a message, it displays a list of the keys in your public key ring and lets you choose. If you don't have the person's public key, then cancel sending the message and get the key (see the section "Distributing Your Public Key" earlier in this chapter for ways to get public keys).

6. If you are signing the message, a PGP dialog box appears (shown here) asking you for the passphrase for your private key. Type the passphrase, verify it, and click OK.

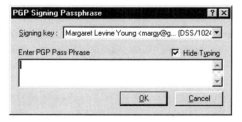

7. If you are sending a signed message that contains your public key, you see another passphrase dialog box that looks exactly the same as the first, only this time it asks permission to add your signature—which includes the public half of your key. Type the passphrase, verify it, and click OK. The e-mail program then sends your message.

Receiving Signed or Encrypted Messages

To receive PGP-encrypted messages with your e-mail program and the PGP plug-in, follow these steps:

1. Download your messages and open your inbox in the usual way.

2. Double-click an encrypted or signed message in your inbox. When the message opens, it looks scrambled—this block of coded words is called a *ciphertext*—as shown in Figure 9-21.

3. Click the Decrypt Message and Verify Signature button on the message window's toolbar.

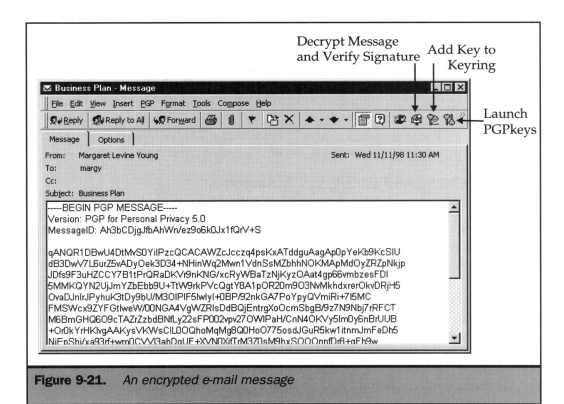

Figure 9-21.   *An encrypted e-mail message*

4. A dialog box asks for your passphrase, to begin the decryption process. Type it, verify it, and then click OK. If the message was signed, PGP displays a dialog box to tell you whether the signature checked out.

5. If the passphrase that you typed is correct, the message and any attachments reappear decoded for you to read.

6. When you close the e-mail message, the e-mail program gives you the option of saving the decoded message by overwriting the original, encrypted message. Click Yes to overwrite the encoded version with the decoded version, or click No to save the message in its original, encoded form.

If an encrypted message has attachments and was sent without using PGP/MIME, you have to decrypt the attachments separately by using Windows Clipboard or Windows Explorer, as explained in the section "Encrypting and Decrypting Files," later in this chapter.

Saving Other People's Public Keys

When you receive a signed message, you can save the person's public key in your key ring by clicking the Add Key to Keyring button on the toolbar of the message window.

Secure E-mail with Other Programs

Even if your e-mail program doesn't support PGP and no PGP plug-in is available, you can send and receive secure e-mail messages. The process is awkward, but it works. To send messages that are signed or encrypted, you copy the text of the message to the Windows Clipboard, use the PGPtray program to encrypt or sign the text, and then copy the text back to your e-mail program. When you receive encrypted messages, you copy the message to the Clipboard and use the PGPtray to decrypt it.

Sending Encrypted or Signed Messages

To send a message that is encrypted, signed, or both, follow these steps:

1. Run your e-mail program and compose a message. Type the text of the message as usual.

2. Using cut-and-paste, cut the text from the message (select it and press CTRL+X in most programs).

3. Click the PGPtray icon in the system tray on the Windows Taskbar (it looks like an envelope with a padlock behind it) and then choose Encrypt Clipboard, Sign Clipboard, or Encrypt and Sign Clipboard from the menu that appears.

4. If you chose to encrypt the text on the Clipboard, you see the PGP Key Selection dialog box, shown in Figure 9-22. Choose the key of the person to whom you want to send the encrypted text, and drag the key from the upper list to the lower (Recipients) list. Then click OK.

5. If you chose to sign the text on the Clipboard, you see the PGP Signing Passphrase dialog box. Type your passphrase and click OK.

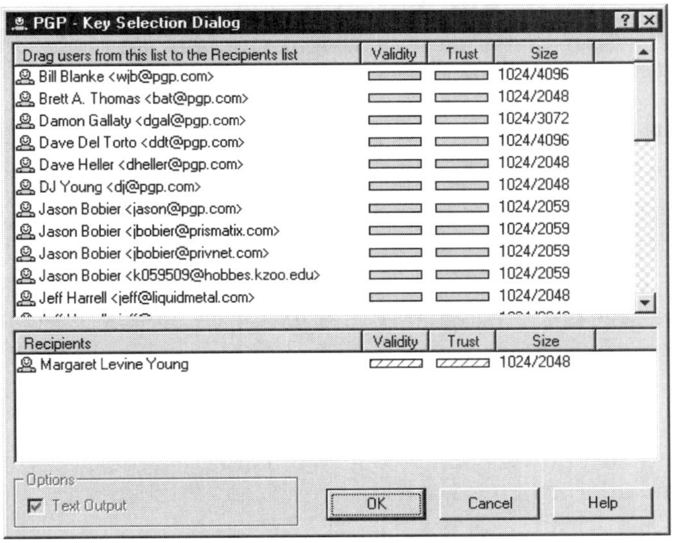

Figure 9-22. *Drag the keys for the recipients to the lower part of the window*

6. Now, the text on the Clipboard is signed, encrypted, or both. Switch back to your e-mail program, click in the message box, and then paste the text back into the message (press CTRL+V in most programs). Encrypted text looks something like this:

```
---BEGIN PGP MESSAGE---
Version: PGP for Personal Privacy 5.0
MessageID: giXuWUZyz/jBJmsvAdfdUBXXmJlU4p2X

qANQR1DBwU4DtMvS0YiIPzcQB/48MW/+K6E2o98ShQy/r3F3Zn5U8et/gh0Xk7UD
jiVKXv+sQtI2mS89JzS1YguuDFwfuYtY+X0K6agivRRthwqX78KoFXCW4rtAIgnf
Y+X1NQLF92kG2WT4uMnMXWp2rc7W13M32BHHUx+SqP1tfit23ppRZziEnH+FqPh/
dAPZOaXD2uVXgxxV3y6TtctpVriOu4FrB1vZa3DhCEY87ppCD9PRGr5JQqvp6RS3
HPMleOQqnslYxbGmH/MaUilzbi823qN2NTVAoi8pwY1X69Evb0cgFCHztE6Qp8AW
RuaxLwXRH8AWsb5sBQq3O2Yb4p6+YEltSb76/7/tUw==
=DB9m
---END PGP MESSAGE---
```

7. Send the message as usual.

Another way to encrypt text is to encrypt a whole file: see the section "Encrypting and Decrypting Files," later in this chapter.

Receiving Signed or Encrypted Messages

If you receive a message that is encrypted, signed, or both, and your e-mail program can't handle it, follow these steps:

1. Run your e-mail program and open the message.

2. Copy the text from the message (select it and press CTRL+C in most programs).

3. Click the PGPtray icon in the system tray on the Windows Taskbar (it looks like an envelope with a padlock behind it) and choose Decrypt/Verify Clipboard from the menu that appears.

4. If the message is encrypted, PGP asks for the passphrase for your private key. Type it and click OK.

5. If the message is signed, you see a dialog box telling you so. Click OK.

6. Click the PGPtray icon in the system tray again and choose either Edit Clipboard Text (to see decrypted text) or Launch Associated Viewer (if the decrypted information is not text).

Saving Other People's Public Keys

A person can send you his or her public key by e-mail or by handing you a diskette. To add the key to your key ring, so that you can use it when sending and receiving e-mail, run the PGPkeys program and choose Keys | Import from the menu. Choose the file that contains the public key that you want to import, and click Open. PGPkeys adds the key to your key ring, and the key appears in the PGPkeys window.

Encrypting and Decrypting Files

You can encrypt, decrypt, or sign an entire file by using PGP. Follow these steps to create a file that is encrypted, signed, or both:

1. In Windows Explorer, choose the file.

2. Choose File | PGP from the menu and then choose Encrypt, Sign, or Encrypt and Sign.

3. If you are signing the file, PGP prompts you for the passphrase of your private key.

4. If you are encrypting the file to send to someone else, PGP displays a list of the public keys in your key ring: drag the intended recipient's public key down to the Recipients list.

5. When you see the Save Signed File As dialog box, choose the folder in which you want to save the file and specify a filename. The PGP program adds the extension .PGP to the filename.

To decrypt an encrypted file that has the extension .PGP, just open it in Windows Explorer. If the PGP program is associated with the .PGP file extension (which the PGP installation program should have done), the PGP program runs automatically and asks you for your passphrase. When you type it and click OK, PGP decrypts the file and asks you where to store it.

To check the signature on a signed file, open it in Windows Explorer. PGP checks the signature and displays a dialog box that reports whether the signature is valid.

The
Complete
Reference

Chapter 10

Other E-mail Topics

227

This chapter covers a potpourri of other useful e-mail topics:

- Handling multiple e-mail accounts
- Sending form letters by e-mail
- Formatting e-mail messages

In this chapter, if the specific details for your e-mail program aren't covered during the discussion of a particular feature—and your e-mail program is covered in the other chapters in this part of the book—then your e-mail program doesn't have that particular feature.

Using Multiple E-mail Accounts

If you receive a lot of e-mail, you may find that filtering your incoming mail (described in Chapter 8) is not enough to keep it organized. You probably need more than one e-mail account, so that you can use different accounts for different purposes. For instance, you may use one account for newsgroups and mailing lists—and you can expect to receive some spam to that address. But if you use filters to find the newsgroup and mailing list messages that you want to view, you can assume that everything not returned by the filter can be deleted (if you haven't given anyone else that address). If you have more than one professional persona—say, you're a yoga teacher and a technical writer—you may want to have different addresses for each business card. For instance, your yoga teacher card might use the address **yogaprof@gurus.com**, while your technical writer card might use the address **writestuff@iecc.com**. Then, when you get e-mail asking for your services, you know immediately from the address that is used which service the writer needs. Additionally, you might want an address that you keep almost completely private and use only for correspondence with friends. With luck, you can keep that address spam-free.

You may also have multiple accounts to manage because you have more than one person using the same e-mail program on the same computer. You can store the messages, signature, stationery, and saved messages for each person in a separate folder.

The types of features that e-mail programs offer to handle multiple users and/or multiple accounts generally fall into one of the following two categories:

- Features that support multiple e-mail addresses for one user
- Features that support totally separate sets of mailboxes for different users

Not all e-mail programs support multiple e-mail accounts. However, if a program supports separate sets of mailboxes, you can use different accounts by setting up the e-mail program as if you were creating accounts for different people, assigning them account names instead of user names.

Many programs refer to the process of setting up the program for multiple users on the same computer as *creating profiles*. Although each user has his or her own set of mailboxes and preferences, and usually can't even tell that someone else has been using the same program to send and receive e-mail, profiles often provide little security. In other words, you have to trust that the other users won't use your profile to enter the program and read your mail.

Not all e-mail programs have both features—for instance, Netscape Messenger lets you create a whole new set of mailboxes for each person using it, but each profile allows only one e-mail account. On the other hand, Eudora allows you to get mail from multiple e-mail accounts, but you have to jump through hoops to set it up to allow multiple users.

If you decide to use multiple e-mail accounts within one profile, you'll usually want to use filters to distinguish which messages were sent to which address. With all programs that support filtering, you can easily filter by using the To line (see Chapter 8).

Eudora Pro

Eudora Pro allows you to manage multiple e-mail accounts by using *personalities*. You can define different personalities to send and receive-mail from different e-mail addresses. However, all the mail that you receive goes to your In mailbox, so if you want to keep the mail separate, you have to create filters that will funnel the mail sent to a particular address to a mailbox that you create for that purpose.

To create a new personality, display the Personalities pane either by choosing Tools | Personalities or by clicking the Personalities tab, shown in Figure 10-1. To start the New Account Wizard, right-click the white space on the Personalities tab and choose New from the shortcut menu. The Wizard asks you for all the information that Eudora needs to retrieve and send mail from the account: the name for the personality (this is what you see on the Personalities tab), your name (the name that will appear on messages that you send), the address for the account, the logon name for the account, the mail server, the type of server, and the outgoing server. Like the initial Eudora setup, you can import the information from an existing Outlook or Netscape account.

To edit a personality, right-click the personality name on the Personalities tab and choose Properties from the shortcut menu. You can then change any of the settings on the Account Settings dialog box.

When you send e-mail, Eudora uses the default personality. If you want to use a different personality to send a message, either select the personality on the Personalities tab and press ENTER or right-click the personality name and choose Message | New Message As. Alternatively, press SHIFT while you click the New Message button on the toolbar: when Eudora displays the Message Options dialog box, choose the personality and click OK.

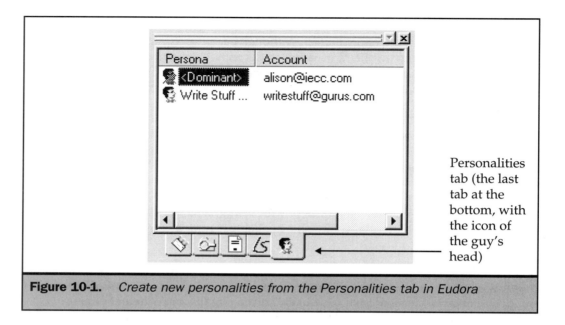

Personalities tab (the last tab at the bottom, with the icon of the guy's head)

Figure 10-1. *Create new personalities from the Personalities tab in Eudora*

To reply to a message by using an account other than the account the message was sent to, right-click the message, choose Change Personality, and choose the personality that you want to use. Then, reply to the message as usual—the address in the From header will be the address of the personality that you selected.

Although Eudora doesn't expressly offer the option of creating entirely separate mailboxes for use by different people who are using the same computer, this option is possible. The easiest way to do it is to install the program twice, in completely different folders. Follow these steps:

1. For each person who wants a separate Eudora mailbox, copy the whole Eudora folder to (usually C:\Program Files\Qualcomm\Eudora Mail) another folder.

2. Create a desktop shortcut for each person, so that you don't get confused about who uses which copy. To create the shortcut, drag the Eudora.exe file from the person's Eudora folder in Windows Explorer to the desktop.

Since Eudora takes up about 8MB on your hard drive, keeping a copy of the entire Eudora program for each user is a waste of hard drive space. If you are tight on space, you can separate the program files from the user files—both types of files usually are stored in the Eudora folder. Follow these steps to separate the user files from the program files, to create mailboxes for different people:

1. Install Eudora normally.

2. Copy the whole Eudora program folder to another place, such as C:*username*\ Mail. This folder will contain only the user's mailbox, without the Eudora program.

3. In the user's folder that you just created, delete all the EXE, DLL, and PDF files (the program and documentation files). What's left is the Eudora.ini file (the master file for the user) and all the mailboxes, signatures, and stationery—one user's Eudora mailbox.

4. Copy this user folder to make a folder for each user.

5. Make a shortcut on the desktop (or in the Start menu) for each user. The command line for the shortcut looks like this (be sure to type the quotes if the pathnames include spaces):

```
"C:\Program Files\Eudora\Eudora.exe" "C:\Fred\Mail\Eudora.ini"
```

Adjust the command line so that the first part is the path to the Eudora program, and the second part is the path to the person's Eudora.ini file.

When you click the shortcut for a person's e-mail, the Eudora program runs and opens the Eudora.ini file in the folder for the user specified in the shortcut.

Outlook 98

Outlook supports multiple profiles and multiple e-mail accounts. Profiles are designed for different people using e-mail on the same computer (although you may find a different use for them); when you combine mail from multiple accounts, you need multiple services in your profile, whereby each service contains settings for one e-mail address.

To set up multiple Profiles, you use the Windows Control Panel rather than Outlook 98. Choose Start | Settings | Control Panel to display the Control Panel, then open the Mail program. You see a window similar to Figure 10-2 (the window may be

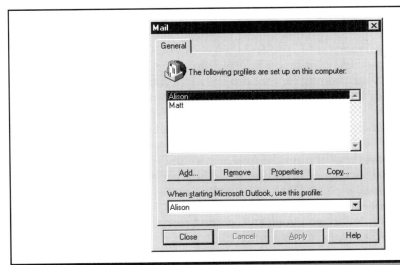

Figure 10-2. *Add a profile to Outlook 98 by using the Mail or Internet Accounts window, accessed from the Control Panel*

called Mail, Internet Accounts, or another name, depending on what Microsoft software—such as Microsoft Office—you have installed).

To create a new profile, click the Add button. Depending on which Microsoft software you have installed, the Microsoft Outlook Setup Wizard may run or you may see another series of dialog boxes. Either way, choose to create an Internet e-mail service or profile, and enter the following information:

- **Profile name** A short name or nickname for the profile—it appears in a drop-down list when Outlook is opened.

- **Mail Account Properties** The name that you want to call the service and the information needed to set up the e-mail account. To display the Mail Account Properties dialog box, you may need to click the Setup Mail Account button. Be sure to click the Servers tab and the Connection tab to fill in the information requested there, also. The Advanced settings generally do not have to be changed. Click the OK button to close the Properties dialog box for the mail service.

If the Microsoft Outlook Setup Wizard runs, it may enable you to browse for your personal address book and personal folder, if you have them on your computer.

When you have multiple profiles set up, you see the Choose Profile dialog box when you open Outlook, as shown here:

Choose the profile that you want to use and then click OK. Outlook opens, showing the folders for the person whose profile was selected, and sends and collects mail according to the mail services defined for that profile. After you define more than one profile, you can define additional profiles by using the New button on the Choose Profile dialog box.

If you want to add e-mail accounts to an existing profile, you need to add a service. To add a service, choose Tools | Services to display the Services dialog box. Click the Add button, choose Internet E-mail from the Add Service to Profile dialog box, and then click OK. On the Mail Account Properties dialog box, provide the necessary information about the e-mail account that you're adding to the profile. Be sure to check the settings on the Servers and Connection tabs.

After you define multiple services, you can send and receive mail for all accounts (services) by clicking the Send and Receive button.

Outlook Express

Outlook Express, the e-mail program that comes with Windows 98, doesn't use the Windows Control Panel Mail program to set up multiple accounts. You can configure the program to send and receive mail from more than one e-mail account, but it's not designed to allow multiple users to read e-mail separately. (You *can* set up an account for each person to collect all the mail into Outlook Express, and then set up filters to sort it out, but other e-mail programs do this better.)

To set up e-mail accounts in Outlook Express, choose Tools | Accounts to display the Internet Accounts dialog box. Click the Mail tab to see a list of mail accounts. To configure Outlook Express to work with a new e-mail account, choose Add | Mail to run the Internet Connection Wizard. The Wizard asks questions about your name, your e-mail address, and the names of the incoming (POP) and outgoing (SMTP) mail servers. If you want to make changes to an existing account, select it and click Properties.

Netscape Messenger

Netscape Messenger 4.5 allows you to set up multiple user profiles (*MUPs*). Separate profiles enable different users to use one copy of Messenger (actually, one copy of the whole Communicator program) and have their own mailboxes, personal settings (including Navigator bookmarks), and preferences. When you open Messenger using your profile, it looks as though you are the only person who uses it—you see only your mail and folders. Profiles are not password-protected, however, and therefore aren't really private. Each profile can use only one e-mail account, but one person can use different profiles to collect mail from different accounts.

See the section "Sharing Navigator with Other Users" in Chapter 19 for directions on how to create and use a new user profile.

Pegasus

Pegasus allows you to run it in multiple-user mode. If you plan to have more that one user, you need to choose this option when you install the Pegasus program. Each user has his or her own folders, address book, and other settings, and can't see any other user's information unless they log in using another user name. Each user can have only one e-mail account (address), so if you want to collect mail from multiple accounts with Pegasus, you need to create a user for each account. This system enables you to keep separate the mail from different accounts, but it also means that you have to change user names to collect, send, and read mail from a different account.

To add users, choose Addresses | User Management to display the Pegasus Mail Users dialog box. Click the Add button. The User Details dialog box asks for the User Name (eight characters or less), Personal Name (the full name that will appear on outgoing e-mail messages), whether the user should have administrative privileges, and whether the new user should receive the default mail messages provided by Pegasus. When Pegasus is in multiple-user mode, you have to provide your user name when you open the program. You can change users without closing Pegasus by choosing File | Change User.

The first time that you use a new user name, Pegasus starts the Pegasus Mail Internet Setup Wizard to get the information about the e-mail account. This Wizard asks for your e-mail address, POP server, user name and password on the POP server, SMTP server, and connection type.

America Online (AOL)

AOL allows each account to have up to five *screen names*. AOL's intention is to provide family access, whereby each family member has their own screen name. You may use screen names for different people or for different personas. Each screen name has its own e-mail address. In addition, each screen name has its own password, which provides some privacy. However, if you are logged on using the *master* screen name, you can change the settings for other screen names. The primary (master) screen name cannot be changed, but you can change the names of the other screen names whenever you wish.

Create a new screen name by logging on to AOL using your primary screen name. Go to the keyword NAMES and double-click Create a Screen Name. If you have five screen names already, you have to delete one before you can create a new one. Screen names must be between three and ten characters, must start with a letter, and must be available. When AOL suggests a screen name for you, you do not have to accept it—keep trying if you don't like the suggested name. Provide a password for the screen name, because each screen name has a separate password.

Sending Form Letters by Using E-mail Stationery

Form letters (or *stationery*) are useful if you receive a high volume of mail on a certain subject and want to send a canned response. Eudora's filter feature (described in Chapter 8) enables you to send a canned response to messages that meet criteria that you set. Other programs require a few extra steps—they allow you to create stationery or import a text file into a message.

You may also find it useful to store in draft form a message that you want to reuse often. And don't forget about cut-and-paste (CTRL+C and CTRL+V in most Windows programs) to copy text from one place to another—in some cases, this may be the easiest way to send a form letter.

Eudora Pro

Eudora Pro enables you to create form letters using stationery. To save any message that you create as stationery, choose File | Save as Stationery when the message is open. You can use stationery that you've already created either by clicking the

Stationery tab or by choosing Tools | Stationery and double-clicking the stationery that you want to use. Or, you can hold down the SHIFT key while you click the New Message button, and then choose the stationery from the Message Options dialog box that appears.

You can reply to a message with stationery by selecting the message in the folder window, right-clicking the stationery name, and then choosing Reply With. Or, hold down the SHIFT key while you click the Reply button on the toolbar.

Eudora is the only e-mail program described in this book that enables you to send a reply automatically to a message that you filter using a particular stationary. To send replies automatically, use the filter feature described in Chapter 8.

Note *If you are going to use stationery to reply to messages, you may want to leave the subject line blank. Then, a reply will have the same subject line as the original message. If you type a subject line in your stationery and then use the stationery to reply to a message, the subject line will appear like this:*

```
Subject of stationery (was RE: Subject of message you're replying to)
```

You also can choose default stationery to use for every new message; select Tools | Options to display the Options dialog box, and then click the Sending Mail icon to display the Select a Default Stationery for New Messages option.

Outlook 98 and Outlook Express

Both versions of Outlook have a stationery feature, but it is meant to allow you to add color and images and set fonts for your messages. Outlook's stationery feature has some limitations—for example, you must use Word or HTML to create messages. People with e-mail programs that can't display formatted e-mail messages don't see your nice-looking formatting, or they see lots of formatting codes. Choose Tools | Stationery to format your messages with the standard "stationery" (formats) that comes with the program (and see the "Outlook 98" and "Outlook Express" sections under "Formatting E-mail," later in this chapter).

To create form letters, you use Outlook's signature feature (described in Chapter 6). Type the content of your form letter to create a signature. Make sure that you don't set the form letter as your default signature. To use the text in a message, open a new message, click the Signature button on the toolbar, and then select the signature that contains the text of your message. You can edit the message before you send it, if you like.

Tip *If you use Word as your Outlook e-mail editor, then you can use Word features such as templates and Mail Merge to create e-mail messages.*

Pegasus

Pegasus doesn't have a "form letter" or "stationery" command, but it does easily enable you to import text from a file into a message. You can create a form letter by creating a text file (using Notepad) that contains the text of your message. If you store the text file in C:\Pmail or your default Pegasus folder and give it a descriptive name, it will be easy to find.

To use text from a text file in a message, open a new message and either press CTRL+M or choose Message | Import into Message. Then, choose the text file from the Select a File dialog box to see the text in your message.

Alternatively, you can use the signature feature to store the text of your message. This works only if the text isn't too long. Pegasus supports up to nine different signatures, so you do have some flexibility as to what you store as a signature. Chapter 6 describes how to create signatures.

Formatting E-mail

Formatting e-mail seems like a cool idea—why limit yourself to plain black-and-white single-font text when you can send messages that are a beautifully formatted as a word processing document or a Web page? The biggest problem with formatted e-mail is that not everyone uses an e-mail program that can display the formatting that you send. The following are the two standards for formatting e-mail:

- **HTML** By adding the same codes that are used to format Web pages, your e-mail messages can include background colors, different-sized fonts, links, and pictures.

- **MIME** By using MIME, the standard for attaching files to e-mail messages, you can send plain-text message with the formatted messages as an attachment.

If you use MIME formatting, most e-mail programs can display your message, followed by an unreadable attachment. But if you use HTML formatting, only HTML-compatible e-mail programs can display anything readable at all—everyone else sees an ocean of HTML codes. Because of this limitation, think hard before you add formatting—do you really need it? Sending formatted messages to people whose e-mail programs can't display them can annoy the recipients.

> **Tip** *Generally, it's safe to send formatted mail to people on the same mail system as you. For instance, you should be able to send formatted mail from work to other people at work.*

Eudora

Eudora provides many text-formatting options on the message composition window's toolbar, including font, font size, bold, italic, underline, color, indent, bullets, hyperlinks, and left, center, or right alignment. However, because you can't control the default font used by the recipient's e-mail program, you can't totally control the look of the message. (You can change the default fonts for your own copy of Eudora by choosing Tools | Options to display the Options dialog box, and then clicking the Fonts category.)

You can turn on or off formatting options. If you don't see the formatting buttons on the message composition toolbar, you can turn them on by choosing Tools | Options to display the Options dialog box, and then choosing Styled Text options.

Outlook 98

Outlook 98 supports four message formats: HTML, Microsoft Outlook Rich Text Format (RTF), Plain Text, and Microsoft Word. When you reply to a message, Outlook should automatically use the same format as the message that you received. If you exchange mail with people who have a variety of e-mail programs, not all of which may support formatting, you should set the format of your outgoing mail to Plain Text. To choose the default mail format, choose Tools | Options to display the Options dialog box, and then click the Mail Format tab. The mail format that you select affects the formatting options that you see in the message composition window.

If you use Word as your e-mail editor, you can use all of Word's formatting capabilities when you create e-mail messages. However, if your recipient's e-mail program doesn't support the formatting that you used, they see only plain text (at best).

Outlook Express

Outlook Express supports only HTML formatting. To control whether you send formatted messages, choose Tools | Options to display the Options dialog box, and then click the Send tab.

Netscape Messenger

Netscape Messenger 4.5 uses HTML formatting, which can result in hard-to-read messages in e-mail programs that don't support it. You can specify in your address book to always send a person HTML text by selecting the Prefers to Receive Rich Text (HTML) Mail option. You can also choose formatting options by choosing Edit | Preferences to display the Preferences dialog box. Click the Mail & Newsgroups category to see its subcategories, and then click the Formatting category.

If you choose to send formatted messages, you can format a message by using the formatting buttons on the message window toolbar.

Pegasus

Pegasus uses Rich Text Format (RTF) for formatting, which not every e-mail program supports. You can format a message by using the formatting buttons on the message window toolbar.

If you want to send plain text messages always, choose Tools | Options from the main menu to display the Options dialog box, click the Sending Mail tab, and then choose the Always Remove Formatting option.

America Online (AOL)

You can format a message by using the formatting buttons on the message window toolbar. However, only other AOL users will be able to see your formatting.

The Complete Reference

Internet

Part III

Chatting and Conferencing on the Internet

Chapter 11

Online Chatting and Conferencing Concepts

The Internet enables a group of people to communicate together—a meeting in which the participants may be anywhere in the world. This group communication can be by text on the screen, by voice, or by video, and messages and responses can be exchanged "live," or they may be read and responded to later. All of these types of online communication are called *online chat* or *online conferencing*.

Forms of Chat and Conferencing

In some types of chatting and conferencing, messages are sent immediately after they are complete (for example, as soon as you press ENTER after typing a message). This type of communication is called *real-time communication*. Other ways of chatting deliver messages more slowly; for example, via e-mail. These other types of communication are also called *asynchronous*, because participants do not all read and respond to messages at the same time (synchronously). Each form of communication has advantages:

- **Real-time chat**   Allows dialog to happen quickly, since each participant sees each message within seconds of when it is sent.

- **Asynchronous chat**   Allows participants to consider their responses, gather information, and formulate a response carefully. It also allows people from different time zones or with different schedules to participate. For example, there may not be a time when all the members of a committee are available for a real-time meeting.

Table 11-1 lists the most commonly used forms of Internet-based chat and conferencing, along with the timing (real time or asynchronous), format of information (text, audio, video, or files), and type of software that you need to participate.

Type	Timing	Format	Software Required
E-mail mailing list	Asynchronous	Text with attached files	E-mail program (such as Eudora, Outlook Express, or Netscape Messenger)
Usenet newsgroups	Asynchronous	Text with attached files	Newsreader (such as Free Agent, Outlook Express, or Netscape Collabra)

Table 11-1.   *Types of Online Chat and Conferencing*

Type	Timing	Format	Software Required
Internet Relay Chat (IRC)	Real time	Text with file transfer	Chat program (such as mIRC or Ircle)
Web-based chat	Real time	Text	Web browser (such as Netscape or Internet Explorer)
AOL chat rooms	Real time	Text	AOL access program (for America Online)
Direct chat programs	Real time	Text	ICQ, AOL Instant Messenger, or other program
Online conferencing	Real time	Text, voice, and video, depending on software used	Conferencing program (such as CU-SeeMe, Netscape Conference, or Microsoft NetMeeting)
MUDs and MOOs (Internet-based multiuser games and worlds, described in the section "MUDs and MOOs" later in this chapter)	Real time	Text	Telnet program or MUD client program

Table 11-1.   *Types of Online Chat and Conferencing* (continued)

CHATTING AND CONFERENCING ON THE INTERNET

E-mail Mailing Lists

E-mail messages are usually addressed and delivered to only one or two people. An *e-mail mailing list* allows messages to be distributed to a large list of people. Depending on how the mailing list is set up, either one, some, or all subscribers can post messages, so that mailing lists can be used to distribute newsletters or press releases or to allow large group discussions. For more information on how to find, participate in, or create mailing lists, see Chapter 12.

Usenet Newsgroups

Usenet is a system that allows messages to be distributed throughout the Internet. Because of the volume of messages, the messages are divided into *newsgroups*, or topics. You use a *newsreader* program to subscribe to a newsgroup, read the messages posted to that newsgroup, and post your own messages. Over 20,000 different newsgroups exist, covering every conceivable topic. For general information about Usenet newsgroups, see Chapter 13. For instructions on the most widely used newsreaders, see Chapter 14.

Internet Relay Chat (IRC)

Internet Relay Chat (IRC) allows thousands of Internet users to participant in real-time text-based chat. When you use an IRC program to connect to a central IRC server and join a conversation (called a *channel*), you see all the messages that are typed in that channel within seconds of when the messages are sent. The IRC program enables you to type and send your own messages, too. For guidance on how to choose an IRC program and use it to participate in Internet Relay Chat, see Chapter 15.

Web-Based Chat

Many people are daunted by the new programs and commands they have to learn to access IRC. Therefore, many Web sites now provide a Web-based way to send and receive IRC messages. Other Web sites provide their own real-time or asynchronous chat pages. For information about how to find and participate in Web-based chat, see Chapter 16.

AOL Chat Rooms and Other Proprietary Services

America Online users spend most of their online hours in *chat rooms*, AOL services that allow real-time chat on a wide variety of subjects. To participate in AOL chat rooms, you must have an AOL account and use AOL's proprietary software to connect to your account. Other Internet users (those with ISP accounts) cannot participate in AOL chat rooms.

Similarly, CompuServe (a business-oriented online service now owned by AOL) offers forums and conferences on many different topics. You need a CompuServe account and CompuServe software to participate. (You can also use telnet, a terminal-emulation program described in Chapter 40, to connect and participate, but this choice is not recommended.)

Direct Chat Systems

ICQ (pronounced "I seek you"), AOL Instant Messenger, and other systems enable you to send messages to other people when both you and they are connected to the Internet. You create a list of the people who you want to chat with. When one of the people on your list connects to the Internet, your direct chat program informs you that your friend is online, and you can then exchange messages. For more information on using direct chat systems, see Chapter 16.

Online Conferencing

If text isn't enough, you can use one of several Internet-based online conferencing programs that enable you to confer via text, voice, and video with one or more other people. To use one of these programs, your computer requires a microphone, speakers, and a video camera. Some conferencing programs also allow all the participants to see or edit a document on their screens and to see or write on a digital *whiteboard* (a shared paint program that all participants can draw on). Chapter 17 describes how to use some of the best-known conferencing programs: Netscape Conference, Microsoft NetMeeting, and CU-SeeMe.

MUDs and MOOs

In addition to unstructured chats and discussions, many multiuser games are in progress on the Internet at any hour of the day or night. *Multiuser dimensions (MUDs)* are text-based chats in which the participants play a game by following a set of rules enforced by the central server computer. The game is usually a fantasy game, but may be an online university or other group event. *MUDs object oriented (MOOs)* are user-programmable games that are similar to MUDs: by programming, participants can create objects in the shared world of the MOO. For more information on how to join MUDs and MOOs, see Chapter 16.

How Does Chat Work?

The following sections provide some general descriptions of how chat and conferencing work.

Identifying Yourself

In mailing lists and newsgroups, you are identified by your name and e-mail address. When you join an IRC channel, Web-based chat, or AOL chat room, you choose a name to go by—variously referred to as your *nickname, handle,* or (on AOL) *screen name.* If someone is already using the name that you planned to use, you must choose another one. On systems that allow you to choose a nickname each time that you join, remember that the person who has a particular nickname today may not be the same person who had it yesterday.

Topics, Newsgroups, Channels, and Rooms

Tens of thousands of people can simultaneously participate in e-mail mailing lists, Usenet newsgroups, Internet Relay Chat, Web-based chat, and AOL chat rooms. The discussions are categorized by topic, enabling people who are interested in a particular topic to communicate with each other. Topics may include hobbies, personal problems, sports, research areas, religious beliefs, or other areas of interest, or chat participants may simply be grouped together by geographical area or age. Some discussions consist entirely of people looking for partners for romance, sex, or simple banter.

Depending on the system, topic groups may be called *newsgroups* (in Usenet), *channels* (in IRC), or *rooms* (in AOL). E-mail mailing lists are already divided by topic (one list per topic), although some mailing lists ask you to include topic keywords in the subject lines of your messages, too.

Following the Discussion

In e-mail mailing lists and Usenet, messages have subject lines. A *thread* is a message on a particular topic, along with all the responses to that message (and responses to the responses, and so forth). The subject lines of responses usually begin with "Re:" (short for *in re*, which is Latin for "on the subject of"). When you read mailing list or newsgroup messages, you can sort the messages by thread and choose which threads to read.

In IRC channels and AOL chat rooms, the discussion consists of short messages from many participants, with each message preceded by the name of the person who sent it. The messages are displayed on your screen in the order in which your computer received them, and several conversations may be happening at the same time.

Following a chat discussion can be tricky. When you join a channel or chat room, stay quiet for a few minutes until your screen fills up with messages. Start by reading one interesting-looking message and then read down through the messages for responses to that message and for other messages from the same person who sent the original message. When you have something to say, jump in!

Chat Etiquette

Here are some general rules of etiquette (or *netiquette*, which is etiquette on the Net) to use, regardless of which type of chat or conference system that you are using:

- *Remember that you are talking to real people, not to computers.* This can be hard to remember when someone says something that you disagree with, and all you know about the person is what you read on a computer screen. Treat people as kindly as you would in person.

- Lurk *(listen without talking) first, and wait until you have something interesting to say.* The definition of "interesting" varies according to the chat system that you use. Mailing list subscribers frown on messages that don't have something substantive to say, while chat room denizens consider "Hello all!" to be an intelligent remark. Be sure that your message is relevant for the group: mailing lists and newsgroups have specific topics that you should stick to. Lists and newsgroups also have *FAQs* (lists of *frequently asked questions* and their answers) that you should read before asking any questions: your question may already be answered in the FAQs.

- *Don't shout.* Typing in ALL CAPITALS is considered shouting. People complain if you use capitals for all of your text. Using only small letters is considered odd but not offensive.

- *Check your spelling and proofread your text before you click Send.* It can be annoying to others (as well as embarrassing to you!) to read text that contains a lot of typos and grammatical errors.

- *Learn the rules.* Many newsgroups, mailing lists, chat rooms, and channels have rules. You may receive a list of them when you join. Be sure to follow them, so that you don't get ejected from the discussion.

- *Precede your remark with the name (or nickname or handle) of the person to whom your remark is directed if several conversations are taking place simultaneously in a channel or chat room.* Otherwise, it is likely that the wrong person will answer your question, or your question will be ignored altogether.

- *In mailing lists and Usenet newsgroups, quote the relevant parts of the message to which you are responding.* Quoting messages is a good idea, so that the people reading your message know what you are responding to. But if subscribers already read the original message, they don't want to read the whole thing again. Delete all but the relevant parts of the quoted message. As a rule of thumb, the message that you write should always be longer than the quoted material in your message. Never quote an entire message and add only "I agree!"

- *Consider whether you really need to post a message to the entire list or newsgroup in which you are participating.* Messages of interest only to the original poster (such as "I agree!") should go privately by e-mail, because the rest of the subscribers aren't interested.

- *Don't try to manage the conversation unless you are the mailing list manager, channel operator, or other person in charge.* Don't send messages complaining about other messages; it's bad enough having to read an off-topic message without also having to wade through complaints about it. If you really have a problem with a message, talk privately to the person who posted it, using e-mail, a private chat room, or a direct chat system.

- *Beware aware of trolls, messages that are intended to provoke a storm of responses.* If someone makes a provocative remark, silence is sometimes an appropriate response. If someone acts obnoxious consistently, the best response is to ignore him or her.

- *Don't post the same message to multiple lists or newsgroups.* Choose the list or newsgroup that is the most appropriate for your message.

- *Don't send copyrighted material to mailing lists or newsgroups.* Doing so is probably an infringement of copyright. Most material on Web sites is copyrighted, as are postings to mailing lists and newsgroups themselves (yes, you own the copyright on your messages!). When in doubt, contact the author of the material to request permission. Of course, quoting a message when you respond to that message is considered polite and proper, as long as the message to which you are replying is posted to the same mailing list or newsgroup to which you send the response.

For all forms of online chat and conferencing, people frequently resort to abbreviations to save typing. These abbreviations may not be familiar. For a long list of frequently used abbreviations, see the Chatter's Jargon Dictionary at **http://www.tiac.net/users/scg/jargpge.htm#Jargon**. This page also includes a listing of *emoticons*, diagrams of faces that are created by using punctuation, which are widely used to add emotion to chat messages (see also **http://net.gurus.com/smileys.html**).

Safety While Chatting

Safety is a consideration when you participate in public chat systems. (Using a conferencing program for meetings with coworkers and clients doesn't carry the same risk, since you already know the participants.) Here are some safety considerations:

- *Remember that what you say is not private.* Other people (or programs) may be capturing all the messages in the conversation. Usenet newsgroup messages are saved in a publicly searchable archive on the Web at **http://www.dejanews.com**. Similarly, many mailing lists maintain searchable message archives.

- *Be aware that your messages are not anonymous.* E-mail and newsgroup messages contain your e-mail address, as well as headers that contain other identifying information. IRC and chat room messages don't contain information that identifies you, but the system operators could, if necessary, trace your messages back to your Internet account, with help from your ISP.

- *Don't believe everything you read.* A person's description of himself or herself may range anywhere from slightly optimistic to totally inaccurate. Many people use online chat systems as a way to experiment with their self-image, and may portray themselves as people with genders, ages, professions, and other characteristics that are different from the ones they have in real life. Others may present themselves inaccurately because they want to defraud you, gain your confidence, or otherwise trick you.

- *Don't reveal more about yourself than you would want everyone in the universe to know.* Specifically, don't reveal your phone number, address, company, school, real name, or other identifying information in an online chat. More than one person has received an unwanted phone call from someone they met while chatting.

- *Never type your password in a chat or conference.* Requests for your password are *always* bogus. Your Internet provider, AOL, or other password-protected system already knows your password, and employees of these systems *never* ask you to type your password in a chat or conference.

- *Don't hang around in sexually oriented channels or chat rooms if you are not interested in sex.* If someone sends you a graphics file, delete it without looking at it, unless you don't mind seeing a more graphic picture than you might enjoy. If someone invites you into a private chat room or channel, consider what kind of chat you are looking for. If you don't like the conversation in one chat room or channel, find another.

- *Don't allow your children to use chat or conferencing systems without supervision.* If you do, be sure that your children know not to give out personal information and never to agree to meet someone in person. Some malefactors offer prizes to kids in return for personal, identifying information; make sure your kids know not to go along with these scams.

- *Take advantage of AOL's guidelines, if you use AOL.* Go to the Parental Controls keyword and click Online Safety Tips, for more information.

- *Be sure to report inappropriate, abusive, or scary behavior when possible.* On AOL, go to the TOS keyword (Terms of Service) to report problems. On IRC, you can ask the channel operator in charge of the channel that you are in to have the person banned from the system. On mailing lists, write to the list manager.

Ways to Use Chat Effectively

Depending on the speed, formality, privacy, and availability you need when chatting online, consider which of the following types of chat to use:

- *For an informal discussion at a specific place and time, with immediate responses, consider an IRC chat (or AOL chat, if all participants use AOL, or Web-based chat).* For an IRC chat, make sure that all participants have access to an IRC program, have installed it, and know how to use it. For a closed meeting, you can create a private channel. Some IRC programs allow you to keep a log of the proceedings. IRC chats are hard to manage with many participants (over about 15). Most Web-based chat systems display ads to support the free service, and many don't allow you to set up your own private chat rooms.

- *For an ongoing discussion that doesn't require everyone to be present at the same time, use an e-mail mailing list.* Mailing lists don't require any special software, and anyone with an e-mail address can participate. If you want to keep minutes of the "meeting," tell the mailing-list management program to save all messages in a searchable archive. If you want to control who can participate, configure the mailing list to be closed. Mailing lists work with small or large numbers of participants.

You might also consider a Usenet newsgroup: creating a newsgroup in one of the standard hierarchies (see Chapter 13) requires a long process of proposals, lobbying, and voting, but newsgroups can be easier for people to find than mailing lists. On the other hand, fewer people have newsreading programs than e-mail programs, and newsgroups cannot be private unless you have access to a private news server.

- *For smaller meetings at which you need to take shared notes, hear or see participants, or see and edit documents onscreen, consider a conferencing program.* Each participant must have the same program (few programs are compatible with each other), along with the hardware to support audio or video. You can control who can join a meeting and who can see or edit shared files.

- *For meeting people, socializing, and hanging around, consider the following programs.* MUDs and MOOs are fun if you like fantasy games. If you don't mind a lot of aimless (and ribald) banter, you might like IRC. If you have specific people to converse with, direct chat programs are probably your best bet.

The rest of the chapters in this part of the book describe each of the ways to participate in Internet-based chats and conferences.

Chapter 12

E-mail Mailing Lists

E-mailing lists enable groups of Internet users to communicate by using e-mail. For example, a group of people working on a project can use a mailing list to plan and track the project, exchanging messages about their progress. A group of hobbyists can exchange tips and answer each other's questions. Or a college professor and her class can conduct an ongoing discussion of the assigned readings for the class. Depending on how a mailing list is configured, it can be an online newsletter, a public forum for open discussion, a moderated discussion, or a private meeting room with a complete transcript of the proceedings. This chapter describes how mailing lists work, how to find mailing lists of interest, how to join one, and how to set up a mailing list of your own.

How Do Mailing Lists Work?

The *mailing list manager* (a person or a program) stores a list of subscribers' addresses in a central location. The mailing list has its own e-mail address, called the *list address*. When a subscriber sends a message to the list address, the mailing list manager distributes the message to all the subscribers' addresses. If subscribers send replies to the list address, replies are also distributed to all subscribers, and a discussion starts.

Each mailing list also has an *administrative address*, which reaches the mailing list manager, not the list subscribers. Subscribers write to the administrative address to join the list, sign off the list, or change configuration settings for their subscription.

For example, to join a list about domestic poultry, you would send a message to the administrative address for the (fictional) CHICKENS-L mailing list, at **CHICKENS-L-request@gurus.com**. You may have to confirm your subscription with a second message, if the list requires confirmations. Once you are on the list, you start receiving all the messages that are posted to the list. When you have something to say, you send a message to the list address for the list, **CHICKENS-L@gurus.com**.

Note *Your e-mail program doesn't have to be configured to work with mailing lists: messages to and from mailing lists are sent and received the same way as other e-mail messages.*

Types of Mailing Lists

The mailing list manager controls who can subscribe, who can post messages to the list, and other list behavior:

- **Open vs. closed subscriptions**   The mailing list manager may allow anyone to subscribe (an *open* list) or may approve only selected subscribers (a *closed* list).

- **Open vs. closed posting**   The mailing list manager may allow anyone to post messages to the list, even nonsubscribers, or may allow only subscribers to send messages to the list.

- **Moderated** Moderated lists have a *moderator* who reviews all messages before posting them to the list. Some moderated lists allow anyone (or any subscriber) to post messages, and the moderator serves as a editor who rejects off-topic postings, repetitive postings, or posting that break some other rule for the list. Other moderated lists allow only one person to post: in effect, the list serves as an online newsletter.

- **Digests** If a list has many postings a day, some subscribers may prefer to receive each day's messages in one big message (a *digest*) rather than separately. Digests are usually sent daily, although they may be sent weekly or some other frequency. See "Receiving Messages in Digests," later in this chapter.

- **Archived** The mailing list manager may save all the messages distributed to the list in an *archive*. If a list is archived, the archives may be available to everyone, to list subscribers only, or to the list manager only. See "Getting Archived Messages," later in this chapter.

- **Reply-to-list vs. reply-to-sender** Some mailing lists distribute messages with a reply-to header that contains the list address: when a subscriber replies to a message, the reply is automatically addressed to the list, so everyone on the list sees the reply. Other mailing lists distribute messages with a reply-to header that contains the address of the person who sent the message: replies are addressed to the original sender, and the rest of the subscribers don't see the response. *Reply-to-list* is better for lists that want to foster discussion. *Reply-to-sender* is better for lists that want to keep chatter to a minimum.

Mailing List Management Programs

Managing a mailing list can require lots of manual labor: each time someone wants to subscribe, sign off, or change configuration settings, the list manager has to make the appropriate changes to the list of subscribers' addresses. In 1986, someone had the idea of writing a program to do all of this work. Now most lists are managed by programs, with help from a human list manager.

How Mailing List Management Programs Work

The mailing list management program (or MLM, for short) responds to all messages addressed to both the list address and the list's administrative address. Messages to the list address are distributed to the subscribers (assuming that the message comes from an authorized address). Messages to the administrative address are processed by the program: for example, a message with the command **subscribe** might add the sender to the subscriber list. Subscribers communicate with the MLM entirely by sending commands to the administrative address for the list.

Popular Mailing List Management Programs (MLMs)

Several different MLMs are in wide use: LISTSERV, ListProc, and Majordomo are the most popular. Unfortunately, each MLM uses a different set of commands. This chapter describes how to use lists managed by these three programs:

- **LISTSERV** Written in 1986 to run on IBM mainframes, now runs on UNIX, Windows 95, Windows NT, and other systems, with a Macintosh version in the works. Over 90,000 mailing lists worldwide are managed by LISTSERV. For more information, see its home page at **http://www.lsoft.com/listserv.stm**. This chapter describes LISTSERV version 1.8c.

- **ListProc (or CREN ListProcessor)** Designed to be very similar to LISTSERV, responding to most of the same commands. ListProc runs under UNIX, and a Windows 95 version is under development. ListProc has added a Web interface to make subscribing and signing off easier. For more information, see its home page at **http://www.cren.net/listproc**. This chapter describes ListProc version 8.2.

- **Majordomo** A UNIX-based mailing list, with the source code available (written in Perl) so that programmers can adapt and customize the system. See its home page at **http://www.greatcircle.com/majordomo** for more information. This chapter describes Majordomo version 1.94; version 2.0 may be available by the time you read this.

Many other MLMs are available, including programs that run on Windows and Macs. To find out about MLMs, start at Yahoo (**http://www.yahoo.com**) and choose Computers and Internet I Software I Internet I Electronic Mail I Mailing Lists.

Of course, some lists are managed manually, by human beings. See the section "Running a Mailing List from Your E-mail Program," later in this chapter, for ways to run a mailing list without an MLM.

List, Administrative, and Manager Addresses

MLMs may run on almost any computer that is connected to the Internet. Once installed, an MLM can manage many lists: for example, a company might install on one computer an MLM that can manage several open discussion lists for the company's customers, an open moderated list for distributing a customer newsletter, an open moderated list for press releases, and dozens of closed lists for company departments and committees.

An MLM has one administrative address, no matter how many lists it handles. The administrative address is almost always the name of the program, followed by @ and the name of the computer on which the program is installed. For example, the administrative address for the Majordomo program installed at gurus.com is **majordomo@gurus.com**. The list address is the list name followed by the same domain name. For example, the list address for the blagues-L list (which distributes jokes in French and English) managed by **majordomo@gurus.com** is **blagues-L@gurus.com**.

*Many mailing lists have names that end with **-L** because this was the standard for naming LISTSERV mailing lists. This naming convention has become a tradition at some mailing list sites, but not all mailing list names end with **-L**.*

Most MLMs also provide an address that reaches the person who is in charge of the list (the *list manager*). LISTSERV and Majordomo add **owner-** to the beginning of the listname, while ListProc adds **-request** to the end of the list name. For example, the owner of the blagues-L mailing list is reachable at **owner-blagues-L@gurus.com**. If a list is managed manually, the administrative address reaches the list manager.

 *To confuse matters, some MLMs provide additional administrative addresses: for example, Majordomo usually allows administrative messages to be sent to the address of the list, by adding **-request** to the end of the list name.*

An MLM also has a *site manager*, who is responsible for running the program. This person may also be the list manager for one or more lists. The address for the site manager is **listmgr@**, **listmanager@**, **list-manager@**, or some other username, followed by the system name on which the program is running.

Subscribing and Signing Off

To subscribe to a mailing list, you need to know:

■ The list name and list address

■ The administrative address for the list

■ The MLM (or human) that manages the list

See the section "Finding Interesting Mailing Lists," later in this chapter, for details on how to find the addresses for mailing lists that might interest you.

For example, a list called **mini-air** with list address **mini-air@air.harvard.edu** has the administrative address **listproc@air.harvard.edu**. The administrative address for MLMs usually uses the name of the program as the username: in this example, the program is ListProc. (Mini-air is the online edition of the *Annals of Improbable Research*, a hilarious pseudoscientific journal).

 Never send subscribe or unsubscribe messages to the list address, because these messages are distributed to all list subscribers. Be sure to use the administrative address for all commands.

If a list is managed by a human being rather than by a program, the administrative address and list manager address are usually the same (since the list manger is the person who processes administrative requests). The administrative address may be the same as the list address, but with the addition of **owner-** or **-request**, or it may be exactly the same as the list address, depending on how the list manager decides to run the list.

Sending a Subscribe Command

To subscribe to a mailing list, send the appropriate command to the administrative address. If the list is managed by a program, the command must be in the text of the message, not on the subject line, which most MLMs ignore. The command must also be structured in a specific format, or the program won't understand it. You must use the exact text, spacing, and punctuation (or lack thereof) described in this section. If you send an incorrect command, the MLM replies with an error message.

For LISTSERV, ListProc, and Majordomo, the command is **subscribe**, but the format differs among the programs. For LISTSERV and ListProc programs, send the following command to the administrative address:

subscribe *listname your name*

(The **subscribe** command can be abbreviated to **sub**.) Replace *listname* with the exact name of the list (just the list name, not the entire list address: omit the @ and the host name). Replace *your name* with your name (not your e-mail address). For Majordomo, omit your name.

For example, to subscribe to the **mini-air** list managed by **listproc@air.harvard.edu**, you'd send a message to **listproc@air.harvard.edu**, with the following line in the text of the message (assuming that your name were Josephine Bloggs):

```
subscribe mini-air Josephine Bloggs
```

The MLM reads your e-mail address from the headers of your message, reads your **subscribe** command, and adds you to the mailing list (if the list is open; if the list is not open, the MLM notifies the list manager or rejects your subscription). The program sends you an automated response. If the list is configured to require a name, and you omit your name, ListProc and LISTSERV complain and reject the **subscribe** command.

For manually managed lists, send a polite note to the administrative address that includes your name and the name of the list that you want to join. Give the list manager a few days to respond (don't nag!): some list managers do things other than managing lists.

Be sure to save the confirmation message that you receive when you join a list. This message usually contains instructions for sending postings to the list, rules for postings, and instructions for signing off the list. The message may also contain a password that you can use to change the setting for your subscription, including changing your e-mail address. It's a good idea to create in your e-mail program a folder called Mailing Lists *and store all of your welcome messages there.*

Tips for Sending Commands

When you send a command to an MLM's administrative address, follow these rules:

- Put the command on the first line of the text of the message.
- Be sure to spell all parts of the command correctly.
- Don't add any punctuation or pleasantries (remember, a computer is reading this message).
- Put the whole command on one line.
- Suppress your signature, if your e-mail program usually adds one. If you can't avoid a signature or other lines being added to the end of the message, type the command **end** on a line by itself after your command. The **end** command tells most MLMs to skip the rest of the lines of the message.

 LISTSERV has the annoying habit of confirming all commands with a message that tells you how much computer processing time your commands took. Just delete these messages.

Confirming Your Subscription

Many lists send you a confirmation message to which you must reply before you are added to the subscription list. This process prevents anyone from forging subscription messages that sign up an unsuspecting victim for lists the victim doesn't want. (Some malefactors have *mailbombed* people by subscribing them to hundreds or thousands of mailing lists so that the victims' mailboxes overflow and are shut down by their Internet providers.)

These confirmation messages are usually poorly written and confusing. Follow the instructions in the message to confirm that you want to subscribe to the list. ListProc requires only that you click Reply and then click Send, to send an unedited reply to the program's administrative address. LISTSERV requires you to reply to the message, deleting the text of the original message and typing **ok** as the new text of the message. Majordomo lists may require you to send the following command back to the administrative address (refer to the message from Majordomo for the exact format and password to use):

auth *password* subscribe *listname youraddress*

Be sure to respond to the confirmation request from the same address from which you send the original **subscribe** command.

If the mailing list has closed subscriptions, the list manager may reject your request to subscribe, or may write to you with a request for information about who you are and why you want to join.

Solving Subscription Problems

If you run into trouble subscribing to a list, send the command **help** to the administrative address to get more information about how to use the **subscribe**

command. If you still need help, write to the list manager at **owner-*listname*@*listsite***
(for most Majordomo lists) or ***listname*-request@*listsite*** (for most LISTSERV and
ListProc lists). Politely ask to be added to the list.

*To find out which mailing lists you are subscribed to at a site managed by an MLM,
send the command **which** to the administrative address (for ListProc or Majordomo
lists), or the command **query** * (for LISTSERV lists). Be sure to include the asterisk
with the **query** command. The program will send you the names of all the lists to which
you are subscribed that are managed by that program.*

Signing Off Mailing Lists

To sign off (unsubscribe) from a list, send a command to the administrative address.
For LISTSERV and ListProc lists, send the command **signoff** *listname*, replacing
listname with the name of the list. For Majordomo lists, send the command **unsubscribe**
listname. For manually managed lists, send a polite note (and thank the list manager
for his or her hard work).

The MLM reads your e-mail address from the message headers, removes your
name from the list, and sends you a confirmation message. For this reason, you must
send the signoff message from the same e-mail account from which you originally
subscribed (except for manually managed lists).

What if your e-mail address has changed, and you can't send a message from the
account from which you subscribed? See the section "Changing Your Address," later in
this chapter, for details on how to provide your new address to the MLM. Once the
program has your new address, you can send a **signoff** command from your new e-mail
account, if you no longer want to subscribe to the list. Alternatively, you can write politely
to the list manager and ask that your old address be replaced by your new address.

*To sign off all the lists managed by a Majordomo site, send the command **unsubscribe** *
to the administrative address. The asterisk tells Majordomo to remove you from all lists.
To sign off all the lists managed by a ListProc site, send the command **purge** password,
replacing password with the password that was assigned to you in the welcome
message that you received when you subscribed to any of the lists. To sign off all lists
managed by a LISTSERV site, send the message **signoff** *.*

Participating in Mailing Lists

To send a message to all the subscribers of a list, address the message to the list address (not
the administrative address). The list address is the name of the list, followed by @, followed
by the name of the computer that hosts the list (for example, the nonexistent CHICKENS-L
list hosted at **gurus.com** would have the list address **chickens-L@gurus.com**). If the list is
unmoderated, the MLM (or human list manager) distributes your message to the subscribers
of the list. If the list is moderated, your message goes to the moderator (or moderators) for
approval.

Replying to List Messages

To respond to a posting with a message of your own to be sent to the entire list, first reply to a message from the list. Then, check the address in the To line of your reply. Some lists are configured so that replies are addressed to the list address, while replies to other lists are addressed to the person who sent the original message. You may need to copy into your reply the list address from the original message, if you want to post your reply to the list.

On the other hand, consider whether the whole list will be interested in your response. Perhaps a private e-mail message to the author of the message would be more appropriate. If the mailing list addresses replies to the list, you can copy the author's address from the original message to the To line of your reply.

If you want to refer to the original message in your response, quote the original message, deleting the parts of the original message that you don't plan to talk about. Don't bore subscribers by quoting the entire original message, which everyone else already read once.

Posting a New Message

You don't have to respond to a message to participate in a discussion by mailing list: you can also start a new topic. Address your message to the list address, choose a specific and informative subject line, and ask your question or make your comment. Remember, however, to read the FAQ (list of frequently asked questions and their answers) for the list first, if there is one, to make sure that your question isn't already answered there (see "Finding Out More About the Mailing List," later in this chapter, for how to read the FAQ).

Do's and Don'ts

Here are some messages never to post to a mailing list:

- Commands intended for the MLM (like **unsubscribe** or **signoff**) or questions intended for the human mailing list manager. Send commands to the administrative address and questions to the list manager address.

- A message that quotes another message in its entirety, with the added comment "Me too!" or "I agree!"

- Chain letters, virus warnings, jokes about Microsoft buying God, get-rich-quick schemes, or other widely distributed e-mail messages.

- Advertisements about products or services. If you sell something of interest to subscribers, you can discuss the technical merits of your product, and include the URL of the product's home page in your signature, but don't try to solicit other subscribers to buy your product.

- Personal attacks on other subscribers. If you have a problem with something a subscriber said, write directly to that person rather than posting an attack to the list. Reply to the list only to discuss what the person said, not to discuss the person.

See the section "Chat Etiquette," in Chapter 11, for general rules of behavior on mailing lists. Some other guidelines for participating in mailing lists include the following:

- *Make sure that the subject line reflects what the message is about.* Make your subject specific: "Trouble Importing Files into OmniData 3.2" is better than "Help!" If you are replying to a message and the topic of your message has drifted from the topic shown in the subject line, edit the subject line to start a new thread.

- *Don't send test messages.* If you're not sure whether you can post messages to a list, wait until you have something to say, then try it.

- *Don't attach files to your messages, unless the mailing list specifically allows attachments.* Instead, send a message describing the file and asking anyone interested in receiving the file to e-mail you privately.

Finding Out More About the Mailing List

Each mailing list should have an informational message about the list. This message may include a FAQ (list of frequently asked questions and their answers). Most lists send you the informational message when you subscribe to the list, but you can get a copy at any time. To receive the informational message about a LISTSERV, ListProc, or Majordomo list, send the message **info** *listname* to the administrative address. To find out about a manually maintained list, write a polite note to the list manager.

Displaying the List Configuration and Subscribers

To see the configuration settings for a mailing list, and possibly find out who is on the mailing list, send the command **review** *listname* to the administrative address (for LISTSERV and ListProc lists). For Majordomo lists, you can't see the list configuration, but you may be able to see who is on the list by sending the command **who** *listname* to the administrative address.

You'll receive a listing of the list's configuration settings, the list's informational message, and perhaps the subscribers list. See the section "Creating Your Own Mailing List," later in this chapter, for an explanation of what some of the list configuration settings mean.

Getting Help

You can send the command **help** to LISTSERV, ListProc, or Majordomo administrative addresses for information about all of your available commands. For LISTSERV lists, you can also send the command **info refcard** for a "reference card" of commands: send the command **info** for a list of information topics that you can request.

Separating Mailing List Messages from Other Messages

Your personal messages and messages from various mailing lists arrive together in your e-mail mailbox. It can be confusing to read them jumbled together. Instead, you can arrange for all the messages from each mailing list to be displayed separately from your personal mail. Two methods work: presorting (filtering) and filters.

Presorting Your Mailing List Messages

Many e-mail programs can sort (or *filter*) your incoming messages into separate folders, so that you have one folder for each mailing list and one folder (usually your In or Inbox folder) for the rest of your incoming messages. Eudora, Pegasus, and Outlook Express can all sort your mail: see Chapter 8 for instructions.

Receiving Messages in Digests

If your e-mail program can't sort your incoming mail into folders by mailing list, the volume of messages from mailing lists can make it hard to find your personal messages. Most mailing lists offer a *digest* option, in which messages are sent out in batches, usually daily. Each batch arrives as one big e-mail message, sometimes with a table of contents at the top. Some MLMs send digests in MIME format, a format that considers each message to be a separate attachment to the digest message. You can control whether the digests that you receive use MIME, depending on whether your e-mail program can handle MIME attachments (as described in Chapter 7).

To switch to receiving digests, send a message to the administrative address for the list. For LISTSERV lists, send the message **set** *listname* **digests**. To tell LISTSERV not to use MIME, send the command **set** *listname* **nomime**. For ListProc lists, send the message **set** *listname* **mail digest** (for MIME digests) or **set** *listname* **mail digest-nomime** (for plain-text digests).

Majordomo handles digests differently than LISTSERV and ListProc: the digest is considered to be a different mailing list, and not all lists have digests. You sign off the mailing list and subscribe to the mailing list as you normally would, but you add **-digest** to the end of the mailing list name (for example, **CHICKENS-L-digest**).

To switch back to receiving individual messages, send the message **set** *listname* **nodigests** for LISTSERV lists, or **set** *listname* **mail ack** for ListProc lists. For Majordomo lists, sign off the digest list and resubscribe to the regular list.

 When you reply to a message in a digest, be sure to quote only the message to which you are replying, not the whole digest. Also, change the subject line of your reply to include the subject of the message to which you are replying rather than the subject line of the digest.

Setting Your Mailing List Options

You can configure some settings that control how and when you receive messages from the mailing list. The settings depend on which program (or human being) manages the list.

Displaying Your Current Settings

To see your current settings for a LISTSERV list, send the command **query** *listname* to the administrative address. For a ListProc list, send the command **set** *listname*. Majordomo doesn't have a command to display your settings. For example, here are the settings for a ListProc list:

```
Current settings are:
ADDRESS = nettcr@gurus.com
MAIL = ACK
PASSWORD = 85396856
CONCEAL = YES
```

> **Note** *For lists that require you to send a confirmation message before your subscription is complete, send the confirmation message before you send a **query** or **set** command.*

These setting show your e-mail address, your mail mode (**ack** means that ListProc sends you copies of messages that you post to the list), your password (use to change your address), and that your name will be concealed (left off listings of subscribers). Manually managed lists usually don't have configuration settings.

Concealing Your Address

What if you don't want your name and e-mail address to appear on the list of subscribers? You may want to prevent e-mail marketers from subscribing to the list and "harvesting" your name along with the rest of the list subscribers. Or the list might be on a personal subject—perhaps a self-help group. You can continue to subscribe to a list, but conceal your name when subscribers use the **review** or **who** command to see the subscribers list. (Note that some lists are configured so that anyone can see the list of subscribers, some allow only subscribers to see the list, and some keep the subscribers list secret.)

For ListProc mailing lists, send the command **set** *listname* **conceal yes** to the administrative address. For LISTSERV lists, send the command **set** *listname* **conceal**. Majordomo doesn't provide a way to conceal your address. Manually managed lists don't usually release their subscribers list.

Holding Your Mail

If you are on several mailing lists and you go away for a week, your mailbox will be full of messages. If you'd rather skip the messages from a mailing list while you are gone, you may be able to ask the MLM to hold your mail (or, more accurately, to throw it away).

For LISTSERV mailing lists, send the command **set** *listname* **nomail** to the administrative address. When you get back, send the command **set** *listname* **mail**. For ListProc lists, send the command **set** *listname* **mail postpone** before you go away. When you return, send the command **set** *listname* **mail ack** (to get individual messages), **set** *listname* **mail digest** (to get plain-text digests), or **set** *listname* **mail digest-nomime** (to get MIME-format digests). Majordomo won't hold your mail for you: instead, just unsubscribe and resubscribe. For a manually managed list, write to the list manager to ask that your name be removed from the list until you notify the manager that you are back.

Getting Archived Messages

Some mailing lists are *archived*, which means that the mailing list manager (human or program) stores copies of all the messages distributed by the mailing list. If the list is archived, the archives can be open to the list manager, to subscribers, or to everyone. If the archives are open to subscribers or everyone, you may be able to search the archives for answers to questions that were asked earlier.

LISTSERV and ListProc can both maintain list archives automatically. Majordomo usually supports list archives for the digest version of a list, which (if it exists) has the name *listname* or *listname*-digest. In addition to archived messages, list archives may include other files that have been put there by the list manager. Manually managed lists don't usually have archives.

> **Note** Not all mailing lists are archived. If a list is intended for informal discussion, subscribers usually don't want their words to be saved in a publicly searchable way.

To read the archives of a list, you use two commands:

- **Index** To see a list of the archive files
- **Get** To request an archive file

To find out what archive files are available for a list, send the **index** *listname* command to the administrative address. For a Majordomo list, use the name of the digest version of the list. In response, you'll receive a listing of the files that are available for that list. For example, a ListProc mailing list might produce the following list of archive files:

```
98-03 (1 part, 58442 bytes) - UUA-L message archive: Mon 03/02, 1998
```

```
98-04 (1 part, 20222 bytes) - UUA-L message archive: Thu 04/02, 1998
98-05 (1 part, 34667 bytes) - UUA-L message archive: Wed 05/06, 1998
98-06 (1 part, 69213 bytes) - UUA-L message archive: Mon 06/01, 1998
98-07 (1 part, 15227 bytes) - UUA-L message archive: Tue 07/14, 1998
98-08 (1 part, 17495 bytes) - UUA-L message archive: Mon 08/10, 1998
```

The first item on each line is the filename (in this example, the first filename is **98-03**, representing the year and month of the archive file).

A listing of archived files for a Majordomo list might look like this:

```
>>>> index kideo-digest
-rw-rw-- 1 majordom  majordom    873 Jun 16 06:05 v01.n001
-rw-rw-- 1 majordom  majordom   4681 Jun 17 06:05 v01.n002
-rw-rw-- 1 majordom  majordom   3715 Jun 18 06:05 v01.n003
-rw-rw-- 1 majordom  majordom  15317 Jun 19 06:05 v01.n004
```

This Majordomo archive list is in the format produced by the UNIX **ls** command; the filename is the last item on each line (for example, **v01.n001**). To get a file from the archive, use the **get** command, like this:

> get *listname filename*

Replace *listname* with the name of the mailing list (the digested version, for Majordomo lists). Replace *filename* with the name of the archive file that you want to get. The MLM will send you the file, which you can read using any text editor or word processor.

Changing Your Address

When your e-mail address changes, the easiest way to update your mailing list subscriptions is to sign off all the lists from your old address, and then resubscribe from your new account. If you no longer have access to your old account, write to the list manager to ask that your address be changed. For Majordomo lists, you may be able to unsubscribe your old address by sending the message **unsubscribe** *listname oldaddress* from your new address.

To change your address for ListProc lists, you can send this command:

> set *listname* address *password new-address*

Replace *listname* with the name of the list, *password* with the password from the welcome message that you received when you first subscribed to the list, and *new-address* with your new e-mail address.

Receiving Copies of Your Own Postings

If you want to receive the messages that you post to the list, send the command **set listname repro** for LISTSERV lists, and **set listname mail ack** for ListProc lists. If you'd rather not receive your own messages, send the command **set listname norepro noack** for LISTSERV lists, and **set listname mail noack** for ListProc lists. Majordomo doesn't give you this option.

Choosing Which Topics to Receive

Some LISTSERV mailing lists require one-word topic keywords as the first word in the subject line of messages that are posted to the list. For example, the (fictional) domestic poultry list might cover topics that include FEED, INCUBATION, CHICKS, LAYING, CULLING, and BREEDS. When you subscribe to the list, you can specify which topics you are interested in, so that the MLM sends you messages only about those topics. ListProc, Majordomo, and manually managed lists don't allow selection of messages by topic.

To post a message about a topic for the subject of the message, type the topic name, followed by a colon, a space, and the subject of your message, like this:

Subject: BREEDS: Are White Leghorns particularly broody?

To find out what topics a LISTSERV mailing list covers, read the FAQ (informational message) for the list. To specify the topics about which you'd like to receive messages, send this message to the administrative address:

set *listname* topics +*topicname*

Replace *listname* with the name of the mailing list, and *topicname* with the exact topic that you want to receive.

To tell LISTSERV not to send you messages about a particular topic, send this message:

set *listname* topics -*topicname*

To receive messages about all topics, send this message:

set *listname* topics all

Summary of Commands

Table 12-1 shows the most commonly used commands to subscribe to mailing lists managed by LISTSERV, ListProc, and Majordomo.

Description	LISTSERV Command	ListProc Command	Majordomo Command
Subscribe	subscribe *listname* *yourname*	subscribe *listname* *yourname*	subscribe *listname*
Sign off	signoff *listname*	signoff *listname*	unsubscribe *listname*
Switch to plain-text digests	set *listname* digests set *listname* nomime	set *listname* mail digest-nomime	unsubscribe *listname* subscribe *listname*-digest
Switch to MIME-format digests	set *listname* digests set *listname* mime	set *listname* mail digest	(not applicable)
Switch from digests	set *listname* nodigests	set *listname* mail ack	unsubscribe *listname*-digest subscribe *listname*
Hold mail	set *listname* nomail	set *listname* mail postpone	(not applicable)
Resume sending mail	set *listname* mail	set *listname* mail ack (or digest or digest-nomime)	(not applicable)
Display list settings	query *listname*	set *listname*	(not applicable)
Get info about list	review *listname*	review *listname*	info *listname* who *listname*
Get help about commands	help	help	help
Get list of archive files	index *listname*	index *listname*	index *listname*-digest
Get specific archive file	get *listname* *filename*	get *listname* *filename*	get *listname*-digest *filename*
Selecting topics	set *listname* topics +*topicname* set *listname* topics all	(not applicable)	(not applicable)

Table 12-1. *Commands for LISTSERV, ListProc, and Majordomo Mailing Lists*

Finding Interesting Mailing Lists

You can find out what mailing lists are managed by a specific MLM by sending a command to the administrative address. For ListProc, Majordomo, or LISTSERV, send the command **lists**.

But what if you don't know where a list is maintained? A Web site name Liszt (our apologies for the bad pun) maintains a huge database of publicly accessible mailing lists, at **http://www.liszt.com**. You can search the Liszt database by keyword. Liszt can tell you the name and administrative address for the list so that you can write for more information about the list. For some lists, Liszt can even display the informational message about the list.

Another searchable database of mailing lists can be found at **http://catalog.com/vivian/interest-group-search.html**. This list is maintained by Vivian Neou, who has been running mailing lists for years.

To find a list managed by LISTSERV, use the form on the Web page located at **http://www.lsoft.com/lists/LIST_Q.html**, which is maintained by the company that sells the LISTSERV program.

The authors of this book maintain a Web page with their favorite mailing lists at **http://net.gurus.com/lists**.

Creating Your Own Mailing List

If you want to create your own mailing list, you have several choices:

- Use your e-mail program as a quick-and-dirty MLM. (See the next section for details.)

- Use a Web site that hosts free mailing lists and pays its bill by adding small advertisements to the e-mail messages distributed by your (and others) mailing list. (See "Free Web-Based Mailing Lists," later in this chapter.)

- Use a fee-based mailing-list hosting service that provides access to an MLM, usually Majordomo. (See "Managing a List Using a Mailing List Management Program," later in this chapter.)

- Install an MLM on your own computer. This approach is beyond the scope of this book. Refer to the Web sites for LISTSERV, ListProc, and Majordomo for information about getting and installing each package. For information on other MLMs, start at Yahoo! (**http://www.yahoo.com**) and click Internet | Mailing Lists | Software. A free license for the Lyris MLM, for example, runs on Windows 98/95, NT, and some flavors of UNIX, and allows an unlimited number of lists with up to 200 subscribers per list (**http://www.lyris.com/lyris.html**).

Here's more information about managing a mailing list by using your e-mail program, a Web-based service, or an MLM.

Before you start a public mailing list, make sure that a similar list doesn't already exist. Search the Liszt Web site for keywords that describe the subject or audience for your list. Over 68,000 lists already exist—yours may not be needed!

Running a Mailing List from Your E-mail Program

If your e-mail program can store a list of mailing lists in its address book, you can use it as a quick-and-dirty MLM. Create an entry in your address book with the name of the mailing list that you want to create, and then store the entire list of subscribers in that entry. (See Chapter 6 for instructions on how to create an entry in your e-mail program's address book.) To distribute a message to the subscribers, simply address a message to your new address book entry. When subscribers want to send a message to the list, they send the message to you (perhaps with a specific keyword in the subject, so that you know that the message is intended for the list), and you forward or redirect the message to the list.

This method has some shortcomings. You have to manually add and delete subscribers' addresses from your address book entry for the list. Also, messages aren't distributed to the mailing list until you read and forward them. If you go on vacation, the list grinds to a halt unless you arrange for someone to handle your mail.

Some e-mail programs can handle the mail-forwarding part of your job as list manager. For example, using Eudora Pro, you can create a filter that first selects all messages that contain a specific keyword in the subject line of the message (the mailing list name, for example), and then automatically forwards these messages to the address book entry for the mailing list, automatically distributing the messages to list subscribers. If you set Eudora to check your mail every few hours, mailing list messages are distributed with little delay and no work on your part. (See Chapter 8 for directions on how to create filters in your e-mail program.)

Even with filters, the job of subscribing and unsubscribing people still falls on your shoulders. Also, your e-mail program can get into a *mail loop* with another program, in which two programs automatically send messages to each other at a dizzying pace, usually an MLM and a vacation program (which responds to messages with a message saying that the addressee is on vacation). If your mailing list gets large (over about 20 subscribers) or has a high volume of messages (more than a few each day), you will probably want to use another method of running the list.

Free Web-Based Mailing Lists

A number of Web sites have sprung up that host mailing lists for free. The catch is that they either display ads on the site while subscribers read their messages or append ads to the end of the e-mail messages that they distribute. This catch may be acceptable, depending on the type of mailing list that you need. Some of these Web sites are listed here:

- **eGroups** (http://www.egroups.com)
- **OneList** (http://www.onelist.com)
- **ListBot** (http://www.listbot.com)

For an up-to-date list of mailing list providers (both free and fee-based), see this Web page:

http://www.cs.ubc.ca/spider/edmonds/usenet/ml-providers.txt

Or send the command **get faq ml-providers.txt** to the address **majordomo@edmonds. home.cs.ubc.ca**. Or start at Yahoo! (**http://www.yahoo.com**) and choose Computers & Internet | Internet | Mailing Lists, and then scroll down the page.

Managing a List Using a Mailing List Management Program

If your organization runs an MLM, or if you want to pay to use a fee-based mailing-list hosting company, you can use LISTSERV, ListProc, or Majordomo to maintain your list. The advantage to using a real MLM is that the program handles subscription and sign-off requests for you, and distributes messages quickly and automatically. For an up-to-date listing of Web sites, see the addresses at the end of the preceding section. Here are the steps to follow to set up a new list:

1. *Create the list.* Unless you can run commands on the host computer, someone else will give the actual commands to create the list, but you'll specify the name and configuration of the list: open or closed, moderated or unmoderated, and other settings.

2. *Write the informational and welcome messages.* Read the informational messages for some other mailing lists, to get ideas of what yours should say. Be sure to include instructions for subscribing and signing off, for switching to and from digests (if digests are available), for postponing mailing list mail (if this option is available), and for contacting the mailing list manager (you). Also provide guidelines for what subjects are welcome, what subjects are to be avoided, and other rules for subscribers. You'll need to install these messages (that is, send them to the MLM) and test that they look OK.

3. *Test the list.* Subscribe to your new list and get a few friends or coworkers to subscribe, too. Then, send a message to the list and make sure that it is correctly distributed to the list, and that replies to the message are addressed to the list or to the sender, depending on how you want the list configured. Check the list configuration, too (see the section "Checking the List Configuration," later in this chapter, for details on how to do this).

4. *Advertise the list.* If the list is open only to a small group (for example, the list is for the board of trustees of your church), let them know how to join. If the list is open to the public, go the Liszt Web site (at **http://www.liszt.com**) and follow the directions to have your mailing list added to the database. Go to the Internet Scout New-List Web site at **http://scout.cs.wisc.edu/scout/new-list** and submit information about your list. Announce the new mailing list on the appropriate existing mailing lists and Usenet newsgroups (but don't overdo it!), and add information about your mailing list to your organization's Web site (if applicable).

5. *Consider making a Web page for the list.* This Web page can explain what the list is about, who the list is for, and how to join. (In fact, you can use the informational message that you write in step 2.) After you upload the Web page to the Web, submit your page to Yahoo!, Excite, AltaVista, and other Web search engines and directories. (See Chapter 33.)

6. *Start managing the list.* Think of a list of topics with which to seed the discussion once the list is running. Handle bounced mail and other problems as they arise.

Sending Commands to the Mailing List Management Program

To manage a list, you send commands to the MLM's administrative address, the same address that subscribers use for commands. To prevent anyone else from changing the configuration of your list, the program needs to know that these commands come from the list manager. The program knows the address(es) of the list manager(s), so you must send list manager commands from the same e-mail address that you specified as the list manager address when the list was created. ListProc and Majordomo also give you a password that you must provide when you issue most list management commands. LISTSERV allows you to create a personal password to use when sending list manager commands.

Checking the List Configuration

To see the configuration of the list, send the command **config** *listname password* for ListProc or Majordomo, or **get** *listname* **(header nolock** for LISTSERV (yes, that's an open parenthesis with no matching close parenthesis). In response, the MLM will send you the configuration settings for the list (and possibly the informational message about the list and the subscribers list).

*The **nolock** part of the **get** command is important for LISTSERV lists: otherwise, LISTSERV locks the settings for the mailing list, which prevents anyone from subscribing or unsubscribing.*

For example, here is part of the configuration for a ListProc mailing list:

```
VISIBLE-LIST
OPEN-SUBSCRIPTIONS
SUBSCRIPTION-MANAGERS [owners] (inactive)
SEND-BY-SUBSCRIBERS
ARCHIVES-TO-ALL
ARCHIVE /var/listmgr/archives/uua-l %h%y uua-l "" messages
MODERATED-NO-EDIT [owners]
DIGEST weekly Friday 0 0
MESSAGE-LIMIT 75
COMMENT "News from the Unitarian Universalist Association"
REPLY-TO-SENDER
OWNERS nettcr@gurus.com
```

The settings for a LISTSERV list might look like this (in part):

```
*   Review= Private
*   Subscription= Open,Confirm
*   Send= Private
*   Notify= No
*   Reply-to= Sender,Respect
*   Validate= No
*   Digest= Yes,/ssa/listserv/notebooks/uus-l,Daily,03:00,size(550)
*   Default-Options= REPRO, DIGESTS
*   Daily-Threshold= 150
*
*   Topics= Introduction, Announcements, Administration, GA, G,
*   Topics= UUA, E, D, C, B, A
*   Default-Topics= Introduction, Announcements, Other
*
*   Owner= nettcr@gurus.com
*   Owner= Quiet:
```

A Majordomo list's configuration might look like this:

```
subscribe_policy = open+confirm
restrict_post = kideo:kideo-digest
admin_passwd     =    kidzvidz
approve_passwd     = kidzvidz
description      =    Videos for children
```

You can change some of these settings by sending **set** or **config** commands to the MLM. For the details of each of these settings, as well as instructions for changing them, refer to the list manager's manual for the MLM that you use (see the section "Getting More Information," later in this chapter).

Helping People Subscribe

If someone needs help subscribing, you can send the message to the administrative address on that person's behalf. For ListProc lists, send this message:

> add *listname password address name*

Replace *listname* with the name of your list, *password* with the list manager's password, *address* with the e-mail address of the person you want to add to the list, and *name* with the person's full name. If you don't want the subscriber to receive a confirmation message, add **quiet** at the beginning of the command. For LISTSERV lists, send this command:

> add *listname address name*

For Majordomo lists, send this command:

> approve *password* subscribe *listname address*

Helping People Sign Off

To sign someone off of your list, send this command for ListProc lists:

> delete *listname password address*

Add **quiet** to the beginning of the command if you don't want to send a confirmation message to that address (for example, if mail to that address bounces). For LISTSERV lists, send this command:

> delete *listname address*

For Majordomo lists, send this command:

> approve *password* unsubscribe *listname address*

Handling Bounced Messages

From time to time (many times a day, for lists with many subscribers and many messages), the MLM may inform you that mail to a subscriber has bounced, including the exact message that it received from the subscriber's mail host computer. Your job as list manager usually includes handling these *bounced messages*.

Take a look at the error message that the subscriber's mail host sent back. Many error messages include the phrase "non-fatal error," which usually means that the mail has been delayed but is expected to get through eventually. Other error messages include the phrase "fatal error": for these messages, continue reading to find out what the error was. Some fatal errors (errors that prevent the message from being delivered at all, ever) are temporary; for example, AOL's mail host produces a fatal error message when a subscriber's mailbox is full. Other fatal errors look permanent, like "Username unknown" or "Mailbox does not exist."

If the error looks non-fatal or temporary, ignore or delete the error messages. If the error looks permanent and fatal, delete the subscriber from your list.

Some MLMs handle bounced mail themselves. Some delete any subscriber whose mail bounces at all, others delete subscribers with fatal mail errors, and others delete subscribers only after a specified number of messages have bounced within a short period of time. You may be able to configure your list to use one of these methods, depending on which MLM you use.

Moderating a List

If you are the moderator for a list, you approve all messages before they are distributed to subscribers. You act as the gatekeeper (or censor) for the list. When someone sends a message to the list address for the mailing list, the MLM sends the message to you. You then send a message to the program to tell it whether to distribute the message or to discard it.

ListProc gives each message a number. You tell ListProc what to do with the message by sending the command **approve** *listname password number* or **discard** *listname password number*. For a LISTSERV list, if the message is okay to distribute to the list, reply to the message without editing the subject, and replace the text of the reply with the single command **ok**. For Majordomo, send the message (complete with the headers of the original message) to the list address for the list, adding the command **approve:** *password* as the first line of the message.

If you choose to reject (discard) a message, be sure to write to the sender to confirm that you are doing so. The sender may want to rewrite the message, to fix the problem that caused you to reject the message.

Editing the Informational and Welcome Messages

Every list should have an up-to-date informational message to tell subscribers how to sign off, how to change list settings, and what the rules of the list are. This message is stored in the *info file* for the list. To see the informational message, send the command **info** *listname* to the administrative address.

Once you receive the informational message, copy it into a text editor or word processor and edit the message. To send the updated message back to the MLM for storage in your list's info file, compose a new message to the administrative address for the list. Turn off your signature or any other text added by your e-mail program. For ListProc lists, type this command as the first line of the message:

put *listname password* info

For Majordomo lists, use this command:

newinfo *listname password*

For LISTSERV lists, type this command as the first line of the message:

put *listname* welcome pw=*password*

Replace *password* with your personal LISTSERV password. (If you haven't created a personal LISTSERV password, before you use the **put** command, send the message **pw add** *newpassword* to LISTSERV to set your password to *newpassword*.)

On the second line of the message, copy the informational message. ListProc, LISTSERV, or Majordomo takes the text from the second line of the message to the end and uses it as the new informational message for the list.

 If you don't tell your e-mail program to suppress your signature when sending the informational file to the MLM, your signature becomes part of the file!

Getting More Information

LISTSERV, ListProc, and Majordomo support many other configuration options. You can get more information about list manager commands via e-mail or on the Web.

- **ListProc**   The list manager's manual is at **http://www.cren.net./listproc/docs/**.
- **LISTSERV**   Get the LISTSERV List Owner's Manual by sending the command **get listownr memo** to **LISTSERV@searn.sunet.se**.
- **Majordomo**   Ask your Majordomo site manager for the list-owner-info file in the Doc directory in the directory in which the Majordomo program is installed.

Summary of List Management Commands

Table 12-2 shows the most commonly used commands for managing mailing lists with LISTSERV, ListProc, and Majordomo.

Description	LISTSERV Command	ListProc Command	Majordomo Command
Get list configuration	get *listname* (header nolock	config *listname* *password*	config *listname* *password*
Add subscriber	add *listname* *address name*	[quiet] add *listname* *address name*	approve *password* subscribe *listname* *address*
Sign off subscriber	delete *listname* *address*	[quiet] delete *listname address*	approve *password* unsubscribe *listname address*
Approve message for moderated list	(reply to message from LISTSERV)	approve *listname* *password number*	approve: *password* (sent to the list *address*)
Reject message for moderated list	(reply to message from LISTSERV)	discard *listname* *password number*	(not applicable)
Install informational message	put *listname* welcome *password*	put *listname* *password* info	newinfo *listname* *password*

Table 12-2. *List Management Commands for LISTSERV, ListProc, and Majordomo*

Chapter 13

Usenet Newsgroup Concepts

One of the oldest Internet services—a decade older than the World Wide Web—is Usenet, a system of thousands of newsgroups that enables people to exchange messages on a huge variety of subjects. This chapter describes what newsgroups are, how they are named, what software you need to read newsgroups, problems that you may encounter, and how to create your own newsgroup. The next chapter gives step-by-step instructions for reading newsgroups, using the most popular programs.

What Are Usenet Newsgroups?

Usenet is a distributed system of messages (also called *articles* or *postings*), like a worldwide chat system. Because so many messages are sent every day, they are divided into *newsgroups*, with each newsgroup concentrating on one topic. You can read the newsgroups' articles, post replies to articles, or post new articles. Like e-mail mailing lists, you can read articles on your own schedule rather than in real time (at the same time that people are writing them). Unlike mailing lists, anyone can read articles, without subscribing to the newsgroup.

Newsgroups are named by using a hierarchical system of words, separated by dots. The first word of a newsgroup name indicates the category (or *newsgroup hierarchy*) into which the newsgroup falls. The following are the original seven hierarchies and their respective topics:

- **comp** Computer hardware, software, networking, and other computer-related topics
- **misc** Miscellaneous topics
- **news** Usenet itself
- **rec** Recreational topics
- **sci** Scientific topics
- **soc** Social topics
- **talk** General discussion

The **alt** newsgroup hierarchy was formed for "alternative" newsgroups (it may stand for Anarchists, Lunatics, and Terrorists, depending on whom you ask). Now there are hierarchies for countries (using two-letter abbreviations), other geographical areas (for example, **ny** for New York and **ba** for the San Francisco Bay area), colleges, ISPs, and other groups (for example, the **biz** hierarchy is for businesses).

Following the hierarchy name, the newsgroup name adds words that specify the topic of the newsgroup. For example, newsgroups about computers start with **comp**, newsgroups about computer systems start with **comp.systems**, and the newsgroup about laptop computers (one type of computer system) is called **comp.systems.laptops**. Newsgroups about social issues have names starting with **soc**, newsgroups about religion have names starting with **soc.religion**, and the newsgroup about Unitarian Universalism is called **soc.religion.unitarian-univ**.

Some newsgroups are *moderated*, which means that all messages are reviewed by a moderator (usually a human being, but sometimes a program) for appropriateness and style. Moderation keeps the content of the newsgroup high, since garbage, repetitive posts, off-topic posts, and general whining is eliminated. However, unless the moderator never sleeps, messages to moderated groups can be delayed, and if the moderator has opinions about the subject of the newsgroup, he or she may slant the discourse.

How Do You Read Newsgroups?

Articles posted on newsgroups are distributed over the Internet by *news servers*, Internet hosts running news server software. These servers store and forward Usenet articles, and provide articles to users running *news clients* or *newsreaders*. News servers and newsreaders communicate by using an Internet protocol called the *Network News Transfer Protocol (NNTP)*. You can use popular newsreaders, such as Netscape Messenger (which comes with Netscape Communicator), Outlook Express (which comes with Internet Explorer versions 4 and 5), Free Agent (a shareware newsreader), NewsWatcher (a Mac newsreader), or one of many UNIX-based newsreaders (the easiest to use is called tin) to read Usenet newsgroups. Chapter 14 describes how to use some of the most popular newsreaders.

Some newsreaders allow you to download all the articles in newsgroups to which you are subscribed, and then read the articles *offline* (when you are not connected to the Internet). If you compose new articles, the newsreader stores the articles and sends them the next time that you connect to the Internet.

An alternative way to read Usenet newsgroup articles is by using the Deja News Web site at **http://www.dejanews.com**. Deja News archives the articles in all the major newsgroups for the past few years and allows you to search them by keyword. See section "Newsreading in Deja News" in Chapter 14 for details.

To begin reading, you usually look at a list of the newsgroups that your news server carries. When your newsreading program displays the list of available newsgroups, you see only the newsgroups carried by your news server. The list may not be complete: most ISPs and others who run news servers choose only the newsgroup hierarchies most likely to be of general interest, to save disk space. If your ISP is in Vermont, it may not carry newsgroups for the San Francisco Bay area. Some companies omit recreational newsgroups (like those in the **alt.sex** hierarchy, for example) from their news servers. Each news server has a *news administrator*, the system manager who makes these decisions. If you don't see a newsgroup that you are looking for and you are sure that it exists, search for it on Deja News. You may also consider asking your news administrator to add the newsgroup to your news server.

Looking at the list of newsgroups, you decide which newsgroups to *subscribe* to. Unlike subscribing to a mailing list, subscribing to a newsgroup doesn't put you on a centralized list of people who read that newsgroup. Instead, subscribing only tells your newsreader that you want to read this group. (See Chapter 14 for specific instructions on how to subscribe to and read newsgroups in many popular newsreaders.)

Next, you instruct your newsreader to show you the headers of some or all of the articles in the newsgroup. The program usually shows you the subject, sender, and posting date for each article. You can select which articles to read (see the section "Choosing What to Read"). After you read articles, you can reply to the sender by e-mail or post a reply to the newsgroup (see the section "Choosing What to Post," later in this chapter).

How Are Newsgroups Different from Mailing Lists?

Technically, newsgroup articles are distributed differently from messages posted to e-mail mailing lists. When you post a message to a mailing list, it goes to the mailing list manager (usually a program), which sends copies of the message to each person subscribed to the list. The messages land in each subscriber's mailbox. When you post a message to a newsgroup, the message is forwarded from news server to news server until the message reaches all the news servers on the Internet. Each news server that carries the newsgroup stores one copy of the message. When people connect to a news server to get newsgroup messages, they see the messages that have arrived in the newsgroups they select. There's no such thing as a newsgroup mailbox: messages for all the newsgroups your news server carries are stored together on the news server. Your newsreader program has the job of keeping track of which newsgroups you subscribe to and which message in each of those newsgroups you've already read.

Once you send a mailing list message to the list subscribers, you can't cancel it (or any other e-mail message). Since newsgroup articles are stored centrally on news servers, a newsgroup article can be canceled by the sender of the message. When you cancel an article that you've posted, a cancellation message is circulated to all news servers, and the servers delete the article from their lists of current articles. If you cancel an article right after you post it ("Oops! What did I just say!?"), the article is deleted quickly, and isn't on news servers long enough for many people to download it.

Another difference between mailing lists and newsgroups is the way that past messages are stored. After mailing list messages are distributed, they are saved only if the mailing list is archived. News servers usually store messages for a specific number of days, typically somewhere between 3 and 30 days, depending on the volume and size of newsgroup messages and the hard disk limitations of the news server. You can browse the past messages that are stored on the news server. Deja News, the newsgroup Web site, stores newsgroup articles for several years.

Finally, mailing lists can be closed (approved subscribers only), while newsgroups that are run on public news servers are all publicly readable. However, some organizations run private news servers, which require a username and password to connect to. For example, some software companies maintain password-protected news servers, so that people who are testing unreleased products can exchange messages in private.

Finding Interesting Newsgroups

Here are some newsgroups to read while you are getting up to speed in Usenet:

- ■ **News.announce.newusers** is a must-read group. Since the newsgroup is moderated, it contains only about 40 articles, with lots of introductory information.

- ■ **News.announce.important** is also a good group to subscribe to. It contains few articles, but the ones that are there are important.

- ■ **News.answers** is a collection of the FAQs (frequently asked questions and their answers) from thousands of Usenet newsgroups—a compendium of the collected knowledge of Usenet.

- ■ **Rec.humor.funny** is a moderated newsgroup consisting entirely of jokes that the moderator (Brad Templeton) thinks are funny (and he's usually right).

After you are comfortable reading newsgroups, try searching for words in the list of newsgroup titles, if your newsreader allows this. Alternatively, go to the Deja News Web site at **http://dejanews.com** and search for words or phrases: when you see the list of articles that Deja News finds, you can also see to which newsgroups the articles are posted. Try subscribing to the newsgroups that have the most useful articles on your topic.

Another source of information about newsgroups and their topics is the Liszt newsgroup listing Web site at **http://www.liszt.com/news**. Liszt can give you a list of the newsgroups whose names or descriptions contain a key word or phrase.

*For more general information about Usenet, see the Usenet Info Center at **http://sunsite.unc.edu/usenet-i**. Many of the regular postings from news.announce.newuser appear on the site as Web pages, along with other Usenet advice.*

Choosing What to Read

When you read an article, your newsreader marks it as read, so that you can tell which articles you have and haven't read. If you decide after a quick scan of the subject lines that all the new articles in a newsgroup look boring, most newsreaders let you mark all the messages in a newsgroup as read. You may also be able to sort the messages by topic or sender and mark groups of messages as read.

*Many newsgroups include periodic postings, which are articles that are automatically posted on a regular basis. Be sure to read these messages the first time that they go by: they usually contain the newsgroup's FAQ, newsgroup rules or other useful information. If you are looking for the FAQ for a newsgroup and you don't see it in the list of articles, try the Usenet FAQ Archive Web site, at **http://www.faqs.org/faqs**.*

Most newsreaders present newsgroup articles in *threads*. A thread is an article, followed by all the replies to that article, replies to the replies, and so forth. These *threaded newsreaders* present the articles in each thread in an indented list, as shown in Figure 13-1, with the replies to each article shown indented below the message to which they reply. You can choose which threads you want to read, mark entire threads to skip, and perform other commands on threads, which combined make zeroing in on interesting topics easier.

Some newsreaders let you create *kill files*, which are files stored on your own system that specify which types of articles you never want to read and which types you always want to read. You can have one global kill file, which applies to all newsgroups, and other kill files that apply only to specific newsgroups. Using kill files, you can *kill* (automatically mark as read, so that you never see them) articles from a particular person, or you might want to kill specific topics in specific newsgroups. For example, you might want to blank all messages from **nettcr@gurus.com** in all newsgroups (if this

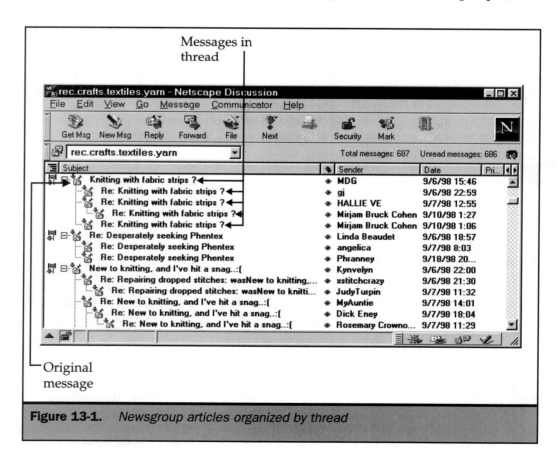

Figure 13-1.   *Newsgroup articles organized by thread*

book annoys you). If you only like to knit and you read the **rec.crafts.textiles.yarn** newsgroup, you could block all articles in that newsgroup that are about crocheting. You could kill a person's posts in one newsgroup but not in another, if the person sends reasonable material to some newsgroups and junk to others. For instructions on filtering messages, see Chapter 14.

| Note | *Not all newsreaders support kill files.* |

Choosing What to Post

When you are reading the articles in a newsgroup, you may find that you have something to say. Or you may start a discussion on a new topic. Either way, you can post a message to one or several newsgroups.

Starting a New Thread

To start a new topic and begin a new thread, just post a message to the newsgroup by using your newsreader. If you think other newsgroups would be interested, too, you can *cross-post* the article to other newsgroups—but do so with caution: cross-posting to lots of newsgroups is considered spamming, and some newsgroups refuse articles that are cross-posted to many groups. Cross-post only if one or two other newsgroups would have a specific interest in your topic. When you cross-post, you can designate one newsgroup to receive *follow-ups* (postings in reply), so that the ongoing discussion happens in only one newsgroup.

Replying by E-mail and Posting Follow-ups

When you compose a reply, think about who will be interested in reading it. If your remarks will be of interest only to the author of the message to which you are replying, send the reply by e-mail. Most newsreaders let you compose an e-mail reply easily. Don't waste everyone else's time, especially if your reply basically states "Me too!" or "I agree!"

On the other hand, if you are answering a question of general interest or have something good to contribute to the discussion, go ahead and post a *follow-up* article to the newsgroup. Quote the message to which you are replying, editing out all but the relevant material. After you send it, the article may take a few hours to appear on the newsgroup. Don't panic, and wait at least a day before reposting the message, because your article is probably just slow to arrive. If the newsgroup to which you posted is moderated, the moderator may delay things (even newsgroup moderators take an occasional vacation!).

Usenet Netiquette

All the usual rules of "netiquette" (listed in the section "Chat Etiquette" in Chapter 11) apply to newsgroups, too. Here are a few additional tips:

- Before you post a question, read the newsgroup's FAQ (if you haven't seen it go by on the newsgroup, check in the **news.answers** newsgroup or the **http://www.faqs.org/faqs** Web site). Also, look through the existing newsgroup messages that appear in your newsreader—someone might have just asked the same question. People get peevish when you ask questions that have already been answered.

- If you are responding to a message, be sure to use the newsreader's command to reply or follow up, so that your message is marked as part of the same thread as the message to which you are responding. If you are starting a new subject, don't use the "reply" or "follow up" command: instead, use the "new article" command in your newsreader, so that your message starts a new thread.

- When you reply or follow up to an article, take a look at the headers of your message before you send it. If the original message was posted to several newsgroups, your reply may be, too. Most newsreaders let you edit the headers of your message so that you can post the reply to only the newsgroups that are appropriate.

- Use just plain text whenever possible, with no special characters, and with lines that are less than 80-characters wide.

- Don't post the same message to many newsgroups: this practice is called *cross-posting*. Choose the one or two most appropriate newsgroups for your message and post it there.

- If you realize that you made a mistake in an article that you posted, cancel it as soon as possible. Instructions for canceling articles for some popular newsreaders are in Chapter 14.

Sending and Receiving Attachments

Like e-mail messages, Usenet articles can contain files. And, like the e-mail system, Usenet was originally designed to accommodate only text, so the files have to be specially encoded to make it through the system. Usenet uses *uuencoding*, one of the encoding systems that e-mail uses, to convert binary (non-text) files to text for transmission. When your newsreader encounters a uuencoded message, it must decode the message to convert it to the original file. If the file is large, it may be split into several (or dozens of) messages, so that your newsreader has to reassemble the file before decoding it. Luckily, most newsreaders are up to the task.

Not all newsgroups allow you to post binary files: many specifically prohibit it. But over 800 newsgroups in the **alt.binaries** hierarchy are dedicated to the exchange of binary files (and not all of them are for dirty pictures). Binary files distributed on newsgroups are mainly graphics files (such as in **alt.binaries.clip-art** and the hundreds of newsgroups in the **alt.binaries.pictures** hierarchy), but some are audio files (such as in the newsgroups in the **alt.binaries.sounds** hierarchy), and even executable program files (almost entirely bootlegged).

To decode and save a file distributed on a newsgroup, refer to Chapter 14, which contains instructions for some popular newsreaders. Some older newsreaders require you to save the messages that contain the file, and run a separate decoding program to turn the messages back into the file. Newer newsreaders perform the decoding for you, and some even display graphics files directly.

 Most of the binary files distributed via Usenet are bootlegged (that is, distributed without the permission of their copyright holders). Please don't use bootlegged material—buy the real thing!

Offensive Postings

Since the early days of Usenet newsgroups, people have posted off-color jokes. To avoid offending innocent readers, *rot13* was born (short for "rotate by 13"). Rot13 is the simplest encryption imaginable: any eight-year-old could easily crack the code. Each letter is replaced by the letter 13 places earlier or later in the alphabet; that is, letters in the first half and the second half of the alphabet are swapped. The letter *a* is replaced by *n*, *b* by *o*, *c* by *p*, *m* by *z*, *n* by *a*, and so forth. The same swapping applies to capital letters.

Rot13-encoded messages contain the word *rot13* in the subject line. When your newsreader displays a rot13-encoded message, it looks like Martian text, and you have to give a command to decode the message. (If your newsreader doesn't support rot13, you have to do the decoding by hand.) If you'd rather not read something offensive, you can just skip decoding the message. To read or post rot13-encoded messages, see Chapter 14.

Avoiding Spam

Spam is a nickname for unsolicited commercial e-mail, but the term is used for Usenet postings, too. Many Usenet readers find advertising offensive, whether it's spam or not. If you want to post a commercial announcement on a newsgroup, make sure that it is directly related to the topic of the newsgroup, contains mainly technical information and no hype, is short, and contains your e-mail address for people who want more information. Also, make sure that you contribute regularly and constructively to the newsgroup, so that participants will feel you've "earned" the right to send an ad. Of course, it's always OK for the signature at the end of your messages to contain a one-line ad.

A pitfall of posting any article to any Usenet newsgroup is that the e-mail address on your article will be "harvested" by programs that scan all postings for e-mail addresses and add the address to a huge database that is sold to spammers (people who send spam). A common experience of people who post to Usenet for the first time is that within a few weeks, they start getting mountains of junk e-mail.

The most common method to avoid getting spammed is to use a garbled e-mail address when you post. Posting articles with fake e-mail addresses is discouraged, but you can easily garble your e-mail address so that a human can figure it out, but a harvesting program can't. For example, if your e-mail address were *nettcr@gurus.com*, you could configure your newsreader to use *nettcr-at-gurus-dot-com* as the return address in your postings. Anyone reading the address could figure out your correct address.

Many people add extra characters to their e-mail addresses (for example, turning *nettcr@gurus.com* into *nettcrZZZ@gurusZZZ.comZZZ*), with instructions in the posted message (usually in the signature) for removing the letters that don't belong. Other people add *REMOVETHIS* or *DELETEME* right after the at-sign in their addresses. Here are a few guidelines:

- Garble the domain part of your e-mail address (the part after @), not just the username part (the part before @). If you garble only the username, spam sent to your garbled address will reach a real domain, and the postmaster at that domain will have to deal with it for years. If you garble the domain, the e-mail will bounce back to the sender, without ever reaching a mail server.

- Don't use the same method of garbling forever. Spammers aren't stupid, and their harvesting programs get smarter every day. When they get wise to the idea of spelling out *at* and *dot*, they will program their harvesting programs to convert *nettcr-at-gurus-dot-com* back to *nettcr@gurus.com*. The programs are already smart enough to remove *NOSPAM* from the middle of e-mail addresses.

- For more ideas, take a look at the headers and signatures of the messages in the newsgroups that you read. Other subscribers may come up with new, creative ways to foil the harvesting programs.

How to Propose a New Newsgroup

To create a new newsgroup, someone must send a special command message on Usenet with a **newgroup** command, a command that instructs news servers to create the newsgroup. However, most news servers ignore newgroup command messages unless the messages are the result of a process that has grown since the early days of Usenet. Specifically, few news servers will create newsgroups in the major hierarchies (**comp**, **misc**, **news**, **rec**, **sci**, **soc**, and **talk**) unless a procedure has been completed that involves proposals, discussion, and voting.

Many news servers will create newsgroups in the **alt** hierarchy at the drop of a hat (as you can tell, if you look at the huge and bizarre list of **alt** newsgroups). However, **alt** newsgroups are not as widely available as newsgroups in the major hierarchies, so your audience may be limited.

Creating a Mainstream Newsgroup

This section gives an overview of the procedure for proposing and create a new newsgroup in one of the major hierarchies. For the details, see the article "How to Create a New Usenet Newsgroup," by Greg Woods, Gene Spafford, and David C. Lawrence, at **http://www.cis.ohio-state.edu/hypertext/faq/usenet/usenet/creating-newsgroups/part1/faq.html**. The article is also posted on **news.groups** and **news.announce.newgroups**.

Although Usenet is not centrally administered, here are the groups involved:

- **group-mentors@acpub.duke.edu**, a committee of volunteers that helps people create newsgroups

- **news.groups**, the newsgroup that discusses the creation of new newsgroups

- **news.announce.newgroups**, the moderated newsgroups that contain the key postings (request for discussion, call for votes, and voting results) for proposed newsgroups

- Usenet Volunteer Votetakers (UVV), at **uvv-contact@uvv.org**, a group of impartial volunteers who conduct the votes for creating newsgroups

Here are the general steps to follow to create a newsgroup in one of the major hierarchies.

1. Contact the group of volunteers at **group-mentors@acpub.duke.edu** to tell them about the newsgroup that you'd like to create. They can help you with the rest of the steps in this process.

2. Write a *request for discussion (RFD)* for the newsgroup, following the format described in the article "How to Format and Submit a New Group Proposal," which is posted regularly on **news.announce.newgroups**.

3. Post the RFD to **news.groups**, **news.announce.newgroups**, and any newsgroups or mailing lists with topics that relate to the new newsgroup. For example, if you want to create a newsgroup about knitting, to be named **rec.crafts.textiles.knitting**, you would post an RFD on **news.groups** and cross-post it to **news.announce.newgroups** and **rec.crafts.textiles.yarn**. Be sure to post the message so that follow-ups are posted to the **news.groups** newsgroup, which ensures that all discussions happen there.

4. Folks on the **news.groups** newsgroup discuss your RFD for 30 days. Topics include the best name for the newsgroup, the group's charter, whether enough people are interested in the newsgroup's topic, whether it overlaps with an existing newsgroup, and whether the newsgroup should be moderated. With luck, a consensus will emerge before your 30 days is up. (If not, conduct a discussion with interested people by e-mail, and try again when you have an RFD that everyone supports.)

5. If a consensus has emerged about the name, charter, and moderation for the newsgroup, contact the Usenet Volunteer Votetakers to set up a vote. UVV posts a *call for votes* (CFV) on **news.groups**, **news.announce.newgroups**, and on the other newsgroups and mailing lists to which you posted the original RFD. UVV also tallies the votes by e-mail. Voting usually lasts from 21 to 31 days.

6. At the end of the voting period, UVV posts the results to all the groups that received the CFV. Then, a five-day waiting period occurs, to see whether anyone complains about the vote process.

7. The newsgroup passes if at least two-thirds of the votes are "yes" (in favor of creating the group), and if at least 100 more "yes" votes than "no" votes are returned (to avoid votes in which few people voted).

8. After the waiting period, if the newsgroup passes the vote, the moderator of **news.announce.newgroups** sends the newgroup command message that creates the newsgroup.

9. If your newsgroup proposal comes up for a vote and loses, you must wait at least six months to bring up the idea again.

Creating an Alt Newsgroup

Creating a newsgroup in the **alt** hierarchy is a lot simpler: you propose the newsgroup in the **alt.config** newsgroup. If the consensus of the group is positive, then you either send the newgroup command message yourself or ask one of the Usenet experts in the newsgroup to send the command for you.

Many other hierarchies work similarly: look for a **config** newsgroup, subscribe to it, read the messages (and especially the FAQ), and ask questions. For example, if you live in New York City and want to create a newsgroup in the **nyc** hierarchy, subscribe to **nyc.config**. If there is no newsgroup called **config**, try **general** (for example, **nyc.general**).

For details, see the article "So You Want to Create an Alt Newsgroup," by Dave Barr, at **http://www.faqs.org/faqs/alt-creation-guide**.

The Complete Reference

Internet

Chapter 14

Reading Usenet Newsgroups

To read newsgroups (described in Chapter 13), you can use a newsreader program. No matter what system you use—PC, Mac, or UNIX—there's a newsreader program to enable you to access newsgroups. (An alternative to newsreaders is the Deja News Web site, described in the last section of this chapter.)

If you use Netscape Navigator as your Web browser, you might want to use Netscape Newsgroup, which is part of the Netscape Communicator 4.5 suite. (In previous versions of Netscape, the newsreader was called Collabra.) Similarly, if you use Microsoft Internet Explorer as your browser, you might prefer Outlook Express, which also comes from Microsoft. You can also use a stand-alone newsreader, like Free Agent for PCs or NewsWatcher for the Mac.

For those of you who connect through a UNIX system (described in Chapter 40), you can read newsgroups through a UNIX program called tin. Many other UNIX newsreaders are available, including rn (the original newsreader) and trn (a threaded version of Rn), but tin is the easiest to learn. Even if you use a text-only browser like Lynx, you can still access newsgroups. Chapter 21 describes the Lynx browser (see the section "Other Lynx Features" for how to read newsgroups).

Common Newsreading Tasks

This section describes the general steps most newsreaders require you to follow for reading newsgroups: connecting to a news server, choosing newsgroups to subscribe to, choosing which articles to read, reading articles, and sending replies. The rest of this chapter gives specific instructions for performing these tasks with the most popular newsreaders: Microsoft Outlook 98, Outlook Express, Netscape Newsgroup, Free Agent, NewsWatcher, and tin, as well as with the Deja News Web site.

Configuring Your Newsreader

When you install a newsreading program, you must tell it your news server (the server from which the newsreader gets Usenet newsgroup articles): if you don't know the name of a news server you can use, ask your ISP or system administrator. If you read newsgroups that are stored on different news servers, some newsreaders let you set up more than one news server (for example, Microsoft, Netscape, and other software companies maintain publicly accessible news servers with newsgroups about their products). You may also need to tell it your SMTP (outgoing mail) server, so that you can reply to newsgroup postings by private e-mail to the author.

Subscribing to Newsgroups

Once you are connected to your news server, you choose which newsgroups to subscribe to. Because news servers can carry 10,000 or more newsgroups, downloading and displaying the list of available newsgroups can take several minutes. Sifting through the newsgroup names can take a while, too. Some newsreaders let you search for newsgroups that contain a word in the newsgroup name.

Selecting and Reading Articles

Newsgroups can contain hundreds or thousands of messages, with dozens or hundreds of new messages every day. You can select which messages to read by thread (topic), date, or sender (using filters or kill files), or you scan down through the message headers to spot messages that look interesting.

If you pay for your Internet connection by the hour, reading newsgroups offline can save you money. Some newsreaders let you download some or all of the message headers in a newsgroup, or some or all of the message text, so that you can read them later, when you are offline. Once the newsreader has downloaded the messages for the newsgroups you want to read, you can read the messages in those newsgroups after disconnecting from the Internet.

Posting Messages

Sooner or later you may want to reply to a newsgroup message. You can either reply directly to the sender of the message by e-mail (if what you have to say is of interest only to the original author) or reply with a *follow-up* posting to the newsgroup so that everyone in the newsgroups can see your response. Most newsreaders let reply either way.

If you want to bring up a new topic, you can post a new message, to one newsgroup or to many. (Don't send the same message to more than one or two newsgroups: choose only newsgroups that are directly related to your topic.)

A few newsreaders let you use HTML formatting when you compose e-mail or newsgroup messages. The messages look great (since you can choose fonts, add lines, and insert pictures), but most people won't be able to see the formatting, since most newsreaders can't display HTML formatting. Some people may even complain that they can't read your messages and request that you use text-only formatting. Use HTML formatting only in newsgroups that explicitly allow this type of message.

If you post an angry message, or one with an error, you might want to cancel the message after you've sent it. Usenet lets you cancel messages that you've posted, by sending out a cancellation message. Anyone who has already downloaded your message will see your message, but your cancellation message deletes the original message from all Usenet news servers. Once the message is deleted from news servers, anyone who downloads messages won't get your cancelled message.

For more general information about reading newsgroups, see Chapter 13.

Newsreading in Outlook Express

Outlook 98, Outlook 97, and Outlook Express are Microsoft's popular e-mail programs (described in Chapter 6). Outlook Express also acts as a newsreader, and Outlook 97 and 98 run Outlook Express when you ask to read newsgroups by choosing Go | News from the menu bar.

When you run Outlook or Outlook Express for the first time, the Internet Connection Wizard helps you set up e-mail accounts and configure the newsreader to work with your ISP's news server.

Finding and Subscribing to Newsgroups

To begin reading newsgroups in Outlook Express (rather than reading e-mail), click the Read News icon (if it appears) or choose Go | News. If you haven't already configured Outlook Express with information about your news server, the Internet Connection Wizard prompts you for the information now. If you want set up another news server later, you can do so by choosing Tools | Accounts and then choosing Add | News on the Internet Accounts dialog box that appears. Then follow the Internet Connection Wizard's instructions.

After you've added your news server, you're ready to begin downloading newsgroups. Outlook Express automatically prompts you to subscribe to newsgroups once you add a server. Downloading the list of available newsgroups can take several minutes. When Outlook Express is done, you see the Newsgroups dialog box shown in Figure 14-1. (You can also display this dialog box by clicking the News Groups icon on the toolbar.)

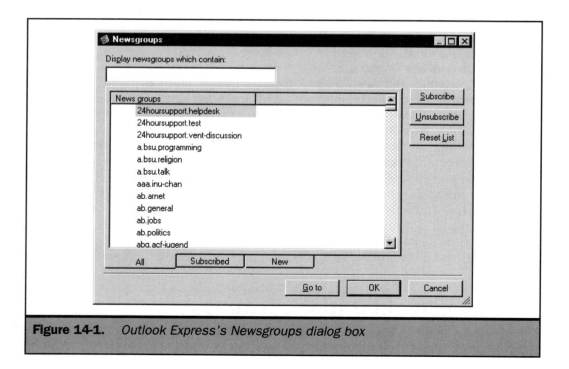

Figure 14-1. *Outlook Express's Newsgroups dialog box*

Once you see the list of newsgroups, you can choose which ones you want to subscribe to by scrolling down the list to the newsgroup you want, clicking the newsgroup name, and clicking the Subscribe button. To see only the newsgroups to which you have subscribed, click the Subscribed tab. When you have finished choosing newsgroups, click OK. The newsgroups you chose appear in the folder for your news server (click the plus button to the left of the news server name if the newsgroups don't appear).

Outlook Express also gives you a way to find specific newsgroups when you see the Newsgroups dialog box. In the Display Newsgroups Which Contain box, type the words you want to search for (for example, if you are looking for a newsgroup that discusses laptop computers, type **laptop**). Outlook Express displays all the newsgroups that contain that string of characters in the newsgroup name.

If you tire of a subscribed newsgroup, you can always cancel it by clicking the Newsgroups button on the toolbar to see the Newsgroups window, clicking the Subscribed tab, clicking the newsgroup name, and clicking the Unsubscribe button.

Selecting and Reading Messages

Once you have selected the newsgroups you're interested in, there are several ways you can read the messages. You can read them while you're online or you can read them offline, without being connected to the Internet.

Reading Articles Offline

To set up newsgroups for offline reading follow these steps:

1. Display the list of newsgroups you are subscribed to by clicking the plus box to the left of the news server name. Outlook Express lists the newsgroups indented below the news server name.

2. Click the newsgroup or newsgroups you want to read offline.

3. Choose File | Properties from the menu bar to display the properties dialog box for the newsgroup.

4. Click the Download tab, and check the When Downloading This Newsgroup Retrieve box. Choose the option you want: New Headers, New Messages (Headers and Bodies), or All Messages (Headers and Bodies).

5. Click OK to dismiss the Properties dialog box.

6. Repeat these steps for each newsgroup you want to read offline.

7. Choose Tools | Download All from the menu bar. If you want to read only one newsgroup, you can select a newsgroup and then choose Tools | Download This Newsgroup.

Outlook Express downloads all the message headers and (if you selected them) bodies (that is, the text of the messages) for the newsgroups you selected. You can disconnect from the Internet and read the articles as described in the next section.

Reading Articles Online

To read newsgroups online, click the plus box to the left of the news server and click the name of the newsgroup you want to read. Outlook Express downloads some or all of the message headers and displays them in the upper-right pane of the Outlook Express window (Figure 14-2). The selected message appears in the lower right pane. You can double-click on specific messages to view them in a separate window.

If you don't like the layout or fonts used when displaying newsgroup messages, you can change them. Choose Tools | Options, click the Read tab, and click the Fonts

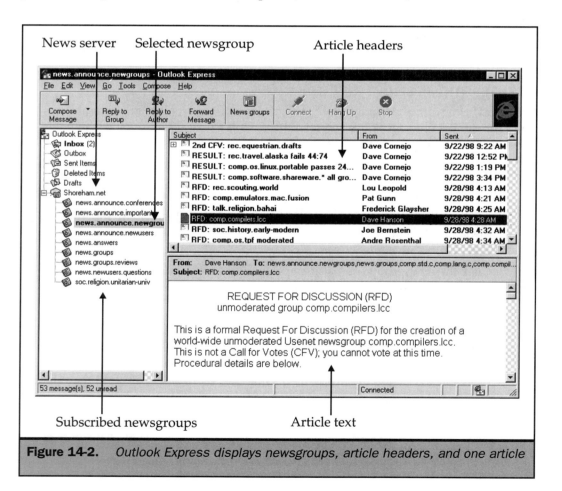

Figure 14-2.   *Outlook Express displays newsgroups, article headers, and one article*

button. Choose the font you want to read your messages in and click the OK
button. When you see the Read tab, you can also set other options that control how
messages appear.

Threading Messages

Outlook Express can sort messages either by *threads* (an original message and all replies
to that message) or by date posted, sender, subject, or several other ways. To keep
threads together, choose View | Sort By | Group Messages by Thread (a check mark
appears by the Group Messages by Thread command when it is selected: to turn this
feature off, give the command again). Outlook Express groups all the messages in each
thread together, and displays only the first message in each thread in the message list.
To see the rest of the messages in a thread, click the plus box by the message.

To sort individual message or threads by subject, sender, or other ways, choose
View | Sort By and select the way you want the messages or threads sorted. You can
also sort by subject, sender, or date by clicking on the column header in the message
list (the upper-right pane in the Outlook Express window).

Selecting Articles and Threads

You can choose whether to see all the unread messages in the newsgroup, or only
replies to your newsgroup messages. To view unread messages, choose View |
Current View | Unread Messages. To see only replies to your newsgroup messages,
choose View | Current View | Replies to My Posts.

To search for messages from a particular person, with a specific subject, within a
specific range of dates, choose Edit | Find Message or press CTRL+SHIFT+F to see the
Find Message dialog box. To search for messages that contain a word or phrase
anywhere in the headers or text, choose Edit | Find Text. To search again, press F3.

Sending Messages

You can reply to an existing messages (adding your voice to an existing thread), reply
by e-mail to the author of a message, or post a message on a new topic.

Replying to Messages

When you want to reply to a message, either by e-mail or by posting a follow-up, click
the message in the list of message headers. To reply to the whole newsgroup, click the
Reply to Group button in the toolbar. You see the message composition window
shown in Figure 14-3. The Newsgroups line at the top of the window shows which
newsgroups the article will be posted to. When you want to reply only to the author of
the message, click the Reply to Author button in the toolbar of the Outlook Express
window. If you haven't sent mail yet with Outlook, the Inbox Setup Wizard guides you
through setting up your e-mail configuration.

Whether you are sending an e-mail reply or a newsgroup follow-up, type your
message in the message composition window. For follow-up articles, click the Post

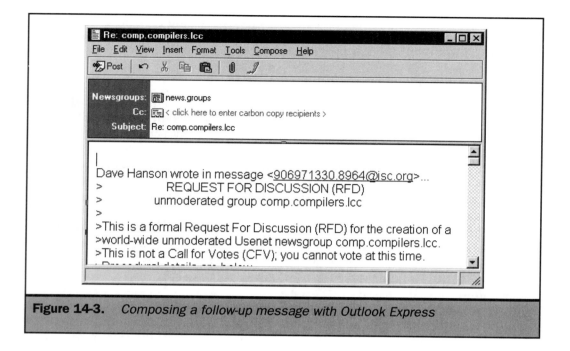

Figure 14-3. *Composing a follow-up message with Outlook Express*

Message button to send the message to the selected newsgroup. For e-mail replies to the author of a message, click the Send button.

Posting a Message on a New Topic

To compose a new message, first click the newsgroup you wish to send your message to. Then click Compose Message on the toolbar. In the message composition window that appears, type your message and the subject, and click the Post button on the message composition window's toolbar.

When you want to post a message to more than one newsgroup, click Tools | Select Newsgroups from the message composition window menu bar. On the Pick Newsgroups dialog box that appears, choose a newsgroup from the list and click the Add button. You can send a message to any newsgroup whether you're subscribed to it or not.

Formatting Messages

When you post a message, you can determine how your message is formatted, as well as adding your signature, a business card, attachments, or links to files or Web site addresses.

You can format your messages using HTML formatting, which lets you change font styles and sizes and indent or center your paragraphs. However, not everyone who participates in newsgroups is able to view HTML documents. To format a message with HTML, select Format I Rich Text (HTML) from the message composition window menu bar. Highlight the text you want to format. If you want to format all the text, select Edit I Select All from the menu bar (or press CTRL+A). Once you've selected the text you want formatted, choose the options you want from the formatting toolbar.

 To ensure that everyone can read your messages, post them as plain text rather than formatted. Choose Tools I Options from the Outlook Express menu bar, click the Send tab, and click Plain Text in the News Sending Format part of the Options dialog box. Then click OK.

Using Stationery

Many e-mail programs let you create form letters (called *stationery*) for messages that you send frequently. Outlook Express lets you use stationery for newsgroup messages, too. You can include a background image, special fonts, signature files, or a business card. Chapter 10 describes how to set up stationery. To use stationary with newsgroup messages, choose Tools I Stationary from the Outlook Express menu bar to display the Stationery dialog box. Click the News tab, click the This Stationery option, and choose which stationery to use. Since stationery uses HTML formatting, most people won't be able to see the formatting.

Canceling Messages

You can't cancel e-mail messages, but you can cancel messages to newsgroups. To cancel a message you've sent, select the newsgroup to which you sent the message, click the message you want to cancel, and choose Compose I Cancel Message.

Printing Messages

To print a message, select the message header or display the message. Choose File I Print or click Print on the toolbar.

Saving Messages

When a message catches your attention and you want to keep it indefinitely, you can save it. Outlook Express gives you two different ways to save messages you want to keep: moving them to an Outlook Express folder or saving them to a text file. To save the message in a folder, drag the message from the list of message headers to a folder in the folder line (in the left pane of the Outlook Express window). To save a message in a text file, choose File I Save As and select the directory and file into which you want to save the message. You can give the message a unique filename or use the subject line as the filename. See the "Filing Messages" section in the Outlook 98 section of Chapter 6 for how to create folders.

Unsubscribing from Newsgroups

As you get more proficient at using newsgroups, you'll find some of the groups you subscribed to either no longer interest you or that they never did. In that case, you can delete them from your folder list. Select the newsgroup from the folder list and right-click it to display up a drop-down menu. From this menu, select Unsubscribe from This Newsgroup. Outlook may ask you to confirm that you want to unsubscribe.

Filtering Messages

Filtering newsgroup messages lets you choose which messages you don't want to see. Outlook Express can filter messages by sender, length, or time of posting. When you choose filtering, Outlook Express doesn't download or display the messages that match your criteria. To filter messages, follow these steps:

1. Choose Tools | Newsgroup Filters from the menu bar to display the Newsgroup Filters dialog box.

2. Click the Add button to see the Properties dialog box shown in Figure 14-4.

3. Choose the newsgroup or newsgroups you want to apply filtering to. You can also filter all newsgroups (for example, you can filter out all messages from a persistently obnoxious poster in all newsgroups).

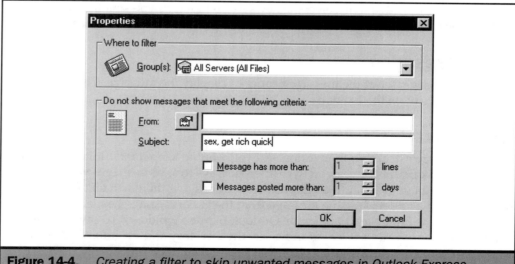

Figure 14-4. *Creating a filter to skip unwanted messages in Outlook Express*

4. Select the criteria you want to filter out or type your criteria, and click OK. The new filter appears in the Newsgroup Filters window. Repeat steps 2 and 3 to create additional filters and click OK.

When you download newsgroup messages, Outlook filters out the messages you specified so that you never have to see them. You can change or delete filters from the Newsgroup Filters dialog box.

Newsreading in Netscape Newsgroup

Netscape Communicator 4.5, which comes with the popular Netscape Navigator as its browser, comes with its own newsreader, Netscape Newsgroup (it used to be called Collabra). Netscape Newsgroup has all the features you need to download, read, and reply to newsgroup messages. You can download Netscape Communicator, including Netscape Newsgroup, from **http://www.netscape.com/computing/download**. (See Chapter 38 for how to download and install programs.)

To open Netscape Newsgroup, click the Read Newsgroup icons in the Netscape component bar that appears in the lower-right corner of Netscape Navigator and Netscape Messenger's window (the icon looks like two balloons). In Netscape Navigator you can also choose Communicator | Newsgroups.

When you run Netscape Newsgroup for the first time, you need to tell the program which news server (or news servers) you plan to use:

1. In the Netscape Newsgroup window, choose Edit | Preferences from the menu bar.

2. In the Preferences dialog box that appears, click the plus box next to the Mail & Newsgroups category if its sub-items aren't already displayed.

3. Click the Newsgroup Servers category to display the news server settings in the right part of this window, as shown in Figure 14-5.

4. Click Add, and type the address for your Internet provider's news server in the Server box. Leave the Port box set to 119 (the default port number for news servers) unless your Internet provider or system administrator specifies another port. If the news server you use requires you to log in with a user name and password before retrieving newsgroup articles, click the Always Use Name and Password box.

5. Click OK. The news server appears in the list of news servers in the Preferences dialog box.

6. Click OK again. Your news server appears in the folder list in the Netscape Newsgroup window, as shown in Figure 14-6.

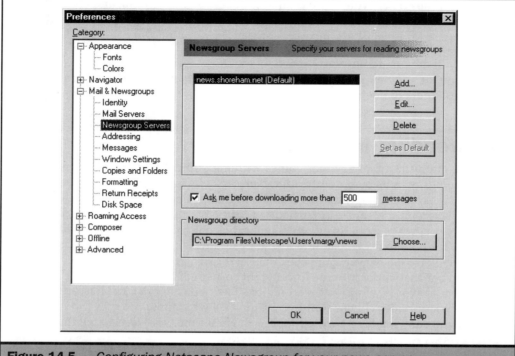

Figure 14-5. *Configuring Netscape Newsgroup for your news server*

Finding and Subscribing to Newsgroups

To subscribe to newsgroups, choose File | Subscribe. You see the Communicator Subscribe to Newsgroups dialog box shown in Figure 14-7. From this dialog box, you can list all newsgroups (by clicking the All tab), search for specific newsgroups you specify with a keyword (by clicking the Search tab), or list any new groups created since you last listed available newsgroups (by clicking the New tab).

When you click the All tab, you see the thousands of available newsgroups on your Internet provider's news server. Each newsgroup hierarchy (like **alt** and **comp**, described in Chapter 13) appears as a single heading, with a folder and plus box to its left. To see the newsgroups within a hierarchy, click the plus box. Hierarchies can contain subhierarchies: keep clicking plus boxes until you see newsgroup names, indicated by two-balloon icons. When you want to see only the top-level hierarchy names again, click the Collapse All button. If you know the beginning of the newsgroup name you want, type it in the Newsgroup box: Netscape Newsgroup scrolls the list of newsgroups down to the newsgroup you type, expanding hierarchies as needed.

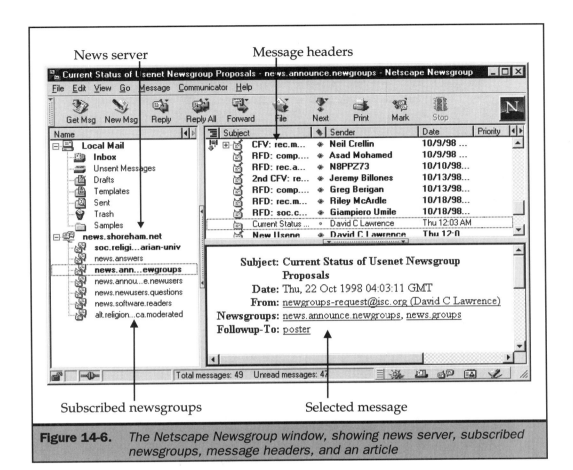

News server

Message headers

Subscribed newsgroups

Selected message

Figure 14-6. *The Netscape Newsgroup window, showing news server, subscribed newsgroups, message headers, and an article*

When you see a newsgroup that looks interesting, subscribe to the newsgroup by clicking the newsgroup name and clicking Subscribe, by clicking in the Subscribe column to the right of the newsgroup name, or by double-clicking the newsgroup. A check mark appears in the Subscribe column next to the newsgroup name.

To bypass downloading what can be a very large list of newsgroups, you can search for specific newsgroups. Click the Search tab, make sure your news server appears in the Server box, type the keyword you want to search for in the Search For box, and click the Search Now button. Netscape Newsgroup displays a list of matching newsgroups. To subscribe to any of the newsgroups listed, click the dot in the Subscribe column to the right of the newsgroup name or double-click the newsgroup. Then click OK.

New newsgroups are added daily. From time to time, take a look at the list of new newsgroups to see if any match your interest. Choose File | Subscribe and click the New tab.

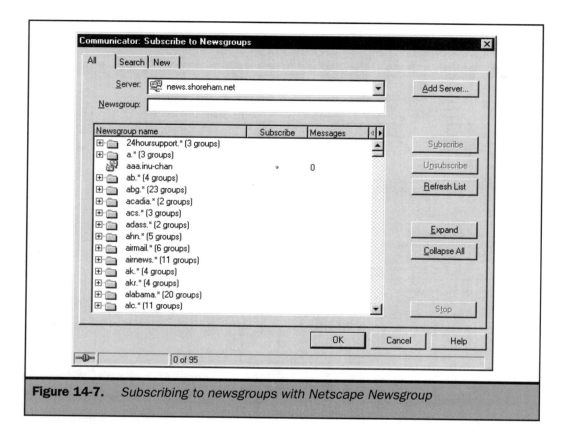

Figure 14-7. Subscribing to newsgroups with Netscape Newsgroup

Reading and Selecting Messages

You can read the newsgroups you've subscribed to either online (while connected to the Internet) or offline (not connected).

Reading Messages Online

If your list of subscribed newsgroups doesn't appear under your news server name in the Netscape Newsgroup window, click the plus box to the left of the news server. Netscape Newsgroup automatically updates all the newsgroups you are subscribed to. This process can take several minutes.

Once you have subscribed to a newsgroup, you can begin reading its messages by clicking the newsgroup you want to read. After the program downloads the list of message headers, they appear in the upper right page of the Netscape Newsgroup window. To read a message, click the message header. The message appears in the lower-right pane, as shown in Figure 14-6.

Reading Messages Offline

If you prefer to read the newsgroup messages offline, follow these steps:

1. Choose File | Offline | Synchronize to display the Synchronize Offline Items dialog box, which controls how you send messages you've composed while offline, and download newsgroup messages that have been posted by others while you were offline.

2. In the Synchronize Offline Items dialog box, click the Select Items button to choose the newsgroups you want to download before going offline, and which you want updated when you go back online. Click the Newsgroup Messages box so that it contains a check mark.

3. Click Synchronize to download the new messages in the newsgroups you selected. Netscape Newsgroup downloads new messages and uploads messages you have composed.

4. Once the download is finished, you can disconnect from the Internet and read the messages from the newsgroups at your leisure.

To tell Netscape Newsgroup that you want to work online again, choose File | Offline | Work Online.

Threading Messages

Reading newsgroups that have hundreds of postings a day can be overwhelming. You can sort the messages by thread, including either only flagged messages or all messages.

To organize a newsgroup's messages, follow these steps:

1. Select the newsgroup you want to read and open it by double-clicking it.

2. After all the messages load, click View | Sort by from the menu bar.

3. Choose how you want to sort messages.

You can sort by date, flags, order received, priority, sender, size, status, subject, thread, unread, ascending, or descending order. You can also combine ascending or descending order with one of the other sort criteria. You just need to determine which is the best way to sort messages to get the best benefit.

Sending Messages

If you have a response to a message, you can either post a follow-up message to the newsgroup or reply by e-mail to the author of the message. When you have something to say on a new topic, post a message to start a new thread.

Replying to Messages

To either reply via e-mail to the author of a message or by posting a follow-up message to the newsgroup:

1. Select the message to which you want to reply.
2. Click Reply on the toolbar.
3. Select the method you want to use for your reply. Choose To Sender Only to send the reply to the author, or To Newsgroup to send the reply to the newsgroup. A message composition window appears with the message addressed either to the author or the group (as shown in Figure 14-8).
4. Type your message and click Send when you're finished.

Starting a New Thread

When you want to compose a message on a new topic (which may start a new thread), click New Msg on the toolbar. When the message composition window opens (as shown in Figure 14-8), type the newsgroup name in the Group box, type the subject line, write the message you want to send to the newsgroup, and click Send on the toolbar.

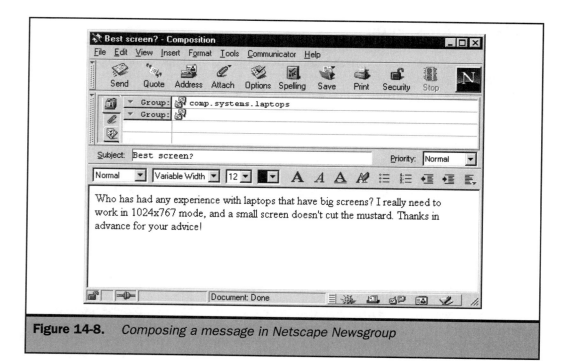

Figure 14-8. *Composing a message in Netscape Newsgroup*

You can check your spelling by clicking the Spelling icon, attach another document or file by clicking the Attach icon, or quote from another message sent to the newsgroup by clicking the Quote icon.

Canceling Messages

If you realize after you sent a message to the newsgroup that you left something out or that you wish you hadn't been so hasty in clicking the Send button, you can cancel the message. Choose Edit | Cancel Message from the menu bar. Anyone who hasn't retrieved newsgroup messages before you canceled the message won't see it.

Printing Messages

When you see the text of a newsgroup message, you can print the message by choosing File | Print or clicking Print on the toolbar.

Saving Messages

To save a message, choose File | Save As | File from the menu bar. Select the directory and file where you want to save the message and type a filename (or let Netscape Newsgroup use the subject of the messages as the filename). Click the Save button when you're finished.

Unsubscribing from Newsgroups

If you don't want to continue to read a newsgroup, unsubscribe from it so that Netscape Newsgroup doesn't waste time downloading its messages. In the list of subscribed newsgroups that appears below the news server name, right-click the newsgroup name and choose Remove Newsgroup from the menu that appears. Alternatively, choose File | Subscribe from the menu, click the All tab, scroll down to the newsgroup name (expanding newsgroup hierarchies as needed), click the newsgroup name, and click Unsubscribe.

Filtering Messages

If there are certain types of messages you'd prefer not to see, Netscape Newsgroup can throw them away before you have to waste your time on them, using *filters*. You can also identify messages that you definitely want to read. To create a filter, follow these steps:

1. Choose Edit | Message Filters from the menu bar. You see the Message Filters dialog box.

2. Choose the newsgroup to which you want the new filter to apply, by selecting the newsgroup name in the Filters For box.

3. Click the New button. You see the Filter Rules dialog box, shown in Figure 14-9.

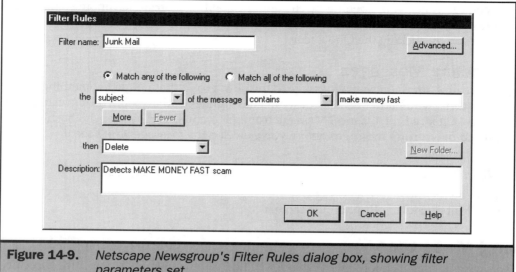

Figure 14-9. Netscape Newsgroup's Filter Rules dialog box, showing filter parameters set

4. Type a name for the filter file in the Filter Name box.

5. Select the criteria to tell Netscape Newsgroups which messages you want to identify.

6. Click OK to save this new filter

7. Repeat steps 2 through 6 for each filter you want to create.

You can indicate which areas to filter: Subject, Sender, Body, Date, Priority, Status, To, CC, or To or CC. You can also indicate how that area contains the filter items; contains, doesn't contain, is, isn't, begins with, or ends with. Then you type in the keywords you want the filter to search for and use to filter out unwanted messages. Next, you choose what you want to do with those filtered messages: delete them, mark the thread that includes the message, ignore the thread, or watch the thread.

Newsreading with Free Agent

Free Agent is a stand-alone program that lets you access and read newsgroups. The latest version of Free Agent is 1.11. You can download a copy from its Web site at

http://www.forteinc.com/agent/freagent.htm

or from shareware sites like TUCOWS at **http://www.tucows.com**. Chapter 38 explains how to download and install programs from the Web.

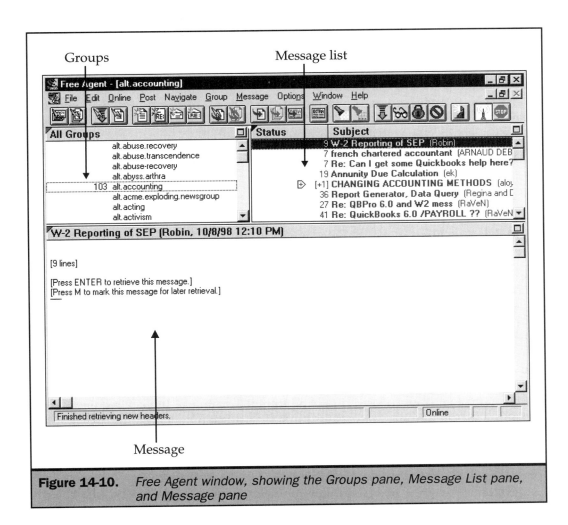

Groups

Message list

Figure 14-10.   *Free Agent window, showing the Groups pane, Message List pane, and Message pane*

Message

The first time you run Free Agent, it asks you for your news server, mail server, e-mail address, and name. Then it connects to the news server and offers to download the complete list of newsgroups. Since this can take a while, you can choose to download them later. Then you see the Free Agent window, which is divided into three panes; the Groups pane, the Message List pane, and the Message pane (Figure 14-10).

Finding and Subscribing to Newsgroups

The Groups pane (in the upper-left part of the Free Agent window) lists newsgroup names. Click the pane header to switch from All Groups to Subscribed Groups (only those you are subscribed to) to New Groups (newsgroups that have been created recently).

Subscribing to Newsgroups

To subscribe to a newsgroup, you can scroll down the list of all groups until you find the newsgroup you want and then double-click the newsgroup name. On the View Empty Group dialog box that appears, you can click

- *Sample Message Headers,* to see the headers of a few messages, to see if this newsgroup might interest you
- *Get All Message Headers,* to see the message headers for all the current messages in the newsgroup
- *Subscribe to Group,* to add the newsgroup to your list of subscribed newsgroups

You can also choose Group | Subscribe, press CTRL+S, or click the Subscribe to Group button in the toolbar to subscribe to newsgroups as you run across them when you're scrolling through the list of newsgroups. No matter which method you use to subscribe, Free Agent inserts a newspaper icon next to the groups you've subscribed to.

Finding Newsgroups

Free Agent lets you search the huge list of available newsgroups for groups by name. You can search individual messages by author or subject. To search for newsgroups with a particular word in the newsgroup name, select the Groups pane. Click the Find button on the toolbar or choose Edit | Find from the menu bar. In the Find dialog box that appears, type a word you want to search for. To find other newsgroups that contain the same word, click Edit | Find and click Find Next in the Find dialog box.

Selecting and Reading Messages

Once you have selected the newsgroups you're interested in, you can read the messages several ways. You can read them while you're online or offline (without being connected to the Internet).

Reading Articles Offline or Online

To set Free Agent to view newsgroup messages online or offline, choose Options | General Preferences and click the Online tab. To configure Free Agent to work online, click the Use Online Defaults button and set your preferences on the Online tab of the General Preferences dialog box, as seen in Figure 14-11. To set Free Agent as an offline reader, click the Use Offline Defaults button and set your preferences.

Downloading Message Headers

To read the messages in a newsgroup, you can tell Free Agent to download the message headers, mark those that interest you, and tell Free Agent to download the

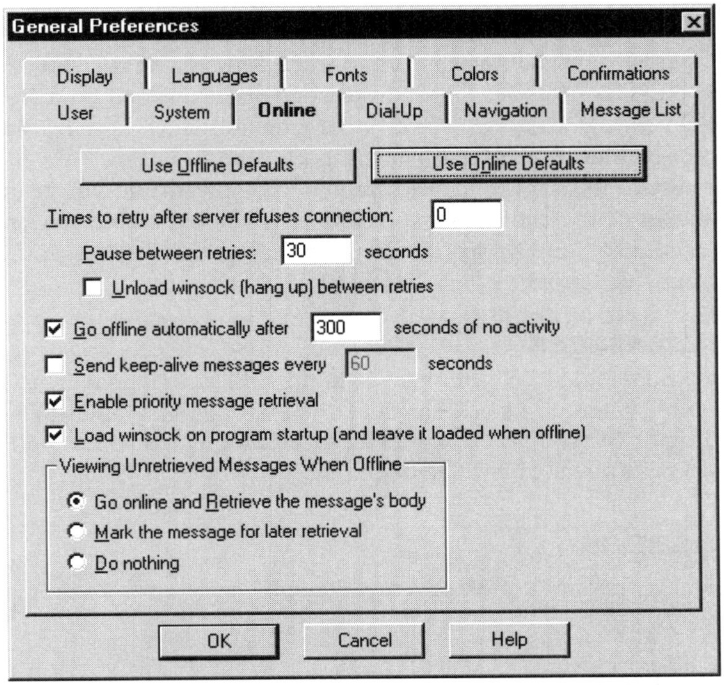

General Preferences

| Display | Languages | Fonts | Colors | Confirmations |
| User | System | **Online** | Dial-Up | Navigation | Message List |

Use Offline Defaults   Use Online Defaults

Times to retry after server refuses connection: 0

Pause between retries: 30   seconds

☐ Unload winsock (hang up) between retries

☑ Go offline automatically after 300   seconds of no activity

☐ Send keep-alive messages every 60   seconds

☑ Enable priority message retrieval

☑ Load winsock on program startup (and leave it loaded when offline)

Viewing Unretrieved Messages When Offline
  ◉ Go online and Retrieve the message's body
  ○ Mark the message for later retrieval
  ○ Do nothing

OK   Cancel   Help

Figure 14-11. *Setting Free Agent for online or offline newsreading*

CHATTING AND CONFERENCING ON THE INTERNET

text of the messages you choose. Click the Get New Headers in Subscribed Groups button (the leftmost button on the toolbar) or choose Online | Get New Headers in Subscribe Groups from the menu bar. Switch the Groups pane to list only the newsgroups you are subscribed to (by clicking the heading in the pane), to make it easier to switch among subscribed newsgroups. For the newsgroup that is selected in the Groups pane, you see the message headers in the Message List page (the upper-right part of the Free Agent window).

You can drag the divider lines between the panes around to change the sizes of the panes. You can also click the Maximize button in the upper-right corner of a pane to maximize it, so that the pane occupies the entire Free Agent window. To return to seeing the three panes (Groups, Message List, and Message), click the Restore button in the upper-right corner of the maximized pane.

Downloading and Reading Messages

New messages appear in red and messages you've already read appear in black. Choose the message you want to read by double-clicking the message, or by pressing

ENTER. Alternatively, you can mark messages for downloading by clicking the message and pressing **M** (an icon appears by the message header), and then downloading all your marked messages by clicking the Get Marked Message Bodies button on the toolbar or choosing Online | Get Marked Message Bodies. When Free Agent has downloaded the message text, a piece-of-paper icon appears by the message header: click the message header to display the message.

To locate a certain message, click the name of the newsgroup you want to search in the Groups pane and click in the Message List pane. Click the Find button on the toolbar or choose Edit | Find to display the Find dialog box. Type a word or name that you want to find in a message.

Threading Messages

Free Agent lets you decide how you want to handle threaded messages. Choose Options | General Preferences and then click the Message List tab. Make sure that the Enable Threading by Subject box is checked. This dialog box also lets you specify how you want threads to appear on the Message List.

Sending Messages

You can start a new thread by posting a message on a new topic, or you can reply to a message you read.

Replying to Messages

Free Agent lets you reply either by e-mail to the author of the message or by posting a follow-up message to the newsgroup. Begin by selecting the message you want to reply to. To respond with a follow-up message to the newsgroup, click the Post Follow Up Message icon on the toolbar, choose Post | Follow-Up Usenet Message, or press **F**. To respond privately to the author of the message, click the Post Reply via Email button on the toolbar, choose Post | Reply via Email, or press **R**.

Either way, Free Agent displays a message composition window. If you are posting to a newsgroup, the name of the newsgroup appears in the Newsgroups box. If you are sending e-mail, the e-mail address of the author of the original message appears in the To box. The message you are responding to is quoted in the text of the message. Edit out the unimportant parts of the original message, add your response, and click Send Now (if you are working online) or Send Later (if you are working offline). If you decide not to send the message, click the Cancel button

Starting a New Thread

To compose a new post to a newsgroup, select the newsgroup in the Groups pane. Click the Post New Usenet Message button on the toolbar, choose Post | New Usenet Message from the menu bar, or press **P**. The name of the current newsgroup appears in the Newsgroups box, but you can change it. Type the subject and your message and click either Send Now or Send Later.

You can send e-mail to anyone, if you don't feel like firing up your e-mail program. Click the Post New Email Message button on the toolbar, choose Post | New Email Message, or press CTRL+M.

Adding a Signature

When you post messages—replies to other messages or new threads you start—you can include a signature at the end of each message. Free Agent lets you set up as many different signatures as you want, so that you can use one (serious) signature on messages to business-oriented newsgroups and another (frivolous) signature on recreational newsgroups.

To set up signature files, click Options | Signatures. In the Signatures dialog box that appears, click the Add button and type a name for the signature (like **standard**) in the Names box. Then type the text you want to appear in the signature line to any messages you send. You can include any information you want, including your e-mail address, your Web site address, and your business name and address.

Canceling Messages

Free Agent also lets you cancel a message after it's sent. To cancel a message, select the message and choose Message | Cancel Usenet Message. When you see the Cancel Usenet Message window, click the Send Now button to send the cancellation message to the news server.

Printing Messages

When you want to print any of the messages you read in newsgroups, begin by selecting the message or messages you want to print. You can print an entire thread by selecting a collapsed thread header (where one header represents all the messages in the thread, and a plus box appears to the left of the header). Choose File | Print or press CTRL+P and click OK to start the print job.

When printing a thread, Free Agent prints all the messages in the thread. If the thread contains many messages, printing can take a while.

Saving Messages

Occasionally you'll want to save messages permanently to your hard drive. To save messages, begin by selecting the message or thread and then choose File | Save Message As. In the dialog box that appears, choose the directory and file in which to save the message(s) and give the file a name. If you are saving more than one message, choose an option in the File Format box: UNIX Message File (with a new-page character separating the messages), Precede Each Message With (and fill in what separator you'd like between messages), or No Separator Between Messages. Then click the Save button.

Deleting Messages and Groups

Free Agent automatically deletes old newsgroup messages for you. You can specify when you want these messages purged: when retrieving new headers, when closing the newsreader, or on demand. You can set these options for all newsgroups, or differently for different newsgroups to which you are subscribed.

To specify when you want old messages deleted for a newsgroup, select the newsgroup in the Groups pane and choose Group | Properties (or press ALT+ENTER). On the Properties for Selected Newsgroups dialog box, click the What to Purge tab to control how Free Agent decides when messages are old enough to delete, and click the When to Purge to control when Free Agent performs the deletions. If you don't like the What to Purge settings that Free Agent suggests, click the Override Default Settings button and check the options you want to use. To purge newsgroups (that is, select old messages for deletion and delete them) now, choose Group | Purge Newsgroups, and choose which newsgroups to purge.

To delete newsgroups from your subscribed list, select the group you want to delete. Then click Group | Delete or click the Subscribe button on the toolbar. Free Agent asks what to do with the messages for the newsgroup from which you are unsubscribing.

Filtering Messages

You can tell Free Agent to ignore threads that you don't want to read or automatically mark other threads for downloading. If you come across a particular thread that interests you, and you want to keep track of all the responses to that thread, click the Watch Thread icon from the toolbar (the little pair of glasses), choose Message | Watch Thread, or press **W**. A pair-of-glasses icon appears next to each message in the thread, along with a download icon, which means that Free Agent will automatically retrieve the bodies of these messages the next time you go online.

Ignoring threads works much the same way as watching threads. When you see a thread you're not interested in, click the Ignore Thread icon on the toolbar, choose Message | Ignore Thread, or press **I**. A circle-with-line icon appears next to the threads you want to ignore. Free Agent then marks those threads as read, whether they've been downloaded or not, so the messages don't appear when you view only unread messages. Also, ignoring threads reduces the number of new unread messages you receive when retrieving messages from the news server.

Newsreading in Tin

Tin is a popular UNIX newsreader. See Chapter 40 for information about how to use UNIX shell accounts. Note that in UNIX, uppercase and lowercase letters frequently have different meanings, so type the commands exactly as shown in this book.

Subscribing to Newsgroups

To run tin, type **tin** at the prompt. Tin begins loading the newsgroups, which may take several minutes. Then tin asks you if you want to subscribe to each new newsgroup in its list of newsgroups:

```
Subscribe to new group alt.binaries.x (Yy/Nn) [n]:
```

Type **y** to subscribe to the newsgroup or **n** not to. If you want tin not to ask you about all new newsgroups, type **N** (that is, press SHIFT+N).

After tin has asked about all the new newsgroups, tin displays a list of all the newsgroups you subscribed to with the number of messages in each group indicated beside them, as shown in Figure 14-12. At the bottom of this screen are the commands you use to access each newsgroup and read the messages. For help in understanding what each command means, type **h** at the prompt.

To subscribe to a newsgroup whose name you know, type **g**. When tin asks for the newsgroup name, type it and press ENTER. Then tin asks where in your list of newsgroups to position this new newsgroup: just press ENTER.

CHATTING AND
CONFERENCING ON
THE INTERNET

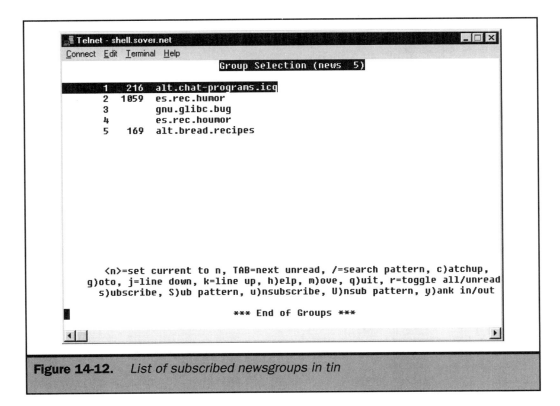

Figure 14-12.   *List of subscribed newsgroups in tin*

When you have finished running tin, type **q** until tin asks whether you really want to quit: and type **y**.

Reading Messages

To read the messages in a newsgroup, use the arrow keys to move up and down to select the group you want to read and type **n**. Tin displays the headers for all the messages in that newsgroup, as seen in Figure 14-13.

Press the TAB key to start reading the messages. Figure 14-14 is an example of a message displayed. Press the TAB key to toggle to the next unread message until you have read all the messages or read all the ones you're interested in. Again, the commands you can use to navigate through messages are listed at the bottom of the screen.

When you want to read all the messages in a thread, first select the newsgroup you want to read and type **n** to open it and see the message headers for that newsgroup. At the prompt, type the lowercase letter **l** to see a list of the threads. Tin displays a list of the headers by thread. Then you can use the TAB key to open and read each of the messages in the thread.

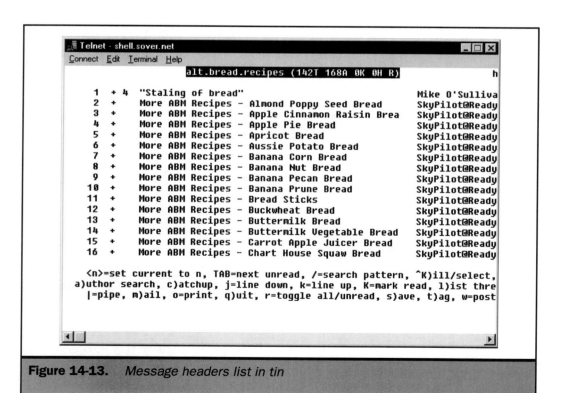

Figure 14-13.   *Message headers list in tin*

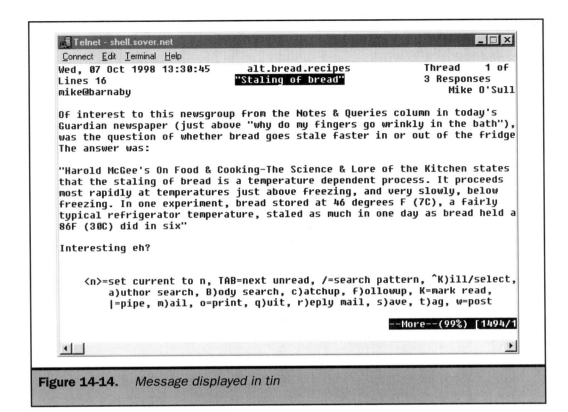

Figure 14-14.   *Message displayed in tin*

Sending Messages

You can reply to a message or post your own message on a new topic.

Replying to Messages

To reply to a message with a follow-up message to the newsgroup, press the lowercase letter **r**. tin opens the reply message and addresses it to the group, as shown in Figure 14-15.

At the bottom of this screen tin displays the available commands. All have a carat symbol beside them, to indicate that you must use the CTRL key along with the letter. For example, ^C means to press CTRL+C.

Type your reply, and delete the unnecessary parts of the message to which you are replying. When you've finished composing your message to the newsgroup, press CTRL+X to exit from the editor. Then press **q** to quit, **e** to go back to the editor, **g** to use PGP encryption (described in Chapter 9) when sending the message, and **s** or ENTER to send the message to the newsgroup.

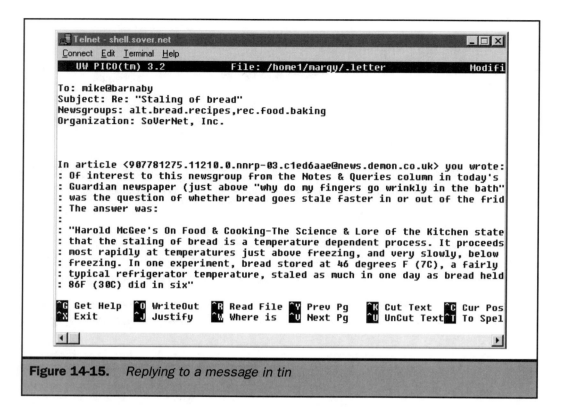

Figure 14-15. *Replying to a message in tin*

Starting a New Thread

When you want to post a message on a new topic, type **w**. Tin asks you to type a subject for the post and press ENTER. Then tin displays the new message screen where you can begin typing your message to the newsgroup. Press CTRL+X to exit the screen and type **s** at the prompt to send your message.

Printing Messages

To print a message, type **o**, the command to print, at tin's prompt. Then select what you want to print: **a** for only the article or **t** to print the entire thread.

Deleting Newsgroups

When you find out after reading some of the posts that you're no longer interested in a newsgroup and want to delete it, you need first to get back to the list of newsgroups.

Type **q** to quit reading messages; then type **q** again to quit reading the newsgroup. Once you see the list of newsgroups again, press the UP ARROW or DOWN ARROW keys to select the newsgroup you want to delete. Type **u** for unsubscribe.

Newsreading with NewsWatcher

NewsWatcher is a stand-alone newsreader specifically designed to work on Macs. The latest version of NewsWatcher is 2.2. You can get a copy of NewsWatcher from TUCOWS (**http://www.tucows.com**), or from the Mac Orchard Web site (**http://www.macorchard.com**). See Chapter 38 for how to download and install programs from the Internet.

When you first install NewsWatcher, you need to configure it with your preferences, including the name of your news server. Then NewsWatcher downloads the list of newsgroups from the new server and displays them in the Full Group List window. You can display the Full Group List window any time by choosing Windows | Show Full Group List.

Finding and Subscribing to Newsgroups

Rather than have to search through a full listing of newsgroups every time, you can create your own newsgroup window. You can include newsgroups in this window that are of interest to you. This is similar to subscribing to newsgroups in other programs.

To create your own group window, follow these steps:

1. Choose File | New Group Window from the menu bar.

2. Select File | Save As.

3. Enter a name for your newsgroup window in the Save Group List As box.

4. Click Save.

Next you can add newsgroups to your newsgroup window. To add newsgroups to this window, highlight the newsgroup in the Full Group List window and choose Special | Subscribe from the menu bar. NewsWatcher adds the newsgroup to your newsgroup window. Repeat these steps to add more newsgroups.

If you want to search for a specific newsgroup, click Edit | Find. In the Find dialog box type the keyword you want to search for.

Reading Messages

To read messages, just highlight the newsgroup you want to read and double-click it. A Newsgroup window opens containing contains all the articles posted to that newsgroup. Double-click any message you want to read. The article appears in a text window (Figure 14-16 shows the top part of a text window containing a message).

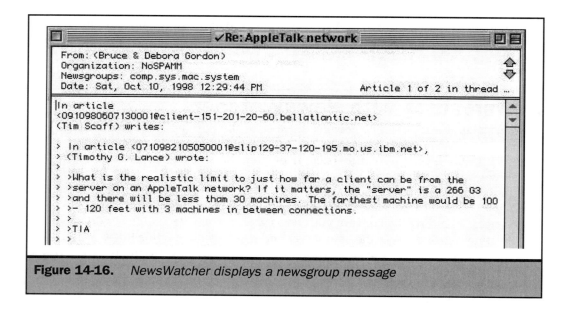

Figure 14-16.   *NewsWatcher displays a newsgroup message*

When a message has had replies, an arrow and a number appear beside that message, indicating that this post is part of a thread. The number represents the number of posts in the thread. To read these threaded messages, simply click the arrow. The arrow turns down and NewsWatcher lists all the posts in the thread below the initial message. To read any of these messages, double-click the message.

Sending Messages

You can reply to a message by posting your own message to the newsgroup, or you can start a new thread by posting a message on a new topic.

Replying to Messages

Highlight the message you want to reply to and choose Message | Reply. In the Article Window that appears, type your message and click Send. Then, click OK when the warning message appears, and the message is sent to the newsgroup. Figure 14-17 shows the top of the window in which you compose a reply.

Posting Messages

To start a new thread, highlight the newsgroup to which you want to send the message. Click News | New Message and type your message in the New Article window that appears. Be sure to type a subject for your message in the Subject line

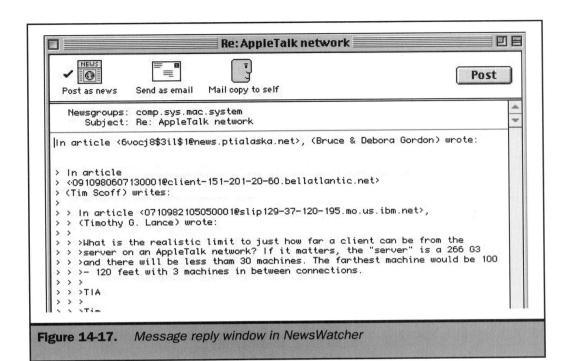

Figure 14-17.   *Message reply window in NewsWatcher*

and click Send when you've finished composing your message. When the warning message appears, click OK to send it on to the newsgroup.

Defining a Signature

In NewsWatcher you can include a signature in your replies and posts. To add a signature to your messages, follow these steps:

1. Click File | Preferences.

2. Choose Topic and highlight Signature.

3. In the NewsWatcher Preferences window that appears, shown in Figure 14-18, enter the signature information you want to include in your messages. When you've finished, click OK.

Printing Messages

When you're ready to print a message, make sure the message you want to print is displayed in foreground, choose File | Print, and click OK. You can also press COMMAND+P if you prefer to use keyboard commands instead.

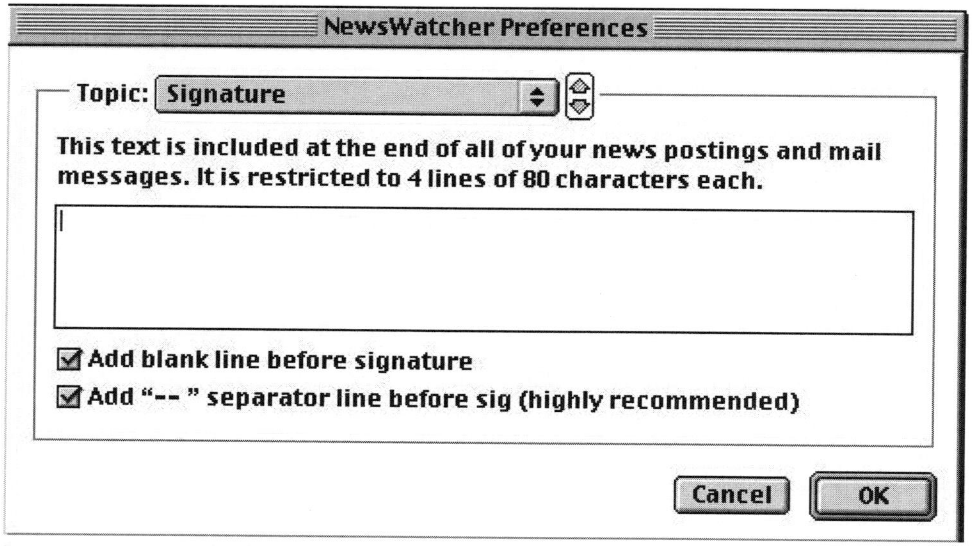

Figure 14-18.   *Signature section of the NewsWatcher Preferences window*

Saving Messages

When you want to keep an article for later reference, begin by highlighting the message. Then select File | Save As and choose the directory and location where you want the file saved. If you want the file to have a different name than the one the program gives it, type the name you want to use in the dialog box. When you've finished with these steps, click the Save button.

Unsubscribing from Newsgroups

If you're no longer interested in a newsgroup, delete the newsgroup from your newsgroup window. Begin by highlighting the newsgroup you want to delete. Choose Special | Unsubscribe from the menu bar. NewsWatcher deletes the newsgroup from your newsgroup window. Repeat these steps for any other newsgroups you want to delete.

Newsreading in Deja News

Deja News is a Web site for searching and displaying newsgroups. It's a handy tool to use when you're looking for specific information in Usenet and don't want to spend hours hunting for it using a newsreader. Deja News maintains a database of all the messages posted to all the Usenet newsgroups in the major news hierarchies for at least the last year. You can search the newsgroup archives for messages that contain words or phrases or messages posted by particular people.

Using Deja News, you can locate the names of newsgroups within your interest areas and then use those names to subscribe to the newsgroups. Once you've found newsgroups of interest, you can read newsgroup articles using Deja News, or you can subscribe to the newsgroups using your newsreader. This process saves you having to hunt through thousands of newsgroups from your news server.

To use Deja News, use your Web browser to go to the Deja News site at **http://www.dejanews.com**. The exact layout of the Web site changes, but you can

- Search for newsgroups that contain a specified word in the newsgroup name or description

- Search all newsgroup articles for individual messages that contain a word or phrase, as shown in Figure 14-19

- Browse newsgroups by newsgroup name

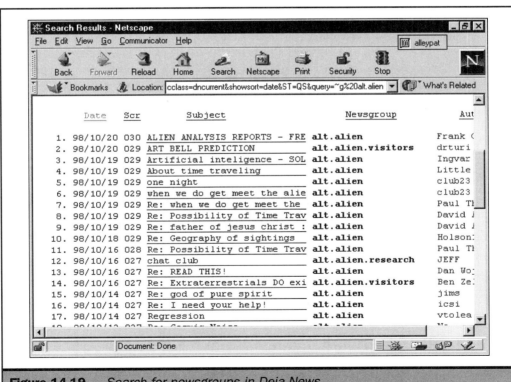

Figure 14-19.   *Search for newsgroups in Deja News*

Once you find newsgroup names, you can click them to see listings of articles. Scroll through the message headers to find an article that interests you. Once you've found an article, click it, and Deja News opens a new window displaying the message. Using the Back button in the browser's toolbar lets you get back to the message headers page so you can locate and read other articles. When you locate a message you want to print, click the Print icon in the toolbar. To save an article or message, click File | Save As and select the directory and location you want to save the file to. Enter a name for the file and click the Save button. You can save any page you access in a browser, so you're not limited to only saving messages.

   Search Deja News's archive for your own name, to see what articles you've posted to Usenet newsgroups, or what other people have said about you.

The Complete Reference

Internet

Chapter 15

Internet Relay Chat (IRC)

*I*nternet Relay Chat (IRC) enables users to type messages back and forth to each other, allowing people from all over the world to communicate with each other any time of the day or night. While using IRC, people can get to know each other without the bias that often occurs when people meet each other in person. Because you can't see the other people, you get to know their personalities through their words alone.

This chapter describes IRC, channels, nicknames, and other IRC-related concepts, and then describes how to participate in IRC by using the most popular chat programs: mIRC, Microsoft Chat, V-Chat, Ircle, and ircii.

What Is IRC?

IRC began back in 1988 and now is used in over 60 countries around the world. It gained international fame in 1991 during the Persian Gulf War, when people around the world gathered on IRC to hear reports from the war. In 1993, IRC users from Moscow typed live reports about the situation during the attempted coup against Boris Yeltsin.

As IRC has gained in popularity, its main use has changed. People still use IRC to discuss current events and news items, but they mainly use it for general social banter and interaction, as well as professional and business communication.

IRC Networks

IRC networks (or *nets*) are the backbone of IRC. IRC networks are groups of IRC servers that are linked together over the Internet, enabling chat sessions to span the globe. All the public IRC networks are accessible via the Internet.

There are many different nets, which are mainly furnished or sponsored by local ISPs, university systems, other organizations, or individuals. The following are the three largest nets:

- **EFnet** (short for *Eris Free net*)   The first and largest net. It was never designed; it just happened. If you are on IRC but unsure which net you're on, chances are good that you're on EFnet. At any time, day or night, you can find almost 40,000 people connected to EFnet, which has no official Web site.

- **UnderNet (http://www.undernet.org)**   This net evolved out of the EFnet in 1992. It formed when a group of EFnet users grew discontented with what they perceived as privacy breaches and slowdowns, and decided to form a new net. Since its inception, UnderNet has grown from 1,000 users in February of 1995, to over 25,000 users at the end of the first quarter of 1998.

- **DALnet (http://www.dal.net)**   One of the older nets, it keeps pace with the UnderNet. It started as a role-playing-game alternative network. Originally, you could find an average of 130 users on this net. However, with the recent growth of the Internet and IRC usage, this net has grown to over 20,000 users during peak hours.

Several dozen other nets are on the Internet. New nets are being added constantly. As more people get connected to the Internet, the older nets can't handle all the traffic effectively.

Already, the UnderNet and DALnet are undergoing many of the same problems that make the EFnet a hassle for users. And, as more and more people get frustrated, the demand creates the supply. Nets come and go all the time on the Internet. Some disappear completely and some divide and evolve into other nets.

*For information about these and other IRC networks, start at Yahoo! (**http://www.yahoo.com**) and choose Computers and Internet | Internet | Chat | IRC | Networks.*

IRC Servers

IRC servers are computers and software that work like IRC switchboards, letting users connect to them by using an IRC client program. Most IRC servers are at universities or ISPs. IRC server computers run the programs that enable you to connect to an IRC net, keep track of users and channels, and make sure that all the messages that all the users type get to the right place. To connect to an IRC net, you connect to a server on that net. Each net has its own group of servers. For example, to access the UnderNet, you connect to an IRC server that belongs to the UnderNet. Each net has its own group of servers. For instance, EFnet has over 100 servers, UnderNet has over 44 servers, and DALnet has about 27 servers.

Each server has its own host name, usually consisting of the location of the server and the net that it accesses. For example, every UnderNet server has a host name ending with *undernet.org*. America Online (AOL) has its own UnderNet server located in Washington, DC., and the host name for the server is *washington.dc.us.undernet.org*.

You may not always be allowed to connect to the server of your choice, usually because the server already has the maximum number of users connected. If this happens, keep trying, or try another server. Several European servers refuse connections from U.S. users, to avoid all of their connections being used by U.S. users.

Widely Used Servers

The following table lists a few servers for each of the three major IRC nets. If these aren't already in the server lists of your IRC program, you can add them. These servers should give you a basis to start exploring IRC.

EFnet Servers	**UnderNet Servers**	**DALnet Servers**
irc.magic.ca	ann-arbor.mi.us.undernet.org	irc.dal.net
irc.colorado.edu	austin.tx.us.undernet.org	irc.services.dal.net
irc.c-com.net	blacksburg.va.us.undernet.org	glass.oh.us.dal.net
irc.blackened.com	chicago.il.us.undernet.org	groucho.ca.us.dal.net
irc.stanford.edu	davis.ca.us.undernet.org	datashopper.dal.net
	newbrunswick.nj.us.undernet.org	

If one server fails to let you on, keep trying the other servers until you find one that lets you connect. As you use IRC, you'll learn which servers work best for you.

Ports on IRC Servers

When you try to connect to a server, you are often asked which port you want to connect to. A *port* is like a line into the server, and each port has a number. The default port for IRC is 6667, and almost all IRC servers let you connect using port 6667. Most servers have additional ports that you can use. If you have a hard time getting connected to a server on port 6667, then try one of the alternate ports. IRC server ports usually range from 6660 to 6670.

For more information on ports, see the section "Servers, Clients, and Ports" in Chapter 1.

Servers for Kids

Many parents are concerned about children being on IRC. You have heard the stories on the news about people who stalk children, including over the Internet. IRC is often a highly uncivilized place for kids or adults. We advise that young children not be allowed on IRC without supervision. All children who use IRC should know the basic safety rules listed in the section "Safety While Chatting," in Chapter 11.

Another option is to let your child connect only to a net that is for children only: Kidlink. Kidlink is a global network for youths up to age 15. Kidlink requires its users to register before using it, it screens its users, and it monitors users' activities to insure that children are safe there. After you or your child registers for Kidlink, you get the server information to let you join. See its Web site at **http://www.kidlink.org** for more information.

Channels

Users meet in *channels*, the IRC equivalent of a chat room. An unlimited number of users can be in a channel, and it takes only one user to open or create a channel. Each channel has a name, usually starting with a pound sign (#). For example, a channel for readers of this book might be called #nettcr.

Each time that a person types a message and presses ENTER, the message appears on the screens of everyone else in the channel. Other people in the channel can then type their replies; this is how conversations occur in IRC.

Each net has its own set of channels. The number of channels varies according to the time of day or night that you log on. The three major nets usually have thousands of channels. Smaller nets may have from ten channels to hundreds during peak hours. The EFnet, for instance, has about 7,000 channels during the day and more than 8,000 in the evening hours. The UnderNet usually has close to 5,000 channels available. DALnet averages between 2,300 and 3,000 channels. The smaller nets average between 250 and 300 channels, no matter what time of day or night you join.

IRC channels frequently have their own topics, styles, and regular participants. Almost every topic imaginable has a channel somewhere on IRC. For example, here are some common types of channels:

- Channels for socializing, such as #teenchat or #teenland for teenagers, and #letstalk or #friends for adults.

- Channels for professionals, such as #writers or #realestate.

- Channels for technical help, such as #techtalk or #WindowsNT.

- Channels for help with IRC itself, such as #newbies, #mirc, and #wastelands.

- Channels for collectors and crafters, such as #coins or #crafts.

- Geographical channels for people from those areas, such as #michigan or #minnesota. These include country channels, in which the discussions take place in the language of the topic country.

Finding a Channel

At any moment of the day or night, IRC users are chatting on over 10,000 different channels. With so many channels available, how can you find a channel that you want to join? After you connect to an IRC server, your IRC program can display an alphabetized list of all the channels available on the net to which you are connected, showing the name of the channel, the number of people in the channel, and the topic that was set for the channel, if there is one.

The list of the channels on a major IRC net can be long and can take several minutes to download. Next to each channel name is a short description of the topic of the channel. Once the list appears, scroll through it to find a channel that interests you.

Some Recommended Channels

The type of conversations that you find on channels varies according to the type of channel you choose. For instance, if you select one of the state or city channels, you are likely to find that most of the people using that channel are from that state or city. The conversation is generally centered around that area, such as things to do, places to go, and current politics or events.

Some channels that you might want to try for fun are #30plus, #40plus, or #webe30+. In these channels, you find people within that age group.

Other channels are strictly for playing games. There are trivia channels and channels for various word games. In some, a *bot* (automated IRC program) runs the game, while in others the participants take turns asking the questions. Listen for a few minutes before jumping in, until you have figured out the rules.

Several channels are available if you need technical help. For help with IRC itself, try #irchelp, #ircnewbies, #wastelands, #mirc (if you use the mIRC program), or #helpcastle. When you need help with other parts of the Internet, try one of these: #webmaster, #html, or #linpeople.

These are just some examples of the channels that you can expect to find on IRC. Each channel has its own regular participants whose personalities give the channel its unique character. Test the waters until you find the channel that feels right for you.

 The vast majority of the channels on most nets consist of people just shooting the breeze or looking for sexual talk. You may have trouble finding much serious conversation.

Creating Your Own Channel

There are a couple of ways to create your own channel. The easiest way is to pick a channel name that isn't already in use and join that channel (that is, joining a nonexistent channel automatically creates the channel). Then, invite your friends to join you on your new channel. When you create a channel, you automatically become the *chanop* (channel operator, or manager) of that channel.

Normally, a channel disappears when the last person leaves the channel. However, a couple of nets (like the UnderNet and DALnet) allow you to register a channel, so that the channel exists permanently—even when you aren't present. When you register a channel, the administrators of that net put a *bot* on your channel, a self-running program that participates in IRC channels. The bot belongs to the net organization and its only purpose is to keep your channel open.

For details on creating and managing a channel, see the section "Starting and Managing a Channel," later in this chapter.

IRC Programs and IRC Commands

To participate in IRC, you need an IRC program (also called an *IRC client*). The original IRC programs were text-based UNIX programs named irc and ircii. These programs required you to type *IRC commands* (all starting with /) to see listings of channels, join channels, leave channels, and other actions. For example, to see a list of available channels, you had to type the command **/list**, and to join a channel, you had to type **/join** followed by the name of the channel.

Newer Windows- and Mac-based IRC programs (including mIRC, Microsoft Chat, V-Chat for Windows, and Ircle for Mac) let you use buttons or menu choices instead of having to remember IRC commands. Most of these programs also let you type the older IRC commands. For specific instructions, see the sections later in this chapter about how to use mIRC, Ircle, Microsoft Chat, V-Chat, and ircii. Many other good IRC programs are available; browse TUCOWS (**http://www.tucows.com**), Mac Orchard (**http://www.macorchard.com**), and Consummate Winsock Applications List (at **http://cws.internet.com**) Web sites for information (and see Chapter 38 for how to download and install programs from these sites).

Nicknames and Chanops

When you connect to an IRC server, you choose a *nickname* (or *nick*) by which you will be known during the session. Only one person at a time on a net can use a particular nickname. However, when you sign off, you relinquish the use of your nickname, and anyone else can sign on and use it. When you use IRC, never assume that a person using a certain nickname today is the same person that used that nickname yesterday.

If you are female and chose a female-sounding nickname, you can expect to get private messages from strangers, which often are sexual in content. To avoid these messages, choose an androgynous nickname. If you choose to stay with a feminine nickname, you have to learn how to handle these kinds of messages.

Some chatters have an at-sign (@) at the beginning of their nickname. An @ signifies that a person is a channel operator or chanop, the person who manages the channel. Chanops have the power to create a topic, give operator status to others, kick people off the channel, and prevent annoying people from coming back (see the section "Starting and Managing a Channel," later in this chapter).

Netsplits and Lags

After you connect to an IRC server and participate in a channel, you may experience two common problems: netsplits and lags.

A *netsplit* occurs when one or more servers split off from the rest of the net, due to a communications problem. Usually, a netsplit is caused by an overload of users. The servers that split from the rest of the net (and all of their users) are still able to communicate with each other, but not with the rest of the net.

IRC nets are similar to a spider's web, with the threads of the web being the IRC servers. When a netsplit happens, it is as though someone swept away or disconnected a part of the web. When the threads are brought back together, those servers rejoin the others, and users on them rejoin the channels they were on.

You can recognize when a netsplit occurs, because a group of people appears to leave your channel simultaneously; a definite sign of a netsplit is if all the people who leave have the same IRC server name. When communication is restored, the people all rejoin the channel. Netsplits generally don't last very long, but if you notice that your server seems to netsplit often in a given session, you may want to change servers.

Lags sometimes are associated with netsplits. The lag is the time that it takes for your message to travel from your server to the net. Before a netsplit, the lag is frequently long, which is an indication that the servers are overloaded and experiencing problems. Sometimes, a lag affects only one or two servers, and sometimes it affects many servers. Your best bet is to try to ride out the storm. But, if your lag is so bad that you are unable to keep up with the conversation or see anything that anyone else might be saying in the channel, change servers. The only drawback to this solution is finding a server that isn't lagged, too: try asking others in your channel which servers are not lagging and then try one of those.

DCC

The *Direct Client to Client (DCC)* protocol enables you to send files or chat with other users by establishing a direct connection between your computer and theirs. This connection bypasses the IRC server and connects you directly from your ISP to the other person's ISP. You can use DCC when you want to hold a private conversation with one other person.

    Don't accept DCC messages from someone you don't know. People have been known to send smutty pictures or computer viruses.

When you send files by using DCC, it is advisable that you and the receiver be on the same IRC server. The lag is decreased, and in the event of a netsplit, you both remain together. When the net is experiencing a significant lag, sending a file may take several tries, or you may have to try again at another time.

Chatting in mIRC

There are dozens of IRC programs to choose from, but mIRC is one of the best. mIRC not only automates most IRC commands, but it also brings information to your fingertips quickly and conveniently. Versions are available for Windows 98/95, Windows NT, and Windows 3.1 (not for the Macintosh). This section describes mIRC version 5.41, but new versions appear frequently.

Getting mIRC

You can download mIRC from several Web sites, including TUCOWS (**http://www.tucows.com**), the Consummate Winsock Applications List (**http://cws.internet.com**), or mIRC's Web site (**http://www.mirc.co.uk**; see Chapter 38 for details). mIRC is shareware; if you decide to use the program, you need to register it and pay the small registration fee ($15 as of late 1998).

After you download and install mIRC, the program prompts you to configure it with your personal information and preferences, including your e-mail address and preferred nickname. Until you register the program, you see a dialog box about the program's author each time that you start mIRC; click anywhere in the dialog box to proceed.

Connecting to an IRC Server

After you complete your setup information, choose a server from the list in the mIRC Setup dialog box (shown in Figure 15-1) and click the Connect to IRC Server button. mIRC tries to connect you to that server. (You can display the mIRC Setup dialog box at any time by choosing File | Setup, clicking the Setup Info button on the toolbar, or pressing CTRL-E.)

After you establish a connection, a status window opens and information scrolls by about the server to which you connected, the net, and general IRC information. The status window in mIRC shows the activity for the server to which you are connected. In the input box at the bottom of that window, you can type commands to the server. Better yet, click buttons on the mIRC toolbar to give commands.

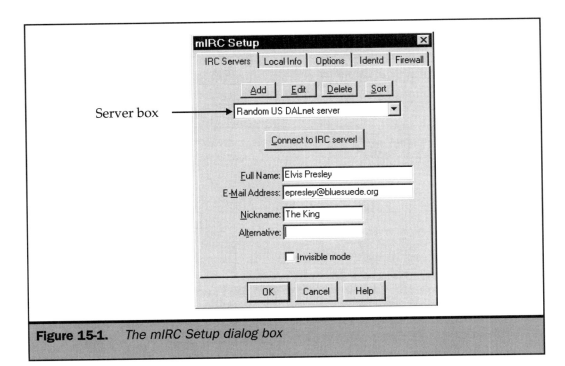

Figure 15-1.   *The mIRC Setup dialog box*

Listing Channels

When you connect to an IRC server, mIRC displays the mIRC Channels Folder dialog box. (see Figure 15-2). You can see this window at any time by clicking the Channels Folder button on the toolbar.

You can also find channels that have either specific text in the channel topic or a designated range of the number of participants. Click the List Channels button on the toolbar to display the List Channels dialog box, in which you can specify the types of channels that you want to see. Then, type the text that must appear in the channel topic, or specify the minimum or maximum number of people in the channel. When you click the Get List button, mIRC displays a window that contains a list of the channels that meet your criteria.

Joining Channels

The easiest way to join a channel is to click the Channels Folder button on the toolbar, choose the channel from the list, and click Join. If you have a listing of channels that meet specific criteria, you can double-click a channel on the list to join that channel. A new window opens for the channel, as shown in Figure 15-3. At the right side of the window is a list of the people in the channel.

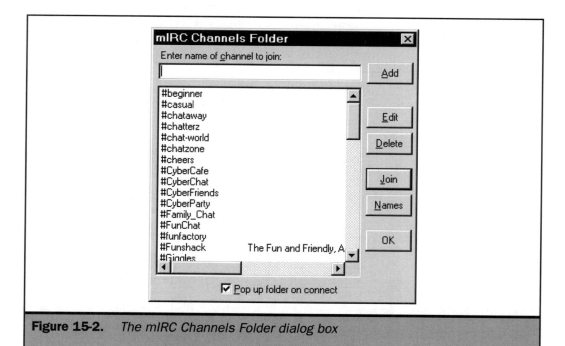

Figure 15-2. The mIRC Channels Folder dialog box

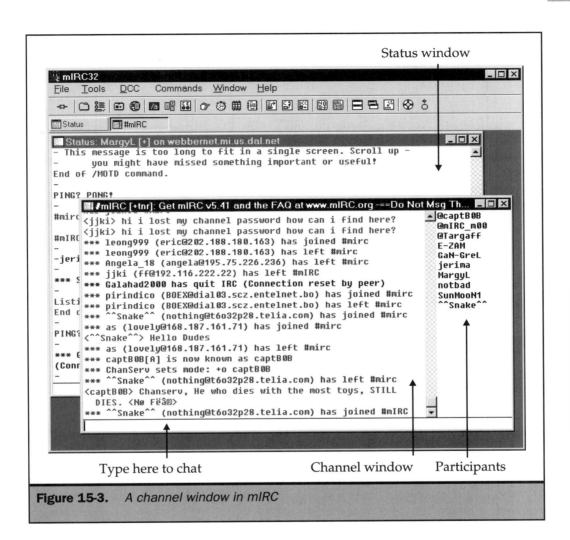

Figure 15-3. *A channel window in mIRC*

Tip   *You can join several channels simultaneously. Display the mIRC Channels Folder again and select another channel. Each channel appears in its own window. Below the toolbar, a row of buttons appears, one button for each open window in mIRC (including the status window). You can click these buttons to select that channel's window.*

Starting to Chat

Once you're in the channel of your choice, you can start chatting. Just type your message in the box at the bottom of the channel window and press ENTER. Within a few seconds, your message appears for everyone on the channel to see, preceded by your nickname in angle brackets. For example, if your nickname is katy and you type "How do you all like mIRC?" everyone in the channel sees:

```
<katy> How do you all like mIRC?
```

You also see reports of people entering and leaving the channel and other events. These lines are preceded by asterisks.

Text messages can seem emotionless. To change the tone of the messages that you send, you can send *actions*, which let you "perform" rather than talk. For instance, instead of sending the message "I'm chuckling," which would appear preceded by your nickname, you can send this message as an action. Type the action command **/me**, followed by the action that you are taking. For example, if you type **/me is chuckling**, then everyone in the channel sees this:

```
katy is chuckling
```

In mIRC, actions appear in a different colored text than normal text.

Whispering

You can carry on a private conversation with someone that you meet in a channel, so that other channel participants don't see your exchange. Some call this *whispering*, some call it *querying*, and others call it *private messaging*. No matter what you call it, there are several ways to initiate private chats with others.

One way to whisper with someone is to double-click the person's name in the list on the right side of the channel window. A separate window appears:

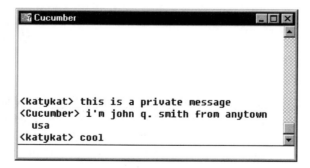

In the input box at the bottom of this new window, type the message that you want to send privately to that user and then press ENTER. The other person's replies appear in this window, too.

DCC (described earlier in this chapter) is another way to carry on private chats. Click a name on the list of channel participants, right-click to see a menu, and then choose DCC | Chat from the menu that appears. A DCC Chat window appears in which you can type messages to each other. An advantage to using DCC is that if a netsplit happens, you two can still chat with each other even if your servers can't communicate.

Sending Files

To send a file (perhaps a picture of yourself or your family) to another user, follow these steps:

1. In the list of channel participants, click the name of the person to whom you want to send the file. The name appears highlighted.

2. Right-click the name and choose DCC | Send from the menu that appears. You see the mIRC DCC Send dialog box.

3. Select the file and click Send. mIRC sends the file to the other IRC user.

You can also start sending a file by clicking the DCC Send button in the toolbar. When you see the mIRC DCC Send dialog box, set the Nick box to the nickname of the person to whom you want to send the file.

Leaving Channels and Disconnecting from Servers

To leave a channel, click the Close button (X) in the upper-right corner of the channel window. To disconnect from the server, click the Disconnect from IRC Server button on the toolbar.

mIRC Tips

Here are a few more tips for chatting by using mIRC:

■ Choose File | Options (or press ALT+O) to see the mIRC Options dialog box with the multitude of options that you can set. In particular, click the IRC Switches tab and make sure that the on Auto-Join on Invite option is not selected. Otherwise, you may accidentally join channels that you would never go to on your own.

■ You can change the colors of the messages that you send. Press CTRL+K to see the mIRC Colour Index dialog box, and then click the color that you want to use for your messages. The colors don't appear until your message is sent; instead, you see codes to mIRC and other IRC programs indicating what color to use for the text that you typed. You can also press CTRL+U to underline text and CTRL+B to make text bold.

For instructions to create your own channel or help manage an existing channel, see "Starting and Managing a Channel," later in this chapter.

CHATTING AND CONFERENCING ON THE INTERNET

Chatting in Microsoft Chat and V-Chat

Microsoft offers you two IRC programs: Microsoft Chat (or Microsoft Comic Chat) and V-Chat. Microsoft also runs an IRC server at **mschat.msn.com**. Both programs work with the Microsoft IRC server and with all the standard IRC nets.

Microsoft Chat lets you choose a comic-strip character to represent you. The messages in the IRC channel appear as a comic strip, showing the participants in the conversation as comic-strip characters, with their messages in word balloons. Figure 15-4 is an example of a channel in Microsoft Chat. (This section describes Microsoft Chat version 2.5.)

V-Chat is a 3-D chat program that lets you use 3-D *avatars* (pictures) to represent you, as shown in Figure 15-5. V-Chat offers several standard avatars, or you can create your own. This section describes V-Chat version 2.

Getting Microsoft Chat and V-Chat

Microsoft Chat comes with Windows 98, and you can download it from Microsoft's Web site either as part of Internet Explorer or as a separate program. V-Chat is also available from Microsoft's Web site. For either program, see **http://www.microsoft.com/windows/ie/chat** for information and downloading. See Chapter 38 for details about downloading and installing programs from the Internet. These programs run under Windows 98/95 and Windows NT. Versions are not available for Windows 3.1 or Macintosh. After you

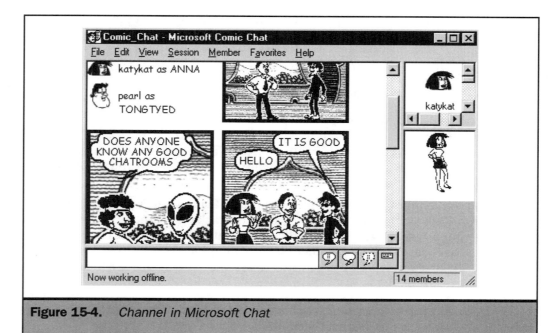

Figure 15-4. *Channel in Microsoft Chat*

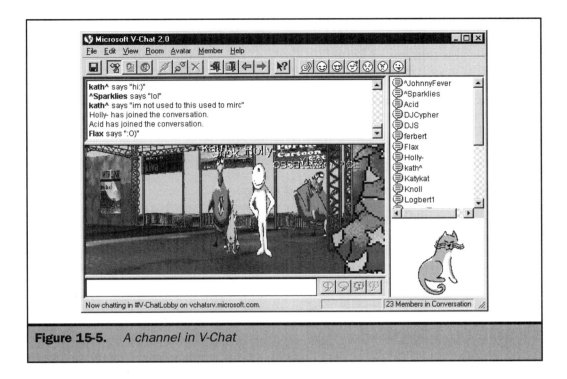

Figure 15-5.   *A channel in V-Chat*

download either of these programs, install and configured it with your preferred nickname and list of servers.

Connecting

When you start either Microsoft Chat or V-Chat, it automatically locates and connects you to the first available network server on its list of servers. Then, you're ready to join a channel and begin chatting.

Listing Channels

With both Microsoft Chat and V-Chat, after you connect to a server, you see a dialog box that lets you choose the channel (or *chat environment,* as it's called in V-Chat). The nets that these two programs connect to are small, and the number of channels or environments available is limited.

Joining Channels and Chatting

To join a channel, simply choose the chat room or environment from the list and either double-click or click the Go To button. Once you're in the channel, type your message and then press the ENTER key, as you do in other chat programs. To create your own channel, see "Starting and Managing a Channel," later in this chapter.

Whispering

When you want to whisper (send a private message) to someone, select their name from the list and click the Whisper button on the toolbar. Then, type your message and press ENTER.

Actions

Microsoft Chat and V-Chat both give you a few options for indicating actions. With either of these programs, select one of the word balloon types: Say, Action, or Think. Then, type your message and press ENTER.

Both programs also offer ways to change the facial expressions of your character representations. With Microsoft Chat, you can choose from a wheel of various expressions. In V-Chat you click one of the face buttons on the toolbar. Select the facial expression option before you type your message.

Chatting in Ircle

There are a few good Mac IRC programs, and one of the best is Ircle. You can download the program from the Mac Orchard (**http://www.macorchard.com**) or Ircle's Web site (**http://www.ircle.com**). This chapter describes version 3 of Ircle.

 You can issue the most frequently used IRC commands by choosing commands from the Command menu. But keep in mind that these shortcuts merely paste the command into the input line. They save you the time and effort of typing the commands yourself.

Connecting

Ircle displays several windows: one window for status information, one for the current users' list, one for DCC status, and a few others. You first need to connect to an IRC server. Choose File | Open Connection or Window | Connections from the menu if you don't already see the Connection window, shown here:

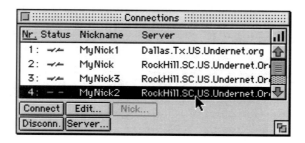

In the Connections window, set your nickname and server preferences. Choose a server, click Edit to set your nickname and preferences in the Connection Preferences window, and then click OK. Click Connect when you are ready to connect to the server.

Listing Channels

After you connect to an IRC server, you see a main message window, which has your nickname in the title bar. To see a list of channels, choose Command | List from the menu, or type **/list** and press RETURN. You can also type the **/list** command with one of the specific minimum, maximum, or public parameters. (See the section "Listing Channels in Ircii," later in this chapter, for details about the **/list** command.)

Joining a Channel and Chatting

To join a channel, choose Command | Join from the menu, or type **/join #***channelname* (replacing *channelname* with the name of the channel that you want to join). A channel window appears with the topic in its title bar (shown in Figure 15-6). In the Inputline box in this window, type messages that you want to send to everyone in the channel. When you press RETURN, your message appears in the chat channel window for the other users to see. To create your own channel, see "Starting and Managing a Channel," later in this chapter.

CHATTING AND
CONFERENCING ON
THE INTERNET

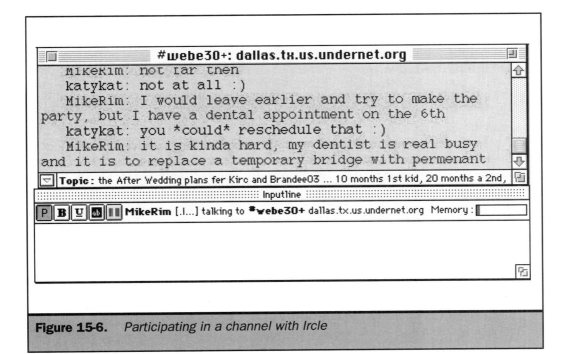

Figure 15-6. *Participating in a channel with Ircle*

Whispering

If you want to chat privately with a user, type **/query** *nickname* (replacing *nickname* with the nickname of the person you want to chat with) or double-click the Query button. Ircle opens a new window. All private messages to and from this user appear in this window.

Remember that the destination of your messages is determined by the window in which you type them. After you open windows in which you are chatting with people, you can press TAB to cycle among the people with whom you are chatting. Pressing TAB automatically sets the input line to **/msg** (the IRC command to send a private message), followed by the nickname of the person who last sent you a message.

Leaving Channels

To leave a channel, either close the channel's window or press COMMAND+W to close the window and leave the channel.

Chatting in Ircii

Ircii is a UNIX chat program that predates the Windows and Mac programs described earlier in this chapter. If you have a UNIX shell account (described in Chapter 40), ircii is the best chat program available. If you see an error when you try to run ircii, try running irc instead (an older version).

Ircii is a text-based program, with no menus or toolbars. You use IRC commands to list channels, join channels, perform actions—everything but send messages after you are in a channel (for which no command is needed). Remember that all IRC commands begin with a forward slash (/).

Starting Ircii

To run ircii, type **ircii** or **irc** at the UNIX shell prompt (you must type this command in lowercase). If you don't want to use your UNIX username as your nickname, type **ircii** *nickname* or **irc** *nickname* (replacing *nickname* with your proposed nickname). Ircii displays its prompt, which usually is an angle bracket (>), to indicate that it is waiting for you to type a command.

Connecting to a Server

Ircii has no built-in menu of IRC servers, so you need to have a list of servers handy to refer to. For information about networks and servers, use a Web browser to start at Yahoo! (**http://www.yahoo.com**) and choose Computers and Internet | Internet | Chat | IRC | Networks. Or, you can start at one of the Web pages for the major IRC networks, listed in the section "IRC Networks," at the beginning of this chapter.

To connect to an IRC server, type **/server** *servername* (replacing *servername* with the name of an IRC server). For example, to connect to an UnderNet server in New Jersey, you can type

/server newbrunswick.nj.us.undernet.org

If someone using your nickname is already connected to the server, ircii prompts you for a different nickname. When you connect, you see the server's welcome message.

Listing Channels in Ircii

Once you're connected to a server, type **/list** to see a list of channels. This list may be so long that most of it flies off the top of the screen before you have a chance to read it. To make the list shorter and eliminate the channels that have only one or two people, you can specify the minimum and maximum number of users on a channel. Type the following:

/list -min #, -max #

Replace # with a number. To limit your search to channels with a minimum of five users and a maximum of ten users, for example, type the following:

/list -min 5, -max 10

Joining Channels and Chatting

To join a channel, type **/join #***channelname* (replacing *channelname* with the name of a channel). Ircii displays a list of the participants in the channel, followed by messages from that channel as they are sent. If the channel didn't exist, you just created it (see "Starting and Managing a Channel," later in this chapter). Ircii lets you join only one channel at a time; when you join a new channel, you leave the channel that you previously were in.

To send a message, type the message and then press ENTER. Figure 15-7 shows the discussion in a channel. Messages from channel participants appear preceded by the sender's name enclosed in angle brackets, like this:

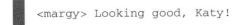

```
<margy> Looking good, Katy!
```

Messages from the IRC server, usually indicating who is joining or leaving the channel, appear preceded by asterisks.

Tip	*To see a list of the participants in the channel, type* **/who** *channelname* (*replacing channelname with the name of a channel*).

```
    chance this year. (And Happy Birthday, Chris-O!)
*** #cuseemeki 11      C13Visit C12http://hightec.com/heaven/index.html C13for
    info on joining our group
*** #sex_sites 21      <?> OPEN <?>     [ List status: 722 working sites
    |Goodlist:392|Bestlist:330| ]
*** margy (~margy@cuseemeki.com) has joined channel #cornwall
*** Topic for #cornwall: bitchland
*** #cornwall W 907005186
*** Users on #cornwall: margy Angie__ Wookster peachyZ @amjoel Gap_Girl
    Christin- canagirl Peachy- @Damnir @notjoel @AlCoHoLiC Recoil @W
*** #cornwall 865791359
<Angie__> I think he is a nice guy!!!
<notjoel> yep... he might summon his demon hordes to eat us
<AlCoHoLiC> I also got a nice buzz going here, so dont mind me.
* peachyZ everybody join 3nick
<AlCoHoLiC> LoL
*** peachyZ has been kicked off channel #cornwall by AlCoHoLiC (DONT
    ADVERTISE!)
<Damnir> PEACHYZ hurry up
*** skitz has joined channel #CORNWALL
<notjoel> hi skitz
*** peachyZ has joined channel #cornwall
[1] margy on #cornwall (+nt) [Mail: 5]
#cornwall>
```

Figure 15-7.   *ircii showing an IRC channel*

Whispering

When you want to send a private message or whisper to another user, type **/msg**
nickname (replacing *nickname* with the person's nickname), followed by the message
that you want to whisper. Because ircii can't display windows, you don't get a separate
private message window. Your private messages appear in your chat channel window,
preceded by stars, like this:

```
**jimbo hi there!
```

  *Make sure that you type the /msg command before any message that you want to send
privately. Otherwise, your private message will appear in the channel that you have joined.*

To initiate a DCC chat session with another user, type **/dcc chat**, followed by the
person's nickname. Messages from the DCC session appear in ircii preceded by the
sender's name enclosed in equal signs, such as the following:

```
=margyL= Can you believe how vacuous this conversation is?
```

After you establish a DCC session with someone, send messages to them by typing
/msg =*nickname* (replacing *nickname* with the person's nickname), followed on the
same line by the message that you want to send to that person. The equal sign before
the recipient's nickname indicates that this message should be sent via the existing
DCC connection.

To close the DCC connection, type **/dcc close chat**, followed by the nickname of the person with whom you were chatting.

Actions

When you want to send an action statement to the channel, type the command **/me**, followed by your action statement. For instance, if you type **/me does a happy dance** and your nickname is *katy*, then everyone in the channel sees this line:

```
katy does a happy dance
```

Sending Files

When you want to send a file to another user, type this command:

/dcc send *nickname pathname*

Replace *nickname* with the person's nickname, and *pathname* with the pathname of the file on your computer. For example, to send a picture to joebob, the command would look like this:

/dcc send joebob c:\gifs\katy.gif

To receive a file that someone is trying to send you, type this command:

/dcc get *nickname filename*

Replace *nickname* with the nickname of the person who is sending you a file, and *filename* with the name that you want to give the file when it arrives on your computer.

Leaving Channels

When you're ready to leave a channel, type **/leave #***channelname* or **/part #***channelname* (replacing *channelname* with the name of a channel). To leave ircii, type **/bye** or **/exit**.

Starting and Managing a Channel

Regardless of which IRC program you use, you can start your own channel rather than join an existing channel. Simply join a channel with a new channel name. Before you join the channel, make sure that a channel with that name doesn't already exist. One way to check for the existence of a channel name is to type the command **/who #***channelname* (replacing *channelname* with the name that you want to create), which lists the participants in a channel: if you get an error message or no response, no channel by that name exists.

After you create the new channel, you are the first (and only) person in it. When you create your own channel, you are the channel operator (chanop), by default. With this power, you can perform chanop commands, such as changing the status of a user on your channel, changing or setting the topic and channel mode, and kicking and/or banning users on your channel. Some of these commands are described in this section.

Many chanop commands are forms of the **/mode** command, which change the characteristics of the channel or another person on the channel.

Setting the Topic

To set the topic for your new channel (the line that describes what the channel is about), type **/topic**, followed by a phrase that describes your intended subject or audience. Unless you plan ahead to meet specific people in your new channel at a specific time, you may have to wait a while for people to join your channel.

Kicking and Banning Users

An inevitable fact of life on IRC is the presence of annoying and abusive personalities. But you don't have to put up with this behavior. You can kick these people out of your channel and ban them from coming back, if necessary.

In mIRC this is easy to do. Highlight the person's nickname in the list of channel participants, right-click the name, and choose either Control | Kick or Control | Ban. In other programs, type **/kick #*channelname nickname*.** For example, to kick joebob out of the #webe30+ channel, you would type:

/kick #webe30+ joebob

Kicking someone out of your channel doesn't prevent that person from rejoining. If someone is persistently bothersome, you can *ban* the person for good by typing this command:

/mode #*channelname* +b *nickname*

For example, to ban joebob from the #webe30+ channel, you would type this command:

/mode #webe30+ +b joebob

Tip *If you want to ban someone from your channel, it is better to ban them before you kick them out. Many users have their programs set up to rejoin a channel automatically after they are kicked from a channel. If you don't ban them first, they can often slip back into your channel before the ban has a chance to take effect.*

Designating Other Chanops

If you are a chanop, you can designate other people as chanops. Every channel should have at least one chanop, so don't leave a channel that you create without creating a chanop to take your place. To make someone a chanop, type this command:

/mode #*channelname* +o *nickname*

That's the lowercase letter *o*, not a zero. To take away chanop status, replace **+o** with **-o** in the **/mode** command.

 It is wise to give chanop status only to people that you know. Some people like nothing better than causing trouble for others by coming to a channel, getting chanop status, and then kicking everyone off the channel.

Other Chanop Commands

Here are some other commands that channel operators can use to control how a channel works:

- ■ **/mode #***channelname* **+m**   Makes the channel moderated, so that only chanops can send messages. This feature is great if you have a guest speaker or use the channel as a classroom: the speakers can talk without interruptions.

- ■ **/mode #***channelname* **+I**   Marks the channel as by-invitation only, which means that no one can join that channel unless they are invited first. To invite someone into your channel, type **/invite** *nickname channelname*.

- ■ **/mode #***channelname* **+p**   Marks the channel as private, which prevents it from appearing on a channels list.

General IRC Tips

Here are some tips and warnings to make your time on IRC more productive, pleasant, and safe:

- ■ When you join a large channel, you may have trouble keeping up with the conversation, because it scrolls by rather quickly. Try concentrating on the comments of just one or two people, ignoring the rest.

- ■ IRC is not case-sensitive; that is, capitalization doesn't matter when you type IRC commands.

- With the larger nets, requesting a list of channels can disconnect you from your server. These lists are so long that some servers see them as *floods* (excessive lines of text being generated by one user).

- If you log on with a nickname that is already in use, the system notifies you. For example, you occasionally may need to change servers due to lag. If you use the same nickname on both servers, when the first server catches up to the second server, you experience *nick collision*—the same nickname in use on two different servers. When this happens, you are disconnected from your server. Simply log back on with a different nickname until your old nickname disappears.

- When you send a private message (whisper) by using the **/msg** command, your message may appear in your main channel window, but with the sender's name enclosed in asterisks. Don't be alarmed. You are the only one who can see your private message.

- If you have a slow connection with your provider, you may experience lag or other problems when holding private chats via DCC.

- To find out more about someone, you can type **/whois** *nickname* (replacing *nickname* with the person's nickname). It's a good idea to try this on your own nickname, to see what other people can find out about you!

- Refer to Chapter 11 for more warnings about etiquette and safety when chatting.

Learning More

Any of the programs described in this chapter can give you hours of enjoyment on IRC. While this isn't a comprehensive guide to IRC, it is a starting point. If you want to learn more, check out Kathryn Toyer's books about IRC, *Learn Internet Relay Chat*, Second Edition, or *Learn Advanced Internet Relay Chat*, both published by Wordware Publishing (Plano, TX, 1998). There are also many Web sites about IRC, and many channels have their own Web sites. Start at the Web site for the IRC net that you use (see "IRC Networks," at the beginning of this chapter) or the Web site **http://net.gurus.com/irc**.

The
Complete
Reference

Chapter 16

Other Types of Chat

Y ou can find a variety of chat forms other than those covered in the last four chapters, as people are continuously developing new ways to communicate by using Internet technology. This chapter describes some of the other ways of chatting—besides mailing lists (described in Chapter 12), Usenet newsgroups (explained in Chapters 13 and 14), and IRC (discussed in Chapter 15). Each type of online chat has unique features and qualities that distinguish it from the others; these types include:

- Web-based chat, both interactive and bulletin-board style chat, accessible via your Web browser

- Direct chat systems, which enable you to send instant messages to online friends

- MUDs, MOOs, and MUSHes, virtual worlds for game playing or socializing

Web-Based Chat

A Web site is often more than simply something to look at or a resource to use; many Web site operators want to provide their users with a community that encourages them to be part of the experience. Web-based chat systems fill this goal, building an online network of people who interact not just with the Web page, but with other users as well.

Web-based chat is accessed through your Web browser (see Chapter 18). In many cases, you may need to enable ActiveX, Java, or JavaScript, or download a plug-in or ActiveX control; these procedures are described in Chapter 22. For a list of some good Web-based chat sites, see the section "Online Communities and Home Pages" in Chapter 25.

Chat on a Web site usually falls into either of two broad types—interactive, immediate chatting that is much like IRC, or threaded discussion boards that are similar to Usenet newsgroups or mailing lists. Unlike IRC or Usenet, no standardized rules exist for how Web chat should look or be used; each new Web site that you visit could present another new system to learn. Fortunately, chatting on the Web is very simple—easier than using an IRC program or newsreader—so learning the basics will enable you to adapt to any system that a Web site operator might provide.

Interactive Web Chat

Web sites that enable you to converse directly with other Web users—in a manner similar to IRC—are providing *interactive Web chat*. Usually, these sites are referred to as *chat rooms*, a concept popularized by America Online. However, America Online chat rooms can be used only by AOL users, whereas anyone on the Internet with the right software can access a Web-based chatting system.

You can find two main categories of interactive chat systems. Some are basically textual in nature—you type something, and what you type appears on the screens of people around the world who are connected to the same site. Others use graphics and even 3-D animation to provide you with a visual *avatar*—your online representation in the chat room, which interacts with other users' avatars as you send and receive messages.

Most chat rooms are written in Java, a computer language that enables programs to be distributed and run over the Internet. To access a Java-based chat room, you need to use a Web browser that can run Java applications, and you must configure it to do so (see Chapter 22 for more information). Other chat sites use auto-loading HTML pages, so that your Web browser doesn't need any extra software. Some chat sites offer both options. Avatar-based chat rooms may require you to install special programs on your computer, to control your avatar.

Text-based chat rooms are very much like IRC (see Chapter 15). You use your Web browser to connect to the Web site, choose a handle, and see the messages in the chat room; when you type messages, anyone using the same chat room can read what you type. For example, Figure 16-1 shows the Yahoo! Chat site at **http://chat.yahoo.com**. This Web site provides all the options previously mentioned: a choice between Java or HTML interfaces, multiple chat rooms, private messages, and room creation.

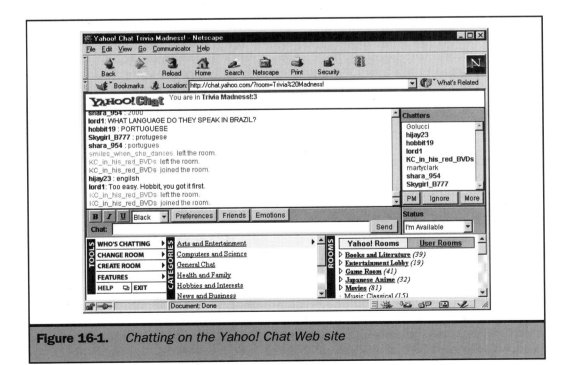

Figure 16-1.   *Chatting on the Yahoo! Chat Web site*

Web Discussion Boards

An alternative to a real-time chat room is a *Web discussion board*, or *Web forum*. Web boards function like Usenet newsgroups or mailing lists—you can read messages, reply to them, and post your own thoughts. A Web board enables any number of people to participate, without having to be online at the same time; the drawback is that discussions are slower than live chatting.

Most Web discussion boards don't require any special software to use them; a normal Web browser is sufficient. Registration is sometimes required to participate on a Web forum, which means that you may have to provide your name and e-mail address to the board operator before you can post messages.

Direct Chat Systems

At times, using the Internet can be a very solitary experience. You're online, you're using the Web or checking your e-mail, but you have no idea whether anyone else is out there. Wouldn't it be nice if you could know when your friends are online, and had an easy way to get in touch with them?

That's what direct chat systems do—they let you keep a list of contacts, in the form of a "buddy list," and when one of your contacts logs on, you're notified. You can then send them messages, chat interactively, e-mail them, or even transmit files directly from your computer to theirs.

Several direct chat programs are popular, including ICQ, AOL Instant Messenger, Yahoo! Pager, and Ding!. Unfortunately, these programs don't work together; if you're using ICQ, you can keep tabs only on your other friends who are using ICQ. If your friend uses AOL Instant Messenger only, then you can't communicate unless you use AOL Instant Messenger, too. ICQ is the most widely used direct chat program.

ICQ

With over 20 million enrolled users, ICQ (pronounced *I seek you*) program is the leader in direct messaging systems. ICQ (from ICQ Inc., formerly Mirabilis) was the first publicly available system to offer buddy lists and instant messages, and it has kept its lead so far as one of the most popular programs on the Internet. ICQ enables you to talk with one other friend or join IRC-style group chats on a variety of subjects. The ICQ Web site lists available topics.

Each ICQ user is issued a number, usually seven or eight-digits long, such as 780498 or 20230642. These ICQ numbers work similarly to telephone numbers: if you want to check whether someone is online or contact someone on ICQ, you need the person's number. ICQ users often include their ICQ numbers in e-mail messages or on their Web pages. ICQ Inc. provides an online database that you can use to look up your friends and associates; individual users can control what information is revealed to the public. A list of users, grouped by interests, is also available, if you're seeking a new friend. You add to your contact list the ICQ numbers of people with whom you want to talk.

Installing ICQ

To download and install ICQ, go to its Web site at **http://www.icq.com**, find the Download link amid the amazing clutter on the page, and follow the instructions. (Chapter 38 describes how to download software from the Web.) The ICQ program is available for Windows 98/95, Windows NT, Windows 3.1, and Mac, along with a Java version that can run on other systems.

After you download the installation file, be sure that your computer is connected to the Internet before you run the installation program. Then, run the program either by choosing Start I Programs I Mirabilis ICQ I ICQ or by clicking the ICQ icon that appears on the screen.

The ICQ program first runs the ICQ Registration Wizard, to help you sign up for an ICQ number. You don't have to enter all the personal information that the Wizard asks for: in fact, only your name and e-mail address are necessary. After you sign up for your ICQ number, the ICQ program starts.

The ICQ program is designed to run all the time, so that whenever someone wants to contact you, the program can alert you. An ICQ flower icon appears in the system tray of the Windows Taskbar: the icon is green when ICQ is online and red when it's offline. When you double-click the icon, you see the ICQ window, shown in Figure 16-2. When you are done using ICQ, minimize it, and it appears only as a flower on the system tray.

ICQ knows when you are connected to the Internet and when you are using ICQ. If you don't use it for a while (usually 10 minutes), ICQ decides that you are offline and lets other users know that you won't respond until you get back and pick up your messages.

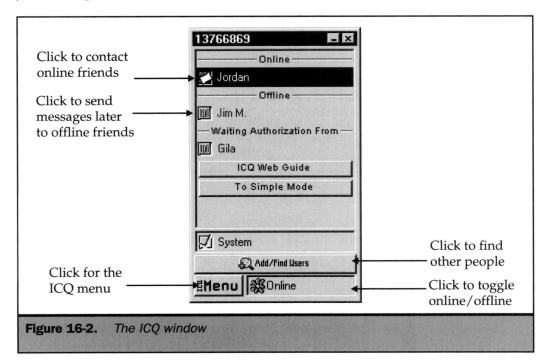

Figure 16-2.   *The ICQ window*

CHATTING AND CONFERENCING ON THE INTERNET

When you receive a message, click the flashing indicator on the ICQ window and choose Receive to read it. You receive an ICQ system message when you start ICQ for the first time, so that you can read information about how it works.

Finding People on ICQ

Before you can use ICQ, you need someone to talk to. The Contact List Wizard, which runs automatically when you start ICQ for the first time, helps you to find people you know (see Figure 16-3). You can run this Wizard any time by clicking the Add/Find Users button on the ICQ window and then choosing Main Search from the window that appears.

The most reliable way to find people is by e-mail address, although you can also search by name. Type some identifying information into the Contact List Wizard window and click Next. If ICQ finds a person who matches what you typed, it displays the person's name and ICQ number. If this information appears to be for the right person, click the person's entry and then click Next to add the entry to your contact list—your list of people you want to talk to. Whenever this person connects to the Internet and runs the ICQ program while you are online, the person's name appears in the Contact List in the ICQ window.

If ICQ couldn't find your friend, it says so and gives you the option of sending the person an e-mail extolling the virtues of ICQ and inviting him or her to get it.

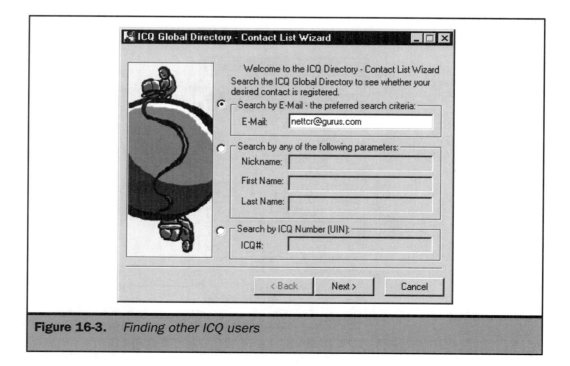

Figure 16-3. *Finding other ICQ users*

Some people have ICQ configured so that they have to approve before you can add them to your contact list. When you try to add those people to your contact list, ICQ asks you to type a message to the person explaining why you'd like to be able to talk to them. (If it's a friend, you can type something like, "Hey, it's me!") When the person approves, you receive a system message from ICQ: click the blinking System icon to read the message.

If you want to prevent people whom you don't know from adding you to their contact lists, you can tell ICQ that you want to approve such requests. Follow these steps:

1. Click the To Advanced Mode button in the middle of the ICQ window to switch from Simple Mode (for beginners). On the window that appears, click Switch to Advanced Mode.

2. Click the ICQ Menu button in the lower-left corner of the ICQ window and choose Security & Privacy from the menu that appears. You see the Security window.

3. On the Security tab, click the My Authorization Is Required option (if it's not already selected).

4. Click Save.

Sending Messages with ICQ

To send a message, double-click the ICQ icon to display the ICQ window (refer to Figure 16-2). The Online part of the ICQ window lists the people on your contact list who are online right now. The Offline part lists your friends who aren't on the Internet right now, or who don't have their ICQ program loaded.

Double-click the person on your contact list to whom you'd like to send a message, or click the entry once and choose Message from the menu that appears. If the person is online, you see the Send Online Message dialog box, shown in Figure 16-4. Type your

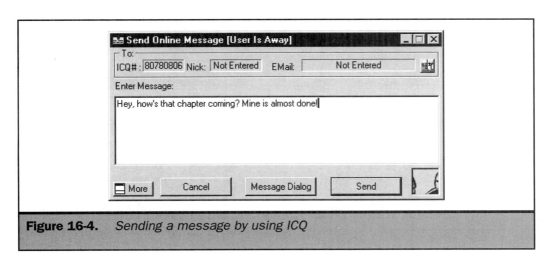

Figure 16-4.   *Sending a message by using ICQ*

message in the Enter Message box and then click the Send button. The message appears on the other person's computer within seconds. If the person whose name you right-clicked is offline, ICQ can hold your message until the person connects.

When someone sends you a message, the ICQ icon in your system tray blinks, or if the ICQ window is already open, the icon to the left of the person's name blinks. Click the icon and choose Receive to see the message.

If you want to have a conversation with someone, you can start an ICQ chat. Click the person's name in your ICQ window and choose ICQ Chat from the menu that appears. When you see the Send Online Chat Request dialog box, type a message to your prospective chat partner in the Enter Chat Subject box and then click the Chat button. If the user is online, he or she gets the message right away; otherwise, ICQ delivers it as soon as the person clicks the blinking ICQ icon. If the other person accepts your chat request by clicking Accept, the ICQ program on both computers sets up a chat window. You can choose whether to chat *IRC style*, with your messages interspersed, or *split-window mode* (shown in Figure 16-5), in which your messages are displayed in one part of the window and the other person's messages are displayed in the other part of the window. As you type messages, they appear character by character on the other person's screen. When you are done chatting, say goodbye and close the ICQ chat window.

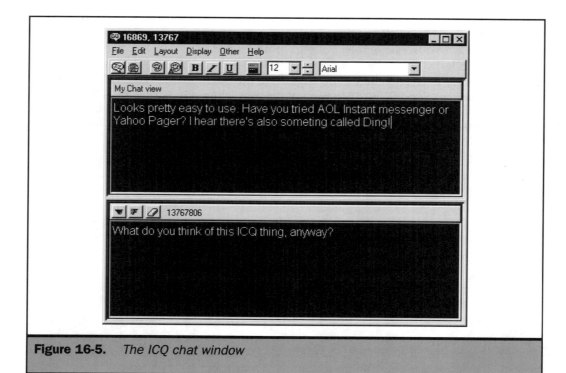

Figure 16-5. *The ICQ chat window*

Other ICQ Features

ICQ can do lots of other things, including voice telephony, file transfer, group chats, and collaborative browsing, in which a group of people can look at Web sites together. For instructions, go to the ICQ Web page and click one of the many links that offer more information about the program.

AOL Instant Messenger (AIM)

AOL Instant Messenger does less than ICQ, concentrating on enabling two people to chat. But AIM has one advantage over all other direct chat systems: it connects to AOL's own messaging system, so that all AOL users are accessible. In fact, AOL users don't even have to sign up for or install AIM, because their AOL software handles it.

Installing AOL Instant Messenger

You may already have AIM, because it comes with many other programs. If you have installed a recent version of Netscape Communicator, Eudora Pro, or many other Internet programs, AIM may have been installed, too. Choose Start | Programs | Netscape Communicator, for example, and you may find an AOL Instant Messenger command there.

If you don't see AIM on your system, you can download it from the following site: **http://www.newaol.com/aim**. See Chapter 38 for information about downloading and installing software. AIM is available for Windows 98/95, Windows NT, Windows 3.1, and the Mac, along with a Java version that can run on other systems.

AIM usually runs all the time, so that whenever someone sends you a message, or one of your friends goes online, the program alerts you. The AIM Sign On window looks like Figure 16-6. The first time that you run AIM, it runs your Web browser and displays an AOL Web page that enables you to sign up for a user name. If you have an AOL account, you can use your existing AOL screen name and password. Otherwise, choose a name—and be creative, because the existing 20 million AOL users have already claimed all the good ones. Make sure that you enter your e-mail address correctly, because AIM sends you an e-mail message to the address that you provide, and if you don't reply to the message, you lose your AIM user name.

To start using AIM, double-click the AIM icon (a person running) in the system tray of the Windows Taskbar. When you see the Sign On window, type your user name and password and click Sign On. AIM signs you on to its central server computer and displays your Buddy List window, shown in Figure 16-7. Like the ICQ contacts list, your buddy list shows the people you want to talk to. AIM alerts you when these people sign on to AIM.

Finding People on AOL Instant Messenger

The Buddy List window has two tabs, one to set up the buddy list (the List Setup tab) and one to see which of your buddies is online. To add someone to your list, click the

Figure 16-6. The AOL Instant Messenger (AIM) Sign On window

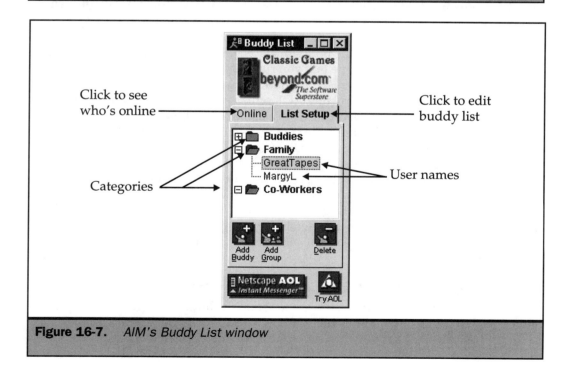

Figure 16-7. AIM's Buddy List window

List Setup tab, click the Add Buddy button, and then type the person's AOL screen name or AIM user name. You can add as many people as you want to add. AOL users can set up a buddy list by going to the keyword BUDDYLIST.

If you don't know someone's AIM user name or AOL screen name, click the Menu or Netscape AOL Instant Messenger button in the lower-left corner of the Buddy List window and choose Find a Buddy | By E-mail Address from the list that appears. Type the e-mail address of your friend, click Next, and follow the directions in the window.

Sending Instant Messages

To send a message (AOL calls it an *Instant Message*) to someone on your buddy list, click the Online tab of the Buddy List window. The list shows only those people who are currently online and running either the AOL software or AIM. The numbers for each category of friend (buddy, family, or coworker) show the number of people online, followed by the total number of people on that part of your list. If the first number isn't zero, click the plus box to display the people in that category, and double-click a person's entry on your list to send a message to them. AIM displays an Instant Message window, similar to the one shown in Figure 16-8. Type your message and then click Send. After your message is sent, the Instant Message window changes to display the messages to and from your friend in the top part of the window, with a box for you to type new messages in the bottom part of the window.

AOL users can send messages to AIM users by going to the keyword BUDDYVIEW.

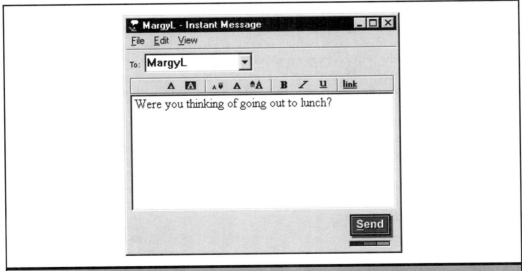

Figure 16-8.   *Sending a message to a buddy by using AIM*

You can set your AIM options by clicking the Setup button on the Sign On window. From the Buddy List, right-click the list. When you see the Preferences window (its name changes as you click its tabs), click the Privacy tab to set options that control who can send you messages.

Yahoo Pager

Yahoo!, the Web portal described in "Portals to the Web" in Chapter 25, has its own direct chat service, called *Yahoo! Pager*. Go to its home page at **http://pager.yahoo.com** to find out about it. Yahoo! Pager comes in two versions:

- **Java**   The Java version runs in your Web browser and downloads automatically when you start to use it. This version runs in any Java-enabled browser, including Netscape Navigator and Internet Explorer, so use this version if you have Windows 3.1, UNIX, or a Mac. You can control whether your Web browser runs Java programs (for Netscape Navigator, see "Managing Java and JavaScript" in Chapter 19; for Internet Explorer, see "Managing Java and JavaScript" in Chapter 20). The Java version of the pager is very confusing to use, because it runs in a special browser window.

- **Windows**   You can download and install a Windows 98/95/NT version of the pager program. Click the link from the Yahoo Pager home page at **http://pager.yahoo.com**. (See Chapter 38 for information about how to download and install programs from the Web.)

Figure 16-9 shows the Windows version of the Yahoo Pager window, with the main window on the right and a message window on the left. Like ICQ and AIM, you sign up for a user name and password, which you verify by replying to an e-mail message. Also, like ICQ and AIM, Yahoo Pager maintains a list (called the *Friend List*) of people you want to talk to. Like AIM, you can put your friends into groups (such as friends, family, and coworkers). To connect to the Yahoo Pager system, choose File | Connect from the opening window. To add someone to your Friend List, click the Add button at the bottom of the Yahoo Pager window. To talk to one of your friends, double-click the person's name on your list

Yahoo Pager can also let you know when e-mail messages arrive in your Yahoo Mail mailbox, when you get responses to your ad in Yahoo Personals, and the current prices of the stocks in your portfolio. For information, see the Yahoo Pager home page at http://pager.yahoo.com.

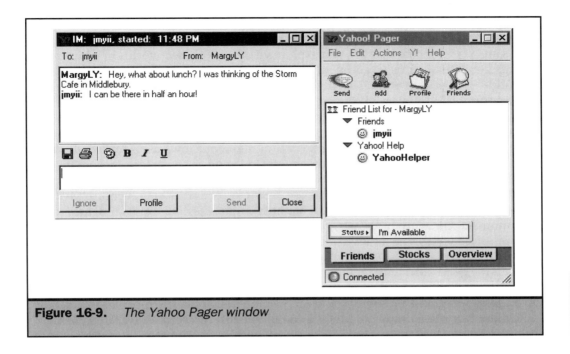

Figure 16-9.   *The Yahoo Pager window*

Ding!

Yet another direct chat service is called Ding!, with a home page at **http://www.ding.com**.
It is similar to other direct chat programs, but Activerse, the creators of Ding!, market it as
a business-productivity tool. The program is free for noncommercial use and $29 for
business users. Activerse also sells the Ding! Switchboard server software (the program
that serves as a switchboard for connections) to larger organizations that want to use
Ding! privately to allow employees to communicate.

Rather than using simple user names, Ding! assigns each person a *WhoDP* that
looks like a URL (Web address). The WhoDP consists of **whodp://** followed by the host
name of the Ding! server, a slash, and a user name. For example, if your user name
were NetTCR, your WhoDP might be whodp://switchboard.ding.com/NetTCR. In
addition to the usual one-to-one messaging and group chat, Ding! also offers file
transfer from one user to another.

MUDs, MOOs, and MUSHes

MUDs are a type of chat that lets you explore virtual, text-based worlds in which you can interact with other users and your environment. The word *MUD* originally stood for *Multi-User Dungeon* and referred to a game in which you braved a dark dungeon to seek adventure, but now MUD encompasses a wide variety of textual worlds, ranging from combat-based adventure MUDs, to online role-playing games, to social/chatting hangouts.

A *MUD server* is an Internet host server program that allows users (called *players*, since MUD terminology reflects its game roots) to log on as characters, explore the rooms that comprise the MUD database, speak to the other players, and interact with objects and programs in the MUD database. Common activities on adventure MUDs include delving deep into the depths of haunted caves, questing for magical artifacts, or hunting ferocious mythic beasts, programmed by experienced players—known as *wizards*—as challenges for other players seeking to win the game.

One branch of the MUD family, known as *TinyMUDs*, is less concerned with winning the game than with telling a good story—or even with just hanging out with some friends. The TinyMUD variants known as MUSHes, MUXes, and MUCKs all have a lesser emphasis on combat, and more emphasis on player-to-player interaction. MOOs, another popular type of MUD, also fall into this category. TinyMUDs are also distinguished by the fact that they generally allow players who aren't wizards to contribute to building parts of the world, a honor that is often reserved only for the most experienced players on adventure MUDs.

To play on a MUD, you need to know the address and have a program that can connect to that address. A *MUD address* consists of an Internet host name (or number) and a port number. Host names (described in "Computers on the Internet" in Chapter 1) may look similar to **muds.idyllmtn.com** or **pern.mccr.org**, or they can be numbers that correspond to a machine's address, such as 206.16.238.103 or 199.2.117.74. Port numbers (described in "Servers, Clients, and Ports" in Chapter 1) are typically four-digit numbers, such as 5000 or 6250. A complete address is in a form similar to **muds.idyllmtn.com port 4201**, which can also be written as a telnet URL, such as **telnet://muds.idyllmtn.com:4201/** (that is, **telnet://** followed by the host name or number, a colon, and the port number).

You can connect to a MUD by telnet or by using a MUD client.

Connecting to a MUD by Telnet

Telnet enables two computers to connect to one another and send commands and information back and forth (see "Logging into Internet Hosts by Using Telnet" in Chapter 40). When you use a MUD via telnet, you specify the host name as you would for any other telnet connection, but you also include the port number. If you find your telnet program to be awkward, consider downloading a different telnet program or a MUD client.

Connecting to a MUD by Using a MUD Client

Most MUD users don't use telnet to connect to their MUDs, but instead use *MUD clients* that offer advanced features beyond the simple telnet interface. (Use of telnet alone, in fact, is often called "raw telnet" as an indication of how basic and difficult it is to use MUD without a client.) A MUD client provides many useful benefits to a player, including:

- Line wrap and better formatting of messages from the MUD
- The ability to highlight designated phrases in bold or in color
- Logging capabilities to save a record of your MUD sessions to a file
- Macros and triggers for automating common responses
- Filters to screen out annoying or unwanted messages
- Managing your character's passwords to log you on automatically when you connect
- Connections to more than one MUD at a time through multiple windows

A wide variety of MUD clients have been created for nearly every computer system. The most popular MUD client, *tinyfugue*, was originally created for UNIX computers, but is also available for Windows 95. tinyfugue (*tf* for short) provides a text-based user interface, somewhat like a DOS window, coupled with a powerful scripting language.

Other MUD clients, with pull-down menus and toolbar buttons for commonly used commands, provide a more familiar look for Windows users. Some of these clients are freeware and some are shareware, requiring a registration fee to be paid to the program author. A list of MUD clients can be found at **http://homepages.together.net/ ~shae/client.html**. Chapter 38 explains how to install new programs from the Internet on your computer.

Chapter 17

Voice and Videoconferencing

The Internet brings people together. As you saw in the preceding chapters on e-mail, newsgroups, and online chat, using the Internet is a great way to communicate with friends old and new. In this chapter, you will find out how to go a step beyond written messages by adding voice and videoconferencing to your kit of communication tools. This chapter describes three programs: Microsoft NetMeeting, Netscape Conference, and CU-SeeMe.

What Are Voice Conferencing and Videoconferencing?

Voice conferencing is talking to another person via the microphone and speakers connected to your computer. *Videoconferencing* is sending your image and voice to one or more other people, through the camera and microphone attached to your computer, and receiving pictures and voices back. You can use one or the other, or both, depending on the peripheral equipment (microphone, speakers, camera) connected to your computer. Instead of typing messages to conduct a conversation, as you do in a chat room, with voice conferencing and videoconferencing, you can talk to other people, see their faces, and transmit your video so that they can see you, too.

How Does Conferencing Work?

When you want to have a conference with someone, you connect to your ISP, start your conferencing software, and log on to one of the *conference servers* (or *directory servers*) listed in your software. The servers are used as the central meeting area. Each server has a *directory*, which is analogous to a phone book, that lists everyone who is logged on to the server. (If you prefer, you can keep your name off the directory list, as explained later in the chapter, in the sections describing how to use specific videoconferencing software applications.)

The person that you want to talk to also has to be logged on. You select the person from the server's directory, and when the other person accepts your call, your conference begins.

 Depending on your software application, you can hold a videoconference with one person or with many people.

What Is Conferencing Used For?

Videoconferencing is an easy way to meet with people when you need to speak face-to-face. Conferencing is becoming a popular business application, to connect a main office with telecommuters, to meet with customers without incurring travel costs and time, and to keep branch offices around the world in visual contact with each other.

You can probably think of many situations in which you would like to talk to someone immediately, without leaving your computer or traveling to where they are located. Here are some examples to give you ideas of how videoconferencing can fit into your life:

- Meet with a classmate before the reunion, and see how you both have changed.

- Show a prospective buyer the latest product that your small business has turned out.

- Hold up the baby to meet her grandparents.

- See the person that you met through an Internet chat room.

Conferencing Sounds Great—Why Don't We All Abandon Our Telephones and Use Videoconferencing?

If this question occurs to you as you read about videoconferencing, you're not alone! Conferencing is very attractive—it saves you the cost of a long-distance phone call, you don't need to leave your desk to see the other person, and you can show your latest invention or interior-decorating scheme to people who are far away.

Before you abandon your telephone and use the Internet for conversations, consider a few factors:

- Does the person you want to talk to have a computer and the hardware and software required for conferencing?

- A computer isn't as portable as, say, talking on a cellular phone; will this lack of portability affect your conferencing?

- Since both parties have to be using their computers at the same time, how will you schedule your conversation?

Note *Using e-mail to exchange messages and set up a meeting time is a convenient way to schedule a videoconference.*

- How private does your conference have to be?

Some people are concerned that other people might eavesdrop on Internet conversations. As with any kind of public communication, you have to remember: absolute security does not exist. Your telephone can be tapped and your cellular phone conversations can be recorded. However, when you use conferencing, the sheer number of transmissions taking place makes it unlikely that your conversation will be overheard. The Internet is as secure as it can be, without limiting how easy it is to use or how convenient it is to access.

*To keep up to date on what's going on with Internet security, bookmark these Web sites: the Electronic Privacy Information Center at **http://www.epic.org**, and the Center for Democracy and Privacy at **http://www.cdt.org**.*

Gathering Your Equipment

To use voice conferencing, you need a microphone and speakers connected to your computer. To use videoconferencing, you need a camera connected to your computer. (Note that a digital video camera that produces output for your computer is different from a video camcorder—and much cheaper.) For either type of conference, you need conferencing software. Lastly, you need a connection to the Internet. Of course, the person who you want to conference with has to have all of these things, too. The following two sections explain how to get the hardware and software you need.

Getting Conferencing Hardware

Your method of installing hardware on your computer depends on your level of expertise. Are you comfortable opening your computer and inserting a sound card, or would you prefer to let someone else do that? Would you rather add peripherals yourself, or buy a computer already set up with speakers, microphone, and a camera?

If you're the do-it-yourself type, use your computer manufacturer's Web page as a starting resource for upgrade information. Most manufacturers list the components that you need for your particular system. Go with a full-duplex sound card; if you use a half-duplex card, in some software applications a pause occurs between when you finish speaking and when the person who you're conferencing with can speak. If you can't locate the information that you need from your manufacturer, try a local, independent computer store.

If you're the give-me-the-computer-already-set-up type, visit the Web pages of mail-order computer makers, or go to your local computer stores to find a system with speakers, a microphone, and camera already installed and ready to use.

If you fall somewhere in between these two types and just need to add a camera and/or microphone to your system, you can buy this equipment either by mail order or from a local computer store. The equipment is easy to install; in most cases, you just need to locate the microphone jack on your sound card and follow the camera's directions for plugging it into your computer.

Getting Conferencing Software

Where do you get conferencing software? You may have it already! Microsoft NetMeeting is included with Windows 98 and Internet Explorer 4. Netscape Conference is included with Netscape Communicator (4, but not with 4.5). Many camera manufacturers include conferencing software packaged with the camera. And, if a friend refers you to a favorite application, check out the company's Web site—you can probably download the software from there.

Conferencing Is More Than Talking and Seeing

Most conferencing software lets you do more than just talk and exchange video. As you can probably tell by the names of the features discussed in this section, software conferencing applications simulate a business meeting where all participants are gathered in one conference room. In Table 17-1, notice that many of the features seem like they are pulled right out of the business world (such as writing on a whiteboard, for example).

Conferencing features may be *named* after actions that take place in business, but that doesn't mean you can't use conferencing software in your personal life, as well. To show how you can adapt conferencing software from a business conference venue to a different setting, suppose, for example, that you are planning a family reunion. Table 17-2 shows some ways to use the business-like features of conferencing when you're not at work.

This Feature:	Is Used to:
Chat	Hold a discussion when you have many people in the conference. Since most conferencing software* allows you to talk to and see only one person at a time, using the chat feature is a way to conduct an online discussion with a lot of people.
File transfer	Send a copy of a file to one or all meeting participants.
Sharing an application	Open an application and let others see it. For example, you can open your browser and jump from link to link in the browser window, or open a word processing or spreadsheet program and make changes to a file, and everyone sees exactly what you are doing.
Whiteboard	Load an existing graphic file for everyone to see, or create your own drawing. Everyone in the meeting sees and can draw on the whiteboard.
Collaboration	Let other meeting participants edit one of your files.

*With CU-SeeMe, you can hold a videoconference with more than one person at a time.

Table 17-1. *Extra Features in Conferencing Software*

Feature	Business Use	Personal Use
Chat	Discuss a project by exchanging typed messages, which everyone in the meeting can see; keep a record of the meeting minutes by saving the chat contents as a text file.	Connect all the cousins on your mother's side of the family and figure out the menu online.
File transfer	Send a hard copy of the meeting agenda to all participants.	Send the recipes that you've organized in text files on your computer to everyone haggling over the menu.
Sharing an application	Show the latest project status report in its original application.	Open your text editor and show everyone the invitations that you sent to be printed.
Whiteboard	Draw your department's organizational chart.	Diagram the best route to the reunion site.
Collaboration	Allow other meeting participants to add input to the project status report.	Allow other family members to edit your written directions to the reunion site.

Table 17-2.   *Business and Personal Uses of Extra Features in Conferencing Software*

Conferencing Using NetMeeting

NetMeeting is Microsoft's entry in the conferencing software field. If you don't already have NetMeeting via Windows 98 or Internet Explorer 4, you can download it from the following Microsoft Web site:

> http://www.microsoft.com/ie/download/w98download.htm

Starting and Configuring NetMeeting

To use NetMeeting, you have to answer some setup questions—things like your name, location, and the server that you want to log on to when you start NetMeeting. The information that you add during setup can be changed later from within NetMeeting.

The first time that you start NetMeeting (by choosing Start | Programs | Internet Explorer | Microsoft NetMeeting, if you use Windows 98), the program displays a series of setup dialog boxes. Select the Log On to a Directory Server When NetMeeting

Starts option and accept the default server listed in the dialog box. Be sure to fill in your first name, last name, and e-mail address. When you use NetMeeting, if someone tries to call you and the call doesn't go through, the caller may be given the option of sending you an e-mail message, using the e-mail address that you specify here.

Tip   *After setup, if your e-mail address changes or you want to change any of the setup information, you can modify the information from within NetMeeting. Either select Call | Change My Information, or select Tools | Options and then click the My Information tab on the Options dialog box.*

Within each directory server are categories that you can choose. These categories group together people with similar interests. The category choices are "For personal use (suitable for all ages)," "For business (suitable for all ages)," or "For adults-only use." Click the down-arrow button at the right end of the Category box and make the selection that best describes how you plan to use NetMeeting. Again, you can later modify this information if you change your mind.

When the setup is complete, you see the NetMeeting window shown in Figure 17-1.

If you plan to let other people edit one of your documents, you need to enable sharing. To do this, on the NetMeeting screen, select Tools | Enable Sharing. Then, restart your computer for sharing to take effect. After your computer restarts, go back into NetMeeting. This time, you don't have to go through the setup screens.

Category box →

Server box ←

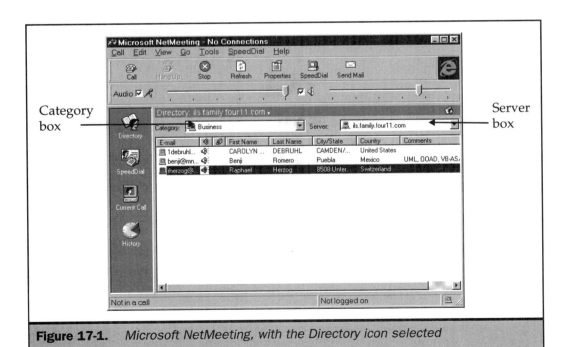

Figure 17-1.   *Microsoft NetMeeting, with the Directory icon selected*

If you don't see the Enable Sharing option on your Tools menu, sharing is already enabled and you are ready to use NetMeeting.

Planning Your Call

Your conference might require a little bit of planning or none at all, depending on whether you want to talk to a friend or to a stranger.

To talk to a stranger, you simply start NetMeeting, click the Directory icon on the left side of the screen, and call someone who is already logged on to the directory server. (The next section describes how to connect to a server.) The person that you call has the option to accept or ignore your call.

To talk to a friend, you need to do a little planning. You and your friend need to be logged on to the same server at the same time. When you see your friend's name, you can call and start your conference.

 If you don't see your friend's name immediately on the Directory screen, click the Refresh button. The Directory list does not refresh itself automatically as people connect and disconnect.

Logging On to Directory Servers

To log on (connect) to a directory server, click the down-arrow button at the right end of the Server box and select the server that you want from the drop-down list. Each NetMeeting directory server shows a list of the people who are logged on to the server. The server to which you are logged on when you start NetMeeting is the server that you selected on the setup screen. If you want to log on to a different server, select Call | Log Off to log off your existing server, and then choose a new server.

 If you don't get connected to the server that you chose on the Server drop-down list, select Tools | Options and click the Calling tab. Click the Server Name down-arrow and select the server that you want. It may take a few moments to connect to the server.

Each server's directory list shows all the people who are logged on to the server *and* have elected to have their name appear in the directory. The names are separated both by server and by category. If you want to see who is logged on to a different category, click the Category down-arrow and make your selection.

 Leaving your name on the directory list is recommended, so that people can locate you quickly, but you can remove your name from the list if you want. To remove your name, select Tools | Options and click the Calling tab on the Options dialog box. Check the Do Not List My Name in the Directory check box. Thereafter, people who want to contact you have to use your e-mail address or IP address (numeric Internet Protocol address, which usually changes each time to connect to the Internet).

The directory list tells you a lot about each person on the list. If the sound icon is next to a person's name, they have audio capabilities and you can have a voice conference with them. If the camera icon is next to a person's name, they have video capabilities and you can have a videoconference with them.

Note   *Even if you do not have a camera connected to your computer, you can still receive video from another person.*

When a red "splat" appears next to a person's name, that person is on a call. You still can call them, but if you try to call, you either are asked to join the meeting they currently are in or your call is ignored and you are asked whether you want to send e-mail instead.

Seeing Yourself As Others See You

Before you start a videoconference, preview your video. (If you don't have a video camera attached to your computer, skip to the next section.) During the preview, you can adjust the position of the camera and the lighting, and make sure that the other person will see exactly what you want them to see. Even small computer cameras pick up items behind you in the background.

To preview your video, click the Current Call icon on the left side of the screen. In the My Video box, click the Play icon. NetMeeting displays your video, and you can move your camera or adjust the lights and background until your video projects what you want the other person to see (see Figure 17-2).

You can choose whether or not to send video automatically at the start of a conference. Choose Tools | Options and click the Video tab to see your choices. If you choose not to send video automatically, send your video during a call by clicking the Play icon on the My Video box. During the conference, you can start and stop your video by clicking the Play and Stop icons on the My Video box.

When you have your video arranged the way that you like it, you are ready to start your conference.

Starting a Conference

Click the Directory icon to display the directory list. To call someone from the directory list, you can either double-click their name, or right-click their name and select Call on the pop-up menu. After you place the call, wait a few seconds. The person that you call has to accept your call (unless they have the Automatically Select Incoming Calls option selected) to establish your connection.

Hearing Voices

As soon as the other person accepts your call, you can begin your conversation. At the beginning of your conversation, you might want to adjust your microphone and

CHATTING AND CONFERENCING ON THE INTERNET

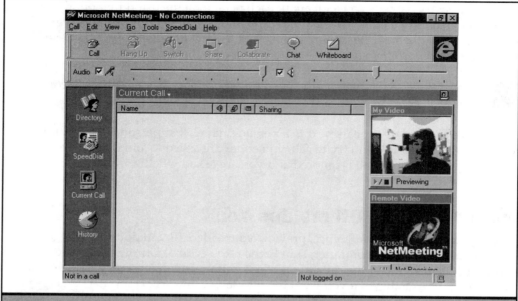

Figure 17-2. *Adjusting your video before a conference*

speakers by using the slider bars in the Audio area of the Current Call screen. If you cannot hear the other person clearly, ask them to adjust their microphone.

If you cannot hear the other person at all, click the Current Call icon and then click the Chat button on the toolbar. This opens the Chat window, in which you can type a message to the other person, asking them to adjust their microphone.

Seeing Faces

You have already seen your own video—now it is time to see what someone else looks like! To see the other person's video (whether you have a video camera or not), click the Play icon on the Remote box on the Current Call screen.

If you have your video options set to Automatically Receive Video at The Start of Each Call, the video may already be playing in the Remote Video box.

You can continue your audio conversation while you send and receive video. Remember, you can have more than two people in a meeting, but you can only conduct a voice or videoconference in NetMeeting with one other person at a time (as of the time this book was written).

How do you get more than two people in a meeting? You can either keep calling people from the directory list or keep accepting calls when people call you. You can always tell exactly who is in your meeting—everyone in your meeting is listed when you click the Current Call icon. To hold a conversation with everyone in the meeting, use the Chat window: click the Current Call icon and then click the Chat button on the toolbar. The Chat window enables you to type messages to the other people in the call.

During your meeting, if you decide that you want to conduct a videoconference with a different person, click the Switch button on the toolbar and select the name of the person who you want to speak to from the drop-down list. (You can also access this list by selecting Tools | Switch Audio and Video.) When you switch from one person to another, your existing conference is terminated and your conference with the selected person begins.

 As a courtesy, before you switch to someone else, you might want to say goodbye to the person in the existing conference and tell them that you are ending the conference.

Sharing a File from Your Computer

You may want to share information from your computer with other people, whether you are meeting with one person or many. Instead of having to read the information into the microphone or type it in the Chat window, you can open the file on your computer in its original format and display it for everyone in your meeting to see.

In NetMeeting terminology, this is called *sharing an application*. When you share an application, although everyone listed in your Current Call window can see the application, you are the only person who can make changes in the file. Everyone sees the changes as you edit the file onscreen.

To share an application, open the application on your computer, and then tell NetMeeting to share it. For example, if you want to share a Word file:

1. Open Microsoft Word.
2. Open the file that you want to share.
3. Click the Current Call button in NetMeeting.
4. Click the Share button on the toolbar.
5. Select Word from the drop-down list of applications that appears.

The file that you open is displayed on the screen of each person in your meeting. Everyone can see the cursor move and any changes that you make to the file, but you are the only person who has control of the cursor.

If you want to take this a step further and let other people make changes to your file, you can start *collaborating*, which permits other people in the meeting to take control of the cursor and edit your file.

Before you can collaborate on a document, you must have the document open on your computer and you must be sharing the application in NetMeeting.

To collaborate, click the Collaborate button on the toolbar. Others who want to collaborate on the file also have to click the Collaborate button on their screens. The Sharing field on the Current Call screen tells you who is collaborating on the document. The initials of the person who is in control of the cursor are displayed on the cursor in the document.

During a collaboration, any collaborator can take control of the cursor by clicking the left-mouse button. As the originator of the collaboration, you can override other collaborators and regain control by pressing ESC.

To stop collaborating, either click your left-mouse button or press ESC, to regain control of the cursor, and then click the Collaborate button on your toolbar.

To stop sharing an application, click the Share button on the toolbar and then click the shared application to clear the check mark.

 Collaborating works better if everyone in the call has their Windows display settings set to similar resolutions, and if no one clicks too fast. If you are collaborating on a file on your computer, be sure to save a backup copy of the file beforehand.

Sending a File from Your Computer

If you have a file to share with meeting attendees (perhaps the minutes of the last meeting), you can send it to them during the meeting. You can send a file to one person in the meeting, or to all people in the meeting.

 If you are on the receiving end of a sent file, a dialog box appears on your screen to inform you that the file is coming, and to give you the opportunity to decline it.

Files sent to you are stored in a subfolder of your NetMeeting folder (usually C:\Program Files\NetMeeting), in the Received Files folder. If you want to change that location, select Tools | Options, click the General tab on the Options dialog box, click the Change Folder button, and specify a new folder.

To send a file to everyone, select Tools | File Transfer | Send File. To send a file to one person, right-click the person's name and select Send File on the pop-up menu.

Drawing on the Whiteboard

Conferences aren't limited to just words and video—sometimes, you need to make your point by displaying a graphic or drawing a picture. In NetMeeting, you can open the NetMeeting Whiteboard and show a graphics file, or create a drawing from scratch.

To open the Whiteboard, click the Whiteboard button on the toolbar. When one person opens the Whiteboard, it opens on everyone's screen, and everyone in the meeting can draw on the Whiteboard simultaneously.

To keep other people from drawing on the Whiteboard, click the Lock Contents button in the Whiteboard toolbox. The same button also unlocks the Whiteboard.

If you prefer to show an existing graphics file, select File | Open in the Whiteboard window and then select the file to display it on the Whiteboard. Displaying an existing graphics file, like a map to your house or your child's latest artwork that you've scanned in on your computer, might be easier than trying to recreate it by drawing it on the Whiteboard.

Exiting NetMeeting Gracefully

Before you exit NetMeeting, be sure to close all the windows that you opened during your conference (such as the Chat window and the Whiteboard).

If you were sharing an application, click the Share button on the toolbar and clear the check mark next to the shared application. If you were collaborating on a document, click the Collaborate button to stop collaborating, and then stop sharing the application. Closing the program safeguards the changes you made during the meeting.

To end your call, click the Hang Up button. To exit NetMeeting, select Call | Exit or close the NetMeeting window.

Getting Together Using Conference

Netscape's conferencing application is called Conference, which is part of its version 4 Communicator suite (but not version 4.5). Conference lets you talk to another person, but it has no videoconferencing feature. The latest information about Conference is available at the following Web site:

> http://www.netscape.com/communicator/conference/v4.0

If you don't already have Communicator, you can download the software from

> http://home.netscape.com/download

Note that you may have to download the entire Netscape Communicator 4 suite.

Configuring Conference

To run Conference, choose Start | Programs | Netscape Communicator | Netscape Conference. Alternatively, if Netscape Navigator is already running, you can choose Communicator | Conference from the menu bar, or press CTRL+5.

The first time that you load Conference, the program asks you some setup questions. You need to enter your name, as you want it to appear in the Web Phonebook, and your e-mail address. This information is stored on a Business Card, and you may include optional information, such as your address, phone number, fax number, or a picture of yourself.

A Wizard guides you through the installation steps. Accept the default DLS (Dynamic Lookup Service) Server and the default Phonebook URL, and leave the List My Name in Phonebook check box selected.

You can change your personal information later from within Conference by selecting Call | Preferences.

Adjust your microphone, following the screen prompts. When your audio is adjusted, the Conference window opens (shown in Figure 17-3) and you are ready to go.

Placing a Call

You have many ways available to place a call in Conference:

- Click the Show Speed Dial button and select someone from your speed dial list.
- Click the Address Book button and call someone from the addresses that you've compiled.

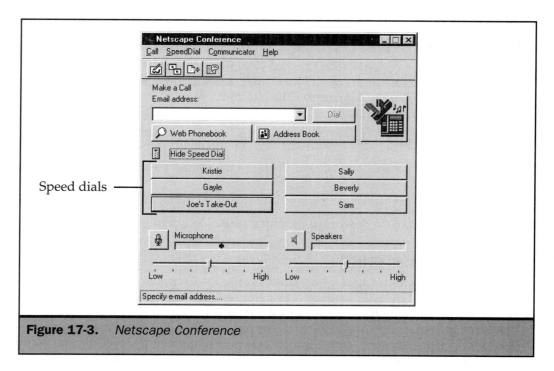

Figure 17-3. *Netscape Conference*

- Click the Web Phonebook button to search the directory.

- If you know the other person's e-mail address or IP address, you can call them directly by typing the address in the E-mail Address box and clicking the Dial button. When you want to conference with a person, the person you are calling must be logged on.

Since most ISPs assign a different IP address each time that you log on, most people do not have one constant IP address. Try using the person's e-mail address first, unless you are sure they have a static IP address.

As you call people, the names are stored in the E-mail Address box. To call someone who you've called before, click the down arrow, select the name from the drop-down list, and click Dial.

Using Speed Dial

You can store up to six speed dial numbers in Conference. To access your speed dial list, click the Show Speed Dial button or click the Speed Dial menu. The first time you open your speed dials, the buttons are labeled Speed Dial 1 through Speed Dial 6. As you add entries, the "Speed Dial" label is replaced by the name of the person on the speed dial entry (as shown in Figure 17-3).

When you see the six speed dials, click the one that you want to edit and type the person's name and e-mail address. To call someone from your speed dial list, click the speed dial button that has their name on it.

Using the Address Book

Click the Address Book button to open the book. You can add your own entries by typing an e-mail address in the Type in the Name You Are Looking For box. If you are not sure of the e-mail address, click the In box and select one of the public directories available on the Internet to search for the name that you want.

You can add entries to your Address Book at any time.

To place a call from the Address Book, select the name of the person that you want to call and then click the Place a Call button on the toolbar. The Pending Invitation dialog box appears and displays the status of your call. If the person is not logged on or does not take your call, you are prompted to leave a voice mail message. You can either leave a voice mail message or cancel the call.

Voice mail works only on Windows and UNIX and requires the Live Audio plug in. On the recipient's side, the voice mail is displayed as an attachment to an e-mail message.

Using the Web Phonebook

The Web Phonebook is located at the URL that you selected when you installed Conference (usually the Four11 Directory Service). To switch to using a different default phone book, choose Call I Preferences.

When you click the Web Phonebook button, the Four11 Directory Service (or other default) phone book opens in your browser window. If you want to converse in a language other than English, click the We Speak button, select a language on the drop-down list, and click Go.

To search for a person, use the fields in the Search Who's Online section of the page. If you just want to see who is online, click one of the letters of the alphabet in the Browse section of the page.

 People log on and off constantly during a session. As you look for people, remember to reload the Who's Online window (by clicking the Refresh button) periodically to update the list of names.

To call a person from the Web Phonebook, locate the person's name and click the Call Now link. The conferencing application that the person is using is displayed on the screen, along with the person's e-mail address and a link to access additional information about the person. Click the Call With button to place the call.

Fine-Tuning Your Audio

As soon as the other person accepts your call, you can begin your conversation. During the conversation, use the slider bars in the Conference window to adjust the volume of your microphone and speakers.

Chatting with Text

If one party's audio connection is not quite up to par, you can always use the Chat window and enter your conversation in text. To open the Chat window, click the Chat button on the toolbar. Type your message in the Personal Note Pad area and then click the Send button on the toolbar. As the conversation goes along, you see a log of the conversation in the Log File area. You can print or save the log (from the File menu on the Conference Text Chat window) to keep a record of your conversation. If you find the log is growing too long, you can clear it by selecting File I New.

If you have an existing text file that you want the other person to see, click the Include button on the toolbar. The file that you choose is loaded in the Chat window.

You can also use the Paste button on the toolbar to load information in the Chat window. When you click the Paste button, the text that has been copied to the Clipboard appears in the Chat window.

If you have trouble tuning your audio, open the Chat window and tell the other person what is happening. You may be able to troubleshoot the problem by exchanging tips and messages in the Chat window.

Viewing and Creating Graphics

Click the Whiteboard button on the toolbar. The Conference Whiteboard opens, and you can open a graphics file (by selecting File | Open) or use the drawing tools to create an illustration.

Tip *A handy feature available on Conference's Whiteboard is the ability to perform a screen capture and show it on the Whiteboard. From the Capture menu, select the area that you want to capture (it can be a Window, the Desktop, or a Region that you specify). Go to the area that you want to capture and click the left-mouse button. If you are choosing a Region, drag the cross hairs to select the region. Go back to the Whiteboard and position your selection.*

If you create something on the Whiteboard and you want to keep it, save and/or print it from the File menu.

Sending and Receiving Files

Relaying all the information that you want to say in the Chat window can be difficult. If you have a file that already contains a lot of what you want to say, send the file to the other person instead of retyping the information in the Chat window.

To send a file, click the File Exchange button on the toolbar. In the Conference File Exchange dialog box, click the Open button and select the file that you want to send. (If you want to send more than one file, repeat this step.) You see a list of the files to send in the Conference File Exchange dialog box. When you have your list of files ready, click the Send button on the toolbar. Depending on the size of the files, it may take a moment for the transfer to be completed.

The Conference File Exchange dialog box also shows the files that you've received. To save a file that has been sent to you, select the file on the list and click the Save button on the toolbar, or choose File | Save from the menu.

Sharing Your Browser

Collaborative browsing enables you to call up a Web page on your browser and let the other person see it simultaneously. As you jump from link to link on the page, the other person sees exactly what you see.

To share your browser screen, click the Collaborative Browsing button on the toolbar. Click the Start Browsing button in the Collaborative Browsing dialog box.

When the other person accepts your invitation to browse, go to your browser and open the page that you want to display.

 The Control the Browser check box should be selected when you start collaborative browsing. You can select and clear this box to share control of the browser.

To stop browsing, click the Stop Browsing button. If you are finished with your browser, close the browser window.

Exiting Conference

Before you exit, close the windows for any of the extra features that you used during the call, after saving any Whiteboard or Chat material you want to save. To exit, either select Call | Exit or close the Conference window.

Voice Conferencing and Videoconferencing with CU-SeeMe

CU-SeeMe is a conferencing application from White Pine Software that enables you to conduct a voice and videoconference with one or more people. CU-SeeMe, which predates both Microsoft NetMeeting and Netscape Conference, is available from White Pine's Web site at **http://www.wpine.com**.

Setting Up CU-SeeMe

When you run CU-SeeMe the first time, a Setup Assistant dialog box appears to ask you for the following information:

- Your name, e-mail address, and location.

- A registration password for the Four11 Directory Server. (You must complete the registration to be listed in the public Four11 Directory Server, which is like a public phone book on the Web for videoconferencing.) You can create any password that you like. If you skip this step, you can register later by selecting Four11 Registration from the CU-SeeMe menu.

- The speed of your Internet connection (which is usually limited by your modem speed, your ISP's modem speed, or the quality of the phone lines between them).

You can also preview your video and tune your audio during the setup process.

Starting CU-SeeMe

Each time that you start CU-SeeMe, you see the Quick Start & Tips dialog box. This screen contains shortcut buttons that access the most commonly used commands in CU-SeeMe. The Quick Start & Tips dialog box includes these options:

- **Visit White Pine**   Connects you to the White Pine Café, which is similar to a chat room. The Café is divided into conversation groups called *conferences*, and you can select which conference you want to join. The name of the conference gives you an idea of what type of conversations you will encounter. For example, if you want to talk about baseball, select a conference with *sports* in the title. When you join a conference, you can see video from all conference participants who have elected to send video.

- **Open Phone Book**   Displays the CU-SeeMe phone book, which shows Contact Cards listed by category. Contact Cards are an electronic business card that shows the name and e-mail address of a person or company. An assortment of Contact Cards is supplied with CU-SeeMe.

 If you just started CU-SeeMe, the phone book is already open and visible under the Quick Start & Tips window.

- **Find a Friend**   Opens the calling list, where you can see who is online. (You can also open the calling list by clicking the Who's Online button on the phone book toolbar.)

- **Test Your Startup**   Takes you to the video and audio tuning dialog boxes, so that you can adjust your settings. (Clicking the Test Setup button on the phone book toolbar also takes you to this dialog box.)

If you prefer not to see the Quick Start & Tips dialog box each time that you start CU-SeeMe, clear the Show This Welcome Screen Next Time You Start CU-SeeMe check box. You can display the dialog box at any time by choosing Help | Quick Start & Tips.

Finding People to Call

CU-SeeMe opens on the phone book (displayed in Figure 17-4), which shows the *Contact Cards* that are supplied with CU-SeeMe. Think of Contact Cards as your speed dial list. The Contact Cards are separated into categories; to select a category, click the down arrow and choose a category from the drop-down list.

When you see the contact who you want to call, select the Contact Card and click the Speed Dial button. You can also click the link on the Contact Card picture (which is shaped like a Rolodex card) to initiate the call.

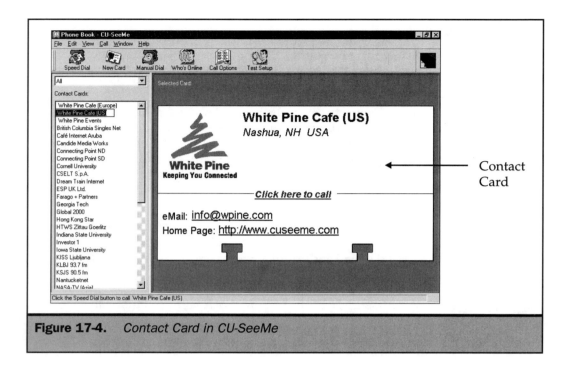

Contact Card

Figure 17-4. *Contact Card in CU-SeeMe*

You can customize your Contact Cards to create your own personalized speed-dial list of the people who you call most often. To create a Contact Card, click the New Card button and follow the prompts displayed in the Contact Card Assistant dialog box.

Searching a Directory

Directories are handy references that you can use to see who is online and potentially available to talk. To access the directory of everyone currently using CU-SeeMe, click the Who's Online button on the phone book toolbar. To place a call from the list, either select the name and click the Speed Dial button, or double-click the name of the person who you want to call.

Note   *To appear on the CU-SeeMe directory, you must be registered with the Four11 Directory Service. The CU-SeeMe directory list changes as people come and go. Click the Refresh button periodically to update the list.*

If you want to expand your search to see who is available on the Four11 Directory Server, click the Web Search button. The Four11 directory lists people who have registered with the service, and who are using all different types of conferencing applications.

The Four11 directory opens in your browser window, and you can search for a person by name, or browse around the directory by clicking a letter of the alphabet. To place a call from the Four11 directory, click the Call Now link next to the person's name and then click the link that specifies the application the person is using.

 The Four11 Directory Server lists the e-mail address of the person that you select. Note the address for future reference or add it to your Contact Cards.

Dialing Direct

If you know the IP address of the person who you want to call, you can call them direct by clicking the Manual Dial button on the phone book toolbar. Direct dialing can be inconvenient to use, as most people don't have a fixed IP address. Calling from a directory is usually easier.

Meeting with One Person

To meet with one person, place your call by using one of the directory lists or by dialing direct. When the other person accepts your call, your videoconference begins. Both of you must send and receive video in order to view each other. You can talk to each other via your microphones and speakers.

Meeting with Many People

To join a conference, select the conference in which you're interested from the Contact Cards list on the phone book screen. When you join a conference, the Conference Room screen is displayed and you see video from many conference participants. To manage the video boxes, you can do the following:

- *Select the people who you want to see.* Click the Video button and select the names.

- *Close some of the video boxes.* Click the Video button and clear the check mark, or right-click the video box and select Hide.

- *Organize the screen.* Drag video boxes until they are arranged as you want them.

- *Resize a video box.* Drag it to your desktop, resize it, and place it back in the CU-SeeMe window.

- *Customize the video window.* Click the Customize button and select Video Layout.

Using Chat

Part of the Conference Room contains a chat area, where you can type messages to people in the conference. Unless you specify otherwise, everyone in the conference can see your chat messages.

If you want only one person to see your message, select Conference | Chat To and then select that person's name from the drop-down list. After you finish your private chat, select Conference | Chat To, and click the name to clear the check mark and return to public chat mode.

Parental Control

Computers around the home are often accessible to children and teenagers. CU-SeeMe has a parental control feature that enables you to limit the actions that a CU-SeeMe user can take. For example, you can restrict the ability to answer incoming calls or the ability to dial out manually. The controls that you set up are password-protected.

To enable parental control, you need to do the following:

■ *Select the areas that you want to restrict.* Click the Call Options button on the phone book toolbar, and select Security. On the Security tab, click the Configure Parental Control Restrictions button, and make your selections from the options lists on the Communications, Usage, and Profiles dialog boxes.

■ *Create a password.* Click the Create Password button on the Security tab, and then enter the password that you want to assign.

■ *Enable the feature.* Click the Enable Parental Control button on the Security tab.

The controls remain in place until you disable them. To disable parental control, click the Call Options button on the phone book toolbar, select Security, click the Disable Parental Control button, and then enter the password.

Exiting CU-SeeMe

After you finish your conversation or conference, click the Hang Up button, or close the CU-SeeMe window.

Summary of Conferencing Applications

Table 17-3 summarizes the conferencing features for each application discussed in this chapter.

	NetMeeting	Conference	CU-SeeMe
Voice conferencing	✔	✔	✔
Videoconferencing	✔	✔	✔
Chat	✔	✔	✔
Whiteboard	✔	✔	See the White Pine Software page at **http://www.wpine.com**
File transfer	✔	✔	
Sharing an application or a browser	✔	✔	See the White Pine Software page at **http://www.wpine.com**
Collaborating on a document	✔		See the White Pine Software page at **http://www.wpine.com**
Videoconferencing with more than one person at a time			✔

Table 17-3.   *Summary of Conferencing Applications*

CHATTING AND
CONFERENCING ON
THE INTERNET

Note   *The features listed in Table 17-3 are current as of the time this book was written. Software often changes, though, so check your software maker's Web site periodically for the latest information on the features included with its conferencing application.*

What's Next in Voice Conferencing and Videoconferencing?

As is the case with most things involving the Internet, conferencing software is in a constant state of change. Applications are upgraded, faster modems appear, and new hardware is released. Chapter 39 discusses future directions in Internet telephony.

To keep up-to-date with what's going on in conferencing, use the Internet as your information resource. In addition to stopping by your hardware or software vendor's Web sites periodically, do a quick search on "videoconferencing" with your favorite search engine, or visit some online computer magazines to see how conferencing is evolving. Also take a look at TUCOWS (described in Chapter 38) for a listing of conferencing programs.

The Complete Reference

Internet

Part IV

Viewing the World Wide Web

The
Complete
Reference

Internet

Chapter 18

World Wide Web
Concepts

389

The *World Wide Web* (usually just referred to as "the Web") is a collection of millions of files stored on thousands of computers (called *Web servers*) all over the world. These files represent text documents, pictures, video, sounds, programs, interactive environments, and just about any other kind of information that has ever been recorded in computer files. The Web is probably the largest and most diverse collection of information ever assembled.

What unites these files is a system for linking one file to another and transmitting them across the Internet. The HTML language allows a file to contain links to related files. Such a *link* (also called a *hyperlink*) contains the information necessary to locate the related file on the Internet. When you connect to the Internet and use a Web browser program, you can read, view, hear, or otherwise interact with the Web without paying attention to whether the information that you are accessing is stored on a computer down the hall or on the other side of the world. A news story stored on a computer in Singapore may link you to a stock quote stored in New York, a picture stored in Frankfurt, and an audio file stored in Tokyo. The combination of the Web servers, the Internet, and your Web browser assembles this information seamlessly and presents it to you as a unified whole.

By following links, you can get from almost any Web document to almost any other Web document. For this reason, some people like to think of the entire Web as being one big document. In this view, the links just take you from one part of the document to another.

Elements of the Web

Following are the hardware, software, and protocols that make up the Web.

Clients and Servers

A *Web server* is a computer connected to the Internet that runs a program (which is also called a Web server) that takes responsibility for storing, retrieving, and distributing some of the Web's files. A *Web client* or *Web browser* is a computer that requests files from the Web. (The word *client* generally refers to a program that causes a computer to request files—a Web browser, for example.) When a client computer wants access to one of the files on the Web, the network directs the request to the Web server that is responsible for that file. The server then retrieves the file from its storage media and sends it to the client computer that requested it.

The Web's Languages and Protocols

The many thousands of computers that make up the Web represent every conceivable combination of computer hardware and software. When a client computer requests a file from the Web, it can assume very little about the server that stores the file, or the various other computers that might handle the file as it is transmitted from the server to the client. For such a system to work, it must have a well-defined set of languages and protocols that are independent of the hardware or operating systems on which they run.

URLs and Transfer Protocols

When the pieces of a document are scattered all over the world, but you want to display them seamlessly to a viewer who could be anywhere else in the world, you need a very good addressing system. Each file on the Internet has an address, called a *Uniform Resource Locator* (*URL*). For example, the URL of the ESPN Sportzone Web site is **http://espnet.sportzone.com**.

The first part of a URL specifies the *transfer protocol*, the method that a computer uses to access this file. Most Web pages are accessed with the *Hypertext Transfer Protocol* (the language of Web communication), which is why Web addresses typically begin with http (or its secure version, https or shttp). The http:// at the beginning of a Web page's URL is so common that it often goes without saying; if you simply type **espnet.sportzone.com** into the address window of Internet Explorer or Navigator, the browser fills in the http:// for itself. In common usage, the http:// at the beginning of a URL often is left out.

The next part of the address denotes the host name of the Web server (see "Domain and Host Names" in Chapter 1). The URL doesn't tell you where the Web server is actually located. Whether ESPN's Web server is in Los Angeles or Bangkok is invisible from the URL. The domain name system (DNS, described in Chapter 1) routes your Web page request to the Web server regardless of its physical location. As users, you don't need to deal with this level of detail, and that's a good thing. The Web would be much less usable if sports fans had to learn a new set of URLs every time ESPN got a new computer.

Some URLs contain information following the host name of the Web server. This information specifies exactly which file you want to see, and what directory it is stored in. If the directory name and filename aren't specified, you get the default Web page for that Web server. For example, the URL **http://net.gurus.com** takes you to the net.gurus.com Web server (maintained by the Internet Gurus, including some of the authors of this book). The URL **http://net.gurus.com/nettcr** displays the home page for this book.

HTML

The *Hypertext Markup Language* (*HTML*) is the universal language of the Web. It is a language that you use to lay out pages that are capable of displaying all the diverse kinds of information that the Web contains.

While various software companies own and sell HTML-reading and HTML-writing programs, no one owns the language HTML itself. It is an international standard, maintained and updated by a complicated political process that has worked remarkably well so far. The World Wide Web Consortium (W3C), at **http://www.w3c.org**, manages the HTML standard. See Chapter 27 for an introduction to HTML.

Java and JavaScript

Java is a language for sending small applications (called *applets*) over the Web, so that they can be executed by your computer. *JavaScript* is a language for extending HTML to embed small programs called *scripts* in Web pages. The main purpose of applets and scripts is to speed up the interactivity of Web pages; you interact with an applet or script that the Web server runs on your computer, instead of interacting with a distant Web server. Java and JavaScript are also used for animation; the Web server sends an animation-constructing applet or script that runs on your computer, instead of transmitting the frames of an animation over the Internet. Typically, this process is invisible to the user—the interaction or the animation just happens, without calling your attention to how it happens.

More-detailed descriptions of how you and your browser interact with Java and JavaScript are contained in "Dealing with Web Pages That Contain ActiveX, Java, and JavaScript" in Chapter 22. Security implications of Java and JavaScript are discussed in the section "Executable Applets and Scripts," later in this chapter. Chapter 34 describes how to create Web pages that use Java and JavaScript.

VBScript and ActiveX Controls

VBScript and ActiveX Controls are Microsoft systems (not Web standards) that work with Internet Explorer.

VBScript, a language that resembles Microsoft's Visual Basic, can be used to add scripts to pages that are displayed by Internet Explorer. Anything that VBScript can do, JavaScript (which Microsoft calls *JScript*) can do, too, and vice versa.

ActiveX controls (AXCs), like Java, are used to embed executable programs into a Web page. When Internet Explorer encounters a Web page that uses ActiveX controls, it checks whether that particular control is already installed on your computer, and if it isn't, IE installs it.

Security implications of VBScript and ActiveX controls are discussed in the section "Executable Applets and Scripts," later in this chapter.

XML and Other Advanced Web Languages

The *Extensible Markup Language (XML)* is a very powerful language that may replace HTML as the language of the Web. Currently, XML is little more than a specification at the W3C, but it is expected to be implemented in the fifth-generation browsers (Navigator 5 and IE 5).

XML is a *language for writing languages* (such as HTML), which is what makes it so powerful. XML gives document designers a greatly increased capability to attach explanatory tags to data. For example, whereas an HTML document might contain a few columns of numbers, the corresponding XML document might contain tags explaining what the numbers represent—that some are prices, for example, while others are quantities, times, or batting averages. The XML-enabled browser can read those tags and offer you choices of ways to view the data that are consistent with what the data represents.

To find out more about XML, go to **http://www.w3.org/XML/#faq**.

Consistent with the vision of XML is the notion of a *style sheet*. The basic idea of a style sheet is to make a distinction between information and the way that the information is presented. A style sheet language describes *how* information is presented, not *what* information is presented. An audio style sheet, for example, might describe the voice and accent of a speaker, and be associated with a text document. Changing the style sheet would change how the text is read, not the text itself. The W3C is working on two style sheet language specifications: the *Extensible Style Language (XSL)* and *Cascading Style Sheets (CSS).* Learn about them at **http://www.w3.org/Style**.

Another extension of HTML is *Dynamic HTML (DHTML),* which consists of three components: HTML, JavaScript, and cascading style sheets (CSS). See Chapter 34 for how to use CSS.

Image Formats

Pictures, drawings, charts, and diagrams are available on the Web in a variety of formats. The most popular formats for displaying graphical information are JPEG and GIF. For more about graphic file formats, see "Elements of Web Pages" in Chapter 26 and "Graphic File Formats for the Web" in Chapter 29.

Audio and Video Formats

Some files on the Web represent audio or video, and they can be played by browser plug-ins (see "Plug-Ins" later in this chapter). Web audio and video come in two flavors: your browser can download either the entire file and play it (which can take a long time, because audio files are large and video files are huge) or only the part of the file that it needs to play next, discarding the parts that it has played already. The second technique is called *streaming audio* or *streaming video.* See "Listening to the Web" and "Web-Based Video" in Chapter 22.

VRML

The *Virtual Reality Modeling Language (VRML)* is the Web's way of describing three-dimensional scenes and objects. Given a VRML file, a browser can display a scene or object as it would appear from any particular viewing location. You can rotate an object or move through a scene, using the controls that a browser provides.

Like Java, VRML moves some computational burden from the network to your computer. Rather than having Web servers store and transmit all the possible 2-D views of a scene, the scene is described in VRML and downloaded to your machine. Your computer then figures out what you would see if you stand in a particular place and look in a particular direction. Given the speed of most Internet connections, computing a view on your machine is much faster than downloading one from a Web server.

Like HTML pages, VRML scenes can contain many kinds of information. A scene of a city square, for example, might contain a kiosk, and each face of the kiosk might display a different picture or text document. The objects in a scene might also be links to URLs, which are accessed when you click the object. The University of Essex, for example, has posted a 3-D campus model on the Web at the following site:

http://esewww.essex.ac.uk/campus-model.wrl

Each building in the model is linked to the directory of the university department that is housed in that building.

Web Pages and Web Sites

A *Web page* is an HTML document that is stored on a Web server and that has a URL so that it can be accessed via the Web.

A *Web site* is a collection of Web pages belonging to a particular person or organization. Typically, the URLs of these pages share a common prefix, which is the address of the *home page* of the site. The home page is the "front door" of the site, and is set up to help viewers find whatever is of interest to them on that site. The URL of the home page also serves as the URL of the Web site. For example, *TV Guide*'s home page is at

http://www.tvguide.com

From the home page, you can get to *TV Guide*'s gossip column, *The Daily Dish,* at

http://www.tvguide.com/dish

A specific story in *The Daily Dish* is at

http://www.tvguide.com/dish/0122b.htm

Special Kinds of Web Sites and Pages

In one sense, Web pages are all the same: they are files on Web servers and are denoted by URLs. Similarly, all Web sites are interlinked groups of Web pages that have certain similarities in their URLs. But as the Web becomes more and more a part of everyday life, our language is expanding to contain words for increasingly more special types of Web pages and Web sites.

Portals

A *portal* is a Web site that wants to be your start page, the page that your browser displays first. That is, the portal wants to be the place where you start your browsing experience—and see every time that you turn on your Web browser. To this end, a portal site such as Yahoo!, Excite, or Lycos provides numerous free services that enhance your Web experience: Web guides, search engines, chat rooms, e-mail accounts, and news services, just to name a few. Competition among the portal sites is intense, and any service provided by one is quickly copied by the others. All portal services are free, but some (such as chat rooms, game rooms, and anything personalized) require you to register and choose a password.

Some ISPs configure their home pages to be your start page when you sign up for an Internet account, so that the ISP's home page serves as your portal. However, few ISPs maintain portal pages that are as complete as Yahoo! or Excite.

Portals, like TV or any other form of free media, are in the business of collecting and selling people's attention. Having drawn you to their site with free services, they try either to entice you to stay so that they can show you advertising, or to link you to other Web sites (such as advertising-supported news services) that have paid the portal to divert attention their way.

Portals developed as competitors to Internet services such as CompuServe and AOL. Not too many years ago, many experts thought that the Web was too chaotic and unmanageable to be a mass market. Most people used structured Internet services, such as AOL, rather than access the Web directly, and only rarely did users stray off their structured ISP's proprietary territory. However, contrary to the expert's doubts about the Web, advertising-supported portal sites have recently brought AOL-like services and structure to the Web. Today, even AOL and MSN are essentially just portals combined with ISP services, because their subscribers spend much of their time viewing nonproprietary Web sites.

For a detailed discussion of portal services and how to choose which portal is best for you, see "Portals to the Web" in Chapter 25.

Web Guides

Web guides are a top-down approach to finding your way around the Web. A *Web guide* is a Web site with a system of categories and subcategories that organizes links to Web pages—much like the Dewey decimal system organizes the books in a library.

Since Web guides were one of the first services provided by portals such as Yahoo! and Excite, many people still confuse the concepts of "portal" and "Web guide."

Search Engines

Search engines are a bottom-up approach to finding your way around the Web. You give a search engine a list of keywords or phrases (called a *query*), and it returns to you a list of Web pages that contain those words or phrases.

Some search engines search only the titles of Web pages, while others search every word. (This takes much less time than you might think.) Each search engine has its own way of deciding which of the Web pages on its list is most likely to be one that you are looking for.

Some allow more complicated queries than others. Keywords can be combined with Boolean (logical) operations, such as AND, OR, and NOT, to produce rather complicated queries. The rules for combining these operations are called the *syntax* of the search engine.

There is an art to designing queries that result in the search engine returning a useful list to you. Given the vast number of Web pages, a query that is too general may yield literally millions of Web pages, most of them useless to you. A query that is too specific may miss many Web pages that you would have liked to see. A more complete discussion of Web guides, search engines, and techniques for using them is contained in Chapter 23.

Home Pages

A *home page* is the front door of a Web site. Technically, the home page is just one of the pages on a Web site, but in common slang, the "home page" and the "Web site" that it introduces are used interchangeably. When a person or organization says "My Web site is at **www.mysite.com**," the URL to which they refer is the URL of the site's home page. The home page introduces the rest of the Web site and provides links that lead to the other pages on the site. Conversely, when a person says, "The directions are on my home page," the directions may not be on the home page itself, but rather somewhere easily accessible from the home page.

PERSONAL HOME PAGES   A *personal home page* is the front door of a Web site that an individual puts on the Web to introduce himself or herself, to share interests with others, and to keep distant friends and acquaintances up-to-date on the course of life. What you put on a personal Web site, or whether you want one at all, depends on how attached you are to your privacy. Home pages (and the other pages they link to) can include such things as pictures of you and your family, a list of hobbies, links to favorite Web pages, writings that you are proud of, causes that you want to promote, directions to your home, Christmas card letters, and so forth.

Beyond simple vanity, a personal Web site serves several purposes. First as you interact with people on the Internet through mailing lists, chat rooms, game rooms, and newsgroups, you will run into some people again and again. Though you have never met them, you begin to develop a sense of community with these people. Personal Web sites are a way for you to flesh out your images of each other, so that you are more than just disembodied words.

Second, when people you knew in high school say "I wonder what ever happened to her?" a search engine can lead them to your home page. They can find out that you have two children, live in Virginia, and can be reached at a certain e-mail address. Many friendships have been reestablished this way.

Finally, a personal Web site is a way to share things with friends. You can easily send 20 people a short e-mail saying "We're back from Hawaii. Check out the pictures on my Web page."

You don't need your own Web server to get a personal Web site. Many ISPs provide customers with free space for Web pages on the ISP's server. Some advertising-supported sites, such as GeoCities (**http://www.geocities.com**), provide free home pages as a way to draw people to their sites.

You can construct and link together your Web pages by using free HTML-editing programs, such as Microsoft's FrontPage Express or Netscape's Composer. (See Chapter 28.)

BUSINESS AND ORGANIZATION HOME PAGES   A *business home page* is the front door to a business's Web site. Like the front door of an office building, it should be attractive, easy to find, and provide enough information to get people quickly to the parts of the Web site that they want to visit.

Similarly, any organization—a church, town, club, government office, school, or whatever—can have a Web site, and the front door to that Web site is called its home page. Even inanimate objects can have home pages; this book's home page is **http://net.gurus.com/nettcr**.

Creating Web sites for organizations has become an industry; a great deal of professional help is available. The basic ideas and tools, however, are more common sense than rocket science. (See Part V.)

Web Browsers

A *Web browser* is a program that your computer runs to communicate with Web servers on the Internet, which enables it to download and display the Web pages that you request. At a minimum, a Web browser must understand HTML and display text. In recent years, however, Internet users have come to expect a lot more. A state-of-the-art Web browser provides a full multimedia experience, complete with pictures, sound, video, and even 3-D imaging.

Because a Web browser has the ability to interpret or display so many types of files, you often may use a Web browser even when you aren't connected to the Internet. Windows 98, for example, uses Internet Explorer to open most image files (unless you specify some other application).

The most popular browsers, by far, are Netscape Navigator and Microsoft Internet Explorer. Both are state-of-the-art browsers, and the competition between them is fierce. Both are regularly upgraded, so it is worthwhile to keep an eye on the Netscape and Microsoft Web sites, listed here, to see when new versions are available:

> **http://home.netscape.com/download**
> **http://www.microsoft.com/ie**

Both Navigator and IE are available over the Internet at no charge. Microsoft designed IE for the Windows operating system, but it is now available for Macintosh and some UNIX systems, as well. Navigator is available for Windows, Macintosh, UNIX, and Linux operating systems.

Navigator is discussed in detail in Chapter 19, and Internet Explorer in Chapter 20. Chapter 21 describes other useful browsers, such as Opera and Lynx.

Browser Concepts

Web browsers interact not just with the Web, but also with your computer's operating system and with other programs, called plug-ins, that give the browser enhanced features.

The Default Browser

Graphical user interfaces (GUIs) such as Windows, MacOS, and various UNIX desktop applications enable you to open a file by clicking or double-clicking an icon that represents the file. When the icon represents a Web page, a local HTML file, or even an image file in a format such as JPEG that Web browsers display well, the operating system runs a Web browser to display the file. Because your click does not specify a browser, the operating system must have a *default browser* listed in its settings. The default browser doesn't have to be the only Web browser installed on your system, and you may use another Web browser to open Web pages, by choosing it specifically. But the default browser is used whenever you specify a Web page without specifying a browser.

Internet Explorer is the default browser in newly installed Windows 98 systems, and in most new home computers of any kind. When you install a new browser, the installation program usually asks whether this browser should be the default. It may even set up the new browser as the default without asking. Whenever you run IE or Navigator, it checks whether it is the default browser, and if it isn't, it asks whether you want to make it the default browser (unless you have told it not to do this).

You can check which browser is your default browser by checking the icon on any HTML documents or Internet shortcuts. In Windows 95 or 98, check the icons of the entries on the Favorites menu.

Browser Home Pages and Start Pages

As if the home page/Web site confusion wasn't bad enough (see "Home Pages," earlier in this chapter), many browsers have a *Home button* on their toolbars, and this has yet another meaning. To a Web browser, "Home" is that place to which you return when you get lost or tired of browsing—your *browser home page*. It is a place to get your bearings, before venturing out again.

A good home page for your browser is one that loads quickly, contains information that you want to check regularly (such as headlines in your area of interest or a local weather forecast), and links to a wide variety of other pages (so that you can quickly go where you want). Portals make good browser home pages, and most let you customize the features that they display. (See "Portals to the Web" in Chapter 25.)

The companies that make Web browsers, naturally, have a biased notion of where your browser home page should be. By default, Internet Explorer's Home button points to Microsoft's portal site **http://home.microsoft.com**, and Navigator's Home button points to Netscape's NetCenter portal **http://home.netscape.com**. In general, these are not bad home pages, and many people never change them. Microsoft and Netscape count on that; the Internet Explorer and Navigator default home pages are some of the most valuable real estate in cyberspace.

Your browser's *start page* is the Web page that the browser loads when you open the browser without requesting a specific page. Internet Explorer automatically starts with the browser home page, but Navigator allows the start page to be different from the browser home page (though NetCenter is the default for both). Your ISP's installation program may have changed your start page to the ISP's home page on the Web.

You can set your start page or browser home page to be any page that you want. (See "Choosing New Start and Home Pages" in Chapter 19 or "Choosing a New Home Page" in Chapter 20.) In fact, you might as well set your browser's Home button to point to somewhere other than its default portal, since IE and Navigator provide you other ways to get to their favorite portals: Navigator 4.5 has a My Netscape button on its tool bar, and IE has an Internet Start button on its links bar.

Your browser's start and/or home page can be a file on your own computer. This gives you complete control over the content, and provides very fast browser startup. A simple page with links to your favorite Web sites may be more useful to you than any outside page—you can create your own customized portal to the Web. You can create a simple Web page by using FrontPage Express, Composer, or any other Web page editor. (See Chapter 28.)

Plug-Ins

Plug-ins are programs that are independent of your Web browser, but that "plug in" to it in a seamless way, so that you may not even be aware that you are using a different piece of software.

Various plug-ins (such as RealAudio for receiving streaming audio, or QuickTime for downloading video) have become standard accessories for IE or Navigator, and are installed automatically when you install the Web browser. To install other plug-ins, download them from the Internet and then follow the directions that come with the plug-in.

For more information about downloading and using plug-ins, see Chapter 22.

Elements of a Browser Window

Most browser windows have the same basic layout. From top to bottom, you find these basic elements:

- Menu bar
- Toolbars
- Address or Location window
- Viewing window
- Status bar

Some Web pages are divided into independent panes, called *frames*. When such a Web page is viewed, the viewing window is similarly divided into independent panes. You can scroll up or down in a frame or even move from link to link, without disturbing the contents of the other frames.

Viewing Pages with a Browser

The purpose of a Web browser is to display Web pages, which may either arrive over the Internet or already be on your computer system.

Viewing Pages on Your Local Drives

You can use your Web browser to view files of any common Web format (HTML, VRML, JPEG, and so on) that are stored on your hard drive or elsewhere on your system. In Windows, Macintosh, and some UNIX desktops, simply clicking or double-clicking the file icon opens the file in the default Web browser.

Viewing Pages on the Web

You can open a Web page by using any of the following methods:

- *Enter its URL into the Address or Location box of a Web browser.* You can type in the URL or cut-and-paste it. Both IE and Navigator have an auto-complete feature—the browser tries to guess what URL you are typing and finishes it for you, by guessing similar URLs that you've visited before.

- *Select it from the list that drops down from the Address or Location box.* Both IE and Navigator remember the last 25 URLs that you have typed into the Address or Location box.

- *Link to it from another Web page.* The reason it's called a "Web" is that pages are linked to each other in a tangled, unpredictable way. Click a link (usually an icon or underlined, blue text) to see the Web page it refers to.

- *Link to it from a mail message or newsgroup article.* Many e-mail and newsreading programs are able to notice when a URL appears in a mail message or newsgroup article. Clicking the URL opens a Web browser, which displays the Web page.

- *Select it from the Bookmarks list (in Navigator), the Favorites menu (in IE), the History folder, or open an Internet shortcut.* See the upcoming section, "Keeping Track of Your Favorite Web Sites."

Using a Browser for Mail, News, or Chat

Web browsers are starting to take over some of the functions of other Internet programs. See "Web-Based E-mail" in Chapter 5, "How Do You Read Newsgroups?" in Chapter 13, and "Web-Based Chat" in Chapter 16.

Keeping Track of Your Favorite Web Sites

Even though URLs are a step up from having to know the exact computer that contains the information that you want, they are still not very easy to remember, and mistyping one can take you someplace totally unexpected. (Some enterprising souls are cashing in on this human fallibility by registering URLs that are frequent mistypings of popular URLs, and selling advertising to be viewed by the accidental visitors to these sites.) Depending on your operating system and your Web browser, you have access to some or all of the following ways to keep track of Web sites:

- **Bookmarks**   An HTML file of links. Navigator establishes a bookmark file when it is installed, and populates it with links in a variety of categories. You can edit this file and add to it when you find a Web site to which you want to be able to return easily. Since a bookmarks file is an HTML file on your computer, any browser can display it and access the linked Web sites.

Navigator displays it as a convenient list that drops down from the personal toolbar, sprouting organized sublists as you pass the cursor over it. (See "Using Bookmarks" in Chapter 19 and "Converting Bookmarks to Favorites and Vice Versa" in Chapter 20.) When Navigator's user profiles are enabled, each user has his/her own bookmarks file. (See "Sharing Navigator With Other Users" in Chapter 19.)

■ **Favorites**   A folder of Internet shortcuts. In practice, favorites behave like bookmarks: you choose one from a menu and your browser goes to the Web page that the favorite denotes. In Windows 95 or 98, the Favorites menu is accessible from the Start menu. In other operating systems, a Favorites folder is created when IE is installed. Although Favorites are easier to add and organize in IE, they call the default browser, even if it isn't IE. (See "Working With the Windows Favorites Menu" in Chapter 19, "Managing the Favorites Menu" in Chapter 20, and "Converting Bookmarks to Favorites and Vice Versa" in Chapter 20.) When user profiles are enabled in Windows, each user has his/her own Favorites folder. (See "Sharing Internet Explorer with Other Users" in Chapter 20.)

■ **Internet shortcuts**   Icons that appear in a GUI, such as Windows, the Mac, or various UNIX desktops. Internet shortcuts resemble file icons, but the file to which they point is on the Web, not on your computer. When you open an Internet shortcut, it starts the default browser (even if another browser is already running) and uses it to open the Web page. Different operating systems give you different methods to construct Internet shortcuts, or you can construct them from within Navigator (see "Creating Internet Shortcuts" in Chapter 19) or Internet Explorer (see "Creating Internet Shortcuts" in Chapter 20).

■ **History**   A list of Web pages that you have accessed recently. IE stores this information in the form of Internet shortcuts that are arranged into a hierarchy of folders inside the History folder. Navigator maintains a history database that can be accessed or edited only from within Navigator. Both methods enable you to return to a Web page with a single click. (See "Using the History List" in Chapter 19 and "Using the History Folder" in Chapter 20.) If other people use your computer, you need to be aware of the privacy implications of having a History list. (See "Privacy Implications of Browser Caches and History," later in this chapter.) When user profiles are enabled in Navigator or Internet Explorer, each user has his/her own History.

Security and Privacy Issues

Interacting with the Web is a little like passing notes across a classroom. You can't know ahead of time what computers are going to handle your messages as they pass between you and a Web server, and you can't be sure that none of those intermediate computers will copy the message, or let someone else read it. Worse, the Web server itself may not be what you think it is. It may be trying to capture sensitive information about you, such as your passwords or credit card numbers. It may be trying to deduce things about your interests or browsing habits. It may even be trying to introduce viruses that will damage the information on your computer.

Each new generation of Web browsers introduces new features to the Web. Some of these features, such as firewalls or the Secure Socket Layer (SSL) protocol, make your Web interactions safer. Others, such as cookies or scripting languages, open new opportunities for mischief in addition to their beneficial uses.

It's important to maintain a balance of caution and confidence. Many of the security issues that make scary headlines or TV plots are totally fanciful or easily avoided while others are theoretical issues that, so far, haven't led to practical problems. Still, some security issues are worth worrying about and taking a few precautions.

Cookies

A *cookie* is a small (at most 4K) file that a Web server can store on your machine. Its purpose is to allow a Web server to personalize a Web page, depending on whether you have been to that Web site before, and what you may have told it during previous sessions. For example, when you establish an account with an online retailer or subscribe to an online magazine, you may be asked to fill out a form that includes some information about yourself and your preferences. The Web server may store that information (along with information about when you visit the site) in a cookie on your machine. When you return to that Web site in the future, the retailer's Web server can read its cookie, recall this information, and structure its Web pages accordingly.

Much has been written about whether cookies create a security or privacy hazard for you. If your Web browser is working properly, the security hazard is minimal. It is, at first glance, unsettling to think that Web servers are storing information on your hard drive without your knowledge. But cookies are not executable programs. They cannot, for example, search for and accumulate information from elsewhere on your system. They simply record information that you have already given to the Web server.

However, cookies do make it easier for advertising companies to gather information about your browsing habits. For example, a company that advertises on many Web sites can use cookies to keep track of where you have seen its ads before, and which ads (if any) you clicked. If this possibility bothers you, both Navigator and IE let you control their use of cookies, including the option to disable the storage of all cookies. (See "Managing Cookies in Navigator" in Chapter 19 and "Managing Cookies" in Chapter 20.)

Turning off cookies entirely makes many Web sites much less convenient. If you have customized a start page at a portal, for example, the customization stops working when you turn off your cookies. Navigator has a setting that we have found to be a good compromise between accepting cookies willy-nilly, and turning off all of them: Accept Only Cookies That Get Sent Back to the Originating Server. Advertisements on a Web page usually come from a different server than the page itself, particularly if an advertiser is attempting to track your browsing across many sites.

Firewalls

A *firewall* is a piece of hardware or software that sits between two networks for security purposes. Typically, an organization might have its own computers linked in an Internet-like network called an *intranet* (described in Chapter 4). A firewall is placed between this intranet and the Internet to prevent unauthorized users from gaining access to all the resources of the intranet. If you communicate with the Internet through a firewall, you must configure your Web browser to request Web pages from the firewall's *proxy server*, the program that filters packets of information between the intranet and the Internet. Ask your intranet or LAN administrator for instructions.

Secure Communications and Transactions

Transactions and communications on the Internet involve more than just your computer and the server of the Web site that you are dealing with. Each message back and forth goes through several other computers along the way, and you can't even predict which computers will be involved. The situation is in some ways analogous to buying a hot dog from a vendor at a crowded football game: Several complete strangers may be involved in passing back and forth the hot dog, your money, and your change. The following are the three major risks involved in any Internet transaction:

- **Eavesdropping** Any information that you transmit may be overheard by other computers—your credit card number, for example.

- **Manipulation** The information that you send or receive may be altered by third parties. For example, the delivery address for your shipment might be altered.

- **Impersonation** You might not be dealing with the entity that you think you are dealing with. Or, conversely, whoever you are dealing with might gather enough information to impersonate you in another transaction.

Servers and Web browsers use complex encryption techniques to guard against these threats. When a server and your browser are acting in a secure mode, the messages transmitted appear to be gibberish to anyone but the designated receiver, tests are done to detect altered messages, and identities are verified.

How Secure Transactions Work

Secure Web transactions use a protocol called the *Secure Sockets Layer (SSL)*. This protocol depends on public key cryptography to establish proofs of identity, called *digital certificates*.

PUBLIC KEY CRYPTOGRAPHY Web transactions (in addition to other secure information, like secure e-mail messages) are encrypted using *public key cryptography*, a system in which pairs of very large numbers are used to encode and decode messages. One number of the pair, called the *public key*, is published; and the second number, the *private key*, is kept secret. When one of the two numbers has been used to encode a message, the other one is needed to decode it.

This technique is useful in two ways. If a message is encoded using the public key, then only the holder of the secret private key can decode it; to anyone else, the message appears to be gibberish. Conversely, the holder of the private key can prove its identity by encoding a message using that key. Anyone who receives that message can decode it by using the public key; the fact that this decoding produces a coherent message is proof that the sender must be the holder of the private key.

Any public key system can be broken by an enemy who has enough time and computing power. However, in a well-constructed system, the enemy's expense would be too great and the result would arrive too late to be relevant. No one is going to spend billions of dollars and wait hundreds of years to discover your credit card number.

The strength of a public key system is measured by the size of the numbers used as keys. Two key sizes are commonly used by Web browsers: 40 bit and 128 bit. As the speed of computation goes up and its price goes down, 40-bit encryption systems are rapidly becoming inadequate, but they are the best systems that American companies such as Microsoft and Netscape can export under current U. S. law. If you live in the United States or Canada, you can download versions of Navigator and Internet Explorer with 128-bit security—and you should! Each added bit in the key approximately doubles the difficulty of breaking the code, so 128-bit encryption is more than a trillion trillion times more difficult to break than 40-bit encryption.

DIGITAL CERTIFICATES   When you give your credit card to a cashier at a Sears store, you have a reasonable amount of confidence that you are really dealing with Sears. No one, after all, would fake an entire store just to get your credit card number.

Web sites, however, are much easier to fake than stores. When you order a computer at **http://www.dell.com**, and the Web site asks for your credit card number, how do you know you're really dealing with Dell? The URL by itself is not evidence enough; clever hackers can fool your browser into displaying a phony URL. Fortunately, there are better ways to establish Dell's identity.

A *digital certificate* (or *certificate* or *digital ID*) is a file that identifies a person or organization. Dell has gone to some certifying authority and gotten a digital certificate (which contains a public key, as described in the previous section). When Dell's server wants to convince your browser that it really is Dell's server, it sends its certificate file. Your browser checks that the certifying authority is on the list that the browser manufacturer programmed into it. (You can add certifying authorities to the list, but you probably shouldn't. Let Netscape or Microsoft do the checking, and just keep your browser up-to-date.) Then, the server and your browser have a short conversation in which Dell's server proves that it knows the private key that the certificate says belongs to Dell. Your browser is then ready to accept that it is dealing with Dell.

You might wonder why your browser hasn't learned enough from this conversation that it could impersonate Dell to someone else. The answer is that the conversation included some random information generated by the browser, so that no two of these conversations are ever quite identical.

See the "Digital Certificates" section in Chapter 9 for how to get your own certificate. Chapter 35's "Digital Certificates" section contains more information about using certificates on your own Web site. You can learn more about digital certificates at the following site:

http://home.netscape.com/certificate/v1.0/faq

SECURE SOCKETS LAYER   The Secure Sockets Layer (SSL) protocol is a method for secure communications and transactions to take place over the Internet. SSL uses digital certificates, as described in the previous section, to verify that the server is what it claims to be. The server and your browser then send encrypted messages back and forth until your transaction is complete.

Executing a Secure Transaction

Fortunately, you don't need to understand or remember how a secure transaction works to execute one. You need only keep three things in mind:

■ *Don't enter any sensitive information into a form until a secure connection has been established.* Most large Web merchants won't ask you to. To check the security level of the form that you're filling out, look at the status bar of your browser window. Both IE and Navigator display a closed padlock icon on the left side of the status bar when dealing with a document that it believes to be secure. In Navigator, you can click the padlock icon if you want to know more about the security of the document and the server it comes from. A window similar to the one in Figure 18-1 appears.

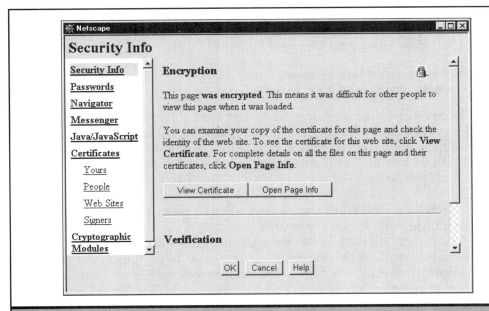

Figure 18-1.   *What Navigator can tell you about a secure connection*

■ *Pay attention to any warning messages that your browser gives you.* Unless you have told it not to (a bad idea), your browser warns you if any of the steps to establish a secure connection fail, particularly if something is wrong with the server's certificate. If this happens, we recommend cutting off the transaction. The problem is probably some technical glitch rather than an attempted fraud, but you shouldn't take the chance.

■ *Remember your common sense.* Don't give these complicated cryptological processes more credit than they deserve. The best that SSL can do is verify that you are dealing with the organization you think you're dealing with. It doesn't promise you that the organization is reputable or that the claims the Web site makes are true.

Executable Applets and Scripts

Java, JavaScript, VBScript, and ActiveX controls (defined in "The Web's Languages and Protocols," earlier in this chapter) are all languages for Web servers to run applications on your computer. Some people are squeamish about the idea of a strange Web server running applications on their machine without their knowledge, and their concerns are not entirely unjustified. These programming systems have security safeguards, but occasionally, bugs are found either in a programming language or in the way that is implemented by a particular browser or on a particular machine. These bugs involve some security risk. You can disable all three systems (see Chapter 22).

Netscape and Microsoft have a strong interest in reacting quickly to fix the security holes that people discover in their browsers, which is a good reason to check their Web sites (listed here) periodically to make sure that you are running the most recent versions of Navigator or Internet Explorer:

http://home.netscape.com/download
http://www.microsoft.com/ie

ActiveX controls involve risks that go far beyond those of JavaScript or VBScript scripts or Java applets. The latter three run in a "sandbox" that limits the accidental or deliberate damage that they can do. Programs running inside the sandbox don't get full access to your computer's resources. With ActiveX controls, Microsoft's philosophy is that if you can trust the author, you can trust the code. Microsoft's Authenticode system goes through a process similar to SSL (see "How Secure Transactions Work," earlier in this chapter) to verify that an ActiveX control was written by the organization that claims to have written it, and that it hasn't been tampered with since it was written.

With the authorship of the control verified, you are left with the decision: Do I trust the author or not? If you say yes, the control can run on your computer, and you may not be able to tell what it's doing. Worse, you are then asked whether to trust code from this author automatically in the future. If you say yes to this, ActiveX controls from that author will install and run without you being made aware that anything has happened.

At the risk of occasionally missing out on some cool feature of a Web page, we recommend disabling ActiveX controls. Or, if you do enable them, don't give automatic trust to any author. Call us paranoid, but we wouldn't let our best friends install new software on our computers without telling us.

For more information about how to include these advanced features in your own Web pages, see "Creating a Page Program with Scripts, Objects, and Events" in Chapter 34.

Viruses

As Web browsers become more complex and new Web technologies such as Java and ActiveX become more powerful, the risks increase of contracting *viruses* (self-replicating programs) over the Web. The most risky thing that you can do on the Web is to download an executable file from someone who you don't know and then run it on your computer. This is no different from letting a stranger put a diskette into your disk drive.

Check regularly for patches, warnings, and new versions at the Web site of the company that wrote your Web browser. Viruses come in through security holes, and many people are working to find and patch those holes before they can be exploited.

Your risk of infection depends in part on how adventurous you are. If all you ever do is read the daily briefing on your company's intranet (described in Chapter 4), your risk of infection is very low. Sticking to well-known Web sites is a safe (if somewhat boring) policy. You can also lessen your risk by turning off advanced features, such as Java and ActiveX. There is a trade-off between risk and functionality, and only you can decide how safe you need to be. (We tend to be fairly adventurous, and haven't found viruses to be a big problem.)

Recognize, though, that a small risk of a virus infecting your computer exists, no matter how careful you are. Everyone should have a virus-checking program, keep it up-to-date, and run it regularly. See "Scanning for Viruses" in Chapter 38.

Privacy Implications of Browser Caches and History

As you browse the Web, your browser may be storing in a *cache* (temporary storage area) the Web pages that you visit, and may be making a list of the Web sites that you have visited. Browsers do so with the best of intentions: cached Web pages can be reloaded quickly when you hit the Back button, and History files enable you easily to find a Web site that you remember looking at last week.

But if anyone else—your spouse, children, boss, or coworkers—have access to your computer, they can find out what you've been looking at, unless you take precautions. Conversely, you can find out what other people have been looking at, unless they take precautions. (See "Managing Navigator's Caches of Web Pages" and "Using the History List" in Chapter 19, or "Managing Internet Explorer's Cache of Web Pages" and "Using the History Folder" in Chapter 20.)

Clearing the History list in either IE or Navigator doesn't clear either the Back menu or the drop-down list under the Location box in Navigator. If you want to be sure to cover your tracks, exit the browser after you clear History—when it restarts, the Back menu is empty, as well. In Navigator, clear the Location drop-down list by deleting the file Prefs.js.

Adjusting Your Security Settings

Navigator and Internet Explorer give you broad latitude about how strict a security policy you want to set. If your policy is too strict, you miss out on some of the cool features of the Web. If it is too loose, you can be defrauded or introduce viruses into your computer system. If you choose too many "ask me at the time" options, your browsing session is constantly interrupted with questions whose implications you may not fully grasp.

Different browsers allow you very different security options, because the companies that make the browsers have very different philosophies about security. For this reason, discussions of specific security options are in the chapters concerned with specific browsers. See "Changing Navigator's Security Warnings" in Chapter 19 and "Changing Internet Explorer's Security Settings" in Chapter 20.

The only cross-platform security advice we give is this: Don't fiddle with your security settings unless you've thought about what you're doing. When you're wading through a blizzard of warning messages that probably aren't important, it's easy to get annoyed and change something (anything!) to make the messages stop. (Internet Explorer is particularly bad about putting a Don't Ask Me This Question Again check box on warning messages. *Don't check that box.* You may not realize the full implications.) The problem is that your browser won't come back to you a day or two later and say "Do you realize that your security settings are still very low?" After you lower your security settings, they don't call attention to themselves.

Anonymous Web Browsing Through Proxies

One way to make sure that Web sites don't accumulate information about you is not to give them any. Unfortunately, just looking at a site leaves a record that someone with your IP address looked at the site. If even this is more information than you want to leave, you can do your Web browsing anonymously, through a *proxy.*

When you use a proxy, you send your Web page requests to the proxy, and it makes the request in its own name. To the server whose pages you are requesting, you appear to be at the proxy's IP address, not at your own.

Two Web sites where you can arrange to work with a proxy are these:

http://www.anonymizer.com
http://www.iproxy.com.

Each site offers a no-frills free anonymous browsing service. An informative how-to piece on anonymous browsing is at this site:

http://www.tamos.com/privacy/anonen.htm

Blocking Offensive or Inappropriate Web Sites

Almost anything that people want to see, hear, or read is on the Web somewhere. You may decide that you want to block your Web browser's access to certain kinds of content, because you either find it offensive, don't want your children to see it, or don't want your workers to waste their time on it. The most recent versions of popular Web browsers, such as Navigator and IE, allow you to participate in a voluntary system for blocking offensive or inappropriate content.

How PICS Site-Blocking Systems Work

The W3C (the same folks who maintain the HTML standards) has created a system called *PICS* for making Web site ratings systems possible. Ratings organizations (such as RSAC and SafeSurf) have created ratings systems based on questionnaires. When Web site owners fill out the questionnaires, the ratings organizations issue ratings labels for their Web sites. The site owners display these labels on their Web sites. Web browsers (such as Navigator and IE) contain software that reads these labels and compares them to your stated standards of acceptability. Web pages whose ratings exceed your acceptable standards aren't displayed unless someone gives the appropriate password. As long as your children don't know the password, they have to ask you before they can see Web sites that might be objectionable. The rest of this section fills in some of the details.

PICS, the Enabling Technology

The *Platform for Internet Content Selection (PICS)* is an Internet protocol that enables ratings to be transferred and understood across the Internet. It was created by Paul Resnick and James Miller at W3C. PICS is a technique for associating an HTML document with a label containing information about its content. A Web browser reads the label first, compares it to criteria set by the user, and then decides whether to display the page.

PICS itself is not a ratings system. It endorses no values (other than, by its very existence, the value of voluntary labeling and filtering) and embodies no standards for Internet content. In theory, anyone could use PICS to rate Web sites according to his or her own values and standards, whatever those might happen to be. (Resnick has given the hypothetical example of rating pages for literary merit.) Ratings systems based on PICS are called *PICS-compliant*. You can find out more about PICS at the Web site **http://www.w3.org/PICS**.

PICS enables rating labels to be attached to a Web page in two different ways:

■ *Labels can be embedded in the page itself.* This technique requires that the Web site owner cooperate by attaching to its pages a label approved by some ratings service. In theory, digital signatures with time stamps can be attached to these labels, to prevent the Web site owner from tampering with them, but we know of no ratings service that currently does this.

■ *Labels can be attached by a label-server.* This technique requires that a ratings service maintain a database of URLs and their ratings that is accessible via the Web. When a browser has been set to work with the labels of a particular ratings service by using this technique, it submits each requested URL to the rating service's label server, and does not display the page until the label has been approved.

The first technique requires the cooperation of Web site owners; the second requires a small army of people to create and maintain the database. Currently, no mechanism to pay the small army exists, so ratings services use the first technique.

Content-Rating Services: SafeSurf and RSAC

Although any organization *could* set up a PICS-compliant ratings system, rate the millions of pages on the Internet, and persuade the authors of those pages to display its rating labels, only a handful of organizations are making a major effort to carry out this plan. The two whose ratings systems are built into Netscape NetWatch are SafeSurf and the Recreational Software Advisory Council (RSAC). Microsoft's Content Advisor includes only RSAC's system. (Microsoft is a founding sponsor of RSAC.)

Other ratings services exist and can be added to NetWatch or Content Advisor by downloading a RAT (PICS rating) file from the service's Web page. W3C maintains a list of the PICS-compliant ratings systems that it knows about at **http://www.w3.org/PICS/raters**.

SafeSurf and RSAC arose in very different ways. SafeSurf is a parents' group trying to make the Internet a safe and useful tool for children. (Its Web site is a good reference for finding links to other kid-friendly and educational Web sites.) RSAC is a nonprofit corporation created by the Software Publishers Association together with computer and entertainment powerhouses, such as Microsoft, Disney, and IBM. RSAC's original mission was to issue a ratings system for computer games, and it later extended its game-rating system to the Internet. What the two organizations have in common is a belief that a voluntary rating-and-blocking system for Web sites is better than government censorship.

You can find out more about these organizations by visiting their Web sites, listed here:

http://www.safesurf.com
http://www.rsac.org

The SafeSurf and RSACi Content Categories

The two most popular ratings systems are called the SafeSurf Rating Standard and RSAC for the Internet (RSACi). The heart of each system is a set of categories of possibly offensive content and defined levels for each category.

The RSACi system (an adaptation of RSAC's computer game rating system) has four categories (language, nudity, sex, and violence) and five levels for each category (from "0–none" to 4). The SafeSurf system has nine categories (profanity, heterosexual themes, homosexual themes, nudity, violence, intolerance, glorifying drug use, other adult themes, and gambling) and nine levels for each category (ranging from "1–subtle innuendo" to "9–explicit and crude or explicitly inviting participation"). The Netscape NetWatch Web site gives the explicit definition of each level in each category for both RSACi and SafeSurf, at these sites, respecively:

> **http://home.netscape.com/communicator/netwatch/b_rsaci.html**
> **http://home.netscape.com/communicator/netwatch/c_safesurf.html**

Web site owners rate their sites voluntarily by going to the rating organization's Web site and filling out a form. To rate a Web site with SafeSurf or RSACI, go to the following sites, respectively:

> **http://www.safesurf.com/classify**
> **http://www.rsac.org**

Once a site is rated, the rating organization e-mails the Web site owner a piece of HTML code to attach to the rated Web pages. This piece of code is the rating tag that is read by Web browsers.

Other PICS-compliant ratings services include the following:

- Adequate.com (**http://www.adequate.com**)
- Safe for Kids (**http://www.weburbia.com/safe**)
- Vancouver Webpages Ratings Service (**http://vancouver-webpages.com/VWP1.0**)

These systems resemble RSACi and SafeSurf in that the Web site owners rate their own sites (though Vancouver's system is unique in having some positive categories, such as educational content and environmental awareness.) None of these systems is pre-installed in Content Advisor or NetWatch, but any can be added by downloading the ratings file (.rat) from the rating service's Web site.

PICS-Reading Browsers: Navigator's NetWatch and Internet Explorer's Content Advisor

PICS-compliant ratings systems would be useless if Web browsers couldn't read the PICS labels. The most recent versions of the two programs that dominate the browser market, Microsoft's Internet Explorer and Netscape's Navigator, do so. Internet Explorer contains a component called *Content Advisor*, and Navigator has a similar component called *NetWatch*. Each lets you set your own acceptable rating levels. After you enable Content Advisor or NetWatch (and choose a password), it blocks Web sites whose ratings exceed your selected level of acceptability, unless the password is given.

Both browsers support both RSACi and SafeSurf. Content Advisor comes with RSACi already enabled, but you can download a file to enable SafeSurf, as well.

NetWatch comes with both RSACi and SafeSurf. You can use more than one ratings system simultaneously.

At present, both Content Advisor and NetWatch suffer from the same deficiency: neither has a memory. If you decide that a particular Web site is sufficiently worthwhile to allow your child to access it, even though it is unrated or has a high rating for some objectionable material, you can't give once-and-for-all permission. Every time that your child wants to return to that site, you have to type the password.

For details on how to operate these two programs, see "Blocking Web Sites with NetWatch" in Chapter 19, and "Blocking Web Sites with Content Advisor" in Chapter 20.

Unrated Web Sites

The most difficult task in establishing a ratings system is to get the cooperation of the Web site owners. Sites that are trying to be kid-friendly, such as Yahoo!'s Yahooligans (**http://www.yahooligans.com**), have a motivation to cooperate with the system. And adult sites, such as Playboy's (**http://www.playboy.com**), are motivated to support voluntary ratings, to avoid government censorship or possible lawsuits. But for the broad range of sites in between Yahooligans and Playboy, the motivation to rate is less clear, and cooperation has so far been erratic. The Weather Channel site (**http://www.weather.com**) has a RSACi rating, while CNN (**http://cnn.com**) does not. Even the Web site of The Children's Television Workshop (**http://www.ctw.org**), creators of *Sesame Street*, was not rated by either RSACi or SafeSurf when we last checked.

RSAC claims that tens of thousands of sites have been rated and that 5,000 more are rated every month. But given the size of the Web and the rate at which the number of Web sites is increasing, it's not clear whether RSAC is gaining or losing ground in the battle to get the Web rated. SafeSurf gave us no estimate, but our own browsing experience convinced us that SafeSurf has rated even fewer sites.

Recommendations for PICS Web Site Blocking

The two biggest decisions that you need to make regarding PICS-compliant Web site blocking programs (such as Content Advisor and NetWatch) are whether to use them at all and, if you do use them, whether to block unrated Web sites.

Currently, so many sites are unrated that if you don't block them, you really aren't protecting anyone. Playboy's Web site may be rated with both RSACi and SafeSurf, but Penthouse's (**http://www.penthouse.com**) wasn't rated by either service when we looked, and neither was Bianca's Smut Shack (**http://www.bianca.com/shack**). And no actively predatory Web site is going to bother getting itself rated. On the other hand, if you do block unrated sites, you make the Web a much smaller place: no CNN, no Library of Congress (**http://lcweb.loc.gov**), no Children's Television Workshop, just to name a few of the many Web sites that were unrated by either RSACi or SafeSurf when we last checked.

Our conclusion is that, at present, Content Advisor and NetWatch are useful mainly for very small children, who are going to want to visit a small list of Web sites over and over. Teenagers would find the blocking of unrated sites very restrictive, and most of the worthwhile content of the Web would be lost to them (unless a sudden upturn in the number of rated sites occurs). Moreover, children who are computer-smart enough to download a second copy of Navigator and install it in an obscure directory are not going to be constrained by the rating systems, unless they want to be.

For children of an in-between age, make a list of the things that you want them to be able to do on the Web, and look for rated Web sites that allow them to do it. (The simplest way to check whether a site is rated is to turn on Content Advisor or NetWatch and try to look at the site.) For example, while many sports sites are not rated (the National Football League's **http://www.nfl.com**, for example), ESPN's site (**http://espn.sportzone.com**) is RSACi rated. So using RSACi will not make it impossible for your 11-year-old to check sports scores on the Web. After you determine exactly what you are giving up by using a rating system, you will be in a better position to decide whether to use one.

Non-PICS Web Site Blocking

While NetWatch and Content Advisor are free components of Navigator and Internet Explorer, respectively, there are other commercial products that filter the Web sites that your browser can receive. A list of the products available, with links to the Web sites of the companies marketing the products, can be found at the Web site of The Internet Filter Assessment Project (TIFAP). TIFAP is a project created and run by librarians, who have a special interest in Internet filtering, now that many libraries contain public-access Internet terminals. TIFAP's Web site is at

http://www.bluehighways.com/tifap

Commercial blocking packages may include access to proprietary databases of "good" and "bad" URLs, and may block pages based on the presence of specific words. (The TIFAP report contains an amusing story about a program that included "XXX" among its objectionable character strings, and so refused to display anything about Super Bowl XXX.)

Opposition to Rating and Blocking Systems

Particular ratings systems such as RSACi and SafeSurf, and even the potential for Internet filtering inherent in PICS, have generated controversy. Many arguments for not rating your Web site and not using filtering software are available on the Web. Many such arguments have been collected by an officer of Electronic Frontiers Australia at **http://rene.efa.org.au**.

Purchasing Products Online with Wallet Programs

Shopping is one of the most popular features of the Internet, for a variety of good reasons: Web sites are open all night, you can move from one store to another in seconds; it's usually easy to find reliable product information; and you never have to worry about over-aggressive salespeople. (For some suggestions on finding good shopping Web sites, see Chapter 25.)

Still, there are a few problems, and most of them have to do with either credit cards or shipping. Typing in credit card numbers is a clumsy process, and if the address you type in doesn't exactly match the billing address on your credit card statements, the transaction may be rejected. (This may sound like a triviality, but it is a serious nuisance. Who wants to have to remember whether their credit card company abbreviates *Street* or whether the correct notation for Apartment 15 is *Apt. 15* or *#15*?)

Credit card numbers, billing addresses, and shipping addresses are things you would like to think about once, get right, and never have to consider again. That's the idea behind *wallet programs*. It works like this: You type your credit card and address information into your computer once, and the wallet program stores it on your computer in an encrypted, password-protected form. When you are ready to pay for something that you want to buy from a participating online merchant, you select a credit card from the list of cards whose information you have entered into the wallet program, and give the wallet program that card's password. You also select a shipping address from a list of addresses that you have entered into the wallet. (You can choose labels for these addresses, like *home, work,* or *Mom's house*.) Your wallet program then establishes a secure connection (see "Executing a Secure Transaction" earlier in this chapter) with the merchant's server and relays all this information. The problem with all wallet programs at this stage of development is that few merchants accept them.

There is one wallet program, called Microsoft Wallet, that you can use with both IE and Netscape Navigator and another, CyberCash Wallet, that works only with Navigator.

Security Issues

The question you have to answer is whether you feel secure letting a wallet program handle your credit cards. The nightmare is that some devilishly clever Web site will be able to trick your credit card numbers out of your wallet without your knowledge, or that someone with access to your computer (either directly or over a network) will be able to break the encryption or guess your password and get your credit card information that way.

Microsoft and CyberCash have done several things to guard your private information. Both wallet programs take the following precautions:

■ They communicate with Web sites by using the Secure Sockets Layer (SSL) protocol (see "How Secure Transactions Work" earlier in this chapter), which makes it unlikely that some third party can overhear your credit card numbers being transmitted.

- They use digital signatures to ensure that they know who they are sending information to, which means that they probably do a better job than you could do of spotting a bogus Web site.

- They store your information in an encrypted, password-protected format, so it is not sitting in a file on your machine, ready for any passerby to open.

How risky it is to keep your private information in a wallet program depends on several factors, including how well Microsoft or CyberCash wrote the wallet program, how accessible your computer is, and whether you choose good passwords and protect them well.

Microsoft Wallet

Microsoft plans for Wallet eventually to interact with electronic cash systems, Internet bank accounts, and whatever other payment schemes people come up with. Right now, it is set up to handle the major credit cards: American Express, Discover, MasterCard, and Visa.

Whether Microsoft Wallet is successful depends on whether merchants set up their Web sites to accept it. (Conversely, Internet merchants may not be motivated to accommodate Wallet until they see whether consumers use it.) At the time of this writing, the list of participating merchants is still a little slim. Popular retailers like Amazon.com and Dell aren't on the list. Microsoft keeps a list of Wallet-accepting retailers at the following site:

http://www.microsoft.com/wallet

Installing Wallet

Currently, Microsoft Wallet runs only under Windows 95/98 or Windows NT 4 or higher. It works with IE 3.02 or higher and is available as a plug-in for Netscape Navigator 3 or higher. The IE version uses ActiveX controls, so you have to leave ActiveX on if you want to use Wallet with IE. (Refer to "VBScript and ActiveX Controls" earlier in this chapter.)

The IE version of Wallet is included on the Windows 98 CD, though you may not have installed it on your system yet. To check, choose Start | Settings | Control Panel, and then select Add/Remove programs. Click the Windows Setup tab and wait while your system takes inventory. When the Add/Remove Programs Properties box appears, select Internet Tools from the list and then click the Details button. A list of Windows 98's Internet tools appears. The check box next to the name of each tool tells you whether that tool is installed. If no check appears next to Wallet, insert your Windows 98 CD into your CD-ROM drive and click the check box next to Wallet. Click OK in each of the open dialog boxes, and Wallet will be installed automatically.

If you are using Windows 95 or NT, or if you want to use Microsoft Wallet with Netscape Navigator, you can download Microsoft Wallet from the following site:

http://www.microsoft.com/wallet/downloads

Follow the instructions on the Web site to install Microsoft Wallet.

Entering Information into Microsoft Wallet

Whether you are using Microsoft Wallet with Internet Explorer or with Navigator, you enter information into Microsoft Wallet from the Internet Options dialog box. Within IE, you can open this box by selecting View | Internet Options. Without using IE, open the Internet Options dialog box by opening the Internet icon on the Control Panel.

The Addresses and Payments buttons are located at the bottom of the Content tab of the Internet Options dialog box. To add, edit, or delete a credit card from Microsoft Wallet, click the Payments button. To add, edit, or delete an address, click the Addresses button. In either case, a dialog box appears containing a list of the credit cards (or addresses) that Microsoft Wallet recognizes.

If you want to delete one of the current entries, select it on the list and click the Delete button. Then click OK. If you want to edit one of the current entries, select it on the list and click Edit. A window appears containing the current information about the entry. Edit it and click OK. To add an entry, click the Add button. If you are adding a credit card, a wizard guides you through the process. If you are adding an address, fill out the form that appears or click the Address Book button to choose an entry from the Windows Address Book.

CyberCash Wallet

CyberCash maintains an impressive list of merchants on its "Go Shopping" page at the following site:

> http://www.cybercash.com/cybercash/consumers/goshop.html

Unfortunately, though, this is not a list of Wallet-using merchants. It seems rather to be a list of merchants who use any CyberCash service, such as its secure transaction and encryption software. We have been unable to find a list of merchants who accept CyberCash Wallet.

Downloading and Installing CyberCash Wallet

You may download CyberCash Wallet free of charge from CyberCash's Web site at **http://www.cybercash.com**. Windows and Macintosh versions are available, though the Windows version includes more features.

Opening the installation file starts an installation wizard. You must be online for this process to work. The first set of screens establishes your wallet identity with CyberCash. You are asked to name your wallet and choose a password, as well as give an address and phone number.

You are also asked to choose a second verification word, in case you forget the first one. This part of the process is handled nicely: your password should be something hard to guess, which naturally makes it harder to remember. Your verification word should be something simpler to remember. If you forget your password, you call

CyberCash, tell them your verification word, and they close your wallet account. (They can't tell you your password, because they don't know it.) No one can get access to your account just by knowing the easier-to-remember verification word.

Entering Information into CyberCash Wallet

After you establish a wallet, you can put credit cards into it. The installation wizard takes you straight to a wizard for entering credit card information. If you want to enter additional cards later, open CyberCash Wallet and click the ReadySetGo! button, as shown in Figure 18-2. The same wizard asks you questions about the credit card type, number, expiration date, and billing address.

Paying with a Wallet Program

When you are shopping with an Internet merchant that works with a wallet program, there is no difference until you get to checkout. Then, instead of typing your credit card information into a form, you click a button. Your wallet opens in a window on your computer screen, and you choose a method of payment. The merchant's payment request is sent to CyberCash or Microsoft, together with the credit card information from your wallet. The information is then sent to your bank or credit card company for approval. The merchant doesn't see your credit card number during this process; unless some billing dispute occurs, the merchant never sees it.

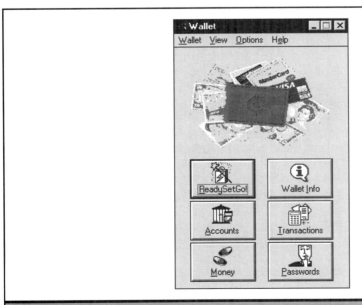

Figure 18-2. *CyberCash Wallet's button panel*

The Complete Reference

Internet

Chapter 19

Netscape Navigator and Communicator

Netscape Navigator is one of the two Web browsers that dominate the browser market. (Microsoft's Internet Explorer—covered in Chapter 20—is the other.) Navigator is the most widely implemented browser, running under Windows, Mac OS, UNIX, and Linux. It is also the most uniformly implemented browser; if you have used Navigator under one operating system you will find that it works very similarly on any other. Navigator is one component of Netscape's complete Internet package, Netscape Communicator, which includes e-mail, newsgroups, HTML composing, and Internet conferencing components, in addition to a Web browser.

This chapter tells you what Navigator can do and gives step-by-step instructions on how to do it. It relies on Chapter 18, "World Wide Web Concepts," and is parallel to Chapter 20, "Microsoft Internet Explorer." In general, issues and concepts that are common to any Web browser are discussed in Chapter 18, while issues and concepts specific to Navigator are discussed here.

Getting Started with Navigator and Communicator

Navigator is a component of Netscape's Communicator suite of Internet programs. You can download either Communicator or a stand-alone version of Navigator free from Netscape's Web site at

http://home.netscape.com/computing/download

You can also order Communicator on a CD-ROM for $10 at the Netscape online store, at

http://merchant.netscape.com/netstore

You may be able to get Navigator or Communicator free without the hassle of downloading a large (10–20MB) installation file. Some new computers (such as the iMac) come with Navigator pre-installed. Some Internet service providers give you Navigator on a CD when you sign up for an account.

Requirements for Installing Navigator 4 and 4.5

Communicator (of which Navigator is a component) is available for Windows 3.1 (Navigator version 4 only), Windows 98/95, Windows NT 3.51 and higher, Macintosh versions 7.5 and higher, Linux 2 and higher, and all the most popular versions of UNIX. Windows and Linux versions require at least a 486 processor. Macintosh versions require at least a 68030 or PowerPC processor. Windows and Macintosh versions need at least 16MB of RAM, while Linux and UNIX versions require 64MB. Once installed, Communicator takes up 10–30MB of hard drive space, depending on the number of installed components. A complete list of supported platforms and their requirements is maintained at this site:

http://home.netscape.com/communicator/v4/datasheet/

Communicator 4.5 (including Navigator 4.5) is available in a preliminary version for Windows 95/98/NT, Macintosh PowerPC, and UNIX platforms as we are writing this book. Its requirements do not differ significantly from those of Communicator 4. We do not know whether the final version of Communicator 4.5 will be available for non-PowerPC Macs or Windows 3.1.

What Else Does Communicator Contain?

Communicator is Netscape's complete Internet package, of which Navigator is only one component. The other components include:

- ■ **Messenger**   An e-mail client, discussed in Chapter 6.
- ■ **Newsgroup**   A tool for participating in newsgroups or collaborative discussions in a newsgroup format, discussed in Chapter 14. (In version 4, this component is called Collabra.)
- ■ **Composer**   An HTML composing program, discussed in Chapter 28.
- ■ **Conference**   A groupware product, discussed in Chapter 17 (version 4 only).
- ■ **Netcaster**   A receiver for pushed channels, discussed in Chapter 24 (version 4 only).
- ■ **AOL Instant Messenger**   A tool for maintaining buddy lists and setting up online chats, discussed in Chapter 16.
- ■ **Calender**   A group calendaring program (version 4.5 only).

Decisions to Make During Download and Installation

If you acquire Communicator by downloading it from Netscape's Web site, you have to decide which components of Communicator you want to install (see the preceding section.) The fewer components that you choose, the shorter the download process is.

One important decision to make before downloading is whether to get the version of Navigator with 40-bit encryption or 128-bit encryption (also called "strong" encryption). If you are an American or Canadian citizen, or a permanent resident of either, you should definitely get the 128-bit version. U.S. law prohibits exporting strong encryption, so you have to fill out an online form affirming that you are a citizen or permanent resident of the U. S. or Canada. (Being Americans ourselves, we don't know what happens if you lie on this form.) The alternative, 40-bit encryption, has become a little bit chancy for secure transactions. (See "How Secure Transactions Work," in Chapter 18.) Choosing strong encryption adds nothing to the length of the download.

During installation, you are asked to choose between Typical Installation and Custom Installation. The main reason to choose Custom is if you are trying to conserve space on your hard drive. Custom Installation asks you to choose whether to install various additional components, such as the Eudora Import Utility or multimedia plug-ins. If you've never used Eudora and have no messages to import, or if your computer has no sound card or other multimedia capabilities, you can save a few megabytes of disk space by not installing these features.

Whether you pick Typical or Custom Installation, in the Windows version you are asked whether Navigator should be your default browser. (See "The Default Browser," in Chapter 18.) If you aren't sure, we recommend saying yes to this question, because it is easier to change the default back to Internet Explorer than to change from Internet Explorer to Navigator. (To change the default back to IE: Open IE and choose View | Internet Options from the menu. Go to the Programs tab of the Internet Options dialog box and check the Internet Explorer Should Check to See If It Is the Default Browser check box. The next time that you run IE, it asks whether you want it to be the default browser.)

Another decision that you are offered during installation is whether Netscape's portal site, NetCenter (**http://home.netscape.com**), should be your start page (the page that comes up by default when you start Navigator). Whatever decision you make can be easily changed. (See "Choosing New Start and Home Pages," later in this chapter.)

If you are upgrading an earlier version of Navigator or Communicator, any preferences, bookmarks, profiles, or passwords are retained by the new version. If you are installing Navigator for the first time, you must set up at least one user profile. The installation wizard guides you through this process. Any decisions that you make at this point can be changed later by using the User Profile Manager utility. (See "Establishing or Changing User Profiles," later in this chapter.) If you set up a password during installation, be sure to memorize it or write it down. (See "Choosing Good Passwords," in Chapter 25.)

Starting Communicator

How you start Communicator depends on your operating system. Be assured, however, that Communicator's installation process sets up every possible option for starting Communicator. In Windows 98, for example, Communicator installs a desktop shortcut, an icon in the task bar, and a folder in the Start | Programs menu. You can click any of these to start Communicator. In addition, if you chose to make Communicator the default browser during the installation process, you can open any HTML document, Internet shortcut, or entry in the Favorites menu to start Communicator.

Communicator can be set up to open any or all of its components when it opens. Select Edit | Preferences from Communicator's menu to open the Preferences dialog box, and then choose Appearance from the Category list to go to the Appearance panel. On this panel is a list of the components of Composer, under the heading On Startup Launch. Check the components that you want to open whenever Communicator starts.

Does Navigator Work with AOL?

Yes. AOL installs Internet Explorer as its default browser, and Web links within AOL pages open automatically in Internet Explorer. But Navigator (and all the other Communicator components) can use the AOL connection to the Internet. Just start AOL, and then open Navigator in a separate window.

In the same way, Navigator works with any ISP. Even if your ISP provided you with Internet Explorer when you signed up, you can use Navigator if you want.

Using Navigator on an Intranet

If your computer is on an intranet or LAN that uses a proxy server (described in Chapter 4), you must tell Navigator to contact the proxy server to get Web pages from the Internet. Contact your intranet system administrator to find out the whether your proxy server uses manual or automatic configuration. For automatic proxy configuration, find out the URL of the Web page that contains the proxy configuration information. For manual configuration, find out the numeric IP address of the proxy server). Then follow these steps:

1. Choose Edit | Preferences in Navigator to display the Preferences dialog box.

2. Click the plus box by the Advanced category, and click the Proxies category. The right-hand side of the Preferences dialog box displays proxy settings.

3. For automatic configuration, click Automatic Proxy Configuration and type the URL in the Configuration Location box. For manual configuration, click Manual Proxy Configuration, click the View button, type the proxy server's numeric address into the HTTP box, type **80** into the HTTP Port box, and click OK.

4. Click OK.

Elements of the Navigator Window

Navigator runs inside a window that provides you with an array of menus, buttons, labels, and information displays. When all of its components are made visible, the Navigator window looks like Figure 19-1. From top to bottom, it contains: Menu bar, Navigation toolbar, Location toolbar, Personal toolbar, viewing window, and Status bar. In Communicator's Macintosh version, the Personal toolbar is not present and the menu bar rises to the top of the screen when the Communicator window is active.

In addition to the standard elements of the Navigator window, you can display a context menu by right-clicking an element of the Navigator window (in Windows) or by holding down the mouse button inside the viewing window (on Macs). The context menu varies, depending on where the cursor is when the mouse is clicked. The purpose of the context menu is to let you choose quickly from among the most likely actions. You can also display the Communicator Floating toolbar, a set of buttons for accessing the various Communicator components. The Communicator Floating toolbar can be dragged wherever you like, or it can exist in miniature on the Status bar.

Customizing the Toolbars

Each visible toolbar has a vertical tab on its left edge. Click the tab to make the toolbar disappear. The tab then turns horizontal and moves to a narrow bar just above the Viewing window, as if the toolbar has been folded up. Click the horizontal tab to make the toolbar reappear. The tab disappears completely if you choose the View | Hide command for that toolbar. (Navigator 4.5 takes a more positive approach by making the command View | Show.)

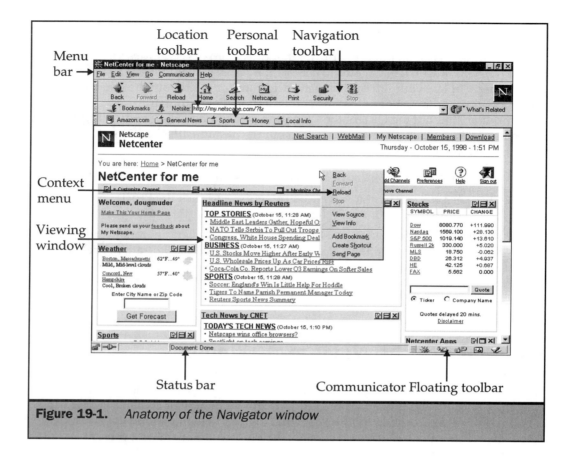

Figure 19-1. *Anatomy of the Navigator window*

To rearrange the toolbars, drag and drop the vertical tab on the left edge of a toolbar. The toolbars can be shuffled vertically, but they can't be placed next to each other on a single row.

The order of the items on the Navigation and Location toolbars is fixed, but the Personal toolbar can be rearranged, and buttons can be added or deleted. (See "The Personal Toolbar," later in this chapter.)

The buttons of the Navigation toolbar can be displayed in three ways: as pictures and text, as pictures only, or as text only. To change the display mode of the Navigation toolbar, open the Preferences dialog box (Figure 19-2) by selecting Edit | Preferences. In the scrolling Category window on the left side of the Preferences dialog box, select Appearance. The right side of the dialog box becomes the Appearance panel. Make your choice of display mode in the Show Toolbar As box.

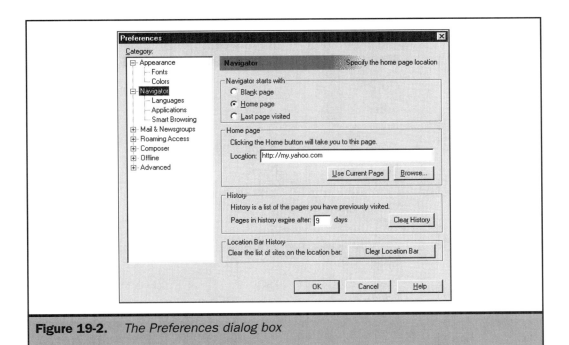

Figure 19-2. *The Preferences dialog box*

The Menu Bar

The menu bar provides Navigator's most complete set of commands. Click any of the words on this bar to see a drop-down menu of options. The menu bar is visible at all times and isn't configurable. In Macintosh systems, the menu bar is at the top of the screen when the Navigator window is active.

When toolbar buttons have been hidden or removed, their functions can be duplicated from the menu bar or the keyboard, as shown in Table 19-1.

Button	Menu	Keyboard (Windows)	Keyboard (Mac)
Back	Go	Back	ALT+LEFT ARROW	COMMAND+[
Forward	Go	Forward	ALT+RIGHT ARROW	COMMAND+]
Reload	View	Reload	CTRL+R	COMMAND+R

Table 19-1. *Menu and Keyboard Equivalents of the Navigation Toolbar Buttons*

Button	Menu	Keyboard (Windows)	Keyboard (Mac)
Home	Go	Home	None	COMMAND+HOME
Search	Edit	Search Internet	None	None
My Netscape	None	None	None
Print	File	Print	None	COMMAND+P
Security (in 4.5)	Communicator	Tools	Security Info	CTRL+I	None
Security (in 4.0)	Communicator	Security Info	CTRL+I	None
Stop	View	Stop Page Loading	ESC	COMMAND+.

Table 19-1. *Menu and Keyboard Equivalents of the Navigation Toolbar Buttons* (continued)

The Navigation Toolbar Buttons

Left to right, the Navigation toolbar contains the following buttons

- **Back**   Returns you to the Web page previously displayed in the viewing window. If multiple Navigator windows are open, each maintains its own list of displayed pages. Hold down the mouse button over Back (or right-click the Back button in Windows) to see a menu of recently displayed pages. Return to any of these pages by selecting it from the menu.

- **Forward**   Undoes what Back has done. After you click the Back button or select a previously viewed page from the Back menu, the pages subsequent to that page are transferred from the Back menu to the Forward menu. Click the Forward button to go through these pages one by one. Hold down the mouse button over Forward (or right-click the Forward button in Windows) to display the Forward menu. To return to any of these pages, select it from the menu. Select a link within the viewing window to erase the Forward menu and cause the Forward button to be grayed out.

- **Reload** Asks the server to send the most recent version of the page currently being viewed. When a page is updated on the server, the new version is not automatically sent out to anyone who might be viewing an older version. Push Reload to make sure that you have the latest version. Also, if a page has loaded improperly or incompletely, Reload tells Navigator to try again. Press the SHIFT key while you click Reload to download the page from the server, regardless of whether a new version exists.

- **Home** Returns you to your start page. (See "Choosing New Start and Home Pages," later in this chapter.)

- **Search** Sends you to Netscape's Net Search page, which contains links to most of the major search engines, Web guides, online white and yellow pages, as well as more-specialized search tools.

- **My Netscape** Links to a personalizable page at Netscape's portal site, NetCenter, which is also the default Home page (see "Portals to the Web" in Chapter 25):

    http://home.netscape.com/netcenter/personalize

- **Images (Mac only)** Loads any unloaded images in the current page. The button is grayed out if all images are loaded.

- **Print** Sends the current Web page to the printer. (See "Printing Pages" and "Saving Pages," later in this chapter.)

- **Security** Takes you to the Netscape security information screen. (See "Viewing a Page's Security Information," later in this chapter.)

- **Stop** Is active only when the browser is in the process of downloading a page from the Web; clicking it stops this process.

Menu and keyboard equivalents of the Navigation toolbar buttons are listed in Table 19-1, earlier in this chapter.

The Location Toolbar

The Location toolbar contains the following objects:

- **Bookmarks button** Opens the Bookmarks menu. (See "Using Bookmarks," later in this chapter.) In the Macintosh version, the Bookmarks button is replaced by a Bookmarks menu on the menu bar.

- **Bookmark icon** Represents the URL of the current page (called the Page Proxy icon in Navigator Help). Drag the bookmark icon onto the Bookmarks button or into the Bookmarks window to create a bookmark for the current page. Drag the bookmark icon onto the desktop to create an Internet shortcut. Drag it onto the Personal toolbar to create a button linked to the current page.

■ **Netsite (or Location) box** Displays the address of the current page. Go to a new page by typing its URL into the box. In Windows, the AutoComplete feature tries to save you keystrokes by guessing which URL you are typing, based on URLs that you have visited before. The drop-down list shows URLs that you recently typed into this box. (On Macs, a similar list appears on the Go menu.) For other ways of opening pages, see "Opening a Page," later in this chapter.

■ **What's Related button** Displays an automatically generated list of Web pages that might be related to the current page. To enable or disable the What's Related button, open the Preferences dialog box (select Edit | Preferences) and choose Navigator/Smart Browsing in the Category list.

The Location box and the What's Related button are the essential pieces of what Netscape calls "Smart Browsing." Smart Browsing integrates the search capabilities of the NetCenter portal into the Web browser itself. For example, if you type key words into the Location box rather than URLs, NetCenter does its best to come up with a Web site. This works well when you are looking for something very specific, such as the home page of a corporation that does a lot of business on the Web. Typing "Southwest Airlines" into the Location box does indeed take you to the Southwest Airlines Web site at **http://www.iflyswa.com,** a URL you might not have been able to guess. It works less well with people's names, even if they are celebrities. At worst, you arrive at NetCenter's Search Results window, no worse off than if you had typed the key words into a search engine.

The Personal Toolbar

The Personal toolbar (not available in the Macintosh version) is the most freely configurable of the toolbars. When you first use Navigator, the Personal toolbar may either be empty or contain a variety of buttons placed there by Netscape (such as a button for AOL Instant Messenger).

Regardless of what you find on the Personal toolbar, never forget that it is a *personal* toolbar—it belongs to you, to use as you see fit. A good use of the Personal toolbar is to fill it with buttons connected to the Web sites that you use most often. Or, you can maintain several different sets of toolbar buttons and switch from one to the other according to the task at hand.

To add a button to the toolbar and connect it to the current Web page, drag the bookmark icon from the Location toolbar onto the Personal toolbar. The new button is created in the place where you set down the icon. You can also drag-and-drop icons from other components of Communicator—a mailbox or newsgroup icon from Messenger, for example. After you drop such an icon onto the Personal toolbar, it turns into a button that opens the corresponding object.

The Personal toolbar is linked to the Personal Toolbar folder on the Bookmarks menu. When the Personal toolbar is hidden, you can still access its contents by clicking the Bookmarks button on the Location toolbar and looking in the Personal Toolbar folder.

To edit the Personal toolbar, edit the Personal Toolbar folder of Bookmarks. (See "Organizing Bookmarks," later in this chapter.) Click the Bookmarks button and select Edit Bookmarks to open the Edit Bookmarks window. From the Edit Bookmarks window, you can do the following:

- *Delete buttons from the Personal toolbar.* Select items from the Personal Toolbar folder and press DELETE on the keyboard. To delete the button but retain the item as a bookmark, drag-and-drop the item from the Personal Toolbar folder to another bookmark folder.

- *Create a button corresponding to a bookmark or a folder of bookmarks.* Select a bookmark or folder of bookmarks in the Edit Bookmarks window and then select File | Add Selection to Toolbar. The bookmark or folder is copied into the Personal Toolbar folder, and a button corresponding to the bookmark or folder appears on the Personal toolbar. For a bookmark, click the button to open the corresponding Web site. For a folder of bookmarks, click the button to display a list of the bookmarks in the folder; select an item from the list to open the corresponding Web page.

- *Rearrange buttons on the Personal toolbar.* Buttons on the Personal toolbar appear in the same order as the corresponding objects in the Personal Toolbar folder. Drag-and-drop items in the Edit Bookmarks window to rearrange the corresponding buttons.

- *Link the Personal toolbar to a folder other than the Personal Toolbar folder.* From the Edit Bookmarks window, select the folder that you want to link to the Personal Toolbar, and then select View | Set as Toolbar Folder. The Personal Toolbar changes to contain buttons corresponding to the contents of this folder, rather than the buttons of the Personal Toolbar folder. To change back, select the Personal Toolbar folder in the Edit Bookmarks window and select View | Set as Toolbar Folder again. In this way, you can have several different toolbar folders and switch among them, depending on the task at hand. (Only one Personal toolbar is displayed at a time, however.)

Space on the Personal toolbar is limited. If you add too many items to the Personal toolbar, those on the far right are pushed off the screen and become unavailable. However, you can increase the number of Web sites available from the Personal toolbar by placing folders of bookmarks on the toolbar, rather than individual bookmarks.

The Viewing Window

Web pages are displayed in the viewing window. The viewing window changes shape only when you resize the Navigator window—it can't be hidden, minimized, maximized, or reshaped in any other way. Many of the things that you see in the Viewing window can be customized, however, including the background color, the size and color of text, and the colors used to denote links. You can also choose whether to download and display images or other multimedia content that may take a long time to download.

Viewing Text

If the text that you see in the viewing window is too big or too small, you can change it. To change the font size in Windows for this session only, select View | Increase Font (CTRL+] on the keyboard) or View | Decrease Font (CTRL+[on the keyboard). You can repeat these commands as often as you like, to make the font as gigantic or teensy as you want it.

To make lasting changes in the way that Navigator displays text, select Edit | Preferences from the menu to open the Preferences dialog box, and then choose Appearance and then Fonts in the Category list. Drop-down lists on this panel enable you to choose the alphabet to display (in English-language versions, the default is Western), and the style and size of the fixed-width and variable-width fonts in which text is displayed. The default fixed-width font is 10-point Courier New and the default variable-width font is 12-point Times New Roman.

Most Web pages don't specify the style and size of the text fonts, leaving that decision up to the browser. Some Web pages do specify fonts, however, and usually the author has some good reason for doing so. For example, the page may have a variety of features arranged in a logical or artistic fashion, and changing the font size may ruin the arrangement. In general, we recommend letting Web pages choose their own fonts when they want to. However, if you simply can't read 10-point type, you may decide to override the font decisions of the Web page author. To do so, check the Use My Default Fonts radio button.

You may also change the color in which text is displayed, though we don't recommend it. (You are more likely to wind up with something hideous or unreadable than something pleasing.) Go to the Appearance/Colors panel of the Preferences dialog box and click the colored box labeled Text. When the Color dialog box appears, follow the process described in the upcoming section, "Changing the Background Color."

Viewing Links

When you pass the mouse pointer over a linked object (including a linked text phrase), the pointer changes from an arrow to a hand, and the URL of the Web page that the object is linked to is displayed on the status bar. Not all links on a page are obvious; a small picture, for example, might just be an illustration, or it might be linked to a larger version of the same picture. Passing the mouse pointer over an object is the easiest way to tell whether it is linked.

Text phrases that are linked to other Web pages are usually displayed in underlined blue type if you have not recently visited the linked page, and in maroon if you have recently visited it. When you are exploring a Web site, this feature lets you know where you've been, and keeps you from going in circles.

You can change these colors from the Appearance/Colors panel of the Preferences dialog box, which you access by selecting Edit | Preferences. The Links section of this panel contains two colored boxes, corresponding to the colors of visited and unvisited links. To change the color, click the corresponding colored box. When the Color dialog box appears, follow the process described in the upcoming section, "Changing the Background Color."

Setting Other Viewing Preferences

Navigator gives you considerable power to customize the way that Web pages appear on your screen. In addition to the font and color choices described previously (see the prior two sections), you can specify the background color of the viewing window, choose whether to download images, and change the default language.

CHANGING THE BACKGROUND COLOR   If you find that the background color of the Viewing window is too harsh or interferes with the visibility of text or images, you can change it. Select Edit | Preferences to open the Preferences dialog box, and then choose Appearance/Colors from the Category list to display the Appearance/Colors panel. The colored box labeled Background shows the current background color. (If you are using Windows and this box is grayed out, uncheck the Use Windows Colors check box.) Click this box to choose a new color. How the new color is specified depends on your operating system, as described next.

In Windows, a palette of colored squares appears in the Color dialog box. If you find on this palette the color that you are looking for, click the square of that color and then click OK. If you want to specify the color more precisely, click Define Custom Colors. The Color box expands to enable you to select a color by one of three schemes: HSL (hue, saturation, and luminescence), RGB (red, green, and blue), or by moving sliders. (Each scheme describes the same universe of colors.) After you specify your color, click Add to Custom Colors. Your new color appears on the Custom Colors row on the left side of the Color box. Select it there and click OK.

On Windows systems, you can set background and text colors for all applications (not just Communicator) simultaneously from the Appearance tab of the Display Properties dialog box. To open this box, right-click an empty place on the desktop and choose Properties from the context menu. To tell Communicator to use Window's background and text colors, check the Use Windows Colors box on the Appearance/Colors panel of the Preferences dialog box. (A small bug: When you install Communicator, the Use Windows Colors box is checked by default, and stays checked even after you change colors to diverge from Windows. To restore Windows colors, uncheck the Use Windows Colors box, close the Preferences dialog box, and then reopen the Preferences dialog box and check Use Windows Colors again. If Communicator is *really* using Windows colors, the Text and Background color bars should be grayed out.)

On a Macintosh, the left panel of the color-specifying window lists six different user interfaces for choosing colors. All six describe the same universe of colors, except for the cutest (Crayon Picker), which restricts you to certain preset color choices. When you click a choice on the left, the right panel displays a user interface for choosing color. By using some combination of sliders, color wheels, and typing, you can make adjustments until the color in the New box is the one that you want. Then click OK.

Some Web pages specify their own background color, and the page's color scheme may become hideous if you insist on your own background color. However, if you really must have your favorite background color, check the Always Use My Colors box at the bottom of the Appearance/Colors panel of the Preferences dialog box.

CHOOSING NOT TO DOWNLOAD IMAGES   Many Web pages have pictures or other graphics on them. These are more time-consuming to download than plain text, particularly if your connection is slow. You can tell Navigator not to bother downloading graphics, from the Advanced panel of the Preferences dialog box. If the Automatically Load Images check box is not checked, Navigator does not download the images on a Web page. If you are viewing a page whose images are not being displayed, you can display them (for this page only, without changing the policy) by selecting View | Show Images, or (on a Mac) by clicking the Images button on the toolbar.

CHANGING LANGUAGE PREFERENCES   Some Web pages are available in multiple languages, and Navigator picks the one that matches your preferences. To define or change your language preferences, select Edit | Preferences to open the Preferences dialog box and then click Navigator/Languages in the Category list.

This panel of the Preferences dialog box maintains a list of favored languages, in order, with your preferred language on top. To add a language to the list, click the Add button and select a language from the list that appears. To remove a language from the Language list, select it and click the Remove button. In Windows, to reorder the Languages list, select a language on the list and click the up and down arrow buttons. On a Macintosh, to reorder the list, drag-and-drop list entries. When you are satisfied with the list of languages, click OK.

The Status Bar

The Status bar sits at the bottom of the Navigator window and cannot be hidden. Left to right, it contains the following items:

- **Lock icon**   Tells you at a glance whether you have a secure connection. If the icon is locked, a secure connection is established, capable of transmitting sensitive information safely. If the icon is unlocked, the connection is insecure, and information that you send could conceivably be intercepted. (See "How Secure Transactions Work" in Chapter 18.) Click the lock icon to open the Security Info page.

- **Connection icon**   Tells whether Navigator is working online or offline. If Navigator is online, the icon's two cables are connected; if offline, the cables are separated. Click the icon to change from one state to the other. This icon isn't present in the Macintosh version.

- **Download bar**   Displays a shaded rectangle, moving back and forth, while Navigator is downloading small files. When larger files are being downloaded, this bar displays the percentage of the file downloaded so far. On Macs, the background of the Status message area turns striped when a file is being downloaded.

- **Status message area**   Keeps you informed about what Navigator is doing. When Navigator is getting a Web page that you have requested, status messages tell you when the Web site has been contacted, and whether it has replied. While the files of a Web page are being downloaded, status messages display the sizes of the files being downloaded and the rate at which they are coming in. When the cursor passes over a link in the viewing window, the status message area shows the linked URL.

- **Communicator bar dock**   Displays a miniature version of the Communicator Floating toolbar when the toolbar's full-size version is not displayed elsewhere.

The Floating Toolbar

The Communicator Floating toolbar contains buttons representing the components of Communicator. Click one of these buttons to open the corresponding component.

When docked, a miniature version of the Communicator Floating toolbar is found on the right side of the Status bar, at the bottom of the Navigator window. This version is fully functional, though the icons on the buttons are hard to discern. To enlarge the bar, click the textured tab on the bar's left edge.

The Communicator Floating toolbar stays on top of whichever Communicator component windows are open when enlarged. You can drag-and-drop the bar to any location. Return the Communicator Floating toolbar to its dock on the Status bar by clicking the close box in its upper-right corner.

Context Menus

If moving the cursor up to the toolbar or the menu bar starts to seem like too much work, you may be able to avoid it by using a context menu. In Windows, right-click inside the Navigator window to display a menu of Navigator's best guesses about what you might want to do. On a Macintosh, display a context menu by holding down the mouse button. Be careful if you are over a link. If you release the mouse button before the context menu appears, Navigator opens the linked page.

The context menu changes depending on where the cursor is located. (That's why it's a *context* menu.) For example, a click inside the viewing window gives you options such as Back, Forward, Reload, Stop, and Add Bookmark, among others, while the context menu over the menu bar gives you choices about which toolbars to make visible.

Viewing Pages with Navigator

Web browsing is more than a passive experience of viewing Web pages. Once a page is open in the viewing window, you may want to search the page for a word or phrase, edit the page in an HTML-composing program, view the page's HTML source code, check the security of the connection with the Web server, print the page, save it, or jump to a related page.

Opening a Page

You may use Navigator to open either pages on the Web or HTML files on your local system.

- **Using the File | Open Page command**   When you select File | Open Page from Navigator's menu bar (File | Open Location in Navigator on Macs), an Open Page dialog box appears (Open Location on Macs). In Windows, you may specify the page to open in either of two ways: Type the page's URL or local file address into the Open Page box, or click the Choose File button to find a file on your computer. After you make your choice, the URL or file address of the page appears in the Open box. Click OK to open the page. On Macs, type the URL into the Open Location dialog box. If you want to open a file on a local drive, select File | Open Page in Navigator, and then find the file in the browse window.

- **Using the Location or Netsite box on the Location bar**   See "The Location Toolbar," earlier in this chapter.

- **Selecting a link on another page, mail message, or newsgroup article**   Any object on a Web page can be linked to any other Web page. Many e-mail and newsgroup-reading programs also support links. Click a link to open the linked page in the viewing window.

- **Choosing an entry on the What's Related menu**   Click the What's Related button on the Location toolbar and select an entry from the list that appears.

- **Choosing an item on the Bookmarks menu**   Click the Bookmarks button on the Personal toolbar to display a list of Web sites that you have bookmarked (plus a few that Netscape has bookmarked for you). On Macs, Bookmarks is a menu on the menu bar, rather than a button on the Personal toolbar. Select any item from this list to display the corresponding Web page. (See "Using Bookmarks," later in this chapter.)

- **Selecting an entry from the Favorites menu**   In Windows, the Favorites menu contains links to Web pages that you have chosen to mark (plus a few that Microsoft has chosen for you). Choose an entry from the Favorites menu to open the corresponding page with the default browser, which could be Navigator. (See "Working with the Windows Favorites Menu," later in this chapter.)

- **Selecting an entry from the History list**   The History list keeps track of the pages that you have opened previously in Navigator. (See "Using the History List," later in this chapter.)

- **Clicking a button on the Personal toolbar**   See "The Personal Toolbar," earlier in this chapter.

- **Opening an Internet shortcut**   If Navigator is your default Web browser, open any Internet shortcut to start Navigator and open your Internet connection. The Mac has no default browser, but any shortcut created by Navigator is linked to Navigator.

Searching Within a Page

To find a word, phrase, or character string within a currently displayed Web page, select Edit | Find in Page from the menu, or press CTRL+F (COMMAND+F on a Mac). A Find dialog box appears. Type what you want to find into the Find What (or Find) box. If you check Match Case (Case Sensitive in the Mac version), the process finds only those strings that agree in capitalization. For example, the word *smith* will not be found in the name *Smith* or *SMITH*. In Windows, choose the Up or Down radio button to search up or down the document. In Mac, the search goes down the page, unless you check the Find Backwards check box; the Wrap Search check box causes the search to continue at the beginning of the document when it reaches the end. After you make your choices, start the search by clicking the Find Next button (Find button on a Macintosh).

Note   *Don't use the Search button to search within a page. The Search button is used to find pages on the Web, not to search within pages.*

Editing a Page for Your Own Use

Navigator itself does not edit documents, but another component of Communicator (Composer) does. After you download a Web page in Navigator, you can edit a copy of it in a new Composer window by selecting File | Edit Page. Naturally, editing your downloaded copy does not change the Web server's copy of the page.

To edit one frame of a Web page, click the frame in Navigator and then select File | Edit Frame. The document displayed in the frame appears in a Composer window.

In Windows, you can open a linked page in Composer (without opening it first in Navigator), open the context menu over the link in Navigator (by right-clicking the link), and select Open Link in Composer.

If you want to use a portion of a Web page in a document of your own, select that portion in the Navigator window with the mouse and then choose Edit | Copy. You may then open another document with Composer or some other program and paste in the copied material.

For more information about editing Web pages by using Composer, see Chapter 28.

Viewing Information About a Page

In addition to the information *on* a Web page, Navigator also allows you to access information *about* the Web page.

Viewing Page Information

To display a Web page, Navigator has to know quite a bit about it, such as how many pieces it has, what servers all the buttons are connected to, where on the Web the page's images are stored, and what method of encoding is used for all the action-generating items in the page.

Navigator hides all this information from you, because you usually don't want to know, and you might not know how to interpret all this information even if you had it. Nonetheless, if you want all this information, Navigator gives it to you if you select View | Page Info. A separate window appears with two panes. The top pane gives the structure of the Web page, with all of its attendant pieces, and the bottom lists facts about the core HTML document addressed by the URL.

If the page was encrypted, the security information is listed at the bottom of the lower pane of the Page Info window. This section contains all the information on the Security Info page, plus information on the method of encryption.

Viewing a Page's Security Information

The Lock icon on the Status bar tells you at a glance whether the current page was obtained via a secure connection. (See "The Status Bar," earlier in this chapter.) For a more detailed look at a page's security status, open a Security Info window by selecting Communicator | Tools | Security Info in Communicator 4.5, or Communicator | Security Info in Communicator 4.

The Security Info window tells whether the page was encrypted. If so, the View Certificates button is available. (For a brief description of encryption and certificates, see "How Secure Transactions Work," in Chapter 18.) Click this button to display the certificates associated with the page, what organization issued the certificate, who owns the certificate, the dates during which the certificate is valid, and a long hexadecimal number called the "fingerprint" of the certificate.

Regardless of whether the page was encrypted, the Page Info button is available, which opens the same window you could have obtained by selecting View | Page Info (see the preceding section). Strangely, more security information is available on the Page Info window that on the Security Info window.

Viewing a Page's HTML Source Code

You can view the HTML source code of the currently displayed page by selecting View | Page Source. In Windows, the HTML code is displayed in a viewing window that has no menu and allows no editing. If you want to edit this text in a word processor and save it for your own use, either select what you want to save with the mouse or press CTRL+A to select all. Then, press CTRL+C to copy it onto the Clipboard. You may then paste the text from the Clipboard into any text editor or word processor.

On a Mac, you can still use the mouse and the menu bar to work with the window displaying the HTML source code. In particular, the Edit | Select All and the Edit | Copy commands work.

Printing Pages

Print the current page by selecting File | Print. The entire current document is printed, not just the portion that currently appears onscreen. Margins are determined by the choices that you make on the Page Setup window, not by the margins that appear onscreen. The position of graphics on the page or the line-wrapping of text may be different on the printed page than what you see on the screen. In Windows, you can preview how the printed page will look by selecting File | Print Preview.

When the current page has frames, choose a frame by clicking in it, and then choose Print Frame. You can't print the framed page as it appears onscreen, as you can with Internet Explorer. At least you can't do this from within Navigator; your operating system may have a Print Screen command.

To set margins, add headers or footers, and make other choices about the appearance of the printed document, open the Page Setup window by selecting File | Page Setup.

Saving Pages

Saving Web pages is a little more complicated than saving text files, because Web pages are more complicated—they may contain images or links, or be broken into frames.

Saving the Current Page

To save the current page, select File | Save As. A Save As window appears in which you can specify a name and location for the file. To save a single frame of the current page, click the frame and choose File | Save Frame As.

To save an image from the current page, display the context menu over the image (right-click it in Windows or hold down the mouse button over it on a Macintosh). Select Save Image As from the context menu.

To save text from the current page, select the text by using the mouse and then select Edit | Copy. You may then paste it into any other application. Links are lost, even if you paste the text into an application that recognizes links, such as Composer.

To save text from a page and keep the links intact, select File | Edit Page to open the page in a Composer window. Then, cut-and-paste the text from the Composer window.

Saving a Linked Page Without Opening It

To save a linked page without opening it, open the context menu over the link (right-click the link in Windows, or hold down the mouse button over it on a Macintosh) and select Save Link As (on Macs, Download Link to Disk).

Copying a Link to the Clipboard

To save a link to a page, locate the link on the current page and open the context menu over the link (right-click the link in Windows, or hold down the mouse button over it on a Mac.) Select Copy Link Location from the context menu. Paste the link into a Composer document to insert the URL into the document as text and link that text to the Web page it represents. Paste the link into the Location or Netsite window to insert the URL into the window.

Opening Multiple Windows

Sometimes, you will find it convenient to open two or more Navigator windows. For example, you may want to compare two Web pages, or bounce back and forth among several browsing tasks, and want each to have its own Back menu.

Select File | New | Navigator Window to open a new window displaying whatever page is specified on the Navigator panel of the Preferences dialog box. (The choices there are Home page, blank page, or last page visited.) Or press CTRL+N.

When the current page contains a link that you want to open without closing the current page, open a context menu over the link (right-click in Windows or hold down the mouse button on a Mac) and choose Open in New Window (on a Mac, New Window with This Link).

Keeping Track of Your Favorite Web Sites

Navigator provides six tools that enable you to return to previously visited Web sites:

- Home button
- Start page
- Bookmarks
- History list
- Personal toolbar
- Location (or Netsite) box

If your operating system supports Internet shortcuts, Navigator enables you to create them, as well. In addition, if Navigator is the default browser in Windows, entries on the Favorites menu open in Navigator.

The Location box and the History folder record Web sites automatically; the Location box remembers the last 15 URLs that you typed into it, while the History list records the most recent URLs that you visited. (Neither of these tools are full-powered in the Mac version: the Location box has no memory, and the History list recalls nothing beyond the current session.) Bookmarks, Favorites, Personal toolbar buttons, and Internet shortcuts are voluntary—they keep track only of the Web sites that you (or Netscape or Apple) have decided to record.

The highest honor you can give a Web page is to make it your start page. This guarantees that you see it whenever you open Navigator. The default start page is Netscape's NetCenter portal, but you can change the start page to be whatever you want. (See the upcoming section, "Choosing New Start and Home Pages.")

The most valuable piece of URL-recording real estate in the Navigator window is the Home button on the toolbar. This also defaults to NetCenter, which is not a bad choice, but if you don't care for NetCenter, you shouldn't waste the Home button on it. Assign the button to a Web site that you might want to check at any time. (See the upcoming section, "Choosing New Start and Home Pages.")

The second most valuable piece of URL-recording real estate is the Personal toolbar (which doesn't exist in Navigator's Mac version). The Personal toolbar comfortably displays only about six links—choose them wisely. Instructions on adding and deleting entries from the Personal toolbar are given in "The Personal Toolbar," earlier in this chapter.

Another handy thing to do with a few frequently accessed URLs (or URLs that you plan to visit soon and then dispose of) is to make Internet shortcuts out of them and put them on your desktop. (See "Creating Internet Shortcuts" later in this chapter.)

Windows 95, Windows 98, and Windows NT have a Favorites menu on the Start menu. This menu is designed to be used by Internet Explorer, but Navigator also works with it. (See "Working with the Windows Favorites Menu," later in this chapter.)

But Navigator's main tool for remembering URLs of Web sites is the bookmark, which combines easy access with the ability to keep track of a large number of sites. (See "Using Bookmarks," later in this chapter.)

Choosing New Start and Home Pages

Navigator regards the home page (which you reach by clicking the Home button on the toolbar) as different from the start page (which opens when Navigator starts up). Change either page by choosing Edit | Preferences. Then, select Navigator in the Category box.

The Navigator Starts With box gives you three choices for your start page: It can be the same as the home page, a blank page, or the last page that you visited in your previous session. To change the home page, either enter a URL into the Location line, click the Use Current Page button (to make the home page the page that Navigator is currently displaying) or click the Browse button (to make the home page a page on your system).

Using Bookmarks

The Bookmarks menu is Navigator's primary place in which to store URLs that you want to revisit. Having a URL bookmarked is only slightly less convenient than having it as a button on the Personal toolbar (see "The Personal Toolbar," earlier in this chapter), and Bookmarks can contain many more URLs. Navigator provides four tools for you to work with bookmarks:

- **Bookmarks button**   Click this button, found on the Location toolbar, to display the Bookmarks menu. (This button is not present in the Mac version of Navigator.) Move the cursor over a folder on the Bookmarks menu to expand that folder. Click a bookmark on this menu to open the corresponding Web page.

- **Bookmarks window**   Select Communicator | Bookmarks | Edit Bookmarks or choose Edit Bookmarks from the Bookmarks menu to open this window in Windows. On a Mac, select Communicator | Bookmarks. From the Bookmarks window, you can delete bookmarks, move bookmarks from one folder to another, create new folders on the Bookmarks menu, reorder folders, put one folder inside another, import other folders of bookmarks, or examine a bookmark's properties. (See "Organizing Bookmarks," later in this chapter.)

- **Bookmark icon**   Represents the URL of the current page (called the Page Proxy icon in Navigator Help). Drag the bookmark icon onto the Bookmarks button or into the Bookmarks window to create a bookmark for the current page. Drag it onto the desktop to create an Internet shortcut on Windows and Mac systems. Drag it onto the Personal toolbar to create a button linked to the current page.

- **Communicator | Bookmarks menu**   Duplicates the functions of the Bookmarks button from the menu bar. If the Location toolbar is hidden, use the Communicator | Bookmarks menu instead of the Bookmarks button. On Macs, this function is served by the Bookmarks menu on the menu bar, marked by a green bookmark icon. (On Macs, Communicator | Bookmarks opens the Bookmarks window.)

Bookmarks is an HTML file, Bookmarks.html (Bookmark.htm in Windows). Each user has his/her own bookmarks file, which sits inside a folder bearing the name of the user profile. In Windows, find this folder in C:\Program Files\Netscape\Users. On Macs, it appears in System Folder/Preferences/Netscape Users.

Adding Bookmarks

To add the current page to Bookmarks, use any of the following methods:

- Drag the bookmark icon on the Location toolbar to the left, onto the Bookmarks button. When the Bookmarks menu appears, continue to drag the icon into whichever menu or submenu of Bookmarks you want this page's bookmark to be located.

- Click the Bookmarks button and choose Add Bookmark or File Bookmark from the menu that appears. Add Bookmark puts the new bookmark at the bottom of the main Bookmarks list; File Bookmark lets you put the new bookmark into a subfolder of the Bookmarks folder.

- Select Communicator | Bookmarks | Add Bookmark or Communicator | Bookmarks | File Bookmark from the menu. On Macs, select Bookmarks | Add Bookmark.

- Open a context menu in the viewing window and select Add Bookmark.

Any of these methods results in a new bookmark icon being added to the Bookmarks menu. This icon is associated with the page that was current when the bookmark was created, and is labeled with the title of the Web page.

You can bookmark a page that is linked to the current page (without opening the linked page) by dragging the link from the current page onto the Bookmarks button or into the Bookmarks window.

Organizing Bookmarks

Most people add bookmarks whenever they find a Web site that they want to return to, but wait until later to decide where to put the bookmarks. When you are ready to organize your bookmarks (and maybe thin them out a little), open the Bookmarks window (shown in Figure 19-3) by clicking the Bookmarks button and selecting Edit Bookmarks from the Bookmarks menu, or by selecting Communicator | Bookmarks | Edit Bookmarks in Windows or Communicator | Bookmarks on a Macintosh.

Folders in the Bookmarks window have +/− boxes next to them; the folder's contents are expanded when a minus sign (−) shows and contracted when a plus sign (+) shows. (On Macs, a right arrow denotes a contracted folder, and a down arrow signifies an expanded folder.) Continue expanding folders until you can see all the bookmarks and folders that you want to organize.

To move bookmarks or folders in the Bookmarks window, drag-and-drop them, or select bookmarks or folders and then select Cut, Copy, or Paste from the Edit menu. To delete bookmarks or folders, select them and press DELETE, or select Edit | Delete. If you delete something by mistake, select Edit | Undo to get it back.

To create new bookmark folders, choose File | New Folder. A Bookmark Properties box appears for the new folder. Use this box to give the folder a name, or even a short description. The new folder appears at the bottom of the Bookmarks menu; move it wherever you want it. You can even put it inside other folders.

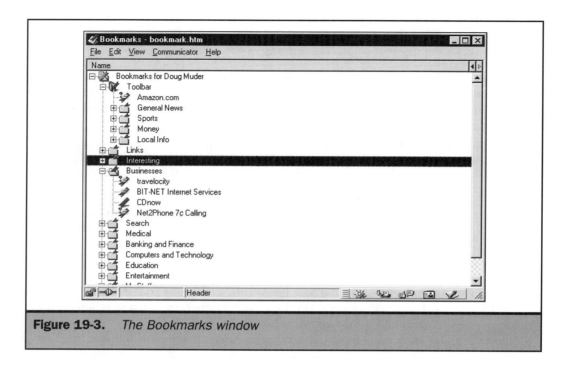

Figure 19-3. *The Bookmarks window*

To organize your Bookmarks menu into sections, add separators. Select the entry that you want to appear immediately above the separator, and then select File | New Separator. To delete Separators, choose the separator's icon in the Bookmarks window and press DELETE. To move separators, drag-and-drop them in the Bookmarks window.

In the Windows version, the View menu of the Bookmarks window provides several automatic ways to rearrange your bookmarks: by name of the bookmark, by location (alphabetical arrangement by URL), by date last viewed, or by the date the bookmark was created.

Using Multiple Bookmark Lists

In addition to building up your Bookmarks file one entry at a time, you may get whole lists of bookmarks simultaneously. For example, you may download a file of bookmarks from the Web, or you may get a file of bookmarks on a disk from a friend or from another computer that you use. You may either open this file (and use its bookmarks) without combining it with your own bookmarks file, or import these bookmarks into your bookmarks file.

To open another bookmarks file without changing your original bookmarks file, select File | Open Bookmarks File from the Bookmarks window menu bar. When the Browse window appears, locate the new bookmarks file and open it. The new set of bookmarks replaces your current bookmarks until you either reopen your old bookmarks file or restart Navigator. (Navigator always starts with the Bookmarks.html or Bookmarks.htm file in your Navigator user profile folder.)

To combine the new bookmarks file with your current bookmarks file, select File |
Import from the menu bar of the Bookmarks window. When the Browse window
appears, find the new file of bookmarks and open it. The new set of bookmarks
appears as a new folder in your current Bookmarks list.

To save the current list of bookmarks under a new name, select File | Save As from
the Bookmarks window menu bar. Choose a name and location for the bookmarks file.
You may use this technique to save your bookmarks to a floppy disk, to give to
someone else.

Finding Bookmarks

Bookmarks have a tendency to accumulate with time, just as index cards and yellow
sticky notes do. When you have only a couple dozen bookmarks, you can just scan
them, but when you have hundreds, it becomes convenient to let the computer help
you find the one that you're looking for.

To find a bookmark automatically, open the Bookmarks window (refer to
Figure 19-3) and choose Edit | Find in Bookmarks from its menu bar. When the Find
Bookmark window appears, type into the Find line a word or character string that you
want to search for. Use the check boxes in the Look In line to specify whether the word
or string should be in the name, URL, or description of the bookmark. (Adding
keywords to a bookmark's description is one way to make it easier to find. (See the
upcoming section, "Editing a Bookmark or Bookmark Folder.") Check the Match Case
check box if the search should pay attention to the capitalization that you use in the
Find line, or check the Whole Word check box to instruct the search to ignore
bookmarks in which the word in the Find line appears only as part of some longer
word or string.

After you specify everything that you want, click OK (Find on a Macintosh) to
begin the search. The process finds bookmarks one at a time. Press CTRL+G (COMMAND+
G on a Mac) or choose Edit | Find Again to find the next bookmark. To examine the
found bookmark in more detail, open its Bookmark Properties dialog box by selecting
Edit | Bookmark Properties in Windows, or Edit | Get Info on a Macintosh.

Editing a Bookmark or Bookmark Folder

You can change the name or URL of a bookmark, or assign a description to it. All these
changes are done from the bookmark's Bookmark Properties dialog box. To open this
dialog box, open the Bookmarks window (refer to Figure 19-3) and select the
bookmark. Then, choose Edit | Bookmark Properties, or Bookmark Properties from the
context menu. On a Macintosh, choose Edit | Get Info.

When you add a bookmark, Navigator automatically gives the bookmark the same
name that the author of the Web page chose as the page title. Usually, that name is
good enough to remind you what the page contains, but sometimes it isn't. If you want
to choose a different name for the bookmark, type the new name into the Name line of
the bookmark's Bookmark Properties dialog box.

You may want to change the URL of a bookmark, either because the Web site it refers to has moved or because you want a different Web site assigned to a bookmark named, for example, "My Girlfriend's Home Page." To change the URL of a bookmark, type the new URL into the Location (URL) line of the bookmark's Bookmark Properties dialog box.

You may decide to add a description to a bookmark, either to remind yourself why you bookmarked this site, or to provide keywords that you can use in a search. (See "Finding Bookmarks," earlier in this chapter.) Type the description into the Description box of the bookmark's Bookmark Properties dialog box.

A bookmark folder also has a Bookmark Properties dialog box. Though the folder has no URL, its name and description can be edited from this dialog box, just as you would do with a bookmark.

Using Bookmark Aliases

Depending on how you organize your bookmarks, you may find it convenient to bookmark the same Web page in several bookmark folders. Keeping several copies of the same bookmark up to date can be tedious, however, so Netscape provides a device that it calls a "bookmark alias." If several bookmarks are all aliases of each other, editing any of them edits all of them.

To create an alias for a bookmark in Windows, open the context menu over the bookmark in the Bookmarks window and choose Make Alias. In UNIX or on a Mac, locate the bookmark in the Bookmarks window and choose File | Make Alias. A new bookmark icon appears under the original bookmark, with the same name (in italics rather than roman type). You may move this alias wherever you like in the Bookmarks filing system, just as you would move the original bookmark.

Updating Bookmarks

You can have Navigator scan a large number of bookmarks to see whether the associated pages have changed since the last time that you viewed them. Select the bookmarks that you want to check in the Bookmarks window and then choose View | Update Bookmarks from the Bookmarks window menu bar. (Choose View | What's New? on a Macintosh.) A window appears, giving you a choice of checking all bookmarks or only the selected ones. Make your choice and click OK.

Navigator then proceeds to contact the Web servers that store the pages to which the bookmarks point, check the dates when the Web pages were last changed, and compare those dates to the dates when you last viewed the pages. After Navigator finishes this task, it displays a window that tells you how many of the Web pages it succeeded in checking, and how many of them have changed.

To see which of the Web pages have changed, look at their icons in the Bookmarks window. An unchanged page has a solid green bookmark icon, a changed page has two gray bars on its icon, and a page that Navigator was unable to check has a question mark next to it.

Working with the Windows Favorites Menu

Windows systems later than Windows 95 provide the Favorites folder as a place to store URLs of Web sites that you want to revisit. Favorites is accessible from the Start menu. Favorites works most easily with Internet Explorer, but Navigator also works with it. If Navigator is your default browser, any Web site that you select from the Favorites menu opens in Navigator. And you can even add Web sites to Favorites from Navigator.

The one thing that you can do from Internet Explorer that you can't do from Navigator is to invoke the Organize Favorites window. The only way to organize the Favorites folder without using Internet Explorer is to manipulate it through the file system; in other words, use Windows Explorer or a My Computer window. The Favorites folder is C:\Windows\Favorites if you don't have user profiles on your system. (We're referring to *Windows* user profiles now, not Communicator profiles.) If you do have user profiles, your Favorites folder sits inside of your user folder in C:\Windows\Profiles.

To add the current page to the Windows Favorites menu:

1. Open Navigator and the Favorites folder in different windows. (The Favorites folder can be displayed in either Windows Explorer or a window descended from My Computer.)

2. Drag the bookmark icon from Navigator's Location toolbar and drop it into the window displaying the Favorites folder. You can also drag a link off the current page and onto the Favorites folder.

The new Favorites entry will be named Shortcut To *title of Web page*. To change the name to something snappier, right-click the new entry, select rename, and change the name. You can also change the icon it displays. Right-click the entry, select Properties, and click Change Icon in the Properties window.

Using the History List

Access the Navigator History list in Navigator 4 by selecting Communicator | History. In Navigator 4.5, select Communicator | Tools | History. The History list appears in its own window, as shown in Figure 19-4. The Mac version of Navigator History looks different and is not nearly so useful: It is a simple list of Web sites visited during this session.

History is organized into six columns: page title, location, when the page was first visited, when the page was last visited, the date when this page is scheduled to be removed from the History list, and the number of times that the page has been visited. Double-click a line in the History list to access the corresponding Web page.

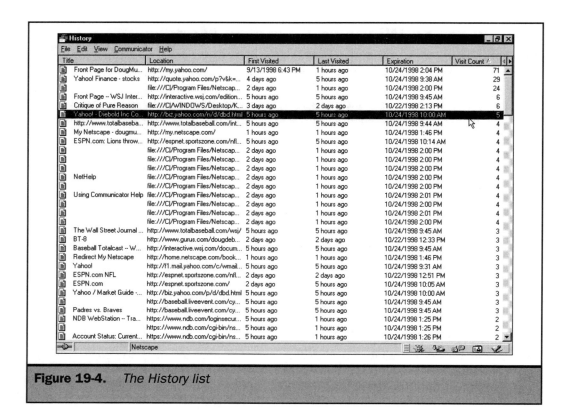

Figure 19-4.   *The History list*

Navigator does not organize its History list into folders and subfolders, as IE does, but it gives more information than IE about the Web pages, which enables you to sort and search the list in more ways than IE provides. Click a column head to sort the list according to that column; click it again to sort the list in descending order.

Searching the History List

Search the History list by selecting Edit | Search History List from the menu of the History window (not the Navigator window). A Search History List dialog box opens, as shown here:

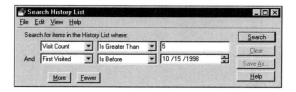

A History search consists of a set of conditions. In the preceding example, two conditions are defined. Define a condition by filling out three boxes on a horizontal line. In the first box, choose (from a drop-down list) the column of the History list to which the condition applies. In the second box, choose from a drop-down list of verbs that go with that column. And, in the third box, type something to compare the column entries against. When you are done, the condition should be a sentence that describes what you are looking for. In the example, the first condition reads "Visit Count Is Greater Than 5."

If you want to enter another condition, click the More button. A second condition-definition line appears. In this way, you can define as many conditions as you want. If you change your mind about the number of conditions that you want to use, click the Fewer button to make the bottom-most condition-definition line go away.

When you are done defining conditions, click the Search button. A list of the entries on the History list that satisfy all the conditions appears at the bottom of the Search History List dialog box. If the list is still too long, refine your search by defining more conditions or tightening the ones that you have. Then click Search again. If what you want is not on the list, refine your search by eliminating conditions (using the Fewer button) or by loosening conditions. Click Search again.

You can save the results of a search by clicking the Save As button. A Save As window appears, giving you the option of saving the resulting list as a text file or as an HTML file. If you save the list as an HTML file, each of its lines is linked to the corresponding Web page.

Changing History Settings

To change the History settings, select Edit | Preferences to open the Preferences dialog box. Select Navigator in the Category list. If you want to delete all entries on the History list, click the Clear History. If you want to change the length of time that entries remain on the History list, type a number into the Pages In History Expire After __ Days box.

Creating Internet Shortcuts

To create an Internet shortcut to the current page on either Windows or Macintosh systems, drag the bookmark icon off of the Location toolbar and onto the desktop. In Windows, the shortcut bears the icon of the default browser, regardless of whether it is Navigator. On a Macintosh, the shortcut is automatically associated with Navigator.

You may also create Internet shortcuts by dragging a link off the current page or dragging a bookmark out of the Bookmarks window. Choosing Create Shortcut from the context menu of the viewing window puts an Internet shortcut on the desktop.

Sharing Navigator with Other Users

On Windows and Macintosh systems, use Communicator's User Profile Manager to create a profile for each Communicator user on your machine. This allows each user to have an independent Bookmarks file, History list, Address book, stored messages, and preferences. On UNIX systems, user profiles are not available within Communicator; instead, use UNIX system tools to create different UNIX accounts for each user.

> **Caution** *Unlike Internet Explorer, Communicator user profiles are different from Windows user profiles. You may have a different user name or password for your Communicator profile than you have for your Windows profile.*

Communicator User Profiles on Windows systems can have passwords that make them unavailable to other users. User profiles on the Mac are not password-protected.

You may even find it handy to have several user profiles just for yourself, if you use Communicator differently for different purposes. For example, you might set up home and work profiles. In this way, family members could use your Messenger program without seeing your work messages, and coworkers could use your Messenger program without seeing your personal messages.

In Windows, each Communicator user profile has a folder inside the folder C:\Program Files\Netscape\Users. This folder contains all the information connected with the user profile, such as its bookmarks file. On Macs, the user profile folders are in System Folder/Preferences/Netscape Users.

Establishing or Changing User Profiles

The User Profile Manager is installed automatically when you install Communicator on Windows or Mac systems. The User Profile Manager is used to create, remove, or rename a user profile, to change the password of a user profile, or to give a profile a password for the first time. This program is separate from Communicator, and can be run only when Communicator is closed. On Windows systems, open User Profile Manager by selecting Start | Programs | Netscape Communicator | Utilities | User Profile Manager. On Macs, find the User Profile Manager inside the Netscape Communicator folder.

User Profile Manager opens by displaying the Profile Manager dialog box, which lists the profiles Communicator has set up already. To change an existing profile, select it on the list. This activates the Rename, Change Password, and Delete buttons, which enable you to rename or delete the profile, or change its password. (Since user profiles on a Macintosh are not password-protected, it has no Change Password button.)

To create a new user profile, click the New button. The Profile Setup Wizard starts. Enter the information that the Wizard requests. You need to know the names of the new user's mail and news servers, and the new user's e-mail address. (In the Mac version, you don't need to know these things; the e-mail address can be skipped, and Communicator doesn't ask for server information until you try to access Messenger or Collabra.

Profiles are easy to delete. Anyone with access to your computer can delete any profile, including password-protected profiles. Deleting a profile destroys access to the e-mail messages stored in that profile's Message Center.

Using Communicator with Multiple Profiles

When Communicator has only a single user profile, it opens automatically with the preferences in that profile. When multiple profiles have been established, however, Communicator must know which profile to use before it can do anything. (Different users, for example, might set up Communicator to open with different components.) Consequently, when multiple profiles are enabled, Communicator starts with the User Profile Manager. Choose the appropriate profile name from the list provided and give that profile's password, if any.

You may also open the Profile Manager dialog box (discussed in the preceding section) by clicking the Manage Profiles button.

Security in Navigator

Navigator is intended to be simple enough for novice users. For this reason, most of what Navigator does is invisible. Some choices that Navigator makes for you, however, have implications for your system's use of disk space or its security—implications that more-advanced users may want to consider. Navigator allows you some limited opportunities to "get under the hood" and make choices about caching Web pages, accepting cookies, and running applets in Java.

The Security Info page enables you to review security information related to the current page (whether it was encrypted, for example) and reset your policies for accepting Java applets, using encryption, passwords, and other security issues. Open this page either by selecting Communicator | Tools | Security Info in Navigator 4.5 or Communicator | Security Info in Navigator 4, or by clicking the lock icon on the left end of the status bar. The Security Info page is shown in Chapter 18, in Figure 18-1.

Managing Cookies in Navigator

Navigator lets you control how it uses cookies. The default option is to accept all cookies. You also have the option to either refuse all cookies, be asked whether to accept or refuse cookies on a case-by-case basis, or accept only those cookies that get sent back to the originating server. For an explanation of what cookies are, see "Cookies" in Chapter 18.

Select Edit | Preferences to open the Preferences dialog box, and then click Advanced in the Category list. The bottom portion of the right panel lists the four cookie policy options as radio buttons. Click the radio button corresponding to your chosen policy. In addition, a check box controls whether Navigator should warn you before accepting a cookie. The warning includes the option to refuse the cookie.

Navigator lists the cookies that it is currently storing in a text file, Cookies.txt. In the default Windows installation, this file is in the folder C:\Program Files\Netscape\ Users*your Navigator user name*. Delete cookies from your system by deleting the corresponding text files.

Managing Navigator's Caches of Web Pages

Navigator stores some of the pages that you view, so that they can be redisplayed quickly if you return to them. In general, this speeds up the browsing experience, but if you are running short of disk space, you may decide to limit or eliminate these caches. You may also empty them if you don't want anyone to find these Web pages on your computer.

Navigator has two caches for Web pages: a small but extremely fast cache in your computer's memory (RAM), and a larger but slower one on your hard disk in the folder C:\Program Files\Netscape\Users*your Navigator user name*\Cache.

To empty or change the size of either cache, select Edit | Preferences to open the Preferences dialog box, and then choose the Advanced/Cache panel from the Category list. The panel contains windows displaying the size of each cache. You can resize a cache by typing a new number into the corresponding window, or empty the cache by clicking the corresponding Clear button.

Managing Java and JavaScript

Java and JavaScript are programming languages that are used to give some Web pages advanced features. They are discussed in more detail in "Java and JavaScript" in Chapter 18, while the security issues they raise are mentioned in "Executable Applets and Scripts," also in Chapter 18.

Turning On or Off Java and JavaScript

The simplest way to avoid any security issue connected with Java is to deactivate it. (The downside: You lose some of the more advanced functionality of Web pages, and you won't be able to use NetWatch.) If you want to deactivate Java and JavaScript, select Edit | Preferences and click Advanced in the Categories window of the Preferences dialog box. The check boxes, Enable Java and Enable JavaScript, turn on or off Java and JavaScript.

Granting Additional Privileges to Java Applets

Java applets run on a "virtual machine," a software construction that prevents the applets from having direct access to the resources on your computer or network. (Some articles refer to this virtual machine as Java's "sandbox.") If your Java virtual machine (JVM) is working properly, even a malicious applet should not be able to do significant harm. (That said, security holes in Java are occasionally found. Netscape patches them as fast as it can. This is a good reason to make sure that you are running the most recently available version of Navigator.)

Some applets may require access to more of your system's resources than the JVM provides. (So far this is fairly rare, though it may become more frequent as increasingly complex applets are written.) Navigator allows you to grant these privileges, should you decide to do so. In general, we recommend extreme caution in granting these privileges (which could be comparable to those enjoyed by ActiveX Controls under IE).

A privilege-requesting applet must be digitally signed and carry a certificate. (See "Digital Certificates" in Chapter 18.) Navigator keeps track of all applets, their certificates, and the privileges they have been granted. To examine these certificates and review or revoke the privileges granted, open the Security Info page by clicking the lock icon on the status bar. Click Java/JavaScript in the left pane of the Security Info. The right pane displays a list of vendors, distributors, and Web sites whose Java applets or JavaScript scripts have been granted privileges. (Our own list is blank. Don't be surprised if yours is also.)

To remove an entry from this list (and thereby revoke the privileges granted), select the entry and click the Remove button. To examine the certificate, click View Certificate. To examine precisely which privileges the vendor, distributor, or Web site's applets and scripts have been given, or to change those privileges, select an entry from the list and click Edit Privileges.

Changing Navigator's Security Warnings

Navigator is set up to warn you whenever you are about to do something that has security implications, such as send unencrypted information over the Internet. Depending on how risky your Web browsing habits are and your general attitudes about security, these warnings may either be important reminders or annoying nuisances. To choose which actions you want to be warned about, open the Security Info page by clicking the lock icon on the status bar. Click Navigator in the left pane of the Security Info window, and then make your choices from the Show a Warning Before check boxes.

Blocking Web Sites with NetWatch

Navigator includes the Web site-blocking application NetWatch, which works with the PICS-compatible ratings systems SafeSurf and Recreational Software Advisory Council for the Internet (RSACi). For a general discussion of PICS and PICS-compatible ratings systems, see "Blocking Offensive or Inappropriate Web Sites" in Chapter 18.

Enabling NetWatch

To begin the setup of NetWatch, choose Help | NetWatch from the menu bar. Navigator then opens the Netscape Web page that explains NetWatch:

http://home.netscape.com/communicator/netwatch

This Web page explains PICS and the two ratings services that NetWatch uses—SafeSurf and RSACi. Near the top of this page is a button labeled Click To Set Up NetWatch.

 Java and JavaScript must be enabled for Navigator to work with NetWatch enabled. To check or change these settings, open the Advanced panel of the Preferences dialog box (select Edit | Preferences and then choose Advanced in the Category list).

Clicking the button takes you to a simple form that sets up NetWatch. The form asks you to set up one or both of the preinstalled ratings systems, and to make choices of ratings levels. These systems and levels are explained in "Blocking Offensive or Inappropriate Web Sites," in Chapter 18, and from links on the page that you view by selecting Help | NetWatch. At the bottom of the form is an Allow Users to See Unrated Sites check box, an option discussed in "Unrated Web Sites," in Chapter 18. After you make your choices, you need to choose a NetWatch password, which is the password that users need to disable NetWatch for a single session or change the NetWatch settings. To turn on NetWatch, check the NetWatch On radio button at the bottom of the form and click the Save Changes button.

Disabling NetWatch or Changing Its Settings

You can disable NetWatch or change its settings by selecting Help | NetWatch. This returns you to the page from which you set up Navigator. Click the Set Up NetWatch button, enter your NetWatch password, and then click the Log In button. If your password is judged to be correct, you are given the Setup form to fill out again.

To change passwords, proceed as in the previous paragraph, but click the Change Password button instead of the Log In button. You will be asked to type your new password twice. Click a Change Password button at the bottom of the form to complete the process.

If NetWatch prevents you from viewing a page that you ask for, you can disable NetWatch for a single session from the NetWatch Protection Alert screen that it displays. Click the Disable NetWatch for This Session link and give the NetWatch password when requested.

 If you forget your NetWatch password, don't call Netscape. They don't know your password and can't help you. See the upcoming section, "Circumventing NetWatch."

Browsing with NetWatch Enabled

NetWatch is invisible as long as the Web sites that you visit either satisfy your acceptability ratings or are unrated (and you allow the viewing of unrated sites). When anyone using your NetWatch-enabled user profile tries to open a page that violates your acceptability ratings or is unrated (and you have not allowed the viewing of unrated sites), the page is not shown. Instead, the NetWatch Protection Alert message is displayed, explaining that the page violates the set standards.

From this screen, you may view the page's ratings, disable NetWatch for this session (if you have the NetWatch password), or change the NetWatch settings (see the preceding two sections).

Circumventing NetWatch

NetWatch settings are maintained separately for each Communicator user profile. This is both a convenience and a hole in the system. You can use this hole to work around NetWatch if you forget the password, but if you have clever children, they also can work around NetWatch.

The user profile dependence of NetWatch is convenient if you are sharing a computer with small children, because you can establish a password-protected user profile for yourself (except in Communicator's Macintosh version) and a password-free user profile for your children. You can then set up NetWatch on your children's user profile without interfering with your own browsing. To gain access to forbidden Web sites, a child would have to know either your user profile password or the NetWatch password.

The hole in the system is that any user can create a new user profile, and the new profile is free from NetWatch restrictions. (See "Establishing or Changing User Profiles," earlier in this chapter.)

Getting Help

Select Help | Help Contents to open the Communicator NetHelp window, shown in Figure 19-5. If you have installed Navigator by itself, without the other components of Communicator, NetHelp goes straight to the Navigator Help files.

The NetHelp window has two main components: a large display window, and a panel of links to its left. Communicator's component icons are at the top of the display window (in Communicator 4 but not 4.5). Click any of these icons to go to the Help files of the corresponding Communicator component. From left to right, the icons represent Communicator itself, Navigator, Messenger, Collabra, Composer, Conference, and Netcaster.

Help's text display is located below the component icons. This is an HTML document with links. You can read it top to bottom, or you can expand one of the links by clicking it.

The links panel has three modes, denoted by the three circular buttons at the top of the panel. The button corresponding to the active mode is enclosed in a square. Change modes by clicking a button, which include the following:

■ **Contents** Contains links corresponding to the different sections of the document shown in the display window. Reading the column is like looking at a table of contents for the document. Click a link to jump to that portion of the document.

■ **Index** Connects to the Look For box just below the buttons. When you first click the Index button, wait a few seconds for the list of topics to be assembled. (It is finished when the box in the scroll bar stops shrinking.) When the list is complete, type a word or phrase into the Look For box. The list of Help topics changes so that only those topic titles are shown that contain the word or phrase that you typed. If any Help topic sounds like the one you are looking for, click it to display the text of the topic in the display window.

■ **Find** Opens a Find window that searches for text in the current document. Type the word or phrase into the Find window; decide whether you want to find the next occurrence or the previous occurrence of the word or phrase and then click the Up or Down radio button; then click Find Next.

In Windows, you can view NetHelp with any browser, because NetHelp is a collection of HTML files on your hard drive. The files are contained in the following subdirectory:

C:\Program Files\Netscape\Communicator\Program\NetHelp

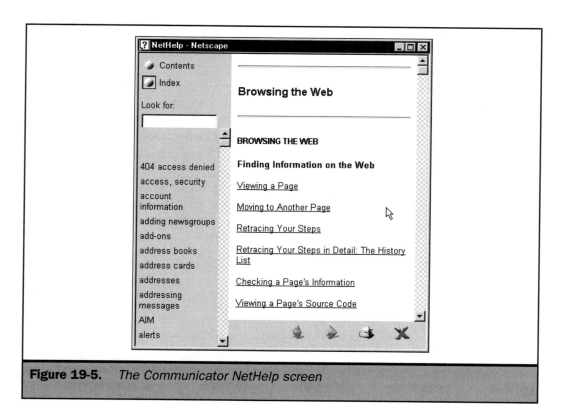

Figure 19-5. *The Communicator NetHelp screen*

The Complete Reference

Internet

Chapter 20

Microsoft Internet Explorer

Microsoft Internet Explorer is one of the two most popular Web browsers—the other being Netscape Navigator. Though originally developed for Windows, Internet Explorer (IE) now is available for a wide variety of platforms, including the Macintosh and some versions of UNIX (currently, no Linux version exists).

This chapter tells you what Internet Explorer can do and gives you step-by-step instructions on how to do it. This chapter relies on Chapter 18 for basic Web concepts, and is parallel to Chapter 19, which covers Netscape Navigator. In general, issues and concepts that are common to any Web browser are discussed in Chapter 18, while issues and concepts specific to Internet Explorer are discussed here.

Acquiring and Installing Internet Explorer

Microsoft Internet Explorer 4 (IE 4) is packaged with Windows 98 and installs automatically during the installation of Windows 98. IE 4 is also available for Windows 95, Windows 3.1, Windows NT 3.51 and higher, the Macintosh operating system (version 7.1 or higher), and two versions of UNIX: Sun's Solaris and Hewlett Packard's HP-UX 10.20 and higher. Internet Explorer 3.01 is bundled with Mac OS version 8, and IE 4 is preinstalled on the iMac (so is Netscape Navigator). Internet Explorer is included on AOL's installation CDs, and installs automatically when AOL installs.

Find the latest information about IE or download new versions—as well as occasional patches and updates—at **http://www.microsoft.com/ie**. (Once you have IE running, you don't have to remember this address—just click the Internet Explorer News icon on the Links menu.)

At the time of this writing, Internet Explorer 5 (IE 5) is available in a test version for Windows 95/98, but hasn't been officially released. The user interface of IE 5 is virtually identical to IE 4. (Most of the improvements in IE 5 are "under the hood," such as the way it handles advanced Internet file formats like Dynamic HTML or Cascading Style Sheets, which are described in Chapter 34.) In the few cases where the two versions behave differently, this chapter describes them both and identifies them specifically with the abbreviations IE 4 and IE 5.

If you have some other operating system, you may be able to run IE through a Windows emulator, or as a remote process running on a Solaris or HP-UX machine over a network.

If you don't already have IE, you can download it for free at **http://www.microsoft .com/ie**, or (at the same Web site) order a CD from Microsoft for a small shipping charge. IE comes with a flotilla of Internet-related programs, including Outlook Express for e-mail and newsreading (described in Chapter 6) and FrontPage Express for HTML composing (described in Chapter 28). The full package (which also includes NetMeeting, a conferencing application discussed in Chapter 17, and Microsoft Chat, an Internet Relay Chat program discussed in Chapter 15) can be as large as 24MB and can take several hours to download over an ordinary phone line. Fortunately, the first thing that you download is a program that manages the rest of the downloading process, so if you are interrupted or cut off part way through, you can continue the download from the point where you left off, rather than starting over. (Netscape could learn something from this.)

Requirements for Installing Internet Explorer 4

If you are running Windows 98 or a late version of Windows 95, you already have IE 4. You don't need to install anything. Otherwise, check the Microsoft Web site for operating system, memory, and hard disk resources that IE requires.

The HP UNIX version of IE 4 requires: HP 9000 Enterprise Server, HP 9000 Workstation or HP Visualize Workstation, English HP-UX Operating System version 10.20, 64MB of RAM (96MB recommended), and 75MB of hard disk space to perform the installation.

After you download the installation file, a setup program takes you through the installation process. Naturally, this process is simplest on Windows systems. Mac and UNIX users should be sure to read the ReadMe file that comes with the setup program.

See Chapter 38 for more about downloading and installing software.

 One difference between Windows 98 and any previous version of Windows is that uninstalling Internet Explorer is no longer a simple matter: do not try it. Install and use another browser if you like, but leave IE where it is. You can, of course, remove IE shortcuts from the desktop by selecting them and pressing DELETE.

Requirements for Installing Internet Explorer 5

As we write this, Internet Explorer 5 is available only in preliminary versions, and only for Windows 95, 98, and NT 4. (Users of NT 4 must install NT Service Pack 3.) Microsoft is committed to Internet Explorer becoming a universal browsing platform, so undoubtedly, Macintosh and UNIX versions of IE 5 will follow after IE 5 for Windows is officially released. These versions may be available by the time that you read this. Check the Internet Explorer Web site at **http://www.microsoft.com/ie**.

Using IE on an Intranet

If your computer is on an intranet or LAN that uses a proxy server (described in Chapter 4), you must tell IE to contact the proxy server to get Web pages from the Internet. Contact your intranet system administrator to find out the whether your proxy server uses manual or automatic configuration. For automatic proxy configuration, find out the URL of the Web page that contains the proxy configuration information. For manual configuration, find out the numeric IP address of the proxy server). Then follow these steps:

1. Choose View | Internet Options and click the Connection tab.

2. In the Proxy Server section of the Internet Options dialog box, select Access the Internet Using a Proxy Server.

3. For manual configuration, type the numeric IP address of the proxy server in the Address box and **80** in the Port box. For automatic configuration, click the Configure button in the Automatic Configuration section of the dialog box, type the URL in the URL box, and click OK.

4. Click OK.

Elements of the Internet Explorer Window

Internet Explorer runs inside a window that provides you with an array of menus, buttons, labels, and information displays. When all of its components are made visible (not all are shown when you first start IE), the Internet Explorer window looks like Figure 20-1. From top to bottom, it contains a menu bar, a Standard Buttons toolbar, an Address bar, a Links bar, an Explorer bar, a viewing window, and a status bar.

Depending on what you are trying to do and how familiar you are with the workings of the browser, the elements of the IE window may be either useful tools or distracting clutter. Fortunately, most of what you see can be customized to display exactly what you find worthwhile. You can display or hide the elements of the IE window, and you can change the amount of space devoted to each element.

IE contains two kinds of separators on its toolbars: simple lines that separate different buttons on the same toolbar, and draggable separators, located between toolbars. The draggable separators are wider than the simple separators and are shaded to give a 3-D effect. When the cursor passes over a draggable separator, the cursor changes to a set of arrows (in Windows) or a hand (on Macs). When this happens, you can click-and-drag the separator. Drag the separator right or left to reallocate the space given to the toolbars on either side of it. Drag the separator up or down to move the toolbar immediately to its right to another row. In this way, several toolbars can be placed on the same row, to save space.

The Standard Buttons Toolbar

Internet Explorer's Standard Buttons toolbar (called the Button bar in the Mac version) enables you to invoke several of the most frequent commands with a single click. It is

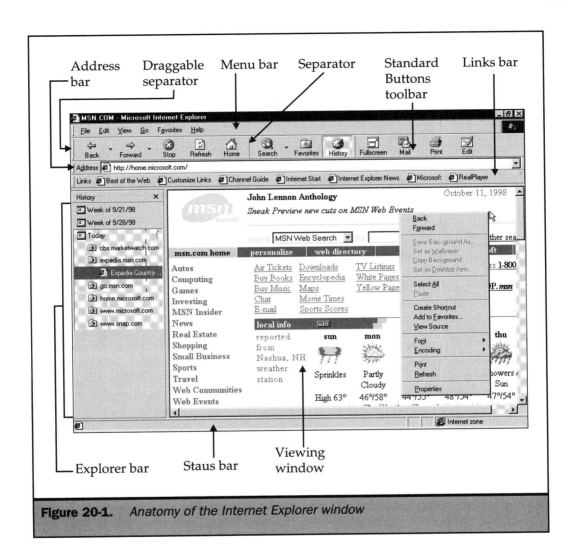

Figure 20-1.   *Anatomy of the Internet Explorer window*

very similar to Navigator's toolbar; if you are familiar with one system's toolbar, the other's is easy to learn. The Internet Explorer toolbar appears above the viewing window, just below the menu bar (or the title bar in the Mac version).

To hide this toolbar, uncheck View | Toolbars | Standard Buttons in Windows versions, or View | Button Bar in Macs. This toolbar can also be displayed in a variety of ways. (See "Customizing the Standard Buttons Toolbar," later in this chapter.)

When toolbar buttons have been hidden or removed, their functions can be duplicated from the menu bar or the keyboard, as shown in Table 20-1. (Asterisks (*) indicate commands unavailable on Macintosh menus.)

Button	Menu	Keyboard (Windows)	Keyboard (Mac)
Back	Go	Back	ALT+LEFT ARROW	COMMAND+[
Forward	Go	Forward	ALT+RIGHT ARROW	COMMAND+]
Stop	View	Stop	ESC	COMMAND+.
Refresh	View	Refresh	F5	COMMAND+R
Home	Go	Home Page		
Search	View	Explorer Bar	Search		
Search (Mac)	Go	Search the Internet		
Favorites	View	Explorer Bar	Favorites		
Favorites (Mac)	Favorites	Open Favorites		COMMAND+J
History	View	Explorer Bar	History		
History (Mac)	Go	Open History		COMMAND+H
Channels	Go	Channel Guide*		
Fullscreen	View	Fullscreen*		
Mail	Go	Mail*		
Fonts			
Print	File	Print	CTRL+P	COMMAND+P
Edit	File	Edit*		

Table 20-1. *Menu and Keyboard Equivalents of the Standard Toolbar Buttons*

Using the Standard Buttons

When fully displayed, the Standard Buttons toolbar contains the following buttons, from left to right (the rightmost buttons aren't displayed if your window is too narrow for the full toolbar):

- **Back**   Returns you to the Web page previously displayed in the viewing window. If multiple IE windows are open, each maintains its own list of displayed pages. Click the down-arrow next to the Back button (or right-click the Back button) to see a menu of recently displayed pages. On a Mac, hold down the mouse button over Back. Return to any of these pages by selecting it from the menu.

- **Forward**   Undoes what Back has done. After you click the Back button or select a previously viewed page from the Back menu, the pages subsequent to that page are transferred from the Back menu to the Forward menu. Click the Forward button to go through these pages one by one. Click the down-arrow next to the Forward button (or right-click the Forward button) to display the Forward menu. On a Mac, hold down the mouse button over Forward. To return to any of these pages, select it from the menu. Selecting a link within the viewing window erases the Forward menu and causes the Forward button to be grayed out.

- **Stop**   Interrupts the process of downloading a page from the Web. The viewing window then displays as much of the page as it can construct from the partial download.

- **Refresh**   Asks the server to send the most recent version of the page you are viewing. When a page is updated on the server, the new version is not automatically sent to anyone who might be viewing an older version, because Web pages are stored temporarily (*cached*) on your hard disk. Push Refresh to make sure you have the latest version. If the page took a long time to load the first time, refreshing may take a long time again.

- **Home**   Returns you to your Start page. (See "Choosing a New Start Page," later in this chapter.)

- **Search**   Opens one of the major Internet search engines in the Explorer bar.

- **Favorites**, **History**, and **Channels**   Display the Favorites, History, or Channels folder trees on the Explorer bar. The Channels button appears in IE 4 but not IE 5. On Macs, Favorites appears after Mail, and History and Channels aren't buttons at all. On Macs, all three of these buttons, along with Search, are tabs on the left edge of the viewing window.

- **Fullscreen**   Shrinks all icons and toolbars, to maximize the viewing area. If the browser window is already in full-screen mode, click the Fullscreen button again to return the browser window to its previous state. The Mac version has no Fullscreen button.

- **Mail**   Opens your designated e-mail client. By default, this is Outlook Express, but if you name another client (such as Eudora) on the Programs tab of the Internet Options dialog box, that program opens instead. (See "Working With Other Internet Applications," later in this chapter.)

- **Fonts**   Lets you increase or decrease the size of all fonts on the Web pages that you view, without changing the default settings. This button is optional in IE 4, and doesn't appear in IE 5. To put it on your toolbar (or remove it) in IE 4, check (or uncheck) the Show Font Button icon on the Advanced tab of the Internet Options dialog box. Macs use two buttons: Font Larger and Font Smaller.

- **Print**   Opens a Print dialog box. (See "Printing and Saving Pages," later in this chapter.) The Mac version has no Print button, unless you choose the Netscape Compatible or Compatible Plus toolbar, which are described in "Customizing the Internet Explorer Button Bar on a Macintosh," later in this chapter.

- **Edit**   Opens the currently displayed page in your designated HTML-composing application. By default, this is FrontPage Express, but if you name another HTML-composing application on the Programs tab of the Internet Options dialog box, that program opens instead. The Mac version has no Edit button.

- **Preferences**   Opens the Internet Explorer Preferences dialog box in the Mac version. Windows versions of Internet Explorer have no Preferences button.

Customizing the Standard Buttons Toolbar

You can display the Standard Buttons toolbar in a variety of forms. You can hide it entirely (or make it reappear) by toggling the check mark located at View | Toolbars | Standard Buttons (View | Button Bar in the Mac version). The toolbar is visible when the check mark is present.

You can change the appearance of the toolbar in several ways: The buttons can have text labels or not, the icons can be large or small (or absent, in the Mac version). The width of the toolbar is affected by two factors: the size of the icons and whether text labels are displayed. The most compact toolbar uses small icons and no text labels. (Even when text labels are not displayed, a tool tip is displayed when the cursor hovers over a button.) These factors are controlled differently in different versions of Internet Explorer.

CUSTOMIZING STANDARD BUTTONS IN INTERNET EXPLORER 4   You can hide the text labels on the standard buttons (or make them reappear) by toggling the check mark at View | Toolbars | Text Labels. Shrink (or expand) the size of the toolbar icons by toggling the Small Icons check box on the Advanced tab of the Internet Options dialog box (which you open by selecting View | Internet Options). The icons are small when the check mark is present, and large otherwise.

The only optional standard button in IE 4 is the Fonts button. (Don't ask us why.) Display this button (or make it disappear) by toggling the Add Fonts Button box on the

Advanced tab of the Internet Options dialog box. The button appears when the check mark is present and disappears when it is absent.

CUSTOMIZING STANDARD BUTTONS IN INTERNET EXPLORER 5 IE 5 gives you considerably more control over the Standard Buttons toolbar than IE 4 does. Access this power from the Customize Toolbars dialog box (shown in Figure 20-2), which you display by selecting View | Toolbars | Customize.

You can hide the text labels on the standard buttons (or make them reappear) with the Show Text check box in the Customize Toolbars dialog box. Shrink (or expand) the size of the toolbar icons with the Small Icons check box in the Customize Toolbars dialog box. The icons are small when the check mark is present, and large otherwise.

Your customized toolbar can contain any collection of the standard buttons, and in any order. The buttons currently displayed onscreen are shown in the Current Toolbar Buttons list of the Customize Toolbars dialog box; the standard buttons that you may add appear in the Available Toolbar Buttons list. Figure 20-2 shows a situation in which the History and Edit buttons have been removed from the toolbar. The buttons in the Current Toolbar Buttons list are shown in the order in which they appear on the toolbar, with the leftmost buttons on top.

To add a button to the toolbar:

1. Select from the Current Toolbar Buttons list the button that you want to appear immediately below the new button (in other words, select the button that you want to be located to the immediate right of the new button on the toolbar).

2. Select from the Available Toolbar Buttons list the button that you want to add.

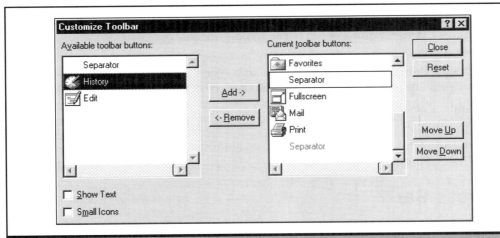

Figure 20-2. *Internet Explorer 5 allows greater control over the Standard Buttons toolbar*

3. Click the Add button.

To remove a button from the toolbar, select it in the Current Toolbar Buttons list and click Remove. This doesn't cause you to lose the button's corresponding function. All buttons have menu equivalents, and some have keyboard equivalents (refer to Table 20-1).

To reorder the buttons, select an entry on the Current Toolbar Buttons list and click the Move Up or Move Down button.

Separators are the small vertical lines that separate one set of buttons from another on a toolbar. Separators are used to group buttons together. You can insert, remove, or move separators in the same way that you insert, remove, or move buttons.

CUSTOMIZING THE BUTTON BAR ON A MACINTOSH In the Mac version of IE 4, you control the appearance of the Button bar from the Internet Explorer Preferences dialog box. Open this box either by clicking the Preferences button (if displayed on your Button bar) or by selecting Edit | Preferences. In the window on the left side of the dialog box, choose Web Browser/Browser Display tab.

The Button Bar Style box on this tab gives you three choices: Text Only, Icon Only, or Icon and Text. The Show Button Bar box gives you a choice of three collections of buttons: the standard Internet Explorer Button bar, a Netscape Navigator Compatible version, and Compatible Plus, a version that has all the Netscape Navigator Compatible buttons, plus a few more. Make your choices and click OK.

The Netscape Compatible and Compatible Plus Button bars provide additional buttons that aren't listed in the "Using the Standard Buttons" section, earlier in this chapter. The new buttons available under these options are listed here:

- **Images** Loads images for the current page, without resetting the preference not to load images. See "Choosing Not to Download Multimedia Content," later in this chapter. Equivalent to View | Load Images, or COMMAND +I on the keyboard.

- **Open** Presents a box into which you can type the URL or local address of a file to open. Equivalent to File | Open Location, or COMMAND+L on the keyboard.

- **Add** Puts the current page on your Favorites list. Equivalent to Favorites | Add Page to Favorites, or COMMAND+D on the keyboard.

- **Source** Displays the HTML source code for the current page. Equivalent to View | Source.

The Address Bar

The Address bar displays the URL of the currently displayed Web page or the file address of the currently displayed local file. Hide the Address bar by unchecking View | Toolbars | Address Bar (or View | Address Bar in the Mac version).

You can open a Web page by typing or pasting its URL into the Address bar and pressing ENTER. The AutoComplete feature tries to save you keystrokes by guessing what URL you are typing, based on URLs that you have visited before. The list that drops down from the Address bar remembers the last 25 URLs that you have typed in; you may select one of these from the list rather than typing it. In UNIX versions of Internet Explorer, AutoComplete doesn't always work for addresses with mixed upper- and lowercase characters.

If the text jumping ahead of your typing in the Address bar bothers you, turn off AutoComplete. In Windows, open the Internet Options dialog box (View | Internet Options) and go to the Advanced tab. Under Browsing, find the check box Use AutoComplete. On a Mac, open the Web Browser/Browser Display tab of the Internet Explorer Preferences dialog box (Edit | Preferences), which includes the Use AutoComplete check box.

 A quick way to launch an Internet search is to type ?, followed by keywords, into the Address bar.

The Links Bar

The Links bar (called the Favorites bar in the Mac version) is a row of icons linked to Web pages. It is the most convenient, easiest-to-access place to put links to Web sites that you visit regularly. Drag the left boundary to expand or shrink this toolbar. Hide Links by unchecking View | Toolbars | Links in Windows, or View | Favorites Bar on a Mac. When the Links bar is hidden, access its Web pages from the Links folder (Toolbar Favorites folder on Macs) of the Favorites menu.

The Links bar comes loaded with Web sites that Microsoft (or Apple) wants you to visit, but it needn't stay that way. If you display the Links bar at all, you can claim it for yourself: remove the original links (or move them to a less prominent location, such as the Favorites menu) and insert new links to the pages that you visit most often. For other ways to store the URLs of Web sites and return to them quickly, see "Keeping Track of Your Favorite Web Sites," later in this chapter.

To delete a link from the Links bar in Windows, right-click the link and choose Delete from the context menu. On Macs, click the Favorites tab (left side of the screen) to display the Favorites Explorer bar, find the link in the Toolbar Favorites folder, and drag the link into trash.

To rearrange the Links bar, drag and drop individual links to their new locations. In Windows, you can do this on the Links bar itself. On Macs, drag and drop within the Toolbar Favorites folder of the Favorites Explorer bar. You can drop a link between other links; when a link is in location to be dropped, the cursor changes to a separator bar.

To add a link to the Links bar, open the page that you want to link, and then drag and drop the Internet Explorer icon from the Address bar to the Links bar. On Macs, hold down COMMAND+SHIFT while selecting Favorites | Add Page to Favorites. If the current page contains a link to the page that you want to add to the Links bar, drag and drop the link to the bar. Or, you can use your favorite technique for adding a page to the Favorites menu, making sure to create the new Favorite inside the Links (or Toolbar Favorites) folder. See "Adding Favorites," later in this chapter.

The Explorer Bar

The Explorer bar displays Search, History, Favorites, or Channels in a pane at the left side of the IE window. In Windows, choose which of these to display from the View | Explorer Bar menu. To hide them, select View | Explorer Bar | None, or click the X in the upper-right corner of the Explorer bar. You can drag the border between the Explorer bar and the viewing window.

The Mac Explorer bar works differently: A series of four tabs (Channels, Favorites, History, and Search) are located on the left side of the IE window. Click a tab to expand it into the corresponding Explorer bar. Click the tab again to collapse it back to the side of the window. Make the four Explorer bar tabs disappear (or reappear) by toggling the check mark located at View | Explorer Bar.

The Viewing Window

The viewing window displays Web pages. The only way to hide this window is to minimize the entire IE window, since the main point of running a browser is to view pages. To maximize the viewing window, click the Fullscreen button on the toolbar. Click Fullscreen again to return to the previous (unmaximized) state. (The Mac toolbar has no Fullscreen button.)

The Status Bar

The status bar displays a variety of useful information. When the cursor passes over a link in the viewing window, the URL of the link appears in the status bar. When IE is looking for or downloading a Web page, the status bar keeps you apprised of its progress. Hide the status bar by unchecking View | Status Bar.

Context Menus

If moving the cursor up to the toolbar or menu starts to seem like too much work, you can use a context menu instead. In Windows, right-click an item in the Internet Explorer window to display a menu of IE's best guesses about what you might want to do. For example, a click inside the viewing window gives you options like: Back, Forward, Print, Refresh, Add to Favorites, and a choice of font sizes.

On Macs, display the context menu by holding down the mouse button. (Be careful if you are over a link. If you release the mouse button before the context menu appears, Internet Explorer opens the linked page.) The menu itself is always the same on the Mac, but different options are grayed out, depending on the context.

Viewing Pages in Internet Explorer

The purpose of a Web browser is to show you Web pages. But once a page is visible, you may want to search it for a word or phrase, edit it in an HTML-composing program, print it, save it, or even view its HTML source code.

Opening a Page

You may use Internet Explorer to open pages on the Web, pages on an intranet, or HTML files on your local system. Internet Explorer supports all the following techniques of opening a page:

- **Using the File | Open command**   When you select File | Open from IE's menu bar (File | Open Location on Macs), an Open dialog box appears (Open Internet Address on Macs). In Windows, you may specify the page to open in any of three ways: Type the page's URL or local file address into the Open box; click the down arrow to select from a drop-down list of recently opened URLs; or click the Browse button to find a file on your computer. After you make your choice, the URL or file address of the page appears in the Open box. Click OK to open the page. On Macs, type the URL into the Open Internet Address dialog box. If you want to open a file on a local drive, click the Open File button in this dialog box, or choose File | Open File.

- **Using the Address bar**   Refer to "The Address Bar," earlier in this chapter.

- **Selecting a link on another page, mail message, or newsgroup article**   Any object on a Web page can be linked to any other Web page. Many e-mail and newsreading programs also support links. Words or phrases that are linked to Web pages are displayed in a different color (usually blue) and may be underlined. If you define a hover color (see "Choosing Colors in Windows," later in this chapter), such linked text changes to a different color when the cursor crosses over it. The sure way to detect a link (whether it's text, a picture, or some other object) is that the cursor icon changes when it passes over the linked object. The default cursor icon for a linked object is a hand with its index finger extended (as if to press a button).

- **Selecting an entry from the Favorites menu**   The Favorites menu contains links to the Web pages that you have chosen to mark (plus a few that Microsoft has chosen for you). See "Managing the Favorites Menu," later in this chapter.

- **Selecting an entry from the History folder**   The History folder keeps track of the pages that you have opened previously in IE. See "Using the History Folder," later in this chapter.

- **Clicking a button on the Links bar**   Refer to "The Links Bar," earlier in this chapter.

- **Opening an Internet shortcut** If Internet Explorer is your default Web browser, open any Internet shortcut to start IE and open your Internet connection. The Mac has no default browser, but if you open any shortcut created by Internet Explorer, IE opens as well.

Searching Within a Page

To find a word, phrase, or character string within a currently displayed Web page, select Edit | Find from the menu, or press CTRL+F (COMMAND+F on a Mac). A Find dialog box appears. Type what you want to find into the Find What box, and check the appropriate check boxes within the Find dialog box. If you check Match Whole Word Only, IE doesn't return words in which your search specification is only part of a larger word. For example, if you specify *book*, IE doesn't locate *bookend* or *bookstore*. If you check Match Case, IE finds only those strings that match the capitalization that you type in the Find What box. For example, IE doesn't find *smith* or *SMITH* if you type *Smith*. Choose the Up or Down radio button to search up or down the document. Click the Find Next button to begin the search, and to continue the search after a match is found.

On a Macintosh, the only check boxes are Match Case and Start from Top. The Mac's Find box and Find button correspond, respectively, to Windows' Find What box and Find Next button.

Don't use the Search button to search within a page. The Search button is for finding pages on the Web, not for searching within pages.

Editing a Page for Your Own Use

After you download a Web page, a copy of it exists on your computer. That copy can be edited like any other file. Naturally, editing your downloaded copy doesn't change the page on the Web server.

Internet Explorer doesn't edit or compose documents. However, in the Windows version of IE, if you select Edit | Page, the default HTML-editing application (FrontPage Express, for example) opens onscreen in a new window. The current page appears in the new window, ready to be edited. (See Chapter 28 for information on editing Web pages.)

If you want to use a portion of a Web page in your own document, use your mouse to select that portion in the Internet Explorer window and then choose Edit | Copy from IE's menu. You may then open another document within another program and paste in the copied material.

Viewing HTML Source Code

You can view the HTML source code of a Web page (described in Chapter 26) and edit it with a word processor. To do so, view the page in IE and select View | Source from the menu. A word processor window opens, displaying the HTML source code. The word processor that is used depends on how your system is set up. In Windows, the most likely choice is Notepad. On Macs, the source opens in an Internet Explorer viewing window, which you can't edit. (If you want to edit the source code for your own use, save the file and open it with a word processor.) In UNIX, you may use emacs or any other text editor.

Printing and Saving Pages

In one sense, printing or saving pages from the Web is just like printing or saving any other kind of document: Select File | Print or File | Save As. The only complicating element is that Web pages themselves are complicated. Web pages often contain images, and may even contain unprintable items, such as sounds or movies. Or, a page may have several frames, each displaying a different document—do you want to print or save all of these documents, or just one?

Printing Pages

To print exactly what is displayed on your screen, select File | Print. If you want to print one frame only, click inside the frame and then select File | Print. In either case, the Print dialog box appears. In Windows, this box looks like Figure 20-3.

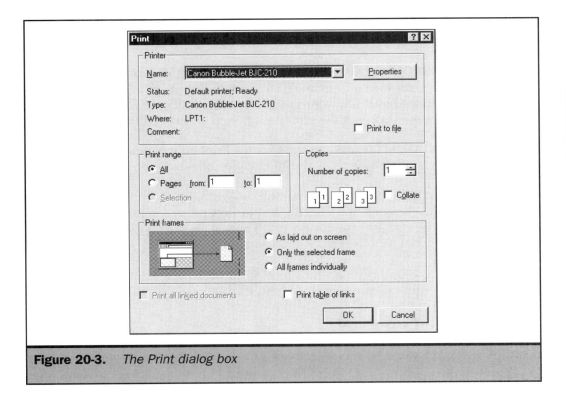

Figure 20-3. *The Print dialog box*

PRINTING PAGES WITH FRAMES   If the page that you want to print is laid out in *frames* (individual panes that you can scroll through separately), you can print it in several different ways, which are controlled by the Print Frames section of the Print dialog box.

To print exactly what you see onscreen, select the As Laid Out On Screen setting. Only the currently displayed portions of a frame will print, regardless of the document's length.

To print the complete document displayed in one frame, select Only the Selected Frame. The selected frame is the frame most recently clicked in. The Print Range section of the Print dialog box controls which portions of the overall document print—as opposed to only the currently displayed screen.

To print all the documents in all the frames, select All Frames Individually. This is equivalent to selecting the frames one by one and printing them with the Only the Selected Frame option.

Both the Only the Selected Frame and All Frames Individually options give you the ability to print information about the pages that are linked to the current one. The check boxes labeled Print All Linked Documents and Print a Table of Links do exactly what they say. The table of links is a boxed table with two columns: the linked text on the printed page and the Web address to which it is linked.

    Don't select Print All Linked Documents and then walk away. The current page may be linked to more documents than you realize, and they may be longer than you think.

PRINTING BACKGROUND COLORS AND IMAGES   You may print a Web page with or without its associated images and backgrounds. To make this choice, open the Internet Options dialog box (View | Internet Options) and click the Advanced tab. Under Printing, check or uncheck the Print Background Colors and Images box.

USING THE PRINT BUTTON   When you click the Print button on the toolbar, *something* prints immediately, without the intervention of a dialog box. That is, the Print button is equivalent to selecting File | Print and then clicking OK in the Print dialog box, without changing any of the default choices.

Since the default choices in the Print dialog box depend on any previous printing that you (or someone else using your copy of IE) have done during this session, you may be surprised if you click the Print button without first checking what the current defaults are set to.

The Print button is useful mainly for situations in which you want to print a series of pages, using the same print choices for each.

Saving the Current Page

You have several options for how to save the current Web page, but all of them begin by selecting File | Save As, to open the Save Web Page dialog box. As when saving any other kind of document, you have to specify a location in which to save the document, and a name for the file.

The Save As Type list in the Save Web Page dialog box provides these three options:

- **Web Page, Complete**   The page is saved exactly as you see it. All associated images, frames, and so forth, are stored, as is the basic HTML file. If you chose to save the Web page under the name Web Page.htm, the associated files that the HTML document calls are stored in a folder named Web Page Files, in the same folder where you stored Web Page.htm.

- **Web Page, HTML Only**   You save the basic HTML document itself: the text, the formatting, and the links to other Web pages. Any additional files that the document displays when you view it on the Web (images, video clips, and so forth) aren't saved. Be careful using this option with Web pages that are broken into frames; sometimes, the basic HTML document does little more than define the frames, and calls other HTML documents to fill them with content—you may see only a page of empty frames.

- **Text Only**   Only the text of the basic HTML document is saved. Formatting, images, and links are all lost.

The Macintosh version of IE replaces the Web Page, Complete option with a somewhat more versatile option called Web Archive. After you select Web Archive from the Format list, click the Options button to obtain the Site Download Options dialog box, in which you can make separate decisions about saving images, sounds, movies, and links.

 If you want to save only a small section of text from a Web page, select the text inside the Internet Explorer window and then cut and paste it into any other text document.

Saving a Linked Page Without Opening It

To save a linked page without opening it, open the context menu over the link (right-click the link in Windows, or hold down the mouse button over it on a Mac) and select Save Target As (on Macs, Download Link to Disk). The Save Target As dialog box behaves similarly to the Save As dialog box, described previously.

Opening Multiple Windows

At times, you will find it convenient to open two or more browsing windows. You might, for example, want to compare two Web pages. Or perhaps you are bouncing back and forth among several browsing tasks, and want each to have its own Back menu.

Select File | New | Window (or File | New Window on Macs) to open a new browsing window. The new window opens displaying the same page as the previous window. To open a new window displaying a particular page, select File | Open and then specify the file, as described earlier in this chapter in "Opening a Page."

If the current page contains a link that you want to open without closing the current page, open a context menu over the link (right-click in Windows; hold down the mouse button on a Mac) and choose Open In New Window.

Keeping Track of Your Favorite Web Sites

Internet Explorer provides four tools that you can use to return to previously visited Web sites: the Favorites menu, the History folder, the Links bar, and the Address bar. If your operating system supports Internet shortcuts, Internet Explorer allows you to create them, as well.

The Address bar and the History folder record Web sites automatically; the Address bar remembers the last 25 URLs that you typed into it, while the History folder records the most recent URLs you visited. Favorites, Links, and Internet shortcuts are voluntary—they keep track only of the Web sites that you (or Microsoft or Apple) have decided to record.

The most valuable piece of URL-recording real estate is the Links bar (called the Favorites bar or Toolbar Favorites in IE's Mac version). The Links bar comfortably displays only about six links. Choose them wisely. Instructions on adding and deleting entries from the Links bar are given in "The Links Bar" section, earlier in this chapter.

Another handy thing to do with a few frequently accessed URLs (or URLs that you plan to visit soon and then dispose of) is to make Internet shortcuts for them and put them on your desktop. See "Creating Internet Shortcuts," later in this section.

Internet Explorer's main tool for remembering URLs of favorite Web sites, however, is the Favorites menu. It provides a nice combination of easy access and high capacity.

Managing the Favorites Menu

The Favorites menu is Internet Explorer's primary place in which to store URLs that you want to revisit. It replaces the bookmark function in Navigator, and enables you to return to a marked Web site with a single click. It is only slightly less convenient than the Links bar (refer to "The Links Bar," earlier in this chapter), and can contain vastly more URLs.

In Windows 95/98/NT, you can use the Favorites menu from the Start menu, even if IE isn't open. If you choose an entry from the Start | Favorites menu, both the default Web browser (whether it is IE or not) and your Internet connection (if the chosen entry isn't available locally) open. This feature eliminates one of the main hassles of changing browsers: losing your bookmarks. Favorites stay with the operating system, not with the browser. (Our preliminary version of IE 5 opens Favorites and shortcuts with

Internet Explorer, no matter what the default browser is. We assume this is a bug that Microsoft will fix before IE 5 is officially released.)

In non-Windows systems, Favorites is an HTML file, not a folder of Internet shortcuts. On Macs, it is System Folder/Preferences/Explorer/Favorites.html. In UNIX, the location of the Favorites file is (relative to where IE is installed) ~/.microsoft/Favorites. When Favorites is an HTML file, any browser that opens it has access to its links.

Adding Favorites

To add a Web page to the Favorites menu, open it and select Add to Favorites from a context menu (or select Favorites | Add to Favorites). On a Mac, this is the end of the process: the new page is appended to your Favorites list. If you want to rename the new favorite or place it inside a folder, see the next section.

In Windows, an Add Favorite dialog box appears. You can either enter a name for the favorite or accept the suggested one. To put the new favorite into a subfolder of the Favorites folder, click the Create In button and choose the subfolder into which you want to put the new favorite. If you want to define a new folder for the favorite, select a folder in which to put the new folder and then click New Folder.

Organizing Favorites on a Macintosh

Click the Favorites tab to expand the Favorites Explorer bar. Drag and drop favorites or folders to wherever you want them. To create a new folder, select Favorites | New Folder. To rename a favorite or folder of favorites, select Favorites | Open Favorites. When the Favorites window appears, click the item's name and type in a new name.

Organizing Favorites with Windows and UNIX

Because Favorites is a folder of Internet shortcuts in Windows, you can organize your favorites either within Internet Explorer, by using its Organize Favorites dialog box, or within Windows or UNIX, by organizing the items in the Favorites folder.

ORGANIZING FAVORITES USING THE ORGANIZE FAVORITES WINDOW   You can organize the Favorites folder from within Internet Explorer by selecting Favorites | Organize Favorites. This opens the Organize Favorites window, shown in Figure 20-4.

When you first open the Organize Favorites window, it displays the contents of the Favorites folder, including its subfolders. To look at the contents of one of the subfolders, either double-click its icon, or select its icon and click the Open button. If you are viewing a subfolder and want to examine the folder that contains it, click the Up One Level button.

The Organize Favorites window offers a choice of either List view, which presents only the icon and name of each item, or Details view, which also tells when the item was created, modified, and last accessed. Switch between the two by using the List View and Details View buttons.

To move, rename, or delete a favorite (or a folder within the Favorites folder), you must first find it in the Organize Favorites window. If the favorite is inside a subfolder

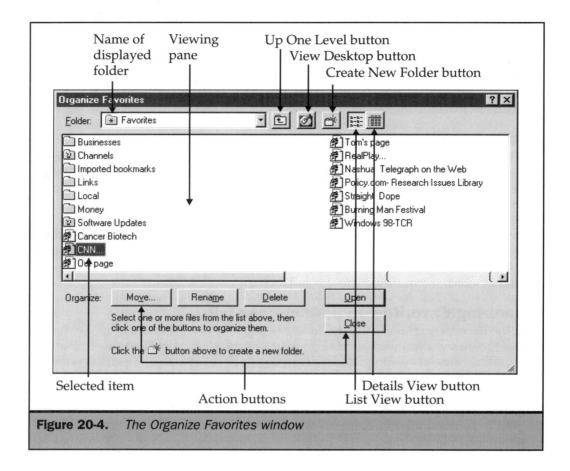

Name of
displayed
folder

Viewing
pane

Up One Level button
View Desktop button
Create New Folder button

Selected item

Action buttons

Details View button
List View button

Figure 20-4. *The Organize Favorites window*

of the Favorites folder, open that subfolder by clicking (or double-clicking) its icon. When you find the favorite's icon, select it.

To delete the favorite, click the Delete button or press DELETE on the keyboard.

To rename the favorite, click the Rename button. A text-editing box appears around the favorite's name. Type its new name.

To move the favorite to another folder within the Favorites folder, click the Move button. A Browse for Folder window appears. Select the folder to which you want to move the favorite and then click OK. Alternatively, you may drag and drop the favorite to the desired location without using the Move button.

To create a subfolder of the Favorites folder, click the Create New Folder button in the Organize Favorites window. The folder is created within the currently displayed folder. The new folder has the default name New Folder, which appears with a text-editing box around it. Type into the box the name that you want the folder to have. After you create the folder, you can rename, move, or delete it, as previously described.

ORGANIZING FAVORITES USING YOUR FILE SYSTEM   Favorites is a folder, so you can organize it as you would any other folder in your file system, without learning how to use the Organize Favorites window.

In Windows, the Favorites folder is located inside the C:\Windows folder, and inside C:\Windows\Profiles\ *your username* if user profiles are set up on your machine. On UNIX systems, the Favorites folder has the address ~/.microsoft/Favorites. The entries on the Favorites menu are Internet shortcuts inside the Favorites folder.

After you find the Favorites folder, you can organize it in the same way that you organize any other folder: create and delete subfolders, move objects from one subfolder to another, or delete objects by using your usual file commands.

Converting Bookmarks to Favorites and Vice Versa

On non-Windows systems, Favorites is an HTML document, just like Bookmarks in Navigator. To change bookmarks to favorites, you simply find Navigator's bookmarks file, move it to the folder in which IE keeps its favorites file, and rename the bookmarks file **Favorites.html**. Changing favorites to bookmarks works exactly the same way, but in reverse.

In Windows, Favorites is not an HTML document, so the process is more complicated. Microsoft has a free utility for Windows 95/98 called *favtool* that converts favorites to bookmarks, and vice versa. We found it on the Microsoft Web site (**http://www.microsoft.com**), but it isn't consistently available there. Another place to look for it is at *Windows Magazine*'s site:

http://www.winmag.com/win95/software.htm

All else failing, put the keyword *favtool* into a search engine; it's bound to be out there somewhere.

IE 5 simplifies matters by adding Export and Import buttons to its Organize Favorites dialog box. Clicking Export saves favorites as an HTML file. Clicking Import opens a browsing window: use it to find the HTML file of bookmarks that you want to import into your Favorites folder.

 A variety of bookmark-and-favorite managing tools for Windows are available either as freeware or shareware at **http://www.winfiles.com/apps/98/url.html**.

Using the History Folder

Clicking the History button on the Internet Explorer toolbar (or selecting View | Explorer Bar | History) opens a new Explorer Bar in the IE window. This pane (shown previously in Figure 20-1) is similar to the left pane of a Windows Explorer window, and it displays the contents of the History folder. Selecting a closed folder expands the

VIEWING THE WORLD WIDE WEB

tree to show its contents; selecting an open folder compresses the tree to hide its contents. Clicking the History button again (or the X in the corner of the History pane) causes the History pane to disappear.

History works differently on Windows systems than on Mac or UNIX systems. In Windows, History is a folder of shortcuts. On Mac and UNIX systems, History is an HTML file of links. On UNIX systems, the location of the History folder is relative to where IE is installed, and has the relative address ~/.microsoft/History.

The History Folder in Windows

The History folder is organized into subfolders—one for each day of the current week, and one for each previous week, going back 20 days. (You can change the number of days that History remembers, which is explained later in this section.) Each day's folder contains one subfolder for each Web site visited with IE. Inside the Web site folders are Internet shortcuts to each of the pages viewed on that Web site.

Return to a Web page by opening its shortcut. Selecting a shortcut displays its title and address in a tool tip window. When you are offline, a symbol displaying a circle with a line through it appears next to the cursor, if the page isn't cached. You can look up the exact time the page was accessed by choosing Properties from the right-click menu.

Delete a shortcut or subfolder from the History folder by selecting Delete from the right-click menu.

To change the History settings, open the Internet Options dialog box (select View | Internet Options). The History settings are on the General tab. If you want to delete all the entries in the History folder, click the Clear History button in the History box of the General tab. If you want to change the number of days that the History folder remembers a Web page, enter a new number into the Days to Keep Pages in History box. Then, click OK to make the dialog box disappear.

The History folder has the address C:\Windows\History if you haven't activated user profiles, and C:\Windows\Profiles*your username*\History if you have. You can edit it as you do any other folder.

The History File on Macintosh Systems

In Mac versions of Internet Explorer, History is accessed by clicking a tab on the right side of the viewing window. The tab expands into an Explorer bar that displays a list of previously visited URLs in the order in which they were visited, organized into daily folders.

An entry in the History file can be clicked to open its corresponding Web site, dragged to the Links bar, or dragged onto the desktop to create an Internet shortcut. The History file has the address System Folder/Preferences/Explorer/History.html.

The History file keeps track of a set number of URLs, not a set period of time. By default, History remembers the last 300 URLs you have visited with IE. To reset this number, open the Internet Explorer Preferences box (Edit | Preferences) and find the Advanced tab under Web Browser. Type a new number into the History box.

Creating Internet Shortcuts

You can easily create Internet shortcuts on your desktop from within Internet Explorer. In the Windows version of IE, just drag the icon from the Address bar to the desktop. In the Mac version, either add it to your Favorites list (Favorites | Add Page to Favorites) or find it in your History list. Then, drag and drop the corresponding entry from the Favorites (or History) Explorer bar to the desktop, or any other folder.

Customizing Internet Explorer

You can customize IE to reflect your tastes, your browsing habits, the other software that you use, and your security policies. For details of how to configure toolbars, refer to "Elements of the Internet Explorer Window," earlier in this chapter.

Sharing Internet Explorer with Other Users

The Windows version of IE inherits its user profiles from Windows. After you set up user profiles under Windows, each user has his/her own start page, Favorites menu, History folder, Links bar, color schemes, and cookies folder.

To turn on Windows' user profile feature, choose Start | Settings | Control Panel and open the Passwords icon. Go to the User Profiles tab and select the radio button labeled Users Can Customize Their Preferences and Desktop Settings.

You can create a new user profile either when you turn on your computer or by choosing Start | Log In As Different User. In either case, the Welcome to Windows box appears, asking for a username and password. By typing an unclaimed username, you establish a new user profile. Whatever password you type (including the possibility of a blank password) establishes the password for the new user profile.

Each user profile corresponds to a folder in C:\Windows\Profiles. The name of the folder is the username. Each user profile folder contains the information specific to that user, such as a Favorites folder.

The Macintosh version of IE doesn't include user profiles. The simplest way for two users to share a Mac and each have their own Web browser settings is for one user to run Internet Explorer and the other to run Netscape Navigator, or to set up user profiles under Navigator.

Linking Internet Explorer to Other Programs

Some hyperlinks on a Web page are intended to launch programs other than a Web browser. For example, a linked e-mail address is better handled by an e-mail program, which can open a message window addressed to the linked address. Similarly, a newsgroup address can be bettered handled by a newsreading program (Usenet newsgroups are described in Chapter 13).

For these hand-offs to happen smoothly, IE needs to know which applications handle various jobs on your system. By default, IE launches the other Microsoft products that are part of the IE package: Outlook Express for e-mail and newsgroup links, NetMeeting for Internet telephone calls, and the Windows Address Book for contact information.

If you prefer to use other programs, you can change these defaults. Open the Programs tab of the Internet Options dialog box, as shown in Figure 20-5. (Open the box by selecting View | Internet Options.) Choose new programs from the drop-down lists. (Unfortuanately, few non-Microsoft products appear as options.)

On a Mac, open the Internet Explorer Preferences dialog box (Edit | Preferences) and go to the Network/Protocol Helpers tab, which lists the various Internet protocols. The protocol mailto invokes an e-mail program, and the news protocol invokes a Usenet newsreader. By default, Outlook Express is listed as the program to handle both e-mail and Usenet newsgroups. To change to another program, select from the list the protocol that you want to reassign, and then click the Change button. When the Edit

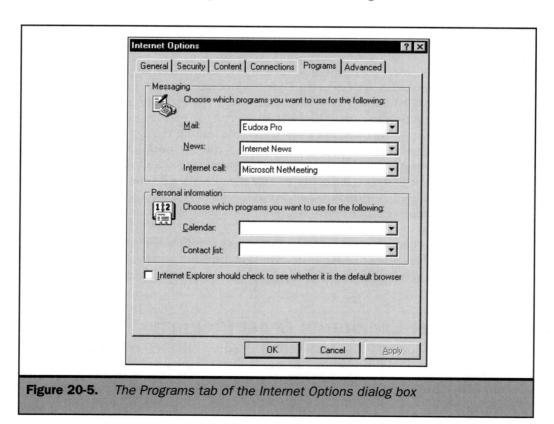

Figure 20-5.   *The Programs tab of the Internet Options dialog box*

Protocol Helper dialog box appears, click the Choose Helper button and browse for the location of the program that you want to handle this protocol.

Choosing a New Start Page

When you open Internet Explorer without specifying a particular Web page, it opens the start (or home) page, by default. You can return to this page whenever you like by clicking the Home button on the toolbar.

When you first install a Windows version of IE, you are assigned the start page **http://home.microsoft.com**, Microsoft's portal site. The initial services this site provides are rather meager: some Web guide categories, a search engine, and some headlines, but Microsoft may have beefed up this site. You have three choices: leave things the way they are (and see this page whenever you start IE), customize Microsoft's start page so that it provides useful information, such as your local weather reports (shown previously in Figure 20-1), or choose another start page entirely.

On Macs, the default start page is **http://livepage.apple.com**, a portal site created for Apple by Excite. It is customizable in the same way that Excite's own portal site is. Chapter 25 discusses the wide variety of portal sites available (including Microsoft's and Excite's), the services that they offer, and how to customize a portal for your greatest convenience.

You can choose a new start page for IE from the Internet Options dialog box, which you can open by choosing View | Internet Options. The Internet Options dialog box opens with the General tab on top. You can type the URL of the new home page into the Home Page box on this tab, or you can click one of the following buttons:

- **Use Current**   The page currently displayed by IE becomes the home page. (If IE isn't open, this button is grayed out.) This can be any page on the Web, on your local area network (LAN), or even on your own hard drive.
- **Use Default**   The home page becomes **http://home.microsoft.com**.
- **Use Blank**   The home page is blank. This is handy if you want Internet Explorer to start up as quickly as possible, and don't necessarily want to open your Internet connection.

Naturally, Microsoft gives you every opportunity to use its portal page. Even after you choose another start page, you can still access Microsoft's page from the Internet Start icon on the Links menu. And if you delete that link from the Links menu, you can still get to Microsoft's portal page by selecting Help | Microsoft on the Web | Internet Start Page. As far as we know, there is no way to delete the Help menu entry.

On a Macintosh, change the start page from the Internet Explorer Preferences box (Edit | Preferences). In this dialog box, select Web Browser | Home/Search, and type the URL of the new start page into the Home Page box. The Use None button is equivalent to the Use Blank button in the Windows version. Use Default restores **http://livepage.apple.com** as the start page.

Choosing Not to Download Multimedia Content

The quickest and easiest kind of information to download is text. Photos, charts, sound, animation, and video are all fabulous in their own way, but if you have a slow Internet connection, you can end up waiting a very long time for this rich multimedia content to download. (Worse, that graphic that you're waiting for may just be an advertisement.)

Telling IE to ignore various kinds of multimedia content may speed up your browsing experience a great deal. In the Windows version of IE, you can do this from the Internet Options dialog box, which you open by selecting View | Internet Options. Click the Advanced tab, scroll down until you see the Multimedia heading, and then remove the check from the check box next to any type of content that you want to ignore.

In the Mac version of IE, choose Edit | Preferences to open the Internet Explorer Preferences dialog box. In this dialog box, open Web Browser | Web Content. The Page Content section contains check boxes for the various kinds of multimedia content.

When you display a Web page without its images or other multimedia content, the areas of the screen that they ordinarily occupy are outlined and contain a word or phrase to hint what the content might be. You can use the context menu over this region to display the content, without changing your policy of not displaying such content. On the Macintosh, if you use the Navigator Compatible or Compatible Plus Button bars, you can click the Images button to display the images on the current page—again, without changing policy.

Setting Other Viewing Preferences

You can control the way Internet Explorer displays fonts and colors, and the default language in which it displays Web pages (when those pages offer more than one language version). These choices are made slightly differently, depending on whether you are using a Windows or Mac version of IE.

Setting Viewing Preferences Under Windows

You control viewing preferences from the Internet Options dialog box, shown in Figure 20-6. To access this dialog box, select View | Internet Options.

CHOOSING FONTS ON WINDOWS SYSTEMS   You can expand or shrink the text size on a Web page—without making any permanent changes to the way that it displays text—by using View | Fonts (View | Text Size on the Mac). The changed font size applies to the current session only, and is forgotten when you exit.

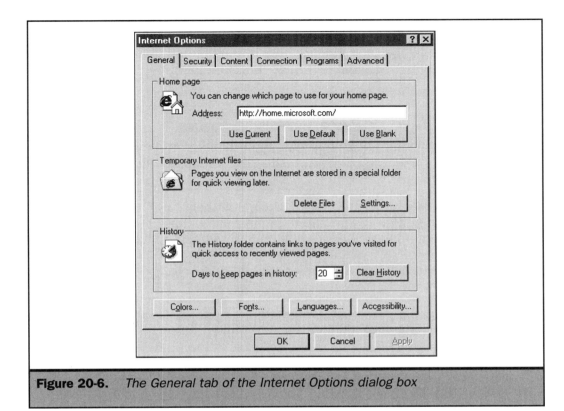

Figure 20-6.   *The General tab of the Internet Options dialog box*

To make longer-lasting changes in the fonts that the Windows versions of IE use to display text, click the Fonts button on the General tab of the Internet Options dialog box (not the Fonts button on the toolbar). The Fonts dialog box opens, shown in Figure 20-7.

The Fonts dialog box contains these basic elements:

- **The Character Sets window**   Lists the alphabets IE supports. The current character set is highlighted. In English-language versions of IE, the default character set is Western.

- **Drop-down lists**   Specifies the proportional font and the fixed-width font for the selected character set. Change the font by picking a new one from the list. Change the font size by choosing from a drop-down list that goes from smallest to largest. The default proportional font for the Western character set is Times New Roman (12 point), and the default fixed-width font is Courier New (10 point). IE lists both of these default sizes as Medium.

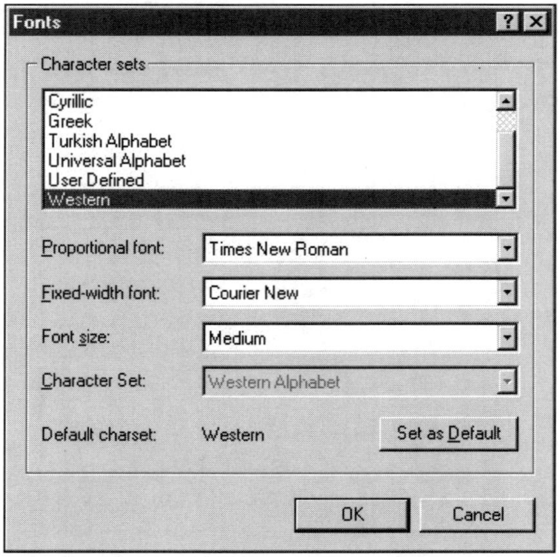

Figure 20-7. *Internet Explorer's Fonts dialog box*

CHOOSING COLORS IN WINDOWS You can change the colors that IE uses to display text, backgrounds, and links. Open the Internet Options dialog box (View | Internet Options), and then click the Colors button. In Windows, the default is Windows colors—that is, the colors defined on the Appearance tab of the Display Properties dialog box, which is opened from the Control Panel.

If you don't want to use the default colors, go to the Colors dialog box and remove the check from the Use Windows Colors check box. Begin the process of choosing your own colors by clicking the colored button next to the Text or Background labels. A palette of colors appears; click the color that you want the text or background to be, and then click OK.

The Colors dialog box also lets you change the colors used for links. Once the Colors box is open, click the colored button labeled "visited" (for the links you've visited) or "unvisited" (for the links you haven't visited). A palette of colors appears, as described in the previous paragraph, and the process proceeds in a similar fashion.

You can also define a *hover color*, a color that links turn when the cursor is over them: Click the Use Hover Color check box in the Colors dialog box and then click the Hover button. A palette of colors appears from which you can choose a color, as previously described.

OVERRIDING SPECIFIED FONTS AND COLORS Some Web pages specify particular fonts and colors, and those choices override the font and color choices that you make in the Fonts and Colors dialog boxes, described earlier. Usually this is a good thing; the Web page author had some reason for choosing those fonts and colors, and you should just go with it. However, if you want your font and color choices to override the choices of the Web page author (as you would if, for example, your eyesight requires very large fonts or very bright colors), you can express this preference in the Accessibility dialog box.

To open the Accessibility dialog box, first open the Internet Options dialog box by choosing View | Internet Options from IE's menu bar, and then click the Accessibility button in the Internet Options dialog box. Check one or more of these check boxes: Ignore Colors Specified on Web Pages, Ignore Font Sizes Specified on Web Pages, or Ignore Font Styles Specified on Web Pages. Then, click OK to make the dialog boxes disappear.

CHANGING LANGUAGE PREFERENCES Some Web pages are available in multiple languages, and IE picks the one that matches your preferences. To define or change your language preferences, click the Languages button near the bottom of the General tab of the Internet Options dialog box, which opens the Language Preferences dialog box.

The purpose of the Language Preferences dialog box is to maintain a list of favored languages, in order, with your preferred language on top. Add a language to the list by clicking the Add button and selecting a language from the list that appears. Remove a language from the Language list by selecting it and clicking the Remove button. Reorder the Languages list by selecting a language on the list and clicking the Move Up or Move Down buttons. When you are satisfied with the list of languages, click OK.

Setting Viewing Preferences on a Macintosh

On the Macintosh, viewing preferences are controlled from the Internet Explorer Preferences dialog box, which you access by selecting Edit | Preferences. This dialog box is divided into a navigation panel and a display panel. The navigation panel has four major headings: Web Browser, Receiving Files, Network, and E-mail. Each of these headings has several tabs under it. In the usual Mac style, click the triangle next to the heading to display or not display the names of the tabs under a heading. Click the name of the tab to show it in the display panel.

CHOOSING FONTS AND LANGUAGES ON A MACINTOSH Change font size on the current page by selecting View | Text Size. To make a lasting change in the size of the fonts that IE uses, go to the Internet Explorer Preferences dialog box, and select the Web Browser/Browser Display tab. Select from the drop-down Text Size list.

To change the fonts that IE uses, open the Web Browser/Language/Fonts tab in the Internet Explorer Preferences dialog box. Use the drop-down lists to select the character set, proportional font, and fixed-width font. Language preferences are also controlled from the Language/Fonts tab. Choose a language from the drop-down list.

CHOOSING COLORS ON A MACINTOSH   Internet Explorer's colors are controlled from the Web Browser/Browser Display tab of the Internet Explorer Preferences box. The page and link section of this tab shows four colored bars, representing the colors that IE is currently using to display text, background, links already viewed, and links not yet viewed, respectively.

To change the color used to display any of these four kinds of objects, click the corresponding colored bar. A color-choosing window appears. The left panel of this window lists five different user interfaces for choosing colors. The five are all equivalent except for the cutest, Crayon Picker, which restricts you to certain preset color choices. When you click a choice on the left, the right panel displays a user interface for choosing color. Using some combination of sliders, color wheels, and typing, you can make adjustments until the color in the New box is the one that you want. Then click OK.

OVERRIDING SPECIFIED FONTS AND COLORS ON A MACINTOSH   If you want your chosen colors for text, background, and links to override the colors specified by a Web page, go to the Web Browser/Web Content tab of the Internet Explorer Preferences dialog box. In the Page Content section of this tab, uncheck Allow Page to Specify Colors and/or Allow Page to Specify Fonts.

Managing Internet Explorer's Cache of Web Pages

Internet Explorer stores some of the Web pages that you view, so that they can be redisplayed quickly if you return to them. In general, this speeds up the browsing experience, but if you are running short of disk space, you may decide to limit or eliminate these caches. IE stores these cached pages in a folder called Temporary Internet Files. On Windows systems, this folder lives in the C:\Windows folder, or (if you are using user profiles) C:\Windows\Profiles*your username*. On UNIX systems, this folder is located in ~/.microsoft/TempInternetFiles, and on Macs, it is System Folder/Preferences/Browser Cache.

If you use Windows, you control IE's cache of Web pages from the General tab of the Internet Options dialog box, shown previously in Figure 20-6. Open this dialog box by selecting View | Internet Options. You can delete all the cached Web pages by clicking the Delete Files button. To set limits on the amount of disk space that can be devoted to temporary Internet files, click the Settings button to open the Settings dialog box. Move the slider to raise or lower the percentage of your hard drive that the Temporary Internet Files folder is allowed to use. Click OK to apply your changes.

On a Mac, the cache is controlled from the Web Browser/Advanced tab of the Internet Explorer Preferences dialog box, which you open by selecting Edit | Preferences. To change the amount of disk space allotted to the cache, type a number of megabytes into the Size box. To delete all the cached Web pages, click the Empty Now button. To move the Browser Cache folder, click the Change Location button and browse for a new location.

Security in Internet Explorer

Web browsers are intended to be simple enough for novice users. For this reason, most of what the browser does is invisible. Some choices that your browser makes for you, however, have implications for your system's vulnerability to viruses or other security lapses—implications that more-advanced users may want to consider. Internet Explorer gives you some limited opportunities to "get under the hood" and make choices about accepting cookies, setting security levels, and running applets in Java or ActiveX (see Chapter 18 for definitions).

For the most part, however, IE's security policy is based on *trust*, and the decisions that you are asked to make involve who to trust and who not to trust. (By contrast, Navigator's security policy is based on *action*, and you are asked to decide which actions to allow or disallow.) For example, when a Web page wants to run an ActiveX control on your machine, IE verifies who wrote the control (Microsoft, for example), and that it hasn't been tampered with by anyone. You aren't told what the control intends to do or what privileges it requests on your system (rewriting files, for example). Instead, you are asked to decide whether you trust its author.

This approach has its pluses and minuses. Trust is an intuitive concept that makes sense to the novice user. Deciding to trust Microsoft or your company's information technology department (or not to trust a Web site offering free pornography) is simpler than deciding a large number of technical issues about your computer's security. On the other hand, more-experienced users may want more direct control over their computer systems than a simple trust/don't trust decision allows. Fortunately, IE does still allow a limited amount of "getting under the hood" to make security policy.

Security Zones

The central concept of IE's security policy is the *security zone*. There are four zones: Local Intranet, Trusted Sites, Internet, and Restricted Sites. To establish your security policy, you assign Web sites to security zones and then choose a security level (High, Medium, Low, or Custom) for each zone. Default settings make this process invisible, unless you choose to tinker with it. As you browse the Web, the status bar displays the security zone of the current page.

What Security Zones Mean

Internet Explorer has the following four security zones:

- ■ **Local Intranet zone**   Consists of Web pages that you can access without going through a proxy server. In general, these are resources on your LAN or within your company or place of business. (You may not have any Web sites in this zone if you are not on a network and connect to the Internet through a modem.) The default security setting is Medium.

■ **Trusted Sites zone**   Consists of sites that you trust as much as you trust the files on your hard drive. The default security setting is Low.

■ **Internet zone**   Consists of Web sites that you have not assigned to any other zone. The default security setting is Medium.

■ **Restricted Sites zone**   Consists of Web sites that you have explicitly decided not to trust. The default security setting is High.

What Security Levels Mean

When you set a zone's security level, you actually are making numerous decisions simultaneously. In general, the security levels have the following effect:

■ **High**   Supposed to exclude content that could damage your computer.

■ **Medium**   Supposed to warn you before running potentially damaging content.

■ **Low**   Not supposed to warn you before running potentially damaging content.

■ **Custom**   Allows you to make the technical decisions one by one, rather than bundling them all together into High, Medium, or Low.

To see a list of the current settings for each security zone:

1. Select the zone from the Zone drop-down list on the Security tab of the Internet Options dialog box (on Macs, the Web Browser/Security Zones tab of the Internet Explorer Preferences dialog box).
2. Choose the Custom radio button
3. Click the Settings button.

After you examine the settings, you may (if you want) reset to one of the default security levels by using the Default Settings section at the bottom of the Settings dialog box.

Security settings are divided into six categories: ActiveX Controls (AXCs) and Plug-Ins, Downloads, User Authentication, Java, Scripting, and Miscellaneous. For each security setting, you choose one of the following:

■ **Enable**   The activity is allowed to happen without warning

■ **Prompt**   Internet Explorer asks you whether to do the activity

■ **Disable**   Internet Explorer will not do the activity

Assigning Web Sites to and Removing Them from Security Zones

Any Web site that you haven't explicitly assigned to some other security zone is, by default, assigned to the Internet zone. Therefore, you can't add Web sites to the

Internet zone explicitly. Removing a Web site from some other zone automatically adds it to the Internet zone.

To assign a Web site to (or remove it from) one of the other security zones:

1. Go to the Security tab of the Internet Options dialog box (View | Internet Options). Macintosh users go to the Web Browser/Security Zones tab of the Internet Explorer Preferences dialog box. The Windows version of this tab appears in Figure 20-8. (The Macintosh version is functionally identical.)

2. Choose the zone name from the Zone drop-down list, and click the Add Sites button. If you are adding sites to (or removing them from) the Trusted or Restricted zones, go to Step 4.

3. If you are adding sites to (or removing sites from) the Local Intranet zone, you are presented with three check boxes: Include All Local (Intranet) Sites Not Listed in Other Zones, Include All Sites That Do Not Use the Proxy Server, and Include All Network Paths (UNCs). (The third choice doesn't exist in the Mac version.) Include or exclude sites fitting these descriptions by checking or unchecking the boxes. To add or remove specific sites, click the Advanced button.

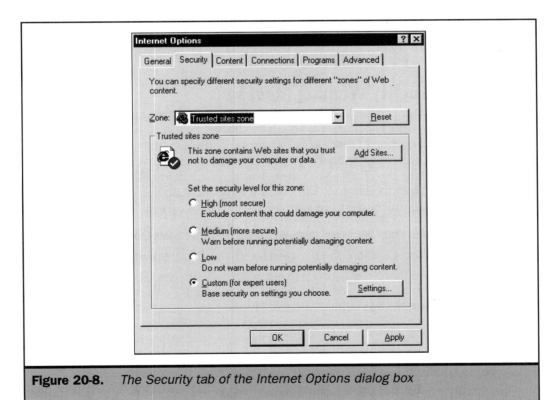

Figure 20-8.   *The Security tab of the Internet Options dialog box*

4. A box appears listing the Web sites assigned to this zone. To remove a site from the zone, select it on the list and click the Remove button.

5. To add a Web site to the zone in Windows, type its URL (complete with the protocol—**http://**, for example) into the Add This Web Site to the Zone box and then click the Add button. On a Macintosh, click the Add button and type the URL into the Add This Web Site to the Zone box when it appears.

Changing a Zone's Security Level

To change the security level of a zone, open the Security tab of the Internet Options dialog box. (On Macs open the Web Browser/Security Zones tab of the Internet Explorer Preferences dialog box.) Select the zone name from the Zone drop-down list and then click the radio button corresponding to the security level that you want.

If you choose the Custom level, click the Settings button to choose the security settings that you want. To know what options you have and how they might differ from the default levels, refer to "What Security Levels Mean," earlier in this chapter.

Setting Other Security Policies

Not all security policies are set by choosing security levels for the various security zones. In IE 4, a cookie policy isn't part of the security levels, though it is in IE 5. Several decisions about Java and ActiveX can be changed without changing security levels, particularly in the Macintosh version.

Controlling Security Warning Messages

Internet Explorer can be set up to warn you before it does anything potentially dangerous. Most of these warnings are set up by choosing Prompt when you customize the settings of security zones. (Refer to "Changing a Zone's Security Level," above.) But a few warnings are controlled from the Security section of the Advanced tab of the Internet Options dialog box. (On a Mac, these warnings are controlled from the Web Browser/Security tab of the Internet Explorer Preferences dialog box.)

In Windows, you can choose to be warned about the following:

- A submitted form is being redirected to a server other than the one it came from.
- Internet Explorer is changing between secure and insecure modes.
- The certificate that a site is using to establish a secure connection is invalid.

On a Macintosh, you can choose to be warned:

- When entering a page that is secure
- When entering a page that isn't secure
- Before submitting a form that isn't secure

- Before submitting a form through e-mail
- Before downloading an ActiveX control

Managing Cookies

Cookies are small files that Web servers store on your computer. The cookie is activated when you return to the Web site that created the cookie on your computer. The information in the cookie allows the Web server to "remember" your previous interactions and provide the appropriate context. (Cookies and the security issues that arise from them are described more completely in Chapter 18.)

Internet Explorer gives you the choice of three policies for handling cookies: accept all cookies (default option); refuse all cookies; accept or refuse cookies on a cookie-by-cookie basis. The Mac version gives you a fourth choice (which we prefer to the other three): accept or reject cookies on a Web-site-by-Web-site basis.

To choose your cookie policy in the Windows version of IE 4, go to the Advanced tab of the Internet Options dialog box and scroll down until you see Cookies. Click the radio button next to the policy that you prefer, and then click either Apply or OK.

In IE 5, cookie management now is part of the security settings, which makes changing policy more difficult, but does allow you to have a different policy for each security zone. The defaults are always to accept cookies in Low and Medium security levels, and to disable them in High levels. If this isn't what you want for a particular zone, you have to customize the security settings for that zone. Refer to "Changing a Zone's Security Level," earlier in this chapter.

In the Macintosh version of IE 4, go to the Receiving Files/Cookies tab of the Internet Explorer Preferences dialog box. The When Receiving Cookies box contains a drop-down list of four options: Never Ask, Ask for Each Site, Ask for Each Cookie, and Never Accept. When you make a choice, a short description of the option appear just below the When Receiving Cookies box. The Cookies tab also contains a list of the cookies currently maintained by IE. To delete an individual cookie, select it from this list and click the Delete button. Disable a selected cookie with the Decline Cookies button. When the selected cookie is already disabled, the Decline Cookies button changes to an Accept Cookies button, which reenables the cookie. You can examine the expiration date of a cookie by clicking the View button.

In Windows, IE cookies are stored as text files in a folder called Cookies, located in C:\Windows (if user profiles aren't being used on your system) or in C:\Windows\Profiles*your username*. Some cookies may also be in C:\Windows\Temporary Internet Files (or one of its subfolders) or C:\Windows\Profiles*your username*\Temporary Internet Files (or one of its subfolders). Reading a cookie as a text file probably will not tell you much, though it may set your mind at ease to realize just how little information is there. Delete cookies from your system by deleting the corresponding text files.

Managing Java and JavaScript

Java and JavaScript are programming languages that are used to give some Web pages advanced features (see "The Web's Languages and Protocols," in Chapter 18.) Some

Java policy is controlled by the security level settings, in the Java and Scripting sections. Refer to "What Security Levels Mean," earlier in this chapter, in which we describe Java settings that can be changed independent of the security levels.

MANAGING JAVA IN WINDOWS   You can deactivate Java and JavaScript in the Windows version of IE from the Advanced tab of the Internet Options dialog box. The check boxes Java Console Enabled, Java JIT Compiler Enabled, and Java Logging Enabled control Internet Explorer's use of Java.

MANAGING JAVA ON A MACINTOSH   In the Mac version of IE, Java is managed from the Web Browser/Java tab of the Internet Explorer Preferences dialog box. Enable or disable Java with the Enable Java check box.

You have a choice between Microsoft's and Apple's Java virtual machine (JVM), with the Apple JVM being the default. We have noticed no obvious difference in how the two JVMs work, though Microsoft's Java implementations are known not to follow the Java standard (an issue which is being worked out in a court battle with Sun, Java's creator).

The Java Options section of the Java tab has check boxes to select whether to log Java output and Java exceptions. It's a good policy to check these boxes. If you use the Microsoft JVM, you may choose to enable the just-in-time compiler, which should speed performance.

If you choose the Microsoft JVM, its security options are controlled by the security level settings. (Refer to "What Security Levels Mean," earlier in this chapter.) The Apple JVM's policies are controlled from the Security Options section of the Java tab. The Byte-code Verification drop-down list gives you three options for verifying Java applets: Check All Code, Check Remote Code, and Don't Check Code. The default, Check All Code, is safest.

The Network Access drop-down list controls whether a Java applet running on your machine can exchange information over the Internet. The default, Applet Host Access, allows the applet to exchange data with the server that it came from. No Network Access is safer, of course, but disables some potentially useful applets. Unrestricted Access lets an applet exchange data with any server on the Internet, which is (for most people) an unnecessary risk.

The Restrict Access to Non-Java Class Files box is checked by default. It prevents Java applets from reading or changing non-Java files on your computer. This is a good safety precaution; unless you know that you want to run a particular applet that needs file access, leave the box checked.

Managing ActiveX Controls

Internet Explorer stores all ActiveX controls (AXCs) in a single folder. In Windows, this folder is called Downloaded Program Files, located inside C:\Windows. On a Mac, it is

System Folder/Extensions/ActiveX Controls. You should check this folder periodically to see what applications IE has downloaded. Deleting files from this folder uninstalls the associated applications. (ActiveX is described in Chapter 18.)

Disabling AXCs entirely isn't a bad idea. You seldom run into them, except on Web sites that are somehow connected with Microsoft (like MSNBC), and because AXCs have fewer restrictions than Java applets, they open a large can of worms. On the Mac, you can disable ActiveX with a single click: On the Web Browser/Web Content tab (under Web Browser) of the Internet Explorer Preferences dialog box, uncheck Enable ActiveX.

Disabling ActiveX on Windows versions of IE is possible, but more difficult, because AXCs are controlled by the security level settings. To disable AXCs for a security zone without affecting anything else, you have to customize the security level of that zone. (Refer to "Changing a Zone's Security Level," earlier in this chapter.)

Blocking Web Sites with Content Advisor

Internet Explorer includes the Web-site-blocking application Content Advisor. Content Advisor works with any PICS-compatible ratings system, and comes with the *Recreational Software Advisory Council for the Internet (RSACi)* ratings system already installed. For a general discussion of PICS and PICS-compatible ratings systems, see "Blocking Offensive or Inappropriate Web Sites" in Chapter 18.

Enabling and Disabling Content Advisor

To set up Content Advisor for the first time, display the Content tab of the Internet Options dialog box (View | Internet Options). On Macs, display the Web Browser/ Ratings tab of the Internet Explorer Preferences dialog box (Edit | Preferences). In either case, click the Enable button.

In Windows, Content Advisor makes you choose a password. On Macs, the default password is blank, and you can set a password by clicking the Change Password button.

IE initially includes only the RSACi ratings system, and the default settings are the most restrictive. If this is what you want, you can click OK and be done. Otherwise, you can use the Content Advisor dialog box to change the settings, as described in the section "Changing Content Advisor Preferences," later in this chapter.

To disable Content Advisor, open the Content tab of the Internet Options dialog box, as you did when you enabled Content Advisor. Click the Disable button and enter your Content Advisor password when requested.

Enabling Content Advisor again (after disabling it) is simpler than setting it up the first time: Click the Enable button on the Content tab of the Internet Options dialog box, and then give the supervisor password when asked. Content Advisor remembers the settings that you were using before you disabled it.

Adding or Removing Ratings Systems

Before you add a ratings system other than RSACi to Content Advisor, you should enable Content Advisor, as described in the preceding section.

Ratings systems are described by files (with the extension .rat); thus, to add a ratings system to Content Advisor, you first need to get a copy of the rating system's corresponding RAT file. (SafeSurf's ratings file, for example, is SafeSurf.rat. Based on SafeSurf's Web page, you might guess that this file works only for Windows versions of IE, but this isn't true.) Typically, the RAT file can be downloaded from the Web site of the ratings organization. After you download the RAT file, save it. In Windows, the installation process is simplest if you save the RAT file in C:\Windows\System folder.

After you obtain the RAT file of the ratings system that you want to install, you need to tell Content Advisor about it. To do this in Windows:

1. Go to the Content tab of the Internet Options dialog box (View | Internet Options).

2. Click the Settings button and then enter your Content Advisor password, to get to the Content Advisor dialog box.

3. Click the Ratings Systems button on the Advanced tab of the Content Advisor dialog box, to access the Ratings Systems dialog box. In this box, you find a list of the file addresses of the RAT files that correspond to the ratings systems that Content Advisor knows about.

4. Click the Add button.

5. When the Open Ratings System box appears, browse until you find the RAT file of the system that you want to add. When you select this file, the Open Ratings System box disappears, and the new RAT file appears in the Ratings Systems dialog box.

6. You may now return to the Ratings tab to set the blocking levels for your new ratings system.

To remove a ratings system from Content Advisor under Windows, access the Ratings Systems dialog box by repeating Steps 1 through 3. Select the corresponding RAT file on the list in the Ratings Systems dialog box and then click the Remove button.

On Macs, you add or remove ratings systems from Content Advisor from the Web Browser/Ratings tab of the Internet Explorer Preferences dialog box (select Edit | Preferences). To remove a ratings system, select it from the Ratings Settings section of the Web Browser/Ratings tab of the dialog box and click the Remove Service button. If you have set a password, Content Advisor asks for it before removing the ratings system.

To add a ratings system on Macs, go to the Web Browser/Ratings tab of the Internet Explorer Preferences dialog box, as directed in the previous paragraph. Click the Add Service button, and find the service's RAT file in the window that appears. Click Open to install the ratings service.

Any smart teenager will figure out that the backdoor way to uninstall a Content Advisor ratings system is to delete its RAT file. No password is required. Internet Explorer then treats sites rated by that ratings service as unrated sites.

Changing Content Advisor Preferences

Content Advisor's default settings are its most restrictive. You can change these settings, change your Content Advisor password, and choose whether to let users see unrated sites.

Changing Content Advisor Preferences in Windows

To makes changes to the ratings levels, open the Content tab of the Internet Options dialog box, as you did when you set up Content Advisor. Click the Settings button and enter your supervisor password, when requested. When the Content Advisor dialog box appears, click the category whose rating you want to change, and then move the slider that appears to the desired level.

To allow (or not allow) users to see unrated Web sites, open the Content Advisor dialog box, as previously explained, and click the General tab. One check box on this tab enables users to view unrated Web sites without the supervisor password; the other check box allows viewing of unrated sites with a supervisor password. Make whatever changes you want and enter your supervisor password when prompted.

To change the supervisor password, click the Change Password button on the General tab of the Content Advisor dialog box. Enter the old password into the first line of the Change Supervisor Password box, and enter the new password into the second and third lines of the Change Supervisor Password box.

Changing Content Advisor Preferences on a Macintosh

To change the Content Advisor rating levels on a Mac, open the Web Browser/Ratings tab of the Internet Explorer Preferences dialog box. Find the category whose rating you want to change, and make a new choice in the corresponding drop-down list.

To make decisions about unrated sites, click the Options button. One check box on this tab enables users to view unrated Web sites without the supervisor password; the other allows viewing of unrated sites with a supervisor password. Make whatever changes you want and enter your supervisor password, when prompted.

To change the supervisor password, click the Change Password button. Enter the old password into the first line of the Change Supervisor Password box, and enter the new password into the second and third lines of the Change Supervisor Password box.

Browsing with Content Advisor Enabled

As long as you are viewing only rated Web pages whose rating is within your acceptability criteria, Content Advisor is invisible. When a user attempts to access a Web site that is unrated or that violates your criteria, Content Advisor displays a dialog box listing the areas in which the site's ratings exceed the criteria, and requests the Content Advisor password before continuing. To allow IE to display the requested page, type the Content Advisor password into the Password box and click OK. Otherwise, click Cancel to return to the previously displayed page.

Getting Help

Since the whole purpose of a Web browser is to give you access to information, you would expect that information about the Web browser itself would not be hard to find. IE does a reasonably good job of fulfilling that expectation. Most situations that arise in everyday use of IE are covered by its internal Help files (accessible using Help | Contents and Index in Windows or Help | Internet Explorer Help on a Mac). And if you come across something too arcane for that (or for this chapter), you can find additional help online.

Select Help | Online Support to connect to IE's online support page. (The Mac version of IE has no comparable menu entry. Go to the Web site **http://support.microsoft.com** instead.) The first time you visit this page, you are asked to fill out a form, to create a profile, and to give that profile a password. When you visit the support site thereafter, enter by giving your e-mail address and the password.

The support Web page (**http://support.microsoft.com/support**) is a search engine to search for relevant information from the Microsoft Knowledge Base (a huge collection of problems and solutions for use with Microsoft products). This search engine offers a variety of methods for entering your question, giving examples of each technique. The search engine outputs a list of titles of articles in the Microsoft Knowledge Base.

Chapter 21

Lynx, Opera, and Other Browsers

A s the Battle of the Browsers wages on, Internet Explorer and Netscape get lots of press. However, these two excellent programs are not the only available browsers. Two other programs—Lynx and Opera—may come in handy. Lynx runs on DOS and UNIX systems, and is very fast, but it doesn't handle graphics, sound, animation, plug-ins, ActiveX controls, or other advanced features. Opera is smaller and faster than the two major browsers and has some neat features. This chapter describes both programs, as well as how to find out about other browsers.

Lynx, the Original UNIX Browser

Lynx is a text-based Web browser that predates Netscape Navigator, Internet Explorer, Mosaic (on which both Netscape and Internet Explorer are based), and almost every other browser. Lynx doesn't display pictures, play sound or movies, or any other advanced features, but it has one big advantage—it's fast. And if you use a UNIX shell account (described in Chapter 40), Lynx may be your only option.

Versions of Lynx (which has a home page at **http://lynx.browser.org**) exist for several systems, including DOS, Windows, and UNIX. For information on a DOS or Windows version of Lynx, see the following Web site:

> **http://www.fdisk.com/doslynx/lynxport.htm**

For a list of computer systems for which versions of Lynx are available, see this site:

> **http://www.crl.com/~subir/lynx/platforms.html**

This chapter describes Lynx version 2.8.

Downloading and Installing Lynx for Windows

If you use Windows 98, Windows 95, or Windows NT, you can download a copy of Lynx from this Web site:

> **http://www.fdisk.com/doslynx/wlynx/lynx_w32.zip**

The installation file that you receive is a ZIP file (a compressed set of files, also described in Chapter 38) named something like Lynx_w32.zip—and it's only 612K, compared to over 5MB for the most popular browsers. To install Lynx after you download the installation file:

1. In Windows Explorer or a folder window, create a folder in C:\Program Files for the Lynx program files by using the File | New | Folder command (for example, create C:\Program Files\Lynx).

2. Run WinZip or another program that can read ZIP files (see Chapter 38), and then open the Lynx installation file that you downloaded.

3. Decompress the files from the installation file into the folder that you created.

4. Read any text files with names like Readme.txt or Install.txt, in case they contain further installation instructions. (If the file extension is .txt, you can double-click the filename to read the file in Notepad; otherwise, run Notepad and drag the filename to the Notepad window.)

5. Create a shortcut to Lynx from your desktop: open Windows Explorer or a folder window, and either click-and-drag the file Lynx.exe (the Lynx program file) to your desktop to create a desktop icon or drag the file to your Start button to add Lynx to your Start menu.

Running and Commanding Lynx

If you use a UNIX shell account (or have installed a DOS version of Lynx), you run Lynx by typing the command **lynx** and then pressing ENTER. Almost all UNIX shell accounts offer Lynx, because the UNIX version is free.

If you use the Windows version of Lynx, run the desktop icon for the program or choose the command off the Start menu. You can also run Lynx by clicking or double-clicking the file Lynx.exe in your Lynx program folder. If you are not already connected to the Internet, Windows may dial the phone and connect to your ISP when Lynx loads, if your Windows installation is configured to connect automatically.

Whichever version you run, Lynx looks something like Figure 21-1. Some versions may use color, but all display a text-only rendition of Web pages. If you use Windows, Lynx appears in an MS-DOS window.

*If you usually type **lynx** to start the program, you can tell Lynx to display a specific Web page on startup by typing **lynx**, a space, and the exact URL of the Web page.*

Lynx commands are almost all one-letter long, and for a few commands, capitalization counts (that is, uppercase and lowercase letters may do different things). For example, to exit Lynx, press **q**. When Lynx asks if you really want to leave, press **y**. If you want to exit without having to confirm, press **Q** instead of **q**.

This book shows commands in uppercase when capitalization doesn't matter.

Browsing with Lynx

Lynx displays the title of the current page in the upper-right corner of the screen or window. If the Web page is too long to fit in the window, Lynx displays something like *p2 of 5* to tell you which part of the Web page you are currently viewing (in this example, page 2 of 5 pages). Press the following keys to move around the Web page:

- Scroll down one page: press either SPACEBAR, **+**, or **3** (or PAGE DOWN for Windows Lynx).

- Scroll up one page: press either **B**, **-**, or **9** (or PAGE UP for Windows Lynx).

■ Return to the top of the Web page: press **7** (or HOME for Windows Lynx).

■ Go to the end of the Web page: press **1** (or END for Windows Lynx).

A menu of commands appears on the bottom two lines of the screen or window. Links are displayed either in *reverse video* (white letters on a black background) or in a different color. One link (the first one on the page) is selected, which is usually indicated by a reverse-video cursor or a special color.

The URLs of the current page and the currently selected link don't appear in Lynx. To see a page of information that includes your version of Lynx, the URL of the current page, and the URL of the currently selected link, press =.

Following Links

Like all Web browsers, Lynx lets you choose a link on the current Web page and display the page to which the link connects. When you first see a Web page, the first

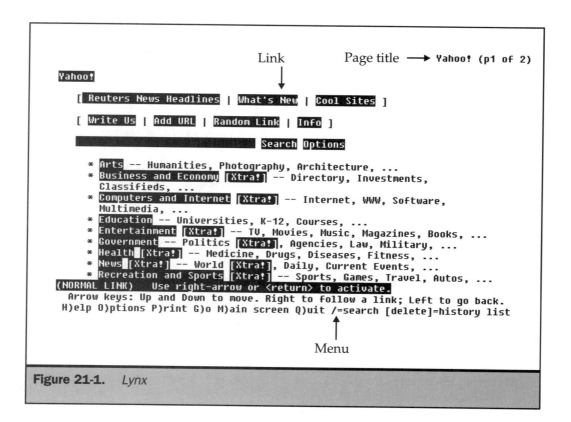

Figure 21-1. *Lynx*

(upper-leftmost) link is selected. To choose a different link, press DOWN ARROW or TAB to move to the next link (moving rightward across the line and down) or press UP ARROW to move to the previous link (moving leftward across the link and up).

 If you can't tell which link is selected, try moving from link to link to see what changes onscreen. Some versions of Lynx can be configured to show a number beside each link, so that you can select links by number.

To follow a link (that is, to display the Web page to which the link connects), press RIGHT ARROW or ENTER. Lynx retrieves and displays the new Web page. If you want to return to the previously displayed page, press LEFT ARROW.

Typing URLs

If you know the URL of the page that you want to see, press **G** (for "go to"). Lynx asks for the URL. Type the complete URL, including **http://**, and press ENTER. If you omit http:// at the beginning of the URL, Lynx rejects the URL. To correct typing errors before you press ENTER, you can press BACKSPACE or LEFT ARROW, or press CTRL+U to delete what you've typed and start over.

To display a file that is on your own computer (or a computer connected to your computer on a LAN), press **G** and then type the full path name of the file.

Using the History Page

Lynx keeps a list of the pages that you have visited. You can view this *history page*, and from it, you can return to previously displayed Web pages. To see the history page, press BACKSPACE (if BACKSPACE doesn't work, try DEL). Figure 21-2 shows a sample history page. Select links from the history page in the usual way. Press **V** (which must be capitalized) to display the Visited Links page, a list of the Web pages that you've visited (excluding non-Web pages, such as Help pages, that are included in the history page).

Returning to the Start Page

To return to the page you saw when you first started Lynx, press **M** (for *main menu*). You can set the starting page (see the section "Configuring Lynx," later in this chapter).

Getting Help

To see Lynx's online help system, press **H** or **?**. Lynx displays a list of topics: browse the topics as though they are Web pages. To exit from Lynx's help system, press LEFT ARROW until you return to a Web page.

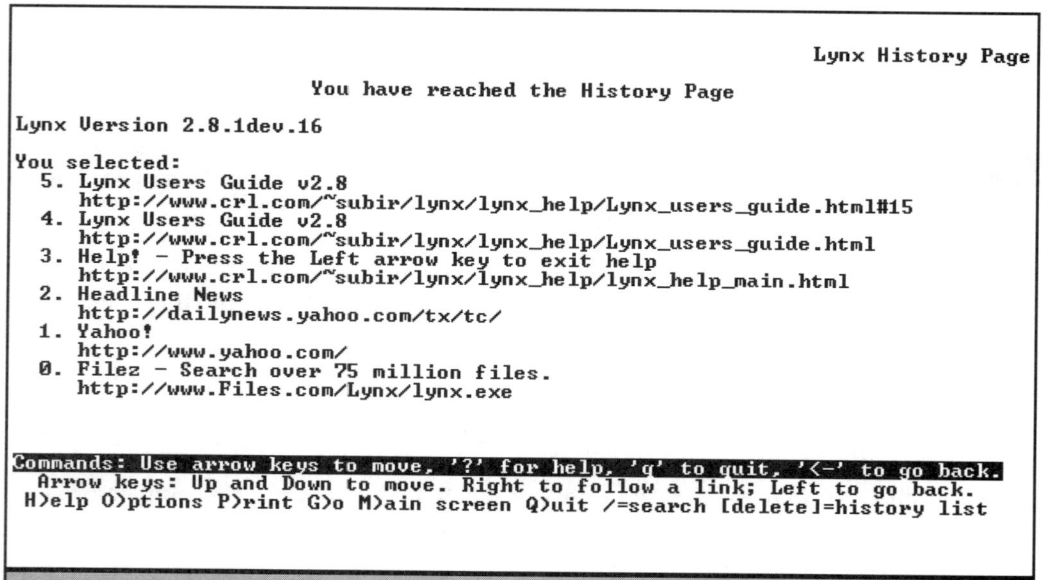

```
                                                          Lynx History Page

                    You have reached the History Page
Lynx Version 2.8.1dev.16

You selected:
   5. Lynx Users Guide v2.8
      http://www.crl.com/~subir/lynx/lynx_help/Lynx_users_guide.html#15
   4. Lynx Users Guide v2.8
      http://www.crl.com/~subir/lynx/lynx_help/Lynx_users_guide.html
   3. Help! - Press the Left arrow key to exit help
      http://www.crl.com/~subir/lynx/lynx_help/lynx_help_main.html
   2. Headline News
      http://dailynews.yahoo.com/tx/tc/
   1. Yahoo!
      http://www.yahoo.com/
   0. Filez - Search over 75 million files.
      http://www.Files.com/Lynx/lynx.exe


Commands: Use arrow keys to move, '?' for help, 'q' to quit, '<-' to go back.
  Arrow keys: Up and Down to move. Right to follow a link; Left to go back.
 H)elp O)ptions P)rint G)o M)ain screen Q)uit /=search [delete]=history list
```

Figure 21-2.   *The history page*

Setting and Using Lynx's Bookmarks

Like other browsers, Lynx can remember the Web pages that you find most interesting, so that you can return to them easily. When you are looking at a Web page that you want to "bookmark" (add to your bookmark list), press **A**. Lynx gives you three choices:

- **Document (press D)**   Add the current Web page to your bookmarks.
- **Link (press L)**   Add the Web page connected to the selected link to your bookmarks.
- **Cancel (press C)**   Cancel the command.

After you choose whether to add the current page or the currently selected link, Lynx displays the title of the page and lets you edit the title that will appear for the page on your bookmark list: press ENTER when you are done.

To see your bookmark list (shown in Figure 21-3), press **V**. (You can't display the bookmark list until you've added at least one bookmark.) Lynx displays a page with a

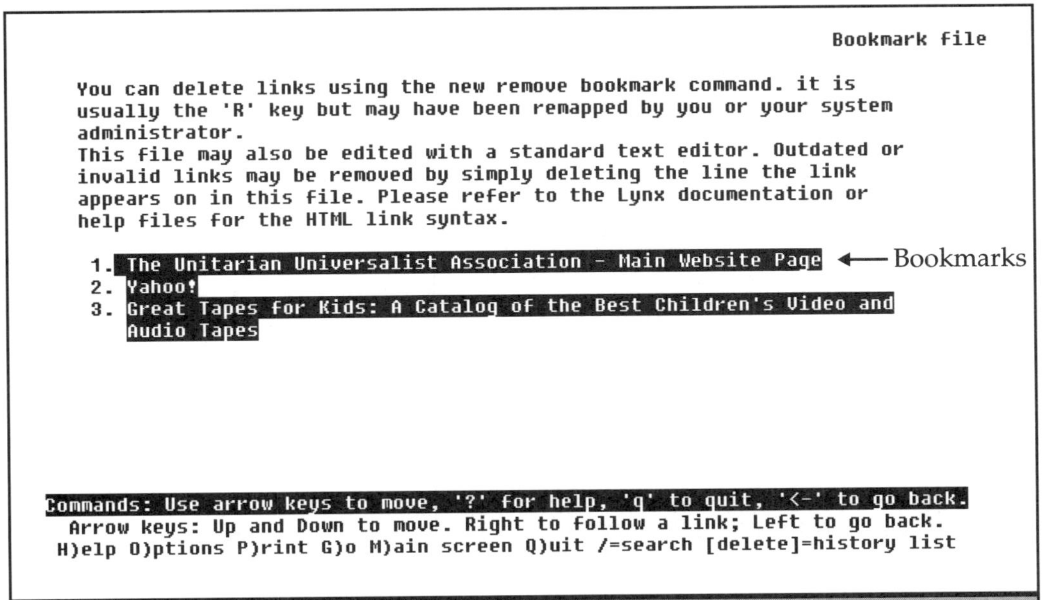

```
                                                         Bookmark file

      You can delete links using the new remove bookmark command. it is
      usually the 'R' key but may have been remapped by you or your system
      administrator.
      This file may also be edited with a standard text editor. Outdated or
      invalid links may be removed by simply deleting the line the link
      appears on in this file. Please refer to the Lynx documentation or
      help files for the HTML link syntax.

         1. The Unitarian Universalist Association - Main Website Page  ◄── Bookmarks
         2. Yahoo!
         3. Great Tapes for Kids: A Catalog of the Best Children's Video and
            Audio Tapes




      Commands: Use arrow keys to move, '?' for help, 'q' to quit, '<-' to go back.
       Arrow keys: Up and Down to move. Right to follow a link; Left to go back.
      H)elp O)ptions P)rint G)o M)ain screen Q)uit /=search [delete]=history list
```

Figure 21-3.   *Lynx's bookmark file*

list of the bookmarks that you've created. Select a bookmark by using the DOWN ARROW and UP ARROW keys and then display the bookmarked Web page by pressing RIGHT ARROW or ENTER.

If you want to delete a bookmark, select the bookmark and press **R**. Lynx asks whether you really want to delete the bookmark: press **Y** or **N** to confirm or cancel the command.

> *Lynx usually stores your bookmark list as a Web page in a file named lynx_bookmarks.html or lynx_bookmarks.htm. If you are familiar with editing Web pages, you can edit this file by hand to add, modify, or delete bookmarks.*

Configuring Lynx

Lynx has various settings that you can change. To see and change Lynx's settings, press **O**. Lynx display the Options menu, shown in Figure 21-4. Your options may differ from those shown in Figure 21-4, which shows the options in Windows Lynx.

VIEWING THE
WORLD WIDE WEB

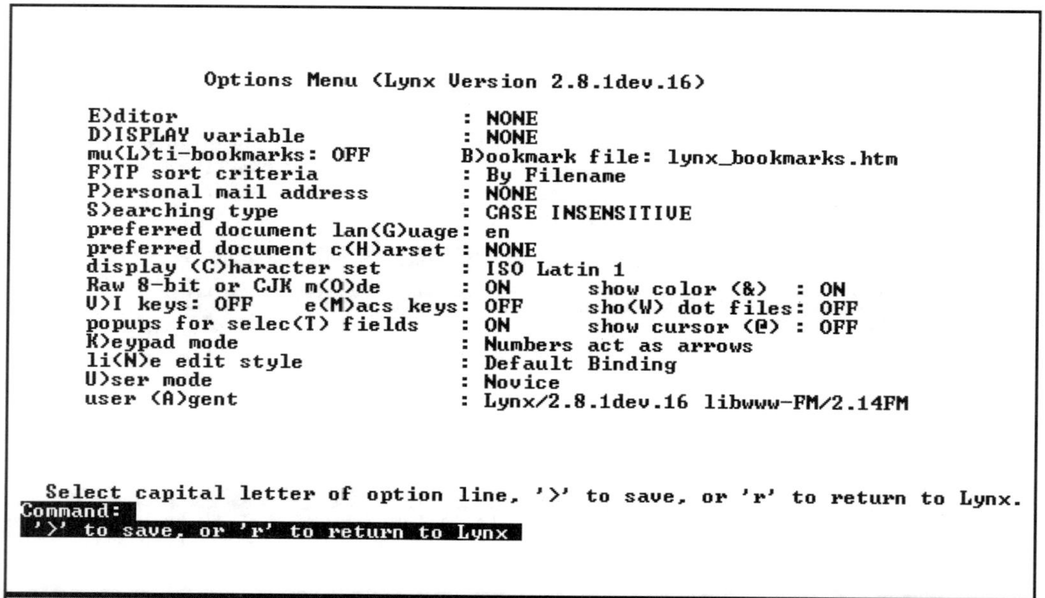

```
                    Options Menu (Lynx Version 2.8.1dev.16)

    E)ditor                        : NONE
    D)ISPLAY variable              : NONE
    mu(L)ti-bookmarks: OFF         B)ookmark file: lynx_bookmarks.htm
    F)TP sort criteria             : By Filename
    P)ersonal mail address         : NONE
    S)earching type                : CASE INSENSITIVE
    preferred document lan(G)uage  : en
    preferred document c(H)arset   : NONE
    display (C)haracter set        : ISO Latin 1
    Raw 8-bit or CJK m(O)de        : ON         show color (&)  : ON
    U)I keys: OFF     e(M)acs keys : OFF        sho(W) dot files: OFF
    popups for selec(T) fields     : ON         show cursor (@) : OFF
    K)eypad mode                   : Numbers act as arrows
    li(N)e edit style              : Default Binding
    U)ser mode                     : Novice
    user (A)gent                   : Lynx/2.8.1dev.16 libwww-FM/2.14FM


    Select capital letter of option line, '>' to save, or 'r' to return to Lynx.
    Command:
    '>' to save, or 'r' to return to Lynx
```

Figure 21-4.   *Lynx Options menu*

To change a setting, press the capital letter that appears in the name of the setting. For some settings, you see a little menu of options, while other settings require you to type a value. To save your changes, press >. To return to Lynx, press **R**. The following are some settings that you might want to change:

■ **Personal mail address**   Specifies the e-mail address to use as the return address for any e-mail messages that you create using Lynx.

■ **Bookmark file**   Controls where Lynx stores your bookmark list. If you turn on the Multi-bookmarks setting on (by choosing either the "standard" or "advanced" setting), you can have up to 26 different bookmark files.

■ **Editor**   Controls which editor Lynx runs when you press **e** to edit the current Web page. For Windows Lynx, specify the full path name of the editor (C:\Windows\Notepad.exe is one example).

■ **User mode**   Controls how much prompting you get while using Lynx. To shrink the menu that appears at the bottom of the Lynx window (leaving more space for the Web page), set the user mode to Advanced.

Other Lynx Features

Here are other things Lynx can do:

■ **Print or save the current page**   Press **P**. Lynx displays a Print menu, which may be different, depending on the version of Lynx you have, the operating system you are using, and other factors. The menu usually has an option to print, save the page to a file, or e-mail the page to yourself. When you save or e-mail a page, Lynx uses the formatted version of the page, not the HTML codes that are included in the page source.

■ **Show the HTML source**   Press \. Lynx displays the HTML codes and text that make up the page. Press \ again to see the Web page. Press **P** to save the HTML version of the page. Another way to save the HTML source code for a Web page is to press **D**.

■ **Edit a Web page**   Press **e** (do not capitalize this command). If the Web page that you are viewing is stored on your own computer and is not read-only (that is, if you have permission to edit the page), you can edit it with Lynx. Lynx runs the editor specified in your options (see the preceding section, "Configuring Lynx").

■ **Search for text within the current Web page**   Press **/** and type the characters that you want to find.

■ **Read Usenet newsgroup articles**   Select a link to a newsgroup, or press **G** and type the URL of a newsgroup (that is, type **news://** followed by the newsgroup name). For more information about newsgroups, see Chapter 13.

■ **Download files via FTP**   Select an FTP link, or press **G** and type an FTP URL. (See Chapter 36 for a description of FTP.)

Table 21-1 lists many of Lynx's commands and what they do.

Keystroke	What It Does
UP ARROW	Selects the previous link
DOWN ARROW	Selects the next link
RIGHT ARROW	Follows the currently selected link to its Web page
LEFT ARROW	Returns to the previously displayed Web page
+, 3, SPACEBAR, or PAGE DOWN	Scrolls down the current Web page
-, 9, B, or PAGE UP	Scrolls up the current Web page
7 or HOME	Scrolls to top of page

Table 21-1.   *Lynx Commands*

Keystroke	What It Does
1 or END	Scrolls to end of page
H or **?**	Displays help information
O	Displays a menu of configuration options
P	Prints, saves, or e-mails the current page
G	Goes to a specific page
M	Displays the start page (the Web page that you see when you start Lynx), which Lynx calls the *main page*
Q or **q**	Quits Lynx (capital **Q** quits Lynx without asking for confirmation)
/	Searches for text within the current Web page
A	Adds the current page to your bookmark file
V	Views your bookmark file
D	Downloads and saves the current Web page
e	Edits the current Web page
K	Displays a list of what each key does in Lynx
BACKSPACE	Displays the history page
=	Displays information about the version of Lynx you are using, the file you are viewing, and the currently selected link
****	Toggles between displaying the Web page and its HTML source
!	Runs a UNIX command shell (in UNIX versions) or MS-DOS window (in Windows versions)
CTRL+R	Reloads the current Web page
CTRL+W or CTRL+L	Refreshes (redisplays) the screen
CTRL+U	Erases the line you are typing
CTRL+G	Cancels input or transfer

Table 21-1.   *Lynx Commands* (continued)

Opera, the Small Browser

Opera is a small, fast browser written by a group of Norwegians. It doesn't have all the features of Netscape or Internet Explorer, but its small size (1.2MB) makes it quick to download, install, and run—and it does have many advanced features, including Java support. If you want a browser that can fit on a diskette, so that you can easily install it on any PC, Opera works fine.

Surprisingly, Opera is not free. You can evaluate the program for 30 days for free, and if you want to continue to use it, you must pay $35 to register your copy. Each time that you run the program, Opera asks whether you want to evaluate it or register. After 30 days, you can use Opera only to see the Opera Software Web site.

The following sections describe Opera version 3.5, which is available for Windows 98/95, Windows 3.1, and Windows NT (version 3.51 or later). Opera is not available for UNIX or the Macintosh.

Getting Opera

To get Opera, you download it from the Internet. Opera is available from the following Web sites (among others):

- Opera Software, at **http://www.operasoftware.com** or **http://opera.nta.no**
- TUCOWS, at **http://www.tucows.com**
- CNET's Download.Com, at **http://www.download.com**

The installation file that you download is only 1.2MB (compared to over 5MB for either Netscape or Internet Explorer). After you download the installation file (a program file with the extension .exe), run the file by clicking or double-clicking its icon in Windows Explorer or in a folder window. The installation program installs Opera, adds it to your Windows Start menu, and adds a shortcut to Opera to your Windows desktop.

Browsing with Opera

To run Opera, choose it from the Start menu (usually by choosing Start | Programs | Opera 3.5 | Opera) or use the desktop shortcut. During your 30-day evaluation period, click the Evaluate button on the first dialog box that you see. When you decide to buy the program, fill out the boxes and click the Register button.

You see several browser windows displayed within the Opera window (shown in Figure 21-5).

Managing Browser Windows

Each browser window shows one Web page. When more than one browser window is open, click in the window (or on its title bar) to select that window, or choose the Window command from the menu and then choose the Web page title from the bottom of the menu that appears.

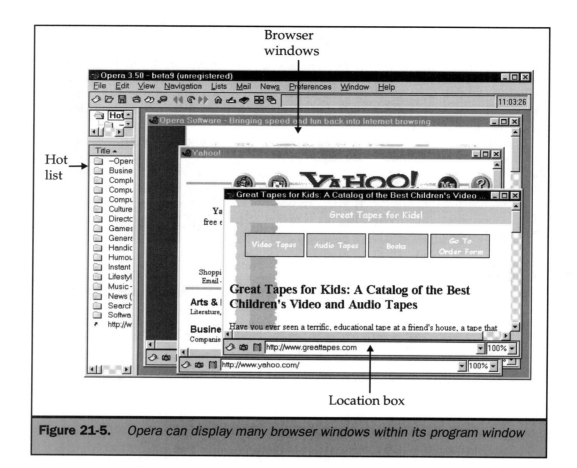

Browser
windows

Hot
list

Location box

Figure 21-5.   *Opera can display many browser windows within its program window*

To open a new browser window, choose File | New from the menu, press CTRL+N, or click the New button on the toolbar. A browser window appears, with no Web page displayed. Another way to open a new window is to SHIFT+click a link on a Web page: Opera displays the linked page in a new window.

To close a browser window, click its Close button (the X button in the window's upper-right corner), or select the window and then either choose File | Close or press CTRL+W.

You can resize browser windows by dragging their borders, clicking their Minimize and Maximize buttons, or choosing commands from the Window menu.

Following Links

Text links are usually underlined and displayed in a different color than normal text, but *graphic links* may be any graphic on the Web page. You can determine which graphics on a page are links by dragging your mouse pointer over them—if a graphic is a link, your mouse pointer changes from an arrow to a pointing hand, and the URL to which the link connects appears in the box at the right end of the toolbar. To follow a link on a Web page, click it. To see a Web page whose URL you already know, type the URL into the location box at the bottom of the browser window.

Returning to Previously Viewed Pages

Opera maintains a list, called a *history list,* of the Web pages that you've viewed in each browser window. To return to the previously displayed Web page in a browser window, either select that browser window, press ALT+LEFT ARROW, and click the Previous button on the toolbar, or right-click in the window and choose Previous from the menu that appears. After you back up to a previous page, you can go forward through Opera's history list either by pressing ALT+RIGHT ARROW, by clicking the Next button on the toolbar, or by right-clicking the page and choosing Next from the menu that appears.

 *You can also display the history list and choose Web sites from it. Press **H** to see the history list, and then use the mouse to choose a site.*

Returning to the Start Page

Unlike most browsers, Opera has more than one start, or *home,* page—the Web page that is displayed when you either click the Home button on the toolbar or press CTRL+HOME. The *global home page* is the default home page for all windows. The *window home page* is the home page that you have set for a specific window, which overrides the global home page for that window.

To specify the global home page, choose Navigation | Set Home from the menu. You see the Set Home Page dialog box:

Set Home Page	✕
Window Home Page	
http://my.yahoo.com	Use Active
Global Home Page	
http://www.operasoftware.com	Use Active
	OK Cancel Help

Type the URL into the Global Home Page text box. To set a home page for a browser window, select the window, choose Navigation | Set Home from the menu, and then type the URL into the Window Home Page text box.

Setting and Using Opera's Hot List

Opera maintains a *hot list,* a feature similar to Netscape Navigator's bookmarks and Internet Explorer's favorites. You can add your favorite Web pages to the hot list and then choose them from the hot list when you want to revisit the pages. The hot list is divided into folders so that you can organize your favorite Web pages by topic. It can appear in several different forms:

- As a menu
- Docked, so that the hot list appears along the left side of the Opera window
- Floating in a separate window

Using the Lists Menu

When you choose Lists from the menu bar, the folders in your hot list appear as submenus. To display a Web page that is on your hot list, choose it from the submenu.

Using the Docked or Floating Hot List

To display or hide the docked or floating hot list, either click the Hot List button on the toolbar, choose View | Hot List, or press CTRL+F2. The hot list appears in two sections: in an upper list and in a lower list. To adjust the width of the lists, or the divider between the upper and lower lists, click-and-drag the divider lines.

The upper section of the hot list displays your folders. When you select a folder, the lower section displays the Web sites in that folder. To see a Web site that is listed on the hot list, double-click its entry or drag it to a browser window.

To switch between showing the hot list docked against the left side of the Opera window and showing the hot list in a free-floating window, right-click the divider between the upper and lower sections of the hot list. From the menu that appears, choose Docking View. When your hot list is floating, you can resize it like any other window (by dragging its borders).

Adding Web Sites to Your Hot List

When you find a Web site to which you want to return, add it to your hot list by using any of these methods:

- Choose Lists from the menu bar, choose the folder to which you want to add the Web site, and then choose Add Current Document Here.
- In the upper section of the docked or floating hot list, click the folder to which you want to add the Web site. Then, choose Navigation | Add Active To Hot List or press CTRL+T.
- In the upper section of the docked or floating hot list, right-click the folder to which you want to add the Web site and then choose Add Current from the menu that appears.

After you give one of these commands, you see a dialog box with information about the Web site; make any edits that you want, and then click OK.

Reorganizing Your Hot List

Opera stores the hot list in the file Opera3.adr, but you can create other hot lists with other names (always using the .adr extension). The following are the ways that you can edit and organize your hot list files:

- **Sort the items in a folder**   Click the Title button at the top of the lower section of the docked or floating hot list. Opera sorts the Web sites from A to Z—click again to sort them from Z to A.

- **Delete an item**   Display the docked or floating hot list, right-click the unwanted item, and then choose Delete from the menu that appears.

- **Change the title or URL of an item**   Right-click the item in the docked or floating hot list, choose Properties from the menu that appears, and then edit the Item Properties dialog box.

- **Move an item or folder to a different folder**   Drag the item from the lower section of the docked or floating hot list window to a folder in the upper section.

- **Create a new folder**   Right-click a folder in the upper section of the docked or floating hot list and then choose New | Folder from the menu that appears.

- **Import Netscape bookmarks**   Right-click a folder in the upper section of the docked or floating hot list and then choose File | Insert File from the menu that appears. Set the Files of Type box to HTML/Netscape Bookmarks, move to the Netscape Navigator program folder (usually C:\Program Files\Netscape\Communicator\Program or C:\Program Files\Netscape\Communicator\Users*yourname*), and then choose the Bookmark.htm file. Opera copies the Netscape bookmarks into the selected folder in your hot list. (Note that Opera 3.5 may be able to import Netscape Navigator 3 bookmarks only, not bookmarks from Netscape Navigator 4 or 4.5.)

- **Import Internet Explorer favorites**   Right-click a folder in the upper section of the docked or floating hot list and then choose File | Insert Internet Explorer Favorites from the menu that appears. Select the Favorites folder from the list that appears and click OK.

- **Create a new hot list file**   Right-click a folder in the upper section of the docked or floating hot list and then choose File | New from the menu that appears.

Configuring Opera

Opera has dozens of configuration settings, all accessible by choosing Preferences from the menu bar. Here are two that you may find useful:

- **Speed up browsing by skipping graphics**   Choose Preferences | Multimedia and click the Show Loaded Images Only option. You can also turn this option on and off for each browser window by clicking the camera icon near the lower-left corner of the window.

■ **Save your browser window settings** Choose Preferences I Save Window Settings. Opera suggests a name for the settings file (with the extension .win). If you leave the Use At Startup option selected, Opera opens the currently displayed windows each time that you start the program, with the windows in their current sizes and positions, and displaying the same Web pages that you see when you gave the command. You can save several different sets of window settings, each set in its own WIN file, and display those windows again by choosing File I Open from the menu and then choosing the WIN file.

Many browser plug-ins, including RealAudio and Shockwave, work with Opera. For information, see the Web page at **http://www.operasoftware.com/config.htm**.

Sending E-mail with Opera

Opera 3.5 can't receive e-mail, only send it, although future versions may come with a complete e-mail program. But the capability to send e-mail from your browser is useful, especially when you run into a mailto link (a link with a URL consisting of *mailto,* followed by a colon and an e-mail address) on a Web page.

To configure Opera to send e-mail messages, choose Preferences I Mail to display the Mail Settings dialog box. Fill in the Name box with your real name, the Mail Address box with your e-mail address, and the Mail Server box with your ISP's SMTP server (the computer that handles your outgoing e-mail messages).

To send e-mail messages, either choose Mail I New from the menu, click a mailto link, or type a mailto link into a location box. You see the Opera mail dialog box, as shown here:

Opera mail	
To:	nettcr@gurus.com
News groups:	
CC:	
BCC:	
Subject:	Your Book

I just opened a new Internet account and I want to test my e-mail. Please respond! Thanks.

Fill in the To, CC (copy to), BCC (blind copy), and Subject boxes; type the message in the large text box, and click the Send button. Opera sends the message right away. (See Chapter 5 for instructions on how to address e-mail.)

Reading Usenet Newsgroup Articles

Opera includes a Usenet newsgroup reader (see Chapter 13 for information about newsgroups). First, configure Opera with the name of your ISP's news server by choosing Preferences | News from the menu. Then, display the News window shown in Figure 21-6 by choosing News | New from the menu.

The first time you open the News window, Opera contacts your news server and downloads a list of all available Usenet newsgroups, which can take several minutes. To switch between displaying the newsgroups to which you are subscribed (a blank list, the first time you use the News window) and a list of all newsgroups, click the leftmost button on the News window toolbar.

When the News window displays all newsgroups, it lists the newsgroup hierarchies (described in Chapter 13). Hierarchies are shown in black, and newsgroups appear in blue. To see the newsgroups in a hierarchy, click the hierarchy.

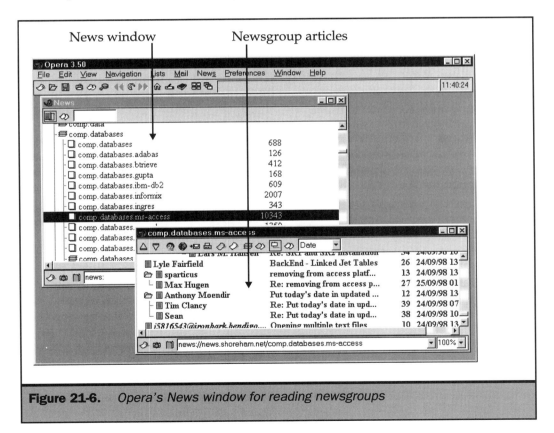

Figure 21-6.   *Opera's News window for reading newsgroups*

To subscribe to or unsubscribe from a newsgroup, click its icon. When you click a newsgroup name, Opera displays a list of the newsgroup's articles in a separate window. To read an article, click the article. To reply to the article's author by e-mail, click the Reply button on the toolbar, or post a reply to the newsgroup by clicking the Post button: either way, you see the Opera Mail window in which to compose your message.

Some Other Browsers

Here are a couple of other browsers to consider:

- **Arachne** From xChaos Software, this browser is useful for DOS users. You can run Arachne on a computer that is as limited as a 286 with less than 1MB of RAM. Arachne is available from the following sites:

  - TUCOWS, at **http://www.tucows.com**

  - CNET's Download.com, at **http://www.download.com**

  - Arachne's home site in the Czech Republic, at **http://www.naf.cz/arachne/xch**

  The software is free for 30 days and thereafter requires registration for $30 if you want to continue to use it.

- **HotJava** From Sun Microsystems' JavaSoft Division, this program is written entirely in Java, Sun's high-level, machine-independent programming language (see "What Is Java?" in Chapter 34). The current incarnation is slow, but it does support Java better than any other browser. HotJava is available from these sites:

  - CNET's Download.com, at **http://www.download.com**

  - JavaSoft's Web site, at **http://www.javasoft.com/products/hotjava**

For a complete list of browsers, see one of these sites:

- TUCOWS, at **http://www.tucows.com**
- BrowserWatch, at **http://browserwatch.internet.com**

Chapter 22

Viewing Advanced
Web Pages

Early Web pages consisted of nothing but text. The first big revolution in Web browsing occurred when Mosaic, the precursor to Netscape Navigator, became the first browser to display pictures right in the Web page. Now, graphics are a familiar part of Web pages, and many Web pages contain other types of non-text information, such as audio files, video files, animated graphics, and moving stock tickers. This chapter describes the technology behind some of these Web components:

- Players, programs that your browser can run to display or play files
- Add-ons (plug-ins and ActiveX controls) to your Web browser that enable it to display new types of information
- Programs that can be contained in Web pages (written in Java, JavaScript, and other languages)
- Programs that play audio and video files from the Web

Finding and Installing Players

A *player* is a program that displays or plays the information in a file. Windows 95, Windows 98, and Macs all come with players for some types of audio and video files, as well as programs that can display many formats of graphics files. If you encounter a file on a Web page that your computer can't play (that is, for which you don't have a player), you may need to get and install a new player. For example, if you want to play MP3 format audio files (described in the last section in this chapter, "Playing MP3 Music"), you need an MP3 player.

Many players are available for free on the Internet. Almost any program can be considered as a player; for example, if a Web page contains a link to a Microsoft Excel spreadsheet file, you could use Excel to display the file. Some programs are available that give you the ability to display files that you might find on Web pages, without giving you the ability to edit or create such files. Here are few of these "display only" players:

- **Microsoft Word documents**   Can be displayed by Microsoft Word Viewer, which you can download from Microsoft's Web site at **http://www.microsoft.com** (try **http://www.microsoft.com/word/internet/viewer/viewer97/default.htm**) or from Download.com (**http://www.download.com**).

- **Microsoft Excel spreadsheets**   Can be displayed by Microsoft Excel Viewer, which is also available for downloading from Microsoft's Web site or from Download.com (refer to the previous paragraph for their URLs).

- **Microsoft PowerPoint presentations**   Can be displayed by Microsoft PowerPoint Viewer, downloadable from the same URLs listed under "Microsoft Word documents."

- **Graphics files** (other than GIF and JPEG files, which browsers can display)   Can be viewed using Kodak Imaging, which comes with Windows 98. You can also use one of several freeware or shareware graphics viewers, available at Download.com (start at **http://www.download.com** and search for "viewer").

■ **Adobe Acrobat documents**   Can be displayed by Adobe Acrobat Reader (see "Recommended Plug-Ins and ActiveX Controls" later in this chapter).

See the section "Watching and Listening to the Web," later in this chapter, for information about audio and video players.

Finding and Installing Plug-Ins and ActiveX Controls

Sometimes, a player can't handle the information on a Web page. Players work only if information is stored in a separate file and you want it to appear in a separate window, not in your browser window. Two other types of programs can handle audio, video, and other information right in your browser: plug-ins and ActiveX controls.

A *plug-in* is a program that can "plug in" to Netscape Navigator, to give the browser a new capability. Most plug-ins work with Internet Explorer, too, and some work with Opera. Plug-ins work with Navigator seamlessly, so that after you install them, you can forget that they are not part of your browser. Netscape originally invented the idea of plug-ins, but Microsoft makes sure that Internet Explorer can use most of them, too.

ActiveX controls are programs that work with Internet Explorer and other programs, but not with Netscape Navigator (see "VBScript and ActiveX Controls" in Chapter 18 for details). Many programs are available as both plug-ins and ActiveX controls.

Note *You can get a special plug-in that lets Netscape Navigator use ActiveX controls, but it is not free. Check Ncompass Lab's Web site at* **http://www.ncompasslabs.com** *for information about its ScriptActive plug-in (click Products or Download).*

Typically, a plug-in or ActiveX control is born when a software company develops a new type of information to play or display on the Web—for example, sound or video. Rather than trying to convince Netscape and Microsoft (and other browser makers) to make their browsers capable of playing or displaying this new type of information, the software company creates a plug-in or ActiveX control (or both) that can handle the task of playing or displaying the new information within the browser. People who want to extend the capabilities of Netscape Navigator can download and install the plug-in, and Internet Explorer users can download and install the ActiveX control. Many plug-ins include a stand-alone player, in case you want to display files when you are not browsing the Web.

Caution *As with any downloaded program, plug-ins and ActiveX controls pose a security risk to your system. Theoretically, a plug-in or ActiveX control could introduce a virus, delete files, or relay information from your hard disk to the Internet. Downloading and installing plug-ins and ActiveX controls from reputable sources—such as Browser Watch, Netscape, and Microsoft—is perfectly safe, but think twice before you use a plug-in or ActiveX control from a site you know nothing about.*

VIEWING THE
WORLD WIDE WEB

Finding and Downloading Plug-Ins and ActiveX Controls

Many plug-ins and ActiveX controls are available for download from the Web: frequently, if a page contains information that requires a plug-in or ActiveX control, the page also contains a link that leads to a page from which you can download what you need. A variety of plug-ins and ActiveX controls are available for Windows, Macs, and UNIX at the following Web sites:

- **Netscape (http://home.netscape.com/plugins)**   Go to this site for plug-ins only.

- **BrowserWatch**   For plug-ins, go to **http://browserwatch.internet.com/plug-in.html**. For ActiveX controls, go to **http://browserwatch.internet.com/activex.html**.

- **TUCOWS (http://www.tucows.com)**   Choose a site that is geographically close to you, choose your operating system, and choose Browser Add-Ons.

- **CWSApps (http://cws.internet.com)**   Click the button for your operating system and then click the Browser Plug-Ins or ActiveX Controls button).

- **Download.com**   For plug-ins, start at **http://www.download.com** and search for "plug-in." For ActiveX controls, start at **http://www.download.com/PC/Activex** and click Browser Enhancements.

For instructions on how to download and install programs (including plug-ins and ActiveX controls) from the Web, see Chapter 38.

Netscape Navigator and Plug-ins

When you are browsing the Web, you may click a link that requires Navigator to have a plug-in. If Navigator knows about the plug-in that you need, you see the Plug-in Not Loaded dialog box. Click the Get the Plug-In button to download the plug-in that the Web page requires. If Netscape isn't familiar with the plug-in that you need, you see the Unknown File Type dialog box, with an indication of the type of data file that requires the plug-in. Click the More Info button to see a page that lists a lot of plug-ins. Pick a plug-in whose description seems to match what you need, and then follow the instructions on the page to download and install it.

You can ask Navigator to display a list of the plug-ins that you already have installed. To see a list, choose Help | About Plug-ins from the menu or type **about:plugins** in the Location box. For information about how to see what ActiveX controls Internet Explorer has installed, see "Managing ActiveX Controls" in Chapter 20.

Recommended Plug-Ins and ActiveX Controls

Here are a few plug-ins and ActiveX controls that you should consider downloading and installing:

■ **Adobe Acrobat Reader**   Displays *Portable Document Format (PDF)* files, documents that are saved with all of their formatting for uploading to the Web (Acrobat Reader is available as a plug-in, an ActiveX control, and a stand-alone player). Unlike with regular Web pages, the author of a PDF file can control the exact formatting of each page of the document. PDF is used for documents that are to be printed (like IRS forms) and documents with formatting too elaborate for HTML. For more information on Adobe Acrobat, see its Web site at

http://www.adobe.com/prodindex/acrobat

■ **Shockwave**   Displays animated graphics, plays sound, and lets you interact with the Web page. For example, games can be programmed to use the Shockwave plug-in. You can download this plug-in from its Web page at

http://www.macromedia.com/shockwave

Check out **http://www.shockrave.com** for the ShockRave Web site, with lots of games that require Shockwave.

■ **Word Viewer Plug-in**   Displays Microsoft Word format document files right in your browser window. You can download this plug-in from the site at **http://www.download.com** (search for "Word Viewer").

■ **Cosmo Player**   Includes a VRML player, which can display three-dimensional "virtual worlds." VRML players not only display a virtual world, they let you move around within the world, viewing it from any angle. You can download the Cosmo Player plug-in (and other VRML plug-ins) from Download.com (start at **http://www.download.com** and search for "Cosmo Player").

Other plug-ins that play audio and video files are described later in this chapter.

Uninstalling Plug-Ins and ActiveX Controls

Uninstalling plug-ins and ActiveX controls is not always easy—in fact, sometimes it's impossible. Some plug-ins come with uninstall programs, but most do not. If you use Windows 98 or 95, you can also choose Start | Setting | Control Panel, open the Add/Remove Programs icon, and see whether the plug-in or ActiveX control appears on the list of installed software that you can remove.

Dealing with Web Pages That Contain ActiveX, Java, and JavaScript

Web pages may contains programs written in Java, JavaScript, and VBScript, which are all described in the section "The Web's Languages and Protocols" in Chapter 18. Programs written in these languages can be stored as part of a Web page and executed on your computer by your browser.

Running programs stored on Web pages is a security risk. You can control whether your Web browser runs these programs (for Netscape Navigator, see the section "Managing Java and JavaScript" in Chapter 19; for Internet Explorer, see the section "Managing Java and JavaScript" in Chapter 20).

Watching and Listening to the Web

The Web has gone beyond text and pictures: many pages also include sound and video. Both audio and video files that contain more than a few seconds of audio or video data can be very large, and can take a long time to arrive over the Internet. Audio and video files are stored in several standard formats. Windows 98, 95, and Macs come with players for many of these formats, and you can use plug-ins and ActiveX controls to play others.

Playing Streaming Audio and Video

To address the large size of audio and video files, *streaming* was invented, which enables your computer to play the beginning of an audio or video file while the rest of the file is still arriving. If the file arrives slower than your computer plays it, the playback has gaps while your computer waits for more data to play. Several streaming formats are widely used on the Web, and you can install plug-ins and ActiveX controls to enable your browser to play them.

When you click an audio link on a Web page, your audio plug-in or ActiveX control runs and plays the file. Some plug-ins and ActiveX controls display a little window with VCR-like controls that let you stop, rewind, or fast-forward the file, as well as adjust the volume of the sound played by the file. When you click a video link, the video appears in your Web browser. Because these video files are highly edited and compressed, the video is usually very small and jerky.

Here are some popular audio and video formats, and the plug-ins and ActiveX controls that can play them:

- **RealPlayer** Plays RealAudio-format audio and video files, including streaming audio. You can download RealPlayer (available as a plug-in or ActiveX control) from **http://www.real.com**—choose the free RealPlayer or the reasonably priced and more powerful RealPlayer Plus.

- **Beatnik Plug-In** Plays a variety of audio file formats, including RMF, MIDI, MOD, AIFF, and AU files. You can download Beatnik from Headspace, at **http://www.headspace.com**. An ActiveX control is under development.

- **QuickTime**   Plays audio and video files stored in the QuickTime format. You can download the Apple QuickTime player from **http://www.apple.com/ quicktime**.

- **Microsoft Windows Media Player**   Plays both regular and streaming audio and video files, including RealAudio, RealVideo, NetShow, and QuickTime streaming files, and AVI and WAV audio files. Download this player from **http://www.microsoft.com** (try **http://www.microsoft.com/windows/ mediaplayer/default.asp**)

- **VDOLive Player**   Plays streaming video; available at **http://www.clubvdo.net** as a plug-in for Netscape and as an ActiveX control for IE.

When you are ready to listen to the Web, here are some Web sites to try:

- National Public Radio (NPR), at **http://www.npr.org**, has today's news and some of your favorite public radio shows

- Broadcast.com, at **http://www.broadcast.com,** lists live radio and TV stations, music, audio books, and other audio and video sources.

- For listings of live and recorded audio and video that is "broadcast" over the Internet, start at Yahoo! (**http://www.yahoo.com**) and click News and Media, and then Internet Broadcasts.

- CDnow, at **http://www.cdnow.com**, is an online CD and audio cassette store that lets you listen to RealAudio clips of many of its recordings before you decide whether to buy.

See Chapter 25 for other sites—including news and sports sites—that provide audio over the Web.

Playing MP3 Music

MPEG3 or *MP3* is a highly compressed audio format that is used for storing audio data, mainly music. Many music files are available on the Internet in MP3 format, which has the file extension .MP3. The problem with most MP3 files is that they are *bootlegged*, recorded illegally without the permission of the copyright holder. Some files are put on the Web by small bands who are just getting their start and use MP3 and the Web as a great way to get wide exposure legally. If your computer has a CD-ROM drive, you can also convert songs from CDs that you own into MP3 files. Converting music CD songs into MP3 files is probably legal as long as you keep the MP3 files that you create and don't give or sell them to anyone else (but no cases have gone to court yet). Not all CD-ROM drives can be used to create MP3 files: the drive must be able to read raw data from music CDs.

To play an MP3 format, you need an MP3 player, which you can download from the Web. Two popular MP3 players are WinAmp (shareware from **http://winamp.lh.net**) and MusicMatch Jukebox (freeware from **http://www.musicmatch.com**). Both are available from TUCOWS (**http://www.tucows.com**) and from **http://www.mp3.com** or **http://www.mp3now.com**, both of which have lots of other MP3-related information. WinAmp allows you to install "skins," which are custom interfaces, to make the program look even cooler than it usually looks.

To find music, start at **http://www.mp3now.com/html/mp3_search.html** and choose an MP3 search site, or try one of these sites:

- Pure MP3, at **http://puremp3.mircx.com**
- Borg Music Search Engine, at **http://electronicshopper.com/mp3/search.html**
- MediaFind, at **http://194.95.209.6**
- Scour.net Media Search, at **http://www.scour.net**

Some of these sites include audio and video files in other formats, but you can identify MP3 files by the filename extension .mp3. Once you find the song that you are looking for (if it is available on the Web), you download the file (which is usually several MB) by clicking an FTP link or using an FTP program (see Chapter 36). You may have trouble getting through to FTP sites that have MP3 files, because they can be very busy: if you get "Document contains no data" or "Site busy" messages, just keep trying. After you download the MP3 file, you can play it as many times as you want by using an MP3 player. If you have a slow computer (for example, a 486), the music may sound terrible, but on faster computers, MP3 files can sound like CDs.

The
Complete
Reference

Internet

Chapter 23

Searching for Information, People, and Companies on the Web

L ooking for information on the Internet without a guide is like searching for a book in a library without a card catalog. This chapter describes how to find what you're looking for on the Internet, whether you're searching for Web pages on a specific topic, the e-mail address of a friend, or information on a particular company.

What Are Search Engines?

Back in the old days (in other words, the 1980s), the Internet was primarily a research medium. Files were stored separately, with no way to go from one file to another easily. In 1991, Tim Berners-Lee developed a network of files connected by hypertext links; this network today is referred to as the World Wide Web. The popularity of the Web exploded when user-friendly browser applications were created to enable people to view text and graphics and jump quickly from page to page. The next thing that was needed was a way for users to find what they wanted, and that's why search engines were created.

A *search engine* is a database application that retrieves information, based on words or a phrase that you enter. How do Web-based search engines work? A Web search engine employs a *search agent* (also called a *spider*) that goes out and looks for information on Web pages. This information is indexed and stored in a huge database. When you conduct a search, the search engine looks through its database to find entries that match the information you entered. Then, the search engine presents to you a list of the Web pages that it determines are most relevant to your search criteria.

Dozens of search engines are available on the Web. Each search engine gathers information a little differently. Some engines scan the entire Web page, others focus on the page title, while still others read keywords and information included in *META tags* (tags that include keywords about the page) on the Web page. That is why you can get different results from different search engines.

Most search engines go beyond just searching for Web pages for you. Many search engines allow you to search for information from Usenet newsgroups (described in Chapter 13) or for specific types of information, such as pictures or sound files.

Tip	*If you are the author of a Web page and want to know how to get your page noticed by a search engine, review the Help file of each search engine. Most search engines provide information that tells you how to code your Web pages so that they will be picked up by the search agent and recognized by the search engine. See Chapter 33 for more information.*

While the way each search engine gathers information is unique, all search engines share a common purpose—to find quickly the information that you're looking for.

What Are Web Directories?

A *Web directory* is a Web site that categorizes Web pages, so that you can browse links to Web pages by topic. For example, the Yahoo! Web directory includes categories for Arts and Humanities, Business and Economy, Computers and Internet, Education, and a dozen others. Each of these major categories contains many subcategories: for example, if you click the Recreation and Sports category, you see Sports, Games, Travel, Autos, Outdoors, and many other subcategories. Keep clicking categories to see their subcategories until you find the specific types of Web pages that you are looking for.

The advantage of a Web directory over a search engine is that human beings have categorized the Web pages, so that all the links in a category usually belong there. Web directories are great for browsing when you don't know the exact name of what you are looking for. For example, if you want to know which gourmet shops sell merchandise online, you can browse to the page that lists online gourmet stores, without knowing the exact name of a store and without stumbling over other cooking-related sites.

On the other hand, search engines are quicker if you are looking for information about a specific, unusual term. For example, if you need pages about fibromyalgia and aspirin, using a search engine to search for the terms gives you pages on your specific topic.

Luckily, several Web sites combine search engines with Web directories, including Yahoo! and Excite, described later in this chapter.

Searching for Information

With tens of millions of pages published on the Web, your goal should be to find only relevant information. Usually, when you search for Web pages by using a search engine, you receive too many results—for example, a list of thousands of Web pages that contain the terms that you specified. The more that you can narrow your search, the better your results. For example, if you're a bird watcher, it's better to search for a specific type of bird (for example, "blue herons") than to search only for "birds."

The key to a successful Web search is to narrow your focus. Search methods are available that you can use to limit your search to exactly what you are looking for, and to obtain productive results. Table 23-1 shows some quick ways to narrow your search. These methods work in most search engines. (For detailed information about the search methods used by a specific search engine, consult the search engine's Help file.)

Searching Using Search Engines and Directories

Each search engine employs a specific set of rules that goes beyond the common search methods, to conduct a focused search. All the search engines described in this chapter

Method	Example	Results
Multiple words	Hawaii vacation	Pages that contain all words, with the most likely matches listed first on the list of results. The words don't have to appear together, or in the order that you specified. Some search engines return pages that contain any of the words, not necessarily all of them.
Phrase in quotation marks	"Baltimore Orioles"	Pages that contain the exact phrase.
Plus sign (+) to include words, and minus (-) sign to exclude words	+penguins -hockey	Pages about penguins, excluding hockey teams named "penguins."
Boolean search	cats AND obedience NOT zoos	Pages about cats and obedience that do not mention zoos. You can also use "OR" to search for pages that contain one word or another; for example, cats OR obedience.

Table 23-1. *Common Search Methods*

have easy-to-use Help files that show you the rules and regulations peculiar to the search engine. If the common search methods don't give you the results that you want, try entering your search terms in the syntax specific to the search engine that you're using. Some of the search engines also include Web directories.

The search engines described in this chapter are listed in alphabetical order.

AltaVista

■ **Web address** http://www.altavista.com

*AltaVista is also available from the Yahoo! home page (**http://www.yahoo.com**) by clicking the Go to AltaVista link on your search results list.*

■ **Getting help** Click the Help link or the Advanced link at the top of the page. You can also click the Help link located at the bottom of the page.

■ **Our favorite feature**   The ability to enter a question such as "Who won the 1956 World Series?" in the search box, and get the answer and a list of related Web pages.

AltaVista is one of the oldest search engines on the Web. To conduct your search, type the word or phrase that you are looking for in the blank box and click Search (see Figure 23-1).

The default search language is English. To conduct your search in another language, click the Any Language down arrow and select a language from the drop-down list. Enter your search words or phrase in the language that you selected.

The AltaVista home page has additional links that enable you to go to the following:

■ Frequently used links, such as Stock Quotes and Yellow Pages

■ Specific categories (such as Business & Finance, or Hobbies & Interests)

■ Current news stories

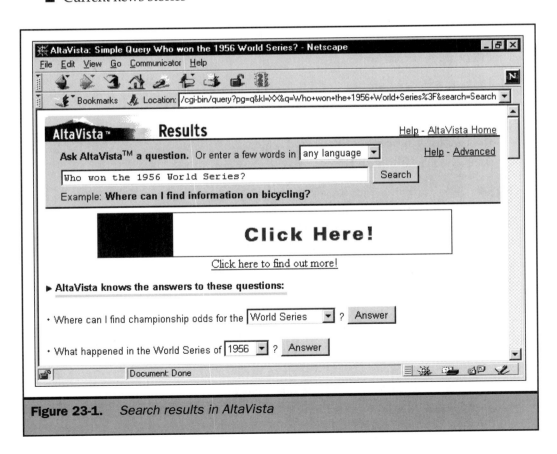

Figure 23-1.   *Search results in AltaVista*

If you have time to browse the Web, using the links on the home page is a quick way to read about a lot of different topics.

Excite

- ■ **Web address** http://www.excite.com
- ■ **Getting help** Click the Power Search link at the top of the page. Excite displays its search form, with a series of drop-down boxes that you can use to customize your search. To access a text Help file and read about the syntax used to conduct a search in Excite, click the Search Tips link at the top of the page.
- ■ **Our favorite feature** Quick access to weather reports, using the search box under the My Weather section of the home page.

The Excite home page contains an abundance of links, to anticipate the most common searches that people perform. You can either use the links and additional search boxes provided on the home page, or enter a word or phrase in the Search box and click Search.

The home page includes:

- ■ Links to top news stories
- ■ A search box for entering stock symbols to get quick stock reports
- ■ A search box for entering your ZIP code, so that you can see the weather forecast for your part of the United States
- ■ A place to enter your birth date, to get your horoscope

HotBot

- ■ **Web address** http://www.hotbot.com
- ■ **Getting help** Click the Help button at the top of the page.
- ■ **Our favorite feature** The Web Developer link. It provides a good starting point for information about developing your own Web pages or enhancing Web pages.

To conduct a HotBot search, type the word or phrase that you are looking for in the search box. Use the drop-down boxes to narrow your search (for example, to indicate whether you're searching for all the words, an exact phrase, and so forth).

Tip *If you want to refine your search, click the More Search Options button.*

When you're ready to submit your search, click the Search button.

In addition to the search bar on the left side of the page, the HotBot home page also provides quick links to Web pages, organized according to the following general groups:

- **Stay Informed** Contains links to news, sports, entertainment, and health stories, as well as links to reference materials such as dictionaries and time zone maps.
- **Manage Your Money** Includes links to business stories, job listings, and education information.
- **Plan a Purchase** Provides links to shopping areas of the Web.
- **Use Technology** Lists links to computer and Web development information, and links to sites where you can download free software or learn more about your favorite game.

Infoseek

- **Web address** http://www.infoseek.com
- **Getting help** Click the Search Tips or the Advance Search link at the top of the page.
- **Our favorite feature** It's a tie between the convenient placement of the Shareware link (it's at the top of the page), and the inclusion of a Women's category, which provides links to women-related issues.

In addition to the search box, the Infoseek home page contains links to current news stories and to categories and subcategories that you can access to find specific information about one topic.

If you want to search in a language other than English, go to the bottom of the page and click one of the language links.

Lycos

- **Web address** http://www.lycos.com
- **Getting help** Click the Help link at the top of the page.
- **Our favorite feature** The Top 5% Web sites link. Web site reviewers pick their top sites; the sites are divided by category. Click the category that interests you to see whether you agree or disagree with the reviewers' critiques.

To conduct a simple search, type the word or phrase in the search box and click the Go Get It button. If you want to refine your search, click the Search Options link and make your selections on the search form.

VIEWING THE WORLD WIDE WEB

Magellan

- **Web address** http://www.mckinley.com
- **Getting help** Click the Search Tips and Help link at the top of the page.
- **Our favorite feature** The Search Voyeur link. This link shows you a list of randomly selected searches that other people are doing, so you can see what other people are looking for on the Web (caution: you may find objectionable content in the words and phrases listed here).

The Magellan search engine not only searches for the words or phrase that you enter, but it also looks for ideas related to your query. To conduct your search:

1. Enter in the search box the words or concept that you are looking for.
2. Select the area of the Magellan database that you want to search. Your options are Reviewed Sites Only, which looks at sites that have been reviewed by Magellan staff; Green Light Sites Only, which includes sites suitable for all ages; or The Entire Web, which searches all Web pages in the Magellan database.
3. Click the Search button.

Your search results are rated according to relevance, with the most relevant site listed first. If you find a site that you like, click the Find Similar link to see related sites.

Northern Light

- **Web address** http://www.northernlight.com
- **Getting help** Click the Help/Hints button at the top of the page.
- **Our favorite feature** The Special Collection. Northern Light acquires information from over 4,500 journals and publications and stores the information in its Special Collection. You can search the Special Collection for free, but if you want to see the full article, you have to pay a small fee (currently from $1 to $4).

Northern Light is a search engine that returns results to you a little differently than other search engines. When you search for words or a phrase, the results are grouped into Custom Search Folders. You can open the folder that most closely matches the type of information you want.

Figure 23-2 shows the results of a search for "gourmet recipes." The search results are ranked and listed on the right side of the screen, and grouped into folders on the left side of the screen.

Tip *To narrow your search, click the Power Search tab and fill in the search form.*

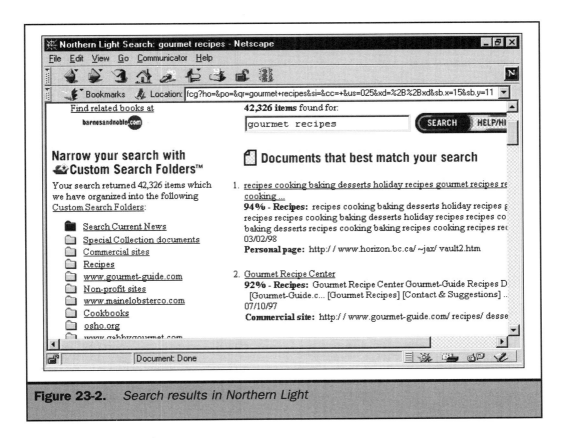

Figure 23-2. *Search results in Northern Light*

WebCrawler

- ■ **Web address**   http://webcrawler.com
- ■ **Getting help**   Click the Help link at the bottom of the page.
- ■ **Our favorite feature**   The Daily Toolbox. This section of the home page provides links to a variety of subjects. The links are updated daily. The subjects are diverse (everything from "free love advice" to "lowering your tax bills") and are fun to browse.

The WebCrawler home page provides a quick way to obtain information about a community. Interested in information about your home town, or another town in the United States? Click the Local Channel link and then enter a ZIP code or select the state (and then the city) that you want to see. You see all kinds of information about the selected city, including schedules of coming events, Arts and Entertainment activities, and lists of Web sites pertaining to the city.

To search using WebCrawler, enter in the search box the words or phrase that you are looking for and then click Search. There are also categories listed on the page that you can peruse to go to Web pages about specific topics.

Yahoo!

- ■ **Web address** http://www.yahoo.com
- ■ **Getting help** Click the Help button at the top of the page.
- ■ **Our favorite feature** Yahooligans! for Kids. This guide provides links to child-friendly categories and Web sites.

In Yahoo!, information is organized into categories. When you conduct a search, your results show the Yahoo! categories that match your search, as well as the Web pages that meet your criteria.

To search in Yahoo!, type in the search box the words or phrase that you're looking for and then click the Search button. If you want to narrow your search, click the Options link and fill out the search form.

The folks at Yahoo! have tried to make it as easy as possible to find information, by creating different sections that you can select. For example, you can select World Yahoo!s to search for information on specific countries, and Local Yahoo!s to find information on specific geographic regions. There are also guides that you can search that are dedicated to one specific topic, such as "Real Estate" or "Computers." The additional Yahoo!s and guides are listed at the bottom of the Yahoo! home page.

Other Search Sites

Web sites have sprung up that try to emulate a good research librarian—you ask a question, and the Web site provides the answer. Here are some examples:

- ■ Answers.com, at **http://www.answers.com**
- ■ Ask Jeeves, at **http://www.askjeeves.com**
- ■ Ask Jeeves for Kids, at **http://www.ajkids.com**
- ■ Electronic Library, at **http://elibrary.com**
- ■ Information Please, at **http://www.infoplease.com**

Searching the Search Engines

When you're looking for information, if you don't like the results that you find, you can always try a different search engine. But wouldn't it be nice if there were search engines available that could search other search engines for you? Well, there are, and this section describes a few of them.

Mamma

The Mamma search engine is available at **http://www.mamma.com**. By default, the Mamma search engine searches Yahoo!, Excite, Infoseek, Lycos, WebCrawler, AltaVista, and HotBot to find the information that you want. To conduct your search, follow these steps:

1. Enter the words or phrase that you want to find. Since you will be searching a lot of data, use the + and - sign to narrow your search, or enter the exact phrase that you're looking for. If you need help forming your search, click the Search Tips link.

2. Select Show Summaries if you want to see a brief summary of each page in your results.

3. Select Phrase Search if you want to search for the exact phrase that you entered.

4. Select Search Page Titles if you want to search the titles of Web pages.

5. Click Find It!

 If you want to select which search engines Mamma searches, click the Power Search link, and select only the sources that you want to use.

MetaCrawler

The MetaCrawler search engine is located at **http://www.metacrawler.com**. To conduct your search, type the words or phrase that you want to find and click Search. If you need to narrow your search, click the Power Search link and make your selections on the search form.

Your search results will show a summary of the pages found by MetaCrawler, with the source (Excite, Yahoo!, and so forth) identified for each page.

 *If you're interested in keeping up with the latest news about search engines, or in reading reviews and comparisons of search engines, visit the Search Engine Watch page at **http://www.searchenginewatch.com**.*

Letting Someone Else Conduct the Search

Sometimes, the information for which you're looking can't be formed into a query that produces the results you want. If you just can't find what you're looking for, you might want to hire someone to conduct the search for you. For a fee of $8.00 per question (as of late 1998), you can receive the answer to a question from a search service called Human Search.

To access this service, go to **http://www.humansearch.com** and follow the onscreen instructions to set up your account. After you establish your account, you can ask a question without using search-engine syntax or operators. For example, you can ask questions such as "Where can I find a list of all newsgroups and mailing lists that discuss dog training?" or "When is the best time of year to plant hydrangeas?" You'll receive a written response from the person who conducts your search.

 *You can look at a list of previously asked questions at **http://www.humansearch.com** for free. On the Human Search home page, enter the keywords that you want to look up, and then click the Submit button.*

Finding People

Looking for people on the Web is an easy way to locate a phone number or address when you don't have access to phone directories. The information that you find in Web-based personal directories is either from public sources, such as yellow pages and white pages, or is added to the directories' databases by the individuals themselves.

A variety of personal directories are available on the Web. You can search for a person's e-mail address, or a phone number and address. The more information that you have available to identify the person when you begin your search (for example, their domain name or the city and state in which they live), the easier it will be to find them.

Personal directories are expanding to provide more information than just personal e-mail addresses and phone numbers. As you use the personal directories, you'll notice that most of them also contain links that you can use to search for companies, maps, stock quotes, and so forth.

Bigfoot

- **Web address** http://www.bigfoot.com
- **Conducting a search** By default, the People button is selected on the Search Bigfoot box when you access the Bigfoot home page. Enter the name of the person you want to find. To search for a person's e-mail address, select the E-mail box; to search for a person's phone number and address, select the White Pages box.

 If you're looking for a white pages listing, you'll have better luck if you click the Advanced Directory Search button and enter the person's city and state of residence.

Click the Search tab to start the search. The results are listed in alphabetical order. If you choose to search both e-mail and white pages entries, the e-mail entries are listed first.

- **Adding yourself to the directory** Click the Join Bigfoot Free button on the Bigfoot home page. Follow the directions on the screen to complete your directory listing.

- **Removing yourself from the directory**   If you are listed in your local white pages, you are probably listed in the Bigfoot directory. To see whether you are listed, and to remove your name from the directory, click the Advanced Directory Search link and enter your name, city, and state. When the listing appears, click the Click Here link on the results screen and follow the directions onscreen to remove your name from the directory.

InfoSpace

- **Web address**   http://www.infospace.com
- **Conducting a search**   Click the Phone Numbers link on the InfoSpace home page. Enter the name of the person you're looking for, select the city, state/province, and country of residence, and then click Find.

If you're looking for an e-mail address, click the Email Search link, fill in the person's name and location, and then click Find Email.

- **Adding yourself to the directory**   Conduct a search for your own name. Locate at the bottom of the results screen the link that enables you to add or update your information. Click the link and follow the instructions onscreen.
- **Removing yourself from the directory**   Search for your listing in the directory. With your listing displayed, click the e-mail link at the bottom of the screen and follow the directions onscreen.

WhoWhere

- **Web address**   http://www.whowhere.lycos.com
- **Conducting a search**   Enter the first and last name of the person you are looking for in the appropriate boxes on the WhoWhere home page. Select either the Email or the Phone & Address button and then click Find. If you don't locate the person, click the Advanced link, enter the city and state, and then search again.
- **Adding yourself to the directory**   On the WhoWhere home page, click the Free Directory Listings link. You can add your e-mail address, home page on the Web, or toll-free number to the directory. Click the link for the item that you want to add, and follow the directions on the screen.
- **Removing yourself from the directory**   Click the Write Us link on the WhoWhere home page and send an e-mail indicating that you want to be removed from the directory. Be sure to include all of your directory information, so that your record can be located and deleted.

Yahoo! People Search

- **Web address** **http://people.yahoo.com** (You can also access Yahoo! People Search from the Yahoo! home page by clicking the People Search link. The URL for an older Web directory called Four11, at **http://www.four11.com**, also takes you to the Yahoo! People Search.)

- **Conducting a search** To search for an e-mail address, enter the person's first name, last name, and domain, and then click the Search button. To search for a phone number, enter the person's first name, last name, city, and state, and then click the Search button.

- **Adding yourself to the directory** According to the Yahoo! People Search FAQ, you currently can't add or edit an e-mail entry in Yahoo! People Search. The e-mail addresses are from previous subscribers to the Four11 directory. The phone numbers are gathered from public white pages information. Revisit the Yahoo! People Search page regularly to watch for an update to this policy.

- **Removing yourself from the directory** Go to the Yahoo! help page at the following address:

    http://help.yahoo.com/help/yps/yps-06.html

Click the E-mail Removal Form link to remove your e-mail listing, or the Telephone Removal Form link to remove your phone number listing.

Finding Companies

Locating company information on the Web is usually as easy as typing **www.***company name***.com**. However, if the company that you're looking for proves more elusive, you can search company directories to find a company's Web site.

You can use a business directory to obtain a Dun & Bradstreet report about a company, or to find the address and phone number of a company.

Companies Online

- **Web address** **http://www.companiesonline.com**

- **Conducting a search** Enter the name of the company that you are looking for on the search form. (You can also search by industry type, stock symbol, or URL.) Click the Go Get It button. A brief company profile is displayed, along with links that you can use to contact the company or find out more information. If you want to pay for additional information, click the Business Background Report button at the bottom of the screen, and follow the directions onscreen to place your order.

The Companies Online Web site gives you access to company profiles compiled by Dun & Bradstreet. You can access a brief company profile for free. More-detailed reports cost $20.

Switchboard

- **Web address**   http://www.switchboard.com
- **Conducting a search**   Click the Find a Business link. Select the category the business belongs to, enter the state where the business is located, and click the Search In button. All companies in that category in that state will be listed, with their addresses and phone numbers. Click the Map button next to an entry to see a map to the location.

If you have more-specific information, such as the company name or an address the company is near, you can enter that information on the search screen, to narrow your search. All search results include the Map button, which you can use to see a map to the company location.

Switchboard is a free directory that helps you to locate businesses by searching categories or geographic areas. Switchboard is a handy Web site to use when you want to find the address and phone number of a company, or when you need to locate a business on a map.

Tip   *Switchboard also has links to help you look for people's e-mail addresses and phone numbers, as well as business entries.*

VIEWING THE
WORLD WIDE WEB

The
Complete
Reference

Internet

Chapter 24

Subscriptions and Channels

The World Wide Web is a vast resource of information, and browsing around the Web is interesting when you have time to look for the information that you need. But what if time is at a premium, or you just want to see updated information without having to search the Web to get it?

Instead of going out on the Web to find what you need, you can have the information delivered to you. This chapter describes how to get information delivered to your computer via a subscription service or the features available with Netscape Communicator and Microsoft Internet Explorer.

What Are Push Technology, Subscriptions, and Channels?

As the Internet, and specifically the Web, have evolved, a new vocabulary has evolved with it. Common words have taken on new meanings in reference to the Internet.

Pull vs. Push

When you browse the Web, you are requesting, or *pulling*, information. You go to the pages that you want to see and jump to the links that you want to visit.

Frequent Internet users and developers didn't take long to realize that information delivery might be more efficient if information could be *pushed* at users, so that Web pages could be delivered without users having to find and request them each time. Subscriptions and channels were developed as a way for users to have information from the Web delivered to their computers.

Subscriptions

With traditional subscriptions, such as magazine and newspaper subscriptions, you sign up and pay to receive information on a regular schedule. Subscribing to a Web page is similar, but no fee is involved. You mark the page to which you want to subscribe, either in Netscape Netcaster or Microsoft Internet Explorer, and set up a schedule to receive downloaded information.

The term *subscription* is also used when you sign up with a broadcast service on the Internet. A *broadcast service* sends information to you from different news sources that you select. Your subscription is free, because advertisers pay for space on the information that you receive. The information is not Web pages, but rather data that the service provides.

Channels

A Web *channel* is a little like a channel on your television set—you go to the channel whenever you want to see what's new. A channel is a Web site that has been set up to deliver information. For example, it could be an intranet site within your company that shows updated employee announcements, or a consumer-oriented site that you like to check when you get home from work, to keep up-to-date on what's going on in the movie business. For your convenience, you subscribe to a channel, have the channel page downloaded to your computer, and read the channel offline whenever you want.

> **Tip** *For both subscriptions and channels, you don't have to download the information to your computer. You can choose to be notified that a site has been updated, by a light that appears next to the Web page name, without having any Web pages downloaded to your computer. However, if you elect only to receive notification, you have to go online to the site to see what's new. To make the best use of the subscription and channel features, we recommend that you download the Web pages that you subscribe to and the channels that you add.*

If you're the author of a Web page, you may wonder how to make your page into a channel: see "Turning Your Web Page into a Channel" Chapter 27.

How to Get Information Delivered

Opinions vary on the best method to use to receive content on your computer, but you basically have four ways available to get information delivered to your computer:

- *Sign up with a broadcasting service*, and have news delivered from sources that you select. (Technically, a broadcasting service is not "push technology," because you don't receive Web pages—the broadcast company sends you news, gleaned from news sources that you pick. A description of this service is included in this chapter nonetheless, to present all information-delivery alternatives from which you can choose.)

- *Subscribe to Web pages* in Netcaster or Internet Explorer and have the pages downloaded to your computer.

- *Use a channel viewer* to see Web sites that are set up to deliver updated information.

- *Sign up with the Mind-It (or similar) Web site.* Mind-It, located at **http://mindit.netmind.com**, asks you for your e-mail address and the URL of a Web page. Whenever the Web page changes, Mind-It sends you the updated page by e-mail.

This chapter discusses how to set up the PointCast broadcasting service, subscribe to a Web page in Netcaster and Internet Explorer, and use the channel viewers in Netcaster and Internet Explorer. These specific products were chosen to show examples of how the information-delivery technologies work; other services and viewers are available. The technology is changing fast; to keep up with the latest offerings, be sure to check periodically with your favorite developer's Web site or computer news resource.

 Mind-It and similar Web sites use e-mail rather than specialized software, but they work almost as well and are easier for most people to use.

Subscribing to a Broadcast Service

Do you want news delivered electronically to you every day? If so, try out a broadcast news service. You can select the news providers who deliver information that you find interesting, and the service is free.

PointCast Network

The PointCast Network has been around for a long time. It was established before channels and push technology became computer buzzwords. This section describes how to sign up with the PointCast Network—from downloading the software to personalizing your selected news sources.

Signing Up for the Service

To sign up for PointCast, go to its Web site at **http://www.pointcast.com** to find everything you need. Click the Download button and follow the steps onscreen to download the EXE file. (If you have a slow Internet connection, you can request a CD from PointCast instead of downloading.) When the download is complete, run or open the EXE file to install PointCast. A setup Wizard guides you through the setup process. During the installation, you are asked to enter your country of residence, age, gender, industry, job, and interests. The Wizard uses your answers to tailor to your tastes the news sources that PointCast proposes. After the installation is complete, click the Update All button to update the information from your default news sources. Updating the information only takes a moment.

Use the buttons on the left side of the PointCast window (shown in Figure 24-1) to move to different categories and view information.

 The download progress is displayed on the title bar of the PointCast window. After all the information is downloaded, you can log off the Internet and read the information offline.

If you don't like the default news sources selected by PointCast, you can always ignore the suggested sources and choose your own.

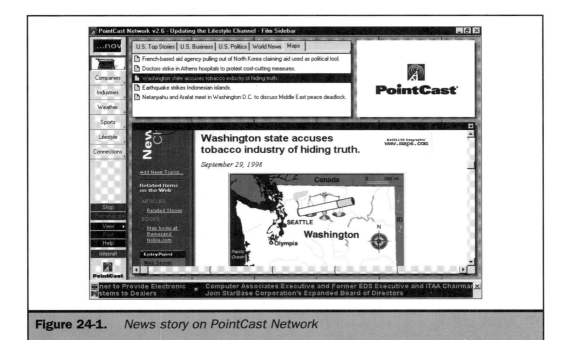

Figure 24-1.   *News story on PointCast Network*

Selecting News Sources

A wide variety of content providers are signed up with PointCast. You can get all kinds of information, including:

- Health news from Johns Hopkins, National Institutes of Health, and others
- Reviews of current music releases
- Headlines from the fashion industry
- Articles from sports columnists
- Worldwide weather reports

To select your own news sources, click the Personalize button and select Add/Remove Channels to see the Add/Remove Channels dialog box, shown in Figure 24-2. Don't be confused by the terminology—"channels" in this case refers to the broadcast information that you receive via PointCast.

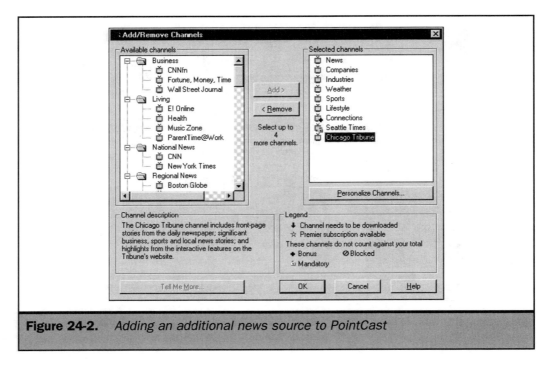

Figure 24-2.   *Adding an additional news source to PointCast*

In the Available Channels box, select the channel that you want to add and then click Add. PointCast adds the channel to your Selected Channels list.

If you are using a dial-up connection, you need to log on to the Internet to download information from the channel that you just added.

If you want to remove a channel from your selections, select the channel in the Selected Channels box, and click Remove.

Personalizing Your Choices

If you want the information that you receive to be more specific than certain channels, each channel is divided into topics, and within each channel, you can select the topics that you want to see.

Suppose that you add the Chicago Tribune channel, but you don't want to see *all* the content that is available. You can personalize your selections to include only topics that interest you.

To pick your topics for a channel, click the Personalize button on the main PointCast screen and then select Personalize Channels to display the Personalize Channels dialog box, shown in Figure 24-3. (You can also choose topics from the

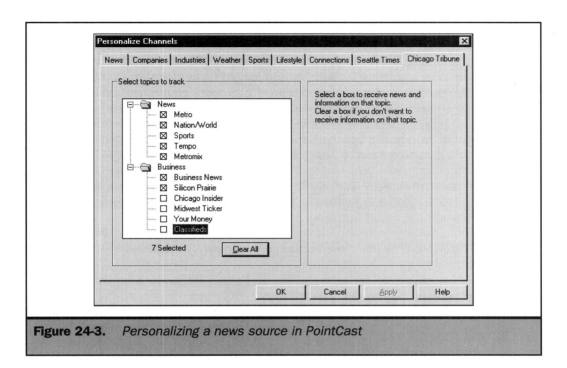

Figure 24-3. *Personalizing a news source in PointCast*

Add/Remove Channels dialog box; select a channel and then click the Personalize Channels button.) Check the boxes for topics that you want to see, and clear the boxes for information that you don't want to see.

Wondering what the air quality is like in a certain city? Add the Health channel, and personalize the channel to include air quality from your selected cities.

Scheduling Updates

You can control how often information is updated in PointCast. Click the Personalize button on the main PointCast screen and select Application Settings. In the Settings dialog box, click the Update tab. The update method that you choose depends on the type of Internet connection you have:

■ If you use PointCast at work and have a constant connection to the Internet, select the All-Day schedule.

■ If you use PointCast from your home computer and connect to the Internet via a modem, select the Update Button option. With this option, whenever you click the Update All button on the main PointCast screen, you are prompted to connect to the Internet.

You can schedule updates at regular intervals for either of these connection types. To set up a schedule, select the Customized Schedule option in the Settings dialog box, and choose the days and time that you want information to be updated. If you use this option, be sure your computer is available and logged on to the Internet at the times you specify. If you're setting up the schedule on your work computer, make sure your network connection to the Internet is available. If you're using your home computer, make sure that you can log on at the time of the scheduled update. Midnight updates sound great, until you remember that's the time of the nightly network backup, or realize that you have to get out of bed to log on to the Internet!

 Before you leave the Settings dialog box, click the SmartScreen tab. If you don't want your current screen saver replaced by the PointCast screen, clear the Replace Your Screen Saver with PointCast check box.

To exit PointCast, click the Close button on the PointCast window.

Subscribing to a Web Site

Subscribing to a Web site eliminates some of the inconveniences of staying up-to-date with the Web sites that you like. When you subscribe to a Web site, you don't have to do any of the following:

- Remember the site's URL, because the site is available from your subscription list.

- Go on the Web and look at the site to see whether it has any new information. The update process does that for you.

- Worry about printing Web pages to read later. You can have the pages downloaded to your computer and read them at your convenience offline.

Both Netcaster and Internet Explorer offer you the ability to subscribe to Web sites. You can subscribe to any site you find on the Web.

Netscape Netcaster

Netcaster is the part of Netscape's Communicator 4 suite of programs that enables you to view channels, customize your channel choices, and subscribe to Web sites. (See Chapter 19 for information about Netscape Communicator.) Netcaster doesn't come with Netscape Communicator version 4.5. You can download Netscape Communicator 4.0 with Netcaster from **http://www.netscape.com**, but you can't download Netcaster separately.

*The Netcaster FAQ is at **http://www25.netscape.com/communicator/ v4.0/faq/netcaster.html**.*

To start Netcaster, choose Start I Programs I Netscape Communicator I Netscape Netcaster. You can also start Netcaster from within Netscape Navigator 4.0 by choosing Communicator I Netcaster on the menu bar.
In Netcaster, you enter subscriptions to Web sites in the My Channels area.

Adding a Web Site to the My Channels List

On the Channel Finder bar, click My Channels and then follow these steps:

1. If you are not already logged on to the Internet, log on now.

2. On the Channel Finder, click New.

3. In the Channel Properties dialog box, fill in the name that you want to assign to the Web site, enter the URL of the site in the Location box, and set the update frequency.

 When you set the update frequency, remember that your computer must always be logged on to the Internet at the scheduled update time. If you don't want to assign a schedule (which means you have to update the site manually), clear the Update check box.

4. Click the Cache tab.

5. In the Download area, indicate how many levels of the Web site you want to download. The main page is level 1, pages linked to the main page are level 2, and so on. The less information that you download, the faster the update takes.

6. If you need to conserve disk space, enter a maximum download size.

7. Click OK. The site is added to the My Channels list, and the initial update begins.

 If you are a frequent Netscape Navigator user, you might wonder what the difference is between bookmarking a Web site and subscribing to a Web site. When you bookmark a site, you have to click the bookmark and go to the site; when you subscribe to a site, the information comes to you—the site is updated, either on a schedule or manually, and the information is downloaded to your computer.

Updating the site may take a few moments. When the red bar is moving across the bottom of the entry, the site is being updated. When the update is finished, click the entry to view the information (Figure 24-4).

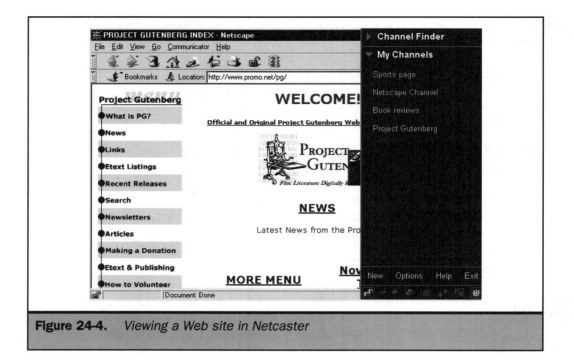

Figure 24-4.   *Viewing a Web site in Netcaster*

 You don't have to be connected to the Internet to view the site after the update is complete. If you are charged by the amount of time that you're connected to the Internet, log off and read the sites in Netcaster.

As you view sites, you might want to hide the Channel Finder bar to see more of the Web page. To toggle on and off the Channel Finder bar, click the Toggle the Netcaster Window icon. This icon, shown here, remains on your screen as long as Netcaster is open:

Controlling Updates

The downloaded information from the site(s) to which you subscribe is updated according to the schedule that you set in the Channel Properties dialog box. To change the schedule, either click Options on the Channel Finder bar and select Properties, or right-click the entry and select Properties.

If the update is in progress and you think it is taking too long, you can right-click the entry and select Stop Update on the pop-up menu to stop the update.

 If an update takes a long time, you might want to set the download to Level 1 to just download the main page of the site.

To bypass the update schedule and update a site manually, right-click the entry, and select Start Update on the pop-up menu. The update starts immediately.

When you are finished using Netcaster, click Exit to close the Channel Finder. Close any Navigator windows that you opened while you were viewing sites.

Internet Explorer

The Internet Explorer Web browser (IE, described in Chapter 20) has options that enable you to subscribe to Web sites. IE is included with Windows 98, and is available from the Microsoft Web site at **http://www.microsoft.com/ie**. To start IE, either click the Launch Internet Explorer Browser icon on the taskbar, run the Internet Explorer icon on your desktop, or choose Start | Programs | Internet Explorer | Internet Explorer.

In IE, you subscribe to Web sites that are on your Favorites list.

Subscribing to a Site on Your Favorites List

Your Favorites list is the list of sites that you've marked as sites you'd like to revisit. You can either enter a subscription when you add the site to your Favorites list, or subscribe to a site that is already on your list.

To subscribe to a site that is not currently on your Favorites list, follow these steps:

1. Type the URL in the Address box and then press ENTER to display the Web page in Internet Explorer.

2. Select Favorites | Add to Favorites.

3. Select the Yes, Notify Me of Updates and Download the Page for Offline Viewing option, and click OK.

The page is added to your list of Favorites, and the subscription is entered.

 When you enter a subscription, the default update schedule is assigned to the subscription. See the following section, "Changing a Subscription," for information on how to change the schedule.

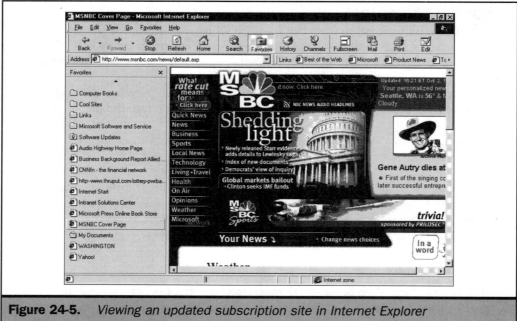

Figure 24-5. *Viewing an updated subscription site in Internet Explorer*

To subscribe to a site that is already on your Favorites list, click the Favorites button on the toolbar to display your list of Favorites. Right-click the entry that you want to subscribe to, select Subscribe on the pop-up menu, and choose the option Notify Me when Updates Occur and Download for Offline Viewing.

Whenever a site you've subscribed to contains new information, a tiny red "gleam" appears next to the entry on the Favorites list (as shown in Figure 24-5). To see the new information, click the entry on the Favorites list.

You must be connected to the Internet while the site is being updated, but as soon as the gleam appears and the information is downloaded, you can log off and read the information offline in IE. Click the page on the Favorites list to display the page in the browser window.

Changing a Subscription

The Daily, Weekly, and Monthly schedules that are preset in Internet Explorer apply to all of your subscriptions. When you add a subscription, the Daily schedule is assigned by default.

If you are using IE from your work computer and are connected to the Internet all day, review the Daily schedule to make sure your computer is available at the hour of day the updates are scheduled to take place. If you are using IE from your home computer, you may need to reset the schedule to coincide with times that you'll be using your computer.

REVISING THE DAILY SCHEDULE   To review and change the Daily update schedule, follow these steps:

1. Select Favorites | Manage Subscriptions.

2. Click the Schedule tab.

3. Right-click one of the subscriptions that is on your Daily schedule, and select Properties on the pop-up menu.

4. Verify that the Scheduled option is selected, and click Edit.

5. Select the schedule you want to edit (Daily, Weekly, or Monthly) in the Schedule Name box.

6. Indicate the frequency and time of day the subscriptions should be updated.

> **Tip** *If you want to create your own schedule under a unique name, do not select one of the preset schedules (Daily, Weekly, or Monthly) in the Schedule dialog box. Instead, click the New button, enter the name you want to assign to the schedule, and set the frequency and time of day for the update.*

CHANGING THE SCHEDULE ASSIGNED TO A SUBSCRIPTION   The changes that you make to the Daily, Weekly, Monthly, or your own custom schedule apply to all subscriptions that are assigned that schedule. In other words, if you change the Daily update schedule, you don't need to modify any of the subscriptions currently assigned to the schedule. The adjusted frequency and time of day are picked up for the next update. However, if you decide to change a subscription from the Daily schedule to the Weekly schedule, you need to revise the individual subscriptions.

To change the schedule assigned to a subscription, follow these steps:

1. Right-click the entry on your Favorites list and select Properties on the pop-up menu.

2. Select the Schedule tab.

3. Click the Scheduled drop-down arrow and select the new schedule you want to assign.

> **Tip** *If you want to review or change the schedule, click the Edit button.*

If you choose not to update a subscription on a regular schedule, you can remove the schedule assignment completely and mark the subscription for manual update. To do this, right-click the entry on your Favorites list, select Properties on the pop-up menu, click the Schedule tab, and choose the Manually option. When you apply this option, you have to update the subscription manually whenever you want to see updated content.

VIEWING THE
WORLD WIDE WEB

Updating Subscriptions Manually

You can update one or all of your subscriptions manually, at any time. If you assign the manual update option, you must update that subscription manually. But, other subscriptions that are assigned a regular update schedule can be updated manually, too.

To update one subscription on the spur of the moment, right-click the entry on your Favorites list and then select Update Now on the pop-up menu.

To update all subscriptions manually (the update may take a while, depending on the number of subscriptions you have), select Favorites | Update All Subscriptions.

 Another way to update all subscriptions manually is to select Favorites | Manage Subscriptions and click the Update All button on the toolbar.

Getting Access to Channels

Channels are Web sites that are set up to deliver constantly updated information. Using channels is a good way to communicate fresh information to a large audience. The audience can be a closed community accessing information on the company intranet, or the worldwide congregation of people who use the Internet to receive information. On intranets, distributing updates via a channel keeps everyone in the company informed about current company events. On the Internet, disseminating information via a channel keeps everyone who tunes in to your channel up-to-date on the latest product or service that you have to offer.

What makes a Web site a channel? The addition of specific HTML tags, or programming that enables channels. Currently, most channel viewers have unique requirements for how channels should be structured. For example, Internet Explorer channels include a *Channel Definition Format (CDF)* file that contains (among other things) the update schedule and abstracts of the Web pages included on the channel. Netcaster channels use JavaScript to enable a Web page as a channel. Marimba channels, which you can access from Netcaster, use Java to define the channel. In the future, a standard might evolve whereby all channels can be read by all viewers, but for now, you need to select a channel that is set up for your browser or channel viewer.

Where do you find channels? Most channel viewer software presents you with a selection of preselected channels. Also, as you browse the Web, you'll likely come across sites that are channel-enabled; these sites are easy to recognize, because most of them present an Add to Channels button, or the equivalent, that you can click to add the site to your channels list.

Channel Finder in Netcaster

If you've added subscriptions to Web sites in Netcaster, you're already familiar with the Channel Finder. The Channel Finder lists the preselected channels that are supplied with Netcaster, and contains an area called My Channels that holds links to the channels that you've chosen to add to your list.

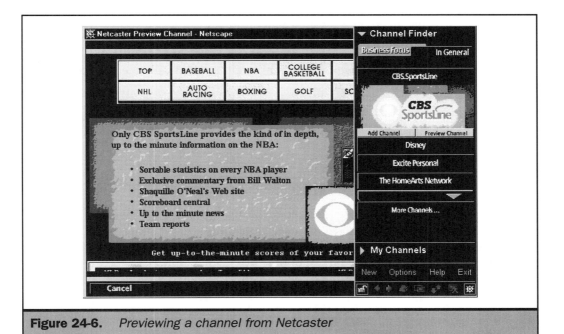

Figure 24-6. *Previewing a channel from Netcaster*

Tip | *The My Channels area also holds the Web site subscriptions that you enter.*

To open Netcaster and access the Channel Finder, choose Start | Programs | Netscape Communicator Professional Edition | Netscape Netcaster. The Channel Finder is displayed automatically. If you don't see it, click the Toggle the Netcaster Window icon, which is the small icon attached to the left side of the Channel Finder.

Preselected channels are listed under the In General and Business Focus tabs. To preview a channel, click the entry on the Channel Finder and then click the Preview Channel button. Channel pages are displayed in a Navigator window, as shown in Figure 24-6.

If you decide that you want to add the channel to your customized list that is displayed under My Channels, click the Add to Channels button on the entry in the Channel Finder.

Adding a Channel

The fastest way to add a channel is to click the Add Channels button on one of the preselected channels, or to click the Add to Channels button provided on a Web site that you find.

If no button is displayed on a site, and you know the site is enabled for viewing in Netcaster, you can add the site to the My Channels area manually. To add a channel, click New on the Channel Finder. Fill in the name and URL of the channel, and the update frequency you want. Remember, your computer must be logged on to the Internet at the scheduled update time.

 If you do not want to assign an update schedule to the channel, clear the Update check box. You have to update the channel manually to receive new information.

Receiving Updated Content

Channels can be updated on a regular schedule, or you can update them manually whenever you want.

To revise the update schedule, right-click the channel and select Properties on the pop-up menu. Select the frequency you want in the Properties dialog box.

To update a channel immediately, right-click the channel and select Start Update on the pop-up menu. You can also start an update by clicking Options, selecting the channel that you want to update, and then clicking Update Now.

 You must be logged on to the Internet when you update a channel. As soon as the update is finished, you can log off and read the information offline.

Deleting Your Downloaded Files

Downloaded information can accumulate fast on your computer. You should clean out the files periodically to free up disk space. To delete all of your downloaded information:

1. Click Options on the Channel Finder.

2. Select one of the channels and then click Properties.

3. Click the Cache tab and then click the Clear Cache button.

All of your downloaded files are deleted.

To quit Netcaster, click Exit on the Channel Finder. Close any Navigator windows that you opened during your Netcaster session.

Channels in Windows 98 and Internet Explorer 4

To access channels in Windows 98, you don't have to go any farther than your desktop. You don't have to do anything special to see the Channel Bar—it is displayed by default when you start your computer.

 You can also access channels from within Internet Explorer. Choose Start | Programs | Internet Explorer | Internet Explorer, and click the Channels button on the toolbar.

Viewing the Preselected Channels

The Channel Bar in Windows 98 or Internet Explorer serves the same purpose as the Channel Finder in Netcaster: It displays channels that you can preview to determine which channels are of interest to you. When you see a channel that you like, add the channel and have information from the channel downloaded to your computer.

The Channel Bar (shown in Figure 24-7) shows channel categories and a few selected channels.

Downloading content from a channel to your computer is a convenient way to keep up-to-date without having to stay connected to the Internet. After the channel's content is downloaded to your computer, you can disconnect and read the information offline.

To preview and sign up for a channel, follow these steps:

1. On the desktop, click the News and Technology category on the Channel Bar.

 To keep the Channel Bar from sliding off the side of the screen, click the pushpin icon at the top of the bar. If you miss the pushpin icon and the bar slides off the screen, click the Channels button on the toolbar to bring it back.

2. In the channel viewer window, click the logo of the channel that you want to preview.

3. If the content looks interesting, click the Add Active Channel button (for an example, see Figure 24-8).

Figure 24-7.   *The Channel Bar on the desktop*

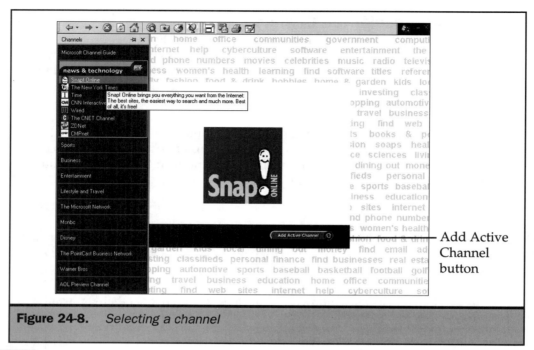

Figure 24-8. Selecting a channel

— Add Active
Channel
button

If you've subscribed to a Web site in Internet Explorer, you're already familiar with this download scheduling process. Channels use the same schedules (Daily, Weekly, Monthly) as the subscriptions to Web sites that you entered.

4. Select the option Yes, Notify Me of Updates and Download the Channel for Offline Viewing.

5. Click No at the prompt Would You Like to Replace Your Current Screen Saver with the Channel Screen Saver, to retain your current screen saver, or click Yes to replace your current screen saver. The channel content is displayed immediately. Click any link to jump to that destination and read the information on the channel.

More channels are available than those listed on the Channel Bar. To search for a channel on a specific topic, click the Channel Guide button on the Channel Bar, and use the search fields to find the channel that you want.

Updating a Channel

Since channels are Web pages that are set up to deliver up-to-date information regularly, we recommend that you accept the publisher's recommended schedule when you add a channel. This is the default schedule selection for channels. Information will be downloaded to your computer on the Web page publisher's timetable.

If you choose to ignore the publisher's schedule, you can override it and assign a new schedule. Click the Full Screen button on the toolbar, right-click the channel that you want to change, and then select Properties on the pop-up menu. Click the Schedule tab and select a different schedule, or mark the channel for manual updates. (If you mark a channel for manual updates, you have to remember to update the channel when you want to see new information. To update a channel manually, right-click the channel and select Update Now on the pop-up menu.)

 If you choose to assign a new schedule, you might want to check the frequency and time of day assigned to the schedule. From the Schedule tab, select the schedule that you want to review, and click Edit.

Cleaning Up Your Downloaded Files

Information that you download from channels you've added and Web sites you've subscribed to is stored in the Temporary Internet Files folder. To delete these temporary files and make room for the next batch of updates, follow these steps:

1. Choose Start | Programs | Internet Explorer | Internet Explorer to open the Internet Explorer browser.
2. Select View | Internet Options.
3. In the Temporary Internet Files area, click the Delete Files button.
4. Click OK in the Internet Options dialog box.

 Clearing your Temporary Internet Files folder also deletes the temporary files stored in IE's history folder. The URLs of the history files are still visible from within IE by clicking the History button on the toolbar, but the actual text and graphics of the files are no longer stored on your computer.

To exit Internet Explorer, select File | Close, or click the Close button on the Internet Explorer window.

Which Delivery Method Is Best for You?

Now that you've sampled different delivery methods, you're probably trying to decide which method is the best one for you to use. Luckily, this doesn't have to be an all-or-nothing decision. You can come up with the delivery combination that you prefer. You might decide to use PointCast for the news briefs you want to see quickly, Netcaster for the Web sites you want to read leisurely offline in Navigator, and Internet Explorer if you find a channel you particularly like.

The
Complete
Reference

Internet

Chapter 25

Making Use of the Web's Resources

Learning to use a browser is not an end in itself. The payoff comes from using the resources of the Web either to do more efficiently the things you already do, or to start doing things that are impossible or impractical with any other medium. In this chapter we suggest what some of those things might be, and describe some Web sites where you can get started doing them.

In particular this chapter tells you about Web sites for portal services, news, weather, sports, personal finance and investing, entertainment, shopping, computers, travel, family and community, health and medicine, religion and spirituality, and reference.

A chapter in a book can only get you started in exploring the Web, but at least we can give you a taste of what is possible and show you a few ways in which you can start using the resources of the Web in your everyday life. We make no attempt to be exhaustive, and the Web sites that we list for a given purpose are not the only ones—or even necessarily the best ones—but they get the job done.

We've taken several steps to make sure the URLs are as useful as possible. Rather than provide URLs for a lot of the specific features of the Web sites we mention (which might change if the site is reorganized), we provide the URL of the home page of the site and explain how to browse from there. Since online links are easier to update than books, whenever possible we tell you where to find a good set of links on a subject. Finally, we've collected the URLs we mention in easy-to-find tables at the end of the sections that mention them. And you don't even need to type in the URLs we've listed in this chapter. Instead, bookmark our Web page at **http://net.gurus.com/nettcr** and look for our set of links, and write to us at **nettcr@gurus.com** about your favorite sites.

What's So Special About the Web?

There has been an enormous amount of hype about the World Wide Web, some justified and some not. This much seems clear: the Web is the first new medium since television. It has a lot of possibilities, most of which are still unexplored or even unimagined.

The Web combines some of the best qualities of other communications media. Like TV or radio (and unlike a newspaper) the Web gives you fresh information; you can get the latest developments on news stories or the current score of an ongoing game. Like a telephone 800 number (and unlike a mail-order catalog), the Web lets you make transactions immediately.

Like a book (and unlike TV, newspapers, or magazines) the Web has unlimited space. The amount of information you can get on a subject is limited by the time *you* have, not by the length of the broadcast or the size of the magazine. Further, the Web is there for you to pick up at your convenience; you don't have to conform to its schedule. Like a library, the Web contains many different points of view, and many different levels of detail. If you don't understand something on a Web page, chances are you can find it explained more simply or in more detail on some other Web page.

To a degree, the Web *contains* other media. Many newspapers and magazines are reproduced in their entirety on the publisher's Web site. Some radio shows can be heard over the Web—including a large number of non-English broadcasts from Europe or Asia. Even television news clips are available, though the quality is not very good unless you have a fast modem.

But the Web does more than imitate other media. It has unique qualities that create new possibilities. Distance has no meaning on the Web. Being in Hong Kong doesn't stop you from following the local news in Billings—or vice versa. If you want to use the Web to communicate with someone who shares your unusual interest or has your rare medical condition, it doesn't matter where they live. The three other players in your Hearts game can be anywhere.

The Web encourages diversity. Even if only a handful of people are going to be interested in your writings, music, or art, you can publish them on a Web page and make them available to the world. On the Web you can find or express opinions that would be considered beyond the pale in other media.

The Web allows quick and comprehensive searches. You can compare prices at a dozen retailers in seconds, or track down that Shakespeare quote. You can find online communities that share your interests. The instant that the season-ending cliffhanger of your favorite TV show ends, you can be online with other fans trading speculations.

Both the strength and weakness of the Web is that anyone can post a Web page. Anyone can express an opinion, and pages appear about all kinds of strange and obscure topics. However, don't believe everything you read on the Web, unless you know something about the organization that hosts the Web page (information on a page at the *New York Times* Web site, for example, is likely to be very reliable). A page about dinosaurs might be written by a research scientist, but it might also be written by a sixth-grader.

Working with Web Sites

You can have a variety of different kinds of relationships with Web sites, depending on whether you tell them anything about yourself or commit yourself to anything. Many Web sites are like billboards—they have their own reasons for providing whatever information they offer you, and you owe them nothing.

Other Web sites invite you to form some kind of relationship. They may want you to register, and tell them something about yourself or your interests. In order to get this relationship rolling, they offer you something for free: a free e-mail account, a free home page, access to a chat room, or maybe just free information like news headlines or a Web directory. The registration process serves two purposes: It allows the Web site to customize its features (including its advertisements) to your interests, and it protects any accounts you've established from being accessed by someone else.

Some Web sites are selling you something directly, like books or airline tickets. This may be a one-time sale or you may have opened a continuing account: you choose a password to identify yourself and they keep information about you on file.

Finally, you can be a paying subscriber to a Web site. They charge your credit card regularly every month, and in exchange you get access to the special information and services that the Web site provides.

Most Web sites that you establish a relationship with want you to choose a password. (Some assign you a password, and allow you to change it later.) What kind of password should you choose? A good password is easy to remember and hard to guess. See "Choosing User Names and Passwords" in Chapter 1.

 If a Web site promises to give you something free and then asks you for a credit card number during the registration process, you might be signing up for a free trial of something that you will eventually have to start paying for.

Portals to the Web

A *portal* is a Web site that wants to be the starting point for your Web-browsing experience. The portal wants to induce you either to make it your start page or simply to bookmark it and visit it frequently. To this purpose, a portal offers free services like personalized news headlines or an e-mail account. Some portals rely on your laziness to get a leg up on the competition: Internet Explorer gives you Microsoft's MSN portal as your default start page, and Navigator gives you NetCenter. You can choose some other portal any time you want (see "Choosing New Start and Home Pages" in Chapter 19 and "Choosing a New Start Page" in Chapter 20), but the longer you wait, the likelier it is that habits, online acquaintances, and accumulations of e-mail messages will keep you from changing. Some of the top portals are shown in Table 25-1.

Yahoo!	http://www.yahoo.com
Lycos	http://www.lycos.com
NetCenter	http://home.netscape.com
Excite	http://www.excite.com
MSN	http://www.msn.com

Table 25-1. *Portal Web Sites*

What Services Does a Portal Provide?

The competition among portals is heated, so new services appear regularly and are copied quickly. At present, you can expect to find some or all of the following services at a portal site:

- **Web directory**   This is a set of categories and subcategories linking you to thousands of Web sites in a structured way. See "What Are Web Directories?" in Chapter 23.

- **Search engine**   NetCenter gives you access to everybody else's search engine, not just its own. Lycos has a special search engine for images. See "What Are Search Engines?" in Chapter 23.

- **News services**   These services are typically national or international services like Reuters, plus everything else you would normally look for in a newspaper: local, national, and international weather reports, stock quotes, sports scores, TV listings, horoscopes, and even cartoons. See "News and Weather" later in this chapter.

- **E-mail**   A free e-mail account with a portal is a simple way to have an e-mail address that doesn't change whenever you switch ISPs or schools or jobs. See "Web-Based E-mail" in Chapter 5. The disadvantage of portal e-mail is that it ties you to a portal, since it is time-consuming to save all the messages to your hard drive.

- **Home page**   At the moment Lycos is offering a small amount of server space for you to post a Web page. NetCenter and Yahoo! let you display a profile, including a picture, and Yahoo! links you to GeoCities if you want a free home page. See "Online Communities and Home Pages" later in this chapter.

- **Chat rooms**   The number of chat rooms and the variety of topics depends on the size of the portal's chatting community. Yahoo! has the largest membership, and so supports about 150 regular chat rooms. Excite displays its current number of chatters, which was over 8,000 the afternoon we looked. MSN's chat rooms currently work only with Microsoft's Internet Explorer or Chat, though Microsoft claims that support for Netscape browsers is planned. See the section "Web-Based Chat" in Chapter 16.

- **Message boards**   These are a portal's internal version of newsgroups. See the next section "Message Boards".

- **Game rooms**   The choice of games varies from one portal to the next, but you can usually find a variety of card games and board games that you play against other real people logged in to the portal. To access a portal's games, look for a Games link on the home page, then follow the instructions given.

- **Clubs**   Yahoo! and Excite both offer you the opportunity to start a "club" online to share ideas and points-of-view with people of similar interests. Excite calls them "communities" and pitches them as a way to share photos. See the upcoming section, "Online Clubs."

- **Investment tools**   These include stock quotes, the ability to track the value of a portfolio, charts, analyst reports, company profiles, and message boards devoted to specific stocks. See "Personal Finance and Investing" later in this chapter.

- **Road maps**   If you enter a street address or zip code, you can get a road map of the area on any scale from national to local. See "Travel by Car" later in this chapter.

- **Shopping tools**   These include bargain-finding programs that allow you to compare prices automatically across many different vendor Web sites. See "Shopping" later in this chapter.

- **Buddy lists**   These make it possible to know when your friends are logged in and available to chat.

- **A personalized start page**   This feature organizes the services of interest to you and presents them in a way that you choose. Your start page, for example, could collect on one page the weather forecast for your home town, the scores of games involving your favorite sports teams, the current value of your stock portfolio, and news headlines in your areas of interest. See the upcoming section, "Creating a Customized Start Page."

Tip   *Even if you have an e-mail account somewhere else, an extra free account is useful as a spam-collector. Whenever you are doing something on the Web that is likely to put you on advertising mailing lists (like ordering products or signing up for a service), give the extra account's e-mail address rather than the address that your friends use when they want to write to you.*

Message Boards

Message boards are a portal's private newsgroup universe. They are organized into topic categories, and within a board the members start new topics (called *threads*), which can then be replied to by other members. (See "Web-Based Chat" in Chapter 16.)

You can only post to a portal's message board if you have registered with the portal, and the portal has the technical ability to screen messages, though we aren't sure how much screening they actually do. They also can unregister a member who is consistently disruptive. This makes a message board a more controlled community than a newsgroup, particularly an unmoderated newsgroup.

Access MSN's message boards by selecting the Web Communities link on the MSN home page. List All Communities opens your newsreader and downloads current messages. Click the Discussion Forums link on the NetCenter home page to find NetCenter's message boards. At Lycos, click the Message Boards link on the home page. The message board subject hierarchy resembles the Web directory hierarchy, so you can find links to the corresponding message board area when you look at a category in the Web directory. At Excite click the People and Chat link on the home page; then look for the Message Boards heading. At Yahoo!, click the Chat link at the top of your Yahoo! or My Yahoo home page.

Online Clubs

An online club is a way to share a common interest with a relatively small group. Starting a club gives you the same kind of control that the portal has over a message board—you can throw people out if they disrupt what you are trying to accomplish. A club is easier to set up and manage than a newsgroup or mailing list, and pulls together a nice collection of features. So far only Yahoo! and Excite offer them, but other portals will surely follow. (Excite calls their clubs "communities," a term this chapter reserves for larger entities like Talk City or GeoCities.)

Any registered user of the portal can establish or join a club. As a member you have the right to post messages to the club message board or participate in the club chat room. In Excite's clubs you can also upload photos (which makes their clubs attractive to extended families).

Access clubs from the top of your My Yahoo page by clicking Chat and Boards and then clicking Clubs. From this page you can either search for a club by name or find it by looking in the appropriate category. To create a club, first find the category it belongs in and then click the Create a Club link. Access Excite's clubs by clicking the People and Chat link on the Excite home page. From the People and Chat page, click the Community Directory link to see a list of available communities or to start a new one of your own. Both Yahoo! and Excite provide Help links that tell you how to start or join a club.

Registering with a Portal

In order to take advantage of any of a portal's personalized services, you have to register and choose a password. Registering for one of a portal's services usually registers you for all of them, and you use the same password. To get started, go to a portal's home page and click any link that has to do with a personalized service: e-mail, personalized start page, games, or chat, for instance. When the Login box appears, look for a New User link to click. (Some portals may have a Login or New User link on the home page.)

The new user sign-up process is fairly simple: choose a login name and a password, and then give some information for personalizing your start page. Your ZIP code, for example, is used to get the right weather report for your page, while your birthday selects your horoscope. Some portals ask questions about interests during the sign-up process, while others minimize the sign-up hassle and let you specify personalized features later. In any case, you can change later any preferences you express during sign-up.

Creating a Customized Start Page

One of the most useful features a portal provides is a personalized start page. A personalized start page like the one shown in Figure 25-1 can pull together on a single screen the information you use most. The personalized start page can tell you if you have e-mail, provide a local weather forecast, show you news headlines in your areas of interest, check the prices on your investments, and/or provide lighter features like a horoscope, TV listings, or lottery results.

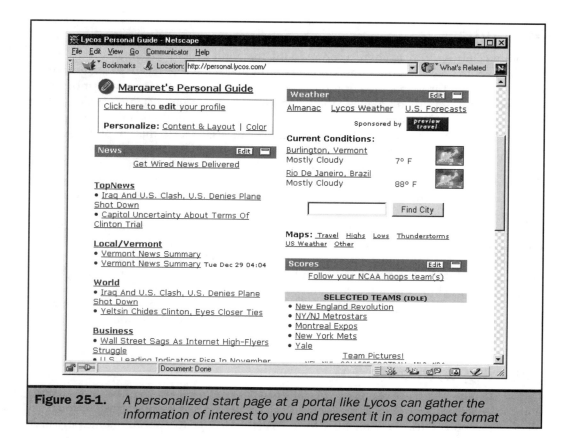

Figure 25-1.   *A personalized start page at a portal like Lycos can gather the information of interest to you and present it in a compact format*

Some portals allow you to detach a section from the start page and let it sit elsewhere on your desktop. Yahoo, for example, lets you detach your sports scoreboard window. If are following an ongoing game while you work, the scoreboard window can sit in a corner of your desktop and refresh itself automatically every 15 minutes.

The customization is based on cookies that the portal's server stores on your machine. If you have set your browser not to accept cookies, your customized start page might not work. (See "Cookies" in Chapter 18.)

No rule says that you can't have accounts on as many portal sites as you like. But in practice, we find that juggling several portal accounts is an unnecessary nuisance. Find one you like and stick with it.

News and Weather

The Web is a very convenient place to get news and weather reports. The biggest names in news coverage—newspapers, magazines, wire services, and networks—all have Web sites that are regularly updated throughout the day. The Web's lack of space constraints lets you keep track of distant or obscure news stories, and to follow links to related stories or background pages. You can even get audio and video news reports, either by choosing the stories you want or by connecting to live network feeds.

Headlines and Breaking News

The easiest place to get current news headlines linked to recent news stories is from your portal (see Table 25-1 earlier in this chapter). Most portals get their news headlines from the same places: mainly Reuters and Associated Press, with some specialized news areas covered by specialized sources, such as technology news from CNET or ZD Net, or business news from CBS MarketWatch. Microsoft's MSN portal gets its news from MSNBC, with some extra features from other Microsoft ventures like Slate or Sidewalk.

Customized News

Some news Web sites (listed in Table 25-2) allow you to be your own editor by specifying your areas of interest. Unlike a newspaper or TV news show, you don't have to see hockey news if you don't like hockey, or hear about the stock market if you don't own stock.

Customized news is a standard part of a customized home page with a portal. (See "Creating a Customized Start Page" earlier in this chapter.) Even if you have a customized start page with a portal, however, you may decide to devote it to general Web resources like Yellow Pages or to light features like horoscopes, and create a customized news page at a site focused on news, such as CNN.

CNN Custom News	**http://customnews.cnn.com**
CRAYON	**http://www.crayon.net**
NewsPage	**http://www.newspage.com**

Table 25-2. *Customized News Sites*

Not all the major news sites offer customized news, but the number that do is increasing. To check, go to the site's home page and look for a link that says "Customize" or "Personalize." When you select this link, you are asked to register (if you have not already done so), and then to choose which of several categories you are interested in. The process is straightforward, though it can be time-consuming if you have a lot of interests.

NewsPage is a customized news service that accesses not only freely available articles but also articles in fee-based services. Its coverage of specific industries is particularly detailed.

CRAYON is an acronym for CreAte Your Own Newspaper. Rather than choosing specific subjects for inclusion in your newspaper, you choose news sources just as when you customize a portal's news headlines. CRAYON includes a large collection of sources to choose from, including local newspapers, opinion columns, and comics.

National Newspapers and Networks

All the major national news organizations maintain Web sites that attempt to be complete news sources (Table 25-3 lists some news organization Web sites). The TV networks, for example, cover many stories on their Web sites that never make it onto the nightly news shows. The newspapers cover breaking news online, and don't just reproduce their once-a-day print versions.

These news Web sites are dominated by text and pictures, but audio and video are beginning to make an appearance as well, especially at the TV network sites. See "Listening to the News Online" and "Watching the News Online" later in this chapter.

Reading Your (or Anybody's) Local Newspaper Online

Most of the best newspapers in America have Web sites (see Table 25-4) that give you access to all the stories in the newspaper—when they are written, not in the morning when the paper appears on your doorstep or in the vending machine. So if you are used to getting your news from *The New York Times* or *The Washington Post* (or if you'd like to get used to it), you can go to these newspapers' Web sites. What's more, unlike the newspapers themselves, the Web sites are free.

USA Today	**http://usatoday.com**	CNN	**http://cnn.com**
PBS	**http://www.pbs.org**	MSNBC	**http://msnbc.com**
Fox News	**http://foxnews.com**	ABC News	**http://abcnews.com**
CBS News	**http://www.cbsnews.com**		

Table 25-3. *Web Sites of National News Organizations*

New York Times	**http://www.nytimes.com**
Washington Post	**http://www.WashingtonPost.com**
San Jose Mercury News	**http://www.mercurycenter.com**
Los Angeles Times	**http://www.latimes.com**
Newspaper Association of America	**http://www.naa.org/hotlinks**
Worldwide News Online	**http://www.worldwidenews.com**

Table 25-4.   *Newspaper Web Sites*

Major city newspapers like *The New York Times* or *The Washington Post* provide the same degree of national and world news coverage on their Web sites that they do in print, with more frequent updates. Even small-city newspapers can provide good news coverage through their links to the larger news organizations.

Local newspapers tend to be the best Web sites for local information of all sorts: movie schedules, live entertainment, local TV listings, and so forth. Often the Web site of a local newspaper contains a great deal more information than you could find in the newspaper itself.

To find the Web site of a local newspaper in the United States, look at the Web site of the Newspaper Association of America. To find a newspaper in another country, check a portal's list of world newspapers, Worldwide News Online, located at **http://www.worldwidenews.com**, or the newspaper links at the Internet Public Library (**http://www.ipl.org**).

News in Depth

Unlike a newspaper, the Web allows stories to have links to whatever background or previous stories are relevant, regardless of the space it takes up. Readers who aren't interested in that background can ignore the links with minimal inconvenience. Linking to competitor's news stories avoids the copyright issues that would be raised by reprinting, so it is possible to construct Web sites that follow evolving stories and issues in great depth and from many perspectives.

What About Comics?

You shouldn't have to give up either comic strips or editorial cartoons just because you get your news online. Look for comic strips in Yahoo! by choosing Entertainment | Comics and Animation | Comic Strips, and for editorial cartoons by choosing Entertainment | Comics and Animation | Editorial Cartoons.

One of the best such sites is Yahoo Full Coverage. The Yahoo! staff identifies significant stories, establishes Web pages devoted to those stories and creates links to relevant coverage available elsewhere on the Web. As the story evolves, the Full Coverage page devoted to that story accumulates links from all over the Web, representing sources from a wide variety of viewpoints. Choose News & Media | Full Coverage from Yahoo!.

If you want to research an issue rather than follow a story, go to Policy.com (see Table 25-5), a Web site that describes itself as "the Web's most comprehensive public policy resource and community." Rather than news stories, you are likely to find links to position papers from influential think tanks of a variety of political philosophies.

Another kind of depth is provided by The Mining Company, a site that *The St. Petersburg Times* has characterized as "Yahoo on steroids." The Mining Company Web site consists of over 500 topics, each of which has its own home page managed by a Mining Company guide. Each of these pages is devoted to the question: How can I best use the resources of the Web to understand this topic? The Mining Company is perhaps the Web's best resource for answering "What is that?" questions. So, for example, if you are reading a news article about clashes between the Hindus and Sikhs in India and want to know "What is Hinduism, anyway?," check it out at the Mining Company. Of special note is the Urban Legends and Folklore: Current Net Hoaxes section at the Mining Company, which is the best place to check out the latest misinformation you run across on the Web.

Listening to the News Online

Radio networks that offer short news programs to their affiliates often put those programs on the Web in either RealAudio or Windows Media Player format. The fidelity you can get with a 28.8K modem is approximately what you would expect from AM radio, which is perfectly adequate for talk programs.

National Public Radio (listed in Table 25-6) offers a short newscast-on-demand updated on the hour. In addition, many of NPR's longer news shows, such as *All Things Considered*, are available either in their entirety or on a story-by-story basis. You can listen to the 13 topic segments (such as top stories or sports) CNN Radio produces for its affiliates, as well as the audio feed of all of CNN's TV networks. Just click the Audio link near the top of the CNN home page. C-SPAN Radio 90 is broadcast live on the Web. For coverage of world news, you can listen to News Now on the Voice of America or BBC Worldservice. Many TV networks also have radio news broadcasts available from their Web sites or audio feeds from television news segments.

Policy.com	**http://www.policy.com**
Mining Company	**http://miningco.com**

Table 25-5.   *Web Sites for In-Depth Coverage and Background on Current Events*

National Public Radio	**http://www.npr.org**
Christian Science Monitor Radio	**http://csmonitor.com/audio**
C-SPAN Radio 90	**http://c-span.org/watch/radio90**
British Broadcasting Corporation	**http://www.bbc.co.uk**
Voice of America	**http://www.voa.gov**

Table 25-6.   *Audio News on the Web*

Watching the News Online

Despite the limitations of video-on-demand at current modem speeds, most of the TV networks are putting at least some of their daily news broadcasts on the Web. At this writing, the cable news channels show the greatest commitment to broadcasting on the Web. All three C-SPAN networks are available live from its Web site (listed in Table 25-7). Video and audio from C-SPAN Events are archived. Fox News Channel broadcasts live on the Web, and Fox News has the most ambitious news-on-demand offering: A list of more than two dozen video news stories is available for assembly into your personal newscast. Just click the boxes next to the stories you want to view, and a video window (either Windows Media Player or RealPlayer) plays the clips in one continuous news show. The stories can also be viewed individually from the Fox News home page (Table 25-3). Another site for assembling stories into your own newscast is Daily Briefing.

CNN also provides extensive video. In addition to the current stories on Headline News and the top stories from CNN's regular newscast, clips are also available from Larry King Live and Crossfire. Click the Video link near the top of the CNN home page. In addition, CNN maintains searchable video archives; look for the Video Archive link on the CNN home page. Even Comedy Central is getting into the act; the headline news segment of The Daily Show is a video preset on Real Player.

C-SPAN	**http://c-span.org**
NBC VideoSeeker	**http://www.videoseeker.com**
Daily Briefing	**http://www.dailybriefing.com**
WorldNet Television	**http://www.ibb.gov/worldnet**

Table 25-7.   *In Addition to Network Web Sites, You Can Watch Video News on These Web Sites*

VIEWING THE
WORLD WIDE WEB

The news divisions of the broadcast networks are also offering video-on-demand. MSNBC puts video clips on the Web, and a number of NBC local stations have local news and weather on the Web as well; you can find them through the NBC Video Seeker site. The CBS Web site asks your ZIP code and then directs you to the Web site of its local affiliate. Video of CBS news programs like the CBS Evening News is then available from the affiliate Web site. The ABC News site also tracks the TV shows it produces, providing video for some of them and transcripts for most of the rest. PBS, for now, is behind the other networks in putting video online. The audio feed of many PBS programs is available at their news site, but little or none of it is available as video. A news show giving an American view of world news is Washington Window from the U.S. government's WorldNet Television. It is available on demand at the WorldNet Web site.

Weather Reports

You no longer have to wait through a half-hour local news show in order to hear what the weather will be for tomorrow's picnic, or whether the latest hurricane is headed your way. The Web gives you access to weather information whenever you want it, including current conditions, today's forecast, five-day forecasts, radar and satellite images, national forecast maps, and storm tracking or other weather service bulletins. You can find information either about your local area or anywhere else in the world. Table 25-8 lists Web addresses for some meteorological sites.

Local Weather

In the United States, most portals can provide today's local weather forecast on your customized start page. If, however, you are not in a major city, you may have to settle for a forecast from a nearby city.

The My Yahoo home page is typical: Today's predicted high and low temperatures are displayed together with an icon depicting weather conditions like sunshine, clouds, or rain. Clicking the city name produces a weather page for that city from Yahoo Weather. This page shows current conditions plus a five-day forecast. Clicking on one of the Maps and Images links takes you to recent satellite and radar images, plus various national prediction maps. Similar information is available through the other portals listed in Table 25-1.

National Weather Service	**http://www.nws.noaa.gov**
World Meteorological Organization	**http://www.wmo.ch**
The Weather Channel	**http://www.weather.com**
WeatherLabs	**http://www.weatherlabs.com**
Weather Web	**http://weather.hypermart.net**

Table 25-8. *Web Sites That Specialize in Weather and Climate*

Local newspaper or TV station Web sites are another source of local weather forecasts. See "Reading Your (or Anybody's) Local Newspaper Online" earlier in this chapter. Most national news sites allow you to input a city name or ZIP code to get a local forecast. Web sites like The Weather Channel, WeatherWeb, and the National Weather Service give local weather reports for any location in the United States and most of the world.

National and Global Weather

CNN's video weather forecasts for the United States, for Asia/Australia, or for Europe/Africa are available at CNN Videoselect; click the Video link near the top of the CNN home page.

You can easily link your way to the national weather service of almost any country from the Web site of the World Meteorological Organization, a service of the United Nations. From their home page, click the International Weather link and then look for your country of interest. Many of these Web sites have English versions, though often they are not as complete as the native language versions.

The Weather Channel and Weather Web offer a full assortment of weather information: local conditions and forecasts anywhere in the world, weather news, large-scale weather maps, radar and satellite images, and storm tracking. For sheer detail and depth, though, nothing matches the National Weather Service of the U.S. government. The NWS Web site keeps track of data from every weather-reporting site in the United States, and links to the most complete collection of satellite imagery, as well as historical climate data. It is also the best site to go to for marine weather.

Sports

All the major news Web sites cover sports, so if you want something as simple as the last night's scores, you can find it wherever you get your news. The quality of sports coverage at portals ranges from a simple list of recent Reuters or AP sports headlines to Yahoo Sports, which is a full-fledged rival of the sports Web sites listed in Table 25-9. If you regularly follow a favorite major league or major college team, you can customize most portal sites to show you that team's most recent score on your start page. See "Creating a Customized Start Page" earlier in this chapter.

CNN/SI	**http://cnnsi.com**
Sporting News	**http://www.tsn.com**
ESPN SportZone	**http://espnet.sportzone.com**
CBS SportsLine	**http://cbs.sportsline.com**

Table 25-9. *Full-Coverage Sports Web Sites*

Finding out last night's major league scores only scratches the surface of the sports coverage available on the Web. You can follow the most obscure teams in the most obscure sports. You can get play-by-play coverage of games in progress, either teletype style or via live audio—no matter how far away from the game you are. Live audio postgame interviews or even video highlights are available at a click. Scheduled chats let you interact with star players or coaches. And fantasy sports leagues simulate the experience of managing a professional sports team.

A few of the major sports Web sites are given in Table 25-9. All these sites have similar formats: The site's home page contains today's headlines and current photos. Buttons on that page link to pages devoted to each of the major sports. On those pages you get even more headlines and links to pages devoted to standings, statistics, teams, and players.

All four of these sites have a large amount of information available free, but charge for certain premium features. ESPN SportZone and CBS SportsLine rely on a subscription model: you can become a Zone insider or a SportsLine member for $5 a month. CNN/Sports Illustrated and The Sporting News do not have members, but require fees for special services like fantasy leagues or contests.

Scores and Schedules

Any news site can tell you the score of major league games played during the previous 24 hours. Finding scores of games weeks or months old, or for a minor league team or a distant alma mater is a bit more challenging.

Finding scores from a week or a month ago is easiest at ESPN SportZone. The scores from the entire current season of any major league sport are available: select a sport from the SportZone home page and then select Scores/Schedules. Click a date on a calendar (or a week number for the NFL) to see the scoreboard for that day. Some kind of recap or box score is available for every game.

CNN/SI maintains pages devoted to most minor league and college baseball teams. *The Sporting News'* or ESPN's minor league and college baseball coverage is more limited. Your best bet for an obscure team is to find a Web page devoted to that team (by putting the team name into a search engine, for example, "Quincy High Blue Devils"), or to find the Web site of a local newspaper (see Table 25-4).

Standings, Statistics, and Records

Major league standings are available at any portal or major news site. Typically, the site has a page devoted to a particular sport, say NFL football, with Standings and Statistics buttons on that page. Online standings are embedded in a rich web of information; a single click can take you from a team's line in the standings to a team page giving past scores, rosters, schedule, and ticket information. Minor league standings are usually not available in newspapers, unless the league has a local team. But you can find them on the Web sites in Table 25-9.

Statistics are far better on a good sports Web site than in the newspaper. The *sortable stats* feature gives you a full listing of a league's player statistics, and lets you re-sort the list according to any single statistic just by clicking on the column header. In addition, each player's name is linked to a page of career statistics. The best sortable stats we've found are on CNN/SI and CBS SportsLine. ESPN has them, but only for paying subscribers. Yahoo! and MSNBC have them as well.

Lifetime individual statistics for current players in major sports are available on all the sports Web sites listed in Table 25-9, as well as Yahoo Sports. ESPN SportZone is typical: go to the page devoted to a particular sport (such as football) and look for the Players link; then search alphabetically for a particular player.

CNN/SI stands out if you're looking for historical baseball statistics. Want to know how many RBI's Ted Williams had the year he hit .406? CNN/SI provides this and many other statistics that you used to find only in *The Baseball Encyclopedia*. To find them, go to the CNN/SI's main baseball page and select Historical Profiles from the links at the top of the page. Settle arguments about awards and records by consulting the online version of the *Information Please Almanac* (**http://www.infoplease.com**). From the home page, click the Sports button and choose the particular sport of interest. In addition to the statistics and awards from the most recently completed season, each sport's section has a Through the Years link to lists of MVPs, lifetime and year-by-year leaders in various categories, and all-time records.

Leagues, Teams, and Players

Most of the major sports leagues have done a good job on their Web sites of collecting the basic information that fans want to know: team and player pages, standings, schedules, statistics, schedules for TV and radio coverage (including online broadcasts), chats with star players, injury reports, and a few news headlines. In addition, you can usually buy official league or team merchandise from the Web site's online store.

The cream of the crop in league Web sites, so far, is the NFL site (see Table 25-10). In addition to everything you would expect from a league Web site, NFL.com has gamecasts

National Football League	**http://nfl.com**
Major League Baseball	**http://www.majorleaguebaseball.com**
National Basketball Association	**http://nba.com**
National Hockey League	**http://nhl.com**
NCAA Football	**http://www.ncaafootball.net**

Table 25-10. *Web Sites of Sports Leagues*

of all ongoing games (see the upcoming section, "Gamecasts") and play-by-play descriptions of every game played during the current season. (Click the week number to get a scoreboard for that week of the season, and then click the Gamebook link under the game you are interested in.) If you have a fast Internet connection, you can get video highlights from NFL Films by choosing Multimedia from the NFL.com home page.

Live Game Coverage

You don't have to live within radio range of your favorite teams to get play-by-play coverage of their games, as shown in Table 25-11. (The Web sites in Table 25-9 also do live gamecasts of many events.) Audio broadcasts of many sporting events are now available through the Web, and sometimes are even archived, so that you can listen to a game on your own schedule. In addition, the Web has developed its own method of covering live events, the gamecast, which takes advantage of the Web's ability to transmit diagrams and statistics quickly.

If you are in doubt about whether or where a given game is being broadcast online, check the Web site of the league (see Table 25-10).

Audio Broadcasts

Live audio broadcasts of all major league baseball games, NHL hockey games, and many other major sports events are available at Broadcast.com. ESPN SportZone has live audio coverage of all NBA basketball games. Typically, the feed from the home team's local radio coverage is uploaded to the Web in a Real Audio format.

We haven't been able to find online audio play-by-play coverage of Sunday afternoon NFL football games, but ESPN Radio does the next best thing: It has correspondents at all the ongoing football games and continuously cycles through them, updating each game every ten minutes or so. If you can't pick ESPN Radio up over the air, you can find it at the ESPN SportZone Web site. (Look for Live Radio/TV

Broadcast.com	**http://www.broadcast.com/sports**
NFL Gameday Live	**http://www.nfl.com**
Monday Night Football	**http://abcmnf.com**
Gamecruiser	**http://www.gamecruiser.com**
Total Sports	**http://www.totalsports.com**

Table 25-11.   *Web Sites That Do Live Play-by-Play Coverage*

in the left column of the SportZone home page.) CBS owns the radio broadcasting rights to all Monday night, Sunday night, and other prime time NFL football games, so you can listen to them either on the air or at the CBS SportsLine Web site. (Look for Live Radio in the left column of the CBS SportLine home page.)

College sports events are often broadcast online, but no central site has all of them. Broadcast.com has many college games, and even archives many of them so that you can listen to them on demand. A number of major colleges have their games broadcast at the Gamecruiser site.

Gamecasts

Another kind of play-by-play coverage, the gamecast, is unique to the Web. In gamecasts, a combination of text and graphics is used to communicate a great deal of information about the current state of the game. Baseball gamescasts are the best developed at present, though football is gamecast as well, and other sports have continuously updated box scores on the Web.

An excellent example of a gamecast is ESPN SportZone's coverage of the 1998 World Series. On a single screen, the following items are easily visible: the score; the score by innings; mug shots and statistics of the current pitcher and batter; a pitch-by-pitch text description of the current inning; game statistics of the line-up of the team at bat; a count of the current balls, strikes, and outs; and a field diagram showing the numbers of the players in the field and icons for the runner on base. Much additional information is available with a click or two. Passing the runner pops up a window that gives his name and tells how he got on base. Similar windows pop up whenever the cursor passes over one of the numbers in the field. Clicking a tab on the page displays the game statistics of the team in the field, an inning-by-inning game log, or an continuously updated box score. Links on the page lead to the team pages of each team or pages devoted to any of the players currently in the game. The Select Another Game window at the top of the screen would display scores of any other games being played at same time and allow you to switch to a gamecast of one of those games by clicking the Go button.

In addition to allowing you to follow a game as it happens wherever you are, a gamecast is an excellent supplement to a game that you watch on television or listen to on the radio (or through an online audio broadcast). You no longer need to rely on an announcer to recap parts of the game you missed, or to tell you who is coming up next or whether he is a good hitter. Most gamecasting sites archive their gamecasts, allowing you to review a game in great detail.

For important events like the World Series or the Super Bowl, any of the major sports Web sites shown in Table 25-9 will have some kind of live coverage. The Web site that gamecasts the widest variety of events, however, is Total Sports. Every major league baseball game is gamecast at Total Sports, and events from many other sports besides. Every NFL football game is gamecast at NFL.com.

Personal Finance and Investing

The Web can not only replace many of your current sources of financial information, it allows you to do things you would never have considered doing with other media. The Web's advantages over other media come from a few main features: it has the ability to tailor the information you receive according to your choices, the ability to compile information in databases and present that data interactively, the ability to do searches based on criteria you set, as well as the ability to input your data directly into preprogrammed calculations. The Web can also provide the following advantages:

- Financial Web sites can give you current (20 minutes old) quotes for precisely the stocks that you own or are thinking of buying; provide links to the previous month's news stories that mention the companies you have an interest in (no matter how obscure they might be); and assemble investment research that used to be accessible only to professional traders, like charts, quarterly reports, earnings estimates, insider trades, stock screens, and analyst recommendations.

- Message boards devoted to a particular stock, industry, or investment strategy let you trade ideas with other investors.

- Online bank or brokerage accounts let you see your balances whenever you want, transfer money between accounts, and download your transactions automatically into a personal finance program like Quicken or Microsoft Money. Stock trades that used to cost hundreds of dollars in commissions can now be done online for less than ten dollars.

- Online calculators can lead you through complicated personal finance calculations.

Keeping Up with the Market and the Economy

A customizable start page at a portal (see "Creating a Customized Start Page" earlier in this chapter) lets you display business headlines and simple statistics, like the Dow Jones average, or even a full stock portfolio. Among the portals, Yahoo! stands out as having assembled a first-rate financial site. The financial weekly *Barron's* chose Yahoo Finance as one of the top financial sites of any kind. Excite's financial coverage comes from Quicken, and is also good.

The Web sites in Table 25-12 are full-service financial information sites. They won't trade stocks for you (see "Online Brokers" later in this chapter for that), but they provide you with financial news, stock quotes, and a variety of tools for researching companies and industries.

Audio and Video Market Updates

If you like to get your information from the radio or television, check out the business page of RealNetworks RealGuide (**http://www.real.com/realguide**) or the Business channel of Broadcast.com (**http://www.broadcast.com**). Access the Morning Business Report and Nightly Business Report from the NBC VideoSeeker site, located at **http://www.videoseeker.com**.

Quotes

Stock quotes for stocks traded on American stock exchanges are easy to find on the Web. Any of the financial Web sites in Table 25-12 provides stock quotes, as do the financial sections of all the national news organizations in Table 25-3 and most major newspaper Web sites.

Submit a request to a quote server by typing the ticker symbol of the stock into a request window and clicking a button. (Most stock quote sites let you look up the ticker symbol.) Some Web sites let you submit several requests at once by typing in several ticker symbols separated by spaces. What you get back also varies from one site to another. A quote may be a simple price, or it can be a summary of the day's trading activity in that stock, together with some statistics related to the stock. Figure 25-2 shows a detailed quote, obtained by submitting the ticker symbol IBM to the quote server on the home page of Motley Fool. The row of links above the quote window lists Motley Fool's tools for analyzing a stock. For example, clicking the Estimates link would produce a list of recent estimates of IBM's future earnings.

REAL-TIME QUOTES AND DELAYED QUOTES   Stock quotes come in two varieties on the Web: real-time quotes and delayed quotes. Real-time quotes tell you the current bid and ask prices. Delayed quotes tell you a price at which the stock traded 20 minutes ago. Delayed quotes are free and widely available. Real-time quotes generally are not.

CBS MarketWatch	**http://cbs.marketwatch.com**
Microsoft MoneyCenter	**http://moneycentral.msn.com**
CNNfn	**http://cnnfn.com**
Motley Fool	**http://fool.com**
Fox Market Wire	**http://foxmarketwire.com**
Quicken Financial Network	**http://www.quicken.com**
S&P Personal Wealth	**http://www.personalwealth.com**

Table 25-12.   *Financial Web Sites*

You can get real-time quotes either from your online broker, or by paid subscription. Recently, the online broker E*Trade (**http://www.etrade.com**) and the financial news Web site S&P Personal Wealth (**http://www.personalwealth.com**) have begun to offer limited numbers of free real-time quotes to anyone who registers. If you don't mind the site's constant efforts to tempt you to subscribe to their premium features, the free quotes are a good deal.

QUOTES FOR OPTIONS, COMMODITIES, AND MUTUAL FUNDS   Most sources of free quotes on the Web do not handle option quotes. CBS MarketWatch has recently begun doing so. First get a quote for the underlying stock, then click the Options Chain link. For quotes on futures for commodities or financial indices, consult the Chicago Board of Trade (CBOT) Web site.

Mutual funds have ticker symbols just like stocks, and many quote engines on the Web recognize them. Look up their ticker symbols just as you would look up stock ticker symbols. (Some quote engines require the prefix MUTUAL: before a fund quote.)

Keeping Track of a Stock Portfolio

If you own (or are otherwise interested in) more than two or three stocks, it can be a nuisance to remember all their stock symbols and type them into a quote server. *Portfolios* are lists of stocks that a Web site keeps for you, so that you can look up the current prices of all of them with a single command.

Once you have created a portfolio somewhere, you can use it as a focus of your financial Web browsing, and get far more information from it than just a list of prices. In the same way that the quote in Figure 25-2 provides a jumping-off point for applying a financial Web site's analysis tools to a particular stock, a portfolio provides a focal point for accessing all of a financial Web site's tools. Examine, for example, the portfolio in Figure 25-3.

You can give the Web site additional information, such as the number of shares you own of each stock, so that it can total up the value of the portfolio whenever it looks up new prices. You can tell the Web site what you paid for each stock, so that it can total up your gains and losses. You can design the display of the portfolio so that it tells you fundamental data about the stock, like its price/earnings ratio or dividend yield, or tells you when new headlines cover this stock. Finally, the portfolio display can provide a convenient set of links to other resources that can help you analyze your investments: charting tools, earnings estimates, insider trade reports, research reports, lists of recent news stories and press releases, brief descriptions of the company's business, balance sheets, and even reports that the company has filed with the Securities and Exchange Commission.

Most sites that track portfolios allow you to set up several of them. If you follow a lot of stocks, you may find it convenient to split them up by industry, or according to some

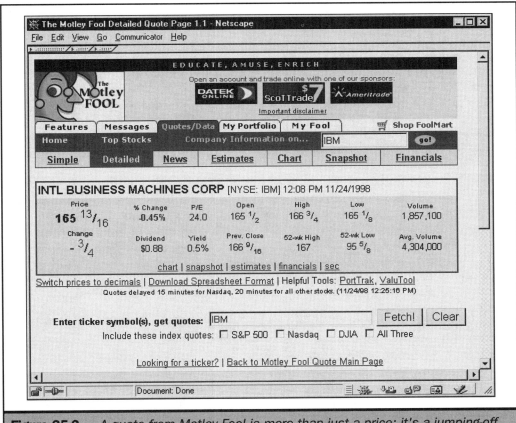

Figure 25-2.   *A quote from Motley Fool is more than just a price; it's a jumping-off point for accessing everything the site knows about a stock*

other scheme. At the very least, we recommend tracking the stocks that you already own in a separate portfolio from the stocks that you are only thinking about buying.

Researching a Stock Online

Once you have given a financial Web site a stock's ticker symbol, either by inputting it to a quote server or including it in a portfolio, you are in a position to make use of the following analysis tools to research the stock:

■ **Company profiles and fundamental data**   A quote like the one displayed in Figure 25-2 already tells you a great deal about a stock. Clicking the Financials

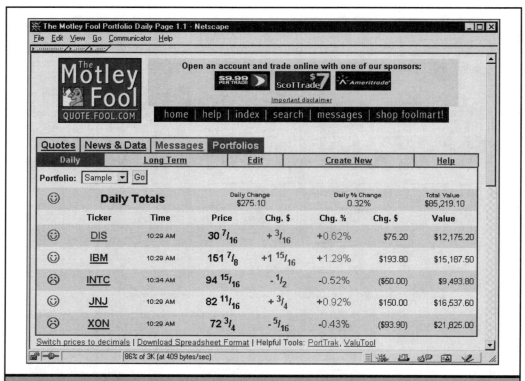

Figure 25-3. *Tracking a portfolio at the Motley Fool. The daily view is shown. This screen is linked to a long-term view of the same portfolio, detailed data for any of the stocks in the portfolio, or other portfolios tracked at Motley Fool by the same user*

link would provide even more information: statistics about sales, earnings, book value, market capitalization, and balance sheet data.

■ **Company news**   Once you have gotten a quote from one of the sites listed in Table 25-12, you can assemble 30 days of linked news stories on that company by clicking a Company News link.

■ **Charts**   At a glance, you can see how a stock has been doing and how volatile its price is. Charts are usually available at a single click from a quote or portfolio display. In Figure 25-2, for example, clicking the Chart link would chart IBM's price for the previous year. You can also chart a stock against an index like the Dow Jones average.

■ **Analysts' estimates and recommendations** Professional analysts make recommendations about whether to buy or sell a given stock, and they estimate how much money the underlying company will make in the coming quarters or years. This information gets collected and averaged by firms like Zack's and I.B.E.S. From the quote report in Figure 25-2, clicking the Estimates link would take you to recommendations and estimates for the quoted stock (IBM). From the portfolio in Figure 25-3, click the Long Term tab and then click Estimates.

■ **Stock screens** Most of the sites in Table 25-12 offer stock screening tools, and each one is a little different from the others. Consult the site's instructions. To find the Yahoo stock screen, click Stock Quotes on the Yahoo! home page, and then find the Stock Screen link under Research. CNN and Excite use Quicken's stock screen. From the Quicken home page, select Investments and then Stock Search. From Fox Market Wire home page, click Stocks and then Stock Screening. Select Stock Screener from CBS MarketWatch home page.

■ **Investment message boards** Individual investors can trade ideas and share information using investment message boards. (See "Message Boards" earlier in this chapter.) Just about any site that has message boards has some area devoted to investments, but the most extensive set of investment message boards are at Motley Fool. Among sites that follow technology stocks, Silicon Investor (**http://www.siliconinvestor.com**) has a large message board community. Motley Fool has boards for discussing individual stocks, investment theories, specific industries, personal finance, recent investment books, problems with brokers, and almost any other aspect of investing. The Ask a Foolish Question board is a good way to check out your understanding of basic investment concepts.

Online Brokers

The main motivation to open an account with an online broker is price. Trades that would cost hundreds of dollars in commissions if placed with a traditional full-service broker would cost less than $30 at almost any online broker, and less than $10 at some. Once they get used to the idea of trading online, however, many people find they prefer its convenience. If you do your financial reading and stock market research online already, it is natural to do your trading online as well. Table 25-13 lists brokerage Web sites (Gomez Advisors is not an online brokerage, but it publishes a scorecard of online brokers).

Choosing an Online Broker

The easiest way to find an online broker is to discover that you already have one. Many popular discount brokers like Charles Schwab or Fidelity let you trade online, often for a considerable discount. Even some full-service brokers now allow online trading. A call to your broker or a visit to your broker's Web site should tell you how you can start trading online, and whether there is any advantage for you to do so.

If you decide to get a new broker, or to open a brokerage account for the first time, read Motley Fool's "How to Select a Discount Broker." Find it by clicking the Get a Broker link on Motley Fool's home page (**http://fool.com**). Some of the more popular and well-reviewed online brokers are listed in Table 25-13. Gomez Advisors maintains a scorecard of top-rated online brokers at its Web site. Publications like *Barron's* (available for a subscription through the Wall Street Journal Online site) or *Money Magazine* (at **http://www.pathfinder.com**) regularly review the top online brokers. Motley Fool has message boards where individuals discuss what they like and don't like about their online brokers.

Opening an Account

As far as we know, there is no paperless way to create a brokerage account. Most online brokerages do have their account application forms online. You find the right form, print it out, sign it, and mail it in. Other brokerages let you request an application at their Web site, but they mail the application to you and you mail it back to them after you have completed it. In a few days you should get mail from your new broker containing your account number and a temporary password.

E*Trade	http://www.etrade.com
DLJ Direct	http://www.dljdirect.com
Discover	http://www.discoverbroker.com
National Discount Brokers	http://www.ndb.com
Fidelity Investments	http://www.fidelity.com
Charles Schwab	http://www.schwab.com
Gomez Advisors	http://www.gomezadvisors.com

Table 25-13. *Online Brokerage Web Sites.*

Placing a Trade Online

Every online broker's Web site is arranged differently, but the process of placing an order is similar on each site. After you log in (and have a secure connection—check the lock icon on your browser), select a link that tells the Web site you want to place an order. The site responds with an online order form like the one in Figure 25-4. Filling out the form specifies the stock you want to buy or sell, the quantity, the kind of order you want to place (Figure 25-4 displays a stop order), and possibly the price at which the order should execute. (A market order executes at the current market price, so you don't specify a price.)

After you have completed the order form, you submit it. (In Figure 25-4 you would submit by clicking the Preview button.) The broker's site then has you preview the order; it repeats the order it received, displays the current bid and ask prices of the stock, and tells you the commission the brokerage charges for this kind of order. You examine the order, and if you are satisfied you enter your password. Entering your

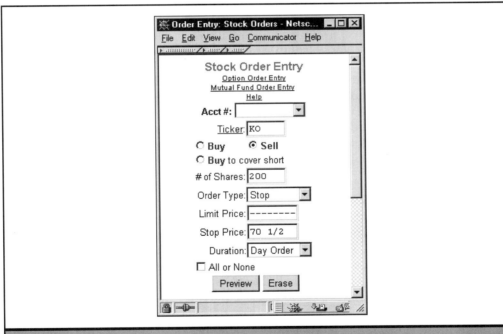

Figure 25-4.   *An online order form at National Discount Brokers. This order would sell 200 shares of Coca-Cola if the price fell to 70 ½ on the day the order was entered*

AAII	http://www.aaii.com
NAIC	http://www.better-investing.org
Investor Words	http://www.investorwords.com
SEC Handbook for Investors	http://www.sec.gov/consumer/weisktc.htm
The Motley Fool	http://fool.com

Table 25-14. *Sites That Teach About Investing*

password is your way of "signing" the order. (It also guarantees that the order isn't being sent by someone who happened by your untended computer.)

When both you and the Web site's computer are satisfied that this is a correct, legitimate order, the order is transmitted to the brokerage's representative at the appropriate exchange, who does the actually buying and selling. This happens very quickly. For heavily traded stocks like IBM or General Electric, a market order executes almost instantaneously.

Orders that have not yet executed are called *open orders*. Orders like the one in Figure 25-5 are not executed until the stock price reaches some preset level. Such orders may remain open for some while, or in fact might never be executed. You may at any time examine your open orders, and cancel them if they no longer fit your plans.

Learning About Investing

Two organizations that have been educating investors for many years now have a Web presence: the National Association of Investors Corporation (NAIC) and the American Association of Independent Investors (AAIC) have good investment primers on their Web sites (listed in Table 25-14). The U.S. government's Securities and Exchange Commission publishes a handbook *What Every Investor Should Know*, which is also available on the Web. A good place to look up what investment terms mean is Investor Words, an online glossary to more than 5,000 terms used in the investment business. Finally, a irreverent, opinionated, but highly useful and amusing place to look for investment education is the Fool's School section of Motley Fool. For specific questions, go to the Ask A Foolish Question message board at the Fool's Information Desk.

Online Banking

Many banks allow you to control a bank account online (see Table 25-15). You can get up-to-the-minute balances on all your accounts (including credit cards), transfer funds

Citibank Test Drive	**http://home.da-us.citibank.com/da**
Bank of America Test Drive	**http://www.bankamerica.com/online/testdrive**
Electronic Banking Association	**http://www.e-banking.org**
Intuit Online Payment	**http://www.intuit.com/banking**

Table 25-15. *Sites for Learning About Banking Online*

from one account to another, pay bills automatically, or even schedule transfers or payments ahead of time. If you have a regular payment like rent or a cable TV bill, you can schedule the payment to go out on the same day each month.

If you already use Quicken or Microsoft Money, you won't have much to learn. Most online bank accounts work with either of those financial packages, or with Managing Your Money. Once you have set up your account, you just enter the transactions you want to make into one of these financial software packages and let it log into your bank's computer system. Your instructions are uploaded to the bank's computer, and the transactions the bank knows about are downloaded into your computer.

You can also communicate with your bank through your Web browser, and not use one of the financial software packages. You may need to upgrade your browser to 128-bit encryption or turn on JavaScript. Other banks provide their own proprietary software.

The best way to understand how all this works is to go through one of the test drive programs that participating banks provide on their Web sites. Table 25-15 includes the test drives at Citibank and Bank of America. Your bank may have a similar online introduction to their service. You can look up institutions that offer electronic banking in your area at the Electronic Banking Association.

If your bank does not offer online banking, and you aren't interested in changing to a bank that does, you can still pay bills online through Intuit Online Payment. You can schedule payments online just as with an online banking account, but the payments come out of the checking account you already have.

Online Calculators for Personal Finance

Financenter.com (listed in Table 25-16) provides online calculators for guiding you through over 100 questions such as Is it cheaper to rent or own?, Should I buy a new or used car?, How much should I be saving for retirement?, and How much life insurance do I need? You answer a series of questions on an online form, click a button to submit the form, and then see the resulting cost/benefit numbers or graphs. If the results look

Savings Bond Wizard	http://www.publicdebt.treas.gov/sav/savwizar
Financenter.com	http://financenter.com

Table 25-16. *Financial Calculating Tools*

wrong to you, go back to the form, change some assumptions, and run it again. These online calculators are also available from the Money section of USA Today Online (Table 25-3). To find out what your U.S. Savings Bonds are currently worth, use the Treasury Department's Savings Bond Wizard.

Entertainment

You can use the Web for entertainment in any number of ways. You can gather information about entertaining activities—TV shows and movies you can watch or concerts you can attend. You can follow news about the entertainment industry and your favorite entertainers. You can use the Web to watch video or listen to audio. You can play computer games online, download new computer games to play offline, or read online magazines about gaming.

Local TV and Movie Listings

Portal sites can display TV and movie listings in your area, but they are not particularly good at it yet. Only a small portion of a complete day's TV schedule can be displayed at any one time, and you don't want to have to wait for your entire start page to refresh just so you can see another hour's worth of TV listings. Movie listings are even more problematic: not all theaters submit their listings to the national services the portals use, so the movie listings in your area may not be complete. The best place to get movie listings online is from the same source you use offline: your local newspaper. Check Table 25-4 to find your local newspaper's Web site.

Your local newspaper may also be the best place to get TV listings, but if not, you can try the TV Guide Entertainment Network (**http://www.tvgen.com**) or Ultimate TV (**http://www.ultimatetv.com**). Just input your ZIP code, and they look up your TV listings, including cable. To see an entire day's (or week's) worth of TV listings on one screen, you'll have to go channel by channel—use either the Web site of the network or of your local station. To find them from Ultimate TV's home page, click the US TV link. You can search by network, by state, or by call letters.

| Digital Cities | http://home.digitalcity.com |
| Sidewalk | http://www.sidewalk.com |

Table 25-17. *Local Entertainment Guides for Major Cities*

Other Local Entertainment

Unless you live in a major city, your best bet for local entertainment news is still the Web site of your local paper. Many of the entertainment news Web sites in Table 25-18 have local pages for major cities. Digital Cities and Microsoft's Sidewalk (listed in Table 25-17) have local Web sites for dozens of cities. The two are clearly competing with each other, and have very similar features. Each city site has an entertainment guide, from which you can find music, art, and movie listings—complete with maps to the theater or club. As so often happens with a Microsoft site, many Sidewalk pages display strangely in Navigator. We didn't have this problem with Digital Cities. Tourist attractions in major cities are covered by destination guides. You can find them in your portal's travel section, or by consulting Table 25-35, later in this chapter.

Entertainment News

E! Online (listed in Table 25-18) is a good all-around source for entertainment news. TV Guide's Web site has expanded to include movies as well as TV, but you'll find better movie coverage at Hollywood Online or at the Internet Movie Data Base.

TV Guide Entertainment Network	http://www.tvgen.com
Ultimate TV	http://www.ultimatetv.com
Ultimate Movies	http://www.UltimateMovies.com
E! Online	http://www.eonline.com
Internet Movie Data Base	http://www.imdb.com
Hollywood Online	http://hollywood.com
Billboard Online	http://billboard.com
MTV Online	http://mtv.com
Rolling Stone Network	http://www.rollingstone.com

Table 25-18. *Where to Find the Latest News About TV, Movies, or Popular Music*

Ultimate TV is the best place from which to follow a current TV show. From their home page, click the TV Season link and then choose a show from the drop-down list. Ultimate TV's page for an individual show gives you the basic information about the network, production studio, actors, and air times, and pulls together links to all the Web resources having to do with that show: episode guides, fan Web sites, mailing lists, Ultimate's own message board on the show, newsgroups, chats, and even related books. Ultimate also maintains a list of links to the official Web pages of current movies at Ultimate Movies.

For coverage of popular music, try Billboard Online, MTV Online, or Rolling Stone Network.

Radio, TV, and Music on Demand

There are two ways to deliver audio or video across the Internet: the entire piece can be downloaded and stored on your hard disk before it is played, or the piece can be *streamed*, that is, later parts of the piece are being downloaded while the earlier parts are being played. (See Chapter 30 for details.) Each format has its advantages. Downloaded audio/video quality is limited only by your patience and your hardware. The quality of streaming media, on the other hand, is limited by the speed of your Internet connection. Audio at 28.8Kbps is adequate to understand speech or to recognize a tune, but that's about all. At 56Kbps music is enjoyable, but still not of the quality of FM radio or a compact disk. Video at 56Kbps provides a small, jerky picture—you can follow the large-scale action, but you cannot read lips.

But streaming media is live. You can watch an event as it happens. You can request a song and start hearing it right away. You can listen to a radio station with no gaps between songs. Watching or listening to streaming media also does not clutter up your hard drive with large files. Further, precisely *because* the quality is low and the files do not persist on your hard drive, streaming media has avoided the copyright issues that have plagued downloaded media. Playing a hit song on streaming audio *advertises* the CD, while downloading an MP3 version of the song might *replace* the CD. Consequently, artists and media companies are reluctant to release downloadable versions of their products.

The result is that streaming media, particularly streaming audio, is an up-and-coming medium. New audio channels are appearing on the Web every day.

Streaming Media

A large number of over-the-air radio stations also broadcast live on the Web. You can link to many of them from Broadcast.com, VTuner, or the RealNetworks RealGuide (listed in Table 25-19). You can also find a number of radio stations on the Preset menu of the RealPlayer program. Many audio channels exist only on the Web, without any broadcast equivalent. The most ambitious of these projects is Rolling Stone Radio, which offers seven different programs, each with its own format. Because Web audio

Broadcast.com	**http://www.broadcast.com**
RealNetworks RealGuide	**http://www.real.com/realguide**
Vtuner	**http://www.vtuner.com**
Rolling Stone Radio	**http://www.rsradio.com**
No Label	**http://www.nolabel.com**
Incredibly Small Concert Hall	**http://www.smallhall.com**
Sony Jukebox	**http://www.sonymusic.com/jukebox**

Table 25-19.   *Streaming Media Sites*

channels are available around the world, and don't need to find their audience in any particular geographic area, channels can target their markets very narrowly. And so, for example, the preset channels on the RealPlayer even include Parrot Radio, the all-Jimmy-Buffet channel.

Broadcast.com's CD Jukebox delivers audio-on-demand, but the selection lacks the most popular CDs. Its Audio Books channel also suffers from limited selection. Sony is selling streaming access to its music catalog through its Jukebox site. For $2.50 you can get 24 hours of access to 10 songs.

Streaming audio offers a way for bands without major recording contracts to seek an audience directly—and for you to listen to music by new, undiscovered musicians. Two Web sites dedicated to independent bands are No Label and Incredibly Small Concert Hall.

The quality of streaming video at current modem speeds has limited its usefulness. At present the main sources of streaming TV broadcasts are news channels. (See "Watching the News Online" earlier in this chapter.) Ultimate TV and Broadcast.com maintain lists of links to streamed TV networks or shows. From Ultimate's home page, click the TV Navigator link, and then click Webcasting. From Broadcast.com's home page, click the Live TV link. Also check the list of TV connections in the left window of Real Player.

Broadcast.com is offering a small number of full-length movies and classic TV shows in a streaming format. From the Broadcast.com home page, click the Video link. The movies are offered at three speeds: 28.8Kbps, 56Kbps, and 100Kbps. Most of the movies offered have little commercial potential, and seem to be more of a proof-of-concept than a serious channel. But you can view a few classics like Frank Capra's *Meet John Doe.*

| WinAmp player | http://www.winamp.com |
| MP3 | http://www.mp3.com |

Table 25-20. *Sites for Downloading Audio*

Downloaded Audio and Video

Due to the size of the video files, downloaded video is available mainly as short clips. The downloadable video files that you find on the Web are usually a samples of some product available in a different medium, like a movie or a video game. The main exceptions to this rule are the sports highlight clips that you can find on many of the sports Web sites in Table 25-9.

For downloadable audio, the obstacles are more legal than technological. The audio MPEG compression schemes produce audio files of CD quality. (The audio files have the suffix .MP3. Technically, this stands for MPEG 1, level 3. You can read all about this in the FAQ at the MP3 site listed in Table 25-20.) At 56Kbps, the download time of a piece of music is roughly three times its play time. Unlike streaming audio, you then have the file; you can play the piece of music whenever you want.

MPEG players can be downloaded and tried out for free. We downloaded the WinAmp player. (It's shareware; if you keep it for more than 14 days you are honor-bound to send in $10.) The Microsoft Windows Media Player (which is free from the Microsoft Web site) also claims to play MPEG files, but it sounded awful when we tried it. Don't give up on the medium until you've tried one of the specialized MPEG players. A large number of sites let you download MPEG music files for free. (Also see the shareware download sites in Table 25-32 later in this chapter).

The catch is that offering music over the Web is not legal unless you have the permission of the music's copyright holder. (If you own a CD, you can convert it to MPEG for your own use, if you have the right software. The copyright violation happens when you trade or give or sell it to someone else.) Sometimes an up-and-coming band allows distribution of an MPEG file of its music to publicize itself. But if a site offers you an MPEG file of the Rolling Stones or Madonna, chances are it's illegal. You can find a collection of legal MPEG files at MP3. Also check the links at the WinAmp site.

Erotica Online

Some of the first Web sites to generate widespread interest were those having to do with sex. Downloading erotica into your computer from the safety of your own bedroom or study has a lot to recommend it over the traditional method of acquiring such material—frequenting seedy bookstores in bad parts of town where people might see you.

Rather than inflict our personal tastes on you (or even tell you what our tastes are) we'll just point you in the direction of Jane's 'Net Sex Guide, located at **http://www.janesguide.com**. Jane's Guide is to online erotica what Yahoo! and Excite are to the Web as a whole. It reviews erotic and pornographic Web sites, both free sites and commercial sites, and provides links.

Jane's is free and supported by advertising. Its opening screen warns you that the site is for adults, but on the whole the site is surprisingly non-sleazy. Its FAQ and Consumer Tips sections help you avoid scams and deal with common problems.

Computer Games

The Internet is the natural medium for people who play computer games. On the Internet, you can

- *Play games online against other people.* Play games like hearts and chess in portal game rooms. MSN's game room includes CD-ROM games like Age of Empires.

- *Download shareware games to install on your computer.* Web directories like Yahoo! and Lycos can lead you to game archives. Also check the shareware sites in Table 25-32, later in this chapter.

- *Order CD-ROM games.* The software retailers in Table 25-23, later in this chapter, handle all the most popular games.

- *Read news about games to be released and reviews of recently released games.* See the sites in Table 25-21.

- *Find game guides that give you tips and tell you secret features of some of the most popular games.* See the sites in Table 25-21.

- *Participate in newsgroups with other users of your favorite games.* Popular games like Doom and Tomb Raider have their own newsgroups. Your newsreader should be able to find a newsgroup for your favorites.

Games Domain	http://www.gamesdomain.co.uk
GameSpot	http://www.gamespot.com
IDG Games Network	http://www.games.net
Videogames.com	http://www.videogames.com

Table 25-21. *Web Sites for Computer Game Players*

Magazines Online

Many magazines publish on their Web sites every word that is in their print versions. Another common practice (used by *Wired*, for example) is to publish back issues of the magazine on the Web site, giving the print version a month of exclusivity. (You may be able to throw away all those clipped articles in your files or piles of magazines in your garage.)

Some weekly or monthly magazines provide more information on their Web sites than their print readers receive. *Newsweek* and *Money*, for example, publish daily news updates on their Web sites. Some magazines, such as *Utne Reader*, focus their Web sites on establishing an online community among their readers, and use their print articles to seed online discussions. Other Web publications, known as *e-zines*, don't have a print version at all. IntellectualCapital.com, a public policy e-zine owned by the same people who do Policy.com, is a good example. Microsoft's Slate (which requires a subscription) is another.

Magazine Web sites are easy to find. Check the Magazines and Serials link on the home page of the Internet Public Library (**http://www.ipl.org**), or pop the name of the magazine into a search engine.

Shopping

The earliest form of retailing on the Web was little more than using the Web to publish a catalog. But after the development of the SSL protocol (see "How Secure Transactions Work" in Chapter 18) made it possible to send credit card numbers safely over the Internet, Web sites began to sell things in earnest. Now Web sites provide many advantages over paper catalogs, 800 numbers, and even physical stores, in fact, offering you many advantages, such as the following:

- **Catalog searches**   Depending on the retailer, you can search for products on retail Web sites by name, model number, category, price, author or artist, or by a keyword appearing in the product description.

- **Bargain searches**   You can search for a product across many retailer Web sites and compare prices.

- **E-mail alerts**   You can define criteria describing a product you are interested in, and receive notification by e-mail when the product is available.

- **Increased selection**   Since online retailers don't have to worry about economizing on shelf space, they can offer a wider selection of products.

- **Good prices**   Because comparison shopping is so easy on the Web, everyone's prices have to stay close to the best available sale price. Discounts from list price typically more than balance shipping costs.

- **Availability**   If you don't live in a major city (and even if you do), the specialized product you are looking for might not be easily available to you. The Web (in conjunction with major shipping companies) makes all places in the world practically equidistant.

Whether you plan to make your purchase online or not, the Web is a great place to look for product information and recommendations. See "Researching a Product or a Merchant" later in this chapter.

How to Shop Online

Shopping at a major online retailer has begun to take on a standard form. From the retailer's home page you either choose a product from a list, work your way through a system of categories and subcategories until you zero in on the product you want, or fill out a search form to find a product. (The search form at Amazon.com is shown in Figure 25-6. Most book, videotape, or CD retailers have a similar form.)

Once you've decided to make a purchase, or at least to think seriously about making a purchase, you click a button that puts the item in your "shopping cart"—in other words, the Web site begins keeping track of the item for you, and reminds you of it when you decide to "check out." Just like using a shopping cart in a real store, putting an item in this virtual shopping cart commits you to nothing. After an item is in your shopping cart, you can forget about it for the rest of your browse through the retailer's site. Any time you want to see what you've put in your shopping cart, just click a Shopping Cart button.

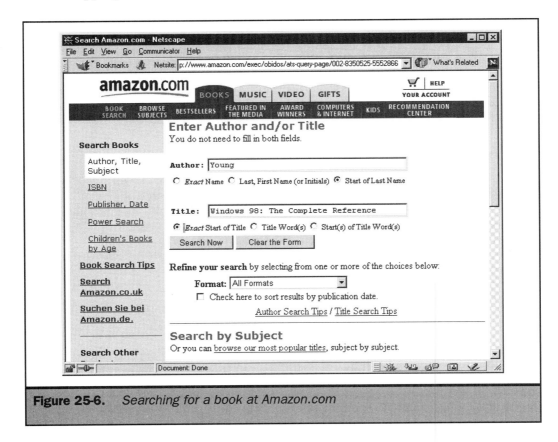

Figure 25-6.   *Searching for a book at Amazon.com*

When you have finished shopping at that Web site, click a Check Out button. The contents of your shopping cart are listed and the prices are totaled. At this point decide how many of each product you want. Setting the quantity to zero removes the item from your cart. When you have the products and quantities you want, click another button to move to the next step in the process. This varies from one retailer to another. Some go straight to the shipping and payment information, while others want you to open an account or give additional information first. A few retailers let you use a program to transfer your credit card information or shipping address from a file on your computer. (See "Purchasing Products Online with Wallet Programs" in Chapter 18.)

The final step in the online shopping process is to give a credit card number. Most online retailers offer a secure connection. (See "How Secure Transactions Work" in Chapter 18.) If you are using either Internet Explorer or Navigator, check the lock icon on the status bar; it should be locked. Usually you must also give the expiration date of your credit card and its billing address. (Online retailers are picky about the billing address; since the verification is done automatically, everything has to match exactly. The verification programs aren't smart enough yet to realize that Apt. 25 and #25 refer to the same place. The surest way to proceed is to have your latest credit card bill in hand.) When you submit the form with the credit card number on it, you're committed to the purchase.

Alternatively, you may have an account with the retailer and they may already have your shipping and payment information. In that case, you'll be shown a screen with this information and asked to give your account's password. When you submit the form with the password, you're committed to the purchase.

In case you're worried about sending credit card information through the Internet, a recent article in Consumer Reports stated: "We were unable to find any instance where a shopper's credit card information was stolen while it was being sent to a merchant."

What You Can Buy Online

A general rule of thumb is that any retailer who has a catalog has a Web site (a few are listed in Table 25-22). Look for a retailer online by checking a search engine or by looking in the Buyer's Index. You can also go to an online mall and look around. For a large list of online malls, go to Yahoo! and choose Business and Economy | Companies | Shopping Centers. Most major department stores have Web sites as well.

Computer Hardware and Software

The most natural things to buy through your computer are accessories for your computer, more or improved software, or even a whole new computer. On the Web you can find product reviews, online retailers, and even computer manufacturers who will build a system to your specifications (see Table 25-23).

PC World Online maintains a Top 400 products list, including various categories of computers and computer products. From the Top 400 home page you can access an

Buyer's Index	http://www.buyersindex.com
iMall	http://www.imall.com
ShopNow Market	http://www.internetmall.com
CyberShop	http://cybershop.com
J. C. Penney	http://www.jcpenney.com
WalMart	http://www.wal-mart.com
Sears	http://www.sears.com
Federated Department Stores	http://www.federated-fds.com

Table 25-22.   *Online Shopping Malls and Web Sites of Department Stores*

interactive buyer's guide to help you select the product that fits your needs, or you can select from a drop-down list of product types to find the most recent PC World reviews. CNET (**http://cnet.com**) and Computer Shopper are also good sources of information on hardware and software products. To compare the current street prices of a number of vendors quickly, go to the Price Watch site. Like PC World and Computer Shopper, it allows you to specify a number of features and then generates a list of products, prices, and vendors.

If you already know what you want, you can go straight to a retailer (some are listed in Table 25-23). The computer retailing Web sites are among the first to

Computer Shopper	http://computershopper.zdnet.com
PC World Top 400 Products	http://www.pcworld.com/top400
Price Watch	http://www.pricewatch.com
Computer Discount Warehouse	http://www.cdw.com
PC Connection	http://www.pcconnection.com
Egghead	http://www.egghead.com
Beyond.com	http://beyond.com
Dell	http://dell.com
Gateway	http://www.gateway.com

Table 25-23.   *Research and Buy Your Computer Equipment and Software Online*

experiment with new retailing models. Some of the sites listed in Table 25-23, Egghead for example, are set up to dispose of their out-of-date equipment through online auctions, where you can get a good price if you don't need the latest version. Some, like CDW, let you set up a *buyer's alert* on a product you are interested in. You automatically receive e-mail if the product drops in price, or if it becomes available after having been out of stock.

You can skip all the middlemen and order your computer direct from Dell or Gateway. Each site lists a few basic models, which you can then configure by adding extra memory, software, a larger hard drive, service packages, peripherals, or other accessories. When you have picked exactly the features you want, the site gives you a price. You can order the system you've designed with a click and have it delivered to your home or office.

Buying Books, CDs, and Videos Online

The main virtue of an online book, music, or video store is that it doesn't have to be selective about what titles to list. Consequently, any of the retailing Web sites listed in Table 25-24 has a larger catalog than could be physically present at any single store. Popular titles are discounted 30 percent or more, and most titles are available at some discount from list price. Shipping costs extra, but typically the price discounts approximately equal the shipping costs for a single book or video, while orders of three or more books, CDs, or videos are almost always cheaper than paying list price at a store.

Retailer	URL	Books	CDs	Videos
Amazon.com	http://amazon.com	Yes	Yes	Yes
Barnes and Noble	http://barnesandnoble.com	Yes	No	No
Borders	http://borders.com	Yes	Yes	Yes
Music Boulevard	http://musicblvd.com	No	Yes	No
CDNow	http://cdnow.com	No	Yes	Yes
Tower Records	http://towerrecords.com	No	Yes	Yes
Reel.com	http://reel.com	No	No	Yes

Table 25-24. *Online Retailers of Books, CDs, and Videos*

Competition has forced these retailers to be more than just a catalog with a Web site and low prices. Each of the retailers would like to draw customers to its Web site even when they aren't looking for any particular title, so they offer a variety of other features: recommendations, reviews, and interviews, for example. Amazon.com and Barnes and Noble each have an automated recommendation feature, in which you pick a category and rate books you have read previously. From your answers a list of recommended books is generated. (Amazon.com's recommendations run more towards the classics of the genre, while Barnes and Noble's are more likely to be new releases.) All these sites are attempting to build some kind of online community; so far Amazon.com seems to be the most successful. Reader reviews are possible on several of the sites, but Amazon.com appears to get more of them than the others, and to feature them more prominently. Borders runs online chats about literary subjects through Talk City (**http://www.talkcity.com**).

All of the retailers listed in Table 25-24 give you the ability to search their catalog by author or artist, title, keyword, or some combination of the three. The Amazon search form in Figure 25-6 is typical. Often these retailers can even find out-of-print books for you. At Amazon.com, you can sign up for two services that send you e-mail notifications: Amazon Delivers sends you reviews of new titles in genres that you specify, while Eyes lets you store a set of search criteria, and sends you e-mail if any new book fills that criteria.

Cars

The Web sites in Table 25-25 are a good place to start your car-buying research, and you can even buy the car online if you like. The process works like this: Look up anything you like about almost any model of car. When you have narrowed down to a few models, specify options, colors, and your ZIP code. The Web site prices the car for you and puts you in touch with a local dealer who will honor that price. You can even negotiate your financing and insurance online. Another approach is to use Priceline (**http://www.priceline.com**) to make a bid on a new car and see if any dealer accepts it. The Priceline process is described in "Online Travel Services" later in this chapter.

CarPoint	**http://carpoint.msn.com**
AutoWeb	**http://www.autoweb.com**
Autobytel	**http://www.autobytel.com**

Table 25-25. *Web Sites for Car Buyers*

HomeScout	**http://www.homescout.com**
Home Advisor	**http://homeadvisor.msn.com**
Apartments.com	**http://apartments.com**

Table 25-26.   *Web Sites for Finding Houses for Sale or Apartments for Rent*

Finding a Place to Live

You can check housing listings online at HomeScout (listed in Table 25-26). Input a city and a maximum price into the HomeScout home page to see a list of houses that fit your criteria. Clicking a listing takes you to the Web site of the real estate agency handling that house. Depending on the agency, you may find a picture of the house or even a map showing its location. You can also search for mortgages on the HomeScout site. Home Advisor leads you through a complete home-buying process: figuring out what you can afford, qualifying for financing, searching for a home, and putting you in touch with the agents handling the homes you are interested in.

Search for an apartment online at Apartments.com. From the home page, click a state on a U.S. map; then fill out a form listing the city, maximum rent, and number of bedrooms. The site returns a list of prospects with more complete descriptions. The site can even generate an e-mail message to the building manager.

Searching for Bargains Automatically

Bargain search engines, such as those listed in Table 25-7, can find similar items on different retailer Web sites and compare their prices. Bargain searches work best for

Bottom Dollar	**http://www.bottomdollar.com**
Yahoo Junglee	**http://yahoo.junglee.com**
Excite Jango	**http://jango.excite.com**
Lycos Virtual Outlet	**http://virtualoutlet.lycos.com**

Table 25-27.   *Search Engines That Compare Prices Across Many Online Retailers*

well-defined products like books or CDs, since they are easy to describe to a search engine—just type in the name of an author or artist, or a title, and the search engine has no trouble recognizing the same product on many different sites.

Each of the search engines listed in Table 25-27 recognizes a different set of categories and searches them in a different way. Lycos Virtual Outlet and Bottom Dollar work by doing a keyword search. Excite Jango is a little more precise: Each product covered by Jango has its own set of specifications which you can choose from drop-down lists. In defining a search for a computer monitor, for example, you can specify any or all of: screen size, manufacturer, and model. And so, while you might find a product using Jango, Virtual Outlet works best when you have already found a product by browsing and you want to compare prices on that make and model.

Online Auctions

One of the more interesting and unique forms of online shopping is the online auction. Products are advertised on the auctioneer's site, and a schedule is given for beginning and ending the auction. Potential buyers submit bids, and the current high bids are displayed on the auction site. (If the seller is offering ten copies of the item, the top ten bids are displayed.) New bidders can submit higher bids, and old bidders can raise their bids. When the closing time passes and/or the length of time between new bids surpasses some set limit (the online equivalent of "going, going, gone"), the auction is closed, and the current high bidders have purchased the items for the prices they bid.

In order to submit a bid, you must register with the Web site and (usually) submit a credit card number. You then choose or are issued a user name and password, and can make a bid by clicking the New Bid button on a product-description page. No bid is valid until you OK it with your password. (This is a situation where you want the most the difficult password you can think of. See "Choosing User Names and Passwords" in Chapter 1.) If you have "won" the auction, you are notified by e-mail.

There are two forms of online auction. In the first, the merchandise is controlled by the Web site; you buy from the site, and the auction is just a method of determining price. OnSale (listed in Table 25-28) is essentially an auctioning department store, with a wide range of products and constant action. Surplus Auction is Egghead's way of getting rid of computer hardware and software that is about to go out of date.

The second kind of auction site is like an online flea market. The community of people who frequent the site buy and sell from each other, and the site itself takes no

eBay	http://www.ebay.com
Yahoo Auctions	http://auctions.yahoo.com
OnSale	http://www.onsale.com
Surplus Auction	http://www.surplusauction.com

Table 25-28.   *Online Auctioneers*

responsibility for the quality (or even the existence) of the products. Yahoo Auctions and eBay follow this model. Each site fosters the community spirit by providing chat space for people to talk about products and the auction experience. The eBay feedback process allows a buyer to comment on a seller after the transaction is completed, and allows a seller to build a verifiable reputation in the eBay online community.

Our hunch is that online auction is going to become a major fad before too long. Our list in Table 25-28 is far from complete, and no doubt new online auction houses have sprung up since we compiled it.

Researching a Product or a Merchant

Consumer World (listed in Table 25-29) is a nonprofit Web site whose purpose is to pull together the best consumer resources on the Web. It links to product reviews,

Compare.net	http://www.compare.net
CSS Bargain	http://consumer.checkbook.org/consumer/bargains/natl/bargtoc.htm
Consumer World	http://www.consumerworld.org
Consumer Guide	http://www.consumerguide.com
BizRate	http://www.bizrate.com
Better Business Bureau	http://www.bbb.org
Consumer Reports	http://www.consumerreports.org

Table 25-29.   *Consumer Resources on the Web Can Evaluate the Products You Buy Offline as Well as Online*

advice on how to shop for services, bargain search engines, consumer protection agencies, and government publications for consumers. Just about any consumer resource you might be looking for can be reached from Consumer World.

Use Compare.net to find products and compare features. The site's search engine gives you a list of products fitting the price range and specifications that you set. (Compare.net compares list prices, not actual retailer prices.) Then you can click any of the products listed to see more detailed information. If you are interested, add the product to your comparison list. When you have examined the listed products, another click sets up side-by-side comparisons of the features of the products on your comparison list. Compare.net generates a recommendation of where to buy the product, or you can input the product name into a bargain search engine to find the lowest online price.

Consumer Reports has a Web site, but most reports are available only to paying subscribers. Subscriptions are $24 a year or $3 a month. A free online product rating service is Consumer Guide. If you know what you are looking for and want to know what a good price for it would be, consult the bargains page of the Center for the Study of Services (CSS). They scan retail ads across the country to get their suggested prices.

If you want to know whether the online merchant you're thinking about dealing with is reputable, see if they have been rated by BizRate Guide. BizRate both surveys customers and has its staff shop a site, then rates the site on categories like price, easy of return, and customer service. You can also consult the Better Business Bureau for both online and offline merchants.

Online Coupons

Retailers now put coupons online and let you print out only the ones you want to use. Typically an online coupon site asks for your ZIP code and then presents a list of coupons that can be used in your area.

Table 25-30 lists a few online coupon sites. To find a larger list of coupon sites, start at Yahoo! and choose Business and Economy | Companies | Marketing | Advertising | Coupons.

Cool Savings	http://www.coolsavings.com
Valupage	http://www.valupage.com
Val-Pak	http://www.valpak.com

Table 25-30. *Sites Where You Can Print Out Coupons*

Computers and Internet

The Web can help you get news about computer and Internet developments, find places to download freeware or shareware for your computer, get online hardware or software support, or look for a new Internet service provider.

Computer and Internet News

The computer and Internet headlines that show up on the portals come mainly from either CNET or Ziff-Davis' ZDNet (listed in Table 25-31). Both cover technology news in depth, and have radio and TV coverage of technology news as well. Check the Business and Technology links at Broadcast.com. ZDTV and TechWeb News are short television news programs available as a preset video link on the RealPlayer program. For investment news about computer and Internet companies, go to Silicon Investor.

Downloading Shareware and Freeware

Much software can be downloaded for free on the Web. Some of it (like Netscape Communicator) actually *is* free—you can download it, install it, and use it as long as you like without owing anyone anything. Some freeware is only a demo for a program that has a price. For example, you can download demo versions of popular games like Tomb Raider. All these kinds of software are known as *freeware*. Other software can be downloaded free, but with the assumption that if you install it and keep it, you will send money to the person or company that made the software. This is called *shareware*.

Many libraries of shareware and freeware exist. The ones listed in Table 25-32 let you search for shareware and freeware either by name, type (for example, FTP or fax programs), or by category. ZDNet and TUCOWS (The Ultimate Collection of Winsock Software) rate software on a 1–5 star (or cow) system. CNET's Download.com includes any kind of downloadable software: shareware, freeware, and commercial software. It publishes reviews, tells you what is popular, and even rates the reliability of the download link. If you don't find what you want at Download.com, go to CNET's lower-rent software site, Shareware.com. The reviews and ratings are gone, but you get a wider selection. See Chapter 38 for how to download and install software.

CNET	http://cnet.com
ZD Network News	http://www.zdnet.com/zdnn
Silicon Investor	http://www.siliconinvestor.com

Table 25-31.   *Sources of News About Computers and the Internet*

CNET Download.com	**http://www.download.com**
CNET Shareware.com	**http://www.shareware.com**
ZDNet Software Library	**http://www.zdnet.com/swlib**
TUCOWS	**http://www.tucows.com**

Table 25-32.   *Where to Look for Shareware and Freeware*

Online Hardware and Software Support

Most hardware and software manufacturers have an FAQ on the Web. If you are having a common problem, you may be able to solve it from the FAQ. The URL of the manufacturer's Web site should be in your manual. If not, start at Yahoo!, choose Business and Economy | Companies | Computer, and look for the manufacturer.

Microsoft, for example, allows you to search the online Microsoft Knowledge Base. From the Microsoft home page (**http://www.microsoft.com**) click the Technical Support link. The first time you access technical support, you are asked to fill out a form to establish a profile and choose a password. Once you have a password, you can log in to Microsoft Support Online whenever you want.

Microsoft Support Online gives you several options for searching for the answers you need. You can search the Microsoft Knowledge Base by product name and keywords, consult FAQs on Microsoft products, download patches for problems if you know the patch you are looking for, access newsgroups on Microsoft products, or consult a Microsoft engineer by e-mail or on the telephone (which may cost you money).

Often you can get your question answered faster or cheaper by posting it to a Usenet newsgroup of users of the same product, rather than asking the manufacturer. Use your newsreader to search for newsgroups devoted to your product or your manufacturer (see Chapters 13 and 14).

Looking for an Internet Service Provider

If you're looking for a new Internet provider (Table 25-33), go to The List. ISPs are listed by area code within the United States or by country. Links from this page take you to the Web pages of ISPs where you can sign up for service. PC World has a similar service. Computer and Internet news sources like those in Table 25-31 frequently publish reviews of national ISPs.

The List	**http://thelist.internet.com**
PC World ISP search	**http://www.pcworld.com/interactive/isps**
The Internet Gurus' Finding an Internet Service Provider Page	**http://net.gurus.com/isp**

Table 25-33. *Information About Internet Service Providers*

Travel

The Web can help you decide what you want to see on your travels, plan your route, and even make your reservations. Online travel agents can show you a list of options for flights or lodging, or do a search to get you the best deal or the most convenient times or location.

Travel by Car

You can use the Web to help you plan your car trips. You can get maps off the Web—detailed, blown up maps that center on your destination and mark it with a star. Or you can have a Web site plan a route for you. You can check where the road construction is and what the weather forecasts are for the cities on your route. In major cities you can get traffic reports, and even call up a Web cam to show you key intersections.

Maps and Directions

If you know an address of any location in the United States, you can map the surrounding area to any scale and get text directions on how to get there from wherever you are. The portal sites listed in Table 25-1 all have their own map-and-direction services. They all work more or less the same way. Access the mapping tool from the portal home page by clicking on a link that has the word "map" in it somewhere. A form for specifying an address, city, or area code appears. When you submit the form, the portal returns a map. The destination is marked in some way, such as a star. Controls next to the map display allow you to ask for a different scale of map. You can usually find a Directions link on the same page that displays the map, or you can use a Directions link from the portal home page and skip getting a map.

Road Conditions and Traffic Reports

Find out where the major road construction projects are at Rand-McNally's Web site (see Table 25-34). Click the Road Construction button on their home page and then specify the city, state, or road, together with the time period (in months) that you want to check out. Rand-McNally also has a convenient weather feature: They generate a list

Rand-McNally	http://www.randmcnally.com
4 Traffic	http://www.4traffic.com
Traffic Spy	http://www.trafficspy.com
SmarTraveler	http://www.smartraveler.com

Table 25-34.   *Map, Traffic, and Road Construction Sites*

of cities along any major U.S. interstate highway (in the order that you pass them on the highway), and you can click any city on the list to get its forecast from The Weather Channel. It's a quick way to get an idea of the weather you are likely to run into during a long trip.

For traffic reports, go to 4 Traffic or Traffic Spy. Both sites collect links to local traffic reports from around the United States. The 4 Traffic site also contains links to other interesting sites like the WWW Speedtrap Registry (which provides state-by-state, city-by-city lists of speed traps and other violations that police are waiting for you to make).

The best local traffic reports we found were by SmarTraveler (which both 4 Traffic and Traffic Spy link to). Their Washington D.C. report lets you click a D.C. area map to get a traffic report on the road you want, while their Boston report is linked to Web cams that let you see for yourself how traffic is moving at key intersections.

Destinations

The Travel sections of most portals have destination guides that direct you to information about major tourist attractions. You can also find online destination guides at Rand-McNally's site, Lonely Planet, and Rough Guides (see Table 25-35). The main virtue of these guides is their links to the Web sites of tourist attractions, museums, public transportation systems, local sports teams, and events calendars. On Lonely

Tourism Offices Worldwide Directory	http://www.towd.com
Disney World	http://www.disney.com/DisneyWorld
Rough Guide to Travel	http://travel.roughguides.com
Lonely Planet Guides	http://www.lonelyplanet.com

Table 25-35.   *Web Sites for Planning What You Want to See*

Planet's Web site, you can access the feedback that they have received from travelers since the most recent printed editions of their guidebooks. The travel service Web sites in Table 25-35 also have resources for you to research a trip, including online destination guides.

Many tourist attractions have their own Web sites. Disney World, for example, has everything you need to plan your Orlando vacation, including making lodging reservations and buying your tickets in advance. We can't hope to list all the major tourist attractions; if you know what you are looking for, you should be able to find it through a search engine or Web directory. Another way to find Web sites of tourist attractions is to look them up at the local tourist bureau. A quick way to find the official tourist bureau of anyplace in the world is the Tourism Offices Worldwide Directory.

If you're trying to decide where to go today, you may be able to check out the view with a Web cam. The Empire State Building, the Kremlin, and the Eiffel Tower are just a few of the Web cam sites you can find through EarthCam, located at **http://www.earthcam.com**.

Reservations for Flights, Lodging, and Rental Cars

You can make reservations on the Web either by using online travel agents or by dealing directly with the Web sites of airlines, hotels, or car rental companies.

Online Travel Services

The Web allows you to be your own travel agent. The process works something like this: Go to the Web site of an online travel service like those listed in Table 25-36, and click a link indicating whether you are looking for a flight, lodging, or a rental car. You are given an appropriate form to fill out. For flights, you fill out a form like the one shown in Figure 25-7. Submit the form, and the site comes back with a list of possibilities and their costs. Looking at the possibilities may lead you to change your search. For example, you might want to see whether it is cheaper to leave or return at a

The Trip	http://www.thetrip.com
Travelocity	http://www.travelocity.com
Expedia	http://expedia.msn.com
Preview Travel	http://www.previewtravel.com
Priceline	http://www.priceline.com

Table 25-36. *Travel Agents on the Web*

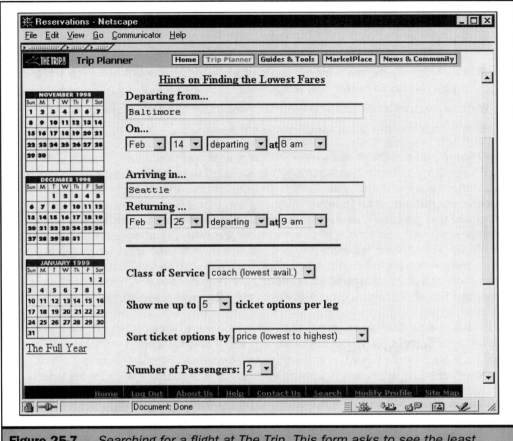

Figure 25-7. *Searching for a flight at The Trip. This form asks to see the least expensive round trip fares between Baltimore and Seattle, leaving Baltimore on the morning of February 14 and returning on the morning of February 25*

different time, to stay a day longer, or to fly out of a different airport. You can iterate this process as often as you like.

For lodging, each of the hotels or motels mentioned is linked to a description, possibly with a picture and/or map. Expedia (listed in Table 25-36) can display a local map next to a list of hotels; clicking a hotel on the list shows you its location on the map. You may also find a link to a Web site for that hotel or motel. For flights, you can click a link to see the restrictions on the tickets. Other information may be available to help you decide among your choices. Once you have made a decision, there may be more questions to answer, to specify the exact seat or room or car that you are reserving.

At this point in the process you have several options:

■ You can let the Web site remember the itinerary for you and go off to think about it.

■ You can try a different travel agent, or go to the airline or hotel Web site to see if you can find a better deal there.

■ You can make reservations with the possibility of canceling them later.

■ You can buy the tickets and have them sent to you.

At some point in the process the Web site wants you to register. Expedia doesn't let you do anything without registering, while some other travel Web sites let you gather information as a guest and only ask you to register if you want to make a reservation or have the site remember an itinerary. Registration is free in any case, and it has the advantage that you can create a travel profile: The Web site can remember than you like aisle seats and kosher meals, or nonsmoking rooms. Members get other advantages as well: On Travelocity, for example, you can use their fare watcher agent to keep an eye on the lowest quoted round-trip airfares between (up to five) pairs of cities. The current low fares are always listed on your Fare Watcher page. When fares change by more than $25, you are sent e-mail. Some of the other travel services have similar services.

Each of the portals is connected with an online travel service, which you can access by clicking a Travel link on the home page. Yahoo! and NetCenter use Travelocity, MSN uses Microsoft's Expedia, and Excite and Lycos use Preview Travel.

One interesting approach to getting good airfares is to make an offer for tickets through Priceline. The process works like this: You fill out a form on the Priceline site, saying where you want to go, what times and airports you are willing to accept, and how many stopovers you are willing to accept. Finally, you tell Priceline how much you want to pay and give them a credit card number. If they can find tickets at your price, they buy them with your credit card; otherwise, no transaction occurs. They send you e-mail within an hour to tell you what happened. The drawback to Priceline is that you can't shop around with it. If you don't like the airline or the timing of the flights—too bad.

 Before making your bid at Priceline, use Travelocity's Fare Watcher to check the lowest quoted fare between those cities. Even if you don't fulfill the conditions for the lowest fare, an airline may accept that price from Priceline.

Other Travel Resources

For most people most of the time, the best way to book your trip is through a travel service like those in Table 25-36. However, if you already know where you want to go and who you want to deal with, it might be faster to go straight to the Web site of that place or organization.

AIRLINES   Most of what you can do from an airline Web site can be done through one of the sites in Table 25-36. Occasionally, however, an airline posts an Internet special on its Web site and doesn't tell the travel agents about it. Also, airline Web sites are usually the best place to check flight arrival times, delays, and cancellations. Some discount airlines, most notably Southwest, don't appear in the flight databases that most travel agents use. If you want to check flights or prices or make reservations on these airlines, you have to use the airline Web site. Navigator's smart browsing feature recognizes the names of all the major airlines; just type the airline's name into the Location box. The airlines are also easy to find through search engines and Web directories.

BUS AND RAIL   The online travel services don't usually handle bus or rail travel; you have to use more specific Web sites. Amtrak lets you make reservations online, as well as examine fares and schedules. Greyhound's site shows you fares and schedules (for non-Greyhound lines as well), but doesn't appear to let you book online. Britain's National Express bus line does allow online booking. We didn't find any universal train-booking system like the one for airlines. You can find the national rail companies of many different countries from Yahoo! by choosing Business and Economy | Companies | Transportation | Trains and Railroads.

LODGING AND CAMPING   As with air travel, the travel services sites of Table 25-36 have lodging pretty well covered. If you just want a place to sleep at one of the standard, well-defined levels of luxury, you don't need to search through individual hotel or motel Web sites. If, however, you know exactly where you want to stay—particularly if it's the kind of unusual place that is hard to describe on a form—you might as well go straight to the Web site the place you want to stay. For example, any of the five treehouse stays that Yahoo! lists when you choose Business and Economy | Companies | Travel | Lodging | Treehouses might be hard to find at Travelocity or Expedia. We also doubt that the online travel services book a lot of RV park reservations. Try the RV Camping Directory site instead.

All the major hotel and motel chains have their own Web sites. You should have no trouble finding them through a Web directory, a search engine, or just guessing their URLs. Best Western, for example, is at **http://www.bestwestern.com**. Navigator's smart browsing feature recognizes most of the major chains, so you can just type a name into the Location box.

The online travel services are also not going to help you find a place to pitch your tent. To find a U.S. national park, discover what services are available there, download park maps, or find out how to reserve a campsite at the park, go to the National Park Service Web site (listed in Table 25-37). This Web site is a good place to gather information, and although the site mentioned the possibility, we could not find a way to make reservations online. The Park Service seems to prefer to do things over the phone. Your best bet to find state park information is to start at the Tourism Offices Worldwide Directory and work your way down. The TOWD is also a good place to start for finding camping options in countries other than the U.S.

Amtrak	**http://www.amtrak.com**
British Rail	**http://www.britrail.co.uk**
Greyhound	**http://www.greyhound.com**
National Express	**http://www.nationalexpress.co.uk**
U.S. National Park Service	**http://www.nps.gov**
RV Camping Directory	**http://www.rvpark.com**
Tourism Offices Worldwide Directory	**http://www.towd.com**

Table 25-37.   *Ways to Travel and Places to Stay That You Won't Find at Expedia*

Kids, Teens, Parents, and Communities

The Web is a great family resource. People at every stage of life can find Web sites that match their interests and abilities, and can get advice and support from others in similar life situations.

Much on the Web can keep kids amused on rainy days, including sites that are both interesting and educational. A child who develops an insatiable interest in dinosaurs or outer space or some other subject can find vast amounts of material, and can interact with other kids who share that interest. Teens can also find good educational sites, as well as ideas and resources for research projects. They can correspond with experts in their fields of interest, and can reach out to other teens to discuss music, games, or the unique issues of their age group.

For parents the Web has online versions of parenting magazines, expert advice on a wide range of family issues, and the support of other parents in online communities. Seniors can find the online companionship of other seniors, as well as a chance to share their experience with younger people. The Web provides resources for finding interesting and worthwhile activities after retirement, and for getting advice and support about the problems of aging.

Guides to the Best Web Sites For Kids

In the same way that the Yahoo! or Excite Web directory is a place to start looking for Web sites on any particular topic, Kids Web and Kids World 2000 (listed in Table 25-38) are places to start looking for kid-friendly Web sites on any particular topic.

Kids World 2000 (shown in Figure 25-8) and the Disney Internet Guide also list a number of good sites for kids, but they take a somewhat different approach than other kids sites: they are children's guides to the Web, not necessarily guides to children's

Yahooligans	http://www.yahooligans.com
Kids Web	http://www.npac.syr.edu/textbook/kidsweb
Disney Internet Guide	http://www.dig.com
Kids World 2000	http://now2000.com/kids

Table 25-38.   *Guides That Get Kids Started on the Web or Get You Started Looking for Kids' Web Sites*

Web sites. The Newspapers link on Yahooligans, for example, doesn't take you to children's newspapers, it takes you to newspapers like *The New York Times* and *The Washington Post*. The sites linked to Yahooligans and Disney Internet Guide have been checked by their respective staffs and judged to be safe for children. The Web is a web, though, and you can't assume that adults-only sites aren't three or four links away. Web directories for kids, shown in Table 25-38, are no substitute for adult supervision.

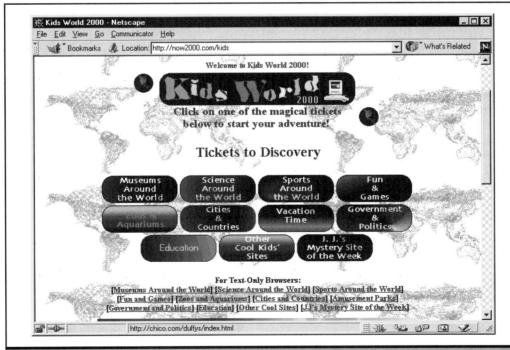

Figure 25-8.   *Kids World 2000 is a kids' guide to Web sites*

Education and Homework Help

One of the best sites for starting any investigation or research project is the Internet Public Library (**http://www.ipl.org**). From its home page are links to its youth and teen reading rooms. Also, look ahead at the education links in Tables 25-39 and 25-40.

The youth room of the Internet Public Library has a story hour. You can have the story read to you via RealPlayer, while each new "page" of the book appears on your screen.

World of Reading (listed in Table 25-39) is a Web site devoted to encouraging children to read. It lets children submit their own book reviews, and posts them after they have been reviewed by an adult. You can look up what children are reading in a wide range of categories, and see how they are reviewing it. The site also includes complete classic texts such as *20,000 Leagues Under the Sea* and *Alice in Wonderland*.

To find lists of the winners of the annual Newberry and Caldecott awards (for best book of children's literature and best children's picture book, respectively) go to the Web site of the Association for Library Service to Children (ALSC), which presents the awards. Click the Other Awards and Notables link to find the Penguin Putnam Books for Young Readers Award, the Coretta Scott King Award, Notable Children's Books, and Notable Children's Websites.

KidPub is a site where children can submit their stories to be published on the Web and (presumably) read by other children. A good place for educational games, including word games and math games, is FunBrain. For example, the site creates puzzles that hide words chosen by the kids in a matrix of letters.

Science and Mathematics Education

A lot has changed since the days when computers used in science and mathematics education were employed mainly as mechanical task masters in addition and multiplication drills. The Web sites listed in Table 25-40 allow a child to send questions to and receive answers from real scientists and mathematicians, find detailed instructions for reproducing the experiments they see on science TV shows, download free software for working with geometrical and other mathematical objects, find lesson plans for independent study, get help planning science fair projects, and compete with other children in designing their own science Web sites.

Children's Literature Web Guide	**http://www.acs.ucalgary.ca/~dkbrown**
World of Reading	**http://www.worldreading.org**
ALSC	**http://www.ala.org/alsc**
KidPub	**http://www.kidpub.org**
FunBrain	**http://www.funbrain.com**

Table 25-39. *Web Sites That Encourage Reading and Writing*

Math Forum	http://forum.swarthmore.edu
Mad Scientist Network	http://madsci.wustl.edu
Newton's Apple	http://ericir.syr.edu/Projects/Newton
Bill Nye the Science Guy	http://nyelabs.kcts.org
School House Rock	http://genxtvland.simplenet.com/SchoolHouseRock
From Mercury to Pluto	http://library.advanced.org/18188
The Nine Planets	http://www.seds.org/nineplanets/nineplanets
NASA Planetary Photojournal	http://photojournal.jpl.nasa.gov
North American Skies	http://www.webcom.com/safezone/NAS
The Tech 10	http://www.thetech.org/hype/tech10
ThinkQuest	http://www.thinkquest.org
The Weather Dude	http://www.nwlink.com/~wxdude

Table 25-40. *Web Sites Devoted to Science and Mathematics Education*

In addition to what it provides for children, the Web connects teachers and parents to the latest ideas in science education, and lets them easily communicate with each other about what works and what doesn't.

New science and math sites appear frequently. The Math Forum has a good set of links to other good mathematics sites. The Youth room at the Internet Public Library (**http://www.ipl.org**) has an excellent set of links to good science and mathematics sites. Also, take a look ahead at the museum Web sites in Table 25-41, and check out the CRC Concise Encyclopedia of Mathematics at the following site:

http://www.astro.virginia.edu/~eww6n/math/math0.html

THE MATH FORUM The Math Forum was created by the National Science Foundation and Swarthmore College to be a center where people interested in mathematics and the teaching of mathematics could share ideas. Math students at every level can find something of use here: online lessons in a variety of mathematical subjects, interesting challenge problems at many levels of difficulty, discussions of the role of mathematics and mathematical educators in society, a guide to the mathematical resources of the Web, organized by grade level and topic, a guide to mathematical software available either free on the Web or for sale from a vendor, and "Ask Dr. Math," an opportunity for K-12 students to ask questions of real mathematicians, together with an archive of past questions and answers.

SUPPLEMENTS TO SCIENCE TV SHOWS   *Newton's Apple* is a science education series on PBS. Teacher's guides to episodes from the last several seasons are available online. *Bill Nye the Science Guy* has his Nye Labs Online—episode guides are arranged by subject. *School House Rock* also has its online equivalent; check out the Science Rock link.

MAD SCIENTIST NETWORK   The Mad Scientist Network collects science questions from kids of all ages and distributes them to scientists for answers. Answers may take several weeks to arrive, as the Mad Scientist Network does not have mad scientists waiting by the phone. Even if you don't have a specific question in mind, you can cruise the archives to look at previous questions and answers, or look at the queue of questions that are waiting for answers. (A good science project for older children and adults is to try to answer the questions in the queue; when the scientist's answer arrives you can see how well you did.)

The Mad Scientist site has a set of links to other ask-a-scientist sites. Also the Mad Scientist Library is a good guide to the Web's science and science education resources, including information about careers in science. MAD Labs is a collection of home science experiments—some of which have edible results. Click the MAD Labs link on the Mad Scientist Network home page to get started.

ASTRONOMY   Astronomy is the most photogenic of the sciences, so it makes for impressive Web sites. A very nice multimedia introduction to the planets, complete with their images, a history of human knowledge about them, and the mythology connected with them, is available at The Nine Planets. NASA's Planetary Photojournal is a collection of more than a thousand space images.

Perhaps the best of the educational astronomy sites is From Mercury to Pluto, put together by two high school students as a ThinkQuest project. It has an attractive interface, beautiful images, and well-communicated information that hasn't been dumbed down for children. If you just want to take your kids outside at night and show them the stars, get a current month's star map from North American Skies.

LINKS TO OTHER SCIENCE SITES   Every month the Tech Museum of Innovation chooses and reviews ten technology Web sites usable by middle school students. Archives of past winners give you hundreds of technology education sites to choose from.

Some of the most interesting educational Web sites are being created by high school students participating in the ThinkQuest contest. Look at the ThinkQuest site to find archives of recent winners, including the From Mercury to Pluto site that we discussed in the Astronomy section.

One interesting place to learn meteorology is from the Weather Dude, a musical TV weather man from Seattle.

Museum Web Sites

The major museum Web sites, shown in Table 25-41, are very good about referencing each other. If you find one good museum site, it should lead you to the others. The most complete list of museum sites we've found is from Kids World. Click the Museums Around the World button on the home page.

Kids World 2000	**http://now2000.com/kids**
Smithsonian Institution	**http://www.si.edu**
San Francisco Exploratorium	**http://www.exploratorium.edu**
Tech Museum of Innovation	**http://www.thetech.org**

Table 25-41.   *A Few of the Innovative Museums on the Web*

Don't miss the San Francisco Exploratorium site. It uses some of the most recent browser technology to create the same kind of "hands-on" exhibits that you expect from a good science museum. In the Changing Illusions exhibit, for example, online users turn dials to change what they see—and fall for the illusions.

Other Sites for Kids

Some other kids' sites we found don't fit into any of the other categories (see Table 25-42). What could be more interesting to kids than a Web site devoted to bugs, worms, farts, and any other yucky subject that comes up? That's the idea behind The Yuckiest Site on the Internet. Play yucky games, send yucky e-mail cards, cook up yucky recipes, and find out the answers to yucky questions.

For more dignified amusement, *The Knowledge Adventure Encyclopedia* is online. Look up a particular subject, or just browse.

It sounds like a joke, but the CIA really does have a home page for kids. Your child can get the official word on what the intelligence business is about, or learn about the CIA's Canine Corps.

Sports Illustrated's SI For Kids site provides child-accessible sports reporting. The Shorter Reporter feature has short articles with large type written with a grade-school reading vocabulary. SI For Kids drops much of the heaviness of regular sports coverage—no stories about athletes' drug problems, gambling, or spousal abuse. It includes some enjoyable, less serious features like Funny Photo, where you are invited to submit your own captions for amusing sports photos.

The Yuckiest Site on the Internet	**http://www.yucky.com**
Knowledge Adventure Encyclopedia	**http://www.letsfindout.com**
CIA Kids Page	**http://www.odci.gov/cia/ciakids**
SI For Kids	**http://www.sikids.com**

Table 25-42.   *Kids' Web Sites That Didn't Fit into the Other Categories*

Teen Web Sites

More Web sites are for and by teen-agers than we can characterize, much less list. As with so many other subjects, a good place to start looking for Web sites for teens is the Internet Public Library (**http://www.ipl.org**); its Teen Room is a jumping-off point to good sites for teens in a variety of areas.

Adolescence Directory Online (ADOL, listed in Table 25-43) is a guide to adolescent issues constructed by the Center for Adolescent Studies at the University of Indiana. The site provides a lot of resources on teen health and mental health issues, and has a good collection of links on its Teens Only page.

National Public Radio's "Teen Diaries" series has transcripts on the Web.

The Student Center is an online community for teen-agers and young adults. They don't check IDs or make you lie about your age if you're older, but their intended clientele is clearly defined. The Student Center offers free e-mail, a free home page (and a very simple wizard for constructing that page), a chat room, and a chance to write your own movie reviews. One advantage for the Student Center over other online communities: the home pages are free of advertising.

Bolt Reporter is the high school newspaper of the Internet. It is a commercial Web publication (with advertising) whose content is by and for teen-agers and young adults. The news, information, and editorial articles in Bolt just get the ball rolling. The real action on the site is in the reader responses and online chats. A word of warning: the teens talk bluntly and explicitly about the issues in their lives, including sex and drugs; you may want to keep younger children away from this site.

Some of the best resource sites are put together by the people who need them. Matt Rodbard assembled all the Web sites that were useful to him in the process of picking a college, getting admitted, and looking for financial aid. The result is Matt's College Admissions Reference Page.

ADOL	**http://education.indiana.edu/cas/adol/adol.html**
Matt's College Admissions Reference	**http://members.tripod.com/~BenoitC**
Bolt Reporter	**http://www.bolt.com**
The Student Center	**http://studentcenter.org**
NPR's Teen Diaries	**http://www.well.com/user/jkr**

Table 25-43.   *Web Sites for Teens*

Portal sites (see Table 25-1) and online communities (see Table 25-46) both house many message boards and chat rooms where teens can meet each other and discuss adolescent issues.

Parenting Support and Advice

Parent Soup (listed in Table 25-44) is the premier online community for parents. Last time we checked, there were more than 200 message boards on every conceivable parenting topic. The site also offers chats with other parents, regular articles on topics of interest to parents, and online experts to answer your questions in such areas as pediatrics and child development. Parent Soup is part of the iVillage online community. See the upcoming section "Online Communities and Home Pages."

Parent Time is the central site for the parenting magazines in the Time-Warner stable, including *Parenting* and *Baby Talk*. The site has resources beyond what is in the magazines, including an Ask an Expert feature with a wide range of subjects.

Clubs and message boards provide a place for parents to support each other and discuss experiences. Yahoo Clubs had 60 clubs and three message boards in the Parenting category when we checked. Excite had 36 clubs and seven parenting message boards. (Excite's parenting topic is hidden under the Lifestyles category.) Other portals have parenting message boards as well. The number of parenting chats varies, but has similar popularity. The topics of the clubs, boards, and chats range from general parenting discussions to those for parents with a special interest, such as single parents or the parents of twins.

The Department of Education's Publications for Parents page has links to complete texts of a number of publications, including the *Helping Your Child Learn ...* series that covers many school subjects. The Education Resources Information Center (ERIC) sponsors a series of resource pages, many of which are of interest to parents, especially the National Parent Information Network and AskERIC, a service that promises to answer education questions via e-mail in two business days.

Parent Soup	http://www.parentsoup.com
Parent Time	http://www.pathfinder.com/ParentTime
Baby Place	http://www.baby-place.com
Publications for Parents	http://www.ed.gov/pubs/parents
ERIC	http://www.accesseric.org:81

Table 25-44.   *Web Sites for Parents*

New or expectant parents should check out the resources at the Baby Place. The site's links deal with pregnancy and childbirth as well as infant care. Parents of teens can benefit from Adolescence Directory Online (ADOL, described in "Teen Web Sites," earlier in this chapter).

Web Sites for Seniors

The AARP has estimated that about 3 million of its members have home computers. A number of Web sites, including those in Table 25-45, target this large and growing market. The AARP's Internet Guide has a good collection of references not just to Web sites, but to mailing lists, newsgroups, and electronic magazines of interest to seniors. If you want to research an age-related issue, start on the AARP's home page and click the Get Answers link.

SeniorNet is a nonprofit group whose purpose is to educate seniors about computers and the Internet. Their site contains an active bulletin board community discussing a wide range of issues—not just computers or aging. An all-around reference page for seniors is Seniors-Site. Research a subject or discuss it with other seniors.

Each of the portals and online communities listed in Table 25-46, in the next section, has a number of message boards or clubs for seniors.

Online Communities and Home Pages

In addition to the communities that gather around the chats, message boards, and games offered by the portals, Web sites exist solely for the purpose of establishing virtual community (see Table 25-46). They offer message boards, chats, articles, and free e-mail accounts and home pages for people of all ages and interests.

The main resource of an online community is the people who participate in it. Each of the major online communities has its own flavor. The best way to figure out where you belong is to stop by and use some of the message boards and chat rooms. Except for the Well, you can join the communities in Table 25-46 for free. And even if you don't feel like registering, you can log in as a guest and use some of the chat rooms.

AARP	**http://www.aarp.org**
AARP Internet Guide	**http://www.aarp.org/cyber/guide1.htm**
Seniors-Site	**http://seniors-site.com**
SeniorNet	**http://www.seniornet.org**

Table 25-45. *Web Sites for Seniors*

IVillage	http://www.ivillage.com
GeoCities	http://www.geocities.com
The Well	http://www.thewell.com
Talk City	http://www.talkcity.com

Table 25-46.   *Online Communities*

Health and Medicine

The Web gives you free access to a level of medical information that used to require an expensive library: detailed medical news, abstracts of current medical journal articles, dictionaries of medical terms, first aid information, descriptions of standard drugs, tests, and procedures, and discussion forums where you can meet others with similar medical problems or interests. Table 25-47 shows addresses of sites with medical information.

Chances are your online source for news headlines has medical news headlines as well, so that you can keep track of major medical advances through Yahoo Health or CNN.

An excellent all-around medical site is Medscape, which includes not only an outstanding range of medical news coverage, but also provides a search engine for finding medical journal articles, plus basic medical references like a medical dictionary and drug handbook. America's Health Network is a cable-TV network devoted to

Medscape	http://www.medscape.com
Healthfinder	http://www.healthfinder.gov
National Health Information Service	http://nhic-nt.health.org
MedicineNet	http://www.medicinenet.com
America's Health Network	http://www.ahn.com
University of Iowa Virtual Hospital	http://www.vh.org
New England Journal of Medicine	http://www.nejm.org

Table 25-47.   *Medical News, Reference, and Research*

health. Its home page provides a good collection of health news and resource links. In addition, you can watch the network live in streaming video.

Another great place to start in searching for health and medicine information is Healthfinder, a service of the U.S. Department of Health and Human Services. Healthfinder is meant to be a clearing house for government health information. From here you can find your way to the appropriate government health Web site or online publication. The Health Media Online link from Healthfinder's home page takes you to a set of links to health news sites on commercial media sites.

The National Health Information Service maintains the Searchable Health Information Resource Database, which directs you to the government organizations who have online information relevant to your search request.

MedicineNet is a network of doctors and other health professionals whose mission (according to their Web page) is "to provide the public with current, comprehensive medical information, written in easy to understand language." The site is organized into the following categories: diseases and treatments, procedures and tests, pharmacy, medical dictionary, first aid, and poison control centers. Each category organizes topics alphabetically, like an encyclopedia. Another source of detailed online information for both patients and physicians is the Virtual Hospital of the University of Iowa.

Many of the most influential medical journals are available online. Yahoo! lists more than 100 medical journal home pages: choose Health | Medicine | Journals. For example, *The New England Journal of Medicine* makes abstracts of articles and some commentary available for free on its Web site, with the full text of the articles available to subscribers. The free portions include almost everything a non-specialist would be interested in, including the ability to search for abstracts of archived articles.

Religion and Spirituality

The Web provides unprecedented access to a wide variety of religious points of view, from ancient texts to chats with current practitioners. You can use the Web to learn about religions, to help you find a church, or to discuss religious issues in an online community.

Learning About Religions

From Yahoo!, choose Society and Culture | Religion and Spirituality | Faiths and Practices to see links to more than 15,000 sites—which gives you some idea of the variety of religions that are represented on the Web. Of these sites, about 10,000 are Christian and another thousand or so are Jewish. Other religions are less well represented, but even some fairly obscure religions have 10 to 20 Web sites.

The virtue of this amazing proliferation is that you can explore almost any point of view from the inside; the problem is to sort through it all. Many of these sites are sectarian and argumentative, but some do an excellent job of assembling links that let the world's religions and sacred texts speak for themselves.

Descriptions of Religious Beliefs and Practices

The Mining Company (**http://miningco.com**) does a good job of collecting material about world religions in its Culture and Beliefs category. The Mining Company's *modus operandi* is to appoint expert guides who give an overview of a subject and assemble pages of links to guide you through the relevant Web resources. The following religions have their own expert guides at the Mining Company: agnosticism/atheism, Buddhism, Catholicism, Protestantism, Latter Day Saints, Hinduism, Judaism, and pagan/wiccan. Everything else is lumped into the "alternative religion" category— hardly encouraging, but once you get over having your faith tossed into the same bin with satanism and voodoo, you'll have to admit that the alternative religion guide does a good, respectful job. You can still find a good set of references on Taoism—it just takes one extra click to get there.

Another good source of links on a variety of religions is Kaleidoreligion (listed in Table 25-48). This site includes an excellent collection of religious art from around the world.

If you want to look deeper into a religion's beliefs and how its history fits into religious history in general, go to the Ontario Consultants for Religious Tolerance (OCRT) Web site. The point of this site is to provide an unbiased source for information about the religions of the world—perhaps in the belief that there would be more religious tolerance if people understood each other better.

Many religions have their own Usenet newsgroup under the **soc.religion** heading. You can learn the basics about the religion by reading the FAQ of the newsgroup. FAQs are available on the Web at the International FAQ Consortium.

Online Religious Texts and Scriptures

The Web makes available a wide range of writings from the religions of the world. The best single jumping-off point we could find was Sacred and Religious Texts, where you

OCRT	**http://www.religioustolerance.org**
Kaleidoreligion	**http://www.intersatx.net/people/curry/gkaleid.htm**
Sacred and Religious Texts	**http://webpages.marshall.edu/~wiley6**
David Washburn's site	**http://www.nyx.net/~dwashbur**
Christian Research	**http://www.integrityonline.com/cenos**
International FAQ Consortium	**http://www.faqs.org/faqs**

Table 25-48.   *Web Sites for Learning About Religions and Studying Religious Texts*

can find links to the *Koran*, the *Book of Mormon*, the *Bhagavad Gita*, and other sacred texts from around the world. The selection of Christian classics is particularly rich, including links to several collections of writings from early and medieval Christian authors.

Biblical scholarship is particularly well represented on the Web. David Washburn has put together a great collection of resources for anyone interested in the original languages and texts of the Bible, and how they get translated into English. Another compendium of scholarly resources on the Bible is Christian Research.

Finding a Nearby Church, Temple, or Synagogue

If you are thinking of attending a new church, or thinking about moving somewhere and wondering what kind of religious community you might find there, you can learn a lot from looking at a church's Web page. At the very least you should be able to find an address, directions, and times for services. You may also find a mission statement, references to the institution's beliefs or philosophy, texts of recent sermons, or a schedule of weekly events. Some churches have online discussion groups or mailing lists that you could join. By the time you make your first appearance at a service, you may have made several friends online.

If you are looking for a church that is part of a larger denomination, you can look for the denomination's Web page, and hope to link from there to a local congregation. Or you can use a Web directory. For example, you could find the Web page of Temple Isaiah in Lexington, Massachusetts in Yahoo! either by choosing Regional | U.S. States | Massachusetts | Cities | Lexington | Community | Religion or by choosing Society and Culture | Religion and Spirituality | Faiths and Practices | Judaism | Congregations | Reform.

Online Spiritual Community

Spiritual and religious discussions happen in every kind of Internet setting: newsgroups, mailing lists, chat rooms, message boards, or clubs. If you participate in chats or message boards at a portal or online community, you can find a Religion category in which to look for specific rooms or boards.

When we last checked the Yahoo Clubs, for example, more than 1,600 had been established in the Religion and Beliefs section, ranging from Christian Teens to Desert Wind Virtual Coven. The most popular of these clubs had more than 400 members. Excite had almost 400 communities under Religion and Beliefs.

Look for religious Usenet newsgroups in the **soc.religion** newsgroup category. Mailing lists are a little harder to find, but you might read about one on a church, denomination, or other religious organization's Web page, or search the Liszt Web site (**http://www.liszt.com**).

The Web as Library

The two most useful libraries on the Web could hardly be more different. The Library of Congress (listed in Table 25-49) was founded in 1800 and has a massive building on the Mall in Washington D.C. The Internet Public Library began in 1995 as a graduate

| Library of Congress | http://www.loc.gov |
| Internet Public Library | http://www.ipl.org |

Table 25-49.   *Useful Libraries on the Web*

students' project in the University of Michigan School of Information and continues as a nonprofit organization with an annual budget of about $100,000. Between the two of them, they cover the two central virtues of a library: the Library of Congress strives for completeness, while the Internet Public Library is selective. Most of the library resources you actually need can be reached from either site, but you can find them much more easily at the Internet Public Library.

If you are a student at a university, your university library may be able to give you access to copyrighted resources (such as the *Encyclopedia Britannica*) that it cannot make available over the Web as a whole. Consequently, you should check your university library site first.

The Library of Congress site has a great set of links to other library Web sites. Go to the bottom of its home page and choose Explore the Internet from the Research Tools drop-down list. From the Topical Guides list, find a list of Library and Information Science Resources on the Web. From this page you can get to almost any other library on the Web.

Standard References

The Web can replace a full shelf of standard references: dictionary, thesaurus, encyclopedia, quotation book, telephone directory, almanac, biographical dictionary, and style manual.

Dictionaries and Thesauri

An online dictionary or thesaurus is a handy tool, especially if you do your writing on a computer. A particular advantage of online dictionaries and thesauri is that links allow you to jump quickly from one word to another. If you don't understand one of the words used in a definition, chances are that one click takes you to the definition of that word.

Some portal sites have dictionaries, but the best single dictionary/thesaurus combination we've found on the Web is the Merriam-Webster site (see Table 25-50). Typical of a number of online dictionaries, Merriam-Webster's WWWebster Dictionary gives you a window into which to type the word or partial word that you want to look up. It returns definitions of the word or words that match your input; the significant words in the definitions are linked to their own definitions.

Merriam-Webster	http://www.m-w.com
Roget's Thesaurus	http://thesaurus.com
OneLook	http://www.onelook.com
Dictionary.com	http://www.dictionary.com
Hypertext Webster Gateway	http://work.ucsd.edu:5141/cgi-bin/http_webster

Table 25-50.   *Online Dictionaries and Thesauri*

The WWWebster Thesaurus works similarly. Roget's Thesaurus is also online and has a similar interface to the WWWebster Thesaurus.

But why restrict yourself to one dictionary when you can look at dozens of them? Input a word into the window on the OneLook Dictionaries home page and get back a list of the online dictionaries that have definitions of it, with links to their definitions. Another combination of online dictionaries is Dictionary.com.

The OneLook dictionary list (accessible by clicking Browse Dictionary List at the bottom of the OneLook home page) is itself an excellent resource for finding links to specialized online dictionaries, including medical dictionaries, slang dictionaries, and dictionaries of computer terms. *The Dictionary of Phrase and Fable*, 1894 edition, is an especially interesting one to browse.

The Hypertext Webster Gateway is a heavily hypertexted version of the 1913 *Webster's Unabridged Dictionary* (conveniently out of copyright). Some university library Web sites have limited licenses for the online version of *The Oxford English Dictionary*. If you access the Web site from within the university computer system, you can use the dictionary; otherwise your request is denied. Check your library Web site to see if it allows access.

Encyclopedias

The Microsoft portal MSN.com provides a link to Encarta Concise, a free condensed version of Microsoft's Encarta encyclopedia. You can also sign up for a free trial of Encarta Online Deluxe (listed in Table 25-51), which is available by subscription. An even more advanced subscription option is the Encarta Online Library, including Encarta as well as other online references, for $60 per year or $10 per month.

The Columbia Encyclopedia can be searched for free from the home page of Information Please, and an earlier version can be searched at Encyclopedia.com.

For a subscription fee, you can access the full Encyclopedia Britannica online. The fee is rather modest when you consider the cost of buying an encyclopedia: either $5 a month, or $50 for the first year and $40 per year thereafter. If you are accessing the

Encyclopedia Britannica	http://www.eb.com
Columbia Encyclopedia	http://www.infoplease.com
Encyclopedia.com	http://encyclopedia.com
Encarta	http://www.encarta.msn.com
Encyberpedia	http://www.encyberpedia.com
CRC Concise Encyclopedia of Mathematics	http://www.astro.virginia.edu/~eww6n/math/math0.html

Table 25-51.   *Encyclopedias on the Web*

Internet through a university system, the university library may have a site license for the Britannica, so that you can access it for free through the library Web site.

Encyberpedia is a cross between an encyclopedia and a Web directory. They didn't write the entries themselves, but they have found very good references to link together.

A variety of specialized encyclopedias are online. Just about any mathematical fact you might want to know is contained in the CRC Concise Encyclopedia of Mathematics, for example. Look for other specialized encyclopedia by starting at Yahoo! and choosing Reference | Encyclopedia.

Telephone and E-mail Directories

Just about any portal has a people-finder utility for looking up phone numbers and/or e-mail addresses. Our favorite is at Excite: From the Excite home page click Reference; then choose from an address-and-phone look-up utility, an e-mail address finder, business yellow pages, and a reverse telephone directory (which tells you who is at a given phone number).

Other Online References

Every reference shelf needs an almanac to answer those questions that are too specific or ephemeral for an encyclopedia, but not quite current enough to be in a recent newspaper or magazine. The Web has the *Information Please Almanac* (see Table 25-52), which is the perfect place to turn if you want to know whether Philadelphia is bigger than Houston, what language they speak in Uganda, or how many times Bjorn Borg won at Wimbledon. (If, on the other hand, you just want to know who Bjorn Borg is, use the biographical dictionary at Biography.com.)

If you specifically want political information, like the names of the seven parishes of Andorra or a list of all the members of the House Judiciary Committee, then you want the *Almanac of Politics and Government* (**http://www.polysci.com**). For concise

Bartlett's Familiar Quotations	**http://www.columbia.edu/acis/bartleby/bartlett**
Information Please Almanac	**http://www.infoplease.com**
CIA World Fact Book	**http://www.odci.gov/cia/publications/factbook**
Elements of Style	**http://www.cc.columbia.edu/acis/bartleby/strunk**
Newspaper Archives on the Web	**http://sunsite.unc.edu/slanews/internet/archives**
Biography.com	**http://www.biography.com**

Table 25-52.   *Other Reference Texts Online*

country-by-country economic, political, ethnic, and strategic information, go to the CIA's *World Fact Book*. If you were wondering how many telephones there are in Afghanistan, the CIA knows and can tell you.

Many newspapers keep archives on the Web, but you should not expect as much out of them as you do from, say, microfiche at the library. Web archives typically only cover the years during which the newspaper has had a Web edition, so the pickings are slim prior to 1995, and nonexistent before 1990. Newspaper archives on the Web are typically not free, even if the current Web edition of the newspaper is. You should expect to pay $1–2 per article, though you should be able to get a list of headlines for free. The Newspaper Archives on the Web site given in Table 25-52 shows a table of newspaper Web sites, the dates for which archives are available, and the price per article. Click the name of the newspaper to go to its archive.

The classic reference for proper English composition, Strunk's *Elements of Style*, is available in its 1918 edition, or you can check the 1901 edition of *Barlett's Familiar Quotations*.

Complete Texts of Classic Books

Once a work's copyright runs out, it can legally be displayed by any Web site that wants to do so. You can download the complete text of many classic books, plays, and poems. (For religious texts, see "Online Religious Texts and Scriptures" earlier in this chapter.)

The best place to begin a search for a book is a library, in this case either the Library of Congress or the Internet Public Library (**http://www.ipl.org**), which maintains at a list of links to Web sites that offer electronic texts, such as those in Table 25-53. Another approach is to search the Literature section of a Web directory like Yahoo! for a title or an author.

Library of Congress Etext Links	http://lcweb.loc.gov/global/etext
Project Gutenberg	http://promo.net/pg
Electronic Text Center	http://etext.lib.virginia.edu
Bibliomania	http://www.bibliomania.com

Table 25-53.   *Sites Containing Complete Texts of Classic Books*

Searching Library Collections

You can search the catalogs of many libraries from a single Web site. A large number of research and public libraries have implemented a standard protocol (Z39.50) that makes it possible for one library's computer to search another library's catalog even if their catalogs are set up differently. A list of these libraries is maintained at the Library of Congress Web site (**http://www.loc.gov**); from the LOC home page, select Access to Catalogs at Other Libraries from the drop-down list under Research Tools; then click the Go button. Choose a library from the list, fill out that library's search form, and click the Submit button.

Information About the U.S. Government

One of the best starting places for finding U.S. government information of any kind is the *Almanac of Politics and Government* (listed in Table 25-54). In its executive branch summary you'll find department-by-department profiles with lists of significant Web pages.

Almanac of Politics and Government	http://www.polysci.com
C-SPAN	http://c-span.org
Project Vote Smart	http://www.vote-smart.org
CQ American Voter	http://voter.cq.com
CQ VoteWatch	http://pathfinder.com/CQ
Center for Responsive Politics	http://www.crp.org
Electronic Activist	http://gemini.berkshire.net/~ifas/activist

Table 25-54.   *Web Sites for Political and Voter Information*

Keep track of your congressman's voting record either at the C-SPAN Web site or at Congressional Quarterly's VoteWatch. From the C-SPAN home page, choose Congressional Votes Library from the drop-down list. You can track votes either by member, by month, or by subject. From a member's voting record, a single click takes you to the full text of the bill or resolution voted on. VoteWatch works in a similar manner. Congressional Quarterly (**http://voter.cq.com**) also lets you rate your representative on its American Voter site by quizzing you on significant congressional votes and comparing your answers to your representative's.

Keep your eye on where the money for political campaigns is coming from at the Center for Responsive Politics.

Project Vote Smart bills itself as "Your one stop for political information on the World Wide Web." The site includes biographies, voting records, and positions of all members of Congress and other major elected officials, as well as their major challengers in election years. In addition, it provides summaries of issues and links to sites representing diverse points of view. The site is an excellent resource for forming your own point of view on major issues and determining what candidates best represent that point of view.

Another Web site devoted to citizen involvement in the political process is the Electronic Activist. On this site you can find e-mail addresses of members of congress and state elected officials.

Information from the U.S. Government

The central U.S. government Web site is FedWorld, listed in Table 25-55 and shown in Figure 25-9. Its home page has several drop-down lists that send you quickly to the most popular government Web sites. The White House provides the Interactive Citizens' Handbook, which is another good jumping-off point. The central location for information relating to Congress is the Congress' own Thomas Web site.

Department of Commerce	http://www.doc.gov
Federal Reserve Board	http://www.bog.frb.fed.us
FedWorld	http://www.fedworld.gov
Interactive Citizen's Handbook	http://www.whitehouse.gov/WH/html/handbook.html
Internal Revenue Service	http://www.irs.ustreas.gov
Office of Management and Budget	http://www.whitehouse.gov/WH/EOP/OMB/html/ombhome.html
Thomas	http://thomas.loc.gov

Table 25-55.   *Guides to Federal Government Resources on the Web*

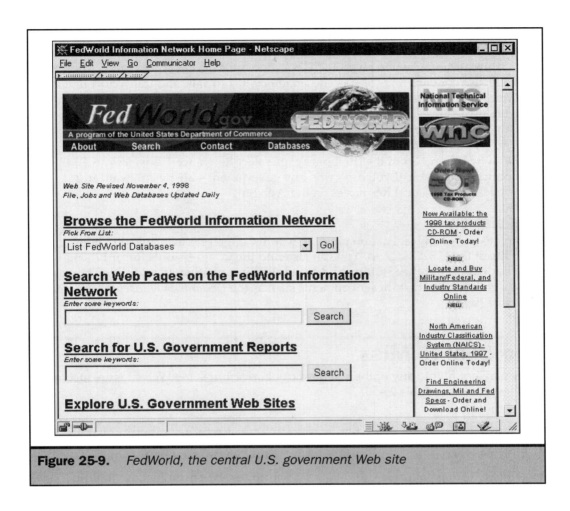

Figure 25-9.   *FedWorld, the central U.S. government Web site*

Tax Forms

The IRS keeps its tax forms and instructions online, so you can always find the form you
need. You can also get to this site from FedWorld: choose Tax Forms and Instructions from
the drop-down list under Browse the FedWorld Information Network.

The IRS maintains a handy list of links to Web sites that offer state tax forms in the
various states. You can access this list from the Tax Forms and Instructions page
mentioned previously.

Government Statistics

The Economics and Statistics Administration is the Department of Commerce office
that oversees both the Bureau of the Census and the Bureau of Economic Analysis, both

sources of voluminous statistical information. The ESA compiles STAT-USA, using statistics from many government agencies.

A source of information about the U.S. economy is the Federal Reserve. The Fed's Web site also contains texts of speeches made by its officials, and transcripts of the Chairman's regular testimony before Congress. Another source of current economic statistics is the Bureau of Labor Statistics. Information about the federal budget is available from the Office of Management and Budget.

You can link to any of these sites from the Internet Public Library, located at **http://www.ipl.org**. From the IPL home page select Reference | Business and Economics | Statistics. If you can't find any government statistic you want from there, click the Statistical Resources on the Web link.

Legislation

Complete text of any legislation pending before Congress is available on Thomas, the Web site of the U.S. Congress. You can also find the Congressional Record there, together with committee staffing and scheduling information. In addition, Thomas hosts a collection of historical documents such as the *Declaration of Independence* and *The Federalist Papers*.

Too Cool to Miss

They may not fit into any of the standard categories, but some Web sites are just too cool to ignore: see Table 25-56.

TerraServer	**http://www.terraserver.com**
Hubble Fantasy Worlds	**http://www.enconnect.net/jdeline**
The Fractal Microscope	**http://www.ncsa.uiuc.edu/Edu/Fractal**
Fractal Archive	**http://fractal.mta.ca/cnam/fractals**
Mind-It	**http://mindit.netmind.com**
Around the World in 80 Clicks	**http://www.steveweb.com/80clicks**
BaddGrrl's CAM-O-RAMA	**http://www.baddgrrl.com/CamORama**
EarthCam	**http://www.earthcam.com**

Table 25-56. *Fantastic but Uncategorizable Sites*

TerraServer

The TerraServer database contains satellite images covering much of the land area of the Earth. Most of the images are several years old, but you probably won't notice—the view hasn't changed all that much since then.

The TerraServer home page starts with a world map and lets you zoom in until you find the location and scale you want. You can look at the Great Wall in its entirety from space, or pick out your house. (You should be able to tell if a car was in the driveway when the satellite went over.) The quantity of data is measured in terrabytes, and Microsoft is using the site to demonstrate its servers' ability to handle large databases—but who cares? The fun thing is what you can see, not how they do it. Click the Famous Places list in the left column and go to the pyramids.

Hubble Fantasy Worlds

Graphic artist Jim DeLine applies the following formula: Start with a particularly striking image from the Hubble space telescope, then use your imagination to create a fantasy world from which the night sky looks that way to the naked eye. He tried this idea about 40 times and came up with some fabulous results.

The Fractal Microscope

The Fractal Microscope lets you start with a fractal image like the Mandelbrot set and keep zooming in on whatever part seems most interesting. The infinite detail of a fractal ensures that you never run out of new sights to discover. Also check out the archive of fractal images. If you find an image you like and are using Navigator on a Windows system, just right-click and choose Set as Wallpaper from the context menu.

Mind-It

Some Web pages don't change very often, but you want to know about it when they do. Maybe you want to know when your sister puts new pictures of your nephews on her Web page, or when the new schedule for the high school football team comes out. You don't have to waste a lot of time checking these pages; you can get Mind-It to do it for you, and send you e-mail when something changes.

Mind-It supports itself by sending you advertising in the e-mails you get from it. But it promises only to send e-mails related to your requests, and never to send e-mails that are just advertising, or to give your e-mail address out to other advertisers.

Web Cams

The Web cam is a simple idea: You set up a video camera somewhere, and periodically upload its picture to a Web site. Enough people have done it that you can check out the current view from all sorts of places. Our favorite Web cam site is Around the World in 80 Clicks, a compendium of 80 Web cams from around the world. You never quite know what you're going to see next. Maybe your next stop is the Eiffel Tower or the Kremlin, or maybe it's the view out the back of a bus in New England. (Think about it: You can sit at home and spy on the Kremlin. The world has changed.) Try taking the 80 Clicks tour as a background activity in an otherwise work-filled day at the computer. The images from the other side of the world can take a while to come in, but every ten minutes or so you can click to your tour window and see what the next stop is.

The indoor Web cam is its own strangely amusing niche—people set up Web cams in their homes or offices. Some are porn come-ons, and the sites want to charge you money to see their Web cams, but a lot of indoor Web cam sites are just people who thought it would be interesting to put a slice of real life on the Web. An interesting compendium of several people's Web cams is BaddGrrl's CAM-O-RAMA. (The name is just to pull your chain; the site promises that there is no nudity, and we have yet to see BaddGrrl do anything bad.)

Finally, the Yahoo of Web cams is EarthCam. They've searched out all the Web cams they could find and categorized them for you. Our favorite category is Weird and Bizarre | Unexplained.

The
Complete
Reference

Internet

Part V

Creating and Maintaining Web Sites

The Complete Reference

Internet

Chapter 26

Web Site Creation Concepts

If you've traveled around the Web a while, you've probably realized there's something refreshing and exciting about being able to access information from anywhere in the world, any time, day or night. The enthusiasm is contagious. Before you know it, you'll want to share your knowledge, feelings, and opinions with the rest of the world.

How do you share all that knowledge? Create your own Web page! Use the Web as the public forum that it is. If that sounds too serious, having your own Web page can also be a lot of fun (a lot of work is involved, too, but don't let that scare you) and a great way to express yourself.

This chapter describes the planning process to help you figure out what kind of content you want to present on your site, and highlights things to keep in mind as you take on the title of Web page author.

The Planning Process

Planning is crucial to the success of your Web site, so you'll know how many pages you need and how the pages will be linked. A *Web page* is each separate text file you format for viewing on the Web; A *Web site* refers to all of the pages you are making available; and your *home page* is the first page visitors see when they visit your site.

The pages of your Web site are connected together by *hyperlinks*, which are the spots on the Web page where users can click to move to another location on the page or to another page. You need to plan your site so that visitors can quickly navigate from page to page, and easily find the information you're providing.

You've probably seen sites where it looks like the author has just added pages at random, without thought to the organization of the site. The last thing that you want is for visitors to your site to get lost, be confused, or have trouble finding information.

The planning process involves answering these questions:

- Why do you want your own Web site?
- What do you need to create a site?
- Who is the audience for the site?
- What tools do you need to develop the site?

Why Do You Want Your Own Site?

There are probably as many different reasons for wanting to publish a site on the Web as there are Web sites. Table 26-1 lists some examples of types of Web sites and the purposes they serve, to help you figure out the purpose of your site. Which category fits your Web site?

Type of Web Site	Purpose
Personal	Share personal interests, hobbies, and activities with friends and family around the world.
Small business	Promote your business, sell products, and establish a presence in the online business community.
Large business	Advertise the company. Give customers 24-hour access for ordering products or receiving customer service.
School	Provide hands-on training for students to learn how to create and maintain a Web site. Give students the opportunity to publish an online school newspaper. Publicize school events.
Church	Furnish information, including the days and times of services and meetings, a map to the church, and dates of special events. Attract young people by promoting church as a hip place to be.
Community groups, clubs, or organizations	Distribute meeting announcements to members. Share your group's information with similar groups on the Web. Announce your presence—other people may be looking for a group like yours to join.
Special interest	Provide information on one interest or activity. For example, if you are a baseball fan, you might want to make your site strictly about baseball. The site could include pages detailing the history of the game, statistics for your favorite team, and links to other baseball resources on the Web.

Table 26-1.   *Purposes of Web Sites*

What Do You Need to Create a Site?

The most important ingredient for a successful Web site is your enthusiasm for the subject matter. If you're truly interested in a subject, chances are good that you'll get other people interested in the subject, too. Visitors to your site should come away with the feeling that you know your stuff and are eager to share it with the world.

In your journeys around the Web, you've probably found sites that impressed you, even if you weren't particularly interested in the subject matter. A well-composed site can bring back visitors who may have just stumbled onto your site, looking for something else. It's like going to a well-kept garden, when you're strictly a city-dweller—even though you are not interested in gardening, you can enjoy the garden and appreciate the time that the gardener spent creating and maintaining the place. By the time visitors leave your Web site, they might not be converted to the subject matter, but they will appreciate the time and care that you put into the production of the site.

To keep people coming back to your site, keep the site fresh by adding new information, deleting out-of-date topics, and updating pages regularly. Occasionally, you'll see sites that haven't been updated in months, or even years. It's disappointing to find a site that you like and look forward to revisiting, and then scroll to the bottom of the page and find the site hasn't been updated in two years.

No shortcuts—it's not fair to your visitors to change the revised date on a page unless you actually update something.

In addition to your passion for the information that you're relaying and your commitment to keep the site up-to-date, you also need:

- A basic knowledge of Hypertext Markup Language (HTML), the language in which Web pages are coded. Even if you develop your pages with an HTML editor that puts all the HTML codes in for you, a basic understanding of how HTML works is helpful. HTML is a markup language—a set of codes for formatting Web pages. For more information on HTML, see Chapter 27.

- Space to store your page on a Web server, to make it available to everyone on the Web. Most ISPs host Web sites for free with a dial-up account, or for a small monthly fee.

- A design layout that enables you to conform to the purpose of your site. Unfortunately, some sites put the most important information three jumps away from the home page, or disguise information under links that have no relation to the topic. Your site layout should be intuitive. Put the information that you think people want the most either on your home page or linked directly to your home page.

Who Is the Audience for the Site?

Defining your target audience helps you to develop the content for your site. To determine your audience, you can start with global audience characteristics (is the intended audience primarily adults or children?) and work your way down to specific characteristics (do you expect visitors to be avid gardeners, home-schoolers, or fans of Grand Funk Railroad?).

You don't have to include a lot of fancy graphics or designs on your Web pages to convey your information. For instance, Figure 26-1 is a personal Web site, Figure 26-2 shows a small business site that makes it easy to order products via the Internet, and Figure 26-3 is a site for a church.

When you figure out who the audience is for your Web site, you can tailor the site to fit the audience. Figure 26-4 shows the home page of a credit union. The audience

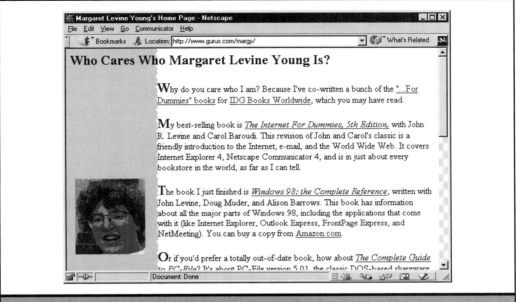

Figure 26-1.   *Example of a personal Web site*

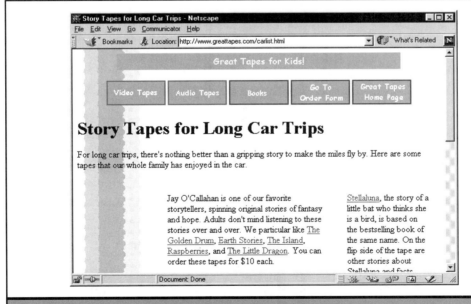

Figure 26-2.   *Example of a small business Web site*

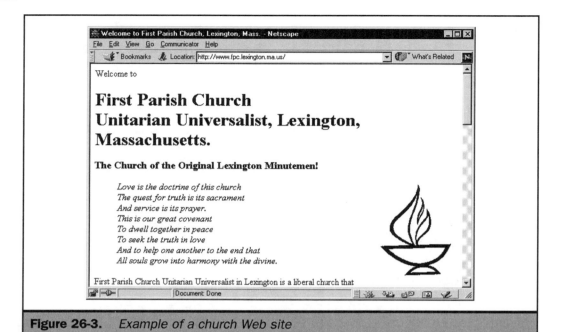

Figure 26-3. *Example of a church Web site*

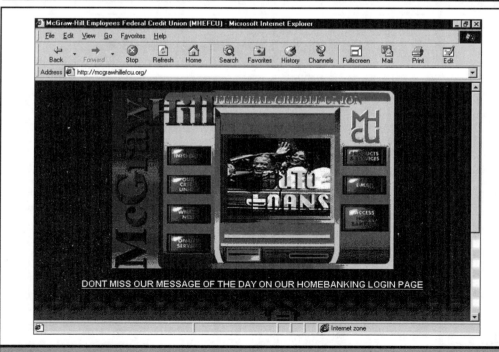

Figure 26-4. *Cash machine graphic at a credit union Web site*

for this site is credit union members. The graphic chosen for the home page is something familiar to most credit union customers—a cash machine.

Your graphics don't have to be as elaborate as the cash machine picture, but you get the idea. Keep your audience in mind when you create your site, and use symbols and graphics that they'll relate to and understand.

With the purpose and audience of your site in mind, the next thing you need to resolve is what tools you need to produce the kind of site you want.

What Tools Do You Need to Develop the Site?

Like any job, creating a Web site is mostly a matter of being interested in the task, implementing a good plan, and having the right tools.

Determining the tools that you need depends on the type of content that you have planned for your Web pages. The components that make up Web pages are the following:

- Text
- Pictures
- Animated graphics
- Audio files
- Video files

Don't worry about including all components on your pages. The first priority is to make sure that your pages are easy to read and well-organized. You don't need to include animated icons to make a page visually interesting; some very nice pages have been created using only well-thought-out text and pictures.

To create Web pages, you need these tools:

- A text editor (if you know HTML), or a Web page editor that adds the HTML codes for you (Chapters 27 and 28 describe both)

- A drawing program, if you want to create your own graphics (Chapter 29 describes creating graphics for Web pages)

- A supply of clip art, if you do *not* want to create your own graphics (lots of clip art is available on the Web)

- Sound or video equipment, if you plan to make audio or video files to include on your site (Chapter 30 describes how to record and format audio files for the Web)

Your site may require more advanced features, such as forms that users can fill in, or a connection to a database of information from which Web pages can be created based on user requests. (A form on your Web page is just like a form on paper. Visitors fill out the form to order products, give you answers to a survey, or any other uses you can think of for a form.) Based on the information your users provide by using forms, your Web site can run *CGI scripts*, programs that process the information visitors fill in on forms. For Web sites with forms and CGI scripts, you'll need additional tools: see Chapter 34.

Navigation and Themes

The "web" analogy is appropriate when you're creating a Web site—visitors should be able to navigate around the pages on your site without retracing their steps or going back to your home page.

You can make navigating your site easier by applying a consistent design to all of your Web pages. Place the navigation buttons or links (such as Next, Previous, and Home) in the same place on each page, so that they are easy to find. Use the same colors, lines, buttons, and icons from page to page so that your pages are easily distinguished as belonging to the same site. For example, the Web site shown in Figure 26-2 uses the same title and row of buttons on all the pages of the site.

Figure 26-5 is the home page of a well-designed book club site. Each specialized book club can be reached via a link from the home page, and every specialized book club Web page retains the same look as the home page, with the same background, layout, and navigation bar (at the top of each page).

If you're not inclined to create your own design or hire a design firm, select a design from the choices included with your Web editor. Many Web authoring software packages contain an excellent selection of themes from which to choose. The themes provide page layouts with matching colors, borders, horizontal lines, and navigation buttons—in short, everything you need to create your Web site. Chapter 28 describes some popular Web authoring programs.

Hunting for Ideas

The Web is a great source of inspiration if you're having trouble choosing a design. By looking at existing pages, you can get an idea of what you do and don't like when it comes to Web page design. Reviewing existing sites on the Web gives you ideas about how you want your Web page to look. Before you construct your site, go to your favorite search engine and search for sites on your proposed topic. Take a look at the existing sites and write down things that you'd like to emulate and things to avoid.

Looking at existing sites to gather ideas is acceptable, but don't copy things from the site without securing the author's permission. There are Web sites that provide buttons, icons, and graphics free for everyone to use, and the authors always state these intentions clearly on the site. See Chapter 29 for more information on clip art.

If you're interested in getting more involved in Web design, articles on that subject are available on the Web, and numerous excellent books are devoted to the subject. To

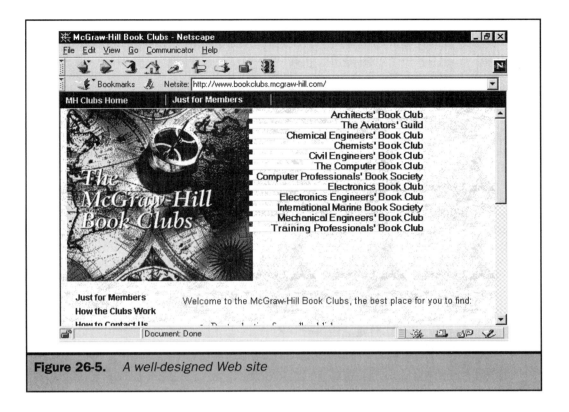

Figure 26-5. *A well-designed Web site*

see what others think of your design, use the Web as an information-gathering medium—consider adding a survey to your site and asking visitors what they think.

Elements of a Web Page

Web page files are text files, including the text that appears on the page and the text commands to format the page, show links, and display pictures. These Web page formatting commands are called *HTML tags*, the commands that are included in the formatting language that Web browsers understand when displaying Web pages. Web page files usually have the filename extension .htm or .html.

Each Web page that you create is stored in a separate file—an *HTML file*. You use a text editor or Web page editor to create HTML files. The main (home) page for a Web site usually has the name index.html, because this is the default filename that Web browsers look for (and that Web servers provide). For example, if a user types **http://www.greattapes.com** into a browser, the Web page that appears is the page named index.html at that Web site.

In additional to HTML files, your Web site will probably include graphics files—lots of them. Each picture that appears on a Web page is stored in a separate file, usually with the extension .gif (for GIF files) or .jpg or .jpeg (for JPEG files). An HTML tag controls where each picture appears on your Web pages. For example, if you use a tiny picture as a bullet for lists on your Web pages, you need only one graphics file, with an HTML tag containing the file name in each place on the Web pages where you want the bullet to appear. You may also have graphics files for page backgrounds. But remember: The greater the total size of all the files required to display a Web page, the longer it takes to view the Web page, especially for users with slow Internet connections. Keep your graphics files small, and don't use too many. For tips on using and creating graphics for your Web pages, see Chapter 29.

For a small site, all the HTML files and graphics files are usually stored in one directory (folder). If you plan a large site, you might want commonly used graphics files to be stored in a separate subdirectory, so that all pages can use the same copies. You might also want a subdirectory for each major section of the Web site.

If your Web site requires forms or other programmable features, you'll also need CGI scripts and other files. See Chapter 34 for more information.

Steps to Creating a Site

Here are the general steps you follow to create and maintain a Web site:

1. Plan the structure of the site, so that you have an idea what information will be on at least the home page and other key pages. Be sure that you've thought about the audience for the site, what your main purpose is, and how often you plan to update the site.

2. Using a text editor or Web page editor, create the pages for your site (or some of them, anyway!) and save them as HTML files. Use a graphics editor to create or view graphics for the pages.

3. Using your own browser, view the HTML files that you created. (In Netscape Navigator and Internet Explorer, press CTRL+O to open a page that is stored on your own computer.) Check that the text is spelled correctly, that the graphics look good, and that links among your pages work. Repeat Steps 2 and 3 until your site looks good enough to publish.

4. Publish your Web site by putting all of its files (HTML files and graphics files) on a Web server (as described in the next section).

5. Using your browser, view the Web pages as stored on the Web server. If you expect a wide audience for your Web site, view the page by using the two most recent versions of the most popular Web browsers (for example, Netscape Navigator 3 and 4.5, and Internet Explorer 4 and 5), because different browsers format pages slightly differently. Also, view the pages from a computer other

than the one on which you created the pages, so that you can spot accidental references to files on your own hard disk.

6. Publicize your site (as described in the section "Publicizing Your Site," later in this chapter), get feedback, get new ideas, and repeat the steps!

Publishing Your Site

Deciding where to store your pages is one of the final steps in creating your Web site plan. To make your site available to everyone on the Web, you need to publish the site on a Web server. You can either set up your own server or post your files to someone else's Web server.

Maintaining Your Own Server

You probably don't want to set up your own server, and here's why: it's expensive. Setting up and maintaining your own Web server requires that you have the following items:

- A computer capable of handling Web traffic, that is up and running 24 hours a day
- Web server software
- A dedicated, high-speed phone line (such as an ISDN or T1 line)
- An ISP that will set you up with a dedicated connection to the Internet

The setup fees and monthly charges required when you use your own server are substantial. Add to that the additional job of being the server administrator—and your ISP's offer to store 2MB to 4MB worth of data for free looks pretty good.

Using Your ISP's Server

Most ISPs include a few megabytes of storage space free of charge with a dial-up account, and most offer additional space at reasonable prices (a few dollars a month). For most people, storing Web files on their ISP's server is the most convenient and economical way to publish a site on the Web.

Some ISPs have special requirements for Web pages that include forms and CGI scripts. If you plan to use a form on your site, get a copy of your ISP's rules for Web sites before you create your site.

File transfer procedures are different for each ISP. Your ISP can give you the instructions that you need to transfer files to its Web server. As soon as the files are transferred, your site is available for viewing on the Web. For more information about transferring Web pages, see Chapter 31.

CREATING AND
MAINTAINING WEB SITES

Using a Web Hosting Service

A *Web hosting service* is a company that rents space on their Web servers. For $10 to $50 per month, you can store your Web pages on the service's Web server. Web hosting companies usually offer multiple Web servers (so that one server is always running, even during system maintenance), a fast connection to the Internet, domain hosting (so that you can use your domain name for your Web pages), frequent backups, unlimited access by the Webmaster (you) to update your pages, and use of standard CGI scripts, such as scripts that display counters that show how many visitors your page has had. Charges may be fixed, or they may depend on how much space your Web pages occupy and how many visitors you have.

To find a Web hosting service, start at Yahoo! (**http://www.yahoo.com**) and choose Business and Economy | Companies | Internet Services | Web Services | Hosting.

Publicizing Your Site

After your site is published on the Web and you've joined the global online community, how are you going to publicize the site? The first step is to register your site with some search engines, so that people doing online searches can find the site. For more information on registering your site with search engines, see Chapter 33.

Aside from telling everyone you see that your site is on the Web, here are some other ways to let other people know about your site—use the method that's appropriate for your site:

- Print the URL of your site on your business cards, stationery, and in your yellow pages ad.
- Add your URL to your signature block in e-mail and newsgroup messages.
- Include the URL in your return address whenever you send greeting cards or holiday cards.
- Have some bumper stickers printed showing your group or club's URL.
- Print the URL in your church bulletin each week.
- Post the URL on all school bulletin boards.

Things You Might Not Have Thought Of

Just when you thought your plan was complete, here are some additional things to be aware of when planning your Web site:

- **Text size**   Try not to use specific fonts or text sizes on your pages, unless it is necessary to the design of the page. Some people like to control fonts and text size via the browser settings, to make the page more comfortable to read.

- **Colors**   Don't use color-coded text to relay important parts of your message. Many people can't distinguish between colors, and might miss the meaning that you intend.

- **Write for an international audience**   Remember that the Web is a worldwide resource, open to people from many different cultures and countries. What is acceptable in your culture might be vulgar in another culture. One general rule: don't use pictures of hand symbols (like a "thumbs up" or the "OK" sign) on your site. Every hand symbol is considered obscene in at least one country in the world. Make sure that addresses, phone numbers, prices, and shipping costs include information for those outside of your country.

- **Required elements**   Always include on your pages the revised date and an e-mail address where people can contact you.

- **Privacy**   Never include personal information about people on Web pages without their consent. For example, if you create a Web site for a church and you include the church's weekly newsletter, omit people's addresses, e-mail addresses, and phone numbers, unless you have their permission to include them. Get the person's permission before mentioning sensitive information; for example, reporting that someone is out of town for a month might be an invitation to burglars, and reporting a wedding date and location invites pickpockets to the event. The Web is much more public than a small printed newsletter!

- **Maintenance**   Don't commit to updating the Web site more than you can actually follow through on. To continue with the church Web site example, it's easy to make a site with information about your church, and the only maintenance the site requires is when staff or contact information changes. However, if you decide to include information about upcoming events, you are committing to updating the Web site often enough to remove events as they pass and add future events. If you decide to publish the weekly church newsletter, you are committing to updating the Web site weekly. The Web is full of sites advertising events that happened in 1997—don't embarrass your organization by doing the same!

- **Accessibility**   Make your Web site usable by vision-impaired people as well as people with all types of software and hardware. For information about designing Web sites for people with disabilities, see **http://www.cast.org/ bobby**. To make sure that your Web pages look good all types of browsers, try viewing your pages on the last two versions of Internet Explorer, Netscape Navigator, and WebTV.

Chapter 27

Creating Web Pages by Hand

ypertext Markup Language (HTML) is the language of World Wide Web pages. The formats that you see applied to text, headings, and graphics on Web pages are controlled by HTML. Entering the world of Web page authoring is like being a traveler in a foreign land—the best way to feel at home and get around easily is to know the language. Even if you plan to use one of the HTML editors that adds HTML codes for you, you'll find it useful to know what HTML is, how it works, and what effect HTML codes have on the appearance of your Web pages. This chapter describes how to enter HTML codes on pages manually to build Web pages by hand.

Where Did HTML Come From?

HTML was developed to provide a way to format text and graphics to be read by Web browsers. HTML is a markup language rather than a programming language: it is a way of coding information so that all types of browsers can read and display the page. HTML is evolving constantly: new codes are added and outdated codes are retired. The evolution of HTML is governed by the World Wide Web Consortium, or W3C. The consortium membership is made up of organizations and companies with an interest in the future of HTML.

> **Tip**   *For information about W3C, see its Web site at **http://www.w3.org**. To see a list of W3C members, visit **http://www.w3.org** and click the link to access the member list.*

Within the W3C are working groups that propose changes to HTML. Most recent changes have involved giving Web authors more control over the layout of Web pages. Consortium members vote on changes, and the W3C develops the approved changes into a specification, which is similar to a user's guide for HTML and is posted in a variety of different formats (plain text, Zip, PDF, tar file, and PostScript) at the W3C Web site.

> **Tip**   *If you want to stay up-to-date on proposed changes to HTML, visit the W3C Web site at **http://www.w3.org/MarkUp** periodically. Creating a new specification is a big undertaking, and proposed changes go through months of review and feedback.*

At the time this book was written, HTML 4 was the current specification, and this chapter describes HTML codes from HTML 4.

Finding Your Purpose

Before you jump in and start coding Web pages, take a few moments to do some site planning. What is the purpose of your site? How many pages do you need to convey the information that you want others to know? What will be the tone of your site—will it be humorous, serious, scholarly, or homespun?

The following are a few of the many reasons individuals post information on the Web:

- To share their knowledge about a favorite hobby
- To create a contact page where friends and relatives can reach them and keep up-to-date with what is going on in their life
- To publish information about their favorite organization or community group
- To publicize their small business

Figuring out what you want to accomplish with your site early in the site's development helps you to determine the composition and layout of your pages and saves you time in the long run.

Structuring Your Web Site

After you resolve the purpose of your Web site, you are ready to start structuring the site. Your site's structure dictates how your Web pages relate to each other, and how visitors locate information at your site. You can start by dividing your information into headings and subheadings, to organize the content that you want to present.

After dividing the information, many Web authors put each topic on a separate Web page and then provide a list of links, similar to a table of contents, that remains visible as the reader jumps from page to page, as shown in Figure 27-1.

Other Web authors opt for a less-structured approach and include only the links that they think their readers would like within the text. Readers jump to the pages that they find interesting, instead of following a hierarchy of heading topics or the outline format of the table of contents.

The purpose of your site should match the structure that you choose. Table 27-1 shows some examples of site structures that suit the Web author's purpose for the site.

No matter what design you develop for your site, keep two overall goals in mind as you write your pages: all pages on your site should be easy to read, and navigating your site should be easy for visitors.

Tips for Making Your Site Easy to Read

To make the text on your Web site easy to read, follow these guidelines:

- *Write short paragraphs.* They're easier to read online, and help readers to focus on what you are saying.
- *Break up the text.* Use bulleted lists or pictures.
- *Keep graphics small and fast.* Use small, fast-loading graphics, so that your pages are displayed quickly. If you have large graphics that you want people to see, include a link that readers can use to go to the full graphic.

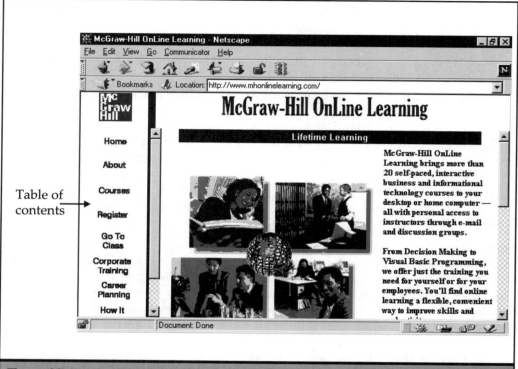

Table of contents

Figure 27-1. *Providing links to information on a site*

Purpose	Structure
To share information about your favorite hobby or interest with other enthusiasts.	Divide your information into short topics under headings and subheadings. If you have too much information for one topic (a reader shouldn't have to scroll more than two or three times to see the full page), create a separate page for the topic and provide a link to it from your home page.

Table 27-1. *Finding the Right Structure for Your Web Site*

Purpose	Structure
To provide instruction on how to complete a task.	Readers should go through instructional information sequentially (first do step 1, and then step 2, and so on). To lead readers through a sequence of pages, you can use navigation links that direct them to the next page, until they are finished with the sequence. Be sure to include a link to the previous page (for those who are interrupted mid-sequence or want to repeat a step), as well as a link back to your home page.
Showcase your business's products or services.	Group your products or services into categories. Provide an overview of your company on the home page, with links leading to more-detailed information about each category.

Table 27-1.   *Finding the Right Structure for Your Web Site* (continued)

Tips for Making Your Site Easy to Navigate

To help visitors find their way from page to page, follow these guidelines:

- *Be flexible.* Resist the urge to apply a strict outline structure to your site. Most sites have a hierarchical structure, starting with general information on the home page with links to more specific pages, which is a great way to organize your information. However, try to limit the number of jumps that a reader has to make to find the information they need. Readers usually follow links three or four levels down into your site; after that, the information on each page should be pretty compelling, to keep the reader's interest. Don't make readers jump to another level just because it fits your outline.

- *Use navigation links to direct readers to other pages.* If you want to direct readers to pages in sequence, use a Next link to point them to the next page (be sure to include a Previous link, too). A link back to your home page is always useful as well. You can include your navigation links on buttons or icons; although most browsers display graphics well, it is still a good idea to provide text links in addition to the icons or buttons, in case some readers are using browsers that do not display icons or buttons. That's why navigation links often are repeated on Web pages, with graphic buttons in the body of the Web page and text links at the bottom of the page.

- *Consider frames.* If you want readers to view pages in any order they choose, consider using frames, to display your page links at all times. Pages constructed with frames usually have the table of contents in a frame on the left side of the page. As readers move from page to page, the table of contents frame remains visible onscreen. When a reader is finished with one page, they select another link. Figure 27-1, shown previously, provides an example of this type of Web page layout (see "Formatting Your Page in Frames," later in this chapter, for how to use frames).

Tip *If you need inspiration as you develop your site, use the Web as a resource. Browse through some sites and note what you like and what you don't like. It's OK to browse, but don't copy any part of someone else's Web page unless you have the author's permission or the site explicitly states that portions (usually graphics or icons) are for public use. Extend to Web pages the same consideration for copyright that you extend to printed pages.*

Starting a Web Page

To start creating a Web page manually, open a text editor. Any text editor will work; the examples in this chapter were created using Windows Notepad.

Tip *Web pages look different when they are displayed in different browsers. The figures you see in this chapter may not match exactly the screen contents you see when you view your pages in your browser. When you make Web pages, test the way they look in various browsers.*

Seeing How You Are Doing

As you create your Web page, you can periodically save what you have accomplished to that point and view it in your Web browser. To display your Web page in a browser, follow these steps:

1. Save the file by using the File | Save command in your Web page editor or text editor.

2. In your browser, choose File | Open Page or press CTRL+O, and then choose the name of the file that contains your Web page. Alternatively, you can type **file://*pathname*/*filename*** in the Location or URL box, replacing *pathname* and *filename* with the exact location and filename of your Web page, and then press ENTER. (Since you are viewing a file stored on your computer or local drive, you do not have to be connected to the Internet.)

HTML Tags

Web pages contain *HTML tags*, the codes that add formatting, pictures, and links to Web pages. Some HTML tags appear by themselves, while others have a beginning tag and an ending tag. Tags are enclosed by < and > symbols.

 If you've used word processing programs, you may already be familiar with the way that tags work. For example, HTML tags are similar to the formatting commands that precede and follow text in WordPerfect. And the heading tags in HTML (Heading 1 through Heading 6) mark important information (Heading 1) down to less important information (Heading 6) in the same way that the built-in Heading styles do in Word.

For example, this line of HTML defines a typical heading on a Web page:

```
<H1>The Book Lovers Book Club</H1>
```

The <H1> tag indicates the beginning of the heading, and the </H1> tag marks the end of the heading. For tags that appear in pairs (such as <H1> and </H1>), the closing tab is the same as the opening tag, with the addition of a /.

 In this chapter, tags appear in uppercase so that they stand out from the text, but you can use any combination of upper- and lowercase in your Web pages (in other words, HTML is not case-sensitive). Because tags always appear enclosed in < and > in HTML, they appear that way in this book, too.

Standard Tags on a Web Page

All HTML pages contain some common tags. The basic structure of a (very short!) page looks like this:

```
<HTML>
<HEAD>
<TITLE>This is the text that will appear on the browser's Title
Bar</TITLE>
</HEAD>
<BODY>
…The substance (text and graphics) of your page goes here…
</BODY>
</HTML>
```

Figure 27-2 shows how this sample HTML would look in a browser. Here is an explanation of each HTML tag in this example:

- **<HTML>**   Every HTML page starts with an <HTML> tag and ends with an </HTML> tag. This tag simply denotes that the page is coded in HTML, the language of Web pages.

- **<HEAD>**   The HEAD section (which starts with <HEAD> and ends with </HEAD>) is reserved for tags that apply to the entire document, including the <TITLE> tag. The HEAD section can also include *<META> tags* (discussed in Chapter 33), which provide keywords and other information about the page.

- **<TITLE>**   The <TITLE> tag is required in the HEAD section. The text that you enter between the <TITLE> and </TITLE> tags is displayed on the title bar of the browser window when you view the page.

- **<BODY>**   The BODY section, starting with a <BODY> tag and ending with a </BODY> tag, contains the content of your Web page. Most of the tags described in the rest of this chapter—including tags to format text, links, and graphics on your page—are included in the BODY section.

Adding Hidden Comments

You can type comments that don't appear on the Web page when it is displayed in a browser. For example, you might want to add notes to yourself, the names of people who worked on the page, or other information to the Web page file, but you might not want this information to appear on the page.

To add a hidden comment, precede the comment text with <!-- and follow it with -->. For example, the following line would not appear in the page when displayed by a user with a browser:

```
<!-- Written for use with the Internet: The Complete Reference
book -->
```

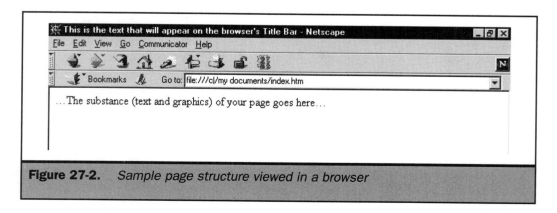

Figure 27-2.   *Sample page structure viewed in a browser*

Controlling the Overall Appearance of the Page

You can include some information in the <BODY> tag to govern the overall appearance of the page. Some tags, like the <BODY> tag, can contain extra information, called *attributes*, just before the closing angle bracket of the tag (for example, <BODY BGCOLOR="blue">). These attributes set the background that is displayed on the page, the color of text on the page, and the color of the links on the page. Each attribute consists of the name of the attribute (such as BGCOLOR), an equal sign, and the value that you want to use for that attribute (such as blue). The value should appear enclosed in quotes, although for many types of attributes, the quotes are optional.

Tip *Setting colors for the background, text, and links is optional. If you omit color choices, the page is displayed in the colors used by each reader's browser. In fact, many browsers give readers the choice of overriding the colors set on the page with the colors used by the browser.*

Displaying Wallpaper in the Background

The background of your page can be either an image or a specific color. To set an image as the background of your page, use the BACKGROUND attribute and place the name of your image file within quotes:

```
<BODY BACKGROUND="image.gif">
```

Like tags, attribute names can appear in upper- or lowercase. For the filename, be sure to use the same capitalization that is used in the actual filename. When a browser displays the page, the image in the file that you specify is *tiled* to fill the background of the Web page: that is, it is repeated across and down the page.

Choosing a Background Color

Instead of using wallpaper, you can specify a solid background color for your Web page. Use the BGCOLOR attribute in the <BODY> tag. For the color, you can enter either a hexadecimal value that represents the color, or one of 16 standard color names. The color names are the following: aqua, black, blue, fuchsia, gray, green, lime, maroon, navy, olive, purple, red, silver, teal, white, and yellow. To indicate a standard color, use this tag:

```
<BODY BGCOLOR="blue">
```

Using a hexadecimal value is safer, if you want your colors to be read by a wide variety of browsers. Not all browsers read the standard color names, but they are recognized by Netscape Navigator and Internet Explorer. The hexadecimal value is six characters that represent the amount of red, green, and blue in the color. The first two characters indicate the amount of red, the next two characters the amount of green, and the final two characters the amount of blue. Hexadecimal values range from white (FFFFFF) to black (000000). For example, this code specifies light aqua:

```
<BODY BGCOLOR="#99FFFF">
```

How do you obtain the six digits of hexadecimal value for a color? Here are two methods to use:

- Consult a conversion chart, such as the chart at the following Web site:

  http://www.geocities.com/SiliconValley/Lakes/3939/hexadecimal.html

  Many conversion charts are available on the Web. To find others, go to your favorite search engine and search for "hexadecimal colors."

- Calculate the six digits of the color, as follows:

  1. Open any graphics program and display the color palette. (For example, in Windows, open the Paint program, select Options | Edit Colors, and click the Define Custom Colors button.)
  2. Move the color indicator until you see the color that you want. Note the Red, Green, and Blue numeric values.
  3. Open a calculator and convert the numeric codes to hexadecimal values. (In Windows, open the Calculator and select View | Scientific. Click Dec, enter the numbers that you wrote down for Red, and click Hex. The result is the first two entries for your hexadecimal value, which can be numbers or letters. Repeat these steps for the Green and Blue numbers. When you have the Red, Green, and Blue hexadecimal values, combine them into one six-character value, and that is your color code.)

Choosing Colors for Text and Links

If you're using an unusual background color, you may need to set the text color so that the text is readable. For example, black text tends to disappear on dark-colored backgrounds; if you're using a dark background, you need to reset the text to a light color that is easy to read against the background.

After you set your colors, test the text and link colors to make sure the text and links are visible. Four attributes in the <BODY> tag set the text and link colors on a page:

- **TEXT**   Controls the color of text on the page
- **LINK**   Controls the color of an unvisited link
- **ALINK**   Controls the color the link turns when a reader clicks it
- **VLINK**   Controls the color of a visited link

The following tag specifies colors for the background, text, and all links. This tag would result in a page with a light-blue background, dark-blue text, green unvisited links, red active links, and hot-pink visited links. When you experiment, the color combinations are not always pretty.

```
<BODY BGCOLOR="#99FFFF" TEXT="#2C148F" LINK="#218F14" ALINK= "#CC0000"
VLINK="#FF00CC">
```

Unless the use of multiple bright colors matches the feeling that you're trying to convey on your page, use colors judiciously, especially on the first pages that you create. You can always go back and add color attributes after the site is developed. If you have a lot of text on your pages, leave the text black and use a white or neutral background. The content on your page is important, and people should be able to read the text without interference from the page design.

Formatting Text

Most of the text on your Web pages is formatted in paragraphs that begin with a <P> tag and end with a </P> tag (the closing </P> tag is optional, and many Web authors leave it out). The <P> tag starts a new paragraph by leaving a blank line and starting at the left margin, without indenting the first line of the paragraph.

Here are some other tags that are used to format text:

■ **
**   Inserts a line break, so that the following text starts on a new line. A single <BR> tag does not leave any vertical space between the preceding and following text. For example, you can use <BR> tags to start each line of a mailing address on a new line:

```
<P>Osborne McGraw-Hill
<BR>2600 Tenth Street
<BR>Berkeley, CA 94710 USA
```

You can use multiple <BR> tags, or <P> and <BR> tags together, to leave various amounts of vertical blank space.

■ **<CENTER>**   Tells the browser to center text across the line, up to the matching </CENTER> tag.

Formatting Headings

An easy way to organize text is to divide it by headings. Six heading tags are available in HTML; it is rare to use all six on one page. The heading tags are <H1> through <H6> and come in pairs (<H1> appears at the beginning of the first-level heading and </H1> appears at the end). The heading numbers indicate the size of the headings, in relation to each other. H1 is the largest heading and H6 is the smallest heading. The exact sizes and fonts that appear depend on the user's browser settings.

Heading text is enclosed between the heading tags. Text paragraphs are marked with the paragraph tag <P> (note that the </P> ending paragraph tag, included in the following example, is optional):

```
<H1>The Book Lovers Book Club</H1>
<P>The Book Lovers Book Club meets online once each month. Books
are selected by a consensus vote of the book club members. We
discuss fiction and non-fiction books.</P>
<H2>Book Suggestions</H2>
<P>We're always open to new book suggestions!</P>
```

To emphasize specific words within a paragraph, you can enclose the words in a <B> tag to mark bold text, or an <I> tag to mark italic text, such as the following:

```
<P>We're <B>always</B> open to <I>new</I> book suggestions!</P>
```

Controlling Fonts

Browsers display text and headings in standard typefaces and sizes, and users can control the default fonts that are used. Web authors can also specify the typefaces and sizes for the text on Web pages, although you never know exactly which fonts are available on users' computers. In most cases, if you specify a font and that font is not available on the user's computer, the browser will display the Web page in the browser's default font.

To specify the font, you enclose the text in <FONT> and </FONT> codes. In the <FONT> tag that you specify the attributes that you want to use:

- **COLOR** Specifies the color of the text, using the same color codes described in "Choosing a Background Color," earlier in this chapter.

- **SIZE** Specifies the size of the text, usually relative to the size it would otherwise be. For example, this code displays one word a little bigger than the surrounding text:

```
Really <FONT SIZE=+1>Big</FONT> Show!
```

  Another way to display text a little larger or smaller than normal text is to use the <BIG> and </BIG> tags or the <SMALL> and </SMALL> tags.

- **FACE** Specifies exactly which typeface you want to use. Using FACE isn't a good idea, however, because you don't know which fonts are installed on users' computers. If you want to control the fonts used in your Web pages, consider using style sheets instead, as described in "Formatting Web Pages by Using Styles," later in this chapter.

Adding Special Characters

HTML is not limited to standard ASCII characters, which do not include special characters such as trademark symbols. You can use *character entities* to create many other characters. Each of these extra characters has both a name and a number. To include a character entity in the text of your Web page, type an ampersand (&), the name or number of the character, and a semicolon (;). If you use the character number, precede it by #. For example, to include a copyright symbol, you can type **©** or **©** in your text. Not all characters have names; some only have numbers.

Table 27-2 lists some useful character entities; you can use the version in either the second or third column of the table (unless only one version is available). For a complete listing of all the standard character entities, see one of the following sites:

> **http://www.natural-innovations.com/boo/doc-charset.html**
> **http://www.owlnet.rice.edu/~jwmitch/iso8859-1.html**

When displaying text, browsers throw away repeated characters. For example, if you include a series of <P> codes (<P><P><P><P>) browsers display the same amount of vertical spaces as one <P> code leaves. Similarly, if you type ten spaces, browsers

Character	Character Entity (Name)	Character Entity (Number)
Less than (<)	&lt;	&#060;
Greater than (>)	&gt;	&#062;
Bullet (•)		&#149;
Em dash (—)		&#150;
En dash (–)		&#151;
Trademark (™)		&#153;
Nonbreaking space		
Inverted exclamation point (¡)	&iexcl;	&#161;
Copyright (©)	&copy;	&#169;
Registered trademark (®)	&reg;	&#174;
Paragraph sign (¶)	&para;	&#182;
One-half (½)	&frac12;	&#189;
Inverted question mark (¿)	&iquest;	&#191;

Table 27-2. *HTML Character Entities*

display only one. To leave extra vertical space, mix <P> and <BR> tags; to leave extra horizontal space, mix regular spaces with nonbreaking spaces (codes).

*If you don't want the paragraphs on your Web pages to be separated by blank space, and want them start with an indented first line, don't use <P> tags. Instead, start each paragraph with the following tags, which start the paragraph on a new line, preceded by four spaces (two regular spaces and two nonbreaking spaces):
    . A better idea is to use styles to control the way that paragraphs are formatted: See "Formatting Web Pages by Using Styles," later in this chapter.*

Presenting Information in Lists

A good way to break up text on a page is to use any of the following lists wherever you can:

- **Numbered lists**   Show a progression of steps in sequence. Numbered lists use the <OL> (Ordered List) tag at the beginning of the list, the <LI> tag at the beginning of each list item, and the </OL> tag at the end of the list.
- **Bulleted lists**   Highlight short sentences, or present a series of items that can be read quickly (like this list). Bulleted lists use the <UL> (Unordered List) tag at the beginning of the list, <LI> for each list item, and </UL> at the end of the list.
- **Definition lists**   Present information in a glossary-type format (one short line, followed by an indented paragraph). These lists use the <DL> (Definition List) tag at the beginning of the list, a <DT> for each term, a <DD> tag for each definition, and a </DL> tag at the end of the list.

For example, the following is code for a numbered list (Figure 27-3 shows how it looks in Netscape Navigator):

```
<OL>
<LI>Select the books and authors you want to recommend.
<LI>Write a brief summary of each book.
<LI>Send your recommendations to the host.
</OL>
```

A bulleted list looks like this (with an introductory paragraph):

```
<P>The most recent books we've read are:</P>
<UL>
<LI>Beloved, by Toni Morrison.
<LI>On The Road, by Jack Kerouac.
<LI>A Moveable Feast, by Ernest Hemingway.
</UL>
```

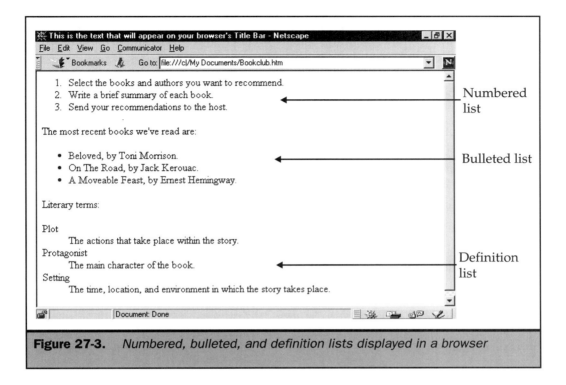

Figure 27-3. *Numbered, bulleted, and definition lists displayed in a browser*

The entries in a definition list look like this (with an opening paragraph):

```
<P>Literary terms:</P>
<DL>
<DT>Plot
<DD>The actions that take place within the story.
<DT>Protagonist
<DD>The main character of the book.
<DT>Setting
<DD>The time, location, and environment in which the story
takes place.
</DL>
```

Presenting Information in Tables

The table layout is an effective way to show statistical data or information that can fit easily into columns. Table data is stored in cells, which are the individual "boxes" that make up the rows and columns of the table. The labels that you put on a column or row to describe the table's content are called *table headings*.

A table can be a simple chart on your page; as you work with tables, you might want to apply additional formatting to align data within cells, adjust the borders, or change the background color of the table.

Laying Out the Table

Tables use the following tags:

- **<TABLE>** and **</TABLE>**   Indicate the beginning and end of the table. All the rest of the tags and text in the table must be between these two tags.
- **<TR>** and **</TR>**   Mark the beginning and end of a row. All the headers and cells in the row come between these two tags.
- **<TH>** and **</TH>**   Mark the beginning and end of a heading.
- **<TD>** and **</TD>**   Mark the beginning and end of a data cell.

The following example shows a table with three columns and two rows. The BORDER attribute in the <TABLE> tag indicates that the table cells will have lines around them. To omit the lines, delete the BORDER attribute.

```
<TABLE BORDER>
<TR>
<TH>Member's Name</TH>
<TH>Hosted the Book Club?</TH>
<TH>Host Dates</TH>
</TR>
<TR>
<TD>Ellen</TD>
<TD>No</TD>
<TD>Not Applicable</TD>
</TR>
<TR>
<TD>Samuel</TD>
<TD>Yes</TD>
<TD>May 10, August 23</TD>
</TR>
</TABLE>
```

In a browser, the table looks like this:

Member's Name	Hosted the Book Club?	Host Dates
Ellen	No	Not Applicable
Samuel	Yes	May 10, August 23

Formatting the Table

If you want to control the appearance of the table, you can use some of the following attributes in the <TABLE>, <TH>, <TR>, and <TD> tags:

- **ALIGN** Controls the horizontal alignment of the row (if you add it to the <TR> tag) or the data in a cell (if you add it to the <TD> or <TH> tag). The most common values are LEFT, CENTER, and RIGHT. For example, this tag starts a table with rows aligned to the right:

```
<TR ALIGN="RIGHT">
```

- **VALIGN** Controls the vertical alignment of the row (if you add it to the <TR> tag) or the data in a cell (if you add it to the <TD> or <TH> tag). The most common values are TOP, CENTER, and BOTTOM. The following tag starts a table with entries at the top of each cell:

```
<TR VALIGN="TOP">
```

- **CELLPADDING** Controls the amount of space between the information within cells and the border. The space is measured in pixels. This attribute is set in the <TABLE> tag. This tag starts a table with five pixels of space between the contents of each cell and its border:

```
<TABLE CELLPADDING="5">
```

- **BGCOLOR** Controls the background color of the entire table (if you add it to the <TABLE> tag), a row (if you add it to the <TR> tag), or a cell (if you add it to the <TD> or <TH> tag). The color can be the name of a standard color or the hexadecimal value for a color. This tag starts a row with the background color of bright aqua:

```
<TR BGCOLOR="#66FFFF">
```

- **BACKGROUND** Displays a graphics file in the background of the table, row, or cell (like the BACKGROUND attribute of the <BODY> tag).
- **WIDTH** Sets the width of the table, either in pixels or as a percentage of the width of the browser window.

Adding Horizontal Lines

You can separate one section of the Web page from the next section with a horizontal line by using the <HR> tag, which moves down a line, inserts a horizontal line, and starts the following material on the next line. You can control the length of the horizontal line relative to the width of the browser window in which the Web page is displayed by using the WIDTH attribute. You can also specify the thickness of the line in pixels by using the SIZE attribute. You can align the line to the left, right, or center by using the ALIGN attribute. For example, the following tag displays a centered, two-pixel-thick line that is 80 percent of the width of the browser window:

```
<HR SIZE="2" WIDTH="80%" ALIGN="CENTER">
```

 # Adding Pictures

A page of all text and no graphics can be a little boring. To spice up your Web page, consider adding some pictures.

Where do you get pictures to add to your Web page? You can use clip art, create your own pictures with a drawing program or graphics program, load pictures from a digital camera, or use a scanner to import a drawing or photograph. There are also many Web sites that offer images free for downloading. Chapter 29 describes how to create graphics for Web pages.

To add a picture, you use the <IMG> (image) tag, entering the tag at the place in the BODY section of the Web page where you want the graphic to appear. You use the SRC (source) attribute to specify the name of the file that contains the picture that you want displayed on the Web page, like this:

```
<IMG SRC="picture.gif">
```

Before you add a picture to your page, you need to determine where the picture will be stored. The filename is either an absolute pathname or a relative pathname.

Absolute vs. Relative Pathnames

An *absolute pathname* includes the full pathname of the file. This means that if you move your files or if you change your directory (folder) names, you have to edit every <IMG> tag in every HTML file that contains the absolute pathname. For that reason, this naming convention is not recommended.

A *relative pathname* indicates the pathname of the image file relative to the pathname of the HTML file. This is the recommended naming convention for graphics files. For example, if your image file is stored in the same directory as your HTML file, you can use just the image filename in your <IMG> tag, with no pathname, as in the example in the previous section. If the image file is in the same directory as your HTML file, but in a subdirectory, include the subdirectory name in the <IMG> tag, like this:

```
<IMG SRC="images/picture.gif">
```

If the image file is stored one directory level up from your HTML file, use two dots (..) in the pathname to move up a directory level, as follows:

```
<IMG SRC="../picture.gif">
```

Some Web authors like to store their frequently used graphics in a directory called *images* or *pix*, so that all the <IMG> tags in all the pages in the rest of the directories of the Web site can refer to one set of graphics files.

Image Attributes

You can add the following attributes to the <IMG> tag to adjust the picture and control how text flows around the picture:

- **HEIGHT and WIDTH**   Control the size (in pixels) at which the graphic appears on the Web page. These attributes are optional; use them only if you do not like the default size and need to resize the picture. The Web browser that displays the Web page adjusts the height and width of the graph to the sizes that you specify. When you use the HEIGHT and WIDTH attributes, make sure that you keep the same proportions as the original graphic; if you don't, the picture looks like you s-t-r-e-t-c-h-e-d it either horizontally or vertically. Resizing a graphic to be larger than the original is rare. The larger the number of pixels, the bigger the picture. For example, the following <IMG> tag displays the picture in the file picture.gif as 30 by 50 pixels, regardless of the size of the stored picture:

    ```
    <IMG SRC="picture.gif" HEIGHT="30" WIDTH="50">
    ```

Using small (but legible) graphics on Web pages is best, because they load faster than large graphics. To make a graphic small, be sure to use a graphics program to reduce the size of the file. Don't just change HEIGHT and WIDTH attributes, which don't change the file size (or speed up downloading time), only the way it is displayed by the browser. For information on resizing Web graphics, see Chapter 29.

- **ALIGN**   Controls how text flows around the graphic. ALIGN has five possible values:

    - **TOP**   Places one line of text even with the top of the image.

    - **MIDDLE**   Places one line of text at the middle of the image.

    - **BOTTOM**   Places one line of text even with the bottom of the image. TOP, MIDDLE, and BOTTOM are useful when you have a *single* line of text that you want placed next to a graphic.

CREATING AND MAINTAINING WEB SITES

■ **LEFT**   Places the graphic on the left side of the page, with your text paragraph wrapped around the right side of the graphic.

■ **RIGHT**   Places the graphic on the right side of the page, with your text paragraph wrapped around the left side of the graphic. LEFT and RIGHT are useful when you have paragraphs of text that you want to wrap around a graphic. For example, the following tag displays a picture on the left side of the Web page, with the surrounding text wrapped around its right side:

```
<IMG SRC="picture.gif" ALIGN="LEFT">
```

■ **HSPACE and VSPACE**   Control the amount of white space around the image. Both values are indicated in pixels. HSPACE sets the amount of space at the left and right of the image; you use this attribute to control the distance between the text that is wrapped around your graphic and the graphic itself. VSPACE sets the amount of space above and below the graphic. The following tag inserts a picture with 25 blank pixels to either side, and 10 blank pixels above and below the picture:

```
<IMG SRC="picture.gif" HSPACE="25" VSPACE="10">
```

■ **BORDER**   Indicates that a border should be placed around the image, and controls the width of the border. The width is measured in pixels. The next tag inserts a picture with a border that is three-pixels wide (a heavy line):

```
<IMG SRC="picture.gif" BORDER="3">
```

■ **ALT**   Contains the text that appears while the picture is loading, or if a user has a browser that does not display graphics, or if the user has opted not to load graphics when viewing Web pages. Always include ALT attributes in all image tags, to make your Web site accessible to vision-impaired users, who use special software to read the text on the screen. For example:

```
<IMG SRC="picture.gif" ALT="Book cover of this week's selection">
```

Note that you can use as many or as few of the attributes as you need. Only the SRC attribute, which specifies the filename, is necessary. All attributes are placed in the same <IMG> tag, separated by spaces. For example, if you decided to use all the attributes listed here, your <IMG> tag might look like this:

```
<IMG SRC="picture.gif" HEIGHT="30" WIDTH="50" ALIGN="LEFT"
HSPACE="25" VSPACE="10" BORDER="3" ALT="Book cover of this week's
selection">
```

You can do other things with graphics besides wrapping text around them. A graphic can be displayed in a table by including the <IMG> tag within the <TD> tag, like this:

```
<TD><IMG SRC="picture.gif" ALT="Book cover of this week's selection"></TD>
```

You can center an image by enclosing the <IMG> tag in between the <CENTER> and </CENTER> tags, like this:

```
<CENTER><IMG SRC="picture.gif" ALT="Book cover of this week's selection"></CENTER>
```

An image can also be a link that takes readers to a new destination, as described in the next section.

Adding Links

The ability to jump from one location or Web page to another has been instrumental in making the Web so popular. No matter what you call them (hyperlinks, hypertext links, or just links), the purpose of links is to help you navigate though a Web site or jump to other, related Web sites.

Links use an <A> tag with an HREF (hypertext reference) attribute to specify the URL to which the link connects. Between the starting <A> tag and the ending </A> tag is the text or graphic that appears on the Web page as the link. A basic link looks like this:

```
Visit the <A HREF="suggest.htm">Book Club Suggestions Page</A>.
```

The value of the HREF attribute ("suggest.htm") indicates what Web page the browser displays when the user clicks the link. The text between the beginning and ending tags is the text that appears on the screen, marked as a link (usually blue and underlined).

Translated by a browser, this link looks as follows to readers who visit your page:

Visit the Book Club Suggestions Page.

The link's destination (the HREF value) can be a filename or the URL of another Web page. If the destination is a filename, the link leads to a Web page stored on your Web site, and you need to decide whether you're going to use absolute or relative pathnames. Relative pathnames are recommended. (For a discussion of the difference between absolute and relative pathnames, refer to "Absolute vs. Relative Pathnames," earlier in this chapter.)

To link to any Web page on the Internet, type the full URL of the destination page in the HREF attribute, like this:

```
<A HREF="http://www.mcgraw-hill.com">McGraw-Hill Books</A>
```

Links that readers click are not confined to text only. You can also use graphics as links. Many Web pages use navigation buttons, such as Next, Previous, Home, or Index, to guide readers through the site. To display an image as a link, include the <IMG> tag between the <A> tag and the </A> tag. The following HTML code displays a link that leads to the schedule.html page on the same site; the link is a picture called next.gif (a small picture that looks like a Next button):

```
<A HREF="schedule.htm"><IMG SRC="next.gif" ALT="Next button"></A>
```

Whenever you use graphic navigation buttons, also include text-only navigation options somewhere on your page, for readers who are not viewing graphics.

Adding a Link That Jumps Within the Page

A link doesn't have to take a reader off the current page. If you have a long page made up of text divided by headings, add links at the top and bottom of the page so that readers can jump to the topics they want to read. To implement a link to a spot on the current page, you add two tags: one tag to mark the destination on the page (called an *anchor*), and one tag to add the link that the reader uses to get to the destination.

To mark the destination on the page, move your cursor to the header or text of the destination and enter an <A> tag that uses the NAME attribute. (You can place the tags around existing text, or add new text between the tags.) The following tag assigns the anchor name "members" to some text:

```
<A NAME="members">Book Club Members</A>
```

To add the link that leads to the anchor, move your cursor to the location where you want to place the link, and enter an <A> tag with an HREF attribute. The value of the HREF attribute uses a # to indicate that it links to an anchor name. For example, the next tag creates a link that jumps to the anchor named "members":

```
<A HREF="#members">list of book club members</A>
```

When readers click the "list of book club members" link, they jump to the Book Club Members location. You can add an anchor name to jump to an existing anchor in any Web page, like this:

```
<A HREF="http://www.sample.com/index.html#members">list of book club members</A>
```

Adding a Link to Your E-mail Address

You've probably noticed that almost all Web pages contain a contact link at the bottom of the page. The link often goes to the Webmaster, or the person responsible for the page.

You can set up the link so that when a reader clicks the link, instead of jumping to a file, an e-mail window opens with your address filled in, so that the reader can simply enter a message and send it to you.

To add a link to your e-mail address, use *mailto:* and your e-mail address in place of the URL in an <A> tag. For example:

```
<A HREF="MAILTO:nettcr@gurus.com">Internet Complete Reference Authors</A>
```

Some people advocate including the e-mail address in the text of the link, so that the address is visible on the Web page. This is probably a good idea, especially if you want to make sure that all readers, including those whose browsers don't support the e-mail form feature, can contact you via e-mail.

Gathering Information in Forms

Up to this point, you have been giving readers information on your page. Now, it is time to receive a little feedback, by using *forms*. A form is useful to your readers because it enables them to send information to you. You benefit because you get answers to the questions that you ask. Forms are used on Web pages for a variety of tasks, including:

- Gathering information from readers (similar to an electronic suggestion box)
- Performing a survey to find out what readers think
- Giving readers an opportunity to order products

Creating a form involves two separate tasks:

- Creating the form page in HTML
- Creating a Common Gateway Interface (CGI) script that processes the responses.

This section describes how to create a form page in HTML. For information on CGI scripts, see Chapter 34. Many ISPs provide CGI scripting services as part of their Web page hosting capabilities.

Creating a Form

The <FORM> and </FORM> tags define the beginning and end of the form. The information that the reader fills in falls within these tags. The following are two attributes that you need to set on the <FORM> tag:

- **METHOD** Indicates how the information from the reader will be sent to the CGI script. Use the POST option on your METHOD attribute, unless your ISP tells you otherwise.

- **ACTION** Specifies the location of the CGI script to run when the user fills in and submits the form.

For example, the following tag begins a form that will be processed by the bookform script stored in the Web server's cgi-bin directory:

```
<FORM METHOD="post" ACTION="cgi-bin/bookform">
```

Fill in the Blanks

The body of a form (between the <FORM> and </FORM tags) contains objects that the user can use to input information. In addition to text boxes in which readers can type information, you can display these other types of controls:

- **Radio buttons** Readers are limited to one selection from the list.
- **Check boxes** Readers can mark as many selections as they want.
- **Drop-down boxes** Readers make a selection from a drop-down list.

You create each of these items by entering an <INPUT> tag. The TYPE attribute of the <INPUT> tag determines what type of box or button you are creating, and the NAME attribute gives the input a name. Depending on the type of input that you are creating, you can also specify other attributes.

Text Boxes

Text boxes are blank boxes into which readers type free-form responses. You create a text box by using an <INPUT> tag with the TYPE attribute set to "TEXT." You can also specify the size of the box (measured in number of characters). The following tag creates an input box named *source* that is 40-characters wide (the top of Figure 27-4 shows how this text box looks in a browser):

```
<INPUT TYPE="TEXT" NAME="source" SIZE="40">
```

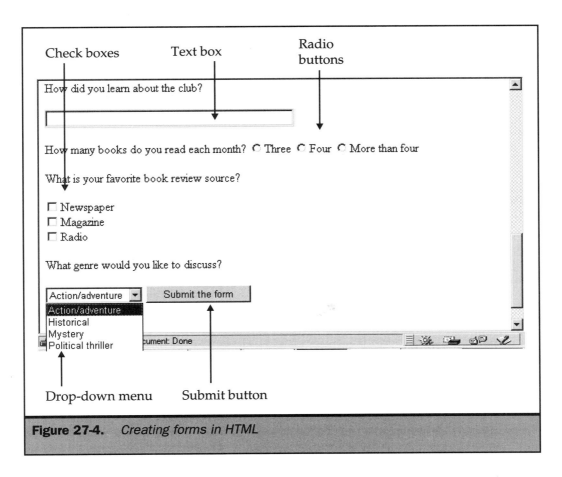

Figure 27-4. *Creating forms in HTML*

To give readers more than one line into which they can type responses, use the <TEXTAREA> tag. You control the size of the text box by using the attributes COLUMNS and ROWS. This following tag creates a large text box that is 25-rows high and 40-characters wide:

```
<TEXTAREA NAME="resource" COLS="40" ROWS="25">
```

Radio Buttons

Use radio buttons when you want to present a set of choices to readers, from which the reader can choose only one. You create each radio button with an <INPUT> tag that sets the TYPE attribute to "RADIO." Each radio button in the group must have the same name (specified with the NAME attribute). If you have more than one set of radio buttons on your form, make up a unique name for each set. The VALUE attribute indicates the value of the button's input if the user chooses that button. When the user submits a form, the browser uses the value of the chosen radio button as the value for the set of buttons.

For example, these three <INPUT> tags create a set of three radio buttons, from which the user can choose only one (Figure 27-4, shown previously, displays the resulting radio buttons):

```
<INPUT TYPE="RADIO" NAME="bknumber" VALUE="three">Three
<INPUT TYPE="RADIO" NAME="bknumber" VALUE="four">Four
<INPUT TYPE="RADIO" NAME="bknumber" VALUE="more">More than four
```

Check Boxes

Use check boxes when the reader can choose more than one of the options in a set of inputs. Sets of check boxes are similar to sets of radio buttons, and the tags contain the same attributes as radio button tags. However, with check boxes, readers can select as many options as they want. For example, this set of check boxes lets the user choose as many media types as he or she wants (Figure 27-4 shows the resulting check boxes):

```
<INPUT TYPE="CHECKBOX" NAME="media" VALUE="newspaper">Newspaper<BR>
<INPUT TYPE="CHECKBOX" NAME="media" VALUE="magazine">Magazine<BR>
<INPUT TYPE="CHECKBOX" NAME="media" VALUE="radio">Radio<BR>
```

 To force each selection on a radio button list or check box list to be displayed on a separate line, add a <BR> tag at the end of each <INPUT> tag.

Drop-Down Menus

Drop-down menus are useful if you need to conserve space on your form. The selections do not appear onscreen; they are displayed only when the reader clicks the drop-down arrow.

Most drop-down menus allow only one item to be selected. However, you can set a Multiple option to allow readers to select more than one item. (To select more than one item, the reader's browser must support this feature, and the reader must know which keys to use to select more than one item on a list. In Windows, you can select more than one item from a list by pressing SHIFT+DOWN ARROW.)

Every drop-down menu that you create on your form must be assigned a unique name.

Type a <SELECT> tag to start a drop-down menu, and type a matching </SELECT> tag at the end of the tags for the menu. The <SELECT> tag must include the NAME attribute, to assign the menu a name. After the <SELECT> tag, enter an <OPTION> tag for each option that you want to appear in the drop-down menu. For example, these lines create one drop-down menu with four options (Figure 27-4 shows the drop-down menu):

```
<SELECT NAME="booktypes">
<OPTION>Action/adventure
<OPTION>Historical
<OPTION>Mystery
<OPTION>Political thriller
</SELECT>
```

Submit Button

Somewhere on your form (usually at the bottom), you need a *Submit button* that the user clicks to send the information on the form to the Web server. (The button doesn't have to say "Submit" on it, but many buttons to submit information do, and readers are comfortable with it.)

Readers click the Submit button (or whatever you call it) when they complete the form and want to send their entries to your Web server for processing. The CGI script specified in the <FORM> tag goes into action when the Submit button is pressed, to process the answers on the form.

To add a Submit button to your form, use an <INPUT> tag with the TYPE attribute set to "SUBMIT." If you don't want the button to read "Submit," enter something else for the VALUE attribute of the tag. For example, the following tag defines a submit button labeled "Submit the form" (as shown in Figure 27-4):

```
<INPUT TYPE="SUBMIT" VALUE="Submit the form">
```

Formatting Your Page in Frames

Frames are a layout innovation used by many Web authors. In the early days of the Web, page layout was secondary to page content. As the Web grew, authors wanted more ways to present information.

Frames let you divide your Web pages into rectangular sections that take up the browser window. The most common use for frames is to add a list of links in a narrow space on the left side of the screen, and present information on the larger, right portion of the screen. The links in the left frame remain onscreen as the reader goes through each page of information. The links serve as a table of contents of the site, although the frame is rarely labeled "Table of Contents." (For an example of a Web page constructed with frames, refer back to Figure 27-1.)

To use frames, the Web page contains tags that define the layouts of the frames on the page. The contents of each frame is stored in a separate file. For example, a Web page that displays two frames is stored in three files: the main file with the frame layout tags, and a file for each frame. The files that appear in each frame are ordinary Web pages, with no special frame-related formatting.

Setting Up Frames

The main file for the Web page contains a <FRAMESET> tag, which specifies the layout of the page, and <FRAME> tags, which indicate the name of the file that appears in each frame. You omit the BODY section from this Web page file, because the body of the page is contained in the separate files for the frames.

Not all browsers are capable of displaying frames, but the last few versions of both Netscape Navigator and Internet Explorer are frames-capable. Whenever you use frames, be sure to include a paragraph of information for readers whose browsers do not display frames. This information is included under the <NOFRAME> tag, so that readers whose browsers can display frames don't see it.

Controlling the Frame Layout

The <FRAMESET> and </FRAMESET> tags indicate whether the page is divided horizontally (by using the ROWS attribute) or vertically (by using the COLS attribute). You can specify the size of each frame either in pixels or as a percentage of the whole browser window in which the Web page is displayed. For example, the following tags divide the page into two vertical frames; the first frame consumes 20 percent of the page, and the second frame uses the rest of the page (noted by the asterisk):

```
<FRAMESET COLS="20%,*">
</FRAMESET>
```

Displaying Web Pages in Frames

Between the <FRAMESET> and </FRAMESET> tags, you add a <FRAME> tag for each frame. The SRC attribute of the <FRAME> tag specifies the name of the file that contains the Web page to appear in that frame. The files that you specify appear in order across and down the browser window. If you define two columnar frames, the first file that you add with the <FRAME> tag is displayed in the left column; the second file that you add is displayed in the right column. (If the <FRAMESET> tag used the ROWS attribute to divide the browser window horizontally, the first file would appear above the second.)

For example, these tags specify the names of files to appear in the two frames:

```
<FRAME SRC="firstdoc.htm">
<FRAME SRC="secondfile.htm">
```

 Tip   *You can set the SCROLLING attribute of the <FRAME> tag to control whether the contents of the frame can scroll—if it's too big to fit in the frame. SCROLLING defaults to "yes" unless you set it to "no".*

Displaying Text for Non-Frame-Enabled Browsers

Finally, enclose text in between the <NOFRAMES> and </NOFRAMES> tags to appear in browsers that don't support frames, as follows:

```
<NOFRAMES>
This page uses frames, which are not supported by your browser.
</NOFRAMES>
```

Putting It All Together

The following is an example of an entire Web page that uses frames:

```
<HTML>
<HEAD>
<TITLE>The Internet Complete Reference Home Page</TITLE>
</HEAD>
<FRAMESET COLS="20%,*">
<FRAME SRC="firstdoc.html">
<FRAME SRC="secondfile.html">
<NOFRAMES>
This page uses frames, which are not supported by your browser.
Click <A HREF="noframes.html">here</A> to see a non-framed version.
</NOFRAMES>
</FRAMESET>
</HTML>
```

Changing What Appears in a Frame

If the Web page in one frame is a table of contents for the Web site, you want links in the one frame to control what appears in another frame. For example, clicking a link in the left frame displays a specific Web page in the right frame. To create this kind of link, you name the right frame and then refer to that name in your link.

To name a frame, add the NAME attribute to the <FRAME> tag. For example, the following <FRAME> tag for the right frame names the frame "Data":

```
<FRAME SRC="secondfile.htm" NAME="Data">
```

Then, include the frame name in an <A> tag in the left frame, using the TARGET attribute to specify the frame in which the linked file should appear. For example, the table of contents Web page displayed in the left frame might contain the following <A> tag, which displays the bookfile.html file in the Data frame:

```
<A HREF="bookfile.html" TARGET="Data">Introduction to Book Clubs</A>
```

When readers click the link in the left frame, the Web page is displayed in the right frame.

 If you leave out the TARGET attribute, the Web page is displayed in the same frame as the link (in other words, the left frame) when readers click the link.

Formatting Web Pages by Using Styles

Web browsers have always had a standard set of styles—the default formats for plain, unformatted text (paragraphs that are divided by <P> tags) and for heading tags (<H1> through <H6>). Individuals can change the default formats for these tags by changing their browser configurations, but few people bother. *Styles* enable Web authors to set the styles used for these standard tags, and create new tags with new formatting.

Newly designed Web pages, which are based on a new version of HTML (HTML 4), include formatting done through styles. In word processing programs, a *style* is a set of formatting commands that dictate how text is formatted. Instead of adding a series of separate commands to text, you apply one style that contains all the commands. In HTML 4, a style sets specific formatting characteristics for tags on your page. For example, if you want all the text of your <H2> (heading level 2) tags to be displayed in bold type, you can use a <STYLE> tag to set the format for all <H2> tags on the page.

HTML 4 supports many types of style sheets, including *cascading style sheets (CSS)*, W3C's proposed way to format text on Web pages, which allows various levels of style sheets to work together. A corporate Web site could use one corporate-wide style sheet to set standard styles for all Web pages on the Web site, for example. The technical documentation department could have an additional style sheet that defines other styles used only in the Web pages for that department. A particular Web page might contain more definitions of styles used only on that page.

This section discusses two ways to use styles on your Web pages: defining styles at the top of a Web page, and linking to a file that contains all of your styles.

 *As with most things associated with the Web, style sheets are changing and being refined. For the latest information on styles or the HTML 4 standard for style sheets, see **http://www.w3.org/TR/REC-html40/present/styles.html**. For details about cascading style sheets, see **http://www.w3.org/Style/css**.*

Defining the Style Sheet Type

Because HTML 4 supports many different types of style sheets, you must specify which type of style sheet you want to use. To use CSS, include this line in the HEAD section of the Web page:

```
<META http-equiv="Content-Style-Type" content="text/css">
```

This tag specifies that the <STYLE> and other style-sheet-related tags in this Web page are CSS. If you leave out this tag, style sheets may work anyway, but as the style-sheet definitions develop, you may run into trouble later. (See Chapter 33 for more information about <META> tags.)

Defining Styles

The <STYLE> and </STYLE> tags, which must appear in the HEAD section of the Web page, enclose the definition of the styles for the Web page. The TYPE attribute of the <STYLE> tag indicates to the browser what system of style sheets you are using: for CSS, set it to the value **"text/css"**.

Between the <STYLE> and </STYLE> tags come the commands that format other tags within your document. For example, the following HTML code changes the definition of the <BODY> tag to set the page background to blue, changes the <H1>, <H2>, and <H3> headings to green, and centers the headings:

```
<STYLE TYPE="text/css">
BODY {background: blue}
H1, H2, H3 {color: green; text-align: center }
</STYLE>
```

Style Sheet Rules

The exact format of the formatting commands depends on the type of style sheet that you are using. With CSS, each style is defined by a *rule*, which consists of a *selector* (the name of the style that you are defining, such as H1) and some formatting within curly braces ({}). The formatting consists of pairs of properties (such as *background*) and values (such as *blue*) separated by a colon. The pairs in the list are separated by semicolons.

For example, this style sheet rule defines the format for <H1> headings:

```
H1 { font-weight: bold;
     font-size: 14pt;
     line-height: 16pt;
     font-family: helvetica; }
```

A complete list of the selectors (styles) that you can define and the types of formatting that you can apply are beyond the scope of this book. For more information, see the HTML Writers Guild's Cascading Style Sheets FAQ at the following address:

http://www.hwg.org/resources/faqs/cssFAQ.html

Storing Styles in a Separate File

You may want more, or all, of the Web pages at your Web site to use the same styles. Rather than adding the same <STYLE> tags to each Web page, store the tags in a separate *style sheet file,* with the extension .css, and link your Web pages to that file so that the Web pages can use the styles defined in the style sheet file.

To link a Web page to a style sheet, add a <LINK> tag at the top of the Web page, before the <BODY> tag. The HREF attribute defines the name of the style sheet file, and the REL and TYPE attributes need to be set to "stylesheet" and "text/css" respectively. For example, the following tag indicates that the styles for this Web page are stored in the style sheet file mystyle.css:

```
<LINK HREF="mystyle.css" REL="stylesheet" TYPE="text/css">
```

Turning Your Web Page into a Channel

In Chapter 24, you learned how to view Web pages through channels. Setting up your Web page as a channel allows visitors to subscribe to your site and receive regular updates, based on the schedule you specify for the channel. If you use Microsoft's Internet Explorer to view channels, Web pages are enabled as channels through the use of *Channel Definition Format (CDF)* files. By creating a CDF file for your Web page, you (and others) can subscribe to it as a channel, and receive updates when the Web page changes.

The coding in a CDF file looks similar to an HTML file, because CDF is based on *Extensible Markup Language (XML),* which, like HTML, is related to *Standard Generalized Markup Language (SGML).* Writing a CDF file is easy because its format is familiar.

Before you create your CDF file, you need to know:

- Your Web page's URL.
- What you want to say in the abstract that briefly describes the page.
- The filename of the logo and icon that you want displayed on the Windows Active Desktop for the channel.
- The channel's update schedule. (In the following example, the channel is updated daily.)

Here's a sample CDF file:

```
<CHANNEL HREF="http://www.mysite.com/news.htm">
<ABSTRACT>The current news page from mysite.com.</ABSTRACT>
<TITLE>My Site's News</TITLE>
<LOGO HREF="http://www.mysite.com/news.gif" STYLE="image" />
<LOGO HREF="http://www.mysite.com/news.ico" STYLE="icon" />
<SCHEDULE>
<INTERVALTIME DAY="1" />
</SCHEDULE>
</CHANNEL>
```

You save the file with the .CDF extension (for example, mychannel.cdf) in the same directory on the Web server as your HTML files. To get people to subscribe to your channel, add a link to the CDF file on your home page. The link tag looks like this:

```
<A HREF="http://www.mysite.com/mychannel.cdf">Subscribe to this
channel!</A>
```

Be sure to test the link to make sure that you can subscribe to the channel.

You can also enable your Web page to be visible in other channel viewers. For information about how to set up your Web page as a NetCaster channel, visit the Netscape Web page at **http://www.netscape.com**. To see how to turn your Web page into a PointCast channel, go to the PointCast Web site at **http://www.pointcast.com**.

Summary of HTML Tags

Table 27-3 lists the HTML tags and attributes defined in this chapter. For more information about HTML, read *HTML: The Complete Reference* (Berkeley, CA: Osborne/McGraw-Hill). The next chapter describes how to create Web pages without having to type all of these tags.

Tag	Definition and Attributes
<HTML>	Indicates the page as an HTML page.
<HEAD>	Provides information about the page.
<TITLE>	Specifies text to appear on the title bar of the browser.

Table 27-3.   *Summary of HTML Tags*

CREATING AND

Tag	Definition and Attributes
<!-- -->	Defines a hidden comment that doesn't appear on the Web page.
<BODY>	Defines the main segment of the page, which contains the content of the page. Attributes:

	BACKGROUND	Image displayed behind the text
	BGCOLOR	Color displayed behind the text
	TEXT	Color of the text
	LINK	Color of unvisited links
	ALINK	Color of active links
	VLINK	Color of visited links

Tag	Definition and Attributes
<P>	Marks a paragraph.
 	Starts a new line.
<CENTER>	Centers text or other information.
<H1> through <H6>	Denotes headings on the page.
<FONT>	Controls the typeface, size, and color. Attributes:

	COLOR	Color of the text
	SIZE	Type size in points
	FACE	Typeface (not recommended)

Tag	Definition and Attributes
<OL>	Indicates a numbered list.
<LI>	Specifies an element in a numbered or bulleted list.
<UL>	Indicates a bulleted (or unordered) list.
<DL>	Shows a definition list.
<DT>	Marks the term being defined in a definition list.

Table 27-3. *Summary of HTML Tags* (continued)

Tag	Definition and Attributes	
<DD>	Indicates the definition paragraph in a definition list.	
<TABLE>	Defines information presented in rows and columns. Attributes:	
	ALIGN	How table is aligned with surrounding text
	BACKGROUND	Image displayed behind the text in the table
	BGCOLOR	Background color of the table
	BORDER	Width of the table border
	CELLPADDING	Amount of space between data and table border
	WIDTH	Width of the table in pixels or as a percentage of the browser window
<TH>	Marks the heading of a table. Attributes:	
	ALIGN	Horizontal alignment of the row
	VALIGN	Vertical alignment of the row
	BGCOLOR	Background color of the table
	BACKGROUND	Image displayed behind the text in the table
<TR>	Indicates a row in a table. Attributes:	
	ALIGN	Horizontal alignment of the row
	VALIGN	Vertical alignment of the row
	BGCOLOR	Background color of the table
	BACKGROUND	Image displayed behind the text in the table

Table 27-3.   *Summary of HTML Tags* (continued)

Tag	Definition and Attributes	
<TD>	Defines a data cell in a table. Attributes:	
	ALIGN	Horizontal alignment of the data
	VALIGN	Vertical alignment of the data
	BGCOLOR	Background color of the table
	BACKGROUND	Image displayed behind the text in the table
<HR>	Adds a horizontal line. Attributes:	
	ALIGN	Controls the horizontal alignment
	WIDTH	Specifies the width in pixels or as a percentage of the browser window width
<IMG>	Adds an image to the page. Attributes:	
	SRC	Filename or URL of the graphic
	HEIGHT	Number of pixels in height
	WIDTH	Number of pixels in width
	ALIGN	Controls text flow around graphic
	HSPACE	Space at left and right of graphic
	VSPACE	Space at top and bottom of graphic
	BORDER	Line around graphic
	ALT	Text displayed while graphic loading, or instead of graphic

Table 27-3.   *Summary of HTML Tags* (continued)

Tag	Definition and Attributes	
<A>	Specifies a link. Attributes:	
	HREF	File, anchor, or URL that is the destination of the link
	NAME	Name of anchor to create at this position on the Web page
	TARGET	Frame in which to display the linked page
<FORM>	Marks a section where readers can enter information and make selections from lists. Attributes:	
	METHOD	How information is sent to the CGI script (usually POST)
	ACTION	CGI script name to run when form contents are submitted
<INPUT>	Defines areas where readers enter information on a form. Attributes:	
	TYPE	Format of input
	NAME	Name of input
	SIZE	Size in characters (for text boxes)
	VALUE	Unique identifier of input (for radio buttons, check boxes, and submit buttons)
<TEXTAREA>	Defines a multiline text box in a form. Attributes:	
	NAME	Name of text box
	COLS	Number of columns (characters) across the text box
	ROWS	Number of rows (lines) in the text box

Table 27-3.   *Summary of HTML Tags* (continued)

Tag	Definition and Attributes	
<SELECT>	Creates a drop-down list on a form.	
<OPTION>	Specifies the selections in a drop-down list on a form.	
<FRAMESET>	Defines the overall format of a page constructed in frames. Attributes:	
	ROWS	Number and size of frames across the Web page
	COLS	Number and size of frames down the Web page
<FRAME>	Contains the name of the file that fills the frame. Attributes:	
	SRC	The filename or URL of the Web page to appear in the frame
	NAME	Unique identifier assigned to frame
	SCROLLING	Controls whether the contents of the frame can scroll if the Web page is too big to fit in the frame
<NOFRAMES>	Information displayed by browsers that cannot display frames.	
<STYLE>	Indicates a series of formatting commands. Attribute:	
	TYPE	Style sheet language
<LINK>	Links another file, such as a style sheet file, to the Web page. Attributes:	
	HREF	The filename to link
	REL	The relationship of the Web page to the file ("stylesheet" for style sheet files)
	TYPE	The type of file ("text/css" for cascading style sheet files)

Table 27-3.   *Summary of HTML Tags* (continued)

The Complete Reference

Internet

Chapter 28

Creating Web Pages by Using Web Page Editors

Web pages are coded using Hypertext Markup Language (HTML) tags to specify the way text and graphics are displayed (as described in Chapter 26). HTML controls the layout and format that you see on Web pages. When you create your own Web pages, you can either type the tags manually in a text editor (as described in Chapter 27) or use a Web page editor to do the coding for you. This chapter describes how to use Web page editors to create pages and build your Web site.

When all of your pages are ready, you upload the pages to a Web server. For more information on uploading files to a Web server, see Chapter 31.

What Is a Web Page Editor?

Although the phrase "Web page editor" sounds like it refers to a person who edits the Web section of a newspaper, in Internet jargon, this phrase describes the applications that Web authors use to code pages in HTML.

Advantages of Web Page Editors

One advantage to using a Web page editor over a plain text editor to write Web pages is that most Web page editors let you see the page as it will appear in a browser. You don't have to go to a completely different application to see the formatted Web page, as you do when you use a text editor.

Another advantage to using a Web page editor is the amount of time that you save by not having to enter all the HTML tags. Because the Web page editor adds the tags for you, you can focus on the layout and content of your page. Most editors also check the tags to be sure that you haven't forgotten the beginning or ending tag, which can be a laborious task to do manually.

The WYSIWYG (what-you-see-is-what-you-get) capability and the amount of time saved by not typing all the HTML tags leads most Web authors to use a Web page editor.

Web Page Editing Tasks

Within a Web page editor, HTML tags are included as options on menus and as buttons on toolbars. Even if you aren't coding pages manually, a basic knowledge of HTML is important, so that you know which button to click. You can also experiment in a Web page editor and see what effect menu options and toolbar buttons have on your text.

All Web page editors deal with the same set of HTML codes and create HTML pages that can be viewed in any Web browser and re-edited with any Web page editor. HTML codes are fairly standard, so the differences that exist between Web page editors are primarily in the way that they arrange their windows and the extra features that they offer. The extra features offered are ways to manage your Web site, usually by verifying links or showing all the files that make up your site. This chapter shows what different Web page editors look like, and explains the extra features that are available with Web page editors.

Microsoft's programs are exceptions to the standard use of HTML. FrontPage and FrontPage Express may use WebBot components, which are supported only by Microsoft's Web server. Don't use these WebBot components unless your ISP's or Web hosting company's Web server supports them.

All Web page editors work remarkably similarly. They all enable you to create a new page, starting with a blank page, a template, or help from a Wizard; edit an existing page; see what your page looks like in a browser; and save the page on disk. When you are done creating or editing a page, you can customize your Web page in many ways, including the following:

- **Text**   Type the text to appear on the Web page and use formatting buttons on the toolbar. Good Web page editors have formatting buttons that are similar to those of a word processor.

- **Pictures**   Insert a picture in the Web page by clicking an Insert Image button on the toolbar and specifying the filename and how the picture should appear.

- **Lists**   Format instructions as a numbered list, or format a list of items as a bulleted list, by clicking a button on the toolbar.

- **Tables**   To format text as a table, most Web page editors have an Insert Table toolbar button to create and format the table. Then, you can type or copy text and insert pictures into the rows and columns of the table.

- **Links**   Add links to other Web pages related to your subject by clicking an Insert Link toolbar button.

- **Lines**   Click a toolbar button to place a horizontal line on the page to mark the end of a section.

Most Web page editors can show you what your Web page will look like in a browser: some have built-in browsers, and others pass your Web page to a browser that you already have installed. Some Web page editors have a built-in FTP program that can upload your finished Web page (and graphics files) to your Web server (see the section "Uploading Pages by Using a Web Page Editor" in Chapter 31).

Where to Find Web Page Editors

Web page editors are available as stand-alone applications or bundled into Internet software packages. This chapter describes how to use some popular editors, including Netscape Composer (which is part of the Netscape Communicator suite), FrontPage and FrontPage Express (from Microsoft), PageMill (from Adobe), and HotDog Professional (from Sausage Software). All run under Windows 98 and some (including Netscape Composer) are also available for the Mac.

Dozens of excellent Web page editors are available. For information about all editors reviewed and/or available on the Web, go to your favorite search engine and search for "HTML editors." Or start at TUCOWS (at **http://www.tucows.com**), choose a location physically near you, choose your operating system, look in the HTML Tools category, and click either Editors Beginner or Editors Advanced. TUCOWS displays a long alphabetical list of Web page editors that you can download (see Chapter 38 for directions on how to download and install programs from the Web).

This chapter describes Netscape Composer in some detail, as an example of how a Web page editor works. The other editors listed in this chapter work similarly, with additional features noted in each program's section.

For more information on creating Web pages, read *HTML: The Complete Reference* (Osborne/McGraw-Hill, 1998).

Netscape Composer

Composer is part of the Netscape Communicator suite and can be downloaded from the Netscape Web site at **http://home.netscape.com**. This chapter describes version 4.5.

To start Composer, choose Start | Programs | Netscape Communicator | Netscape Composer. You can also start Composer from within Navigator, by clicking the Composer button on the right side of the status bar at the bottom of the Navigator window, or by choosing Communicator | Composer.

When you are in Navigator and choose File | Open Page to see a Web page, you can specify whether to open the page in a Navigator window or a Composer window. Also while in Navigator, you can choose File | Edit to switch to Composer to edit the page that you are looking at.

Creating a New Page

To make a new Web page, you can start either from scratch, with a template, or with help from a Wizard. To make a new page from scratch, you just run Composer and start typing.

Creating a New Page by Using the Wizard

To start a new Web page quickly, you can use a Wizard or a template from the Netscape Web site. To use a Wizard, select File | New | Page From Wizard. (You need to be connected to the Internet to access the Wizard.) When the Wizard window appears, click the Start button at the bottom of the window. The window has three parts: instructions in the left part, a preview of your page in the right part, and a place to type your text at the bottom (see Figure 28-1). Click each link in the left part of the window, and type the information that the link requests.

After you enter all of your information, click the Build button. In the Navigator window, select File | Edit Page to view the document in Composer. In Composer, select File | Save As and save the file to your local drive.

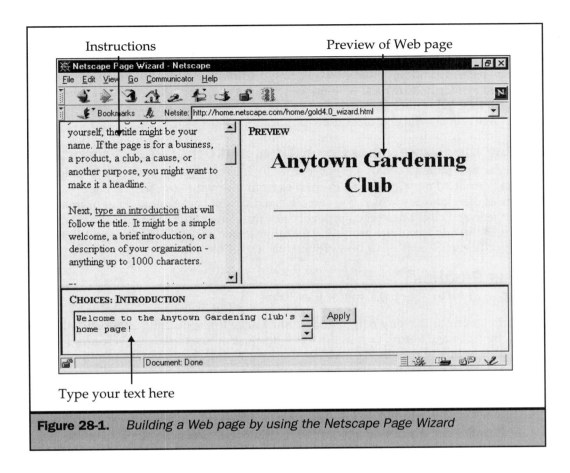

Figure 28-1.   *Building a Web page by using the Netscape Page Wizard*

Using a Wizard gives you the basic structure of your Web page; you can then modify the page by using the menu commands and toolbar buttons in Composer.

Creating a Page from a Netscape Template

Another way to create a page quickly in Composer is to use one of the templates available at the Netscape Web site. In the Composer window, select File | New | Page from Template. Click the Netscape Templates button (you have to be connected to the Internet to access the Web site) and select the template that you want to use.

A blank page using the template that you chose appears in a Navigator window. Select File | Edit Page to view the page in Composer. In the Composer window, select File | Save As to save the HTML file and the graphics files to your local drive.

With the basic page in place, you can use Composer to modify the page to suit your needs.

Modifying Your Page

Common ways to edit a Web page include setting the background color and title for the page, entering and formatting text, adding pictures, formatting instructions as a numbered list, formatting a list of items as a bulleted list, formatting text as a table, adding links to other Web pages related to your subject, and placing horizontal lines on the page to mark the end of sections.

Setting the Background Color, Title, and Other Page Properties

One of the first things that you probably want to do is change the background color. Choose Format | Page Colors and Properties from the menu. You see the Page Properties dialog box, in which you can select a different background color or image, or change the color of links on your page. Click the General tab to change the title that appears in the title bar of the browser. To change the colors of the background or text, or to specify a graphic file as a background, click the Colors and Background tab.

Adding Pictures

To add a picture to your page, follow these steps:

1. Position the cursor where you want the image to appear, and either click the Insert Image button or select Insert | Image. You see the Image Properties dialog box, shown in Figure 28-2.

2. Click the Choose File button, select the image file, and click Open.

3. In the Text Alignment section, select one of the options to indicate how text wraps around the picture.

4. In the Space Around Image section, indicate the number of pixels of white space that you want on the left and right side of the picture, or at the top and bottom of the picture. If you want a border around the picture, indicate the border width in pixels.

5. Click the Alt Text/Low Res button and enter the alternate text to display while your graphic is loading.

6. Click OK to close all the dialog boxes. The Composer window shows the graphic in the Web page.

 To see how your text wraps around the graphic, click the Preview in Navigator button.

Formatting Lists

Formatting text as a list is a good way to make instructions, short paragraphs, or a series of items easier to read. Numbered lists work well for sequential items or instructions. Bulleted lists work well for short, related paragraphs or to highlight items that you would normally separate by commas in a paragraph.

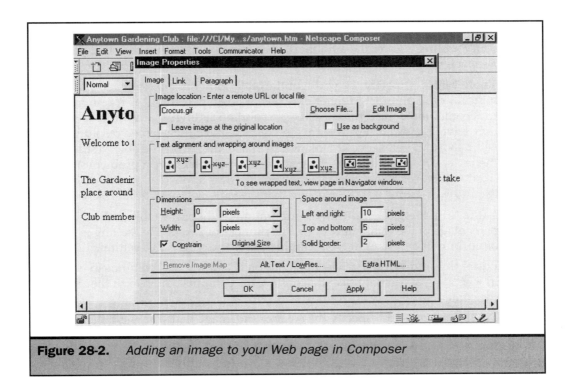

Figure 28-2.   *Adding an image to your Web page in Composer*

To add a numbered list, click the Numbered List button or select Format | List | Numbered. To add a bulleted list, click the Bullet List button or select Format | List | Bulleted.

Inserting a Table

The table format is useful when you need to present information so that it is aligned in columns and rows. Web page designers also use tables to leave blank space to the left of their text. To insert a table, click the Insert Table button or select Insert | Table | Table. In the New Table Properties dialog box that appears, specify the number of rows and columns that you want and whether the entire table should be placed at the left, center, or right on the page. Fill out any of the following optional fields that you want to use:

- **Include Caption**   Indicate whether you want the caption above or below the table. A caption area is displayed on the Composer window after you fill out this dialog box; type the caption in the designated area.

- **Border Line Width**   Enter the number of pixels that you want as the width of the border around the table. Enter 0 if you do not want a border around the table.

- **Cell Spacing** Type the amount of space (in pixels) that you want between cells.

- **Cell Padding** Enter the amount of space (in pixels) within cells that you want between the text and the border of the cell.

- **Table Width** Specify the width of the table, either as a percentage of the total window or as an exact number of pixels. Using a percentage is recommended, to accommodate the different screen-resolution settings that visitors to your site may have. For example, if visitors to your site have their screen resolution set at 640 × 480, and you set your table width at 800, they won't be able to see part of the table. If you use the percentage option, you won't have a problem with a fixed number of pixels, because the percentage is applied as a percentage of each viewer's screen, thus ensuring that the table will fit within all screens.

- **Table Min. Height** Indicate the minimum height of the table, either as a percentage of the total window or as a number of pixels. This setting is not used often, but if you do use it, you should opt for the percentage setting.

- **Equal Column Widths** Select this option if you want all columns to be equal in width. If you do not select this option, the columns adjust to fit the size of the contents.

- **Table Background** Specify the color or the image that you want displayed as the background of the table.

> **Note** *You can also specify a background color or image for a specific row or cell, instead of the entire table. After the table is displayed in Composer, right-click the row or cell, select Table Properties, click the Row or Cell tab in the dialog box, and select a color or image.*

Adding Links

To insert a link to another Web page:

1. Position the cursor where you want the link to appear in the text. If the text or graphic that you want to use as a link is already in your Web page, select the text or graphic.

2. Click the Insert Link button or select Insert | Link. You see the Character Properties dialog box. (If you selected a picture as a link, you see the Image Properties dialog box.)

3. Unless you selected text or a graph as the link, enter the text of the link as it will appear on your page in the Link Source area of the dialog box.

4. In the Link To area, enter the URL or filename of the page to which you want to link. Click OK.

To insert a link to another spot on the same Web page:

1. Position the cursor at the destination spot.
2. Click the Insert Target button or select Insert | Target. You see the Target Properties dialog box.
3. Type the name of the target and click OK.
4. Position the cursor where you want the link to appear in the text.
5. Click the Insert Link button or select Insert | Link. You see the Character Properties dialog box.
6. In the Link Source area, enter the text of the link as it will appear on your page.
7. In the Link To area, select the target that is the destination of the link.

Adding Horizontal Lines

Horizontal lines divide your page into readable sections. To insert a horizontal line, click the Insert Horiz Line button or select Insert | Horizontal Line.

The line is placed at the cursor position. The default size of the line is 100 percent of the window. To resize the line, right-click the line and select Horizontal Line Properties.

Saving and Publishing the Page

After you complete your page, save the file on your local drive. Select File | Save As and enter a filename. To upload your Web page to a Web server, you can use the Publish button on the toolbar (see the section "Netscape Composer" in Chapter 31).

FrontPage and FrontPage Express

FrontPage and FrontPage Express are two Web page editors from Microsoft. FrontPage Express is available as part of Windows 98 and Internet Explorer 4.0. FrontPage is a stand-alone application that you purchase separately. FrontPage Express is best suited for creating pages quickly. FrontPage has many more features than FrontPage Express and allows you to view and manage the overall structure of your Web site and create Web pages.

For more information about FrontPage and FrontPage Express, see the Microsoft Web site at **http://www.microsoft.com**.

FrontPage Express

To start FrontPage Express, choose Start | Programs | Internet Explorer | FrontPage Express. If the command doesn't appear and you use Windows 98, you may need to install FrontPage Express. Choose Start | Settings | Control Panel, open Add/Remove Programs, click the Windows Setup tab, and look at your list of installed Windows components.

FrontPage Express comes with templates and Wizards to help you create Web pages. Using the Personal Home Page Wizard is an easy way to get your Web page up in a hurry. To start the Wizard, select File | New and choose Personal Home Page Wizard in the dialog box. The Wizard windows prompt you through steps to create sections on your Web page. When you're finished with the selections, you see the Web page (shown in Figure 28-3).

In addition to the usual formatting buttons on the toolbar, the Standard toolbar contains the Insert WebBot Component button. A *WebBot component* is a dynamic object that works only if your server is running Microsoft's FrontPage software. Check with your server administrator before including WebBots on your page. Three WebBots are available:

- **Include** Allows you to put a file on your Web page by referencing the filename

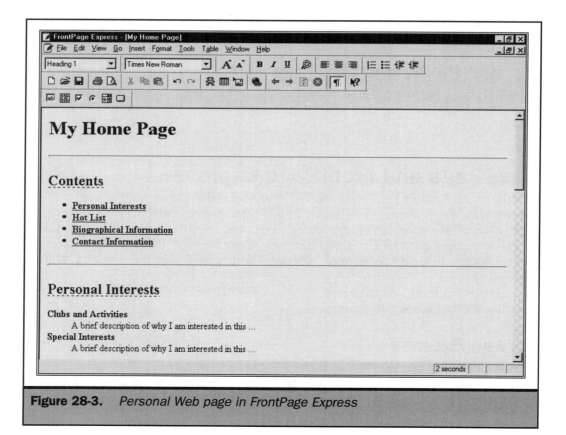

Figure 28-3. *Personal Web page in FrontPage Express*

- **Search**   Places a search form on your page
- **Time Stamp**   Displays the date and/or time on your page

The Forms toolbar contains buttons that you can use to create a form. Implementing a form is a two-step process: you create the form as an HTML page, and then you assign a CGI script to process the information that visitors enter on the form. Before you create a form, contact your ISP to make sure it processes CGI scripts. Many ISPs supply the scripts for you.

When the page is finished, select File | Save As. You can either save the file to your local drive or publish it directly to the Web server. To save it to your local drive, click the As File button in the Save As dialog box, and enter a filename. To publish it directly to the Web server, click OK in the Save As dialog box, and go through the Web Publishing Wizard windows (see the section "FrontPage Express" in Chapter 31).

FrontPage

You can construct a Web page by using FrontPage Express, but if you want more features than just quick HTML coding, you might want to try FrontPage. To start FrontPage, choose Start | Programs | Microsoft FrontPage. Accept the default selection in the Getting Started dialog box.

FrontPage Explorer

In addition to an editing window, the FrontPage window includes an area called *FrontPage Explorer*, which enables you to manage your Web site. From FrontPage Explorer, you can view all the files that make up your site, check hyperlinks, and get an overview of the navigation paths on your site. You can also look at the preset themes that are supplied with FrontPage, and choose an overall theme for your pages.

To preview the themes supplied with FrontPage, click the Themes icon on the Views bar, as shown in Figure 28-4. When you see a theme that you like, click the theme name. The background, images, and buttons that you see in the preview will be available on all of your pages.

If you have your own theme and simply want to start creating pages, select Tools | Show FrontPage Editor to access the editing window. You can start from a blank page, or use one of the FrontPage templates (by choosing File | New and selecting a template). Use the toolbar buttons and menu commands to format the text and graphics on the page.

Additional toolbars for formatting tables and graphics are available in FrontPage. To view a toolbar, select the toolbar from the View menu.

Formatting a Page by Using Frames

In addition to themes and templates, another formatting option that many Web authors use is to structure their Web pages in frames. Frames enable you to divide a Web page

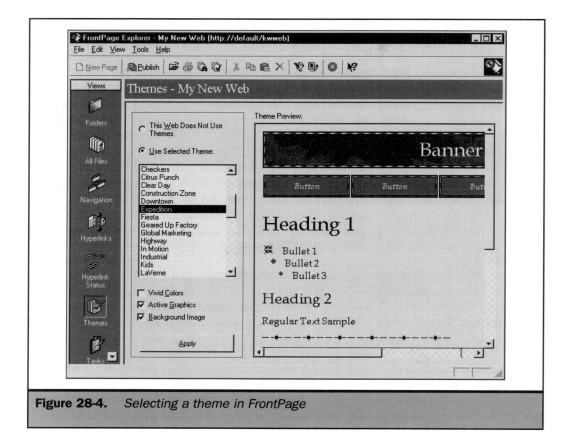

Figure 28-4.   *Selecting a theme in FrontPage*

into sections. Each section, or *frame,* is a separate HTML file (see Chapter 27 for a description of frames). For example, if you want your page to have a list of links on the left side of the window, and the content of pages displayed on the right side of the window, you have to create a minimum of three HTML files:

- One file defining the overall frame structure
- One file containing the links that appear on the left side of the window
- One file containing the initial content loaded on the right side of the window

Create the links file and the content file first. These files are regular Web pages, and no special formatting is necessary. When you create the frame structure file, FrontPage asks you to enter the filenames of the links file and the content file.

To create the frame structure file:

1. Select Frame | New Frames Page | Contents. The Contents structure sets up two vertical frames on the page.

2. Click the Set Initial Page button in the left frame and enter the name of the links file.

3. Click the Set Initial Page button in the right frame and enter the name of the content file.

When you display the page in a browser and click one of the links in the left frame, the contents of the destination page will be displayed in the right frame (as shown in Figure 28-5).

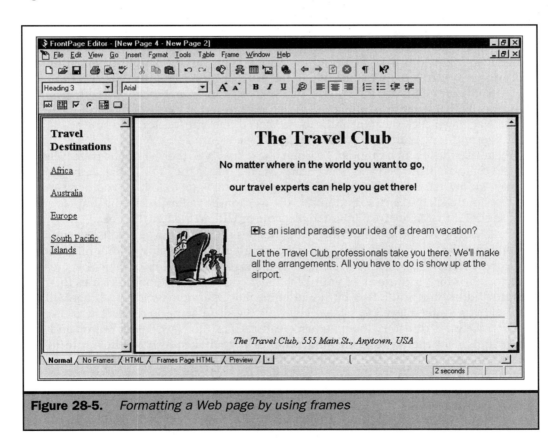

Figure 28-5. *Formatting a Web page by using frames*

If you're interested in seeing what the HTML tags look like for the pages that you create, click the HTML tab at the bottom of the FrontPage window.

Frame-structured pages have some extra tabs at the bottom of the FrontPage window. The No Frames tab shows what visitors whose browsers don't support frames see when they access your page. The Frames Page HTML tab shows you the HTML tags used on the frame structure page.

PageMill

PageMill is a Web page editor from Adobe. For information about the program, see the Adobe Web site at **http://www.adobe.com** (try **http://www.adobe.com/prodindex/ pagemill**). PageMill is not shareware or freeware: you can purchase the program from the Web site or from a store. A downloadable demo may be available at the Web site.

To start PageMill, choose Start | Programs | Adobe | PageMill | Adobe PageMill. When PageMill opens, you see the edit window. Type the title of your page in the Title box and press ENTER to go to the body of the page. Type the text that you want to include on your page. Use the buttons on the toolbar to format the text, add tables, insert horizontal lines, or add pictures. To change the appearance of many of the items in the Web page, click the item and choose View | Show Inspector; you see the Inspector window, with settings for the object (see Figure 28-6).

A link can be text or a graphic. To insert a text link, type the text on the page. Select the text that you just typed and select Edit | Make Link. In the Link To box at the bottom of the window, enter the filename or URL to which you want to link. (If you don't know the filename, click the Browse button.) To use a graphic as a link, select the graphic and then select Edit | Make Link. Enter the filename or URL in the Link To box.

PageMill helps you to keep track of all the files that make up your site. As you expand your site, you might find yourself managing HTML files, graphics files, audio files, and video files. Before you use the site management features of PageMill, create a directory in which to store all of your Web files. You can create subdirectories for images, videos, and audio files from within the Site Overview window in PageMill.

To create a site, select Site | New Site. Give the site a name, and select as the location the main directory that you just created. Click the New Folder button and create folders for each type of file that you have at your site, as shown in Figure 28-7. The numbers in the In and Out columns indicate the number of incoming and outgoing links that are on a page. To see the linked filenames, click the number.

You can keep the Site Overview column on the screen as you edit Web pages. To do this, close the directory window (the window on the right side of the window). The edit window appears in its place, in which you can create additional Web pages.

Figure 28-6.   *Formatting a picture in PageMill*

Leaving the Site Overview column open onscreen gives you easy access when you want to include graphics, video, or audio files on a Web page.

HotDog Professional

HotDog Professional is a full-featured Web page editor from Sausage Software (**http://www.sausage.com**). A simplified, less-expensive Web editor is available, called HotDog Express, but it has fewer features. If you simply want to create a page in a hurry, HotDog Express probably fits your needs. If you have an interest in learning HTML and intend to have an active site, you probably want HotDog Professional. Both programs are shareware that can be downloaded from Web software libraries.

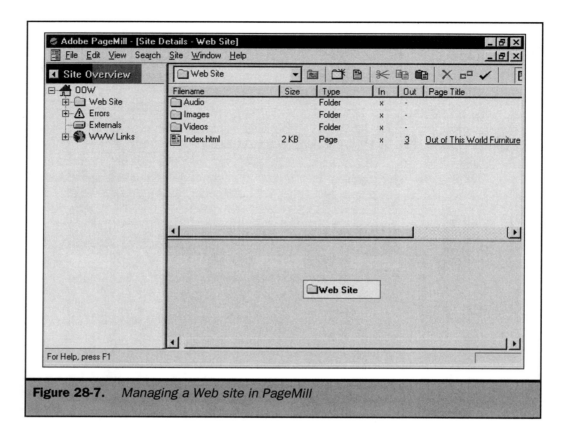

Figure 28-7.   *Managing a Web site in PageMill*

To start HotDog Professional, choose Start | Sausage Software | HotDog Professional. If your computer has sound enabled, you'll know when the application is ready, because the dog stops barking.

The HotDog Professional window is divided into the following two sections, as shown in Figure 28-8:

- **Rover View**   The top section, which shows you the HTML tags in your document

- **Web View**   The bottom section, which shows you the formatted page as it will appear in a browser

You can maximize either view by clicking the Rov or Web buttons at the bottom of the window. As you enter text and graphics in Rover View, Web View shows you what the page will look like in a browser.

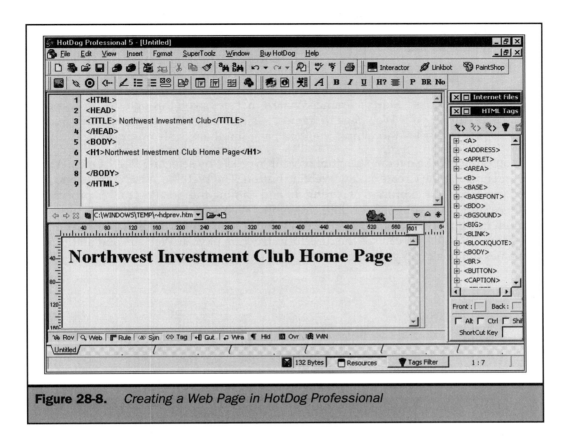

Figure 28-8.   *Creating a Web Page in HotDog Professional*

Tip *Viewing the codes on a split screen is a good way to learn HTML. More HTML resources are available: To open a window that displays all HTML codes onscreen, select View | Resource Manager | HTML Tags. To display an HTML Reference Guide, select Help | HTML Reference.*

The Insert and Format toolbars contain most of the buttons that you need to format text and insert graphics on your page. In addition to the usual buttons, you can use the following toolbar buttons:

■ **Insert Comment**   Comments are text that isn't displayed when the page is opened in a browser. Web authors often use comments to add notes on a Web page. Even though comments are not displayed in regular view in a browser, they are visible when the page source is viewed in a browser. In other words, don't enter comments that you don't want other people to see.

- **Insert Forms**   Starts a Forms Wizard that steps you through the process of creating a form.

- **Insert Embedded Item**   Used primarily by Netscape to embed audio and video controls on a Web page.

- **Insert Frames**   Starts a Frames Wizard that steps you through the process of structuring your Web page in frames. (Using frames is a way to divide screen space to display more than one Web page simultaneously onscreen.)

You can view the overall structure of your Web site by selecting File | Open Web Site and clicking the Create a New WebSite button. The WebSite Wizard starts and steps you through the process of setting up and naming the site. Part of this process involves setting up your site for publication on a Web server, so you need the file location information that you received from your ISP or server administrator. After you create the site, you can see the directory structure of your Web site and all the filenames that make up your site.

The Complete Reference

Chapter 29

Creating Web Graphics

Graphic images have helped make the Web an increasingly exciting place. You can brighten up your Web pages with nearly any image, simply by storing the image in one of the graphics file types (*formats*) that browsers can display. For the fastest-downloading, highest-quality images, however, you may need to do some fine-tuning. This chapter tells you how to use popular graphics programs to create, fine-tune, compress, and then add popular special effects to your Web graphics.

Perhaps the most important fine-tuning that Web images need is for their files to be made as small as possible (in kilobytes), so that the images download quickly. You can keep file size small by saving an image in the file format that is best suited for its content. The quality of Web images doesn't need to be as high as the quality for printed images, so you also can keep down file size by compromising quality where you don't need it. Where image quality is important, you can adapt images to the special needs of Web browsers and computer displays.

You may also want to add popular special graphics features common on the Web. You can animate an image, similar to a movie, make selected areas transparent so that the image appears to be pasted on the page, or make the image come into focus gradually (display it *progressively*).

You control some graphics features by how you design the Web page, not by doing anything to the image. You use tags on the Web page to position or align images on the page, turn images into clickable hyperlinks, or assemble them into an array. You control such features either by writing HTML code or by using a Web design tool (discussed in Chapters 27 and 28). Some special graphics programs, discussed in this chapter, also help you to control those images on the Web page.

Graphic File Formats for the Web

Computer graphics are stored in many different file formats, which fall into two main types:

- **Vector images**   Consist of lines and various shapes, outlined and filled with colors or shadings.

- **Bitmap images**   Consist of colored dots, or *pixels*. Web documents commonly use only bitmap images, and in two principal formats: *GIF* (CompuServe's Graphics Interchange Format) and *JPEG* (Joint Photographic Experts Group); a third bitmap format, PNG (Portable Network Graphics) is also used.

This chapter concentrates on creating GIF and JPEG files for Web pages. Choosing the best format can give you better-looking or faster-downloading graphics. Because smaller files download faster, all Web graphics formats rely on *compression*, a way to pack more information into a smaller file. Each format compresses data in its own way, and some ways trade off image quality for a smaller file size.

Using GIF

For drawings and artwork created on a computer (including clip art, icons, screen captures, and text), use GIF. Specifically, when an image consists of uniformly colored pieces—colored lines and shapes, for instance—GIF is the best format for getting smaller, faster-downloading files, without losing image quality.

GIF also gives the best quality for scanned-in photographs and artwork (although GIF files of photos may be huge). The main alternative, JPEG, may distort certain parts or qualities of the image in the process of making the file smaller.

GIF is also the only choice if you want to do special effects, such as animations and images with transparent areas. (See the discussions of those features later in this chapter.)

Using JPEG for Color Photographs

For color photographs, JPEG files are much smaller than GIF files. (For black-and-white photographs, JPEG doesn't offer any big advantage over GIF.) Even if an image is not actually a photograph, try using JPEG when you can see (under magnification) that most regions of the image are made up of dots of many colors. (Some drawings that have undergone *dithering*—a process of simulating a color by mixing dots of other colors—are also more efficiently stored in JPEG than in GIF.)

JPEG is not perfect for all photographs. JPEG is a *lossy* format, meaning that it discards some data to create a small file. Most graphics programs allow you to trade off JPEG quality for image size, but even the highest-quality JPEG image loses some image quality. JPEG images have small distortions, especially around sharp edges, such as the edges of text characters.

Other File Formats

Most of today's browsers display only a few file formats other than GIF and JPEG. Some browsers can display PNG format, which offers good compression and better color fidelity than GIF, and also supports transparency and progressive delivery (discussed later in this chapter). Many browsers also support the UNIX graphics file format, XBM (X Window BitMap), and some browsers support portable bitmap (PBM) formats.

Other image formats can be used on the Web for specific applications. Browsers display other formats (such as multimedia formats) if the file format is supported by special browser options. By installing a *plug-in*, which typically displays images directly in the browser window or embedded in the Web document, or a *player*, which displays an image by itself in a separate player window, you can "teach" your browser to display other graphic formats (see Chapter 22 for information about plug-ins and players).

In the future, browsers may support other file formats *intrinsically* (without plug-ins or players). In particular, Netscape and Microsoft browsers may soon support vector images, such as those created by drawing programs or that come with clip art collections. Currently, you can use vector images on conventional Web documents only if you first convert them to bitmap formats such as GIF or JPEG. If vector files could be used directly, they would download much faster, because of their smaller size. Two major vendors of Web graphics software, Adobe and Macromedia, support Web vector formats, and Microsoft's IE 5 may support an unnamed vector format. Macromedia promotes its Flash format, and Adobe promotes its Precision Graphics Markup Language (PGML) format, but both apparently are seeking a common standard.

Getting GIFs and JPEGs

How do you create images in GIF or JPEG format? The latest versions of nearly all graphics programs can output graphics to GIF or JPEG formats. If you don't already have a graphics program on your computer that outputs GIF or JPEG, you can easily download one from the Internet. This section offers a few suggestions for graphics editing programs.

Creating GIFs and JPEGs with Word Processors

The latest versions of many word processors can create Web pages with graphics. If you are using a word processor to create your Web pages, it may generate GIF or JPEG images from inserted pictures, drawings, charts, or other non-text objects on your page.

If, for instance, you use Microsoft Word or Corel WordPerfect to create a Web page, and that page contains images, the images are saved as GIF files. Equations and other inserted objects, such as spreadsheets and charts, may also be translated into GIF files. (Note that the HTML file that results, the newly-generated GIF files, and any folders that contain them must be copied to your Web server without changes—otherwise, the documents may not display the images.)

Some word processors provide additional support for Web graphics. In WordPerfect's Web view, for instance, you can right-click a graphic, choose HTML Properties, and on the Publish tab of the dialog box that appears, choose JPEG or GIF. You can choose Interlaced GIF to make the image gradually fade in, or you can choose Transparent color and then select a color in the image to be displayed transparently. WordPerfect also translates symbols, text boxes, and TextArt into bitmapped graphics.

Common Programs for Creating GIF and JPEG Files

Graphics programs come in three main varieties:

- **Paint and photo programs** Enable you to read different image files and customize them for Web use, or create a Web image of your own by using a paintbrush and other tools (an example is Adobe's Photoshop).

■ **Illustration programs**   Focus on creating images, principally vector graphics, and thus typically have fewer features for optimizing the bitmap files (such as GIF and JPEG) used on the Web (examples include Corel Draw and Adobe Illustrator).

■ **Graphics utilities**   Designed as small programs with simple features that focus on converting images from one format to another and fine-tuning those images.

The following are just a few graphics programs that are widely available:

■ **Microsoft Paint** (Windows 98 version)   The most recent version of Microsoft Paint, enables PC users to paint a simple image or read in an image in Windows bitmap (BMP), PCX, JPEG, or GIF format and then edit it. You can then save the image in GIF or JPEG rather than Paint's native PCX format.

■ **Adobe Photoshop**   A professional-level, general-purpose graphics program that enables you to scan, edit, paint, and enhance images on PCs and Macs. Photoshop also reads a variety of graphics file formats. It enables you to fine-tune your images and then output them to GIF and JPEG, as well as many other formats. Photoshop Limited Edition (LE) does the same basic tasks and often comes bundled with scanners.

■ **Paint Shop Pro**   A popular and inexpensive PC program that is similar in many respects to Photoshop. As in Photoshop, you can read various image files, scan images with a scanner, and edit, paint, add text, and enhance images. Paint Shop Pro offers a free evaluation period. You can download an evaluation copy from the Web site **http://www.jasc.com**.

■ **Lview Pro**   Another popular and inexpensive PC paint and photo tool (similar to Paintshop Pro) that also offers a free evaluation period. Its help files are a little less helpful than Paintshop Pro's, but it offers some special features for Web images. You can download a free evaluation copy from the Web site **http://www.lview.com**.

■ **GIFConverter**   An image utility program for Macs that supports many popular graphics formats, such as GIF, JPEG, and PICT. It can be downloaded from **http://www.shareware.com** and many other sites on the Web.

■ **ImageMagick**   A free image utility for X Window systems (UNIX systems) that supports JPEG conversion from and to many formats. It is created and distributed by the Independent JPEG Group, **http://www.ijg.org**.

■ **XPaint**   A well-regarded paint program for X Window systems, supporting GIF, JPEG, PPM, TIFF, XBM, XPM, and XWD formats. It can be downloaded from **http://www.shareware.com** and many other sites on the Web.

Dozens of other excellent graphics programs are available on the Web. In general, two good places to look for downloadable graphics software are **http://www.download.com** and **http://www.shareware.com**. TUCOWS, at **http:///www.tucows.com**, also lists graphics programs used for the Web. For more information on downloading and installing programs from the Web, see Chapter 38.

Creating a GIF or JPEG Image File

How do you actually create a GIF or JPEG image file with a graphics program? You can either paint or draw an image from scratch, scan an image, or convert an existing file to GIF or JPEG with a paint program or graphics utility.

■ *Paint or draw an image from scratch.* Use a paint program, such as Photoshop or Paint Shop Pro, to create your own GIF or JPEG image. Start with the File | New command. In some paint programs, you then proceed through a dialog box in which you can choose image size, number of colors, and other attributes that are described in this chapter. In other paint programs, these choices are made for you by default.

■ *Scan a paper image.* If you have a scanner installed on your computer, you can use a paint program to acquire the image. Choose File | Acquire (or a similar command) to begin the scanning process.

■ *Convert an existing file to GIF or JPEG with a paint program or graphics utility.* Open an image in the drawing program's native (vector) format and then save it as a GIF or JPEG image:

1. Select File | Open or a similar command. In the dialog box that appears in most programs, you generally must either specify which type of file you want to open (such as an Adobe Illustrator AI file or a Windows BMP file) or choose "all types," to see list of file types from which you can choose.

2. Choose File | Save As or a similar command to save a copy of your image. In the dialog box that appears, choose a file type of GIF or JPEG.

3. Look for an options button in that dialog box to control some of the attributes that are discussed in this chapter. (See the next section, "Issues in Converting Images to GIF and JPEG," for a discussion of conversion issues.)

Even if you are using a text-based UNIX connection, you may be able to do graphic file conversions.To use text-based UNIX graphics utilities, you type a command line to convert a file to GIF or JPEG. Display the program's help files for details, but the command line usually consists of the program's name, the name of the file to be read, the name of the file that you want to create, and then various "switches" (options), consisting of dashes, slashes, and letters. The switches tell the program which file type to create, and any special attributes that the file should include.

Issues in Converting Images to GIF and JPEG

Converting an image from its original format into GIF or JPEG can require you to make certain choices that involve tradeoffs. Some programs make those choices for you, unless you find the controls for those variables. Look for a Tools | Options, View | Options, or Edit | Preferences command in your program, and then look for settings that relate to file types. Here are a few of the choices that you or the program may make:

- **Colors**   Fewer colors means smaller files, but may mean poorer quality or poor fidelity to the original image. If you change the number of colors, you may have the option of telling the program how to choose new colors: use dithering or the nearest color. See "Optimizing Images for the Web," later in this chapter, for more details about color depth and palettes.

- **JPEG quality**   Many programs offer an image quality control for JPEG output. Lower quality creates a significantly smaller file, but can introduce unwanted color blurs, especially near the abrupt color changes that occur at sharp edges and text.

- **GIF version and interlacing**   Choose GIF89a if you want to use interlacing (progressive display), and then also choose interlacing. See the upcoming section, "Special Effects: Progressive Display and Transparency," for details.

If you have an image in a program that can't store the image in GIF or JPEG format, copy the image from that program's window to your computer's Clipboard (in Microsoft Windows, select the file and press CTRL+C). Then, open a new, blank image in a program that can output to GIF or JPEG (such as Microsoft Paint in Windows 98) and paste the image (CTRL+V in Windows). Now you can save the file as a GIF or JPEG file.

Getting Web Clip Art from the Internet

An amazing amount of artwork is available free of charge on the Internet. You must be careful to ensure that you obtain any such art from its legal owner (the person or entity who has the authority to give rights), and that you have the owner's permission to use it on the Web. Ask for non-exclusive worldwide rights to use the artwork on your Web site, along with rights for any derivation from the Web site (such as pictures of or articles about the Web site). Some amateur collections that are offered free are collections of other people's work, obtained without permission. Do not use art from such collections without first obtaining the true owner's permission.

Free sources come and go quickly on the Internet, so the best way to explore the world of Web clip art is through a search engine or Web guide. At Yahoo!, (**http://www.yahoo.com**) for instance, choose Computers and Internet | World Wide Web | Page Creation | Design and Layout | Graphics.

*Art Today, at **http://www.arttoday.com**, requires you to register to access its collection of clip art, but the fee is small ($30 per year) and the collection is huge (over 750,000 images).*

Special Effects: Progressive Display and Transparency

The Web uses many special effects involving graphics. Some special effects require that you do something in the Web page, such as write HTML code or use an advanced Web page development program. Two of those special effects, however, are special options of the graphics file itself: progressive display and transparency.

What Is Progressive Display?

Progressive display is one way of coping with a long download time. On many Web pages, the images don't appear until after they have been completely downloaded, or they appear gradually from top to bottom. With progressive display, the image starts blurry and gradually becomes more detailed over the entire image area as it is downloaded. Some people simply like that effect better.

A GIF file that the browser displays progressively is called an *interlaced* GIF image. Interlacing is an option only in files in the latest GIF format, called GIF89a. (The other common GIF format is GIF87a). Most tools that create GIF files give you the option of creating an interlaced GIF89a file.

A JPEG file that displays progressively is simply called *progressive JPEG*. Progressive JPEG is a fairly new effect, so only more recent browsers and graphics programs support the effect. (If a program does not support progressive JPEG, it doesn't just fail to display the file progressively; it won't be able to display the file at all.)

The PNG file format also supports progressive display. Most of the commonly available browsers and graphics programs don't yet support PNG well, however.

What Is Transparency?

Transparency is a way of making graphics look like they are drawn directly on a Web page, rather than drawn on a rectangular piece of paper and then pasted on. How does that effect work? Web pages often have a background color, image, or pattern. When an image on a Web page has transparent portions, that page background shows through the image's transparent portions. Without transparency, the image appears in a rectangular area with its own background color. Transparency is only available for GIF (and PNG) images, not JPEG images.

The alternative to transparency is to match background colors exactly between the image and the Web page, but that can be tricky. Where there is a background pattern or image on the Web page, matching is next to impossible, because you can't align the graphic precisely enough with the page background.

Setting a GIF Color to Be Transparent

The way to make a GIF image file transparent is to designate one of the colors in that image as the *transparent color*. Any part of the image that is in the color you choose then disappears entirely when the image is viewed in a Web browser. Although you usually use transparency for image backgrounds, the chosen color can be any color in the image, not just the background color. Many graphics programs that output GIF 89a file formats give you some way to choose one color as transparent.

Note that many graphics programs don't automatically show the transparent color *as* transparent! You may need to look for a special viewing option (usually in the program's View menu) actually to see the transparency. You can also open the image in your Web browser to check its transparency, with the File | Open or similar command. See the upcoming section, "Avoiding or Fixing Transparency Problems," if you have troubles with transparency.

The following two sections provide detailed instructions of two typical ways to create transparency, using Microsoft Paint and Paint Shop Pro, respectively.

Using Microsoft Paint

You can use Microsoft Paint (Windows 98 version) to create transparent GIF images. You must first save the image as a GIF file, if you haven't already done so. (Choose File | Save As and select GIF as the file type.) To make your job easier, click a distinctive color in the color palette, such as bright orange, that doesn't appear to be used anywhere in your image; then, use Paint's fill tool (the spilling-bucket icon) to fill the background area with that color.

After those preparations, choose Image | Attributes, and in the Attributes dialog box that appears, click the check box for Transparency. Click the Select Color button to choose the color in the palette that will become transparent. Microsoft Paint does not show the transparent area as transparent! You must save the image and then open it in a Web browser (choose File | Open) to see the result.

Using Paint Shop Pro

The simplest way to create a transparent GIF in Paint Shop Pro is to designate one color as the *background* color and then specify that the background color should be transparent. The following are the steps to take:

1. Click the dropper icon on the Tool palette, on the left side of the window.

2. In the image, *right*-click the color that you want to become transparent.

3. Choose Colors | Set Palette Transparency (or press CTRL+SHIFT+V). If a dialog box informs you that Paint Shop Pro must decrease the palette, click Yes. Read the upcoming section, "Optimizing Images for the Web," to make the best choices in the Set Palette Transparency dialog box that appears after you click Yes. (Or, simply click OK in that dialog box to accept the default settings.)

4. In the Set Palette Transparency dialog box, choose Set the Transparency Value to the Current Background Color, then click OK. To view the result of your transparent color selection, choose Colors | View Palette Transparency (or press SHIFT+V).

5. Choose File | Save As, and in the Save As dialog box, select CompuServe Graphics Interchange (GIF) as the file type.

6. Click the Options button in the Save As dialog box, and in the Save Options dialog box that appears, make sure that Version 89a is chosen. Click OK.

7. Click Save in the Save As dialog box.

Avoiding or Fixing Transparency Problems

Several problems can afflict your transparent image, including pinholes, ragged edges, and incomplete (spotty) transparency. You can avoid or fix many such problems.

The root of the problem is that GIF uses a *palette* (limited selection of colors) of no more than 256 colors, and each color may be used in many pixels throughout the image. If a color in the palette (distinguished not actually by its color, but by an index number in the palette, 0 to 255) is designated transparent, any pixel anywhere in the image that uses that index number will be transparent—even those outside of the area that you want to be transparent. The opposite side of the problem is that pixels in the area that you want to appear transparent may remain opaque. They may only be *similar* to your designated transparent color, not actually *of* the color whose index number you chose in the palette.

The first step in avoiding such problems is to choose a color for transparency that appears only in the area that you want transparent. You can then use that color to fill (replace) or paint the color in the area that you want to become transparent. One way to ensure that a palette color is not used in the image is to add a unique color to the palette. See the next section, "Optimizing Images for the Web," for more information on palette control.

Transparency sometimes leaves rough edges or unwanted, fuzzy borders around objects. The problem is caused by a gradual color transition along the edge, instead of a sharp one, or by a nonuniform background color. Several causes, to be avoided if possible, exist for this problem:

■ *Objects in the image (typically text) have been anti-aliased. Aliasing* is the staircase-like edge that appears around slanted or rounded edges on computer screens. *Anti-aliasing* is the removal of that staircase-like edge by making the edge less distinct: blending the object and the background colors in the pixels along the edge. Avoid anti-aliased images where transparency is needed.

■ *The image originated as a JPEG image.* JPEG images invariably have subtle color variations around edges. Try to obtain an original image in another format, or plan to spend a lot of time editing the colors in the image.

- *The image was scanned from a drawing or photograph, or is the result of a realistic computer rendering of a 3-D scene.* Realistic or hand-drawn images invariably have blurred edges, which means less color uniformity. Try rescanning (or rerendering) the image with fewer colors selected in the scanning or rendering software, and anti-aliasing turned off.

- *The image was dithered.* In *dithered* images, dots of different colors in the palette are sprinkled near each other, to give the illusion of a color that isn't in the palette. You get holes in your image in places where dots appear on the otherwise-opaque object and happen to be in the transparent color, and you get spots where dots appear on the background and are not transparent.

Dithering has a positive side, however. If you want an image either to fade gradually to a transparent background or to be partially transparent, you need dithering. No matter how close in color value a pixel is to the chosen transparent background color, that pixel will not be partially transparent. Dithering allows you to sprinkle transparent pixels in various proportions among the opaque pixels, to achieve partial transparency. The image palette, however, must not have any colors available between the foreground and background color for this effect to work, or else an intermediate, nontransparent color will be introduced.

Dithering is a double-edged sword for transparency. If given a dithered image, try to obtain the undithered original, so that the option to dither is yours. You can avoid dithering an image by careful palette control, as described in "Optimizing Images for the Web," or by changing settings in your graphics program.

If you have problems with an image because it has nonuniform colors, because of dithering or any of the other reasons just listed, you may be able to clean up the image. See "Optimizing for Quality," in the next section, for suggestions.

Optimizing Images for the Web

Creating good Web graphics is mainly a matter of balancing download speed and image quality. If you aim for speed, you reduce the number of colors and the amount of detail an image can contain. If you aim for color fidelity, use a highly detailed image, or add certain special effects, you may actually diminish image quality slightly for certain viewers of your Web graphics, and will almost certainly worsen downloading speed. Certain optimizations help minimize the tradeoff, and some graphics programs can do much of the optimization process for you.

The quality problems that you get in the normal course of creating Web graphics are subtle. (Too subtle, even, to be visible in illustrations in this book.) For casual Web sites, sizing your image properly and choosing GIF or JPEG appropriately is enough. Only for professional or business Web sites do you usually need to consider doing more.

Optimizing for Speed

Images need to download fast, or people won't wait for them before moving to another page. Download speed is essentially a matter of small file size and reusing images where possible. Four principal factors affect file size, as follows:

- Choice of format (GIF, JPEG, or PNG), and JPEG "quality" (refer to "Graphic File Formats for the Web," at the beginning of this chapter, for a discussion of format issues)
- Image dimensions
- Image content
- Number of colors

This section focuses on the last three factors in file size: dimensions, content, and colors.

 Reuse images where possible to save download time. Browsers don't download the same image file more than once in any given browsing session, even if the image (such as a button, bullet, or icon) is repeated within or among your Web pages. Some Web page development tools (especially word processors) may, however, create a separate file for each instance of an identical bullet or icon. You may need to edit the HTML file to ensure that only one of those image files is used for each instance.

Minimizing Image Dimensions

One important way to keep files small is to use the smallest practical image height and width (in pixels). If you reduce both height and width by half, for example, most image files diminish in size by at least half. A photograph in GIF format might reduce to nearly one-quarter of the original file size and download from the Web in one-quarter of the time. For drawings, where images are stored in vector format, image dimensions don't matter until you convert the image to bitmap format (GIF or JPEG).

You obtain best results by making the image the right size from the start, although you can also reduce a larger image. (Going the other direction, enlarging a smaller image, usually results in unacceptably poor quality.) Most graphics programs provide a resize, stretch, shrink, or size attribute control that you can use to reduce image size. (You usually find the sizing commands in the Image menu, if you use Photoshop, Paint Shop Pro, or one of the many other popular PC and Macintosh graphics programs.)

 To avoid distorting an image any more than necessary, don't crop, shrink, or otherwise edit an image that is in JPEG format. In some programs, doing any of these things may make the image dimmer, as well as distort it. Save the image to another format before you edit it.

Only one kind of dimension is relevant in Web images: *pixels*. Some graphics programs show image dimensions in inches or centimeters (cm), by default (look on the status bar, in many programs, to see which scale it uses for image dimensions). If you can set dimensions in pixels in your program, don't be concerned with dimensions displayed in other units, or with resolution. If your graphics program does not show dimensions in pixels, you can calculate pixel dimensions. Multiply the dimensions in inches (or cm) by the resolution in pixels per inch (or cm) that the program displays. Adjust image size in such a program by adjusting either the dimension in inches (or cm) or the resolution; the result is the same. Some drawing programs may not even discuss pixels until you try to save your file in a GIF format.

If you are using a program to create your Web pages, and shrinking the graphics in that program doesn't seem to make them download faster, try reducing the image size in a graphics program. When you're creating a Web page, you may be able to force an image into a space smaller than its pixel dimensions, but forcing won't reduce the file size and it will hurt the image quality. For instance, the following HTML code forces Image.gif to be displayed in a space 126 by 126 pixels, regardless of its actual dimensions:

```
<img src="Image.gif" width="126" height="126">
```

The file is still transmitted in its entirety, so it takes just as long to download as if it were not forced into smaller dimensions. The browser receiving this document will perform the job of reducing the image size to 126 by 126 pixels on the screen. Browsers are not as good as most graphics programs at this kind of task, so you achieve better quality and a smaller file by reducing the image size in a graphics program rather than in a browser.

Reducing a GIF image's size affects its quality, because the program must eliminate pixels, a process that can distort or eliminate small features and introduce rough edges. Some programs can smooth the result by anti-aliasing. Anti-aliasing can become objectionable, however, if the background color is transparent or if the image is displayed on computer hardware or browser software that has only limited color range. See the upcoming section, "Optimizing for Quality," for information on controlling anti-aliasing.

Minimizing or Avoiding Certain Types of Image Content

Images with less detail (or, more precisely, more uniformity among its pixels) create smaller files. All graphics formats for the Web rely on data compression, and uniformity aids compression. In data compression, if a group of pixels is identical in color, each pixel doesn't require its own color value in the file—the group can be represented by a single value. The fewer color changes that occur in a row of pixels, the fewer groups that are needed, and thus the smaller the file. For that reason, certain image attributes are costly in file size, such as the following: horizontally graduated fills (where a color changes gradually from left to right), patterned backgrounds, dithering, speckling, high-resolution photographs, images with printing screens applied, images scanned from coarsely screened media such as newspapers, and scanned image files for which the color palette is larger than the original number of colors in the artwork.

The best solution is to seek better original artwork. Failing that, you need to make the image's colors more uniform, blur or despeckle the image, or choose a different way to minimize file size, such as reducing the number of colors, described in the following section. To make colors more uniform, see the upcoming section, "Optimizing for Quality." To blur or despeckle the image, look for a blur or despeckle filter in your graphics program. Photoshop, Paint Shop Pro, Lview Pro, and other common graphics programs offer a variety of filters for removing excessive detail and color variation. Some scanner software also offers descreening settings.

Minimizing and Flattening Colors

Usually, the fewer colors your image uses, the smaller the file. If you are drawing a picture, use as few colors as possible right from the start. In addition, many graphics programs let you reduce the color palette of an existing image, which is called *flattening* the colors. Reducing the palette reduces the size of the image file, but not because the file has less palette data (palette data is a small part of the image file). When the program removes colors, it gives the affected pixels new colors. It has fewer colors to choose from, so a pixel is more likely to match a neighboring pixel's color. The pixels are then part of a same-color pixel group, and no longer require their own data in the file.

If you use a graphics program to reduce colors, be aware that how it reduces the colors is important. If a program removes a color from the palette, the image file gets smaller only if the program simply reassigns the next-closest color to the pixels that had the removed color. If the program compensates by dithering, the file may not get significantly smaller, because dithering makes pixels different from their neighbors, thus requiring each pixel to have its own data in the file.

Most graphics programs that offer color reduction let you choose a reduction process. Look for options in the dialog box that appears when you reduce colors. The process that helps to minimize file size is often called *nearest-color* substitution. The other process, dithering, goes under various names, but a common one is *error diffusion*.

Optimizing for Quality

Rapid downloading is important, but you also need to maintain a level of quality. Given a certain size and content, the way to ensure quality is to choose the file format well and control the depth and uniformity of color in the image.

Choosing Color Depth and Palettes in GIF and JPEG

The number of different colors an image file can contain is called its *color depth*. GIF files have a maximum color depth of 256 colors, which is called *8-bit color*, but can also have depths of 7 bits (128 colors), 6 bits (64 colors), 5, 4, 3, 2, or 1 bit. JPEG files have a fixed color depth of 16.7 million colors, called *24-bit color*, a depth that makes JPEG images generally better for color photographs. Within a given depth, the actual number of colors used in the image (the *palette*) can be fewer than the color depth allows. An 8-bit GIF image (256 colors possible), for instance, might use only 200 colors.

But GIF files aren't as limited as they seem, and JPEG files are not as high-quality as they seem. The quality of both depends on the computer that displays them. Most older computers (those with VGA display adapters) can display only 256 different colors (which is why GIF images use only 256 or fewer colors). Today, some computers can display 16.7 million different colors. Many computers can still display only 256 or fewer colors, but those can now be *any* 256 colors out of 16.7 million, 64,000, or some other very large number.

GIF images today are equally flexible. You (or your graphics program) can *choose* the 256 colors out of 16.7 million colors that best match the colors in your original image. You can also choose a smaller palette or color depth, to save file size, or choose a specific palette, to match better the palette of a broad range of computer displays (as described in the following section).

So-called *true color* formats, such as JPEG or 24-bit PCX, do not use a palette: each pixel can be any color out of 16.7 million. However, if a computer cannot display a particular color in a JPEG image, it either chooses the closest color it can display or approximates the missing color by dithering other colors, depending on the browser. To minimize quality problems caused by such compromises in the browser, create your image in (or convert your image to) a palette format such as GIF and then convert the file to JPEG.

If your Web page has several images on it, make sure that all images use the same palette. Computers that use screen palettes can display the colors of only one palette at a time. If you have images with different palettes, you may force the computer to substitute or dither colors.

Choosing Between Quality and Control

Web images sometimes look worse when they are viewed in a browser or on someone else's computer than they looked originally. This problem arises because either the browser, the computer's display adapter, or its operating system doesn't have as many different display colors as the original hardware and software. To compensate for the colors that it doesn't have, the displaying system must either dither the image by mixing dots of colors that it does have, or substitute colors for the original ones. The result can be speckled images or peculiar colors.

To avoid having some other computer dither or substitute colors in your image, you need to use the smallest commonly used color palette. That minimal palette, sometimes called a *Web-safe* or *Netscape palette,* consists of 216 specific color values that were chosen by Netscape years ago. (An even more minimal palette is the set of 16 fixed, so-called *Windows colors.*)

If you choose to create images in this limited palette, you sacrifice the maximum quality that your image could provide in order to gain control. You, not the system on which your image is viewed, now control how the dithering is done and what colors appear where. In gaining that control, you reduce your image to the lowest common denominator. You lose the quality that a larger palette offers: a crisper, richer, higher fidelity image.

Should you make the tradeoff? The decision depends on how much you care about delivering top image quality to the viewers in your audience, but with lower graphics capability. The Web-safe, 216-color standard assumes people are running the lowest color quality commonly available in Microsoft Windows: 256 colors (8-bit color). Some systems, however (certain UNIX systems, for instance), actually use even lower color depth than that. The majority of computers and browsers today use much higher color depth. Many run at least 16-bit color (32,000 or 64,000 colors). By adopting Web-safe colors, you deprive those viewers of higher quality. Many Web sites now optimize their graphics for this higher color depth.

USING A WEB-SAFE PALETTE   If you decide to use the Web-safe colors, for maximum control, how do you do so? All but the most basic graphics programs let you construct a palette, load a palette from a file, or customize a palette of an existing image by removing, adding, or adjusting colors. Some programs offer Web-safe palettes, downloadable from the vendor's Web site. Adobe, for instance, offers a Web-safe Photoshop palette developed by Lynda Weinman (whose Web site is at **http://www.lynda.com**) at its download center at the following site:

http://www.adobe.com/supportservice/custsupport /download.html

One practical way to get a Web-safe palette is to obtain an image in Web-safe colors, save the palette as a separate file (if your graphics program allows it), and then apply that palette file to your own images. An example of such an image file is **http://the-light.com/netcolpc.gif**, created by Victor S. Engle. You can find other examples on the Web by searching for the phrase "Web-safe palette." Open a Web-safe image in your graphics program and look for a menu pick that lets you save the image's palette as a file. In Paint Shop Pro, for instance, choose Colors | Save Palette. In Photoshop, use Mode | Color Table. Once you have this palette as a file, you can load it either before you create a new image or after you open an existing image, to convert that image to Web-safe colors.

To create a Web-safe palette manually, first determine whether your graphics program lets you edit palette colors. Then, you need the list of Web-safe colors from Netscape. The list currently is available on Netscape's Web site, in the document entitled "Netscape Navigator's color palette on Windows," in a file named 960513-14.html; searching for "palette" at **http://help.netscape.com** should locate this document. After you obtain this document, you manually type some or all of the values that it lists for red, green, and blue (R, G, and B) into your palette and then create your image. To edit colors in the palette of an existing image, you must change each existing color's set of R, G, and B values to the closest Web-safe set, which is difficult to determine.

Eliminating Problems with Photographs in GIF

The GIF format sometimes displays photographs poorly. If a photograph in GIF format is blotchy or speckled, uses unrealistic colors, or has bands of color instead of gradation, it may have been scanned using too few colors, or its palette may have been reduced too far. Repeat the scan or palette reduction from the original image, using a larger palette. You can also reduce a speckled or banded area to a uniform color. (See the following section.) A more attractive way to replace blotches, pools, or bands of colors may be to "smudge" certain areas of the image or apply a "blur" filter, if your graphics program provides those tools.

Reducing Mixed Colors to a Single Color

Reducing an area of mixed colors to a uniform color can improve image quality, minimize file size, and help you get uniform transparency for that color with no unwanted holes or spots. The simplest approach is to paint over a nonuniform area with a single color, using the painting or drawing tools common in many graphics programs. Click a distinctive (and for transparency, unused) color in the palette that your program displays, click a paintbrush or other drawing tool, and then drag across the area of the image that you want to paint.

If the area that you want to repaint has irregular edges, however, such as the background behind a flower, manually repainting the area is difficult. If the mixed colors in that area are similar to each other (say, a variety of lighter and darker greens), you can sometimes improve uniformity by reducing the number of colors in the image palette.

More advanced programs, such as Photoshop and Paint Shop Pro, offer tools that allow you to replace a range of colors with a single color. The next two sections tell you how to do it.

PHOTOSHOP   Photoshop provides a "magic wand" that lets you select an area of similar colors and then fill that area with a single color. Click the Magic Wand button on the toolbar and then click the area of the image that you want to reduce to a uniform color. To adjust the range of colors selected, choose Window | Palettes | Show Options to display the Options palette. In the Tolerance box, enter a larger value to expand the range of colors, or a smaller value to reduce the range, and then click the image again. You will need several tries to select the pixels that you want. To expand or contract an area, choose Select | Modify | Expand (or Contract). To add individual areas to the selection, press CTRL while clicking areas of the image; to remove areas, press SHIFT while clicking. To fill the selection with a single color, choose a foreground color on the toolbar, click the Fill tool (the spilling paint can), and then click the selected area.

PAINT SHOP PRO   Paint Shop Pro has magic wand and fill functions very similar to Photoshop's. To select a range of colors, click the Magic Wand tool and then click the image. To adjust the range of colors that the wand selects when you click, use the Controls palette. If that palette is not on your screen, either click the Toggle Control Palette button on the toolbar, or choose View | Toolbars and click to place a check mark in the Control Palette check box.

In the Control Palette, as in Photoshop's Options palette, is a Tolerance box for adjusting the range of colors selected. You will need several tries with different tolerance values to select the pixels that you want. Between tries, remove your previous selection by pressing CTRL+D; then, adjust the tolerance value and click the image again to try your new tolerance. Paint Shop Pro's Magic Wand allows you to select pixels by *hue* (color, such as blue, regardless of brightness or darkness), brightness, or *RGB value* (color and brightness combined). Choose one of these methods in the Match Mode selection box of the Control Palette.

Animating GIF Graphics

Animated graphics for the Web take various forms, but they are usually *animated GIF* files, a single file containing multiple images that your browser can play in succession. You can place animated GIF images on a Web page just as you would regular GIF images. Each image is a frame of the animation, like a frame of a movie. You can set the time between frames and make the animation loop either indefinitely or a fixed number of times. Netscape Navigator and Microsoft Internet Explorer display animated GIFs without additional software. Some graphics utilities and paint programs designed for single images, however, display only the first or last frame of the animation.

Other forms of animated graphics may use Java, which you can code by hand or use a development tool that outputs Java, such as Microsoft's Liquid Motion or Corel products using Corel's Barista technology. Such tools can often help you to convert standard presentations, done in Microsoft or Corel presentation formats, into Web slide shows or animations. The person viewing the file needs a Java-compatible browser to see the animation. Java does not, as a rule, transmit multiple images the way animated GIF does, but instead transmits code that draws a sequence of images on the browser screen. The code can be extensive and require long download times. In addition to Java, vector graphics file formats, such as Macromedia's Flash and Adobe's PGML, can provide animation, but (as of this writing) also require special browser plug-ins.

Animated GIF graphics often come as part of the clip art bundled with graphics programs and Web development tools. They are also available for free from the same Web sites that offer other free clip art. Sources to search for on the Web include "GIF Animation Station." At Yahoo!, to see a listing that includes free clip art sites, choose Computers and Internet | World Wide Web | Page Creation | Design and Layout | Graphics.

Animations are very easy to create—with the right graphics tools. Among the commonly used tools for animations are the following:

- **Animation Shop** (distributed with Paintshop Pro 5)   An inexpensive, capable, and easy-to-use program available from **http://www.jasc.com** on the Web (the same company that makes Paint Shop Pro). Animation Shop helps you assemble multiple GIF images into an animation, generate animated special effects from single images, and optimize your palette.

- **Adobe Image Ready**   A professional Web development tool that runs on a variety of computers and includes animated GIF output, palette optimization, and special effects. Image Ready integrates tightly with Adobe Illustrator, which you can use to create the original artwork to be animated.

- **CorelDRAW 8**   A high-end graphics suite that is available for a variety of computers. The drawing module enables you to create images for animation, and the paint module can assemble and output the images as an animated GIF file with optimized palettes. See **http://www.corel.com**.

- **GifBuilder**   A popular and simple freeware GIF animator for the Macintosh, developed by Yves Piguet, and available at **http://www.download.com**.

- **GIF Construction Set**   An inexpensive program that is available as shareware from Alchemy Mindworks at **http://www.mindworkshop.com**. It includes clever GIF animation wizards, performs palette optimization, and can create animations by generating transition effects (such as wipes or fades) between individual GIF images.

- **Ulead GIF Animator**   A program that offers a variety of inexpensive and nicely featured Web graphics tools at its site, **http://www.webutilities.com**. One such tool, GIF Animator, provides animation and optimization wizards, plus a variety of transition effects for creating animations based on one or two original images.

- **Xanim**   A multipurpose utility for X-Window UNIX workstations that provides GIF animations from a variety of animation and video formats, including AVI, FLC, FLI, and MOV files.

- **Imaging Machine**   A remotely located program that you run from your Web browser, not on your computer. If you have a way to upload your individual GIF images to a Web site or FTP site (as described in Chapter 36), you can use the Imaging Machine at Visioneering Research Laboratory, Inc.'s Web site, **http://www.vrl.com/Imaging/animate.html**, to create an animated GIF file.

Creating and Animating Image Sequences

The best way to create the series of images that you need for an animation usually is with a drawing program, not a paint program. With a drawing program, you can move and adjust shapes very flexibly. (A paint program with multiple layer capability, such as Photoshop, can also suffice.)

Drawing programs, however, normally store their images as vector-format (drawing) files, not as GIF files. (See the first section of this chapter, "Graphic File Formats for the Web.") Some professional drawing programs intended for Web development may directly create animated GIF files from a sequence of vector images, but most drawing tools will not. In most drawing tools, the process involves creating a series of drawing files (one for each frame), converting each one to a GIF file, and then using a GIF animation tool to assemble those GIF images into a single animated GIF file. In more detail, the process usually looks like this:

1. Using your drawing program, draw the image that you want to animate. Group together any shapes that make up an object that you want to animate. Save your starting image (the first frame) as a drawing file.

2. Create a single frame of your animation by slightly moving, rotating, resizing, or changing the coloring or shape of the object(s) that you want to animate. Do not change the dimensions or palette of your drawing, however. If your drawing program offers a motion-blur feature, apply that feature to your moving object to enhance the illusion of motion between frames.

3. Save your modified image as a separate drawing file.

4. Repeat Steps 2 and 3 until you have finished all the frames of your animation and saved them as separate files.

5. If your GIF animation program can't directly read the format in which you have stored your frame drawings, convert each frame drawing file to a separate GIF file by using a graphics utility or paint program. (Photoshop, for example, can read Adobe Illustrator, EPS, or PICT drawing files and output GIF files.)

6. Run your GIF animation software to assemble the frame images into a single GIF file. The details of this process vary from program to program, but most make the process simple. Some programs, such as the PC-based Animation Shop, provide a wizard that steps you through the process. In other programs, such as the Mac-based GifBuilder, you can simply drag the frame files into the Frame window of the program.

Your GIF animation software may offer a variety of options for your animation. It can let you set the time interval between frames and how many times the animation repeats before it stops. The better programs provide automatic features that can optimize the palette for speed or image quality. In addition, a good program can often apply to your animated images the same features of transparency and interlacing that you use in still GIF images.

Some GIF animation software, including Ulead GIF Animator and Jasc's Animation Shop, can also convert movies (such as Microsoft's AVI files) and other animations (such as AutoDesk's FLC or FLI files) to animated GIFs. Animated GIFs offer the advantages of not requiring special software and downloading faster than many movie formats. The usual tradeoff is lower image quality.

The following are some tips for creating a GIF animation:

- Some drawing programs can output directly to GIF, possibly saving you a conversion step (Step 5, earlier in this section). You may, however, get better conversion results by converting the file to GIF in a paint program or graphics utility.

- A word processor that has drawing features and writes text and graphics to HTML, such as Corel WordPerfect (and to a lesser extent, Microsoft Word), can be a simple animation tool. In a blank document, draw an image or insert clip art and then copy the image repeatedly, moving or changing some object each time that you copy, to animate the object. When you output to HTML, you get a series of GIF images that you can animate with a GIF animation tool (and a blank HTML document that you can discard).

- Use images that are all the same size and from the same palette. Changing palettes in mid-animation can cause peculiar coloring effects.

- If your drawing program does not output a format that your graphics utility or paint program can read and convert to GIF, try using your computer's copy and paste techniques to copy each image between your drawing software and your graphics utility or paint program.

- Continuous looping is an option, but is distracting and usually annoying to watch.

- Time intervals between frames do not apply while the image is being downloaded to someone's browser. As a result, the first playing of the animation will be uneven.

- Keep it short! People generally don't wait for long graphics downloads, and the longer the animation, the bigger the GIF file.

Animating with JavaScript: Rollovers

JavaScript is slightly off the topic of creating Web graphics, because it is part of the HTML document, not part of an image. Nonetheless, you can use JavaScript to animate graphics interactively (in response to user activity). The user must have a Java-enabled browser, however.

JavaScript can load and unload images in response to a variety of events. A common use of JavaScript is the *rollover*, which calls attention to an HTML link by replacing the linked image with another image when the cursor passes over the link.

(See Chapter 34 for more details on JavaScript rollover code.) A simple (but slow-responding) example is the following:

```
<A HREF="nextpage.html"
onmouseover = "document.mysymbol.src = 'image2.gif' "
onmouseout = "document.mysymbol.scr = 'image1.gif'"
<IMG SRC="image1.gif" WIDTH="100" HEIGHT="100" BORDER="0"
NAME="mysymbol"></A>
```

As the user passes a cursor over the link to nextpage.html, the image1.gif image is replaced by image2.gif. The downloading time for image2.gif makes the effect slow when it is first used.

Advanced Features of Graphics Programs

Many graphics and drawing programs today have various advanced features that are useful for Web graphics. Many of the graphics programs already mentioned, such as Photoshop and Paint Shop Pro, offer some or all of these advanced features. Here are two other professional-level programs for creating Web graphics:

- **Macromedia Fireworks**   Macromedia's tool for Macintosh and PC computers offers slicing, optimization, image mapping, JavaScript rollovers, paint tools, animation, and *tweening* (animation transition effects). You can download a trial version of Fireworks from **http://www.macromedia.com**.

- **Adobe ImageReady**   This Adobe tool for Macintosh and PC computers offers palette optimization, animation, image maps, image slicing, and tiled backgrounds.

The following sections describe some of the advanced features that you will find useful for Web graphics in the preceding programs and other programs.

Anti-Aliasing

Anti-aliasing is a method of reducing the "jaggies," a staircase-like effect more properly called *aliasing*, that appears along slanted lines on computer images. Anti-aliasing works by creating color values that are intermediate between the object color and the background color, and then using those values to fill in the steps of the staircase. Anti-aliasing also helps display fine detail, such as the *serifs* (small protrusions) that many fonts have. Where a serif or other detail is smaller than a single pixel, anti-aliasing uses a faded version of the object color to give the illusion of less than one pixel.

The disadvantages of anti-aliasing are that file size increases and you get unintended intermediate colors along the edges of your objects. If you create a transparent background, you get an opaque fringe around the edges of objects.

Some programs do anti-aliasing automatically. The process is used in two common circumstances: to reduce the dimensions of an image and to apply text or other sharp-edged objects. Some tools refrain from automatically anti-aliasing GIF and other palette-based images, but only anti-alias 24-bit, "true color" images. If you are converting a 24-bit image to a palette (GIF) image, convert it before you shrink it or apply text to it, if you want to avoid anti-aliasing. On the other hand, if you want maximum image quality, do the conversion last and make sure anti-aliasing is turned on.

Image Slicing

Many Web page designs let the visitor click graphics, instead of text, to navigate to various documents of the site. (The images may still contain text, but in some font or graphical treatment that regular HTML document text would not allow.) You can accomplish the incorporation of graphics as links in two ways:

- Use a single image linked to an *image map*, a special feature of the HTML document, in which clicking different parts of an image links the viewer to different URLs

- Slice the image into several pieces, arrange them seamlessly in a table, and then link them separately

In the second method, you can give each piece of the image *alternate text* that appears if the image hasn't yet downloaded or the visitor has disabled browser graphics. The visitor can then explore your site without a long wait or a special effort. The second method also enables you to substitute a new piece of the image (in a different color, perhaps, to indicate a previously explored link) without requiring the visitor's browser to download an entire image. This method requires a graphics program that can *slice* an image into several parts and save each part as an image.

Background (Seamless) Tiling

Web pages can have an image for a background (a feature coded into the HTML page, not the image itself, as described in Chapters 27 and 28). That image automatically *tiles*—repeats itself in rows and columns—across the width and height of the browser window. Only one copy of the image file is downloaded; the browser does the repetition. To make the background image into a continuous surface, especially a textured surface, such as pebbles, flocked paper, or granite, the image must not appear to repeat; or if it does appear to repeat, like wallpaper, it should not show seams. Some advanced programs offer special features for *seamless tiling,* matching the left side of an image to its right side, and its top to its bottom, so that no obvious border appears. Such background images can be quite small, requiring little download time, yet still fill the page.

Advanced Compression and Optimization

Optimizing an image for speed and quality is no easy task. You must consider the different computers and browsers viewing the image, the image content, the palette, and more. Some Web graphics optimizing tools can help you trim file size in half, even after your best manual efforts. Many of the tools already mentioned include optimizations of various sorts. More-advanced tools are available, either in the form of programs or filters. Filters often conform to the Photoshop plug-in filter standard, which means that a wide variety of programs can use them. Some advanced tools may require that you have a good comprehension of computer graphics issues to use the tool properly. The following are two examples of filters especially designed for compression and optimization:

- **Boxtop Software**   Offers a variety of Photoshop-standard filters for the Mac and PC. Image Vice is one such filter that performs advanced palette optimization as well as *clipping, smoothing,* and *convergence* operations that reduce areas of mixed colors into sets of uniform colors, for better compression. A small preview is offered.

- **Ulead SmartSaver**   A PC Photoshop-standard filter that lets you create GIF, JPEG, and PNG images with optimized palettes, and provides a useful preview of the image and its file size as you make adjustments.

Using Special Effects to Create Animations or Enhance Graphics

Animation programs often can create a GIF animation from individual images either by *tweening* (creating transition frames between images) or by expanding upon a single image, using such special effects as wipes, fades, dissolves, and explodes. Some programs contain all that you need to do text-only animations using those effects. Figure 29-1 shows a waving "flag" animation of text in Animation Shop.

Multimedia Graphics

Multimedia generally refers to movies, animations, audio, and *interactivity* (response to user input). You can think of multimedia on the Web as coming in two forms: *standard* video, audio, and animation files in formats supported by more than one vendor, and *proprietary* multimedia that requires acquiring a particular vendor's proprietary

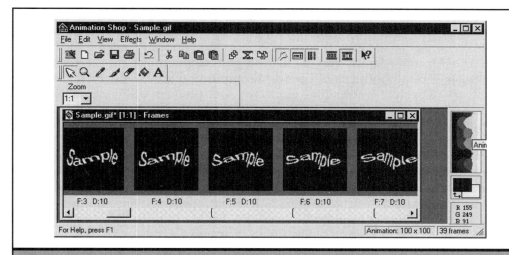

Figure 29-1. *Some animation programs offer complete text animation and transition effects*

software to either create or play. (This book discusses audio in Chapter 30, and certain advanced Web concepts related to multimedia in Chapter 34.)

Standard multimedia graphics include animation in GIF and Java, and video in several forms: MPEG (Motion Picture Experts Group), AVI (Microsoft's audio/video format, Audio Video Interleave), and QuickTime (Apple's audio/video format). Exactly *how* standard these formats are is open to debate. In earlier Web browsers, you needed additional plug-ins to view all of these formats. Gradually, browser vendors are including in Web browsers the capability to view these formats (or to use the operating system's ability to view them). Yet, not all users can view all of these formats or their variants without adding plug-ins or players, particularly UNIX users. Unsurprisingly, AVI works most reliably under Windows and in Internet Explorer, and QuickTime works most reliably on Macintosh computers. UNIX users can obtain players, such as Xanim, to view these formats. Chapter 22 discusses viewing issues further.

Standard animation on the Web currently is achieved by using GIF (discussed earlier in this chapter) or Java and Dynamic HTML (DHTML). Java is a programming language that runs within Java-capable browsers and that can animate graphics in various ways. The programs, called *applets*, are downloaded to your browser by a Web page and then executed. Chapter 34 discusses Java applets and DHTML further. In addition, new formats are always being proposed for the Web. The vendors of two vector formats, Macromedia's Flash and Adobe's PGML (discussed in the first section of this chapter), are making these formats open to the public. If the formats are adopted as standards by the World Wide Web Consortium (W3C) or by browser and development tool vendors, they will enable yet another form of standard animation.

Preparing standard Web video formats requires a video source (a camera, VCR, and a video capture card or a digital video disk) with video editing software—or an animation program. Most video or animation programs (Adobe Premier, Caligari Truespace, or Macromedia Director, for instance) can output movie files in standard video formats. Video requires significant data compression to be useful on the Web, and uses various compression engines (software). One problem with video is that the browser or player requires the same compression engine that the creator program used, and not all computers have access to all the different engines. Even with compression, most video files require significant download time.

The most well-known proprietary multimedia software on the Web is by Macromedia. Macromedia distributes its Shockwave players (plug-ins) aggressively, so many people have the ability to view Macromedia's multimedia formats. Macromedia's principal formats are its movie and Flash (vector graphics) formats. You can create Macromedia video movies and animations with audio by using either Macromedia Director or Macromedia Flash (see its Web site at **http://www.macromedia.com** for details.

Chapter 30

Creating Web Audio Files

The Web includes every sort of interesting combination of sound, video, synchronized photo slide shows, animated graphics—there's a new variation every week. Audio is perhaps the most useful medium beyond ordinary text and graphics, the most practical for ordinary modems, and essential to mixed media productions. A good knowledge of Web audio also carries over directly to other multimedia that you may tackle in the future. This chapter concentrates on how to create audio files for inclusion on Web pages.

Because most people were introduced to digital audio with compact disks, they tend to think that any digitized sounds must be of very high quality. The truth is that *digital* audio simply refers to any sounds stored as a series of numbers, and the quality varies tremendously. Essentially, the better the quality, the more numbers that are required: a three-minute popular song, for example, consumes about 30 million bytes on an ordinary CD. This is far too much data to place on the Web for transfer to modem users. The data size becomes manageable only by starting with recording format options that give less than CD quality. Often, you can then further reduce the size with *encoding* software.

Types of Web Audio Files

Audio comes in a variety of file formats, just as graphics do. Different formats use different *encoding* methods (methods of translating sound information into digital data). A program that stores audio (or video) data is called a *codec* (coder-decoder). Your choice of format depends on what degree of sound quality you want, the audio software tools that you have available on your computer, and the degree to which various formats are supported on the Web.

Static vs. Streaming Audio Files

Web audio formats generally fall into two categories: static and streaming. Ordinary audio files are also called *static* files, and can be of various formats and quality. You upload these files to your Web server much as you would your own Web pages, and then link to them. The user links to your audio file and waits for the *entire file* to download. Then, an associated sound program begins to play the file. Commonly used formats include WAV, AIFF, AU, and MP3 files.

Streaming audio files allow the user to start hearing the sound within a few seconds of the beginning of the download. After several seconds, during which the user's streaming player program *buffers* (stores temporarily) the first part of the data (the *preroll* time), the audio begins playing and continues as the program downloads further portions of the file. If the downloading data is not interrupted, the audio can continue to play indefinitely as the audio data *streams* into your PC, keeping just ahead of what you're hearing.

To implement streaming, your Web pages link to a *metafile,* a small text file that contains the name and location of the actual audio file. Why this complication? If you link directly to the audio file, the browser program dutifully downloads the entire file before turning it over to the player program, defeating the purpose of streaming. By first linking to a tiny metafile, your browser hands the metafile over to the player, which can then stream the actual sound file. However, if the average throughput of the user's Internet link is less than required for your stream, either the player refuses to play it or inevitable tiresome pauses occur during playback while the player rebuffers.

This chapter describes the two most prevalent audio streaming standards: RealNetworks' *RealSystem G2* (also called *RealAudio*) and Microsoft's Windows Media Services (formerly *NetShow*). For more information about RealSystem G2 and RealAudio, see **http://www.real.com** on the Web; the RealNetworks Developer Zone is at **http://www.real.com/devzone**. For information about Microsoft Windows Media Services, see one of these Web sites:

> **http://www.microsoft.com/ntserver/nts/mediaserv**
> **http://www.microsoft.com/windows/windowsmedia**

The following are the advantages of using ordinary static audio:

- **Quality** Because larger files simply mean longer downloads, you can send short amounts of high-quality sound if the user tolerates the wait. Musicians' Web sites sometimes include 20-second clips of some of their songs in static audio, wanting their visitors to sample the full richness of their work.

- **No midstream pauses** A static file may take a long time to download, but once it does, the static file should always play perfectly, and you can save it and play it again and again.

- **No plug-ins to download** The programs to play many formats may already be part of the user's operating system. (Windows and Macs come with audio software to play many static audio file formats.)

- **No need for a special server** Streaming audio may work without a special streaming server program running on the Web server, but it usually works better through such a server.

The following are the advantages of streaming audio:

- **Long programs are practical** People can listen to a three-hour presentation with only a few seconds of initial delay—truly a remarkable advantage. With static audio, even the delay for a three-minute clip may be more than most of your users will tolerate. Streaming audio also allows live feeds, in which the Web site creates the audio stream on-the-fly and serves the audio just a few seconds after it happens.

- **More features** The same encoder and player that you use for your streaming system may allow many additional features, such as merging video, graphics, and slide shows. Because streaming audio formats are of adjustable size and quality, just like static audio, you can choose to serve a high-quality audio file without streaming to modem users—it being no worse than—and often faster than—other static audio formats.

CREATING AND MAINTAINING WEB SITES

Types of Audio Files

Audio files can contain sound with varying degrees of quality, with higher quality coming at the cost of slower downloading. Some audio file formats in popular use are shown in Table 30-1.

One consideration in your choice of format is quality. The basic factors that affect audio quality are the following:

- **Sampling rate, given in samples per second (or hertz [Hz], which means the same thing)**   Most common audio files deliver *"sampled"* audio (with the notable exception of MIDI), which means that they represent sound waves by a series of numbers, called *samples*. The more samples recorded per second, the higher the quality and fidelity of the sound file.

- **Sample depth (in bits per sample, such as 8, 16, or 32)**   The more bits per sample, the more closely the sample represents the original (or intended) sound wave, and the higher is the audio quality.

- **Number of channels**   One channel gives monaural sound, two channels allow stereo, and more channels can be used for a variety of purposes.

- **Compression**   The more efficient the compression, the greater the sample rate and depth that is possible for a given download time. MPEG audio is generally considered to offer the best compression/quality tradeoff.

Most tools for developing static audio files offer a variety of file types. In general, however, you will find that audio tools on the PC tend to favor the WAV format, tools on Macintoshes favor the AIFF format, and tools on UNIX workstations favor the Mu-law format. The RealSystem G2 (RealAudio) streaming file format is supported on a wide variety of computers. (For more on RealSystem G2, see the following section.)

How to Create Audio Files for the Web

The typical steps in putting sound recordings on the Web—whether they are in static or streaming format—are the following:

1. Capture the audio with a recording device, such as a cassette, minidisc, or DAT (digital audio tape).

2. Generate an uncompressed audio file on your computer by using its sound card.

3. (*optional*) Edit and process the uncompressed audio.

4. Encode the file into a different audio format, which usually compresses the file size in the process.

5. Load the resulting audio onto your Web server and add links to the audio files from your Web pages.

Name	File Extension	MIME Type/Subtype	Features
Apple's Audio Interchange File Format	AIF, AIFF	audio/x-aiff	Regular and stereo (multichannel), varying sample rates; not compact.
Windows Media (NetShow)	ASF, ASX	video/x-ms-asf	Wide range of sampling quality, multichannel. Designed for audio and video streaming.
Mu-law (U-law)	AU, SND	audio/basic	Telephone quality audio, sampled at 8Kbps; fairly compact; commonly used.
Modules	MOD	audio/x-mod	8-bit sampled audio at various rates, plus data for special playing effects; fairly compact.
MPEG Audio Layer 3	MP3	audio/x-mpeg	Wide range of quality, multichannel; quite compact.
RealSystem G2 or RealAudio	RA, RM, RAM, RPM	audio/ x-pn-realaudio	Wide range of sampling quality, multichannel; quite compact. Designed for audio streaming, not static audio.
Resource Interchange File Format, Waveform Audio Format	WAV	audio/x-wav	Wide range of sampling quality; regular and multichannel audio, similar to AIFF.
MIDI (Musical Instrument Digital Interface)	MID, MIDI	audio/x-midi	Not for sampled audio, but a music description language. Far more compact than sampled music.

Table 30-1.   *Some Popular Web Audio Formats*

Step 1. Capturing the Audio

The secret to creating successful Web audio is to start with a good, clean recording. While many books are available regarding audio recording techniques, the following few pointers can help you to get your digital audio project off to a good start:

■ *Always obtain rights to post your recording.* Don't just ask "May I record your speech?" Instead, be specific: ask "May I have your permission to place a recording of your speech on my organization's Web site? You would retain copyright, and I'll note that on the Web page." Written releases are even better. Remember, obtaining permission to use a recording for one purpose doesn't necessarily give you rights to use it for other purposes. Even though you may be making a nonprofit use of a recording, you are still subject to copyright laws. Be especially careful when posting music on the Web, because performers, composers, and publishers may all have rights to grant.

■ *Don't rely on post-processing to clean up recording deficiencies.* If the original recording is muddled, distorted, or noisy, a good final product may be impossible to obtain.

■ *Suit the tools to the task.* A recording of a PTA meeting for the Web doesn't require the same degree of attention to detail as does a music recording intended for both the Web and a demonstration CD. You don't need to spend lavishly to obtain very acceptable Web audio.

■ *For speech or singing, place the microphone within a foot of the performer's mouth.* In general, your ears can perceive sound cleanly at a much greater distance than can your microphone. (A microphone *too* close, though, can result in pops, distortion, or excessive breath sounds.) Remind the speaker to repeat comments made by anyone who is not at one of your microphones.

■ *Get a feed.* When an existing public address system or professional music-mixing board is already set up at the recording venue, in most cases, you'll benefit by obtaining a direct feed (that is, a cable connection) from the board to your recording device. Be certain that you have a compatible adapter and line levels, and obtain permission in advance.

■ *Monitor your recordings.* As you record, listen with headphones and trust your ears. With a setup that you've used before, and where volume levels don't change greatly, perhaps you don't need to monitor the entire recording, but listening is your best insurance against Murphy's Law foul-ups. Headphones that cover the ears completely are best, so that you can distinguish the recorded sounds from the live sounds: even an inexpensive pair can save you from audio disaster. Test all of your gear, and have backup plans for critical events.

Recording Devices

While it's possible to record directly from a microphone or sound system to your computer's hard disk, for most situations, a separate audio recorder is more practical. Portable minidisc recorders are ideal for capturing Web audio, combining a very low noise level with quick, random access. A DAT recorder is another choice that eliminates tape noise. Without venturing into expensive commercial recording equipment, consider not only a home cassette deck (use Type II cassettes) as a recording device, but perhaps your 8mm video camera—just ignore the video portion and use an external microphone. (The soundtracks of non-Hi-Fi VHS or non-HiFi VHS-C recorders are not as capable.) For many types of Web audio, ordinary portable cassette recorders, or, in a pinch, even microcassette units, may be sufficient. Depending on how much you compress the audio files later, much of the frequency response and subtleties that high-grade recorders preserve may be sacrificed anyway.

Set, and preferably monitor, your recording volume levels carefully. With ordinary analog recording devices, don't be so conservative with a low recording level that you increase noise needlessly. With digital devices, don't be so liberal with high recording levels that you cross over into their unforgiving distortion overload range.

Microphones

The trick to capturing a clear recording for the Web is not so much that you have an expensive microphone as that you position your microphone correctly. Using a recorder's built-in microphone is often a bad idea, because you risk three things: pickup of tape motor noise, muddled sound resulting from improper positioning, and overzealous analog compressor circuits that may raise the volume far too much during quiet passages.

Unless you're using a sophisticated shotgun or parabolic microphone, be sure that your microphone is 6 to 12 inches from the speaker's lips. Even a $20 to $50 microphone can often give you clear speech recordings, but if you run long extensions of 25 feet or more of unbalanced cables, which are used on most such consumer microphones, you may pick up hum. You can avoid long cables and free up your presenter by using a wireless microphone. If you do so, however, plan to spend at least a few hundred dollars for decent quality, remember to check with your venue to be sure that your microphone's radio frequencies won't conflict with existing equipment, and bring a wired microphone, just in case the wireless mike doesn't work. Whenever possible, though, take the easy way out and obtain a direct-feed cable from an existing professional sound system, and save your microphone as an emergency backup.

Sound Card

You need a sound card to get audio in and out of your computer. You may not require an expensive sound card—give any existing card a tryout with your intended application. Older sound cards sometimes advertised "CD quality recording," referring to the rate of sampling, but their background noise levels were not good for critical music recordings. Many newer cards offer about 70dB (decibels) of quieting (a high ratio of signal to noise) and are quite good. Some sound cards, when recording in mono, discard the right channel. If your card does this and you have stereo input, be sure to mix the left and right channels into a mono signal when you specify mono output.

Step 2. Generating a Digital File

When you have a good, clean audio recording, you can store it on your PC in digital form by using either of the following methods:

- Encode it directly into the ultimate format that you want to use on the Web, which is usually a compressed format.

- Convert it first to an uncompressed format, usually a WAV file on PCs or an AIFF file on Macs, and then encode it into a compressed format.

By encoding your recording directly into the final format, you need a lot less disk space, you save a bit of time, and you don't need an audio processing program (apart from your streaming encoder, if you plan to use streaming audio). However, after your audio file is in a compressed format, editing the file is hard. On the other hand, by first converting your recording to a WAV file, you can edit and process the audio before you commit it to its final format. To encode directly, connect your sound source to your sound card, and then skip to "Step 4. Encoding the File into a Compressed Audio Format."

To capture an uncompressed audio file on your hard disk, you can use a sound utility program included in your operating system (for example, Windows comes with the Sound Recorder program) or bundled with your sound card. The built-in sound programs on laptops usually work fine as well. If you recorded the sound in an analog format, you digitize the sound in this step. Typically, you connect the LINE OUT connector on your recording device to the LINE IN jack on your computer's sound card. If you consistently get low recording volumes, try the MICROPHONE input on your sound card and check for distortion. Monitor the audio transfer with headphones, at least until you're confident of the sound levels.

If you're transferring sound from a digital device (DAT or minidisc) into a high-end sound card, the sound has already been digitized, and you simply need to move it to your PC and store it in standard format. You may be able to connect the recording device to your PC with a digital wire or fiber optic cable: consult your manuals. A digital connection eliminates the need to convert the signal to analog and then back to digital (redigitizing), with a resulting loss in quality. If your sound card is at all worthy, though, you won't lose noticeable quality on the Web by redigitizing.

Most sound formats—not only compressed formats—give you many choices that enable you to balance quality and file size. Choose a quality that is considerably higher than your target users' modem rates can handle, so that you have more options later when you process the data. Digitizing at around 22,000Hz at 16-bit resolution is sufficient for a modem-using audience.

Tip   *More precise recommendations are contained in the RealSystem G2 Production Guide (available free from **http://www.real.com**). This document also contains a table of RealSystem G2 codecs (coder/decoders) that denotes which codecs are backward-compatible, suggests ideal sampling frequencies, and provides a host of other helpful information.*

Step 3. Editing and Processing the Uncompressed Audio

Numerous audio processing programs are available, and you don't have to use one from the maker of your streaming software. PC and Mac users can find downloadable audio programs at repositories such as **http://www.download.com** or TUCOWS, at **http://www.tucows.com**. UNIX users have a fine resource at **http://sound.condorow.net**. Look for programs for your operating system, and then for multimedia programs. (See Chapter 38 for more information about downloading and installing programs from the Internet.)

The most useful processing functions for Web preparation are the following:

■ **Editing**   Most often, you just edit out a few seconds of leading and trailing time. Attempting to edit out coughs or profanity is much more time consuming—avoid such editing if possible. Most streaming formats also provide tools that enable you to perform simple editing later, if needed.

■ **Removing direct current offset**   Also called removing *DC bias*, this process centers the waveform around the zero line.

■ **Automatic normalization of volume**   The audio processing program can seek out the loudest portion and adjust the volume of the entire recording, so that the loudest portion is just below the distortion level. RealNetworks recommends normalizing to 95 percent or –0.5dB.

■ **Volume (dynamic) compression**   If you haven't used an analog compression device in front of the recorder, compression can help bring all parts of the recording to within a narrow range of volume. This process is terrible for a fine CD music recording, but is often wonderful for Web audio that is to be delivered via modem. The *RealNetworks G2 Production Guide* suggests adjusting the volume to a threshold of –10dB, a ratio of 4:1, and attack and release times of 100ms (milliseconds). Then, adjust the input volume level until you get about 3dB of compression, and set the output level to around 0dB.

Step 4. Encoding the File into a Compressed Audio Format

Now that you have a digitized and processed, but uncompressed, audio file, it's time to get small. Which format you choose depends on whether you want a static or streaming file, and which particular static or streaming format best suits your sound. If your target is a high-fidelity, nonstreaming MP3 file, several downloadable encoders are available at the shareware sites listed in the preceding section. If streaming audio is your goal, use the RealProducer G2 Authoring Kit (several versions are available at **http://www.real.com/products/tools**), or the Microsoft NetShow Encoder or Windows Media On-Demand Producer (try the page at **http://www.microsoft.com/ntserver/nts/mediaserv** or **http://www.microsoft.com/windows/windowsmedia**, but because Microsoft reorganizes its Web site regularly, you may need to start at **http://www.microsoft.com** and search the site). RealNetworks has several versions of its RealProducer G2 program, including the free authoring kit and the commercial RealProducer Plus G2 package that includes additional publishing tools. All these encoders are free.

In general, remember that audio compressed with a newer encoder version may not be playable by an older player. Usually, the user can simply upgrade the player for free, but sometimes the new technology player may actually require a hardware upgrade. Check the specs: you may need to restrict your encoding options so that compatibility is maintained, or perhaps simply download an earlier encoder version.

The simple secret to encoding good audio for modem users is to be conservative with your *target bit rate*, the connection speed at which you expect users to be able to download the file. RealSystem G2 and Windows Media (NetShow), the two streaming methods, are in fierce competition and each company wants to showcase its higher bit-rate modes. You may also want every bit of increased fidelity that you can produce. But if you can reign in your optimism about how high a throughput your users can obtain, you'll have much smoother sailing. You may think that you're through with picking formats, but each encoder supports several *codecs* (coder/decoders), low-level software engines that do the real encoding work and determine the final bit rate.

If you are creating a streaming file, consider that both Microsoft and RealNetworks enable you to encode a single file at more than one bit rate, so that during playback, the server can choose a different encoding if the user connection is slower than expected. RealNetworks calls this feature *SureStream*. Before you choose this option, though, make sure that:

- Your Web site includes a true RealSystem G2 or NetShow server, because ordinary Web server streaming (HTTP streaming) can't handle the combined streams

- You don't need to support users with RealSystem G2, RealAudio, and Windows Media Players that are older than the ones that support this option

If you're encoding from a file to a streaming format, you may find that you encode much faster than real time. This makes sense when you consider what the encoder must accomplish if you encode directly from a sound source! (Compare this to MP3 encoders, which are sometimes *much* slower than real time.) Encoding at higher bit rates may take *less* time, because less compression work needs to be done. The multiple-bit-rate mode understandably takes much longer, so recording to a WAV file first is often better.

When you run your encoding program, configure the program (by choosing Options or Preferences from the menu bar) to specify the speed at which most users will connect to the Internet ("network bandwidth"), whether the user can save the file for later replay, and where the audio input will come from (a sound card or a previously recorded file). Try choosing Options or Preferences from the menu bar, depending on the program. When you begin encoding an audio file, you specify the file that contains the audio data, the name to give the encoded file, network bandwidth, copyright information, and whether the audio contains voice, music, or both.

Here are some tips for successfully encoding an audio file:

- If you're encoding directly from an external sound source, experiment a few times until you get the recording volume level just right. Be sure the appropriate inputs are selected, and then adjust the volume to the level at which the loudest passages light the red bars on the encoder's level meter but don't activate the overload indicator.

- Avoid frequent overloads, which cause lots of ugly distortion.

- When using a Microsoft encoder, unless you're encoding for an intranet application, stay with the MetaSound, MetaVoice, or MP3 codecs for your audio. These are the *core codecs* included with your users' Media Player program. Otherwise, you may produce some great audio that many in your intended audience can't decode.

- If you're in a hurry to encode a lot of material, turn off automatic indexing. Although this feature allows users to use rewind and fast-forward, by turning it off during encoding, you save time, and you can use other utilities to set index points later.

Step 5. Linking the Resulting Audio File to Your Web Pages

Chapter 31 describes how to upload Web pages to a Web server so that people can see your pages over the Internet or an intranet: you use a file transfer program to copy the files to the Web server. You load audio files similarly, but check with your ISP or server administrator for the correct directory location.

When you offer audio files on the Web, it's polite to include a link on your Web page to a Web site from which the user can download the player that your audio file requires. For example, if you include a RealSystems streaming audio file, include a link to **http://www.real.com**, *where the user can get the RealPlayer program.*

Linking Static Files to Web Pages

If you created a static audio file, just upload it to your directory on the Web server, and be sure to specify that it is a binary (not ASCII) file; otherwise, the file transfer process garbles the file in transit.

On the Web page from which you want the static audio file to be accessible, add a link with the name of the audio file. For example, you could add a sentence like this:

```
Fred Smith's <A
HREF="http://www.myisp.com/mydir/conference/speech.wav">State of
the Club Report</A> has details about next year's plans.
```

Linking Streaming Files to Web Pages

If you created a streaming audio file, you need to perform an extra step before you upload the file. Instead of linking directly to the file that contains your audio (usually an RM file for RealNetworks, or an ASF file for Microsoft Windows Media/NetShow), you link to a *metafile*, a small text file—located on the Web server—that contains the name and location of your audio file. However, if you link directly, your listener's browser downloads the entire sound file before the player program gets a chance to play it, totally defeating the purpose of streaming.

Tip   *Consult your encoding program's documentation for situations in which metafiles may not be necessary.*

Whether you have a RealSystems or NetShow/Windows Media streaming audio file, here are the general steps for creating a metafile, linking to it from your Web page, and uploading the files:

1. Using Windows Notepad or any text editor, create a tiny, text-only metafile containing the name of the actual audio file that you want to play. The line contains the URL of the streaming audio file. For the streaming to work, the URL must start with the protocol used by your streaming file (RealSystems or Windows Media). The exact format for the line contained in the file depends on your streaming format: see the next two sections for the exact format. Most people use the same name for the metafile that they use for the audio file (except for the extension) to avoid confusion.

2. Using your Web page editor or any text editor, add a link to the Web page from which you want the streaming audio file to be accessible. This link is a normal <A> tag link to the metafile that you just created. For example, you might add this line to your Web page:

```
Click <A HREF="mysong.ram">here</A>to hear my singing!
```

This link uses relative addressing, because the metafile (a RealSystems RAM file in this example) is stored in the same directory as the Web page, but you can also use a complete URL identifier, like this:

```
Click <A
HREF="http://www.myisp.com/mydir/showersong.ram">here</A> to hear
my singing!
```

3. Upload the large audio file to your ISP's RealSystems or Windows Media or NetShow server directory, and upload your tiny metafile to the directory that contains your Web pages. When using FTP to transfer your RAM metafiles, be sure to use ASCII transfer.

4. Test your new audio file to be sure that it plays the audio file that you intend. If it's the correct file, then you're ready to wow the world.

> **Tip** *If your ISP or Web hosting service doesn't provide you with a RealSystems or Microsoft Media or NetShow server to transmit the streaming files to your users, you can still stream your audio (with less performance) simply by specifying the ordinary Web transfer protocol, HTTP, in the metafile. Your ISP or Web hosting service needs only to define the proper MIME types (that is, types of multimedia files) on its Web server: contact them to ask. Then, upload both the metafile and the audio file to your directory on the Web server.*

Linking RealSystems Files

For a RealSystems audio file, you create a metafile with the extension .ram. The metafile contains a single line indicating the URL of the audio file. If you are using a regular Web server, the URL starts with the usual *http://*. If your Web server runs the RealServer program to provide streaming audio, the URL starts with *rtsp* instead of http. The *rtsp://* at the beginning indicates that this is a RealSystems file. If your ISP runs an older, version 5 Web server, use *pnm://* instead of *rtsp://*. RTSP, *RealTime Streaming Protocol*, was introduced for the version G2 servers. You can have multiple lines (with one URL per line) if you want to play several audio files in succession.

For example, if your ISP's domain is myisp.com, your audio file is named mysongs.rm, and your ISP's RealSystems directory is named myaudio, you would create a RAM file named mysongs.ram containing this line:

```
rtsp://www.myisp.com:554/myaudio/mysongs.rm
```

The 554 port identifier can vary with your ISP. When the port number is 544, which is the default port for RealSystems, you can omit the :554. Note that your Webmaster must configure your server for the RealAudio MIME type before your Web page will work properly. Ordinary Web servers cannot deliver many RealAudio files at once, so your Webmaster may impose constraints on your use of RealAudio unless the server is a streaming server.

To can also "embed" the RealAudio file in your Web page, so that the RealPlayer program runs in the browser window: see "Embedding a RealAudio File in a Web Page" in Chapter 34.

Linking Microsoft Windows Media Files

For a Windows Media/NetShow streaming file with the file extension .asf, the metafile has the extension .asx. The latest ASX format uses an XML (*Extended Markup Language*) structure. For example, if your ISP's domain is myisp.com, your audio file is named mysongs.asf, and your ISP's Windows Media directory is named myaudio, the ASX file would look like this:

```
<ASX Version="3.0">
<Entry> <Ref Href="mms://www.myisp.com/myaudio/mysong.asf" />
</Entry>
</ASX>
```

ASX files have tags that look similar to HTML. The protocol to specify at the beginning of the second line (in place of the usual http://) is *mms://* (Microsoft Media Server protocol).

Note   *If you ever work with RealSystems SMIL files, you'll find them similar in structure to ASX files.*

Chapter 31

Uploading Web Pages

Creating Web pages is great fun, but you need a public place to put the pages to make them accessible to everyone on the Web. Unless you are on an intranet, and other intranet users can access your hard disk, the Web pages that you've stored on your local drive need to be transferred to a Web server, so that other people can see your work.

Maintaining a Web site demands that you establish a procedure to update pages quickly and easily. This chapter defines the process of uploading Web pages, and details how to use applications to upload files and directories for your site.

The Uploading Process

You first need to find a Web server on which to publish your pages. Where do you find a Web server? Contact your ISP, shop for a Web hosting service, or (if you are on an intranet) ask your system administrator. Most ISPs offer Web hosting services either with the cost of the dial-up connection or for a low monthly fee. (See "Publishing Your Site" in Chapter 26 for more information.)

You next need to consider the resources that you have available. If you code your Web pages in a text editor (as opposed to a Web page editor), you need to upload the pages to the Web server either manually by using an FTP program or automatically by using an uploading application, such as NetLoad. To learn how to upload files using FTP, see Chapters 36 and 37. If you use a Web page editor to create pages, you can use the publishing feature in the editor to upload your files.

The third thing that you need to do is prepare your files to be uploaded, so that they have the right filenames and folder structure.

Administrative Preparation

The Web server's owner can give you the host name of the Web server computer, the name of the base directory in which to store your files, and a user name and password to use to log on to its system. If you are going to use the uploading feature of a Web page editor, ask for the information in the form of a URL (Internet address), which will look like one of the following:

ftp://ftp.hostname.com/directory

http://ftp.hostname.com/directory

To avoid confusion, when you store your Web page files in directories on the Web server, use the same structure as the set of folders on your hard drive. Most uploading programs do this for you.

Most ISPs use UNIX-based systems, so it helps to know at least some basic UNIX commands so that you can manage the files in your directories. (See Chapter 40 for information on basic UNIX commands.)

File Preparation

Before you upload your pages, verify that everything is in place and looks the way that you want it to on all pages:

- Make sure that your directory structure is sound. You should have a main directory, with subdirectories for images, video files, and audio files. Your home page, usually named index.html, should be in the main directory. Unless you have a large number of HTML pages, the rest of your HTML files can also stay in the main directory.

Note

If you have a large site with many HTML files, you might want to set up subdirectories to organize the HTML files. Just make sure that the index.html file (the starting page) remains in the main directory.

- Check the spelling on every page.
- Verify that graphics are displayed properly.
- Test all the links to be sure that you arrive at the proper destination when you click the link. If you coded your pages manually or if your Web page editor does not verify links, open the HTML file in your browser and make sure that all the links work.

When you have the administrative information from your ISP or server administrator and your files have been checked, you're ready to upload your pages to the Web.

Tip

In your Web pages, make sure that the names of files in links (<A> tags) and images (<IMG> tags) are relative to the location of the Web page. That is, if the linked file or graphics file is in the same folder as the Web page that refers to it, type only the filename in the tag rather than the full pathname of the file. If the linked file or graphics file is in the parent folder of the folder that contains the Web page, type ..\filename to specify the file.

Uploading Pages by Using FTP

You can use an FTP program to upload your files to the Web server. Windows 98 and 95 come with an FTP program, or you can download one from the Web (from TUCOWS, **http://www.tucows.com**, among other places). See Chapters 36 and 37 for how to use an FTP program to upload files.

Uploading Pages by Using NetLoad

NetLoad is an FTP program that is designed to transfer entire folders from one computer to another. If you create your Web pages manually, NetLoad is an excellent way to upload the pages to a Web server. When you transfer files to a Web server, the NetLoad application re-creates your local directory structure on the server. Then, as you update your Web page files, you can tell NetLoad to *synchronize* your files with the files on the Web server. NetLoad examines the filenames and creation dates and tells which files need to be transferred to the Web server for the first time, which files need to be updated on the Web server, and which files need to be deleted on the Web server. When NetLoad is done, the folder and files on the Web server match those on your hard disk.

You can download a copy of NetLoad from the Aerosoft Web page at **http://www.aerosoft.com.au/netLoad**. The program is also available from TUCOWS and other software libraries (see Chapter 38 for instructions). To use NetLoad, you need FTP instructions from your ISP or Web server administrator and the name of the directory in which your files should be stored on the Web server.

Configuring NetLoad

To start NetLoad, choose Start | Programs | NetLoad | NetLoad. To tell NetLoad about a set of Web pages on your own computer and the corresponding Web server to which you want to upload them, follow these steps:

1. Choose NetLoad | Setup to display the NetLoad Setup dialog box, shown in Figure 31-1.

2. Type a Nickname (the name that you use to refer to this Web site), the FTP Server (the host name of the server to which you are uploading the pages), and the User Name and Password that you need to log in to the FTP server, using the information that you received in your FTP instructions.

3. In the Local Directory box, type the path to the folder on your computer in which your Web pages are stored. In the Remote Directory box, type the directory name that your ISP or Web hosting company provided.

4. Click the Add button to add this information to the list of FTP servers.

5. Close the NetLoad Setup dialog box.

Note *If you do not want files marked with the trash icon to be deleted, click the Settings tab in the NetLoad Setup dialog box, and clear the Delete Files/Directories When Marked with Trash Icon option.*

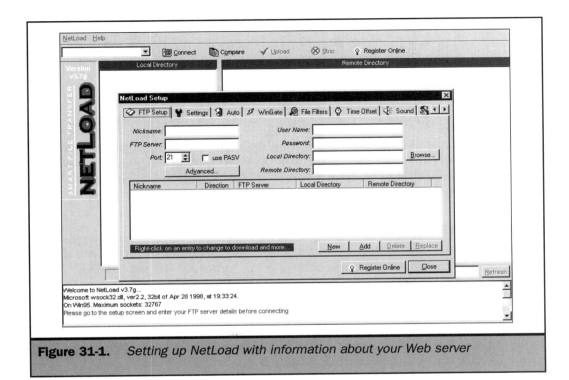

Figure 31-1.   *Setting up NetLoad with information about your Web server*

Uploading Your Files

In the main NetLoad window, click Change to specify the directory on your computer where the Web pages are stored. (You have to do this even if you specified the local directory on the NetLoad Setup dialog box.) Verify that the correct Web server directory is listed in the box at the bottom of the Remote Directory column. To upload your files, follow these steps:

1. Click the Connect button to connect to the Web server. NetLoad connects to the Web server and displays the files on your computer in the Local Directory window (on the left) and the files on the Web server in the Remote Directory window (on the right).

2. Click the Compare button to see whether the two lists of files are the same. If this is the first time that you are uploading the files, lots of files will be on your local computer and not on the Web server. NetLoad displays little icons next to each file to tell you whether it needs to be uploaded, and why. To see a list of what the icons mean, choose Help | Icon Legend.

3. Check that NetLoad is right about which files need to be uploaded, and then click the Upload button to upload the files.

The great advantage of using NetLoad is how easy it makes updating the Web site later. After you update your Web page files on your own computer, NetLoad can figure out which files have changed, been created, or been deleted, and make exactly the same changes to the files on the Web server.

Uploading Pages by Using a Web Page Editor

Most Web page editors (described in Chapter 28) include a publishing feature that you can use to upload pages and publish them on the Web. The following sections describe how to upload your Web pages from a variety of Web page editors, including Composer, FrontPage Express, FrontPage, PageMill, and HotDog Professional.

Netscape Composer

To start Composer, choose Start | Programs | Netscape Communicator | Netscape Composer. You can also start composer by opening Netscape Navigator and clicking the Composer button in the lower-right corner of the screen. Then, follow these steps to upload your Web page files:

1. Open the main file for your site (usually named index.html).

2. Choose File | Publish (or click the Publish button on the toolbar) to display the Publish dialog box, shown in Figure 31-2.

3. In the HTTP or FTP Location to Publish To box, type the HTTP or FTP location to which you are publishing the page. Also enter your user ID and password. (This information comes from whoever runs your Web server.)

4. In the Other Files to Include section of the dialog box, select the files that you want to transfer. You can transfer the current page and all files associated with it, which includes all the graphics and objects that you inserted in the file, or all files in the current folder. Composer displays a list of files to be transferred, and you can select or remove files from the list manually. If you are in doubt about which files to transfer, it is better to transfer too many files than to leave out a file that's needed for your page.

5. Click OK to start the file transfer. The names of files are displayed onscreen as the files are transferred, and you can monitor the progress of the transfer onscreen.

FrontPage Express

To start FrontPage Express, choose Start | Programs | Internet Explorer | FrontPage Express. To transfer files to a Web server, open the page that you want to transfer and choose File | Save As. Enter the page location that you received and then click OK to start the Web Publishing Wizard. The Wizard prompts you through the information that is needed to publish your pages.

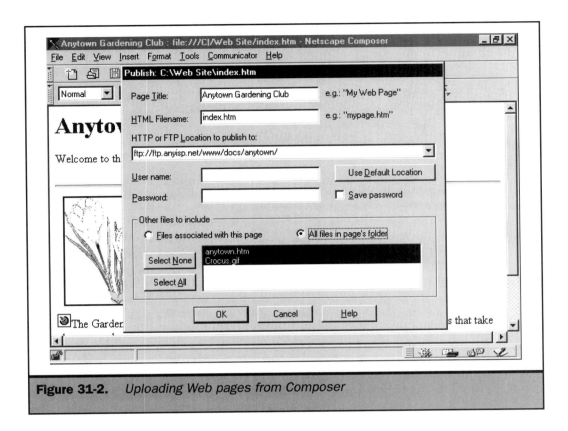

Figure 31-2.   *Uploading Web pages from Composer*

CREATING AND
MAINTAINING WEB SITES

> **Note**   *The Web Publishing Wizard comes with Windows 98. If you haven't installed this Wizard,
> you see an error message when you try to publish Web pages. To install the Wizard, insert
> your Windows 98 CD-ROM in the drive and choose Start | Settings | Control Panel, open
> Select Add/Remove Programs, click the Windows Setup tab, and choose Internet Tools on the
> Components list. Click Details, and select Web Publishing Wizard.*

FrontPage

To start FrontPage, choose Start | Microsoft FrontPage. In the FrontPage Explorer
dialog box, open the Web site that you want to publish. Before you upload the Web
page files for your site, make sure that the links are valid. In FrontPage Explorer
(shown in Figure 31-3), click the Hyperlink Status icon in the Views list. Broken links
are displayed in red and show the status as Broken. To verify links to external pages
that are not on your Web site, you need to be connected to the Internet. To repair a
broken link, double-click the link and enter the new URL, or edit the page on which the
link is displayed.

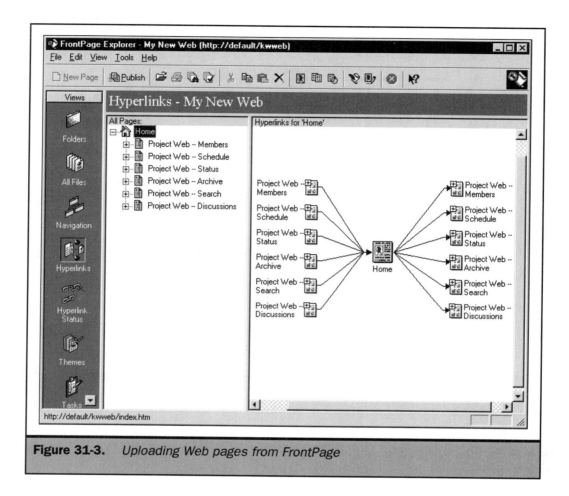

Figure 31-3.   *Uploading Web pages from FrontPage*

When you are ready to publish your pages, click the Publish button. The pages are published at the location that you specify in the dialog box.

PageMill

To start PageMill, choose Start | Programs | Adobe | PageMill | Adobe PageMill. Select Site | Load and open the site that you want to publish (see Figure 31-4). In the Site Overview panel, click the Errors folder. Repair any errors before you upload your files.

To start uploading files, select Site | Upload. In the Edit Site Settings dialog box, enter the host name, remote folder, user name, and password that you received from your ISP or server administrator. Click OK to upload the files.

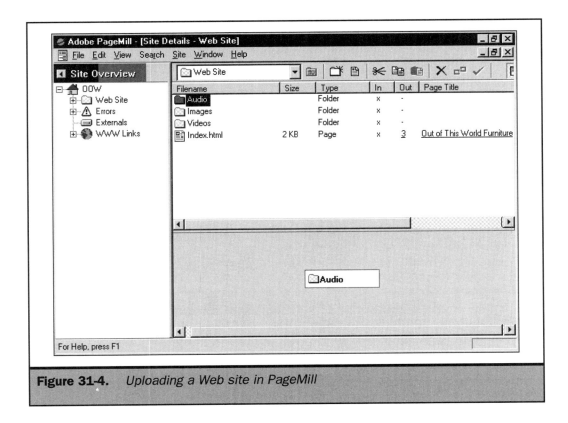

Figure 31-4.   *Uploading a Web site in PageMill*

HotDog Professional

To start HotDog Professional, choose Start | Programs | Sausage Software | HotDog Professional. Select File | Open Web Site, and select the site that you want to upload. Maximize the WebSites window (as shown in Figure 31-5) and follow these steps to upload your files:

1. Click the Check Errors button on the toolbar. If HotDog finds broken links, fix them before you upload your Web pages. To fix a broken link, click the Check tab on the WebSites dialog box. Double-click the error that you need to fix and then either edit the link or edit the file that contains the link.

2. Click the WebSites Properties button on the toolbar. Click the Directories folder and specify where your files are stored locally.

3. Click the Web Server folder and enter the Web server, directory, user name, and password that you received from your ISP or server administrator.

4. Click the Upload Your Web Site button on the toolbar.

HotDog transfers your Web pages to your Web server.

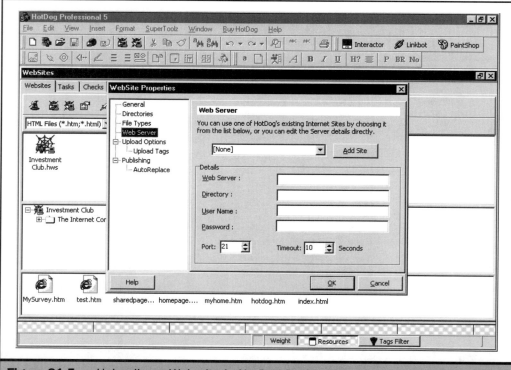

Figure 31-5. Uploading a Web site in HotDog Professional

Chapter 32

Analyzing Web Traffic

Once your Web site is up and running, you'll probably have an ongoing interest in knowing how well it is attracting visitors. The Web server (whether it belongs to your own organization, your ISP, or a Web hosting company) not only serves Web documents to users, but it also serves you by saving data about everything it does. The Web server program creates an entry in a log file every time the server responds to a request for an HTML document, graphic, form, or other service. This means that every user is tracked during every visit to your site.

These log files become quite large very quickly. A number of traffic analysis programs on the market can crunch these huge files to produce tables and graphics that summarize a Web server's activity. But getting the most value from these reports requires that you understand the raw data that is collected—and what is not collected in the logs.

This chapter describes the data collected by Web servers, what the data means, and lists various popular analysis programs that you can use to monitor your Web site. We also cover the shift from storing traffic data in traditional text files to using databases. Many ISPs and most Web hosting companies have analysis programs that you can use to track traffic to your site.

Web Traffic Analysis Jargon

Web marketers frequently boast about the size of their audience, the number of "hits" their Web sites receive, and their great banner ads. But just what are they talking about, and what are they really saying?

The term that is most thrown around—and most abused—is the word "hits." The following are a few commonly used terms and definitions used to describe Web traffic, including *hit*:

- **Hit**   Commonly thought of as the number of times a page on a Web site is requested by a browser—but this is not accurate. "Hits" also includes the number of times all other files, such as graphic images, are viewed. For example, if your home page has nine graphics on it, each time someone views your home page, the log file registers one hit for the HTML file and nine hits for the graphics, for a total of ten hits. Because the term "hits" has such an ambiguous meaning, most people are now measuring traffic in terms of *page views*, described next.

- **Page view**   The viewing of one specific HTML file—without counting any graphics or other items on the page. If one person views a page, moves to another page, and then comes back to the page, only one page view is usually counted, because the person's browser typically stores (caches) the page and doesn't request it again. Some ISPs and online services cache Web pages on their own servers, so that if 100 America Online users see your page, your Web server may experience only one page view.

- **Visit**   All the pages viewed by a user within a continuous session, which can include a single HTML file or a visit that lasts for an hour or more on heavy content sites. Standard Web server logs include the IP (numeric) address (see Chapter 1) for each computer that requests files from the server, so traffic analysis programs use this identifier to determine the starting point and ending point for each visit or session. Because users don't "log out" from a Web site, assumptions have to be made about when the user actually leaves the site.

- **Visitor**   Represents, theoretically, each unique individual who comes to a Web site, which means that the total visitors to a site should be the unduplicated count of visitors. Unfortunately, IP addresses are reused by ISPs as different people dial into their networks. This means that two different people could visit a Web site using the same IP address. Also, when an individual disconnects and reconnects to an ISP, the user is usually issued a different IP address, which appears in the log as a different visitor. These problems make it hard for log analysis programs to determine the exact number of visitors coming to a Web site. The use of cookies (defined in Chapter 18) to identify when a particular computer returns to a site can help improve accuracy of these regulations, but that requires extra database programming (and not all users accept cookies).

- **Organization**   Represented in a Web server's log as the domain name used by each visitor, which is frequently the user's ISP's domain.

Log File Data

Many Web servers use one of several standard log file formats when creating their logs. These standards enable commercial log analysis programs to read the log files of all popular Web servers.

The original Web server programs create logs in a *Common Log Format* that uses several files to store all the information collected about files served. These log files include:

- **Access_log**   The main log file that captures filenames, IP addresses, dates, times, and other data.
- **Referer_log**   The file that captures URLs of the Web sites from which users came.
- **Error_log**   The file that includes requests for files and system error messages.

Data in the Access Log File

The access_log file in Common Log Format has eight fields of information for each HTML and graphic file served:

- **Address field**   Either the IP address or domain name from which the request came.
- **ID field**   Generally not used, for security and privacy reasons.

- **AuthUser field**   Used when username and password authentication is required of the user to see the page.

- **Date and time field**   Date, time, and time offset from Greenwich Mean Time (GMT).

- **Method field**   HTTP command that the user's Web browser sent to the Web server to make the request; usually either the GET command, for requesting static HTML and graphic files, or the POST command, for data supplied from a form. Can also be the HEAD command, for requests from certain agents, such as search engine spiders.

- **File name field**   Name of the file served.

- **Status field**   Status or error code, indicating whether the request was successful.

- **Size field**   Size of file served, in bytes.

The following sections explain some of these fields in more detail.

The Address Field

The address field in the Web server log file contains either the user's IP address or the domain name for the organization providing the user's connection to the Internet. Many system administrators prefer to store only the IP address, because extra processing and bandwidth are required to look up domain names. When domain names are needed, that processing can be done either by another computer or by the Web server in non-prime time.

The address field is used to tabulate such things as how many different people are visiting a Web site. As an individual user requests each file, the Web server stores the IP address in each log entry. This allows log analysis programs to determine how many different sessions have occurred, by counting how many different IP addresses have been logged.

Before online services and ISPs provided dial-up services and started reusing IP addresses, it was easy to determine the number of distinct users who were coming to a Web site. Now, several factors make this tabulation less accurate:

- Dial-up users are typically assigned a different IP address each time they connect to their ISP.

- Users of online services (for example, America Online, Prodigy, and MSN) access the Internet through a relatively small number of gateways, each with its own IP address.

- Corporate users and some online users connect through proxy servers, each with its own IP address.

- Community terminals and kiosks in libraries and cafes allow many people to access the Web using the same computer.

Increasingly, the IP address can be used to identify only a current session, instead of providing any information about the individual accessing a Web site.

Many traffic analysis programs can determine the order in which pages are accessed by each individual IP address. By understanding the various paths that people take through your Web site, you can learn more about their interests and their decision making during the visit. For instance, if more people leave the home page and go to a product summary page rather than a services page, then they clearly are mainly interested in the products sold by that company. If more people leave the products page and go to the services page rather than the pricing page, then they probably want to learn about the support services before checking out the price.

Of course, this type of analysis requires a clear understanding of the content associated with each filename, and how pages are displayed to your users. Knowing how pages are displayed—using various sizes and resolutions of screens—is important, because that placement of links onscreen can affect what people click as much as their interests affect this decision. In the example of people choosing the products page followed by the services page, knowing whether the link to the pricing page is clearly visible onscreen or hidden "below the fold" (where the user has to scroll down to see it) would be helpful.

The length of time that people typically stay on certain pages is another valuable piece of information that can be determined by re-creating sessions with the IP address. In general, the longer viewers are exposed to your message, the more likely they are to accept the information presented. In the case of a commerce site selling products, longer viewing times can translate into higher sales.

The Date and Time Field

The date and time field in the log file shows when the server sent the requested material onto the Internet. This field's obvious use is to calculate the elapsed time between two page displays, so that you can calculate how long the user viewed the page. However, this calculation can be thrown off by the following factors:

- *When serving large graphic files.* Sometimes, the *latency* of the Internet (the delay in transmitting bits from the server to the browser) is large enough that an entire file can be served to the Internet before a user's browser has received even a portion of the file. If you try to make any inferences about such things as the connection speed of a user by calculating time differences for graphics on a Web page, the results will undoubtedly be incorrect.

- *Large Web sites that use multiple servers.* High-traffic Web sites commonly use multiple servers, either to serve different pages within a site or to serve multiple items on the same page. For instance, during the release of a large, popular government document, CNN balanced the load on its servers by moving parts of its site to different Web servers, with graphics files and HTML files on different servers.

When you analyze the log files to re-create sessions for a Web site that has multiple servers, be sure that the clocks on all servers are synchronized so that hits to the various files that make up pages can be studied in the proper order.

The Method Field

In general, the method field provides little information, because most Web pages are served using the GET command (the standard command for requesting a Web page in HTTP, the language in which browsers and Web servers communicate). Whenever a user clicks a link to request a static Web page or a page generated by a database application using a template file, the method field contains GET.

Form data, on the other hand, can be submitted using either the GET or POST method, and the log indicates which was used. The more obvious difference between the GET and POST methods is that forms submitted using POST pass their data "behind the scenes" to the server, while forms that use the GET method pass their data as part of the URL to the server.

In most cases, displaying data in the URL is not a problem. However, form data can get passed to other Web sites, which may be a security problem. Specifically, when the user links to another Web site, the URL of the current page—including the form data that was used to create the current page—is passed to the other Web site in the referrer field (described in the upcoming section, "The Referrer Field"). If the form data contains user IDs, passwords, or other sensitive data, this information is stored in the log files of the site being linked to—probably a bad idea! If your site uses forms to pass sensitive information to the Web server, be sure to use the POST rather than the GET command in the scripts that run the form. (See Chapter 34 for information about how Web page forms work.)

The Status Field

Users expect Web servers to complete each request for a file that the browser requests from a server. As Web users all know, sometimes things don't work right and the user sees an error page. Sometimes the error occurs because the requested page doesn't exist. Sometimes the network stops delivering files while they are being served.

The status field contains a code that indicates whether the server successfully delivered the requested file or something happened to keep the file from being delivered. The typical status codes that appear in the log include:

200 Successful delivery of the file
302 Redirect to another file
400 Bad request
401 Password required
403 Forbidden to access the file
404 File not found
500 Server error

The redirect status code indicates that the server has been directed to serve one page in place of the requested page. Often, you can use this feature to track hits from a particular source. For instance, you might have a banner ad that directs people to a particular page, which, in turn, redirects users to your home page. By having the ad link people to the redirect page, you can easily track how many people clicked your ad, without having to actually maintain a separate home page.

The Size Field

The size field typically is used by Web server software to report the size of the file served. The size of a file shouldn't be ambiguous, but sometimes, the size reported isn't really the size. Some Web server programs always use the actual size of the file, while others report the actual amount of data served.

As you can imagine, if users are stopping large graphics before they are finished, or if they are leaving a page before the graphics have finished downloading, then a server that always reports the file size—instead of the amount of material actually served—provides misleading information. If you use large graphics on your Web site, be sure to check with your system administrator to learn what is included in the size field in the log files.

Data in Other Log Files

Over time, knowing where visitors come from has become important, and additional log formats have been created with additional fields of information that combine into one record the log data that originally was stored in multiple types of log files. The exact location of this additional information depends on which Web server program you use. The two main pieces of additional data that are added are the referring URL and a description of the browser software being used.

The Referrer Field

The referrer field in the log file shows the URL of the page that contains the link that was used to access the current page—which is how you can tell which Web site your traffic is coming from.

The referrer field contains a lot of useful information, such as the URL of the referring site and the page containing the link to your site. When people link to your site from a search engine, you can usually see the search phrase contained in the referring URL, which can help you determine how to target the content on your site.

If you are running banner ads on other Web sites, the referrer field may contain useful information about the site that displayed the ad. In most cases, however, the company serving your ads uses a redirect program to monitor the ads served, so your referrer field shows only the ad-serving company's server.

The Browser Field

The browser field contains a piece of text that describes the browser and version of the software used. Web developers frequently want to use the latest features that are only supported by the most recent version of browsers from Netscape or Microsoft. You can review a tabulation of this field to find out whether most users have upgraded to browsers that can display Web pages that use these features. Generally, users are slow to upgrade, and the browser field usually shows that to accommodate most visitors, your Web pages must work with the two or three most recent versions of the most popular browsers.

Another use of the browser field is to determine which features of JavaScript can safely be used with that user.

Analyzing Log Files

With the knowledge of what data is collected in the server logs, you are ready to explore the variety of ways to use that information to learn about your audience and their information needs. For instance, if your Web site is not generating inquiries through its inquiry form, you can use the log file to identify potential problems. The first question you might have is whether a significant number of people are actually seeing the inquiry form. If people aren't seeing the form, they can't respond. By following the path that people take through your site, you can locate pages that have links to the inquiry page—but low traffic to the inquiry form—and spot pages that don't motivate people to move on to the inquiry page. On the other hand, if many people are viewing the inquiry form—but are not completing the form—then you can focus on making the form more attractive and compelling.

Tracking Interest in a Topic

You can use log files to determine the level of interest an audience has in a topic. By breaking a long story or promotional page into multiple Web pages that are linked from the first page through to the last page, you can determine how interest decreases as people move through the story. For instance, if a three-part article receives half as many hits on the second page as on the first page, you clearly are losing people very quickly. On the other hand, if the second page receives almost as many hits as the first page, but the third page drops off, then you know that people are interested through most of the story.

Applications for Tracking

Analyzing your log files helps you to understand how visitors use your content—and which content to enhance—but it can also help you to understand how to group together and link various content items in ways that you may not have thought of.

For instance, assume that you have a Web magazine that has a variety of news and feature articles for families, with topics ranging from health and parenting to financial planning and retirement issues. You group each set of articles under section headings, with index pages for each section linking to the articles within their section.

If you use a log analysis program (described in the section "Products for Analyzing Web Traffic," later in this chapter) to determine the frequently used paths through your site (as shown in Figure 32-1), you might be surprised to find people moving from the health pages to articles in the retirement section—indicating that a group of people are interested in both topics. You can take advantage of this information in several ways.

You could add a short "sidebar" article at the side or bottom of the main article that promotes links to articles in another section. You could also develop "in-house" banner ads and schedule them to run in one section while promoting articles in the other section. Whatever method you use to inform your readers of other articles in which they might be interested, be sure to add codes to your links that will create entries in your access log, so that you can trace the effectiveness of this internal promotion.

In addition to using log analysis data to promote additional content within your site, you can spot targeting opportunities on your site for advertisers. If a potential advertiser is looking for opportunities to increase the frequency of exposure to a particular group of people, your log analysis information can help you to recommend multiple sections of your site that are read by their target market—increasing your potential advertising revenue.

On the other hand, if your advertising prospect is interested in reaching the broadest possible audience—with a minimum of repeated exposures—then your log analysis can help by showing places where different people go within your site.

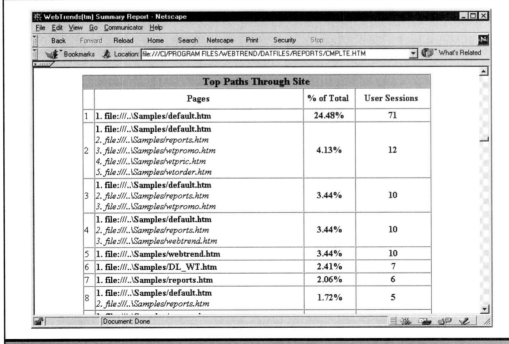

Figure 32-1. *Traffic analysis report showing popular paths through a site*

Test Marketing

One way that traffic analysis can help you to identify which benefits of your product are most attractive to your target market is to create multiple pages on your Web site, each explaining a different feature, function, and benefit. These additional *entry pages* should link to a more complete description within your Web site, or to your home page.

For example, when Sevio Software (**http://www.sevio.com**) introduced its MarketView marketing analysis software, it was unsure of whether marketing executives were more interested in analyzing their competition in a market or comparing the potential of different markets. To learn the interests of their target market, Sevio created multiple entry pages to their Web site, each focusing on a different benefit of using their software. To begin the market test, Sevio submitted each page to major search engines that update their indexes quickly.

Soon, hits were coming to several of the pages—with practically no hits to other pages. By reviewing the referrer field of the log files to spot the search phrases used to find certain pages, a market map was created that associated certain search phrases with the benefits promoted on certain entry pages.

Of course, it's important to know whether those hits resulted in downloads of its demo software and subsequent sales, which is where the IP address in the log file helps. The inquiry form used to register the demo captures the IP address of each person requesting a demo. This IP address is correlated with the IP address captured in the server log—which allows the marketing department at Sevio Software to know several things:

- Which search engines produced hits that resulted in demos and sales
- Which search phrases generated the best hits
- Which entry pages led to demos and sales
- Which days of the week and times of the day are popular for people to surf the Web that later result in sales
- How many pages are seen—and for how long—by customers versus noncustomers

Since a few of the popular search engines (for example, InfoSeek and AltaVista) currently update their databases rather quickly, you can run tests like these without having to wait months, as is common for traditional market research testing.

Tracking Individuals

A frequent request from Web marketers is to identify individual people and spot them as they return to a Web site. The two methods for identifying specific people are to use *cookies* (described in Chapter 18) that store unique identifiers on a person's computer, and to have people save a bookmark to your site that contains a unique identifier.

Privacy advocates have generated a considerable amount of debate about whether cookies invade an individual's privacy by sending personal information to Web servers. Fortunately, because of the way cookies are handled by Web browsers from companies such as Netscape and Microsoft, this is not a problem, because the format of the cookie file is designed to store codes to recognize individuals—not to store actual personal information about individuals.

Still, many people configure their browsers to *not* accept cookies, so including ID information in bookmarks is a good way to track individuals who return to your Web site. Personalization software used on your site can provide members of your audience with useful functionality—and provide you with significant traffic data that you can use to understand the information needs of individuals who frequent your Web site.

Products for Analyzing Web Traffic

Log analysis programs have been around since the beginning of the Web, so it's not surprising that there are a wide range of products that you can use to analyze traffic on your Web site. However, what may be surprising is the complexity of deciding on a log analysis program. There are three categories of products and services from which to choose, based on where the processing is performed:

■ Software that runs on the Web server itself, processing files locally and generating reports, usually in HTML files, for display with a Web browser over the Internet

■ Software that runs on your local PC, which requires that the log files be transferred over the network and stored on your PC before processing can begin

■ Services that copy your server data to their data center for processing, and then e-mail reports to you or permit you to view the reports over the Internet

All three methods are effective, and software products (and services) are available in all three categories that can do a very good job of providing you with useful information. Usually, one category of products is best for you, so here are questions that can help you to decide which category of products to focus on:

■ *Is the traffic to the Web server high, medium, or low?* High traffic sites create very large log files that are difficult to move to a PC for processing.

■ *Where is the Web site hosted?* If your Web site is on a dedicated server housed at your company, then it will be relatively easy for you to use a PC-based program, because it can probably access your server easily. If your site is on a dedicated server located at an ISP, then it may be more difficult for you to move very large log files to your PC, so you should look at server-based software or an outside service. If your site is on a shared server with other sites at an ISP, then your ISP can probably provide you with traffic reports, using software it provides, or you can download the log files to your PC over the Internet for processing.

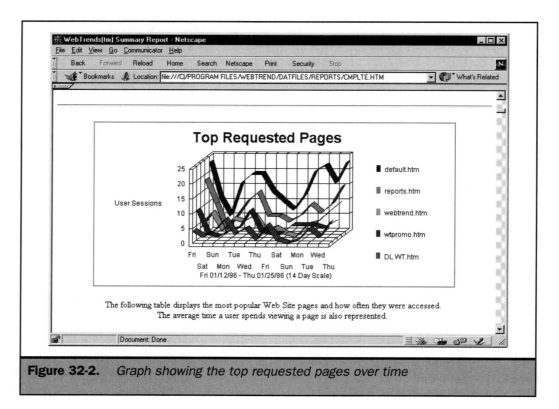

Figure 32-2. *Graph showing the top requested pages over time*

■ *Do you sell a significant amount of advertising on your Web site?* Many ad agencies require sites to use an outside traffic analysis service to monitor traffic.

■ *Who sees the Web traffic reports?* If you need traffic analysis for internal Web site management—and not to show to top management or advertisers—you may want to use one of the shareware/freeware products that are available for download rather than a more expensive commercial product (which can cost hundreds or thousands of dollars). On the other hand, you may need a product that produces attractive reports and summary graphics, such as the graph shown in Figure 32-2.

Log Files vs. Log Database

As Web server companies have expanded the capabilities of their products, one of the features that has become common is the use of a traffic database instead of ASCII text log files. When you hear that data is available in a "database," you may think of complex searching, sorting, and reporting—and that is exactly what these databases allow. The problem, of course, is that you are still dealing with practically the same data that has always been available in the log files.

Most of the traffic analysis programs that create databases work with servers that can write entries to a relational database as people visit the site.

Traffic Analysis Reports

As you compare your traffic analysis needs to the features and capabilities of the products available, one of the factors to consider is how well the set of reports available meets your needs. The following list of typical reports found in many traffic analysis products can help you to decide which reports you need and, therefore, which products will meet your needs:

- Top requested pages
- Top referring sites
- Visits by day and time
- File activity by day and time
- Most active countries
- Most active organizations (that is, domains)
- Errors and abandonment
- Most used browsers and versions
- Most used platforms (that is, operating systems)
- Average number of pages displayed per visit
- Average length of visit
- Top entry pages of people coming to the site
- Top exit pages of people leaving the site

Products to Consider

Now that you understand the traffic data stored in the logs and methods that you can use to analyze your traffic, you are prepared to find a product that can generate the reports and tables that you need. Here are a few popular traffic analysis products and services on the market that you should consider:

Accrue Insight	http://www.accrue.com
Andromedia, Inc.	http://www.andromedia.com
Aquas, Inc.	http://www.bazaarsuite.com
ILux	http://www.ilux.com
Internet Profiles Corporation (I/PRO)	http://www.ipro.com

Marketwave	**http://www.marketwave.com**
net.Genesis	**http://www.netgen.com**
Netrics	**http://www.netrics.com**
WebTrends	**http://www.webtrends.com**

As you visit the Web sites of these companies, compare your needs to the list of features and standard reports that each offers. Also, look for opportunities to download trial versions of the software, so that you can get a feel for how they perform when using your data. Then, you'll be able to gain insight into individual behavior on your Web site—and increase the effectiveness of your Web site.

The Complete Reference

Internet

Chapter 33

Building Traffic to Your Web Site

A ttracting people to your Web site is the key to making a Web site successful, and this chapter shows a few of the most efficient ways to accomplish this. Because Web surfers learn about Web sites from a variety of sources, you need to make sure that you are seen in many different media—and this chapter shows you how to use the promotion techniques that have proven most successful.

Online promotion not only generates attention, but also encourages people to click their way straight to your Web site. As you probably know, people often enter a Web site from pages other than the home page, so you must make sure that each page in your Web site tells its story well to a first-time visitor. This is especially true for people finding your site with a search engine.

Search Engines

One of the most popular ways that people find Web sites is through search engines, such as AltaVista, InfoSeek, and Excite. In addition to these search engines, many people use Web directories such as Yahoo!, which are different from search engines in that people—not software—determine which sites should be indexed. No matter what you call them, these starting points are important to the success of any Web site (see Chapter 23).

The key to having search engines generate significant traffic to your Web site is to understand both how people use search engines and how the search engines rank sites in their index. In general, people enter only a few words on the search form and expect the search engines to provide links to meaningful Web sites. Unfortunately, most people don't use the full selection of searching capabilities offered by search engines, such as the form for advanced searching capabilities that is found on most search engines. This means that when you craft your Web pages, you have to anticipate that your audience enters only two to four words to describe what they are looking for.

After a user submits those few words to a search engine, the search engine software tries to select Web pages that match the user's interests and needs. Although the exact formulas used by search engine software is highly confidential, specialists in search engine submissions conduct experiments on a regular basis to try to understand the formulas being used.

Most search engines look at a combination of attributes and apply different weightings to calculate rankings, which is one reason why different search engines provide different results when using the exact same search phrase. The attributes that are commonly used by search engines include:

- <META> tags for both description and keywords
- The <TITLE> tag
- Content of the page
- Popularity of the Web page

Writing for Search Engine Optimization

To get the best listing for your Web site in search engine results, when you write text for your Web pages, consider both the search engine formulas and the needs of your audience. *<META>* *tags* are hidden tags (the information in <META> tags doesn't appear on the Web page) that enable you to specify additional information about the page. *<TITLE>* *tags* specify the title that appears at the top of the page. For example, the following <TITLE> and <META> tags are taken from the Backyard Nature Web site:

```
<TITLE>Bird feeders and bird houses for garden birds</TITLE>

<META NAME="description" CONTENT="Bird feeders and bird nestboxes
for backyard and garden birds. ShelterHut is a modular birding
station with nature habitats for wrens, bluebirds, hummingbirds,
purple martins.">
<META NAME="keywords" CONTENT="backyard, common birds, bird, bird
feeder, bird house, nesting box, birding, wild bird, nature,
songbirds, bluebird, purple martin">
```

This example specifies the title for the Web page, a description of the page, and a list of keywords that describe the content of the page.

Adding <META> Tags

Each <META> tag contains a NAME attribute, which controls the type of information the tag contains, and a CONTENT attribute, which contains the actual information. The two types of <META> tags that guide some search engines are the keywords <META> tag and the description <META> tag.

The Description <META> Tag

The *description <META> tag* (a <META> tag with the attribute NAME="description") enables you to enter a description of the page in a few sentences, and is used by many search engines to describe the content of the site on the page of hits that is displayed to the user. The text in the description <META> tag should contain concise use of important, descriptive words, because the text in the description <META> tag counts in more when weighting search results than the same text within the body of the page.

This means that you need to write—and rewrite—the description <META> tag until it is as short as possible, yet still describes the essence of that page and uses all the important keywords. The reason to make the <META> tag short is so that the important words in the description represent the highest possible percentage of the total number of words in the description. For example, if an important keyword for you is "database," and your description is 50-words long, then this keyword represents only two percent of the description <META> tag. On the other hand, if your description is only ten words, the keyword "database" represents ten percent of the description.

Search engines compare the words in the description <META> tag to the words used in the body of the page, to make sure that the words in the description <META> tag are actually used in the body. The search engines do this to prevent people from using popular search words to generate traffic even though their Web page has nothing to do with that popular search word. (Sleazy Web site operators have tried inserting many different keywords unrelated to their sites in attempts to have their Web pages appear on search results for which their sites are totally inappropriate.)

The Keywords <META> Tag

The *keywords <META> tag* (a <META> tag with the attribute NAME="keywords")contains keywords that may be used throughout the body of the Web page. The list of keywords helps you to increase the weight applied to the ranking by the search engines, by indicating that certain words in the body are important.

Analyzing Your <META> Tags

Each search engine that uses <META> tags has its own set of requirements, such as the maximum number of characters that it looks at. Because the formulas used by search engines change periodically, you need to use an online automated service to analyze your Web pages, to help ensure that they are formatted properly for the majority of search engines. Web-based services that you can use include:

- Web Site Garage, at **http://www.websitegarage.com**
- SiteOwner.com, at **http://www.siteowner.com**

Submitting Your Site to Search Engines

If you've been on the Internet for more than just a few days, you know what "spam" is—advertising that you didn't request that arrives via e-mail—and you've probably received spam from people saying that they can make your site show up high in search engine results. Another frequent claim by these spammers is that they will submit your site to over 200 search engines.

These claims have two major flaws: no one can guarantee to make a site show up high in the search results of a search engine, and very few search engines generate significant amounts of traffic. In reality, most traffic comes from the top six to eight popular search engines—not from the specialized search engines and lists that these promoters talk about.

Although the Web is truly a targeted media with targeted content, most people using the Web don't use the specialty search engines to find sites, probably because the general Web user doesn't even know about these specialty search engines. Also, the popular search engines do an adequate job of helping people find sites of interest, so most people don't need to seek out these specialty search engines. You benefit most when you focus your search engine submission resources on the following search engines and directories:

- AltaVista, at **http://www.altavista.com**
- Excite, at **http://www.excite.com**

- InfoSeek, at **http://www.infoseek.com**
- HotBot, at **http://www.hotbot.com**
- WebCrawler, at **http://www.webcrawler.com**
- Yahoo!, at **http://www.yahoo.com**

Each of these sites (which are described in "Searching Using Search Engines and Directories" in Chapter 23) has a link that takes you to a form on which you can easily submit the URL of a Web page, for inclusion in the directory or search engine database. Because submitting a Web page manually to all of these search engines takes less than ten minutes, submit your own pages manually, instead of paying someone to submit them for you.

If you have many pages with different topics, you need to submit the section pages—or perhaps every page within your Web site—to obtain complete coverage with search engines. If you are in this situation, you may want to contract with a professional Web submission firm to handle this task for you on an ongoing basis. Some of the firms to check out are the following:

- WebPromote, at **http://www.webpromote.com**
- AAA Internet Promotions, at **http://www.websitepromote.com**

Search engine submissions must be redone frequently, because search engines periodically delete pages from their indexes. Consequently, experienced Webmasters (Web site managers) review their search engine placement about once a month. Because some search engines take two to three months to list a site, you need to maintain a log showing the pages submitted, the search engines, and the date submitted. The log helps you to remember each month, as you review your placements, exactly how long it's been since you submitted your site. If a site takes longer than normal to index a page, then you know that you need to submit the page again.

Because the formulas used by the search engines change periodically, you may want to check out the following online resources to keep updated:

- A link to many search engines and directories, at **http://www.mmgco.com/top100.html**
- Helpful information about <META> tags, at **http://www.tips-tricks.com/ announce.html**

Improving Your <TITLE> Tags

Because search engines strive to provide more relevant results to their users, the <TITLE> tag has taken on greater importance for Web developers. Several search engines assign a relatively high weight to the words used in the <TITLE> tag, so be sure to include the most important keywords in short, descriptive text.

One way to improve your ranking with the search engines is to use a different description in the <TITLE> tag for each page, which enables you to match the <TITLE>

tag more closely with the exact content on that page. Not only does this improve the chances for that page to show up higher in the priority list for search results, it also increases the number of different search words and phrases that will produce a listing for your site by the search engines.

Links to Your Site

From its very beginning, the Web has been built on pages of links to other Web sites, and this still can provide a great deal of traffic to your Web site. The techniques for obtaining links to your site has changed a bit over the past few years, but the value of having links to your site has increased, because search engines now include the "popularity" of Web sites when they calculate the ranking of hits for their users. This means that links to your site not only bring traffic to your site, but they also help improve your ranking with the search engines.

Several methods are available to obtain links to your site:

■ Obtain a listing on the "link list" page of other sites
■ Use Web rings that link from one site in a group to the next site
■ Exchange services that facilitate sites linking to one another

Requesting Links on Other Web Sites

Many Web managers are now reluctant to include on their sites a list of links to other Web sites, for fear of losing visitors to their own Web site. This fear is common with retail e-commerce sites that are selling products. On the other hand, many business-to-business sites are designed to be information sources and lead generators, so those sites frequently include a link list that includes noncompetitive companies that serve the same target market.

The process of obtaining links to your site requires a considerable amount of research, e-mail, and monitoring the results of your efforts. In addition, you probably need to maintain a links page on your own Web site, to obtain links from people who only provide reciprocal links.

One of the best ways to identify candidates from which to request links is to use a search engine, such as AltaVista or InfoSeek, to identify Web sites that are compatible with yours, and to locate the links page within those sites. For example, if your Web site sells bird feeders, use a search phrase that includes the quoted words "bird feeder" and "link list" (both sets of words enclosed by quote marks). Because search engines such as AltaVista and InfoSeek can handle multiple quoted phrases—and search for the actual phrase in quotes—you can easily narrow your search to Web pages that use both search phrases. If the quoted phrase "link list" doesn't produce a sufficient number of appropriate hits, you have to substitute other words, such as "resources" or "list of links".

After you identify several candidates from which to request links—and bookmark them for later reference—you are ready to begin your campaign of requesting links. Before you request a link from a site, adding that site to your list of links first is very helpful, so that you can demonstrate that you intend the linking to be reciprocal. Whether you use the bookmark tool within Netscape Navigator or a stand-alone bookmark manager, maintaining a links page is easy by using the bookmarks feature. Just add descriptions for each site in the notes area, and then export that folder of links to an HTML file. You can then paste the bookmarks and notes into an HTML template designed for your site, thus creating your links page.

After you publish a links page on your Web site, you are ready to e-mail the Webmaster at each site to request that they link to your site from their links page. Be sure to describe why you think their audience will find your site beneficial. If they link to other product-oriented companies, then you can mention your similar products. If they link only to articles and other reference material, be sure to direct them to those types of pages on your site. Give them the URL of your links page to demonstrate that you have already linked to their site.

For an example of how one site handles its link list, view the links page at the LABMED site, at **http://www.labmed.org/lnk_startingarescue.html** (see Figure 33-1). The page lists links, including the page title and the URL.

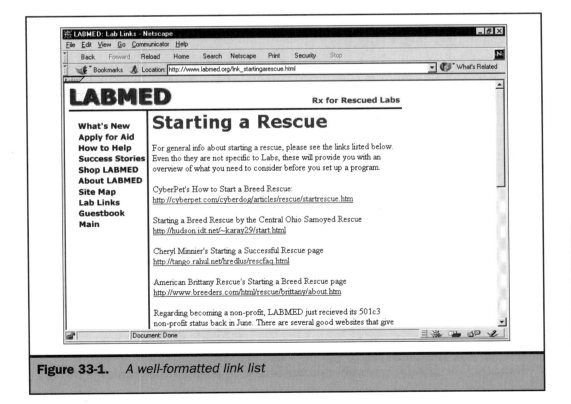

Figure 33-1. *A well-formatted link list*

Web Rings

One of the more innovative approaches to obtaining links to a Web site is through *rings*, groups of sites with similar audiences that agree to link to other sites in the ring. The concept targets visitors who are interested in the *topic* of a Web site rather than the specific Web site. The Web managers in the ring are comfortable letting these visitors link to other sites in the ring, to obtain reciprocal overflow traffic from the other sites in the ring.

Promoting your site through a Web ring has several benefits, such as not having to research and continually maintain a links list. Most Web rings use special software that directs users to the next Web site in the ring, so that Webmasters generally are assured that all the links in the ring are up-to-date. The potential downside to using a Web ring is that sites in rings are generally less professional-looking than large, high-traffic Web sites, which poses a potential image problem. In addition, many Web rings have very few members, so the amount of traffic generated may be rather low.

The following are a few central clearinghouses for rings that you may want to investigate:

- LoopLink, at **http://www.looplink.com**
- WebRing, at **http://www.webring.org**
- The Rail, at **http://www.therail.com**

Link Exchange Services

The Web began as a text-only service that used hypertext links to guide readers from one page to another, and from one site to another. Later, the ability to display graphics and turn graphics into hypertext links led to many sites switching from text links to graphic links. As Web managers have had a chance to study how people use Web sites, they have realized that some people feel graphics are just for looks, or are banner advertisements that are not related to the content of the page. The result is that text links—those mundane, blue-underlined pieces of text—are used by readers for navigation at least as much as the fancy graphical links are used.

To take advantage of this for marketing, a few services now facilitate matching Web sites that link to each other. Because no easy way exists to monitor the effectiveness of these text links, this area of Web marketing has not developed as fully as the graphical side of Web advertising. One Web site serving this area is Missing Link, located at **http://www.igoldrush.com/missing**.

Banner Advertising

Many methods of generating traffic-building links to your site have limits, because the marketing message is either not targeted to interested individuals or reaches only a small audience. The *banner advertisements* that appear at the top of many high-traffic Web sites can generate a significant number of new visitors to the advertiser's site.

These ads are called "banner" ads because they stretch across the tops of Web pages in horizontal strips, much like traditional print banners. Once you create an effective banner ad, there are two general ways to obtain banner advertising for your site—free and paid.

Creating Compelling Banner Ads

Whether you are using a free banner ad service or paying for advertising, you want to create as effective an ad as possible. The objective for most banner ads is to attract the attention of people interested in the product being advertised, and motivate them to click the ad so that they receive the entire marketing message.

Banner ads are too small to deliver an entire message, but they can convey the essence of a headline—similar to the function of a headline in a magazine ad. A banner ad combines the text of a headline with a small amount of art, enabling it to deliver more than just a text message.

The first step to creating an effective banner ad is to list all the words that can be used to describe the benefits of the product. Keep in mind that the benefits to the customer are not the same as the product's features and functions: every customer doesn't benefit from every feature. In fact, different people may receive different benefits from the same product, so you need to select a target audience and understand the reasons why they may be interested in your product.

As you might imagine, to get the attention of different target audiences for the exact same product, you need to use different banner ads. For example, desktop computers are used for a wide variety of purposes, from educating children to performing accounting functions at large companies. Clearly, the same desktop computer would benefit from a different ad for each audience. For other products, spotting the difference between benefits and features can be hard, because they are intertwined. For example, the message beeper carried by many people delivers messages anywhere the owner is located. Is that a feature or a benefit? If you look at the reason someone would want to receive messages anywhere, then you can more easily spot the true benefit of using a beeper.

If you are creating a banner ad for a beeper, your list of descriptive words would include both the feature "receive messages anywhere" and the benefit "spend more time with your family." By combining and condensing such words and phrases, you can generally create a descriptive headline that works well in a banner ad.

After you create the text of your banner ad, you need to apply creative graphics to help attract attention. Many graphic designers can create appealing banner ads, so consult with your design firm or advertising agency. Before you invest in having a professional create your banner ad, you may want to develop the initial test ads yourself. Many graphics programs can create banner ads, from the basic paint programs that come with many computers, to Adobe PhotoShop, which is used by most professional designers.

In addition, various Web sites provide templates that enable you to create banner ads automatically, simply by putting your text into a Web form. Although you may not want to use an ad based on a template that many other people have used, these services provide a quick and easy way to visualize the text of a banner ad in a variety of formats. A few of the Web-based banner-creation services that you may want to use include:

- Media Builder, at **http://www.mediabuilder.com**
- Prescient Code Solutions, at **http://www.coder.com**
- Web Animator, at **http://web-animator.com**

One technique used on almost every banner ad is to animate the graphic in a way that displays multiple lines of text—or creates a moving image—that attracts attention and delivers a longer message to the viewer. Although these animations are not movie-quality, they do use the same method that animators have used for centuries—displaying a series of "cells" one after the other. Each cell consists of the entire graphical image that is displayed at that point in time, so each cell must be created individually and then assembled one by one into a file format that supports this technique.

The GIF89 file format (created by CompuServe in 1989) is used by browser software for animation. This format allows multiple pictures to be downloaded and displayed as they are received by the client software. For example, a series of pictures contained in an animated banner ad can ask a question, and then show the viewer how to answer that question—which involves clicking the banner (see Figure 33-2). See the section "Animating GIF Graphics" in Chapter 29.

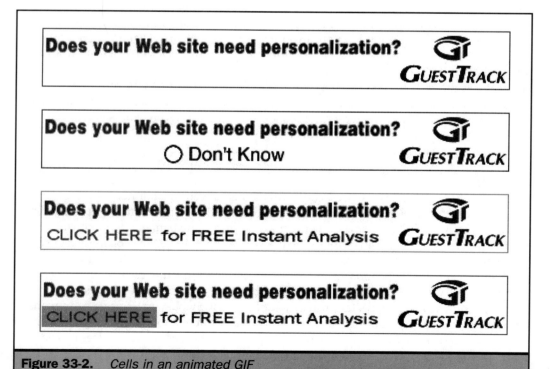

Figure 33-2. *Cells in an animated GIF*

Banner Exchange Services

Web managers who do not have an advertising budget for banner ads have found that *banner exchange services* enable them to convert traffic to their site into credits worth advertising exposure on other Web sites. Most banner exchange services display your ad on another Web site once for every two times that you display ads for other Web sites. This two-to-one ratio has become common in the banner exchange arena, but you can find other ratios, too.

When you use a banner exchange service, you provide it with a banner ad that promotes your site and your URL, and agree to display the banner ads of other Web sites on your pages. Sometimes these services require everybody to display ads near the top of the page, so that users don't have to scroll down, but other services allow you to place ads anywhere on a Web page.

You might ask how these companies can provide this service for free, and what becomes of the other half of the Web exposures. The more successful banner exchange services are able to sell advertising to larger companies, which use the other half of the advertising inventory available to them. This means ads that appear on your site might be traded for ads promoting sites similar to yours, or they might be paid ads from companies trying to reach your audience.

Many banner exchange services are in operation, so you should review several, to select one that can deliver a quality audience for you. The biggest advance in banner exchange services is the ability to target which types of sites display your ads. Unfortunately, many banner exchange services still don't offer targeting based on the types of ads that a particular Web site displays, so unless you sell a very general product, you probably want to avoid those with such generic placements.

One method generally used to target ads is to maintain one giant pool of Web sites, and allow each Web manager to specify which category they feel best describes their site. The other method is to restrict membership in a banner exchange service to sites that appeal to just one particular audience.

Some of the banner exchange services to explore are the following:

- LinkExchange, at **http://www.linkexchange.com**
- SmartClicks, at **http://www.smartclicks.com**

Another benefit of a banner exchange service is that traffic reports may be available to you. These reports can sometimes replace the traffic reports generated from your log files, which could reduce your time and cost to generate these reports.

Media Buying Networks

Several good reasons exist to invest funds in online advertising instead of using free banner swap networks, such as improved targeting and increased exposure, as well as eliminating the need to run banner ads on your site.

The online advertising industry has grown from nothing a few years ago to over $700 million spent annually. Although this is a small amount compared to any other mass medium, the tremendous growth indicates where this industry is headed. Today, the best approach for buying banner ads is to work through one of the leading ad networks that can serve a banner ad on hundreds, and sometimes thousands, of Web sites. Many of these networks provide a very good level of targeting to specific demographic characteristics based on the content of the Web site.

Some of the large ad-buying networks include:

- BURST! Media, at **http://www.burstmedia.com**
- FlyCast, at **http://www.flycast.com**

Measuring Advertising Effectiveness

When spending large sums of money on advertising, measuring the effectiveness of the ad campaign is important. Several measures of effectiveness are available:

- Clickthrough rate
- Inquiry rate
- Close rate
- Cost per sale

Clickthrough Rate

Each of these metrics uses reported data for the number of exposures, the number of times that people click a banner add, and various dollar amounts that you have available. The measurement that typically receives the most attention is the *clickthrough rate*, the percentage of people who see a banner and click an ad. Using this consistent metric across all banner ads and Web sites that are running your ads provides a convenient way to compare how one ad performed versus other ads, and enables you to measure the effectiveness of each Web site that is running your ads. When you run ads on very similar Web sites—with similar audiences—you can easily draw conclusions about the Web sites and eliminate those that are not performing.

Calculating a clickthrough rate for each Web site sounds easy, but the technical challenges of measuring how many times a Web site actually delivers an exposure to each ad has proven difficult for the online advertising industry. Because banner ads are generally served by a central ad server, and Web pages are served by the publisher of that material, those two pieces of content travel over different paths to reach the viewer. Combine this with the differences in Web server software technology that cause some servers to report a fully served ad when it starts, while others log a completion only when the file has been completely served onto the Internet, and you start seeing differences in reporting. Additional discrepancies in reporting are caused by the latency of the Internet that delays the receipt of files over the Web.

Since the reports from an advertising network's server are at least consistent across Web sites, the online advertising industry now relies on this source of data to compare the effectiveness of ads and Web sites. To calculate your clickthrough rate, you can combine the reported number of ad exposures provided by your media-buying service or advertising agency with the data from your server indicating the number of times people came to your site by clicking banner ads. Of course, you should calculate a clickthrough rate for each banner ad and each Web site running your ads. This is easy when each ad at each Web site has a code appended to the end of the URL.

If you run static Web pages, then you can simply have your media-buying service add codes such as "?ad4site9" to each ad. In this example, the code might indicate ad number four running at Web site number nine. As people click your banner ad and come to your site, your Web server log records the ad's code, which you can tabulate by using a traffic-analysis program (described in Chapter 32).

Inquiry and Close Rate

After you perform a clickthrough rate analysis and are comfortable that your ads are performing well, you can analyze the behavior of prospects as they view your Web site. Because you can track each person's page views during a session, you can track how many people click an ad, complete an inquiry form, or make a purchase, and thus calculate an *inquiry rate* and a *close rate*. Some Web sites, and some banner ads, will attract people to your Web site who really have no interest in your product. This may be caused by a creative look that is especially appealing or by benefits promised in the ad that don't match your offer. Sometimes, the audience of a Web site is more "click happy" than other Web audiences and just likes to click things.

Obviously, if you evaluate your advertising campaign only by the clickthrough rate, you could miss an opportunity to improve its overall effectiveness. By tracking viewers all the way as they see an ad, click the ad, view your Web site, and then take an action, you obtain a complete end-to-end analysis that can improve your Web marketing success.

Cost Per Sale

Another way to measure the effectiveness of online advertising is to calculate a cost-per-sale rate for each ad and each Web site. This requires that you apply a complete end-to-end tracking to calculate both the total cost of buying ads—segmented either by individual ad or by Web site—and the number of sales resulting from those ads. Sometimes, the cost of buying ads at a particular Web site will seem like a bargain, but when the actual advertising cost of each resulting sale is higher than your average Web sale, its effectiveness may be too low to remain on your advertising schedule. The reverse can also occur, whereby a Web site with a high advertising rate and a very low clickthrough rate delivers an exceptionally qualified audience that results in a high sales rate.

Since so many variables can affect the final performance of banner ads, periodically run small tests on new Web sites, and with new ads. The results of these tests enable you to continually improve the effectiveness of your advertising.

Traffic Retention

After you start attracting people to your Web site, consider ways to keep them coming back. The key to bringing people back to a Web site is to continue to have new and helpful information that they can use to improve their lives.

You can do a number of things to achieve this, from the type of content that you place on your site, to sending e-mail to past visitors.

Compelling Content

Since the Web was created, we've often heard the expression "content is king," but very seldom do we hear exactly what that means. Several aspects of creating Web content are compelling enough to cause people to return to a Web site on their own. The big news organizations have enjoyed a tremendous amount of repeat traffic to their Web sites, because people expect updated material daily—and sometimes hourly—that is well researched and well written. Unfortunately, most Web managers cannot afford a large staff of writers and artists, especially when the focus of the business is selling products.

To create a content-development plan, you can combine the success of these large news sites with what you know about how people look for information about products. For example, stories about how customers use a company's products can be the biggest source of new content for that company's Web site. Each time that a new customer starts using your products, consider whether their application might be "newsworthy" and worth promoting on your Web site. Not only does this help attract customers similar to the one profiled in a case study, it also can improve the relationship with your existing customer.

Case studies, sometimes called success stories, usually include a fixed set of sections using a fixed format. These sections usually include:

- The Need (sometimes called "The Problem")
- The Solution
- Our Approach

E-mail Newsletters

People who want to return to a Web site often simply forget to look in their bookmarks for sites to visit. The best way to remind people to return is with an informative e-mail newsletter that contains short summaries of new articles on your Web site and links to those articles.

Newsletters that promote a product Web site should contain at least one moderately long summary of an article that is available on the Web site, and short summaries that contain links to new announcements on the Web site, or links to news articles found on other sites. By limiting the amount of content that has to be created specifically for the newsletter, it's easier to maintain a regular publishing schedule.

If you are undecided on a format for your e-mail newsletter, take a look at the newsletters sent out by news organizations, such as CNET, ZDnet, and CMPnet. You'll find a variety of formats, even within the same organization, so you'll have a variety of formats to pattern your newsletter after.

The strong interest in distributing e-mail newsletters has resulted in several companies that provide free or low-cost distribution to lists of people in return for placing advertising within the newsletter (these sites also support discussion mailing lists, and are described in "Free Web-Based Mailing Lists" in Chapter 12). For many purposes, accepting advertising by these newsletter services does not detract from the content, so you may want to investigate placing ads in these newsletters.

Companies that serve a wide range of customers should consider the use of one of the personalized e-mail products that can tailor the master content template to match the interests and needs of each subscriber. By adding special codes to a master newsletter template, the software can select which pieces of content to include for each person. For instance, if you sell golf products on your Web site, you may have several different groups of prospects, such as novices, experienced players, and professionals. Even though members of each audience may look at the same product pages in your Web catalog, they have different needs and buying motives that you can appeal to with a personalized e-mail newsletter.

A personalized e-mail system can also be used by your salespeople, to respond quickly to prospects making inquiries at your site. By reviewing the profile created in the database by prospects, and selecting product information from a library, your Web server can send a series of personalized e-mails that can motivate prospects to return to your site—and purchase your products. However, make sure to send only appropriate information to visitors who have made inquiries, to avoid the appearance of being a spammer.

Some personalized e-mail products to review include:

- UnityMail (Revnet), at **http://www.unitymail.com**
- GT/Mail (GuestTrack), at **http://www.guesttrack.com**

The Complete Reference

Internet

Chapter 34

Advanced Web Page Options

The advanced options possible for Web pages are growing at a phenomenal rate. New concepts and technologies include cascading style sheets, object models, dynamic HTML, scripting languages, Java, ActiveX components, multimedia embedding, and others. The simplest way to use most of these technologies is to obtain one or more of the advanced Web page development tools now commercially available. Yet you can still achieve useful results by simply writing code by hand, using a text editor. This chapter explores only the tip of the iceberg, providing very simple examples of each technology.

Many of these advanced Web page options are made possible by the efforts of the World Wide Web Consortium (W3C), which researches, designs, negotiates, and recommends the standards by which Web pages are created and displayed. For the most complete, accurate picture, explore the documents at the W3C Web site, **http://www.w3.org**. Many of the core documents are highly technical in nature and use a specialized terminology, but the site also offers an increasing number of introductory articles and links to other highly readable articles elsewhere.

Adding Clickable Graphics by Using Image Maps

A popular feature of Web pages allows the user to click various parts of an image to go to various pages. These so-called "clickable graphics" rely on *image maps* in the HTML document or on the Web server. The image is associated with the map by the HTML code that inserts the image in the document. The image file itself has no map information in it.

In the latest HTML standard (HTML 4) you can apply image maps to other objects besides images, such as multimedia, if those objects are embedded using the <OBJECT> and </OBJECT> tags. See "Adding Multimedia," later in this chapter.

The Future of Web Pages: XML

In the future, an increasing number of Web pages will probably be written in XML, not HTML. *XML*, or eXtensible Markup Language is HTML's younger but bigger and more capable brother. Both languages are derived from SGML (Standard Generalized Markup Language), a language designed for describing pages that has extensive capabilities unrelated the needs of the Web. XML is a recommendation of the World Wide Web Consortium.

XML will allow Web pages to more easily and efficiently handle certain complex tasks, including passing data between unrelated programs, handling more of the processing load at the browser instead of the server, presenting different views of data to different users, and adjusting content according to the historical preferences of different users.

Overview of Image Maps

An image map is code that is either part of a Web page's HTML (and is therefore called a *client-side* image map) or it is in a separate file on the Web server (a *server-side* image map). Most developers today use the client-side image map, because it's easier to implement, gives users faster response, and reduces demand on the server. Some less-sophisticated browsers, however, can only handle server-side image maps.

Image maps do two things: they identify areas of the image (often called *hot spots*), and link these areas to different URLs. Each hot spot consists of a shape (circle, rectangle, polygon, or point), and a location on the image.

For example, an automobile manufacturer could place hot spots on the image of an automobile, so that users clicking on a portion of the car would be shown a document about that portion. The manufacturer might use circular hot spots for the wheels, a rectangular hot spot for the rear passenger compartment, and a polygon for the front compartment (to extend under the dashboard).

Client-Side Image Maps

Following is an image map coding for an image of an automobile as the map might appear in client-side form (in the HTML of a Web document):

```
<MAP NAME="car">
<AREA SHAPE=CIRCLE COORDS="86,144,36" HREF="AWD.html" >
<AREA SHAPE=CIRCLE COORDS="481,144,36" HREF="AWD.html">
<AREA SHAPE=RECT COORDS="168,31,261,138" HREF="passenger.html">
<AREA SHAPE=POLY
COORDS="266,33,266,82,296,137,386,139,383,71,331,33,266,33"
HREF="frontseat.html">
</MAP>
```

As this client-side code shows, the image map code is bounded by <MAP> and </MAP> tags, which use the NAME attribute to name the image map ("*car*" in this example). Hot spots are defined by <AREA> tags with SHAPE and COORD (coordinate) attributes, as follows:

- A circle shape (CIRCLE) uses the following coordinates, in order: column (or X position) of circle's center, row (or Y position) of circle's center, and radius.

- Rectangle shapes (RECT) use two column, row coordinate pairs to define diagonally opposite corners (X_1,Y_1, X_2, Y_2).

- Polygon shapes (POLY) list any number of X,Y coordinate pairs in a connect-the-dots scheme.

- The default shape (DEFAULT) is not really a shape; it gives an URL for the rest of the image, outside of the hot spots. If it is used, clicking outside of a hot spot takes the visitor to that default URL.

The image map must in some way be associated with the image (which can be in GIF, JPEG, or PNG format). That association takes place in the Web document, in the <IMG> tag that places the image. For client-side image maps, you use the USEMAP attribute, as follows:

```
<IMG SRC="car.gif" USEMAP="#car" BORDER=0 WIDTH=600 HEIGHT=200>
```

This example would use the image map code just listed, which is part of the same document and is tagged with the name "car".

In HTML 4, you can include alternate text with each <AREA> tag: text that appears in the hot spot if the Web site visitor's browser is not displaying images. Write the attribute in this form: ALT="*Your alternative statement here*". The browser must support this HTML 4 feature for the visitor to see the text, however.

Server-Side Image Maps

Server-side image maps are text files containing one hot spot per line, analogous to the <AREA> tags of client-side image maps. Creating and using server-side maps involves several complications, however. The exact format of each line depends on the Web server type (Web servers fall into two types, CERN and NCSA). Also, the correct HTML code you need in the Web page to associate an image with a map varies with server type. Finally, you often need high level access to the Web server to use server-side image maps. On NCSA-type Web servers, for instance, such maps must be "registered" (entered on a line) in a special configuration file. Often you must have access to directories typically restricted to the Webmaster. Contact your Webmaster for specific details of server-side image maps on your server.

Creating Image Map Code

You can write image map code using any text or HTML editor, but using image-mapping software is easier. Figure 34-1 shows how a PC image mapping program, LiveImage, lets you draw hot spots on the image and define their URLs. Such tools then output the map code—either by writing the code into a separate file or by inserting the code directly into your existing HTML file. LiveImage, for instance, can do the entire job: create the map, insert it into the HTML file, and link the image to the map.

A few representative image mapping tools (and the Web addresses where you can find them) are the following:

- LiveImage (PCs), at **http://www.liveimage.com**
- Web Hotspots tool suite, the Imagemapper tool (PCs), at **http://www.1automata.com**
- Adobe PageMill (PC/Macintosh), at **http://www.adobe.com**
- Imaptool (X Window System), at **http://www.debian.org/Packages/unstable/web/imaptool.html**

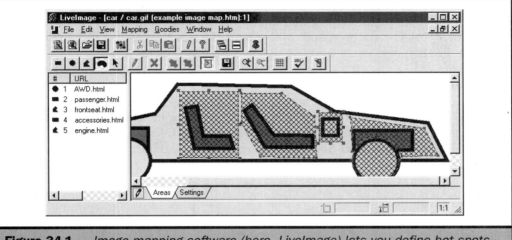

Figure 34-1.   *Image mapping software (here, LiveImage) lets you define hot spots graphically*

Using Cascading Style Sheets

A recent feature of HTML is the *cascading style sheet* (CSS). The creation of the CSS standard has revolutionized the way Web pages are conceived and structured, and opened up worlds of flexibility for the Web page designer. CSS has many attractive features, but two of the most attractive benefits of CSS are:

- The ability to change appearance of text and other objects throughout a Web site without editing all the pages
- The ability to position and even animate text and other objects on a Web page

To get the full story on CSS, go to **http://www.w3.org** and follow the link to Cascading Style Sheets information. The following two sections provide details on how to create and use styles, and how to use them in positioning objects.

Creating and Applying Text Styles

The ability to change the appearance of text and other objects throughout a Web site easily stems from using named styles. With CSS you begin by creating a description of how something should look, the font or color of text, for instance, and giving that description a name. You can make up your own name or use any of the standard HTML tags (such as <H1> and <H2>). If you make up your own name, you then apply that name to other text. Subsequently, if you want to change the appearance of all text having that name, you only need to edit its definition.

You don't have to hand-code the HTML to use CSS. The most recent versions of many popular Web page design tools employ CSS, or at least the most important features of styles. For example, both Macromedia DreamWeaver and SoftQuad HotMetal Pro help you create and use styles.

Creating Styles in HTML

If you do hand-code your HTML, here's how to create the definition. Use the *STYLE element* (the <STYLE> and </STYLE> tags and everything in between them), and place it in the header of a Web document (between the <HEAD> and </HEAD> tags). The following example illustrates how to assign a style to a standard HTML tag, <H3>, and how to define a custom style called "sidebar":

```
<HEAD>
<STYLE TYPE="text/css">
<!-
H3 { font-family:Desdemona, Cursive; font-style:normal; color:green }
.sidebar { font-family:Arial, sans-serif; font-style:italic;
color:blue}
->
</STYLE>
</HEAD>
```

What's going on in this STYLE element? The tag <STYLE TYPE="text/css"> indicates that you are defining CSS styles. The comment lines <!-- and --> keep earlier browsers that don't recognize style sheets from being confused by the definition lines. The definition lines (called *style declarations*) begin with a style name, like H3, and the definition follows in curly braces, { and }. When you declare a custom style, like sidebar, you begin with a period. Within the curly braces are the various *properties* of the style, such as font-family or font-style, separated by semicolons. Those properties can have certain values. You can provide alternative values to cover the case where the browser cannot implement a particular value by listing the alternative after a comma. In this example, if the browser does not have the Desdemona font family, it may use any font in the Cursive family. (You can find the allowable properties in the CSS1 W3C Recommendation at **http://www.w3.org**.)

Applying Styles in HTML

The styles you define (in this example, custom style sidebar and standard style H3) will apply automatically to all instances of like-named tags throughout this document. For instance, any headings formatted with the <H3> tag appear in green, Desdemona font, or a cursive font if the computer doesn't have Desdemona. To apply a custom style (technically called a *class*) to any tag, you add the style name by using the CLASS attribute as in the following example:

```
<P CLASS=sidebar>Sidebar style.</P>
```

In this example, the style is applied to an ordinary <P> tag. You can apply a style to any tag of the appropriate type (as in this case, where text styles are being applied to text tags). To apply a style to just a portion of text, use the <SPAN> tag especially designed for this purpose, as in the following example:

```
This text is normal, but <SPAN CLASS=sidebar>this text is in
Sidebar style.</SPAN>
```

Defined styles can apply either to a single document or to any set of documents. Defining a style in the header of the same document where you use it is called *embedding* a style sheet. You can also have a separate Web style sheet that controls any document on your site that references it. Just create an ordinary text file containing only the style definition lines, give the file a name with the extension .css (say, mystyles.css), and place it in the directory with your Web pages. In the header of Web pages that you want to reference this style sheet, use a <LINK> tag as shown in the following example:

```
<LINK REL=StyleSheet HREF="mystyles.css" TYPE="text/css">
```

Replace "mystyles.css" with the name of your style sheet file. Any style that you apply locally to text (or any other object) takes precedence over the applied style. For instance, even if the style is not in boldface, you can apply bold style locally with the <B> tag.

Positioning and Animating Objects

One valuable aspect of styles is that not only can you, from one central location, set such properties as font, color, and size for any set of objects on the page, but you can set any individual object's position, too. With the aid of JavaScript or some other scripting language, you can also make that position vary in time, which animates the object.

Absolute Positioning

Objects can be positioned either absolutely, with respect the edges of the page, or relative to other objects. If you are hand-coding your HTML, the following example shows you how to write the style declaration code for positioning an object absolutely:

```
#textA { position:absolute; left:4in; top:2in; width:3in;
height:3in}
```

As you read in the preceding section, style declarations go either within the STYLE element in an HTML document's header, or within a separate CSS file.

What's going on in the style declaration? First, notice that the style declaration in this case begins with a hash mark (#), which indicates that the style's name (here, textA) is linked to the object on the page by an ID attribute, instead of the CLASS attribute, as described in the preceding section. For instance, here is the HTML code for a paragraph that uses the style defined in the preceding example:

```
<SPAN ID="textA">This text is 4 inches from the left, and 2
inches down.</SPAN>
```

The attribute ID is set to textA. The ID attribute should be used instead of the CLASS attribute when you are applying position or any other style to a single object on the page, not a group of objects. The CLASS attribute will work, technically, for the same purpose, but is intended to supply style information for a whole set of objects, such as the text formatting of all the sidebars in a Web site. The ID attribute might then be used to set the position or other properties of an individual sidebar.

The other properties, left, top, width, height, define the position and size of a rectangular area in which the text (or other object) appears.

Relative Positioning

If you want to position text or something else (call it object "B" for the purposes of discussion) relative to other text or another object (call it object "A"), you use a slightly different style declaration. Set the position property for Object B to relative instead of absolute in the style declaration, as in this example:

```
#textB { position:relative; left:2in; top:2in; width:3in;
height:3in}
```

To position Object B relative to ordinary HTML text, you can simply begin Object B following that text, as in this example:

```
Here is the ordinary text we call Object A<P>

<SPAN ID="textB">This text is positioned relative to the preceding
text.</SPAN>
```

To position Object B relative to other positioned text, however, you must nest Object B within Object A, as in the following example:

```
<SPAN ID="textA">Here is the positioned text we call Object A<P>
    <SPAN ID="textB">This text is positioned
    relative to the preceding text.</SPAN><P>
</SPAN>
```

Animating an Absolutely Positioned Object

You can animate objects on your Web page by using JavaScript, ECMA Script, or another page scripting language. Using that language, you can give control of the position value to a script that varies the value. See the following section, "Adding Programming to Pages" for more information on scripting.

As of this writing, different browsers handle Web page objects differently. Most notably, Microsoft's Internet Explorer differs from Netscape Navigator. These distinctions should disappear now that a standard Document Object Model has been recommended by the World-Wide-Web Consortium (W3C) and ECMAScript has emerged as a standard JavaScript-like language. Until those standards are commonly supported, however, your script must be able to cope with distinctions by checking which type of browser is displaying the text and defining the positions accordingly.

Adding Programming to Pages

Ordinary Web pages are simply documents. They have clickable hyperlinks to other documents, and they might contain singing, dancing multimedia, but they never get beyond simply displaying information to you. Computer programs, however, are usually much more interactive. Program screens change immediately in response to your actions, without downloading an entire new page: a menu drops down, text appears, a window opens, or an image changes. Or perhaps you type information into the program, and the computer stores that information, computes an answer from it, or uses it to retrieve other information for you from a central database. Ordinary Web pages don't do that.

The missing element that keeps an ordinary Web page from being as interactive as a computer program is, simply, programming: actions that occur in response to various events, like passing a mouse cursor over something, or entering a password. To add action to a Web page, you must add some form of program—by writing it yourself, by using a program-writing tool, or by using an existing program.

You can add programming in one of two main ways:

- Place programs on the Web server, called *CGI scripts* or *server extensions*, and add commands to your Web pages that run those programs. CGI scripts are usually written in one of two computer languages, Perl or C. Server extensions are special programs created by companies that sell Web software (such as Microsoft).

- Add programs to the page itself, using any of several technologies such as JavaScript, Java, VBScript, or ActiveX.

Programs on servers can do things that page programs cannot; in particular, only server programs can enter data into, or distribute data from, a central source. You cannot create an online store or visitor registration (guest) book, for instance, without employing server software of some kind. Programs on Web pages cannot (by themselves) send or receive data that is not on a Web page. By themselves, they are limited to using whatever data is stored within a page or entered into the page by the user. They can, however, communicate with server programs to transmit or receive data.

Programs on Web pages can also perform some stunning and useful interactive effects. Rather than a Web page being a fixed combination of text and graphics, every element of the page can be generated or modified by the program. Anything can be animated or can respond to any action, and text and graphics are almost entirely unrestricted. This way of creating the content of a Web page from its programming is called *Dynamic HTML*, or *DHTML*.

Adding programs to the Web page is generally much easier than adding them to the server. However, if your Web server already has certain programs or server extensions installed, running server programs from commands in your Web page can be quite easy. (For instance, if your server has Microsoft Front Page extensions installed, by using Microsoft Front Page you can insert Microsoft WebBots. *WebBots* are commands to run Front Page extensions to perform standard operations like Web searches or automatic date and time display. See "FrontPage Express" in Chapter 28.)

Page programs take several forms. The easiest form of program to write for a Web page is a page *script*. The standard language for page scripts is JavaScript. Microsoft also offers its VBScript language, which as of this writing is fully supported only by Microsoft's Internet Explorer. More sophisticated programming requires Java programs (not JavaScript), usually found in modules called *applets*. You don't need to write your own applets, you can use prewritten applets that allow easy customization (without programming). In addition, some advanced Web development tools will output Java for you. A browser must be able to understand the programming language (be *Java-* or *JavaScript-enabled*) in order to run Java applets or JavaScript. Current releases of Netscape and Microsoft browsers are able to run JavaScript and most Java programs.

Creating a Page Program with Scripts, Objects, and Events

Page scripts are created by adding script language such as JavaScript to the HTML of a Web page to manipulate the various items on the page. As the browser downloads the page, it reads and interprets each line of code in order, and the script executes. That aspect of scripts resembles the way conventional programs execute, and will seem logical to you if you have done any programming.

Writing page scripts that respond to user actions, however, requires a unique way of thinking about how actions happen, because of the *object* and *event model* used by browsers. Browsers consider each item they display (or hold hidden within the HTML code of a page) to be an *object*. When scripts execute, they can create, change and read objects. The various languages that manipulate these objects, such as Java, have abstract objects of their own, and are therefore broadly termed *object-oriented* (although a programmer might object to calling scripting languages like JavaScript truly object-oriented). To program by using objects, whether they are Web page objects or the abstract objects of Java, requires a very different way of thinking from programming in Basic, C, or other languages. To get a hint of just how different object-oriented thinking is, consider the following attributes of objects:

- Objects have a *name*, either inherently or assigned by you. The entire Web page is named *document*, for instance. A browser window is named (unremarkably) *window*. You might create additional objects of the window type (new browser windows) with names assigned by you.

- Objects have *properties*. A property of a window object, for instance is the text that appears in its title bar. That property would be referred to by *window.title*. Properties can have subproperties of their own.

- Objects are capable of actions, called *methods*. A document can write (on itself), for instance. That action occurs when a script executes the method, document.write(HTML code), where HTML code is the content of the document, like <P>Hi, Mom!</P>. (A different method would require something different in the parentheses.)

The objective of scripting is to make a page respond to user actions. A user action–in fact, any change that the browser can detect, including the time-out of a timer—is called an *event*. Moving the mouse cursor over an object, for instance, is called the *mouseover* event. By associating a property of an object with an event, that property will change when the event happens. By associating the filename of an image object with a mouseover, for instance, the image content can change when the cursor passes over the image area.

What Is JavaScript?

JavaScript is a scripting language that reflects the object orientation of Web pages. *ECMAScript,* named after the European standards body, ECMA, is a standardized version of JavaScript. Microsoft's version of ECMAScript is *JScript*; Netscape's version is still called JavaScript. Just to make matters confusing, JavaScript is the name still in common use for all these variants. With JavaScript you can do a variety of actions on a Web page, such as the following:

- Read what kind of browser and display the user has and adjust the page accordingly
- Open additional browser windows and write content, title, and status bar text to them
- Control frames and the documents within them
- Provide mouseover feedback with images and sounds
- Create forms, set form defaults, read and check form input, and change the page in response
- Create and read "cookies," and respond according to the cookie data
- Read and write the date and time
- Execute Java applets with varying parameters depending on user input or on which browser is displaying the page
- Animate objects by sliding document layers over each other

The JavaScript language offers features common to other programming languages. Features include variables, loops, conditional statements, various numeric and string operators (such as +, −, /, ++, --), user-defined functions (similar to subroutines), and comments.

Using JavaScript in Web Pages

JavaScript code can be embedded in the HTML document, or contained in a separate, associated file. If JavaScript code is written within a document, it can appear within conventional HTML tags, or within a separate script area. A separate script area may appear in either the head or body of the HTML document, and is usually written as follows:

```
<SCRIPT LANGUAGE="JavaScript">
<!- A line that causes non-JavaScript browsers to interpret
following lines as comment, not display them.

Your JavaScript code goes here.

// A single comment line to a JavaScript browser; an end-of-comment
to non-JavaScript browsers ->
</SCRIPT>
```

For non-JavaScript browsers, which cannot interpret the <SCRIPT> tag, two special lines are added to make the JavaScript code appear to be a comment. Comments are ignored by browsers.

The following "mouse rollover" code gives you a simple example of JavaScript objects, events, and properties in action. The JavaScript in the example signals the user that the mouse cursor is over a hyperlinked image by changing the image.

```
<HTML>
<BODY>
<SCRIPT LANGUAGE="JavaScript">
<!- This line begins protection for non-JavaScript browsers
image1 = new Image
image2 = new Image
image1.src = 'firstpicture.gif'
image2.src = 'secondpicture.gif'
// This line ends protection for non-JavaScript browsers ->
</SCRIPT>
<A HREF = "somedoc.html">
     <IMG SRC = "firstpicture.gif" WIDTH="100" HEIGHT="100"
               BORDER="0"
NAME="picture"
     onmouseover = "document.picture.src = image2.src"
     onmouseout = "document.picture.src = image1.src">
</A>
</BODY>
</HTML>
```

The lines of code added to conventional HTML to implement the rollover are shown in boldface. The JavaScript within the <SCRIPT> tags creates two objects (image1 and image2), assigning each to a different image file. The browser downloads the two image files to its cache (storage), but does not yet display them. The JavaScript within the <IMG> tag makes the tag sensitive to the mouseover event. The NAME attribute (picture) for the <IMG> tag enables the mouseover code to control the image by its object and property name (document.picture.src). When the event occurs (onmouseover), the image changes, and returns to the original image afterward (onmouseout).

Using Microsoft Languages and Technologies

Microsoft has its own technologies for making Web pages more interactive. Because Microsoft's Internet Explorer is widely distributed, Microsoft technologies are widely used. They are by no means universally supported, however, by all browsers or servers.

Microsoft's fully-proprietary scripting language for Internet Explorer is *VBScript*, an extension of Microsoft's Visual Basic language. You can use VBScript in Web pages for many of the same functions you might perform in JavaScript, but the language is very different. VBScript is not, at this writing, intrinsically supported by Netscape products. Microsoft's *Jscript* is a scripting language that is an extended variant of the ECMAscript standard.

ActiveX is a technology called an *application programming interface (API)* that lets Web developers use certain preprogrammed components, and gives them access to certain Windows features. For instance, your Web page can employ the same buttons and other controls that Windows programs use. ActiveX also allows browsers to execute Windows programs using Microsoft Windows Object Linking and Embedding (OLE) features. For example, Netscape Communicator provides a built-in ActiveX API that lets users open an Excel spreadsheet from within Netscape Navigator. As a Web page programmer, you can use ActiveX features by using special terms within JavaScript or VBScript. Microsoft's ActiveX Control Pad is an authoring tool that lets developers add ActiveX controls and features (as well as JavaScript and VBScript code). ActiveX is in many respects a competing technology with Java, offering developers advanced features in return for adopting a proprietary technology.

Microsoft Front Page allows you to add *WebBots*, Microsoft's term for their proprietary Web page features. Many WebBots work by running programs on the Web server. The server must be equipped with those programs, called *Microsoft Front Page extensions* for those Web page features to work. WebBots can do tasks like searching the Web, automatically displaying the last date and time, or adding forms and navigation bars. (See "FrontPage Express" in Chapter 28 for how to add WebBots to Web pages.)

Getting Pre-Designed Scripts

Many people make their scripts available for your use or education on the Web. A good starting place to find these scripts is Yahoo!. From **http://www.yahoo.com**, choose Computers & Internet | Programming Languages | JavaScript (or choose Visual Basic | VBScript for that language). Following are some specific Web sites to visit for JavaScript examples or useable samples:

- A good starting place for documentation and examples is developer.com at

   http://javascript.developer.com

- A related site with introductory information and downloadable samples is at

   http://www.javagoodies.com

- Netscape offers sample JavaScript code on its developer Web site at

   http://developer.netscape.com/docs/examples/javascript.html

- For highly advanced examples that also employ cascading style sheets (CSS), see the Template Studio's Web site at

   http://tstudio.usa.net

What Is Java?

Java is an advanced, standardized, object-oriented programming language that can be used for many applications, not just Web pages. Java has a unique quality, however, that has made it particularly useful for Web pages: programs written in Java can run without modification on a broad variety of computers (*platforms*). This quality is referred to as *multiplatform* or *platform-neutral*. In order to run on any computer at all, however, that computer must have software that can understand Java, called a *Java engine*. Today, most computers don't have Java engines built into their operating systems, but the major vendors of Web browsers (notably Netscape and Microsoft) have built Java engines into their Web browsers for various platforms. (The browsers are said to be *Java-enabled*). As a result, you can equip your Web pages with Java programs and when users with Java-enabled browsers download your pages, your programs will run. Java programs on Web pages are limited by the browser's Java engine, however, which, to prevent security problems, has very limited access to the user's hard disk drive and software resources that are sufficiently powerful to cause damage. Java programs on the Web cannot, therefore, do everything a regular program or application can do.

Java programs on the Web can, however, do everything a scripting language like JavaScript can do—and more—and can generally do it faster, too. Java usually runs faster because the programs that are attached to Web pages are in binary form (machine-readable only). Java can do more principally it is designed to work across the Internet (and across networks in general). Java programs can use Internet services such as e-mail, file transfer, and telnet, as well as Web services to interact with server programs around the world.

What Are Java Applets?

A Java program for a Web page usually comes in a form called an *applet* (because it is a small *application*). Applets are contained in separate binary files called *class files* that must be downloaded to your browser in addition to the HTML Web page. (Sometimes, the applet relies in turn on other binary files, called *library class files,* that must also be downloaded.) Special instructions in the HTML code of the Web page file (the <APPLET> tag) associate applet files with the Web page, and transmit data to the applet that tells it how to operate.

How Do You Get Applets?

To write a Java applet, you must have good programming skills and understand how to use a compiled object-oriented language. You also need the same sorts of special tools that developers in other sophisticated languages like C or C++ require: compilers, linkers, libraries, debuggers, documentation, and the like. The original collection of tools for this purpose is called the Java Development Kit (by Sun Microsystems, who pioneered the Java language) and is available at **http://java.sun.com**. Many other vendors offer development software of various kinds, containing similar tools.

Rather than write Java applets, you can obtain them free or buy them. Java applets are available at various sites on the Web. A starting place is Yahoo!: choose Computers & Internet I Programming Languages I Java I Applets. You will find a variety of links to Web sites offering applets. Another good starting point sites offering applets and instructions on using them is **http://www.javasoft.com/applets**.

Applets themselves are files generally ending in the extension .class. Often they are contained in compressed files, such as ZIP or TAR files, that also contain documentation.

How Do You Use Applets?

To use an applet with your Web page, you must add tags to your Web page and place the class file (the applet file) on your Web site, usually in the same directory as your Web page. Following is an example of one way the code is often written, using the <APPLET> and </APPLET> tags. The example uses a hypothetical applet called sitemap.class that creates a graphical image displaying a table of contents ("site map") for your Web site:

```
<APPLET CODE="sitemap.class" WIDTH="400" HEIGHT="400">
<PARAM NAME="bgcolor" VALUE="white">
<PARAM NAME="font" VALUE="medium | bold">
<PARAM NAME="url" VALUE="http://yoursite.com/">
</APPLET>
```

Depending on the applet, you may need no <PARAM> (parameter) tags, or you may need many. This example requires only three such tags.

The HTML code for the applet always appears between <APPLET> and </APPLET> tags. (The code including <APPLET>, </APPLET>, and everything in between is called the *APPLET element*.)

Within the <APPLET> tag, the CODE attribute is required, because it gives the applet file name (sitemap.class in the example). The width and height attributes are optional, but usually included to give the dimensions (in pixels) of the area of the page where the applet is allowed to write.

Other optional attributes that can go inside the <APPLET> tag are the following:

- **CODEBASE**   The URL where the applet file resides, if it is not in the same directory as the Web page
- **ALIGN**   Horizontal alignment, for example, center
- **VSPACE** and **HSPACE**   The vertical horizontal whitespace, respectively, around the applet's writing area

Most applets allow the page developer to choose details about how the applet operates. You give those details by using <PARAM> tags that contain name and value attributes. In the preceding example, the Web page developer has set three parameters named bgcolor (background color), font, and url to various values. You must have the applet's documentation to know how to set its parameters properly.

In HTML 4, the <APPLET> tag is "deprecated," meaning for practical purposes that you should stop using it once you expect everyone to have an HTML 4 browser. Instead, you use the <OBJECT> tag. The <OBJECT> tag is described in more detail in the section, "Object Embedding" later in this chapter. To upgrade to the <OBJECT> tag for a simple instance like the examples shown, you can just replace <APPLET> tags with <OBJECT> tags. The first line (now the <OBJECT> tag line) is now written as follows:

```
<OBJECT CODETYPE="application/java" CLASSID="java:sitemap.class" WIDTH="400"
HEIGHT="400">
```

The CODETYPE attribute is optional, but helps browsers that are not Java-enabled to avoid downloading the applet. As with the <APPLET> tag, <PARAM> tags follow the <OBJECT> tag and are written the same. You close the code with </OBJECT> instead of </APPLET>.

Within both the <APPLET> and <OBJECT> tags, you can include alternate text by including an ALT = "*some text*" attribute. In this case, "*some text*" appears on the visitor's screen if the visitor's browser can't process the applet.

Making Pages Interact with a Server Program

Depending upon what you are trying to accomplish with your Web page, an alternative to putting a program (a script or Java applet) in a Web page is to put a program on the Web server and run the program from a command in the Web page. Such a server program is essential, for instance, if you want to enter data from your Web site visitors into a central database or allow them to read data from that database. Pages that you see on the Web that use forms for registering, signing in, or for placing orders are communicating with a server program to do those tasks. In fact, the original intent of forms, and still one of the most common uses for forms, is to gather information and pass that information to a server program. (Today, forms may also be used in conjunction with Web page programming such as JavaScript.)

For some Web applications, you may need programs talking to each other at both locations: on the Web page and on the Web server. If the Web page program is a Java applet, it is even possible to make your Web page communicate with an e-mail or chat server instead of the Web server.

Web pages run your server programs through a server feature called the *Common Gateway Interface* (*CGI*). The programs that run on the server under this feature are called *CGI scripts* for historical reasons, not because they have anything to do with Web page script languages such as JavaScript or VBScript. CGI scripts are generally written in the languages of either C or Perl, although other languages are also used to create the executable script file.

Creating a CGI script for a Web server is not a simple task. Even installing the CGI script can require high-level access to the Web server that only your Webmaster may have. Most Internet service providers require that you submit such scripts to them and pay for them to review it before you (or they) install it on the server. This precaution is to make sure the script will not cause problems for others. For most Web page developers, attractive alternatives include using predesigned or preinstalled scripts that their Webmaster has already approved and has provided easy access to. Another alternative is to buy special tools that create the scripts for you.

How Do You Make Web Pages Run Server Scripts?

To write a Web page command that runs a server script, you must know a few things about that script. Pages that run server scripts refer to the scripts by the *script's* URL. To run a server script, therefore, you must know the script's URL: its name and the subdirectory where it is located on your Web server. (Note that it must be *your* Web server—the server the Web page comes from. You are not usually permitted to run a script on a different server.) You must also know what kind of data the script wants passed to it, and what method must be used for passing the data.

There are two basic ways of running a CGI script located at a particular URL, depending on how that script requires data to be passed to it. (The way you pass data is officially called the *method*.) The two methods of passing data that a script may use are as follows:

- **GET**   For transmitting a line of data
- **POST**   For transmitting data from forms

Some scripts require one particular method to be used. Others can use either method.

The GET method in its simplest form uses a conventional HREF (hyperlink reference) tag in HTML, but instead of another Web page's URL, it uses the script's URL. Following is an example of a link you click to run a program using the GET method. Although this example runs a script when the user clicks a link, your page could alternatively use JavaScript to run a script. In this hypothetical example, the script receives data about what Canadian province is being discussed and what language is to be used for script output.

```
<A HREF="/cgi-bin/myscript.bin?province=quebec&language=french">
Click here to run the script.<P></A>
```

The URL is cgi-bin/myscript.bin. (The script file's name is myscript.bin, and it is in the cgi-bin directory of the Web server.) Not only is the URL given, but in the same line, following a question mark symbol (?), values (*parameters*) are passed to the CGI script for it to act upon. The parameters in the example are named province and language, and they are given the values quebec and french, respectively, in this case. The ampersand (&) separates the two values.

The CGI script and the HTML code that runs the script must both be designed to work together, as they must both use the same method and variables. To read the data in the example, for instance, the CGI script must know or ascertain that the GET method was used to transmit the data. It then looks within a special variable (an *environment variable*) reserved for this purpose that usually has the name QUERYSTRING (or QUERY_STRING) to find the data that was passed. The data is passed as a single string of characters, so the script must separate (*parse*) the data. It does so by looking for the variables by their names (in this example, province and language) or by their position in the string, and reading whatever data follows each variable's equal sign (=).

How Do You Pass Data from Forms to Server Scripts?

To pass data from forms to server scripts, you use special attributes within the various form tags. Following is an example of the HTML for a Web page in which a form is used. The example acquires and transmits the same data as the example in the preceding section. The user fills out a form (this one happens to use radio buttons) and then clicks a button labeled "Submit your choices" to run the CGI script and transmit form data to it. (See Chapters 27 and 28 for more details on forms, form tags, and attributes.)

```
<FORM ACTION="/cgi-bin/myscript.bin" METHOD="post">
    Choose your province and language:<P>
<INPUT TYPE="radio" NAME="province" VALUE="New Brunswick" CHECKED>
    New Brunswick<P>
<INPUT TYPE="radio" NAME="province" VALUE="Quebec">
    Quebec<P>
<INPUT TYPE="radio" NAME="language" VALUE="english" CHECKED>
    English<P>
<INPUT TYPE="radio" NAME="language" VALUE="french">
    Francais<P>
<INPUT type="submit" value="Submit your choices">
</FORM>
```

The ACTION attribute gives the URL of the script file. As in the example of the preceding section, the name of the script file is myscript.bin, and it is located in the Web server's cgi-bin directory. The METHOD attribute in this instance is POST, not GET. The script, as in the script described in the previous section for the GET method, receives the data from the QUERYSTRING variable, and must parse the contents to extract the values submitted for province and language. Each value has the same name as the form input field that acquired the value. For instance, clicking the top radio button assigns the value New Brunswick to the variable province.

Writing Scripts

Writing CGI scripts requires a knowledge of some compiled language such as C or C++, or a script language the server can interpret, such as Perl. You must understand how data is passed between the Web page and the server script, as the preceding sections describe. You must understand how to perform processing in the UNIX or other environment in which the server runs. You must understand how to write HTML to a Web browser from a CGI script. This section provides an overview, describing in general terms the actions of a simple CGI script that reads data from a form and writes the data back as a confirmation page. To actually write the CGI script, you must translate this overview into the language of your choice.

1. Perform any initial tasks that enable the server to execute your program, such as telling it what directory the language interpreter is in.

2. Parse the environment variable QUERYSTRING (or its equivalent) into its separate data values, breaking the string at ampersand (&) characters.

3. Perform any processing necessary on the Web server, such as writing to a file or handing database transactions.

4. Begin outputting the Web document to the standard output (*stdout*): Output a header giving the Web document MIME type: "content-type text/html" followed by a blank line.

5. Output "<HTML>" to begin the Web document.

6. For each variable, write "You chose", then the variable name, then the variable value, and end with "<P>" to terminate the line.

7. Output "</HTML>" to end the document.

Obtaining and Using Prewritten CGI Scripts

To avoid writing your own CGI scripts, you can obtain prewritten CGI scripts, which are written in various languages, on the Web. Generally, however, scripts still require customization before they will run on your Web server, so you will have to understand something about the program's language and your Web server. You may also need a compiler and programming skills to recompile that modified script if it is in C, C++, or another compiled language. Finally, once you obtain a script, someone still needs to install it on the server. (See the next section, "Installing Server Scripts.")

The most common scripts that are in an easily changed format are still those in the Perl language, although server-side VBscript and other languages are also available on some servers. The Perl language is interpreted, not compiled, so if your server can interpret Perl, you don't need a compiler or any other tools besides a text editor to customize the script.

To start looking for CGI scripts, go to Yahoo!, and choose Computers & Internet | WWW | CGI-Common Gateway Interface.

A popular kind of CGI script is one that takes information your Web site visitors enter into a form and transmits the information to you by e-mail. Some of these scripts limit you to asking for only certain information. Various commercial forms-to-e-mail scripts exist, but one of the most flexible free versions is an MIT script called cgiemail, created by Bruce Lewis. You or your Webmaster can obtain it and its documentation at **http://web.mit.edu/wwwdev/cgiemail/**. Your Internet Service Provider may already have installed the script. Once cgiemail is installed on your Web server, create your

Web page with a form whose ACTION attribute is the URL of the cgiemail script on your server. Then, as the documentation describes, create a simple text template file listing the form fields used on your Web page, and install both your Web page file and the template file in your regular Web document directory on the server. The cgiemail script takes it from there.

Installing Server Scripts

Server script files usually cannot be placed in the same directory as your Web page files. They must be placed in a directory to which, typically, only the Webmaster has access (for security reasons). The Webmaster must configure the server to recognize this directory as the place where scripts live. Moreover, either you or your Webmaster must set "ownership" of your script files (a UNIX file attribute) in a particular way (world-readable and world-executable).

Using Microsoft's Active Server Pages (ASPs)

Microsoft has a proprietary technology called *Active Server Pages* (*ASP*) that can add interactivity to your Web pages, including such server-side tasks as running databases, without CGI scripting. The limitation is that your server must use Microsoft software. Microsoft's Windows NT Server and Personal Server include this software, which is called the Microsoft Internet Information Server (IIS).

If your server has the necessary Microsoft IIS software, you can create pages that mix ASP code and HTML. If you save the result with a file extension of .asp, the server knows to pass that code to the IIS. The IIS can then run scripts either on the server or contained in other Web pages you may have created. The scripting language for using ASP code is, by default, Microsoft's VBScript. ASP commands and scripting language are contained within special symbols, <% and %>, in the Web page.

If your server has a database that conforms to Microsoft's standard, the Open Database Connectivity (ODBC) standard, you can even include commands to write to or read that database. Those commands are in yet another language, *SQL* (Structured Query Language).

Adding Multimedia

Many Web developers would like to include multimedia, such as video, audio, and animations of various kinds, on their Web sites. There are two basic ways to include multimedia: linking and embedding.

The simplest way to include multimedia is to add a hyperlink to your multimedia file (just as you would link to another Web page). When your Web site visitor clicks the hyperlink, the multimedia file is either played directly by the browser, or the browser passes the job to separate plug-in or viewer software. Most browsers inherently support a limited variety of common video and audio files, and rely on a plug-in to display other multimedia file types such as Macromedia's Shockwave files.

Usually, however, Web page developers prefer to include the multimedia automatically as part of a page, called *embedding* the multimedia. With embedding, you can allow the Web site visitor to experience embedded multimedia immediately, without clicking anything; and if the medium is visual, like video or an animation, it appears right on the Web page itself.

Object Embedding

The current HTML specification, 4, includes a standard way of embedding multimedia, called *object embedding*. Of course, an HTML 4 browser is necessary for it to work. Prior to HTML 4, the usual way to include multimedia was Netscape's invention, the <EMBED> tag, which is still in common use today. Another still-common method is to run the multimedia from a Java applet, which uses the <APPLET> tag (see "How Do You Use Applets?" earlier in this chapter). Object embedding uses the tags <OBJECT> and </OBJECT>. The *OBJECT element* includes <OBJECT>, </OBJECT> and everything in-between.

Object embedding is not only used to include multimedia in HTML 4, it can be used to include nearly anything, including multimedia, images, applets, and even other HTML pages. All of those things are considered objects. Object embedding is the preferred way, in fact, to include applets in a page, and in the long run may also replace the <IMG> tag as the way to include images.

Exactly how you write the object embedding statement in HTML depends on whether or not you need the browser to download a plug-in, viewer, or other resource such as an ActiveX control in order to display your multimedia (these are described in Chapter 22).

Embedding Objects That the Browser Can Handle Without Downloading Additional Viewing Software

Many browsers can handle objects in a variety of multimedia formats intrinsically (without special additional software). Here are some of the types of multimedia files that popular browsers commonly support without help:

- Microsoft video (AVI files)
- Apple Quicktime (QT, movie, MOV, or MOOV files)
- MPEG (Motion Picture Experts Group) video (MPG or MPEG files)
- Audio (AU, WAV, AIFF, MID, or MIDI files)

In addition, browsers are often already equipped with the plug-ins, viewers, ActiveX components, or other technology needed for viewing various types of multimedia. If you expect the browser to be able to display the multimedia object without downloading additional software (either because the browser can handle the multimedia intrinsically or because you expect the user has previously downloaded whatever plug-in or viewer is needed), you can write the OBJECT element as simply as in the following example:

```
<OBJECT WIDTH="500" HEIGHT="500" DATA="glennlaunch.mpg"
TYPE="application/mpeg">
</OBJECT>
```

The attributes of the <OBJECT> tag in this example provide the following information:

- **DATA** The location and name of the multimedia file. If a relative address (which, like the one in the example, does not begin with http://) is used, the location is assumed to be the same as for this Web page, unless the optional CODEBASE attribute is used.
- **WIDTH** and **HEIGHT** The size of the area in which the multimedia appears (optional).
- **TYPE** The file's MIME type (optional). (See the upcoming box, "Understanding and Using Multimedia MIME Types.")

An additional and useful optional attribute to add to the <OBJECT> tag if your multimedia file is large is the STANDBY attribute, in the form of this example: STANDBY="Please wait". The text in quotes is displayed while your object downloads.

Embedding Objects with the <EMBED> Tag for Older Browsers

For older browsers that do not process the OBJECT element properly, you can use the <EMBED> tag. This tag was originally extended HTML developed by Netscape. An example of the <EMBED> tag is as follows:

```
<EMBED width="500" height="500" src="glennlaunch.mpg">
```

To ensure that your page is usable by older browsers and yet is HTML 4-compliant, you can include the <EMBED> tag within an OBJECT element as described in the upcoming section, "Alternative Media for Browsers That Can't Display Your Type of Multimedia." The <EMBED> tag can also use the ALIGN, BORDER, VSPACE, and HSPACE attributes that are used in the <IMG> tag. See Chapter 27 for more about the <IMG> tag. Depending upon the plug-in or viewer handling the multimedia, other attributes may include AUTOSTART="true" or "false" to determine whether the multimedia begins to play immediately or not, CONTROLS=*value*, and CONSOLE=*value*, where value is determined by the plug-in or viewer.

Embedding Objects That Need Additional Browser Software

Multimedia that the browser can't play on its own requires the user to download a viewer, plug-in, or ActiveX control (described in Chapter 22). In that case, you need to add the CLASSID attribute to the <OBJECT> tag , as in the following example, which gives the URL where the viewer (in this case, 3d_games, a hypothetical viewer) can be found:

```
<OBJECT WIDTH="500" HEIGHT="500"
CLASSID="http://www.radviewers.com/3d_games"
DATA="wheykewl.gam">
</OBJECT>
```

If the browser has not already downloaded the viewer or other software identified in CLASSID, it begins to download (with the user's approval) that software. In this example, the viewer is presumably designed to read the developer's own GAM file format, and it is located at the URL given by CLASSID.

If you are using Java applets, ActiveX controls, or other popular add-on software, you do not give the URL (which begins with http:) for the software as the preceding example describes, but instead use special URI (Uniform Resource Identifier) code within the CLASSID attribute, as follows:

- For Java applets, the CLASSID URI begins with java:, as in classid="java:myjavathing.class"

- For ActiveX controls, the CLASSID URI begins with csid: and continues with the ActiveX component's very long unique code, as in the following code for a Macromedia Director ActiveX control:

```
classid="clsid:166B1BCA-3F9C-11CF-8075-444553540000"
```

If the Java or ActiveX component is not in the same directory as the Web page file, you need to include a CODEBASE attribute inside the <OBJECT> tag to give its URL, as in the following example:

```
<OBJECT CLASSID=="java:myjavathing.class"
CODEBASE="http://www.radviewers.com/java">
```

The CODEBASE might not even be on your own Web site. For instance, if you were embedding a Shockwave Director ActiveX control, your CODEBASE attribute might look like the following line, which points to the URI at Macromedia for a Shockwave player:

```
CODEBASE="http://active.macromedia.com/director/cabs/sw.cab#version
=6,0,0,0"
```

CREATING AND
MAINTAINING WEB SITES

Objects That Use Parameters

Some objects (most notably, Java applets) allow the Web page developer to specify *parameters*—values that tell the object exactly how to run. Parameters might, for instance, tell the object what colors to use, what fonts to use, or which of various types of animations to use. The <PARAM> tag appears after the <OBJECT> (or <APPLET>) tag, and before the </OBJECT> (or </APPLET>) tag, and sets parameters by using the following form:

<PARAM *name=value   name=value* ...>

Each parameter has a *name* and can take various *values* as determined by the object's designer. See the discussion earlier in this chapter of Java applets for additional examples.

Understanding and Using Multimedia MIME Types

Each kind of media file commonly used on the Internet has a MIME (Multimedia Internet Mail Extension) type. You can find a good, readable list of MIME types at

http://www.ltsw.se/knbase/internet/mime.htp

Browsers differ in their intrinsic capabilities for handling various MIME types. If a browser cannot intrinsically display a certain MIME type, it tries to turn the job over to an additional chunk of software like a viewer, plug-in, or ActiveX control. If it has no such software to display the embedded media, it then either displays any alternative text that you have included in the <OBJECT> tag using the ALT attribute, or proceeds to display an alternative object, as described in the next section, "Alternative Media for Browsers That Can't Display Your Type of Multimedia."

In the <OBJECT> tag, you can identify the MIME type of your multimedia file by using the TYPE attribute. The TYPE attribute is optional, not required, but by including it, you allow the browser to avoid wasting time downloading the file if it has no way of displaying the file. If you don't include the TYPE attribute, the browser uses the file extension to figure out what kind of file it is.

MIME type names have two parts, the type and subtype, separated by a slash in the MIME name as in application/x-msvideo. Common multimedia types are application, audio, and video; application is a catch-all type that simply implies that the file's format is generally native to a particular application.

MIME subtypes are of two varieties: registered and unregistered. Registered subtypes are registered by the Internet Assigned Numbers Authority (IANA), after a formal process. Unregistered sub-types can be anything at all—in fact, you can create your own—but the subtype must begin with x-. Audio files in WAV format, for instance, are of the MIME type audio/x-wav.

Alternative Media for Browsers That Can't Display Your Type of Multimedia

The HTML 4 OBJECT element is designed so that you can accommodate Web site visitors whose browsers don't have any way to display your multimedia, or that don't even handle HTML 4. For instance, if a visitor doesn't have MPEG movie capability (or has it turned off), your page could automatically show the visitor a GIF image instead. The following example shows how it's done:

```
<P>
<OBJECT DATA="Thebrain.mpeg" TYPE="application/mpeg">
        <OBJECT DATA="Thebrain.gif" TYPE="image/gif">
           The human brain during recall displays specific
           active regions.
        </OBJECT>
</OBJECT>
```

Simply list your alternative objects between the top-level <OBJECT> and </OBJECT> tags, in order of preference. In this example, three levels of contingency are provided: first, an MPEG movie is shown; if the browser can't handle MPEG movies, a GIF image is displayed; if the browser has images turned off, the text is displayed. Text in an OBJECT element, as shown here, serves the same purpose that alternate (ALT) text does. (Remember, however, that the OBJECT element is an HTML 4 feature, so this way of allowing for contingencies will only work for HTML 4-compliant browsers.)

To ensure that older browsers can also handle your embedded multimedia, you can add the <EMBED> tag within the top-level OBJECT element. For instance:

```
<P>
<OBJECT DATA="Thebrain.mpg" TYPE="application/mpeg">
    <OBJECT DATA="Thebrain.gif" TYPE="image/gif">
    The human brain during recall displays specific
    active regions.
    </OBJECT>
    <EMBED SRC="Thebrain.mpg">
</OBJECT>
```

Adding Audio to Web Pages

Audio is increasingly popular on Web pages as a way to bring music and narration to site visitors, both for the sake of variety and to improve site accessibility to visually impaired visitors. Many computers today come equipped with audio capability (either built-in or by means of a sound card hardware option), so you can simply plug a microphone into the proper jack and run the computer's (or sound card vendor's) audio accessory software to create an audio file from your own performance. You can also acquire content (audio files) from the Internet, or from CDs if your computer has a CD-ROM drive, but you must be certain to obtain the rights to use the content from the owner. See Chapter 30 for details of creating different kinds of audio, as well as choosing the best audio format for your application.

You deliver audio in your Web page in one of two ways: by causing the browser to download, then play, an audio file, or by *streaming* the audio: playing it as it arrives at the Web site visitor's browser. The former, called *static* audio, requires the visitor to wait. Because audio files are large, the wait can be quite long. Streaming provides more immediate audio (usually involving a few seconds of delay), but sometimes at the expense of audio quality. See "Static vs. Streaming Audio Files" in Chapter 30.

As with other media, the browser recognizes the MIME type of the audio file from its file extension, and if it can play the file on its own, does so. If it cannot play the file on its own, it hands the job to a plug-in, audio player, or ActiveX component.

Linking and Embedding Audio

For either static or streaming audio, as for other types of multimedia, the file can either be linked from a Web page (exactly as other Web pages are linked) or embedded in a Web page (exactly as other objects are embedded). When you link to an audio file, the player control panel appears in a separate window. Following is the HTML code for simply linking to an audio file:

```
<A HREF="http://www.animalsounds.com/cows.au">Mooing sounds</A>
```

The user clicks the link to start downloading the file. The viewer launches and begins to play the audio—within a few seconds if you are using streaming audio, or after the file downloads if you are using static audio.

The main advantage of embedding is that it allows the player controls to appear on the Web page instead of in a separate window. It also allows the audio to start automatically, rather than waiting for the Web page visitor to click a link. (Linked files can, however, also start automatically if you use Javascript or other advanced tricks to execute the link.) Embedding can be done using the OBJECT element or <EMBED> tag, as described in the earlier section of this chapter, "Object Embedding."

Adding Streaming Audio

Streaming audio is generally accomplished using proprietary technology from one of several software vendors. Those vendors include RealNetworks, Inc., Xing Technology Corporation, GEO Interactive, Microsoft, and VDOnet. In general, these vendors offer not only streaming audio, but also streaming video. Many vendors offer their most basic players and encoders for free. The sections "Step 4. Encoding the File into a Compressed Audio Format" and "Step 5. Linking the Resulting Audio File to Your Web Pages" in Chapter 30 describe how to create a streaming audio file and link to it from your Web page.

Note *An open-standard (nonproprietary) solution exists for streaming audio and video, called MBONE, but is comparatively rare and is not particularly well-suited to the low-speed dial-up connections used by many Web users. MBONE was developed by the Internet Engineering Task Force (IETF).*

Embedding a RealAudio File in a Web Page

You can either link to the RealAudio RAM or RPM file or embed the RealPlayer object in your Web page. With a link, which looks like the following code, the user clicks the link and the RealPlayer program runs in a separate window:

```
<A HREF="cows.ram">Audio from the barnyard</A>
```

To embed the RealPlayer control on your Web page, so that the RealPlayer runs in the browser window, use the OBJECT element or <EMBED> tag described in the section, "Object Embedding," earlier in this chapter. As that section indicates, until all browsers fully support the HTML 4 OBJECT element, an approach that covers all contingencies is to include an <EMBED> tag within the OBJECT element. If the browser cannot process the OBJECT element, it proceeds to the <EMBED> tag. Here is an example of the RealPlayer control in an HTML page:

```
<OBJECT CLASSID="clsid:CFCDAA03-8BE4-11cf-B84B-0020AFBBCCFA"
HEIGHT=140 WIDTH=312>
<PARAM NAME="src" VALUE="sample.ram">
<PARAM NAME="controls" VALUE="Default">
<PARAM NAME="autostart" VALUE="true">
<EMBED SRC="sample.rm" CONTROLS="Default" AUTOSTART="true">
</OBJECT>
```

Notice that the example does not quite follow the usual form for an OBJECT element in HTML 4. Instead of using the DATA attribute of the OBJECT element to identify the audio file, as would be conventional in HTML 4, it uses the <PARAM> tag with a SRC attribute. The example reflects the current state of affairs for RealAudio as of this writing: the DATA attribute (and the CODEBASE attribute) of the OBJECT element are not used.

You can choose a variety of RealPlayer controls with the CONTROLS attribute of the <PARAM> tag. By setting CONTROLS to ControlPanel, PlayButton, StopButton, InfoVolumePanel, and other values, you can place various controls for the audio on your Web page. See the technical support Web pages at **http://www.real.com** for details.

The AUTOSTART parameter allows you to start the audio flow immediately. Otherwise, the user must click the Play button on the control panel to begin the sound.

Other Streaming Audio Alternatives

Streaming audio is a growing field, with new vendors being added regularly. Two such vendors are Xing Technology and Geo Interactive. Like RealNetworks, both now offer streaming audio as a subset of their video capability.

XING TECHNOLOGY'S STREAMWORKS   Xing Technology's Streamworks products include both client (browser) and server solutions, plus software and hardware for video and audio conversion to streaming digital formats. Xing relies on the industry standard, MPEG, for its streaming audio and video. (Although MPEG is essentially a video format, its Layer 3, called *MP3*, carries audio and can be used alone.) Xing offers various MP3 encoders, servers, and players either free or inexpensively through its Website, **http://www.xingtech.com**.

You link to an Xing streaming audio file as you would to any other media file, for instance:

```
<A HREF="http://yourISP.com/myjokes.xdm">Click here to hear my
jokes.</A>
```

If you use an Xing server, your streaming audio files have the extension .xdm; otherwise, they have the standard MPEG layer 3 extension, .mp3.

GEO INTERACTIVE'S EMBLAZE PRODUCTS   Geo Interactive takes a different approach to streaming audio and video than do RealNetworks and Xing. Geo Intereactive's Emblaze technology does not use special servers, nor does it use a conventional viewer, plug-in, or ActiveX component. Instead, Emblaze uses Java applets to play specially-formatted media files, which you create with Emblaze tools.

You put the media file and the Java applet or applets in a directory, link to the applet from your Web page, and your visitor's browser downloads the Java applet to play the audio (or video). The applet code in your Web page uses a parameter to point to the media file, as the following audio example code shows:

```
<APPLET CODE="EmblazeAudio.class">
<PARAM NAME="soundfilename" VALUE="thesound.ea">
</APPLET>
```

This example simply plays the file thesound.ea immediately as the page is loaded. You can include a playing console in the EA media file when you create it.

You can obtain free trial copies of Emblaze products from Geo Interactive's Web site at **http://www.emblaze.com**.

Adding Video to Web Pages

Video is popular for multimedia presentations on CD, but is not yet very popular on the Web. The main reason is that the Web generally cannot handle the rate of data transmission that quality video requires. Also, the Web does not transmit data at a steady rate, leading to gaps, pauses, and quality lapses in the video. This variable rate is also a problem for audio, but less so. Finally, getting video from the video source and into the computer usually requires an additional expenditure in hardware at this time. Unlike audio boards, video boards are rarely included with the computer.

As with Web audio, two approaches are used to get around the bandwidth and variable data rate problems. One approach is to use static video, which requires the user to download a file (which typically makes use of advanced data compression to shorten download time), then play it. The alternative is to use *streaming video*. Streaming video not only uses advanced compression in the data stream to overcome the bandwidth problem, but must also solve the problem of variable transmission rate. Solving the latter problem usually involves a special streaming Web server, although technologies from Geo Interactive and others can deliver streaming video without special servers.

To date, broadcast- or CD-quality streaming video cannot be delivered over typical dial-up connections to the Internet. The quality of streaming video possible today over a typical dial-up connection is limited to color images a few centimeters square, with audio.

Adding static video to a Web page is identical to adding static audio. Simply embed or link to a file that is in one of the standard video formats. The video file formats most commonly supported by Web browser are as follows:

- Apple QuickTime
- Motion Picture Experts Group (MPEG)
- Microsoft WAV

The big technical achievement of video file formats is compression. All these formats offer varying degrees and types of compression, which they implement by using different compression and decompression *engines*—software that encodes or decodes the format. One practical challenge for Web developers is ensuring that the type of compression engine used for creating the video clip is also available in browsers or viewers. AVI files, for instance, can use compression types of Microsoft Video, or any of several variants of Intel Indeo, Cinepak, and others. QuickTime movies can use Video, Compact Video, Animation, or Raw (uncompressed) compressors. QuickTime files also come in two forms: the native Macintosh file and a "flattened" file used by other computers. MPEG videos come in a variety of flavors, as well, and the standards are progressing rapidly, with MPEG-4 being the latest in the progression.

Streaming video today usually involves using proprietary solutions, just as streaming audio does. The example vendors in the preceding section also do streaming video with the same technologies. To date, most of applications for streaming video have been on corporate intranets, not the Internet, because of the generally higher bandwidth available on an intranet. New streaming technologies and faster modems are gradually making Internet video more attractive to a broader base of users and developers.

Chapter 35

Web Commerce

No business can survive unless its potential customers know it exists. The World Wide Web offers you a unique opportunity to get the word out about your company, let your audience know what products and services you offer, and give them a way to order your goods over the Internet.

Doing business over the Web is quite a bit like doing business in a physical store: you need to let folks know who you are, what you do, and where you can be found. Creating a Web presence does have certain advantages over establishing a physical location, however. Instead of leasing a store, buying a sign, and printing marketing literature you'll have to live with for months, you can set up a presence that is reachable by anyone with Web access, can be found through the search engines discussed in Chapter 33, can accept orders from Web site visitors, and can be updated as often as you like.

Types of Commercial Web Sites

How much functionality you build into your Web site depends on your goals for the site. For instance, if you expect visitors to make purchase decisions (and purchases!) based solely on the information on the site, you construct a very different site than if you saw your site as an invitation for visitors to contact you by phone, fax, or in person.

There are three basic types of commercial Web sites you can set up for your business: a public relations (PR) site, a marketing site, and a sales site. You can think of these three types of sites as a logical progression. A PR site presents your company in its best light, a marketing site tells them about your products, and a sales site lets them buy the perfect product from a company they respect.

PR Sites

The goal of a PR Web site is to make your business' best qualities known to anyone who visits the site. New product announcements, significant hirings, expansions, Web site redesigns, price changes, and alliances are all great candidates for inclusion on a PR Web site. While you should stay away from the "everything's news" mind set, whenever you make a change that affects your customers, you should announce it on your site.

Create a special area on your Web site that contains your press releases and, when possible, invite your visitors to receive the releases by e-mail. Running mailing lists is described at the end of this chapter (and general mailing list topics are discussed in Chapter 12), but for now you should bear in mind that most of your customers would appreciate monthly summaries of what's new with your company and not daily updates on every change you've made.

You should definitely have all of your company's contact information prominently displayed on your site, including an e-mail address so visitors can ask any questions that occur to them while they are at your site. Including your company's general contact e-mail address at the bottom of each page is a good idea—that way your potential customers won't need to dig through your site to find your e-mail address and can ask their question while it is fresh in their mind. You should also avoid making your press releases into sales documents. Remember, the object of a press release is to attract attention; nothing raises the defenses of editors, journalists, and potential customers like a sales pitch disguised as a news release. Get your potential customers to the site; then sell them your goods.

A number of sites offer advice on how to write a press release, though you should remember that many of the sites are maintained by marketing companies that would be happy to write your release for you. Hiring an outside firm to write your first few releases or more, if you are happy with their work or don't have the time to write them yourself, is a viable option. Remember that you will be paying for a specialized service and, as when you hire any outside firm or individual contractor, you should ask to see samples of their work and to speak with some of their clients. A few firms to consider are

- Charles Kessler & Associates, at **http://www.net-market.com/howto.htm**
- GroupWeb, at **http://www.groupweb.com/your/ejournal/how_to_press.htm**
- BizHub, at **http://www.bizhub.com/products_services/press_release.shtml**

Marketing Sites

A PR site is the basic corporate Web site; it gets your name out there, lets potential customers know what's going on with your firm, and gives your audience enough information to contact you in person or over the Internet. A marketing site goes beyond the basic Internet presence of a PR site by providing detailed information about your products and services, comparing your offerings to those of other companies, and listing prices.

The most important part of a marketing Web site is the information about your products and services. Rather than focus on the glossy, newsworthy side of your company, your marketing information should be written like printed one-page fact sheets. Those fact sheets should list the name of the product or service and the specific function of the equipment (or the problem the service solves), as well the product's internal tracking code, stock number, dimensions, configuration options, and additional equipment (like cables, batteries, and toner) required to operate the product. If you have a digitized photograph of the product or can represent the service with a graphic, you should certainly include those images in your online fact sheet.

The next part of your Web presentation for this product or service should describe your product's attributes and advantages. How you market your product depends on the type of product or service and how what you are selling is distinct from your competitors' offerings, but one easy way to present your product is in a feature/benefit format. In a feature/benefit presentation, you list the qualities of your product and how the user will benefit from each of those features. For instance, if you build custom computer systems for businesses and home users, you could describe one or more of your typical designs, catalog the components that make up the system, and list the benefits of the components individually or as a part of the system.

You might also want to compare your products to those of your competitors in terms of features, performance, price, warranties, and so forth. If you're comparing your products and services to industry norms, you should list the feature, the average implementation of that feature in your area, your implementation, and explain how your approach is superior. For instance, if custom computer builders in your area only include a 300MHz chip in their $1,000 computers and you offer a 333MHz chip (and similar or better components like RAM, storage, and video cards), you should point that out in your presentation.

Sales Sites

Just as a marketing site is one step up in complexity from a PR site, a sales site extends the capabilities of a marketing site by allowing visitors to purchase your goods or services over the Web. Your site should include all of the information a visitor needs to evaluate your products and the tools for them to purchase your products.

You have a number of options in setting up your sales site, though you should keep in mind that the security of the transaction is extremely important. It is far more likely that a customer's credit card number will be stolen by a store clerk making minimum wage than by a hacker intercepting your e-mail, but you should still take every reasonable precaution to ensure your customers' information is safe while in transit and when stored on your computers.

The easiest way to establish a sales site is to hire a Web-hosting company to host the site for you. You'll need to provide the contents for the site and fulfill the orders yourself, but the hosting company will take care of your Internet security needs. In the following section, you'll learn enough about Web security to evaluate a hosting company's services.

A number of software programs are available that allow you to set up your stores with a minimum of original programming. Web sites of companies that offer this type of software include

- Alpha Software, at **http://www.onlinemerchant.com**
- IMSI, at **http://www.imsisoft.com**
- Multiactive Technologies, at **http://www.ecbuilder.com**
- Sitematic, at **http://www.sitematic.com**
- Storesonline, at **http://www.storesonline.com**

Selling via Secure Servers

The best way to ensure that your Web-based transactions are safe is to use a *secure server*. A secure server is a computer connected to the Internet with software that allows visitors to establish a secure (encrypted) link to your server, safeguards user information on the server, and is difficult for even a determined attacker to break into. For a secure connection to be possible, both the user and the merchant must have the appropriate software in place.

The Internet and its transmission protocol, TCP/IP, were designed for efficiency and not security. Packets of information are sent "in the clear" and can be read by any computer, intended recipient or not. Since Web commerce entails sending sensitive financial information over a public network, some care is required.

Server-Side Security

Enter cryptography. Using public key encryption (described in Chapter 9), secure servers have built-in software to establish encrypted connections with other computers. The protocol used to establish these connections is the *Secure Socket Layer* (*SSL*) protocol as described in the section "How Secure Transactions Work" in Chapter 18. You can find out about secure Web server software by visiting the sites of these manufacturers:

- Microsoft, at **http://www.microsoft.com**
- Netscape, at**http://www.netscape.com**
- Stronghold, at **http://www.stronghold.com**
- O'Reilly & Associates, at **http://www.oreilly.com**

When a home user visits your Web site using Netscape Navigator or Microsoft Internet Explorer, how do they establish an SSL connection? Fortunately, recent versions of Netscape Navigator and Microsoft Internet Explorer can establish SSL connections with secure Web servers without the user needing to take any action.

Digital Certificates

As a user, however, you might want assurances that the people operating the secure server somewhere else on the Web and asking for your credit card number are who they say they are. Just as there's no foolproof way to guard against fraud in the real world, there's no 100 percent effective way to guard against fraud on the Web. To assure your visitors that you are a legitimate enterprise, you use digital certificates, described in the section "Digital Certificates" in Chapter 9.

A *digital certificate* is a key pair created using public key cryptography. Unlike with PGP (Pretty Good Privacy, a widely used system for encrypting e-mail also described in Chapter 9), which allows anyone to create a key pair, digital certificates can be created and issued only by *certification authorities*, bodies that verify the identity of the person or company requesting a digital certificate. Once generated, a digital certificate guarantees the identify of the certificate holder, and is used like a key in the encryption process. The recipient can tell the message was signed by the certificate holder and can check the message against the public half of the key, maintained in a database by the certification authority.

Several levels of digital certificates are available, with the level depending on the amount of proof offered to establish the applicant's identity. One common scheme is as follows:

- **Level One** A certificate tied to an e-mail address. The only check made is a return e-mail to that address to ensure it is valid. This level does not necessarily tie the e-mail address to an identifiable person or company.

- **Level Two** At this level, the certification authority asks for proof of an individual's identity, such as a driver's license, passport, or credit card. The information provided in the application is checked against common databases, such as those maintained by credit rating firms.

- **Level Three** The highest level of assurance, normally reserved for companies and other permanent organizations. The applicant must supply three forms of identification to an authority, such as a notary. Acceptable documents include a group's articles of incorporation and other public records.

If you are implementing your own Web commerce site, you should seriously consider purchasing a Level Three certificate from a well-known certification authority. Having taken the time to register with a certification authority marks you as a serious company, not a fly-by-night organization. You should require the same of any company you hire to host your sales site for you.

A number of well-established certification authorities have Web sites describing digital certificates in general and their products and services in particular. They include

- VeriSign, at **http://www.verisign.com**
- Thawte, at **Consulting http://www.thawte.com**
- GTE Cybertrust, at **http://www.cybertrust.gte.com**
- Entrust, at **http://www.entrust.com**

Selecting a Secure Hosting Service

The most confusing step in selecting a secure hosting service is finding one. Fortunately, a number of easily accessible resources can help you find a hosting service. Once you have a list of candidates, you can ask them pointed questions 'about what they will do for you.

Finding a Secure Hosting Service

One place you can find hosting services is on Yahoo: choose Business and Economy | Companies | Internet Services | Web Services | Hosting. From that starting point you can search for hosting firms by region or get a complete list. Not all of the companies listed offer secure Web sites, so visit each firm's Web site or contact the company in person to determine whether they offer the basic services you need to run your business on the Web. You can also find advertisements for hosting companies at the back of Internet industry publications.

Questions to Ask Potential Secure Host Providers

Now that you have a list of companies that might host your sales site, ask the following questions to make sure they have sufficient resources to host your site.

- *Does the company offer a secure server?* If not, move to the next company on your list.

- *How is the company connected to the Internet?* The best type of connection is a T3, an extremely high-capacity line, though multiple T1 lines are also acceptable. Choose a company with redundant connections, so if a line to one provider goes down, plenty of bandwidth is still available from other sources.

- *Does the company have a digital certificate from a known certification authority?* Well-established companies have a certificate from a certification authority. Not having one would not necessarily disqualify a firm from hosting your site, but it is better to find a company that does offer that extra level of assurance.

- *Does the company offer 24-hour live technical support?* Many smaller hosting companies do not have a live person answering phones around the clock, but your visitors may not always arrive during normal business hours. It is vital that your hosting company has someone on hand to receive calls informing them the site is unreachable or that something is broken.

- *What is the monthly fee?* The going rate for secure hosting services at the time of this writing is $20–$40 per month. That price should include access to the secure server, enough storage for your Web site, and enough bandwidth so you can transfer your site's contents to your visitors without incurring additional charges.

- *How much storage is included?* The minimum amount of storage you should request for your site is 20MB, which should be enough for most smaller and medium-sized businesses. Additional storage can usually be purchased for a few dollars per month, so ask about that rate as well.

- *How much bandwidth is included?* In other words, what is the amount of data you can send and receive before the host starts charging extra? Most hosts allow from 3–6GB of bandwidth usage, which should be plenty for the average business. If your site has lots of graphics or offers streaming audio or video, you might need to purchase more bandwidth.

- *Can I use my own domain name?* If your firm has its own domain name, which it should, your provider should allow you to use it on your site. There may be a one-time setup fee to transfer your domain name to the hosting firm, but you should be able to negotiate it away.

- *Can I update my site at any time?* You should be able to update your site at any time and as often as you like with no extra charge.

- *How many e-mail addresses are included with the base price?* Many hosting firms provide ten or more e-mail addresses with your domain name, so you can receive mail as **info@*yourdomain*.com**, **sales@*yourdomain*.com** and other addresses.

- *Can I upgrade my account at any time?* Rather than paying for extra bandwidth or storage, the hosting company should allow you to upgrade your account and reserve more storage and bandwidth for your site.

- *How often is the site backed up?* Whether the site is backed up should not be an issue; the only question is how often. Many providers back up their sites every two or three days, though daily backups are preferable. Keep copies of everything you upload to your server.

- *How are site statistics kept?* Your hosting company should make your site's visitor logs available to you, preferably in both raw and analyzed form. At the very least, your provider should tell you the number of times each file was accessed, the number of page views, and the number of visitors for a given day. These statistics should be updated every day.

- *How long will it take to set up my site?* If you are uploading your own content, the site should be available the same day. If you are contracting the firm to design and implement your site as well, the amount of time needed will depend on the complexity of your design.

- *What CGI scripts are included? Can you run your own?* Most hosting companies have a library of CGI scripts, such as shopping carts and guest books, for you to use in your site. If you are confident you can write your own CGI scripts, ask if you will have the ability to augment your site with them.

Shopping Cart Software

While your visitors are at your site, they will probably want to browse around and see everything before "checking out." Of course, if they see something they want to buy, they should be able to keep it on hand and purchase it when they leave. In other words, they need an electronic *shopping cart* to carry the items they want to purchase with them until they are ready to leave.

Most secure site providers include shopping cart software in their Web commerce packages, though you might need to provide your own if you can't find a provider that meets all of your other needs and offers that software. A number of companies offer shopping cart software for Web commerce, including these:

- Mountain Networks, at **http://www.mountain-net.com**
- AHG, at **http://www.ahg.com**
- Americart, at **http://www.cartserver.com/americart**
- Oakland Group, at **http://www.oaklnd.com**

Interacting with Your Customers

Beyond establishing the technical infrastructure to do business online, you need to make a commitment to providing excellent customer service. In the online world, that means giving your customers a means to ask questions, offer opinions, and interact with your staff and other customers.

Several tools are available for interacting with your customers, but the most useful are guestbooks, Web-based discussion groups, and mailing lists. Regardless of the tool you choose, the most important aspect of customer service is responding to your customers' questions and complaints promptly. A recent study from Jupiter Communications (**http://www.jup.com**) discovered that 42 percent of top-ranked Web sites took longer than five days to reply to customer e-mail inquiries, never replied at all, or were not accessible by e-mail. Responding to user inquiries and comments quickly is vital so that your current and potential clients don't become frustrated at a perceived lack of response. By responding promptly to your customers' inquiries, you can set yourself apart from the crowd.

Setting Up a Guestbook

A guestbook is one of the simplest ways to encourage feedback from your site's visitors. Users can access your Web site and fill out a form; the guestbook program appends the information to an existing HTML file for subsequent visitors to read. Several good guestbook scripts are available on the Web, though your ISP or Web hosting provider is likely to have a script for you to use. If not, check out the following sites:

- Extropia, at **http://www.extropia.com/scripts/guestbook.html**
- MSA, at **http://www.worldwidemart.com/scripts**

Setting Up Discussion Groups

Web-based discussion groups are similar to guestbooks, but they have the advantage of *threading* messages (displaying messages and their replies together). For instance, a visitor could post a message with the subject heading "Need story tapes for long car trips." Every reply to that message would be maintained as a part of the series of messages, or *thread*, associated with that post. With many discussion group scripts, the messages a user has already read either are not shown or are displayed in a different color. See Chapter 16 for a users-eye view of Web-based chat.

Discussion groups are handy because they let your visitors ask questions or make comments that can be identified and responded to easily, rather than requiring your users and staff to page through a single document as in a guestbook.

You can find discussion group software at the following sites:

- O'Reilly & Associates, at **http://webboard.oreilly.com**
- Extropia, at **http://www.extropia.com/scripts/bbs.html**
- The CGI Collection, at **http://www.itm.com/cgicollection**

E-mail

As you read in the section, "Creating Your Own Mailing List," in Chapter 12, you can set up mailing lists for your organization. One use of a mailing list is for sending out news to your customers. Tread with care, though, so that your messages aren't regarded as spam (unsolicited commercial e-mail, described in Chapter 8). Make sure that your messages are regarded as an e-mail based newsletter, with useful and interesting content, rather than unwanted ads.

Another use of mailing lists is to create a discussion group for your customers or prospective customers. If you have complex products with which your customers need ongoing help, a mailing list can let a users group share information and advice about your products. Be sure to monitor the mailing list, though, to keep discussions on topic and to make sure that questions are answered promptly. A user's group mailing list can be a valuable source of feedback and ideas for improving your products—almost like a free focus group.

The Complete Reference

Internet

Part VI

File Transfer and Downloading

Chapter 36

File Transfer Concepts

Y ou transfer files all the time on the Internet, without even thinking about it! When you browse the Web, files are transferred to your Web browser. When you send e-mail, files are transferred across the Internet to the message's recipient. Web and e-mail programs, however, are specially designed to handle a few particular file types, types that they know how to display or create. They also use special communications languages, called *protocols*, designed specifically for efficient transfer of those files.

Sometimes, however, you just want to get or send "any old file." It might be a word processor document, a spreadsheet, a photograph, or a program. To transfer the file across the Internet, you have several choices:

■ Transfer the file using one of the commonplace Internet services: e-mail or the Web.

■ Use software specially designed to transfer "any old file," software that speaks a special protocol called *File Transfer Protocol* (*FTP*).

This chapter discusses how these different ways of transferring files work, and the differences in using these methods. It also discusses some of the questions and issues that arise around file transfer on the Internet: ensuring proper transmission of files, avoiding viruses and other file contamination, and observing property rights.

Using File Transfer Protocol (FTP)

FTP is designed for distributing files to a number of users. It is not designed for communicating files between individuals. FTP uses a *client-server* system, in which files are stored at a central computer and transferred between that computer and other, widely distributed computers. The central computer runs software called an *FTP server*, and the software at the other, widely distributed computers runs software called an *FTP client*. Using File Transfer Protocol, the client requests that a file transfer be initiated, and then the client and server exchange data.

Like FTP, Web clients request files from Web servers. Using HyperText Transfer Protocol (HTTP), Web clients (browsers) request files from Web servers (Web sites). The big difference is that FTP service goes both ways: "up" to the server, as well as "down" to the client.

Just as you need Web client software (a browser, which speaks HTTP) so that you can receive files from a Web server, you need FTP client software to exchange files with an FTP server. Note that FTP communication is always between clients and servers, never between clients: just because two people have FTP client software doesn't mean they can exchange files with each other. One person might send a file to a server and the other person might then download that file, but a server must still be in the middle.

FTP Clients

FTP client software can be a separate, stand-alone program, such as Ipswich Software's popular WS_FTP for Windows computers, or Dartmouth College's shareware program, Fetch, for the Macintosh. FTP client software can also be built into other software. In fact, FTP client capability is incorporated in popular Web browsers from Netscape, Microsoft, and others, and is included as a utility program in various operating systems, such as UNIX and Windows 98 and 95.

The FTP client capability that is incorporated into Web browsers is usually fine for downloading files from public (so-called *anonyomous*) file servers. It even works for uploading files to FTP servers, as long as the servers are set up in a certain, standard way.

Stand-alone FTP client software, whether a commercial program or an FTP utility provided as part of the operating system, generally offers more flexibility. Such programs can help you deal with the less conventional configurations of FTP servers, with the various types of files, and with managing the files and directories at both ends of the transfer. FTP utilities generally rely on text commands, whereas commercial FTP clients usually offer a graphical user interface with buttons and windows. Commercial programs sometimes also offer useful non-FTP utilities such as *Ping*, *Finger*, *Whois*, and *Lookup* that help you connect to the server you want and troubleshoot the connection.

FTP Servers

As with Web servers, the Internet contains thousands of FTP servers. Many organizations that run Web servers also run FTP servers, which they use to handle the distribution of various files: free programs, product documentation, or data files. Often, when visitors to a Web site click a link to download something, the link actually redirects the visitor's browser to an FTP server. (You can tell that such a redirection has happened if you notice that the address your browser is using for the download begins with *ftp://* instead of *http://*.) For most Internet users today, such subtle redirections are their only exposure to FTP.

FTP servers are, however, independent of the Web, and supply other files besides those listed on Web pages. In general, the other files on FTP servers support the needs of the more technical users of the Internet, such as UNIX users and software developers.

Public ("Anonymous") and Private FTP Service

Some files on FTP servers may be accessible to the general public, while others are accessible only by private users such as customers or members of the organization that runs the server. On many FTP servers at educational and non-profit organizations, public access is a service due only to the generosity of that organization.

To separate the general public from the more private, privileged users, every user of an FTP server must log on to that server. If the server supports public access, the public logs on using the login name *anonymous*, with either no password required, or the user's e-mail address required as the password. For that reason, public servers are usually called *anonymous FTP servers*. Private users log on using assigned names and passwords, which gives them various degrees of privileged access to private folders (directories). When you use a Web browser to access an FTP server, it automatically performs an anonymous login for you unless you direct it to do otherwise.

FTP servers put files in a variety of folders. When you connect to a server, you see whichever folders your level of privilege permits you to see and use. Depending upon how you log on, you may be permitted to do various things: simply see the files listed in a folder, download the files, put new files into the folder, or change existing files. Commonly, you will find a folder named pub (for *public*) that contains files for public downloading.

Transferring Files of Different Types

FTP doesn't need to know much about what type of file you are transferring. It does have two modes of sending files, however: *binary* and *text* mode. Binary mode sends the file exactly as it is, with no changes at all. You can send any file in binary mode.

Text mode was designed for plain ASCII text. ASCII is the common standard for text, but one feature is not standard: how the end of a line of text is represented. UNIX and Macintosh systems differ from PC systems in how they end a line of text. If you use binary mode to transfer a text file that originated on a UNIX system to your PC, the lines won't end properly. Text mode solves that problem; your client program substitutes the correct line endings for your system. Text mode, however, does not correctly transmit anything but a text file.

Finding Files on FTP Servers

You can find files on FTP servers by using Web search engines, because of the links to FTP files now offered on Web pages. FTP servers have, however, been on the Internet much longer than Web servers. So, before the Web, a separate system called *Archie* arose to help people locate material on FTP servers, much the way Web search engines help people locate material on Web servers. Archie allows you to search for files by file name only on FTP servers. You might, for instance, search for a file with the name quadrathlon.sit, or containing "*quad.*"

Archie is an entire client-server system dedicated to supporting FTP servers: there are Archie servers and Archie clients. You can obtain Archie client software as a stand-alone program or integrated with an FTP client program. Alternatively, you can use the Web to submit search requests to any of the various Archie servers around the world. One starting place to find such Archie "request forms" and "gateways" is Yahoo! at **http://www.yahoo.com**. Choose Computers and Internet | Internet | FTP Sites | Searching | Archie.

Running Your Own FTP Server

Most Internet users do not have a sufficiently broad audience for their files to need to run an FTP server of their own. Instead, they generally distribute their files by e-mail. While it is possible to obtain FTP server software for most computer systems, unless you are permanently connected to the Internet, your users would have to know when you were connected. Also, there are security issues with allowing other people access to your computer. To maintain security, an FTP server allows you to limit access to certain folders for certain users.

If you do need to be able to make files accessible to other people on demand, your Internet Service Provider (ISP) may allow you to maintain a folder on the ISP's FTP server. An alternative is to place files on your Web site, if you have one. To understand the issues in distributing files from a Web server, see the upcoming section; "Downloading Files from the Web."

Transferring Files by E-mail

E-mail is a method of transferring files between individuals on the Internet, or sending them to a specific list of people. Most e-mail programs make attaching files to messages very simple; the sender or receiver of the file rarely has to know much about what is happening. There are, however, different ways to attach files, and both the sender and receiver must use the same method. Three methods are commonly used:

- **Multimedia Internet Mail Extensions (MIME)**   Increasingly, MIME is the Internet standard.
- **Uuencoding**   A method with roots in UNIX.
- **BinHex**   A method commonly used on Macintosh computers.

These methods are necessary because e-mail protocols were originally designed to handle only plain text messages. When a file is "attached" to an e-mail message, it is actually appended to the text message with a header that tells the receiving e-mail program how to decode it. The e-mail program trims off the remaining data and converts it to the appropriate file. If your e-mail program doesn't have the ability to handle the encoding method, or is set up to use another method, you may appear to have received a message with vast amounts of random text at the end.

If you do receive such a file, examine the first few lines of text that follow the e-mail message for the words *uuencode* or *binhex* as a clue to the encoding method. Then check to see if your e-mail program allows you to choose that method. Ask the sender to resend the message. Another alternative is to download from the Web one of the uudecode or binhex decoding utility programs available. Save the e-mail message as a text file, open that text file in your decoding utility, and the utility will reconstruct the original file. For the full details of transferring files by e-mail, see Chapter 7.

Downloading Files from the Web

By far the most popular form of file transfer is to download files from the Web, especially free or trial software. (For the full details on downloading software from the Web, please see Chapter 38.)

How does your Web browser handle this file transfer process? Sometimes the link you click to begin downloading a file actually redirects your browser to an FTP server, as you read earlier in the section in this chapter on FTP servers. The browser then turns over the job to its internal FTP client software (or to the operating system's FTP client utility). You can proceed to browse other sites on the Web while the download happens, although your browsing may be slowed by the ongoing download process.

If the link you click to download a file does not redirect your browser to an FTP server, the Web server delivers the file. When a Web browser begins to receive a file from a Web server, it examines the file's type. It either looks for information from the server as to the MIME type of the file (for example, text/HTML for Web page files), or it looks at the file's extension (for example, GIF). Browsers are principally focused on displaying files, not saving them, so if the browser knows how to display a given type of file, it does so. If it does not know how to display the file, it checks to see if it has any helper software that can display the file: a plug-in or a viewer program. Failing that, it asks you if you want to save the file. If you choose to save the file, you can proceed to browse other sites while the file downloads.

Browsers are increasingly clever about recognizing file types, however, so they attempt to take action on a file rather than simply save it. Some browsers can recognize a file as being a plug-in or other add-on component for the browser itself. They can then automatically install that component, given your approval, or they recognize that they are receiving a file that is executable (a program) on your computer, and ask you if you wish the program to be run once it downloads. Some browsers can check with your computer about what program it associates with certain file types, and run that program—even within the browser window itself. Increasingly a browser, recognizing that it lacks the necessary viewer or plug-in to display a file, offers to download the required software.

If you have a Web server (or have the use of one), you can use it to distribute files. For instance, you can use it as a drop-box for other people to pick up a file at their leisure. Transfer the file to the site by using FTP. Then you can either link to the file from a Web page, or simply give people the filename and URL for the file.

Quality, Security, and Ownership Issues

The ability to transfer files across the Internet raises a number of technical and other issues. Among them are ensuring the quality and integrity of the file, maintaining the security of your computer, and observing copyright ownership rights.

Ensuring File Quality and Integrity

In nearly all circumstances, if a file has downloaded in its entirety, it is error-free. Various schemes in the software that transfers files detect any errors that occur during transmission. When problems occur, they are usually the result of sending a binary file as a text file, or vice-versa, in FTP. The best way to check for those problems is to obtain from the original source exactly what size the file is supposed to be, and make sure the file you downloaded is exactly that size.

Ensuring Security

Security problems do arise, but not from the areas that people worry most about. One common concern is, could someone introduce a virus or trojan horse during the file's transmission from computer to computer across the Internet? (A *virus* is an unauthorized program that is slipped into your computer, usually with malicious or mischievous intent, and which may also reproduce itself and spread to other computers. A *trojan horse* is a program that is likewise copied to your computer by stealth, but its intent is to allow further access to your computer at a later time.) Although the scenario of introducing rogue program code during a file's transmission seems plausible, intercepting and modifying a file that is being transmitted, without causing the transfer to fail due to error checking, and without the perpetrator being exposed, is extremely difficult.

More likely than a file being corrupted while in transmission is a file that is corrupted at the source. Someone may intentionally or accidentally create a file that is not what it appears to be, and distribute it by posting it on an FTP or Web server, e-mailing it, or submitting it to a newsgroup.

Acquiring a computer virus from e-mail is a common concern (and the subject of many an Internet myth). Most e-mail readers, to date, are themselves incapable of transmitting a virus to your computer because they do not execute the material they receive, nor do they cause any other program to execute that material. They only display text and store any attached files. Viruses and Trojan horses can only infect your computer when some program code or file executes.

Although reading e-mail messages is (to date) fairly safe, someone could knowingly or unknowingly send you a file containing a virus as an e-mail attachment. If you run or open an infected file, your computer may be infected. To avoid problems, you should obtain virus scanning software and let that software examine any files you receive as e-mail attachments. At the very least, be certain that the sender has checked the file for viruses.

Strictly speaking, you cannot catch a virus from a data file (such as a word processor or database file) that you receive, only from a program file. The exception to that rule is that some files cross the line between data and program. In particular, popular word processor programs and spreadsheets can contain "macros" and run them without asking your permission. Increasingly, vendors of such programs take steps to alert you when macros are present, and allow you to avoid loading or running the macros. In addition, most virus-scan software can check files for known macro viruses.

As e-mail programs become increasingly sophisticated, and do things other than simply displaying plain text and storing files, there may be occasional releases of e-mail software in which it is possible to catch a virus by simply reading a message. In 1998, for instance, a release of Microsoft's Outlook Express allowed this possibility, although no instances of abuse were recorded and a "patch" to Outlook Express was quickly distributed. Another example is that some e-mail programs can be set to automatically run any attached program file when the message is read—an extremely bad idea, as it leaves you no way to check the trustworthiness of the sender or virus. Scan the file before running the program.

The best steps to take to avoid downloading corrupted programs or macro viruses are the following:

- Avoid downloading programs—or file types capable of containing macros—from anyone but reliable sources: the trusted originator of a file, or any responsible organization that is likely to have the expertise and a sufficient vested interest in your security to avoid posting a corrupted file.

- Check the file's exact length in bytes against published file length, if available. If the file you download is not the size it is supposed to be, do not use it. You either downloaded it incorrectly (say, as a text file in FTP) or it is corrupted. Note that some computers normally display file size rounded off to the nearest 1K. In Windows 95/98, for instance, you must right-click a file and choose Properties to see the exact file size.

- Scan the file for known viruses, using commercial virus scanning software.

Observing Property Rights

Copyright ownership and property rights are issues that arise because it is so easy to copy and distribute computer files. Even though it may be easy to send a copy of a computer file to a friend, you may have no right to do so. Rights apply to any and all kinds of materials that can be sent as a file on the Internet: images, programs, data, text, scripts, applets, movies, sounds, and animations. That includes all the components of a Web page, from the cute graphical bullets and bars to the hidden JavaScript that makes the page sing and dance. Even if you don't copy the material but instead link to the original file from your Web page (for example, making a picture appear on your Web page by linking to a graphics file on another Web site), you may well be violating a copyright.

Creators of text and graphical materials retain their rights, whether or not someone else scanned the work from a magazine or other publication into a computer file. Just because someone e-mailed you an article and the author is unknown, you don't have the right to distribute the article. The same is true of cartoons, drawings, and photographs.

Even if a file appears to be free, the material that file contains can have any number of constraints on how, when, where, and how often it is used. You may be required to give credit on the page where you use it, for instance, or abstain from using it in print. Finally, even if a file appears to be offered for free on a Web or FTP site, it may not have been acquired legally. Some amateurs have been known to collect other people's image files and offer them for downloading (usually out of ignorance) on the Web. To avoid property rights issues, make sure that you have an explicit agreement with the actual author or authorized distributor of the work before using or copying a work.

The
Complete
Reference

Internet

Chapter 37

File Transfer Protocol (FTP) Programs

F*TP* (File Transfer Protocol) lets you transfer files over the Internet. An *FTP server* stores files, and *FTP clients* connect to FTP servers, either to download files from or upload files to the server. See Chapter 36 for more information about the basic concepts of FTP and other means of file transfer.

What Kind of FTP Software You Need

To use FTP, you must have FTP client software, which is available in several forms:

- **Web browsers** Most Web browsers, including Microsoft and Netscape browsers, include basic FTP client capability. You can use this capability to transfer files in both directions, but only if the server is set up in a conventional way. To cover all circumstances, or to get additional file management features such as file renaming or folder management, you need a separate FTP client program.

- **Command-driven programs** Some operating systems such as UNIX and Windows 98 come with a more capable FTP client program, called Ftp, but they are *command-driven* (that is, to use them you must type text commands).

- **GUI programs** If you plan to do much file transfer, especially uploading, you might want a commercial FTP client program, such as Ipswich's WS_FTP (for Windows), that uses a graphical user interface or *GUI* (an interface that uses windows and clickable buttons). A popular Macintosh client GUI program is Dartmouth College's shareware Fetch program. Vendors of UNIX systems often provide their own GUI-based FTP software

This chapter gives instructions for a FTP clients of each variety: command-driven, GUI, and Web browser, as well as for finding files on FTP servers using Archie.

Basic Procedure for Using Any FTP Client

Whatever FTP client you use, you begin by connecting to the server. Then transfer files and disconnect.

Connecting to the FTP Server

To connect to an FTP server, you give the host name of the server (for example, **rtfm.mit.edu**) to your FTP client software and then you log in. You can log in to an FTP server in one of two ways:

- If you have an account on the FTP server, you log in with a user name and password. You can access all the files that your user name gives you permission to use.

■ If you don't have an account on the FTP server, you can log on anonymously. (Connection without an account on the FTP server is called *anonymous FTP*.) In anonymous FTP, you supply **anonymous** as your user name and your e-mail address as your password (as a courtesy for the server's log records).

Once you have logged in to an FTP server, the server may display welcoming and instructional text about using the server. Your client program might or might not display that text.

FTP servers transmit messages to let you (or your client program) know what's going on. You might see those messages, which start with three-digit numbers, or your client program may ignore them or intercept them and substitute its own messages or other indicators. For example, when you have transferred a file, you might see the message 226 Transfer Complete, or you may see a dialog box saying the same thing in different words.

Transferring Files

FTP servers typically contain many different directories (folders). Once you are connected to an FTP server, you select a particular folder, called the *current working directory*, from which you will download, or to which you will upload, files. If you have permission to do so, you may be able to create additional folders, rename folders, or delete them.

Note   *FTP is the usual means of transferring files from your personal computer to your own Web site, or a Web site on which you are a permitted contributor. Such transfers use private, rather than anonymous FTP: they require a user ID and password. A unique characteristic of these transfers is that the site name often begins with www, not ftp, as is common for ftp sites. If you share a Web server with other users (as is often the case for dial-up ISPs), you may be assigned a directory on that server in which only you have the ability to add, delete, or rename files or folders. The Web server may allow you to give other people permission to change the files in your directory (see Chapter 40).*

When you transfer a file—by either uploading or downloading—you use one of two modes. Your client program may choose the mode automatically, based on the file's extension, or you may need to choose the mode yourself. The choices are the following:

■ **ASCII mode**   When transferring text files (including HTML files), use ASCII mode. Different computer systems use different characters to indicate the ends of lines. In ASCII mode, the FTP software automatically adjusts line endings for the system to which the file is transferred.

■ **Binary (or Image) mode**   When transferring files that consist of anything but unformatted text, use Binary mode (also called Image mode). In Binary mode, the FTP software does not make any changes to the contents of the file during transfer. Use Binary mode when transferring graphics files, audio files, video files, programs, or any other kind of file other than plain text.

Disconnecting from the Server

When you have finished using an FTP site, you disconnect from that site (or your client program disconnects when you exit the program). Some FTP client programs allow you to connect to several FTP sites at once; disconnecting from one site doesn't affect your connection to other sites.

Using Command-Driven Clients (UNIX and Windows 98/95)

UNIX, Windows 98, and Windows 95 come equipped with command-driven FTP client software, which means that you control the software by typing command lines. For each command line, you type a command (word) that may be followed by additional information (called *arguments*), and then press ENTER. For example, once you are connected to a server and have opened a directory, to download a file, you type the **get** command, followed by the name of the file you want to download, and then press ENTER.

An Overview of the Session

Windows 98 and many UNIX workstations provide a graphical user interface (GUI) comprised of windows, buttons, and menus. When you run command-driven client software, you type commands to perform most tasks instead of using the GUI's menus or buttons. To type commands in a UNIX GUI environment, open a command shell window (for example, an xterm window). To type commands in Windows 98, choose the Start | Run command. Then, whichever operating system you are using, take the following steps to run the FTP client:

1. Type **ftp**, followed by a space and the host name of the FTP server, and press ENTER. (In Windows 98, if you are not connected to the Internet, you see the Dial-Up Networking window; click Connect. When you are connected to the Internet, the Ftp program window appears.) You see a message confirming that you are connected to the server. If your attempt to connect fails, you may instead see a message saying that the host name is unknown or that the maximum number of connections to this host are already in use.

2. The FTP server prompts you for a user name. If you have an account on the server, type your user name when prompted, and then press ENTER. If you don't have an account on the server, type **anonymous** to use anonymous FTP and press ENTER.

3. The FTP server prompts you for a password. Type your password if you have one, or else (for anonymous FTP) type your e-mail address. Your typed characters may not appear, for security reasons. Press ENTER again. If your account and password are acceptable to the server, you see an introductory message. Some FTP servers display a long introductory message. At the bottom of the message (if any) the program displays the prompt ftp> to indicate that it is ready for you to type a command.

4. At the ftp> prompt you may type any of the FTP commands described in the remainder of this section. At a minimum, you type commands to set the directories from which (or to which) you wish to transfer a file; then, you give commands to download or upload files. Before each transfer, you may need to type commands to check or set the best transfer mode (ASCII or binary) for the kind of file you are transferring.

5. When you have finished transferring files, unless you want to connect with another server at this point, type **quit** or **bye**. This command disconnects you from the FTP server and closes your FTP client program. A message confirms that you have disconnected. (If you want to leave your FTP client open and connect to a different server, type **close** or **disconnect** instead of **quit** or **bye**, and then press ENTER. Next, type **open**, followed by a space, the host name of another FTP server, and then press ENTER to connect to the other server.)

Changing Directories on the FTP Server

Once you are connected to an FTP server, you must move to the directory on the server from which you want to download a file (or to which you want to upload a file). To change directories, type **cd** (which stands for Change Directory) followed by the name of the server directory to which you want to move. (As it does when any FTP command executes, the server sends a confirmation message such as "250 CWD command successful.")

To find out the name of the current directory, type **pwd**. (PWD stands for Print Working Directory, but the "printing" in this case only takes place on your screen.) For example, you might see the following (what you type appears here in boldface; what the FTP server types appears here in regular type):

```
ftp> pwd
257 "/usr/home/george" is current directory.
```

The information in quotes gives the name of the file directory (folder) to which you are currently connected at the server. Several names usually appear, separated by slashes as in the preceding example, which give you the folder's full, or *pathname*. The pathname gives the folder's place in the *directory structure* at the server: how folders are contained within other folders. The last name (george, in this example) is the folder to which you are connected. The name preceding it (home, in this example) is the folder containing *that* folder, and so on. If folder A contains folder B, A is B's *parent* folder. The top folder, called the *root* folder, is indicated by the initial slash (/).

Each FTP server has its own directory structure. On many public (anonymous) FTP servers, the downloadable files are in a folder called pub. Here are a few tips for changing directories:

- To change to the parent directory of the current directory, type **cd ..** (that is, the **cd** command followed by two dots).

- To move to the top-level directory on the FTP server, type **cd /** (that is, the **cd** command followed by a forward slash).

- You can move directly to a directory by typing its full path name, starting at the root; the full path name starts with a / to represent the root directory.

- If the FTP server runs the UNIX operating system, capitalization is important. When typing directory or filenames, be sure to use the correct capitalization—most names use lowercase letters.

Listing Files and Folders in the FTP Server's Current Directory

To see a list of files and subdirectories in the current directory on the FTP server, type the **dir** command for a full listing of all details, or **ls** command for a shorter listing. (Not all FTP servers support the **ls** command.) The exact appearance of the listing depends on the FTP server's operating system. Figure 37-1 shows a typical listing for the **dir** command.

If the **dir** command produces a long listing, you can use wildcards to limit the files and directories that are included. The wildcard character * matches any number of characters. Some useful examples of using the wildcard character follow here:

- **dir c***   Lists the file and directory names that begin with C

- **dir *.txt**   Lists all text files, which often contain helpful information about the directory contents

- **dir index***   Shows any file beginning with *index*, which is a name sometimes used for files containing information about the FTP site

- **dir *.zip, dir *.tar, dir *.hqx**   Lists compressed files for PC, UNIX, and Macintosh computers, respectively

Selecting the Current Folder on Your Computer

Before you upload or download files, set the *current local directory*, the currently selected folder on your computer (not the server's computer). This is the folder from which your FTP client can upload files and to which it can download files. Often the

FILE TRANSFER AND
DOWNLOADING

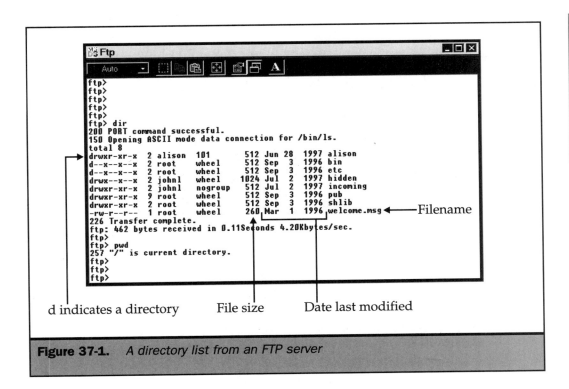

Figure 37-1. *A directory list from an FTP server*

FTP client program is already set up to use a particular folder, usually within the program folder.

Note that some command-driven FTP clients do not accept folder names or filenames that include spaces. Consider renaming the local folder or creating a new folder with a name that does not use spaces. If you are using the Windows 98 FTP client, however, and the pathname of the folder contains spaces, the spaces will be okay if you enclose the pathname in quotes.

To change the current local directory, type **lcd** (which stands for local change directory), followed by the pathname of the folder on your computer. To move to the parent folder of the current folder, you may type **lcd ..** (the **lcd** command followed by two dots). (Using the dots is a way to avoid typing a parent folder name if it includes spaces!) To move to a subordinate (child) folder of the current folder, you may type **lcd**, a space, and then just the folder name.

For example, the command **lcd xfers** selects a subordinate folder (named xfers) of whatever the current folder is. Typing the command **lcd c:/myfiles** would select the folder myfiles on the C drive of a PC.

You can't see what files or folders are in the current local directory by using FTP; you use your regular operating system commands or controls to browse that folder. On a PC, for instance, you would use Windows Explorer or a My Computer folder window.

Uploading Files

You can upload files to folder on an FTP server if you have write permission in that folder. If you are replacing a previous version of a file, you also need permission to write to that file. Most anonymous FTP servers don't accept uploads, however, or they accept them into only one specific directory. Read the server's welcome message to find out the rules for the server you are using.

To upload a single file, use the **put** command. To upload a group of files, use the **mput** command. To upload a file, follow these steps:

1. Connect to the FTP server, change to the directory on the FTP server in which you want to store the file, and then set the current local directory to the folder on your computer that contains the files you want to upload.

2. If the file or files you want to upload contain anything but unformatted ASCII text, type **binary** to select Binary mode. To switch back to ASCII mode to transfer text files, type **ascii**.

3. Type **put**, followed by a space, followed by the filename on your computer, followed by a space, followed by the filename to use on the FTP server. Then press ENTER. For example, to upload a file named firstdraft.doc from the current local directory and call the uploaded version report.doc, the command is **put firstdraft.doc report.doc**.

4. You see a series of messages; the message Transfer Complete appears when the file transfer is done. Note that if a file with the name that you specify already exists on the FTP server, the **put** command may overwrite the existing file with the uploaded file.

If you want to check that the file is really on the FTP server, type **dir** to see a listing of files in the current directory.

You can copy a group of files to the FTP server by typing the **mput** (multiple put) command in place of the put command. Type **mput**, followed by a wildcard pattern that matches the names of the files you want to upload. (See the earlier section, "Listing Files and Folders in the FTP Server's Current Directory," for examples of wildcard patterns.) The pattern * indicates that all files in the current directory on your computer should be copied. For example, to upload all the files with the extension .html, you would type **mput *.html. As it copies the files, the mput** command asks you about each file. Type **y** to upload the files or **n** to skip it. If you don't want the **mput** command to ask you about each file before uploading it, type the command line **prompt** first before typing the **mput** command line. The prompt command line turns off filename prompting (and, if you type it again, turns prompting back on).

Downloading Files

To download files from the FTP server to your computer, follow these steps:

1. Connect to the FTP server, change to the directory on the FTP server that contains the file that you want to download, and then set the current local directory to the folder on your computer in which you want to store the files you download.

2. If the file or files you want to download contain anything but unformatted ASCII text, type **binary** to select Binary mode. To switch back to ASCII mode to transfer text files, type **ascii**. If, after downloading, you discover that a file you have downloaded is unusable, you probably forgot to issue the **binary** command before downloading the file.

3. Type **get**, followed by a space, followed by the filename on the FTP server, followed by a space, followed by the filename to use on your computer. Then press ENTER. (You can't use filenames with spaces.) For example, to download a file named bud99_12.doc and call the downloaded version budget_dec1999.doc, type the command line **get bud99_12.doc budget_dec1999.doc**.

4. You see a series of messages; the message Transfer Complete appears when the file transfer is done. To interrupt the file transfer, try pressing CTRL+C or CTRL+Z. Sometimes that doesn't work, and the only way to interrupt the transfer is to close the FTP window.

5. If you want to check that the file really is downloaded, don't try to use FTP. Browse the current local directory using the normal folder-browsing features of your computer. On a PC, for instance, use Windows Explorer or a My Computer folder window to see a listing of files on your computer. On a Macintosh computer, open the hard drive and navigate to the folder.

You can copy a group of files from the FTP server by typing **mget**, followed by a wildcard pattern that matches the names of the files that you want to download. The pattern * means that all files in the current directory on your computer should be copied. For example, to download all the files with a file type of zip, you would type **mget *.zip**. As the **mget** command copies the files, it asks you about each file. Type **y** to download the files or **n** to skip it. If you don't want the **mget** command to ask you about each file before downloading it, type the command line **prompt** first before typing the **mget** command line.

Using Common FTP Commands

FTP clients and servers use a variety of commands, many of which have only little use to the casual user, and many of which are redundant (like bye and quit). Table 37-1 lists commands commonly found on FTP clients and servers.

Function	Command	Description
Start FTP	FTP *hostname*	Starts FTP and connects to the FTP server named *hostname*.
Server connection	close	Disconnects from the FTP server, without exiting the FTP client software.
	disconnect	Disconnects from the FTP server, without exiting the FTP client software.
	bye	Disconnects from the FTP server and exits the FTP client software.
	quit	Disconnects from the FTP server and exits the FTP client software.
	user *name password*	Logs into the same FTP server using a different user name. If you omit *name* and *password*, FTP prompts you for them.
	open *hostname*	Used after disconnecting, connects to a new FTP server named *hostname*.
Transfer mode (type)	ascii	Transfers files in ASCII mode (used for text files).
	binary	Transfers files in Binary or Image mode (used for all files except text files).
	type *transfertype*	Sets the transfer type. *Transfertype* must be ascii, binary, or image.
Directories	cd *dir*	Changes to the *dir* directory on the FTP server. If you omit the *dir*, FTP prompts Remote Directory, and then waits for you to type the directory name and press ENTER.
	dir *pat*	Lists the files in the current directory on the FTP server that match the wildcard pattern *pat*, with full information about the files. Omit *pat* to list all the files.
	ls *pat*	Lists only the filenames of the files in the current directory on the FTP server that match the wildcard pattern *pat*. Omit *pat* to list all the files.

Table 37-1. *Listing of Common FTP Commands*

Function	Command	Description
	lcd *dir*	Changes to the folder *dir* on your computer.
	mkdir *dir*	Creates a directory named *dir* on the FTP server (assuming that you have permission to do so).
	pwd	Displays the current directory on the FTP server.
	rmdir *dir*	Deletes the directory *dir* on the FTP server (assuming that you have permission to do so).
File transfer	get *old new*	Downloads the file *old* to your computer and names it *new*. Omit *new* to use the same name.
	mget *pat*	Downloads the files to your computer that match the wildcard pattern *pat*.
	recv *old new*	Downloads the file *old* to your computer and names it *new*. Omit *new* to use the same name.
	put *old new*	Uploads the file *old* to the FTP server and names it *new*. Omit *new* to use the same name.
	mput *pat*	Uploads the files to the FTP server that match the wildcard pattern *pat*.
	send *old new*	Uploads the file *old* to the FTP server and names it *new*. Omit *new* to use the same name.
	append	Uploads a file and appends it to an existing file. Type **append**, followed by the name of the file on your computer that you want to upload, and then the name of the file on the FTP server to which you want to append the file.
Feedback	verbose	Turns verbose mode on and off. When verbose mode is off, FTP displays fewer messages.
	?	Displays a list of the commands that the FTP client can perform.
	help	Displays a list of the commands that the FTP client can perform. Type **help**, followed by a space and a command name to get a short description of that command.

Table 37-1.   *Listing of Common FTP Commands* (continued)

Function	Command	Description
	remotehelp *command*	Displays the help information provided by the FTP server. Omit *command* to see a list of the commands the FTP server supports.
	status	Displays the status of the FTP client software, including the name of the FTP server to which you are connected, the file transfer mode (ASCII or Binary), and the bell mode.
	debug	Turns on and off debugging mode (which displays more information about what FTP is doing).
	glob	Turns on and off metacharacter expansion of local filenames. When on, the FTP client software replaces wildcard patterns with the list of filenames they match. When off, the client passes wildcard patterns along to the server.
	hash	Turns on and off hash mode (in which FTP displays a # for each block transferred).
File management	delete *name*	Deletes the file *name* on the FTP server. If you omit the *name*, FTP says Remote File, and then waits for you to type the filename and press ENTER. Most publicly accessible FTP servers don't let you delete files.
	mdelete *pat*	Deletes the files that match the wildcard pattern *pat* on the FTP server.
	rename *old new*	Renames the file named *old* on the FTP server, using the filename *new* (assuming that you have permission to do so).
	literal *command*	Sends a command to the FTP server that the Windows 98 FTP program doesn't support. Type **literal**, followed by a space and the command you want to send.

Table 37-1. *Listing of Common FTP Commands* (continued)

Function	Command	Description
	mls *dir filename*	Stores a listing of the contents of the *dir* directory on the FTP server, and all of its subdirectories, in the file *filename* on your computer. Type * as *dir* to list all files.
	prompt	Turns on or off filename prompting for **mput** and **mget** commands. When prompting is on, FTP asks before transferring each file.
Beyond FTP	trace	Turns Internet packet tracing on and off.
	!	Runs a DOS command shell and displays a DOS prompt. You can type DOS commands, such as **dir**, which displays the contents of a folder. To exit from DOS and see the ftp> prompt again, type **exit**.
	quote *command*	Sends a command to the FTP server that the FTP client software doesn't support. Type **quote**, followed by a space and the command you want to send.

Table 37-1.   *Listing of Common FTP Commands* (continued)

Using GUI-Driven Clients

FTP client programs that use a graphical user interface are quite common, but they generally are not included with a computer's operating system. They can be acquired in various forms, including commercial and shareware products from a variety of sources. Two popular programs are WS_FTP for the PC and Fetch for the Macintosh.

You can get either of these programs from TUCOWS (at **http://www.tucows.com**). See the next chapter for how to download and install programs.

WS_FTP

WS_FTP is an FTP client program offered by Ipswitch, Inc. (**http://www.ipswitch.com**), for PCs under Microsoft Windows. Two versions of the program are available: WS_FTP LE, available free for certain government, academic, and personal users, and WS_FTP Pro (not free) for business users. Both versions have an identical user interface that Ipswitch calls the "classic" interface. WS_FTP Pro also has an alternative interface that turns Windows Explorer into an FTP program. For more information about both versions, see

http://www.ipswitch.com/Products/WS_FTP

Using the Windows Explorer Interface

The latest versions of WS_FTP Pro (release 6.0 and later) comes with a WS_FTP Pro Explorer feature that allows you to use Windows Explorer as an FTP program. Run Windows Explorer as you normally do (choose Start | Programs | Windows Explorer, for instance). In the left-hand panel of the Windows Explorer window, as Figure 37-2 shows, you may click WS_FTP Pro Explorer, revealing a number of folders.

You may view the contents of folders under the WS_FTP Pro Explorer icon just as you would any other folder in Windows Explorer. Each WS_FTP folder, however, instead of containing files on your computer, contains FTP sites (servers) such as the LucasArts site shown in Figure 37-2. Each site is represented by a computer icon.

To view an FTP site, click that site's icon. Your PC should begin to go online to the Internet. (If it does not, you must connect to your Internet account manually.) After a delay, the site's files and folders appear in Windows Explorer, as Figure 37-2 indicates.

Windows Explorer allows you to treat the folders and files on an FTP site exactly as you would the files and folders on your own computer, but subject to the permissions that site allows you. Hardly ever, for instance, are you permitted to create, rename, delete, paste, or cut a file or folder on an anonymous server. You may, however, copy that file or folder to any folder or disk drive on your PC by using the Edit | Copy and Edit | Paste commands or by dragging and dropping, just as you would a file or folder on your own PC. You may also double-click the file, and WS_FTP downloads the file to a temporary folder on your PC and then opens the file in whatever application is registered on your PC to handle that file type.

WS_FTP requires that your connection to an FTP site be "configured" in WS_FTP before that site appears in Explorer. The sites shown in Figure 37-2 are preconfigured by Ipswitch. You may add an FTP site just as you would add a new folder to your PC: Click the WS_FTP Pro Explorer icon (or any folder subordinate to it) and choose File | New from the menu. (You may also simply add a new folder for FTP sites by using the same command.)

A wizard then steps you through the process of "creating" (configuring) an FTP site (or, alternatively, simply adding a folder to organize sites). At each step of the wizard, you enter information about the site, then click the Next button. You are prompted by the wizard to do the following (in order): choose to create an FTP site or a folder; give the site a name of your own choosing; type the FTP server's name (such as **ftp.*yourisp*.com**); and enter a user ID and password (or choose Anonymous and enter your e-mail address for a password). Click to enable the Save Password check box to avoid being prompted for a password when you next browse this FTP site. Click the Finish button to complete the task.

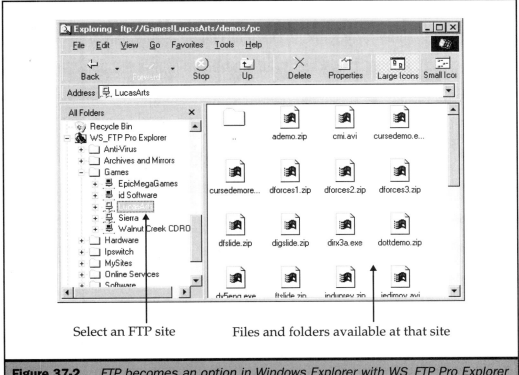

Select an FTP site   Files and folders available at that site

Figure 37-2.   *FTP becomes an option in Windows Explorer with WS_FTP Pro Explorer*

Using the Classic WS_FTP Interface

The conventional, or *classic* user interface for WS_FTP is illustrated by the window shown in Figure 37-3. The window has two panels. The left-hand panel displays files and folders on your PC (the *local system*); the right panel displays files and folders on the FTP server (the *remote site*).

LAUNCHING AND CONNECTING   The following steps launch WS_FTP and connect it to an FTP server. WS_FTP comes preconfigured with connections to a variety of FTP servers. If you want to connect to a different FTP server, see the next section, "Adding a New Site."

Launch WS_FTP LE (or WS_FTP Pro using the classic user interface): Click Start | Programs | WS_FTP Pro (or WS_FTP LE), unless you installed the program differently. The main window of Figure 37-3 appears.

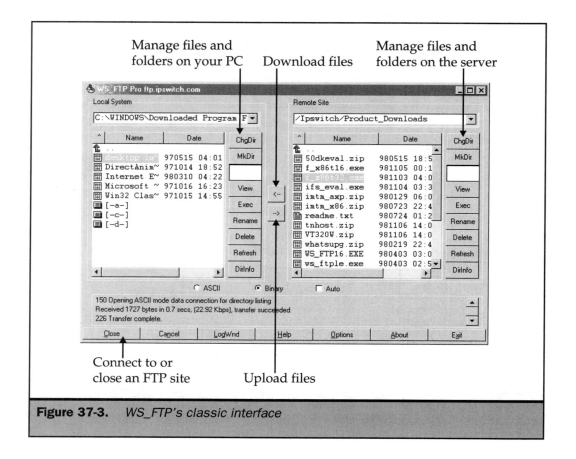

Figure 37-3. WS_FTP's classic interface

On top of the main window appears a dialog box—one of two possible dialog boxes that may appear, depending upon which version of WS_FTP you are using, as follows:

- The Session Properties dialog box of Figure 37-4, or
- The WS_FTP Sites dialog box of Figure 37-5

Both dialog boxes perform the same functions: to allow you to choose which FTP site you wish to connect to, or to add another site to WS_FTP's list.

To connect to a site in the Session Properties dialog box, click the DOWN ARROW for the Profile Name selection box and choose from the list of sites. Click OK in that dialog box.

To connect to a site using the WS_FTP Sites dialog box, click to open the folder containing the site in the Configured Sites box, click the site icon (such as Ipswitch in Figure 37-5), and click the OK button.

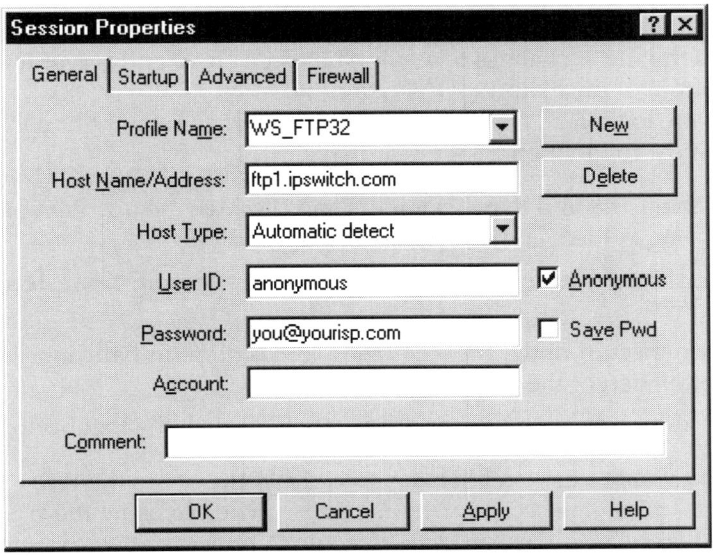

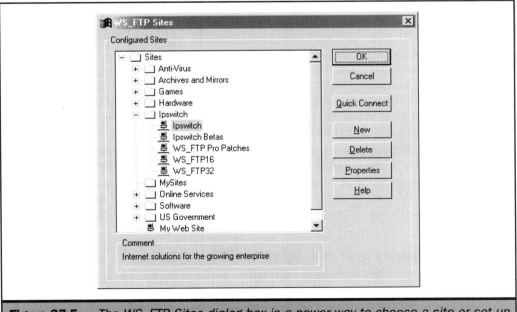

Figure 37-4.   *The Session Properties dialog box lets you choose a site or set up a new site*

Figure 37-5.   *The WS_FTP Sites dialog box is a newer way to choose a site or set up a new site*

Whichever dialog box you use to make the connection, your PC dials up a connection to the Internet, and WS_FTP logs you into your chosen site. You can watch the various command exchanges take place between client and server in the scrolling area at the bottom of the main WS_FTP window.

Once you are logged in, the FTP site's folders appear in the right panel. You might now do any of the following:

- To open folders and manage folders and files, see the upcoming section, "Choosing Folders and Managing Folders and Files"

- To transfer folders and files, see the upcoming section, "Transferring Folders and Files."

- To disconnect from the site, click the Close button (initially labeled Connect) at the bottom left of the WS_FTP window.

- To disconnect from the site and exit WS_FTP, click the Exit button.

If a site you want to use isn't listed, you can add the site to the WS_FTP list as described in the following section. Alternatively, if you are using the WS_FTP Sites dialog box of Figure 37-5, you can click the Quick Connect button to simply connect without adding the site to the list. The Quick Connect dialog box appears, in which you enter the FTP site's name (such as **ftp.ipswitch.com**), and a user ID and password where indicated in the dialog box. For anonymous FTP, click the Anonymous check box and enter your e-mail address in the Password text box.

ADDING A NEW SITE   To add a site to WS_FTP's list of sites, click the New button (in either the Session Properties dialog box of Figure 37-4 or the WS_FTP Sites dialog box of Figure 37-5). You can then enter the site's name and your user ID and password.

If you are using the Session Properties dialog box of Figure 37-4, the key boxes of that dialog box are now cleared so you can enter the site information there. For Profile Name, enter any name you like. For Host Name/Address, enter the server's name such as **rtfm.mit.edu**. If the site's manager has given you a user name and password, enter those where indicated; otherwise, for anonymous FTP, click the Anonymous check box and enter your e-mail address for the Password. Click the Save Pwd check box to avoid being prompted for a password when you log in to this site. Host Type is best left set to Automatic Detect (the default), and Account is best left blank, unless you are told otherwise by the site's manager.

If you are using the WS_FTP Sites dialog box of Figure 37-5, a wizard steps you through the process. See the earlier section, "Using the Windows Explorer Interface," for a description of this wizard.

CHOOSING FOLDERS AND MANAGING FOLDERS AND FILES   Before transferring files, you must open the source and destination folders you want to use at the server (or remote system, in the right-hand panel of the WS_FTP window) and on your PC, (or local system, in the left-hand panel). Each panel has its own column of buttons along the panel's right side. Use the buttons as follows:

Open a folder either by double-clicking it or by clicking it once and then clicking the ChgDir button. To open the parent folder of the currently displayed folder, double-click the green up arrow (which is followed by two dots). To open a different disk drive on the local system side, double-click the drive letter.

Create a new folder by clicking the MkDir button (on either the local system or remote system side). Enter a new folder name in the Input dialog box that appears, and click OK.

Rename a folder or file by clicking it, then clicking the Rename button. Enter a new name in the Input dialog box that appears, and click OK.

Delete a folder or a file by clicking it and then clicking the Delete button. To delete a folder on the server side, however, the folder must first be empty.

To return to a directory you have used previously (at either the local or remote system), click the down arrow for the selection box at the top of each panel. Choose the directory from the list that appears. Or, in WS_FTP Pro, you may click in that same box, type a path into it, and press the ENTER key.

TRANSFERRING FOLDERS AND FILES   In WS_FTP, you transfer individual files, groups of files, or folders and their contents (including other folders). Transferring files in WS_FTP requires three steps, as follows:

1. Select the files or folders to be transferred. (To upload to a server, select files on the left side; to download, select files on the right.) Click a folder if you want to transfer the folder and its entire contents. To select multiple folders or files, drag across them.

2. Choose the transfer mode (ASCII or Binary). Use Binary for anything but plain ASCII text files. Choosing Auto causes WS_FTP to choose a mode based on the file extension; ASCII mode for .txt extensions, for instance. To program the Auto mode for certain extensions, click the Options button, then the Extensions tab of the WS_FTP Properties dialog box that appears. Follow the directions there.

3. Click one of the two arrow buttons between the local (left) and remote (right) panels. The arrow points in the direction of file transfer: left for downloads to your PC, right for uploads to the server. If you have selected a folder, WS_FTP displays a dialog box confirming that you want to transfer the folder (which it may describe as a "directory structure") as well as the files; click Yes.

A dialog box appears during the transfer. When the files or folders are transferred, the destination display is updated. To update the display manually, click the Refresh button.

Fetch

Fetch is a Mac program offered by Dartmouth College (**http://www.dartmouth.edu**). (The Fetch page is currently at **http://www.dartmouth.edu/pages/softdev/fetch.html**.) A license is available free for users closely affiliated with an educational or non-profit charitable organization, and at low cost (approximately $25) for other users. In addition, many Internet service providers are licensed to distribute Fetch to their Macintosh subscribers. The latest release as of this writing is release 3.03.

Fetch offers different ways to connect to an FTP site. You may manually type in the site's address and your log in information, or you may choose a site from a list of sites that Fetch knows about.

Once Fetch is connected to a site, a window opens for that site. You may open multiple windows at once, if necessary, and close windows as you are done with a site. You may transfer files or entire folders of files, as well as manage folder and files on the remote site. When you are done with Fetch, choose File | Quit. Fetch's behavior can be customized through selections on the Customize menu.

Connecting Manually to a Site

To connect manually to an FTP site, you use the New Connection dialog box. The New Connection dialog box opens automatically when you first launch Fetch. You can also open that dialog box at any time by choosing File | New Connection. In this box you fill in the blanks as follows:

- **Host** The name of the FTP site you wish to connect to, such as **ftp.dartmouth.edu**.

- **User ID** The user ID the site manager has given you, or for anonymous FTP, type **anonymous**.

- **Password** The password the site manager has given you, or for anonymous FTP, type your e-mail address.

- **Directory** The folder (directory) you wish to connect to at the site, such as pub, if you know it. Otherwise, leave this space blank.

Connecting by using Shortcuts and Bookmarks

The FTP site you wish to connect to may well already be known to Fetch. Confusingly, however, Fetch has multiple lists of FTP sites it knows about: the *shortcuts* list and one or more *bookmarks* lists. Shortcuts are the way Fetch originally kept a site list. Bookmarks are newer and intended as a more general list of FTP and other sites on the Internet. You can use either feature.

The list of shortcuts that Fetch is equipped with is small. You can choose a site in the shortcuts list by clicking the down-arrow labeled Shortcuts in the New Connection dialog box, or by choosing File | Open Shortcut. To add a site to the Shortcuts, choose Customize | New Shortcut. In the Bookmark Editor dialog box that opens, enter your choice of name in the Name text box, and choose Folder for the Type. Fill out the User ID, Password, and Directory boxes as you would in the New Connection dialog box.

Fetch also maintains bookmark lists, each list being stored as a file. Fetch comes with one file, called Bookmarks and located in the Fetch folder, that contains a long list of anonymous FTP sites you can connect to. You can add your own sites to that file or create other bookmark files. To open a bookmark file, choose File | Open Bookmark File, and use the standard Macintosh file-opening dialog box that appears. For instance, open the file named Bookmarks in the Fetch program folder. In the bookmarks window that appears, double-click any of the sites listed to connect to that site. The Customize menu choice provides commands for editing and adding new sites to this list. To create your own bookmarks list, choose File | New Bookmark File, use commands in the Customize menu to add or edit bookmarks, and save the bookmark list with File | Save.

Downloading and Uploading Files

Once you are connected to an FTP site, Fetch displays a window listing the site's folders (and files). Open the folder you intend to use on the site (whether for uploads or downloads) by double-clicking the folder.

Download a file by double-clicking the file, or selecting the file and clicking the Get File button. Fetch prompts you for a filename to use for the downloaded file on your Macintosh. To download multiple files or a folder full of files, select the files and/or folder and click the button that now reads either Get Files or just Get. Fetch will prompt you for further details.

Upload a file by clicking the Put File button. Fetch then prompts you for the current name of the file you intend to transfer. A dialog box also prompts you for the name to use on the FTP server. FTP servers are often more restrictive about filenames than Macintosh computers; avoid lengthy names, spaces, and punctuation other than the underscore mark (_). To upload a folder full of files, choose Remote | Put Folders and Files; navigate to the folder in the dialog box that appears, and click the Add All button.

Transferring Different Types of Files

FTP servers transfer all files in one of two ways: either as ASCII (text) files or as binary files. Macintosh computers, however, keep track of many different kinds of ASCII and binary files. Fetch is aware of many of these varieties, and can in many instances take care of the details necessary to not only choose the correct transfer mode, but also properly store downloaded files.

Fetch handles these details in its *automatic* mode of transfer, in which it determines the file type on the server by the file's extension. (It is guided by a table you can find by using the Customize | Suffix Mapping command.) Fetch uses the automatic mode by default, but you can choose Binary or ASCII mode by clicking the Binary or Text buttons, respectively, in the connection window. Fetch uses Text mode if it cannot discern the file's type from its extension. Fetch can also transfer downloaded archive files, such as StuffIt (SIT) files, to the appropriate program, guided by settings you can access with the Customize | Post-Processing command.

Because the Macintosh does not rely on file extensions to signify file types, Fetch automatically appends extensions on uploads of certain files. It appends .hqx for binhex files and .bin to MacBinary II files, as determined by the Format tab of the Preferences dialog box (choose Customize | Prefererences).

Using Web Browsers to Transfer Files

Many Web browsers, including Netscape Navigator and Microsoft Internet Explorer, include FTP client software that can be used for downloading files from most FTP servers. Some browsers can also upload files. Browsers do not, in general, provide any means of managing your content at an FTP site, such as renaming or deleting folders or files.

Connecting to FTP Servers

To connect to an FTP server, enter the URL of the FTP server as you would the URL of a Web server. Type the URL into the Location box near the top of the Netscape Navigator window, or the Address box of Internet Explorer, for instance.

To use anonymous FTP, you create the URL by simply prefixing the server name with **ftp://**, as in **ftp://rtfm.mit.edu**. The browser supplies a user ID and password that satisfy the server's anonymous login requirements.

For private FTP servers, where you are given a user ID and password, type the URL in the following form:

ftp://*userID:password@servername*

In this URL, you type what is shown in bold, then substitute text for the text in italics, as follows: *userID* is the user name assigned to you by the site manager, *password* is your assigned password, and *servername* is the name of the FTP server. For instance, if you had private FTP privileges on a fictional server **ftp.whatever.edu**, your assigned user name was *reader*, and your password was *readit2u*, you would enter the URL **ftp://reader:readit2u@ftp.whatever.edu**.

Note that this entire URL, including your password, is stored in the browser's history file, so that someone else using your computer could conceivably access your FTP site. To avoid placing your password in the URL, Netscape's and certain other vendors' browsers let you omit the password, as in **ftp://reader@ftp.whatever.edu**, and prompt you for the password once the server is contacted.

If you know the folder to which you want to connect at the server (whether you are using private or anonymous FTP), you can append the folder with a slash to the end of the URL. For instance, **ftp://rtfm.mit.edu/pub** connects you to the pub (public) folder of that MIT server.

Once you are connected, your browser displays directory names and file names as a list of links. To open a directory, click it as you would any link on a Web page.

Downloading Files

To download a file, click it. The browser prompts you for a name and location on your computer. If, however, the file is a type normally displayed by the browser or any of the viewers or plug-ins with which it is configured, the browser will download and display the file, rather than prompt you for a filename and location.

Uploading Files

Netscape Navigator and certain other browsers can also upload files (assuming you have permission to do so at the FTP server). After you have opened the folder to which you want to copy a file, simply drag and drop the file into the browser window. The browser displays a prompt asking you if you want to upload the files; click Yes and the browser performs the operation. (As of this writing, Microsoft's Internet Explorer does not support this feature.)

Finding Files by Using Archie

An Internet service called *Archie* helps people locate material on FTP servers around the world. To use Archie, you connect to an *Archie* server and perform a search. Archie derives its name from *archive*, as it serves as a tool for searching file archives. It uses a client-server system, like FTP and the Web. One drawback of the Archie service is that demand often exceeds server capacity; you may have to wait for results.

A few Archie servers are **archie.rutgers.edu**, **archie.internic.net**, **archie.uquam.ca**, **archie.doc.ic.ac.uk**, **archie.luth.se**, and **archie.nz**. Archie servers are search engines to files, especially program files, on anonymous FTP servers. Unlike Web search engines, Archie searches only for filenames or parts of filenames, not content.

You can access Archie servers in several different ways:

- Obtain Archie client software as a stand-alone program
- Use the Archie client software integrated into certain FTP client programs.
- Use the Archie request forms and Archie gateways on the Web to submit search requests to any of the various Archie servers around the world.
- Send e-mail to an Archie server.
- Connect to an Archie server by using yet another client-server system, telnet, that allows you to log in to remote systems. (See Chapter 40 for a description of telnet.)

If you prefer using the Web, you can find Archie request forms and Archie gateways through Web search engines like Yahoo!. Starting at **http://www.yahoo.com**, choose Computers & Internet | Internet | FTP Sites | Searching | Archie. A few of the request form sites are the following:

- **http://archie.rutgers.edu/archie.html**
- **http://www.thegroup.net/AA.html**
- **http://cuiwww.unige.ch/archieplexform.html**

If you prefer a client program, two commonly used programs are WSArchie for Windows PCs by David Woakes, and Anarchie for the Macintosh by Stairways Software (at **http://www.stairways.com**). Bunyip Information Systems, which commercialized the Archie server, maintains an FTP directory of Archie clients (including WSArchie and Anarchie) for a variety of operating systems at the following site:

ftp://ftp.bunyip.com/pub/archie/clients/

The WSArchie program for Windows 95 and Windows 98 strongly resembles the file-finding window of those operating systems. Likewise, Anarchie strongly resembles the Macintosh Finder.

If you have access to a telnet client, you may telnet into certain Archie servers (such as **archie.rutgers.edu**) and use text commands to control the server; use *archie* as your login ID. Once you are connected to Archie, type **help**, **help find**, or **help set** to get command information. (Typing **help** enters you in conversation with the help feature, in which a prompt of help> appears; press ENTER to return to the archie> prompt.) You may e-mail an Archie server with your request and your results will be e-mailed back to you.

Whichever method you use to access the Archie server, you give Archie certain information:

- What characters to look for in the file's name and how to use them in the search.
- What limitations to apply, including the maximum number of "hits" (incidences of found files) and "matches" (incidences of identically named files). This information is optional.
- What Archie server to use (client programs come with lists to choose from).
- What *domains* (countries) you wish to search for the file (optional).

To begin with, you have in mind a series of characters that you expect to be in the name of the file you are looking for. You can tell Archie to interpret these characters in different ways as it searches. Look for controls in the Archie Web page or client software as follows. (The text commands that you type if you use telnet are in parentheses):

- **Substring (set search sub)** Look for this exact sequence of characters, but in any case (upper- or lowercase letters), anywhere in the file's name.
- **Substring, case-sensitive (set search exact_subcase)** Like substring, only exactly in the case you type.

- **Regex (set search regex)**   Allow the wildcards that are part of UNIX "regular expressions," in which, for example, * means any set of characters, ? means any single character, and more.

- **Exact (set search exact)**   Look for this exact sequence of characters, no more, no less, and with the same case that you type.

Look for other controls in your client program for the other settings listed in the preceding bullets. Client programs are often set up with certain defaults, so you may not need to set these controls yourself.

When your settings are complete, enter the string of characters you want Achie to search for, and then click the Search or Find button. (In a telnet session, type **find** followed by the string, and press ENTER.)

Archie produces a list of files and their locations, which you can then set your FTP client to download. Some Archie clients (such as WSArchie) are integrated with your computer's FTP software and can download automatically when you double-click the file. Other Archie clients such as Anarchie, already include FTP (and Web) functionality and can perform the download themselves.

Archie servers do have time limits. If your search exceeds those time limits, the Archie server does not return anything except a message to that effect. Archie also lets you set a priority for your search at the expense of other users, but changing this priority rarely gains a faster return. A better solution is to reduce the number of "hits" or matches you want.

Once you find the file you want by using Archie, you can use any of the FTP programs described in this chapter—or a Web browser—to download the file.

The Complete Reference

Internet

Chapter 38

Downloading and Installing Software and Other Files

One of the most popular uses for the Internet is downloading files. The files can contain programs, pictures, movies, documents, data, sounds, or multimedia. Programs can be offered for free (called *freeware*), or the supplier may allow you to try the software and pass it along to friends, with payment due only if you like it (called *shareware*). Vendors commonly offer time-limited trial versions of their software, too (sometimes called *trialware*), as well as updates, patches, and other additions to software you have already purchased.

The Web is usually your best source for finding the files you want. Nearly every commercial Internet site, and most university or college Internet sites, offer a public downloads section. Within these download sections, if you are seeking software, you must find the subsection for your particular system. Documents, images, and other media files are generally not system-specific. The section "Downloading Shareware and Freeware " in Chapter 25 suggests a number of Web sites where you can find useful files to download.

Today most Internet users download files from the Web, but FTP servers (described in Chapters 36 and 37) are also a common source. Many people also receive files by e-mail. Although the process by which files are downloaded to your computer using the Web, FTP, or e-mail is complex, the more recent your Internet software, and the more conventional your requirements, the more this complexity is hidden from you.

If you are using the latest Web browsers and are downloading popular software, for instance, the process may be fully automated.

If you are downloading something other than a program, however, or a file that originated on (or is principally intended for) a different kind of computer than you use, the underlying complexities can become very apparent. This chapter can help you surmount the difficulties involved.

No matter how you download files, however, the security of your computer system must be maintained. Computer viruses, "trojan horses," and other forms of malicious software are rare, especially when a file is downloaded from a software vendor, but are a finite risk for anyone who downloads files. Files received by e-mail from an unknown source (or forwarded by a well-intentioned friend), in particular, should always be checked for viruses before they are opened or otherwise used. See "Scanning for Viruses" at the end of this chapter.

Downloading Files from the Web

In most instances, if you are downloading software from a Web site, you simply click a link on a Web page. Take note of any description provided for the file, such as self-extracting, StuffIt, or ZIP, as you may need that information in order to know what to do after the file downloads.

You can click Web page links to download and save other types of files, too. If you are downloading a file other than a program file, however, simply clicking a link to that file may cause the browser to display the file's contents rather than saving it on your system. For instance, if a link takes you to an Adobe Acrobat PDF file, and your browser is equipped with an Acrobat reader, your computer downloads and displays the file rather than allowing you to save it. To ensure that the browser downloads a file, right-click the link (or, on the Macintosh, press the Option key and click) and look for a "'Save *something* As" menu choice, where *something* depends on the browser and on what you are clicking. In Internet Explorer, look for Save Target As, while in Netscape products, look for Save Link As. Select that choice.

If you do not have a link to click, but you do know the Internet address (URL) of a file, you may type that URL (or copy and paste it) directly into your Web browser. For example, you might read that **ftp://ftp.jrandomserver.org/coolprog.exe** is the URL of a program you want. Type that address into the Location, Netsite, or Address box of the browser.

When downloading certain software, some browsers (notably Internet Explorer) display a dialog box giving you the option of running the software, rather than downloading it. If you trust the source of the software completely, or do not intend to virus-check the software anyway, you may choose that option. In general, however, it is best to download the file instead, so it may be virus-checked. The browser may also display a dialog box that gives you the option of clicking a check box if you wish to always trust the source of the software you are currently downloading. Click that check box if you don't want to be asked again if you wish to download or install software from this vendor.

On most systems and browsers, a dialog box prompts you for the filename and folder you wish to use for storing the program on your computer. (On other systems and browsers the file is immediately downloaded to a particular folder or to your desktop, as defined in the Preferences or Options settings of the browser.) You can choose any folder you wish; if you are downloading a program, the best choice is usually to put the file in a folder by itself. Usually any filename works, although caution dictates using the name your browser suggests. A few downloaded files do not work if you change the filename. Do not change the file extension. Note the chosen folder so you can find the file later, and note its filename and extension. Click the Save button in that dialog box when you are ready. You see a dialog box that displays the progress of the download.

The time required for downloading large files can be quite long (especially for a dial-up connection); possibly longer than you are willing to spend online. Depending on the server that supplies the file, your browser may be able to estimate download time and displays it in the dialog box that appears during downloading. Otherwise, if the Web page that describes the file gives the file's size, you can calculate download time. Most browsers, in the dialog box that appears during downloading, display the rate at which data is being received once downloading begins. Wait 30 seconds or so for the data rate to appear and divide the file size by the data rate (being careful to recognize that a megabyte is millions of bytes, and a kilobite is thousands of bytes). For example, a six megabyte (6MB or 6Mbyte) file received at a data rate of two kilobytes per second (2KBps) will take 3000 seconds (about 51 minutes) to download.

  Most browsers allow you to continue browsing the Web (or even exit the browser) while a file is downloading. Pages appear much more slowly, however, while the download continues.

Finding Files on Your Computer After Downloading

When some programs download files, they don't always tell you where they put the files; nor do they ask you where you would prefer them to be stored on your computer. This problem is especially true for files you receive by e-mail.

One solution is to use your computer's find capability to search either for the file name, or for a file with a recent creation date. In Windows 95 or 98, for instance, choose Start | Find | Files or Folders; choose the Date Modified tab in the Find dialog box that appears; click During the Previous 1 Day(s), and then click the Find Now button.

Another solution is to check your program to see what location it is configured to use for attachments or downloads. The Eudora e-mail program, for instance, stores attachments in a folder named Attach, within the Eudora program folder (unless you have configured it otherwise). Under Windows 98, Microsoft's Outlook Express generally stores attachments in C:\Windows\Temp, from which you should move them if you want to keep them.

Determining What to Do with Downloaded Files

Usually, you know what you have downloaded, and therefore know what to do with it: run it, open it with your word processor, or view it in a graphics program, for instance. Before doing anything, however, make sure your computer has checked the downloaded file for viruses, even if the file is only a document (see the section "Scanning for Viruses" later in this chapter).

Often, the file is not quite ready to use. It may require decoding or decompression before you can use it. See the following section, "Dealing with Compressed and Archive Files."

If, after consulting the following section, you still don't know what to do with the file, your computer may know what to do. In a Windows, Macintosh, or UNIX windowing environment, after you virus-check the file, try simply double-clicking the file; your computer might launch a program that can open the file. If no program is currently associated with that type of file on your computer, your computer might instead display a dialog box listing all the programs you have and then ask you to choose a program in which to view the file. If you do choose a program, that program will thereafter be associated with that file type. If you are not sure which program to choose, press the ESC key to exit the dialog box and try opening the file from within various programs. If the file is supposed to be a document file, for instance, launch your word processor program and try opening the file in your word processor with the File | Open command.

Dealing with Compressed and Archive Files

Downloaded files are not always ready to be used. A file is often *compressed* in order to minimize downloading time and storage space on the computer where the file resides. In addition, if you are downloading a program, the file is probably an *archive* file: it contains several different files. Finally, the file may be *encoded* in a way that makes it easier to transfer across the Internet. You may have to decode, decompress, and unbundle a file in order to use its contents. As complicated as that sounds, the process is only rarely complicated and gets easier every year. Often, a single tool can do all tasks. In addition, many of the newer e-mail, FTP, and Web browser programs either automatically process these files into ready-to-use files, or automatically turn over the task to software that can handle the task. Finally, there is a trend towards *self-extracting* files: program files that bundle the compressed data with a decompression program.

Compressed file formats are often referred to as *archive* formats because compression is desirable for archival storage. Another reason they are called archive formats is because, in most instances, they allow compressing multiple files into one file. An entire folder of program and program documentation files, for instance, can be compressed into a single archive file.

Table 38-1 lists the archive and compression file types most commonly found on the Internet, by file extension. File extension is the best indicator of what kind of file you have, although you should also pay attention to descriptions found on the Web site or in the readme.txt or index.txt files of an FTP site's folder.

Some files may have two extensions, such as .tar.z. Multiple extensions usually imply that the contents have undergone two or more steps in creating the file: perhaps an initial process to create a single archive from multiple files, and then another to compress the archive file.

File Extension	File Type	Explanatory Section in This Chapter
BIN	Binary file, usually referring to a Macintosh MacBinary file if downloaded from a Macintosh folder	"Decoding and Decompressing Macintosh Files"
EXE	PC program or self-extracting file (binary file)	"Using Self-Extracting Files" and "Installing Programs"
HQX	BinHex encoded Macintosh file (text file)	"Decoding and Decompressing Macintosh Files"
SEA	Macintosh Self-Extracting Archive (binary file)	"Using Self-Extracting Files" and "Decoding and Decompressing Macintosh Files"
SIT	Macintosh compressed file (StuffIt) (binary file)	"Decoding and Decompressing Macintosh Files"
TAR	UNIX TAR archive (binary file)	"Unpacking TAR Archive Files"
UUE	Uuencoded UNIX or PC file (text file)	"Decoding UUE files"
Z, GZ	UNIX or gzip compressed (binary file)	"Unzipping ZIP Files"
ZIP	PC compressed file (ZIP) (binary file)	"Unzipping ZIP Files"

Table 38-1. *Types of Files Most Commonly Downloaded*

Compressed Files for Different Computers

Dozens of different file types (file *formats*) exist for compressed files. Fortunately, in each of the most popular operating systems, only one or two formats are commonly used:

- **Windows** ZIP format predominates; files end in .zip or, (if self-extracting) .exe. The tool most commonly used to both create and decompress ZIP files is Nico Mak's WinZip program, which is available in evaluation form at

http://www.winzip.com. (The ZIP format should not be confused with files stored on Iomega's Zip disks, which are not in ZIP format.) Other tools exist for PCs, Macintosh computers and UNIX workstations that can also decompress (unzip) ZIP files. Not all programs that use the ZIP format are entirely compatible; some decompression software is limited to earlier versions of the ZIP format, or else cannot handle certain advanced features.

- **Macintosh** StuffIt format predominates; files end in .sit or (if self-extracting), .sea. The tool most commonly used to decompress files in SIT format is Aladdin's StuffIt Expander, Aladdin Expander, and other tools available free or as evaluation software at **http://www.aladdinsys.com**. PC versions are also offered.

- **UNIX workstations** Predominant formats are the standard UNIX **compress** format, with the .z extension; or gzip format, with the extension .gz. To uncompress Z files, use the UNIX **uncompress** command, which takes the form **uncompress** *filename*.**z**, where *filename.z* is your downloaded file. Another format commonly used in UNIX is gzip (GNU zip, not to be confused with the Windows ZIP format), designed to replace the UNIX compress utility. Files in the gzip format end in .gz. GZ software can be obtained from **http://www.gzip.org**. WinZip decompresses GZ files for PCs and Aladdin Expander decompresses GZ files for Macintoshes or PCs.

Although you cannot use program files that are intended for a system other than yours, you can often use document, image, or other files. For that reason, you may need to decode a file in a format other than the predominant format for your system: ZIP files may contain useful files for Macintosh users, for instance.

Using Self-Extracting Files

Today, much of the software and other material available on the Web for downloading is in the form of self-extracting files. A *self-extracting file* is a combination of an extraction program and a compressed archive; when you run the program file, it extracts its own data into ready-to-use files. For the PC, self-extracting files have the extension .exe, and for the Macintosh they end in .sea. (The EXE file extension is used for nearly all programs on the PC, not just for self-extracting files, so you must rely on the documentation at the site from which you downloaded the file to tell you that the file is self-extracting.) Self-extracting files are created by tools such as Nico Mak's WinZip and Aladdin tools. To use self-extracting files, do the following:

1. Virus-check the file you have downloaded unless you are absolutely certain it does not contain a virus (see "Scanning for Viruses" later in this chapter).

2. Move the file into a folder of its own, if it is not already in such a folder.

3. Double-click the file. The self-extracting file creates a series of files; it may ask you to tell it where to put the files, or it may just place the files in the same folder as the self-extracting file. (If the file contains a program and is both

self-extracting *and self-installing*, it may ask you where you want to install the program. Extracting simply unpacks the files; installing informs your operating system that you have the program.)

4. Virus-check the extracted (or installed) files unless you are absolutely certain they do not contain a virus.

If this file is supposed to contain a program, and in Step 3 nothing indicated to you that the program was installed, you may now have to install that program. See the section, "Installing Programs," later in this chapter. If the file contains a document, multimedia, or something other than a program (or program enhancement), it is now ready to be used.

Unzipping ZIP Files

The most common compression format for files originating on the PC is the ZIP format. A variety of tools are available for decompressing the ZIP format, but the most commonly used program on the PC is WinZip. Other popular tools include ZipMagic for the PC and PKUNZIP and UnZip for PC, Macintosh, UNIX and other computers.

WinZip

You can obtain WinZip from Nico Mak Computing, at **http://www.winzip.com**. (The program itself comes as a self-extracting, self-installing file; download it, and then double-click it. The installation program inquires whether you wish to use the classic or wizard interface; choose the classic interface if you intend to follow the steps in this section.) Once you have installed WinZip, to extract files from a ZIP file using WinZip (release 7), take the following steps:

1. Double-click your downloaded ZIP file to launch WinZip and open the downloaded file. The WinZip window displays the files contained in your downloaded file.

2. If you see a file that appears to contain instructions, such as a file named readme.txt, double-click that file to read its contents in WordPad or whatever other program your PC uses for that type of file. Read the instructions.

3. If you want to extract all files, proceed to Step 4; otherwise, CTRL-click on the individual files you want to extract, to select them.

4. Click the Extract button in the WinZip window. The Extract dialog box appears. You may choose an existing folder into which you want to extract the files, or create a new one. For extracting downloaded software, a new or empty folder is best unless you are updating existing software. If you are updating existing software, open the folder where that software is installed, or whatever folder you may have been instructed to use.

5. To create a new folder by using the Extract dialog box, begin by opening the disk drive and folder where you want the new folder to be created. (Double-click disk drives and folders in the Folders/drives window to open them.) Type the name of the new folder you want to create in the Extract To text box.

6. Click the Extract button in the Extract dialog box. The files are extracted to the folder you chose. You may exit WinZip by choosing File | Exit.

ZipMagic

ZipMagic, by Mijenix Corporation, is particularly useful if you use a lot of ZIP files. ZipMagic runs continuously in the background, where it causes ZIP files to be displayed as folders in nearly all Windows windows, within Netscape or Internet Explorer windows, and within Eudora or Microsoft Inbox, Exchange, or Outlook. You open the ZIP "folders" to display and use the files (and folders) contained within exactly as you would any other file or folder on your PC. You may also convert actual folders and their contents into ZIP folders (actually ZIP files).

The left-hand window in Figure 38-1 shows three folders in a folder window; the two folders with ZIP icons are actually ZIP files that ZipMagic displays as folders. Double-clicking the ch37figs.zip folder in Figure 38-1 opens the window shown on the right in Figure 38-1, displaying the contents of that folder (ZIP file). Note that each window is equipped with a tiny Zip button at the upper right; clicking that button allows you to disable the ZipMagic display in that window or to change ZipMagic's properties.

You can download ZipMagic from **http://www.mijenix.com**. The program comes as a self-extracting, self-installing file; download it, and then double-click it to begin the installation process. Once ZipMagic is installed, you may control it by double-clicking the Zip icon ZipMagic places on the Windows taskbar. ZipMagic appears within your browser window when you download archive files, and after the file is downloaded, gives you a choice of saving, installing, or (if the file is a document), viewing it.

PKUNZIP and UnZip

PKUNZIP (which comes with a companion program, PKZIP) and UnZip are two programs for unzipping ZIP files on a very broad variety of computers and operating systems. Both programs allow you to view and extract TAR, GZIP, BinHex, and uuencoded files as well as ZIP files. A number of other programs for the ZIP format are also distributed on the Internet (mostly on FTP sites), with varying degrees of ability to handle the full variety of ZIP file variants. Both are DOS programs that also run with Windows.

PKZIP and PKUNZIP are available from **http://www.pkware.com**, and UnZip is available at many sites worldwide, such as the FTP site **ftp.cdrom.com** in the United States and **http://www.hensa.ac.uk** in the United Kingdom. You must download the correct binary (program) for your computer and operating system; look for a folder or links at these sites named after your type of system.

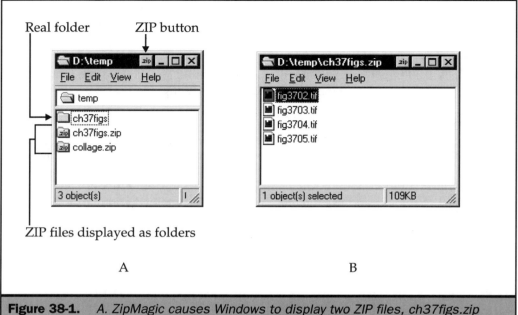

Real folder   ZIP button

ZIP files displayed as folders

A   B

Figure 38-1.   *A. ZipMagic causes Windows to display two ZIP files, ch37figs.zip and collage.zip, as folders. B. Double-clicking the ch37figs.zip folder opens a window displaying the files in the ZIP file.*

PKZIP for Windows is Pkware's version for PCs running Windows, and it both zips and unzips. The program downloads as a self-extracting, self-installing file. Download the file, then double-click it to both decompress and install the program. You can then launch PKZIP for Windows by choosing Start | Programs | Pkware | PKZIP for Windows. To extract files from a ZIP file (or self-extracting ZIP EXE file) in PKZIP 2.6 for Windows, you then take the following steps:

1. Choose File | Open, and in the Open dialog box that appears, choose the ZIP file from which you want to extract files.

2. If you want to extract only selected files, CTRL+click them; otherwise, go to Step 3.

3. Choose Extract | Extract files from the menu bar. The Extract menu appears.

4. Click the Browse button in the Extract dialog box, and in the Browse dialog box that appears, select a disk drive and folder for your files. Click OK in the Browse dialog box.

5. Click the Extract button to extract the files.

6. Click the Done button after the last file is extracted.

For DOS PCs and UNIX workstations, most versions of PKZIP and UnZip use command lines, rather than windowed interfaces. To run those programs, change to the directory where the program file unzip (or unzip.exe) is stored, copy your ZIP file to the same directory, and then type the command **unzip** *filename*.**zip**, where *filename*.zip represents the name of your ZIP file.

On Macintosh computers, Aladdin's StuffIt Expander opens ZIP files, as well as other archive formats used primarily on PCs.

Decoding UUE Files

Some files are stored in a coded form in which binary files (including programs, images, documents, and other media) are turned into text files (containing only ASCII characters). This text encoding allows the file to be transmitted and received by programs capable of handling only text, including the Internet e-mail system. Text encoding is becoming less necessary as more users employ the latest Internet tools, which are capable of handling binary files without requiring the user to be involved in decoding.

The oldest method of encoding binary files as text for e-mail transmission is called *uuencoding*. Uuecoded files have the extension .uue. Program files specifically for PCs are rarely encoded as text, and if so are usually uuencoded.

If you receive a message with a uuencoded section, or download a uuencoded file, the message or file must be converted back into its original binary form. If you use an e-mail program that does not automatically decode a file, save the message as a text file and use a uudecoding program, such as the UNIX decoding command. (If a file is long, it may be broken up into multiple e-mail messages. In that case, you must use text editing tools to combine the messages into a single text file before decoding.) The UNIX command to decode takes this form: **uudecode** < *yourfile.uue*.

Uuencoded files available on the Internet may have undergone several preparatory steps which you must then undo before you can use the contents. When you uudecode a uuencoded file, it may reveal a Z (compressed) file. When you decompress the Z file, it may reveal a TAR (archive file). You must then un-tar the TAR file to unpack the component files.

Upacking TAR Archive Files

In the UNIX operating system, archiving and compression are handled separately. In UNIX the term *archive* most commonly refers to files in the TAR format, which are created by the tar program. (TAR stands for Tape ARchive, but Tape in this context is irrelevant.) The TAR format simply allows a group of files to be combined into one file, which ends in .tar.

If you use a UNIX workstation, the command to extract files from a TAR file in UNIX may vary with the particular operating system. The following form, however, works with most systems:

tar xvf *filename*.**tar**

A TAR file may be compressed (using the UNIX compress command or gzip) into a Z or GZ file, and usually has the extension .tar.z, .tar-z, .tar.gz, .tar-gz, or .tgz. To obtain the files contained in such a compressed archive file, you first decompress the TAR file, then extract its files.

If you use a PC or Macintosh, the program you use to decompress ZIP or SIT files may be able to perform both operations: decompression of the Z file into a TAR file, and unpacking of the TAR file into individual files. That program may require you to know (or guess) what file or files are contained in the Z file. For example, if you open a compressed TAR file (TAR.Z, TAR-Z, TAR.GZ, TAR-GZ, or TGZ) with WinZip, WinZip asks for the filename you wish to extract. The safest choice is to keep the name WinZip suggests, but change the file extension to TAR. WinZip then offers to unpack the TAR file into the final, ready-to-use files.

Keep in mind that the files contained in a TAR file are most likely intended for use on a UNIX system. If so, you will be unable to use any program files that are unpacked, although you may be able to read the documentation.

Decoding and Decompressing Macintosh Files

For most Macintosh users, files download, decode, and decompress without much fuss. Macintosh files are unique, however, which can occasionally complicate the downloading process. Macintosh files have a two-part (or *two-forked*) file format comprised of a *resource fork* and a *data fork*. UNIX and PC systems do not support such a file format, and most servers of downloadable files are UNIX or PC systems. Therefore, when Macintosh communications software transmits a file to a non-Macintosh system or across the Internet, it uses one of two schemes to preserve the full Macintosh file structure: MacBinary or BinHex.

When a binary file is placed on the Internet, the Macintosh software handling the transfer generally attaches a *MacBinary header* to the file, which contains the resource fork information. Such files are often denoted by a BIN extension attached to the file.

An alternative approach is to encode the binary file in *BinHex* format, which not only preserves the resource fork but also stores the file as ASCII (text) characters. BinHex files carry an extension of .hqx. BinHex format, like unencoded format, was intended to allow binary files to be carried by simple Internet programs, such as UNIX mail, that could handle only text. Even though most contemporary e-mail, Web browser, and other programs can now handle binary files through the use of MIME, HQX files are still very common on the Internet.

Decoding BIN and HQX Macintosh Files

Files in either MacBinary (BIN) or BinHex (HQX) format cannot be executed directly on the Macintosh; they must be decoded first. Software to decode these formats is available on the Internet, but because that software itself must be in either MacBinary or BinHex, Macintosh users faced a "chicken-and-egg" dilemma. The dilemma is today solved by the built-in capability of most Web browsers and other Internet programs for the Macintosh.

Many contemporary Internet programs for the Macintosh, including browsers from Netscape and Microsoft, and the popular Fetch FTP client program, handle MacBinary and HQX decoding automatically. A few, such as Netscape Navigator, rely on auxiliary "helper" software on the Mac, generally StuffIt Expander or one of Aladdin's other products. Netscape products currently come with StuffIt Expander.

When Macintosh Internet software downloads a file from the Internet and decodes it, you generally (by default) end up with two (or more) files on your desktop: the original file and the decoded file or files. You may discard the HQX and SIT or SEA files once you have a usable file. You can set many programs to delete the compressed file automatically, but that might not always be a safe idea.

If your copy of Netscape Navigator or Communicator does not decode HQX files, it may be attempting to refer the job to a helper application that is not present. Take the following steps in your Netscape browser to decode the HQX file:

1. Choose Options | General Preferences; a Preferences dialog box appears.

2. Click the Helpers tab, and a Helpers card is displayed.

3. Scroll down the list on the Helpers card until you see Macintosh BinHex Archive in the leftmost column.

4. Double-click Macintosh BinHex Archive, and an Edit Type window appears.

5. At the bottom of the Edit Type window, change the Handled By preference from Application to Navigator (or Communicator, if you are using Netscape Communicator.)

6. Click OK.

If you receive a downloaded file (say, from another Internet user) that is supposed to be a valid Macintosh file, but you cannot open or run the file, it is probably still in MacBinary or BinHex format. You can convert the file into a valid Mac file by using StuffIt Expander, by choosing Extract | MacBinary (for a BIN file) or BinHex (for an HQX file) | Decode. A standard Open dialog box allows you to select the file; do so, and then click Open. You will find the decoded file in the same folder as the original.

Decompressing (Expanding) SIT and SEA Macintosh Files

The process of decoding a Macintosh file may involve several steps, including decompression. If you download and decode an HQX (BinHex) file, for instance, it may yield a compressed SIT (StuffIt) file, which must then be decompressed into a valid Macintosh file. Such files are sometimes indicated by a filename ending in .sit.hqx. In some instances, your software both decodes and decompresses the file automatically. If your Macintosh is equipped with StuffIt Expander, for instance, it both decodes and decompresses SIT files that are encoded in HQX format, leaving you with the original file HQX file, the SIT file, and the final, ready-to-use file.

StuffIt or SIT is the most common compression format used on the Macintosh. Aladdin Systems makes the expansion software for SIT files available for free on its

Web site at **http://www.aladdinsys.com**, in both HQX and MacBinary format. Aladdin's software can also decode a variety of other formats, including ZIP files.

Another common format, especially for program downloads, is the SEA format, the Self-Expanding (or -Extracting) Archive format. Downloaded files in SEA format require no special software to expand. They can be used as described in the earlier section of this chapter, "Using Self-Extracting Files." Files in SEA format are binary files, so they come with a MacBinary header. Fortunately, most contemporary browsers can decode the MacBinary header, leaving you with an executable SEA file. If, however, you obtain a SEA file from another source (such as on a floppy disk, downloaded by a PC user) you need to convert it to a valid Macintosh file, as described in the preceding section.

Using StuffIt Expander

If your Macintosh uses System 7.0 or higher, you may decode and expand files by selecting them and dragging them on top of the StuffIt Expander icon. Otherwise, to use Stuffit Expander to open a file that has been downloaded to your desktop:

1. In Stuffit Expander, choose File | Expand.
2. In the dialog box that opens, click the Desktop button, highlight your saved file, and click Expand. One or more new files appear on your desktop.
3. Choose File | Quit.

For PCs using Aladdin software, the process is similar. If a PC (or UNIX workstation) receives a BinHex or MacBinary file, however, the resource fork is either discarded, saved as a separate file, or used by the program to construct an appropriate file extension. Usually, the lost information is not crucial, but some Macintosh file types (certain QuickTime movies and Macintosh sound files) put important information in the resource fork. These files generally do not work on a PC or UNIX workstation. Instead, you must find the QuickTime movie in a format called *flattened*, or the audio file in a format recognized by your computer.

Installing Programs

Once you have obtained a program file, either by decompressing or extracting the file from an archive (as the preceding section describes), or by downloading it in a ready-to-use form, you take the following steps.

First, on any system, unless you completely trust the source from which you downloaded the file, virus-check the file or files you downloaded or extracted from an archive file. Perform the virus check, even if you already virus-checked the archive file from which the files were extracted. (Many virus scanners cannot examine the files within an archive.) See the next section, "Scanning for Viruses."

If you are using a Windows system, unless the software arrived in a self-extracting, self-installing form, and has already been installed, look for an Install.exe or Setup.exe file among the files you have downloaded or extracted from an archive. If you find such a file, double-click it. An installation program launches, and steps you through the process of installing the software. After the installation finishes, it is important to virus-check your entire computer before running the new application. To run a newly-installed Windows 95 or 98 program, choose Start | Programs and look for a new command with the name of your installed software.

On a Macintosh system, after virus-checking the program file or files, double-click the program file. The program launches and in most cases steps you through an installation process. Follow the installation process as you normally would for a new application installed from any other source. If an installation does not take place, simply move the program file and its associated files to a new folder in the Applications folder on your hard disk drive. To use the program, double-click it.

On a UNIX system, copy the program file to your bin directory. To run the program, type its name, followed by any switches or arguments the documentation directs you to use, and press ENTER.

Scanning for Viruses

It is important that all downloaded files, unless they come from an absolutely trustworthy source, be checked (*scanned*) for viruses before they are used in any way or stored anywhere but in a separate folder on your system. You should check all files, even document files, because of the possibility of *macro viruses*—viruses that make use of a word processor's or spreadsheet program's ability to execute instructions (macros), as well as display a file. For the most complete virus checking, obtain commercial virus-checking software, such as McAfee VirusScan (available from **http://www.mcafee.com**). Often such software comes with an online service that automatically briefs the software with the latest virus developments. Besides detecting viruses, antivirus software may also help you remove the viral infection from file.

Although antivirus software cannot guarantee that it will find a virus that it is not specifically aware of, the better software contains "heuristic" capability that will alert you to files it deems suspicious. Such capability can become annoying if it is too conservatively designed, because it finds nearly everything suspicious.

Commercial virus-checking software does its job at various times, depending upon how you set it up: when you start your computer, at a particular time (such as every Friday), or continuously in the background. When it runs in the background, it checks whenever you download files through a specified browser or e-mail program, or attempt to move them to a specified "safe zone" of your computer. You can determine how the software does its job when you install it, or by setting your preferences from the program window when the program is running.

Background virus-checking has good and bad points. It is safest if you are forgetful, and is convenient if you download often. Background checking also provides the best protection against the subtle (and rare) viruses that arrive, not as files, but as infections of your computer's memory that can arrive through your Web browser. However, in some instances, background checking can slow down your system, cause conflict with other background programs, or cause other erratic behavior. Background checking may also not guard against viruses that arrive through Internet tools that are not specifically checked by the software. For instance, your virus scanner may check only files that arrive through Netscape Navigator, and not check files that arrive through Microsoft Internet Explorer or an FTP client program. Manually running your antivirus software after downloading files is usually the most practical option.

Quite a few good antivirus programs are available. You can find listings, reviews, and additional background on virus-scanning by submitting the term *virus* to any good search engine or Web guide. All virus-scanning programs work differently, so rather than go into the specifics of how to check downloaded files in each program, the following instructions provide an example of how to use one of the more popular programs: Symantec's Norton Anti-Virus, available for both PCs and Macintoshes, currently in Release 5. Take the following steps to check a downloaded file with Norton Anti-Virus (NAV) 5:

1. Launch NAV. (On a Windows system, for instance, either double-click the NAV icon on the Taskbar if it is present, or choose Start | Programs | Norton AntiVirus | Norton AntiVirus.)

2. In NAV, choose Scan | Folder, and in the Scan Folders dialog box that appears, choose the folder containing your downloaded file. (If you have already expanded a downloaded archive file into a folder, choose that folder.)

3. NAV not only checks the downloaded folder, but also checks the contents of your computer's memory (RAM) and the crucial "system-level" files that are used to start up your computer. The Scan Results dialog box appears. If NAV finds any viruses, it reports them and suggests ways to deal with the problem.

4. When NAV has finished checking, click the Close button in the Scan Results dialog box and click the Exit button in the NAV window.

On the Macintosh, NAV uses *Safe Zones* when running in the background. Any files moved or downloaded into a Safe Zone are checked. The default Safe Zone in the latest releases is the Macintosh desktop. You may also have StuffIt Expander or other Aladdin program automatically launch your virus-scanning program. You can find the control for doing so by choosing Edit | Preferences in the Aladdin program.

Viruses are not common in downloaded files, especially if you stick to popular and reputable software libraries. Be sure to keep your virus-checking software up-to-date by checking its manufacturer's Web site: many virus-checkers allow you to download updates that contain information about newly-discovered viruses.

Watch for Scams

Viruses are not the only malevolent programs lurking on the Internet. For example, several years ago, a pornography site in Moldova (a former Soviet republic) required users to download a special viewer program. Unbeknownst to those who downloaded the program, the "viewer" also reconfigured their computers to connect to the Internet via a long-distance call to Moldova! Presumably, the perpetrators arranged with the Moldovan phone company to receive a cut of the astronomical phone charges. AT&T noticed the strange increase in calls to Moldova and contacted the authorities. The moral of the story: download software only from reputable software libraries.

The Complete Reference

Internet

Part VII

Other Internet Topics

The Complete Reference

Internet

Chapter 39

Internet Telephony

885

*I*nternet telephony or *IP telephony* is the hardware and software needed to carry telephone calls over the Internet. Internet telephony requires specialized hardware and software, and raises many legal and tariff issues, described in the later sections of this chapter. This chapter starts by describing how the current telephone system works, including the details of ISDN digital phone lines, because Internet telephony borrows heavily from ISDN.

 Tip   *If you want to experiment with Internet telephony now, see Chapter 17, which describes several programs that allow voice conferencing over the Internet.*

Background: The Integrated Digital Telephone Network

The *Public Switched Telephone Network* (*PSTN*)—the global phone system you use every day—is one of the very few human achievements that has worked its way into the lives of people in a comprehensive and uniform way. Like flush toilets and cars, telephones work the same way no matter where you go. If you find an antique phone with cloth-covered wires, a mouthpiece mounted on a wooden box, and a separate earpiece, chances are it will work when connected to a telephone line. The same voltage and power levels used to move the clapper and ring the bells mounted on an antique phone are used today to signal an incoming call to the most modern electronic phone.

Compare this with electrical service. Electrification has been around approximately as long as telephones have, but electrical service is plagued by incompatible voltages and frequencies from one country to the next. Television has three incompatible transmission standards, not counting digital TV. Telephony, by comparison, is the most unifying of all basic utilities with a global reach. And, while the telephone central office equipment, fiber-optic cables, and telephones themselves have advanced in technological development, the electrical standards and interfaces that make it possible to connect telephone instruments to telephone switches in any city to any other have not changed since those early phones made of wood, wire, metal, and cloth.

Digital Telephony

The telephone network is a success, but it has problems: making an electrical circuit that reached from one telephone to another, or that was relayed over long distance circuits, was too unreliable and expensive to permit the telephone network to grow. So, while the phones at the ends of the network remain the same, the guts of the network began to use digital technology. The electrical circuit would end at the telephone company switch, and a digital virtual circuit would exist inside the telephone network.

By the 1960s and 1970s, when digital technology began to be widely used in telephone central office switches and the long distance network that ties local switches together, momentum gathered to move the customer's experience of telephony forward. The logical next step after converting telephone switching equipment and transmission lines to a globally standardized digital technology was to bring that technology all the way to the ends of each phone line. This would make the telephone a digital terminal for the global digital telephone network.

ISDN

Integrated Service Digital Network (*ISDN*) is the name of a family of standards and technologies for bringing the flexibility and power of the global *integrated digital network*, the network that carries phone calls all over the world, all the way to the end of the wire where the telephone is attached. ISDN is important to an understanding of IP telephony because many of the standards for IP telephony have an ISDN heritage. Many of protocols used by IP telephony software are lifted directly from ISDN and ISDN applications. Chapter 3 describes how to connect a computer to the Internet by using ISDN.

ISDN brings the integrated digital network to your home or office over the same pair of copper wires your plain old telephone uses, but the similarities end with the physical copper. Instead of a voltage that will knock you over if you ever have the misfortune to be holding the bare wires in a telephone line when the phone rings, ISDN uses packets of digital data to tell ISDN phones when to signal an incoming call by ringing. ISDN phone lines for connecting individual telephones are called *Basic Rate Interface* (*BRI-ISDN*) lines. These lines carry enough data to perform the aforementioned signaling, plus two voice circuits, a configuration known as *2B+D*, for two *bearer* (B) channels, plus one data (D) channel. ISDN phones use the D channel to signal off-hook, phone number, and other information used in placing a call. The central office switch at the phone company uses the D channel for signaling new incoming calls, or that the other end of a call has hung up, among much other information.

ISDN B channels carry phone calls. These channels bear a stream of bits to and from the telephone company's switch. This bit stream carries your voice in a normal telephone conversation. A single BRI-ISDN line accommodates two logically separate digital channels suitable for bearing voice calls. The logical separation of the ISDN line into two B plus one D channels is accomplished by dividing the bits going down that line into frames. These frames are like rail cars coupled into a never-ending train, always moving at a constant speed. When your voice is digitized by an ISDN phone, the bits representing the analog voltage your voice created in the phone's mouthpiece microphone are put into a frame belonging to the correct logical channel on its way to the telephone switch to which the ISDN phone is connected. The frames, like the rail cars of our never-ending train, move in lockstep. The rate of bits moving over the ISDN line never varies. The frames alternate between channels so that there is never a missing frame, or a lack of a place to put the bits from the output of the device digitizing your voice.

At the telephone switch, the bits are switched onto another line, probably one carrying more than the two bearer channels of a BRI-ISDN line. It might be a *Primary Rate Interface ISDN (PRI-ISDN)*, which is divided into 23 B channels, plus one D channel (of higher capacity than the D channel in a BRI-ISDN line). PRI-ISDN lines, too, are divided into frames moving in lockstep. As the bits move deeper into the global telephone network, even higher capacity lines, some capable of carrying thousands of B channels, keep the bits representing your voice moving in lockstep. This hierarchy of increasingly fast lines and the switches that connect them, all moving bits in lockstep, is the integrated digital network. Parts of this hierarchy are now no longer quite so lockstep, and use a technology called *Asynchronous Transfer Mode (ATM)*. ATM enables breaking the lockstep of frames for superior efficiency, especially in mixing voice and data traffic, while retaining the ability to move voice within a predictable interval. The result of all this is that when the bits representing your voice go in one end, they come out the other with minimum delay, with no gaps, and always at the same rate as they went in.

ISDN Applications

The idea of applications of the telephone network is part of ISDN. Because ISDN specifies applications as well as the network that carries them, its name includes *Integrated Services*. The telephone companies and equipment manufacturers designed ISDN to make it possible to sell more services than just voice circuits connecting one telephone instrument to another. These applications are defined as part of ISDN. So, with ISDN at both ends of a phone call, you can do more than just talk. You can:

- Have a videoconference
- Have a "data conference" and exchange digital images, documents, and other files
- Use compressed speech for "subrate" communications, saving money by using a fraction of a long-distance circuit, for example
- Use compressed high-quality speech to link a radio station's remote broadcast to the station's transmission facility
- Use compressed high-fidelity audio to link a live broadcast from a concert hall to a radio station's transmission facility
- Transmit faxes several times faster than the fastest non-ISDN fax machine

These applications never gained wide use, though the niche-market for ISDN in radio remote broadcasts is well established. The largest use of ISDN in the U.S. is for Internet connectivity, where ISDN lines are used because they carry data faster than modems over analog lines. But the ISDN applications are still important because they form the basis of what you can do with IP telephony.

ISDN Protocols and Standards

ISDN brings a large array of protocols and standards to the problem of connecting voice calls from one telephone to another and connecting more complex calls from one terminal supporting ISDN applications to another. ISDN telephone sets use these protocols to set up calls, exchange data, and convey the contents of the telephone conversation. ISDN protocols are also important because they enable ISDN to work without the telephone system knowing what kind of equipment is attached to the phone line. As long as the equipment understands ISDN protocols, the connection works. Protocols are even more important when application-specific equipment is replaced by a general-purpose computer and software. For example, ISDN conferencing applications use standards for compressing voice and video for transmission over ISDN lines.

The *Q.931 standard*, also known as *Digital Subscriber Signaling 1* (*DSS1*), is used on an ISDN line's D channel to negotiate a mutually compatible set of capabilities when two pieces of equipment meet in a call. Q.931 is used to set up calls, control calls and change their state, be notified of changes in the call (for example, the other party hung up), and to release or close calls. H.320 is the set of standards enabling video, audio, and data conferencing over ISDN. Several other standards define how voice and video are compressed and uncompressed (using *codecs*—coder/decoders).

IP Telephony Software

IP telephony is, in general, any means of having a phone conversation over an IP network. However, lack of standards means chaos and lack of connectivity. H.323, the standard for IP telephony, is based on ISDN, and that relationship enables IP telephony to integrate with conventional telephony.

H.323 Is IP Telephony

H.323 is the name applied to a family of standards and protocols that enable conferencing—video conferencing, audio conferencing, data conferencing. In order to make conferencing possible, the H.323 standard uses the standards and protocols that make ISDN phone calls possible, among them Q.931 for call setup, and G.711 and G.723 for encoding voice.

H.323 is part of the same family of standards as H.320, the set of ISDN conferencing standards. So an IP telephony "call" is not so much like an ordinary ISDN phone call as it is like an ISDN conference, whether you use software that supports only voice or a program that supports multimedia add-ons. Even a call from an analog telephone, passing through a telephony server or IP telephony gateway device, becomes an H.323 conference on the far side of the gateway.

The ISDN versions of these protocols (such as H.320) differ from their IP versions (such as H.323). When an ISDN phone digitizes your voice, the bits traverse the telephone network in lockstep from one end of the call to the other. The same is true for all the content of an ISDN conference: the video, the data bits, everything travels through the telephone network in a virtual circuit of frames. This guarantees that the bits come out exactly as fast as they went in, that there are no gaps or overruns at any point in the network, and that delay, or *latency*, is minimized. If you remove this lockstep mechanism and replace it with Internet Protocol (IP, described in Chapter 1), you get IP telephony. The difference between H.320 (ISDN telephony) and H.323 (IP telephony) is the difference between the way the bits move. Almost everything else is the same. The Q.931 protocol for setting up the call, the various compression formats for voice and video, and the data conferencing standards are all the same.

The fact that the protocols for setting up calls and controlling them are the same simplifies the integration of IP telephony into a telephone network using ISDN standards. Because the codecs and application layer standards are mostly the same, voice calls, video calls, and most types of data conferencing can interoperate between IP telephony software like NetMeeting and ISDN conferencing equipment like conference room video systems. The difference is that the Internet makes no guarantee that the contents of your call will arrive in lockstep, and that you will have all the bandwidth you need. However, the lack of this guarantee does not mean that IP telephony is inherently flawed or unreliable.

H.323 Client Software

Lots of H.323-compatible Internet telephony programs are available. The best known is NetMeeting, Microsoft's telephony program that comes with Windows 98. Installing Internet telephony programs is no harder than installing other Internet applications: Chapter 17 describes how to install and use NetMeeting.

H.323-based IP telephony bears a striking resemblance to making an ISDN phone call. But ISDN phones are connected to telephone switches, and IP telephony works without telephone switches. Telephone switches connect phone calls and, when you dial a number, know where the phone belonging to that number is, and what switches your call must traverse to get there. When you make a Internet telephony call (using a program such as NetMeeting), you must either know the network address of the person you are calling, or use a directory server to find that person. Then, the NetMeeting software on your computer contacts the NetMeeting software on the computer of the person you are calling, and data, including voice, flows between the two computers just as it does for any Internet application.

Telephony Server Software

But using NetMeeting (or another Internet telephony program) to contact another NetMeeting user isn't the whole answer. What if you wanted IP telephony to be more like using a phone? What if you wanted to be able to use NetMeeting to call a regular phone number on the Public Switched Telephone Network? What if you wanted to be able to receive calls on NetMeeting from phones on the PSTN, so other people could reach your Internet telephony program by dialing a phone number? To achieve these goals, you need *telephony server software* that works with your H.323 software. The telephony server software you would need consists of two main components: a gateway, and a gatekeeper.

A *gateway* enables calls from the PSTN to enter your IP telephony system, and lets you use your IP telephony system to call numbers on the PSTN. A gateway can be used without a gatekeeper, in order to bypass the phone system. If your company has a branch office in India, it might be much more economical to install IP telephony gateways at your U.S. office and the branch office in India and run phone calls between the two over the Internet. In this case, the gateways form a closed system, and once the gateways are configured to talk to each other, making a call is the same as if you were using a leased phone line or alternative long distance carrier for those calls.

But if you really want IP telephony to look and act like a telephone system so that people calling you have no idea you are answering your calls on your PC, you need a gatekeeper. The *gatekeeper* enables computers running H.323 programs to have extension numbers assigned to them, just like phones attached to a PBX (private branch exchange). The gatekeeper translates addresses and phone numbers. It also manages which H.323-enabled computers are part of the simulated PBX environment, and it can redirect calls, so that if you are not at your PC to answer a call, it gets sent to a voice mail system. The gatekeeper enables a collection of PCs running IP telephony software to look like conventional telephone extensions attached to a PBX.

By using gatekeeper and gateway software on an Internet server, you can also attach special telephones to the server and make the server act like a telephone switch. You can attach outside phone lines and make calls to the outside from phones on the inside, and the IP telephony part begins and ends inside the server. If you install H.323 client software on networked PCs and configure the gatekeeper to know about them, you have a mix of PCs and phones behaving like phones to unsuspecting callers from the outside. You can also connect the system to the Internet and enable your conventional phones to call H.323 users on the Internet, or, through other gateways, call other conventional phones, using the Internet for part of the distance to the other phone, as shown in Figure 39-1.

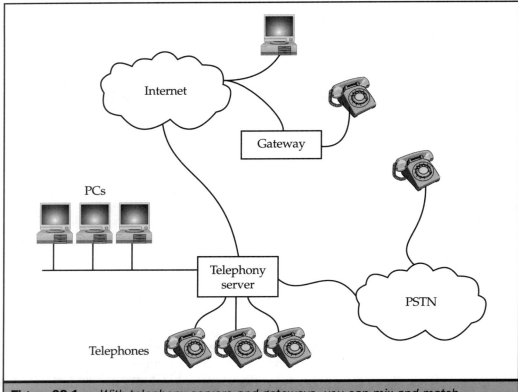

Figure 39-1. *With telephony servers and gateways, you can mix and match telephones, PCs, the Internet, and the PSTN*

Multipoint Conferencing

Support for *multipoint conferences* (conference with people in more than two locations or using more than two computers) is a large part of the H.323 standard. But it isn't a very important part of IP telephony servers. Multipoint conferencing requires software services called *Multipoint Control Units* (*MCU*) and *Multipoint Processors* (*MP*). These manage and process the streams of voice and video data, mixing the voice data so that it should sound roughly as if all the people in the conference call are in the same room and can hear each other as they speak. Multipoint Processors use a lot of computing power and complete implementations of them are scarce. NetMeeting includes software for multiuser conferences for the data part of a conference, but does not provide an audio/video MCU or MP.

IP Telephony Hardware and Systems

Depending on how you want your Internet telephony system to work, you may need voice processing cards and other hardware. Figure 39-2 shows the hardware and network connections for an Internet telephony system.

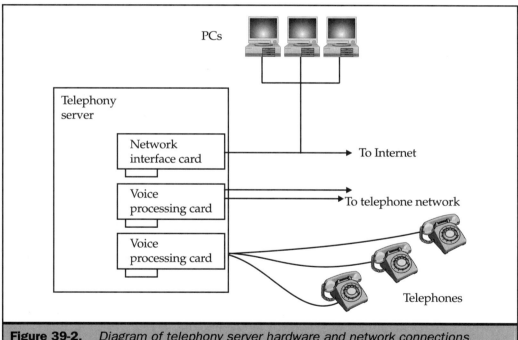

Figure 39-2.   *Diagram of telephony server hardware and network connections*

Voice Processing Cards in IP Telephony

If you are thinking of building an IP telephony system, you will need to connect it to the telephone network. This is where *voice processing cards* come in handy. Voice processing cards are used, primarily, in computers that run voice mail systems and *interactive voice response* (*IVR*) applications. If you have called a bank-by-phone system or the "movie line" to find movie show times and locations, you have used an IVR system. Voice processing cards are used for these applications for two reasons:

- You can plug phone lines into a voice processing card. Voice processing cards can digitize your voice, so voice mail systems can then store the message you leave. They can play back voice over the phone, which is how you hear your voice mail. Some voice processing cards connect to digital phone lines, like ISDN lines, so they do not need to digitize an analog signal. Some connect to high-capacity lines like PRI-ISDN lines, and some leave off the telephone network interface so that it can be put on a separate card, which is useful when building really large systems.

- Voice processing cards have *digital signal processors* (*DSPs*). These cards can listen for touch tones, so that they can tell which movie you want to find the show time for, or which extension you are trying to reach. They can tell when you are talking, and when you are silent. They can compress your digitized voice so that your voice messages take up less room on disk.

Voice processing cards enable computers to replace a human answering a phone. They also replace the phone itself. This means that voice processing cards can be put between the telephone network and an H.323 IP telephony system. When a phone call arrives from the telephone network, the voice processing card digitizes the voice from the phone line and compresses it, so that IP telephony gateway software can then send it on to a phone or H.323 client program. When a call originates in the Internet telephony system, your voice is digitized at your PC under the control of NetMeeting, is sent to the gateway, and is uncompressed and played on the phone line by the voice processing card.

Other IP Telephony Gateway Hardware

Not all IP telephony gateways are built out of general-purpose voice processing cards. IP telephony gateway functions require different amounts of DSP power than IVR or voice mail applications, and it might be more economical to run the higher-level gateway functions on a special-purpose processor than on the CPU of a PC server. You can buy hardware designed specifically for the purpose of IP telephony gateways. This hardware can come in the form of cards that plug into PCs, like voice processing cards, or in the form of an external box which contains all the hardware and software of an IP telephony gateway.

IP Telephony un-PBXs

Can you buy an IP telephony phone system? Yes, you can, but only just. You can buy telephony server software, plus hardware that interfaces a computer to the telephone network, and build something that more or less works the way a telephone switch, or PBX, works. You can even buy devices that look for all the world like a telephone, yet they plug into an Ethernet network and communicate with an H.323 telephony server. Even with all the buzz surrounding IP telephony, the day when you can buy an IP telephony system that can replace a conventional telephone system in real-world use is only now dawning.

Companies like NBX, Cisco, and COM2001 make Internet telephony products that can wholly replace a PBX. These companies approach telephony servers mostly from the network software point of view. None have ever made conventional phone systems. Some established PBX makers, like Ericsson, Lucent, and Mitel have also created telephony server systems. But there is a general feeling in the industry that nobody knows yet what the successful approach to this category of products will be.

IP Phones

Part of the reason for the slow dawning of IP telephony phone systems is that PCs make lousy phones. If you have a pressing need, like avoiding otherwise unaffordable international long distance rates, using NetMeeting in place of a phone is acceptable. But imagine the uproar if, at your office, your phones were removed and you and your colleagues had to use NetMeeting, with speakers and a microphone, or a headset, for all phone calls. Some telephony server makers have introduced IP telephony phones, but even these are not a complete solution. Put an IP telephony phone next to a PC, and you end up using one for "normal" calls, and the other for multimedia calls involving video, document sharing, and text chat. The trouble is, when an incoming call arrives, has it been directed to the right H.323 client? So, in addition to IP phones, hybrids that make calling using a PC easy also have to be developed.

Unified Messaging and IP Telephony

E-mail integrated multimedia messaging is often referred to as *unified messaging*. In this type of messaging, voice messages, and sometimes faxes, are delivered to the user either through a conventional voice mail touch-tone interface, or through e-mail. Since IP telephony is the unification of the Internet with the telephone network, using an IP telephony system should, at the very least, imply that your voice messages will arrive in your e-mail. This means IP telephony systems should be able to handle calls when the users of those systems are not present, record a voice message, and e-mail that voice message to the user who missed the call.

However, to exploit the full potential of unified messaging in IP telephony, some aspects of unified messaging, especially those copied directly from voice mail, have to be reconsidered:

- IP telephony is H.323 multimedia conferencing. This means the notion that unified messaging is just voice mail in your e-mail has to be expanded to include the other media types that can be part of an H.323 call. So your message might contain voice, video, images, and files containing data.

- It isn't only the message that should take on multimedia dimensions. The greetings and prompts a caller hears and sees (if the caller is using a PC or a videoconferencing system) should also be a multimedia presentation. For example, a caller using H.323 conferencing software to make a call might be presented with your calendar if you are unavailable to take the call. In addition to leaving you a message, the caller might use the calendar interactively to make an appointment with you. HTML documents, Java applets, and other active content might well become part of your unified messaging "greeting message."

- The way multimedia messages are composed is different than the way voice messages are composed: in voice mail, the voice mail system provides the hardware and software for recording the voice message. Some voice mail systems enable callers to edit their messages. But there is no reason for an H.323 unified messaging system to do these things for callers using PCs. Those callers should compose their messages on their own systems, and mail those messages from their own "home" mail server. There are numerous issues in this area in terms of presenting callers with prompts and choices during the process of composing a message that have to be worked out using a blend of server-based and client-based software.

- A voice mail system answers your calls because your calls are transferred to the voice mail system if you don't answer. The voice mail system looks to the telephone network like a bunch of telephones that answer calls on your behalf. That is what a voice processing card does: it enables the voice mail system to answer calls, interpret the signaling—such as touch tones—on the phone line, and record the caller's voice. H.323 calls don't have to terminate at a telephone. They terminate in H.323 software. While there remains the need to interpret touch tones and other audible signals, since calls can originate from conventional phones, it isn't exactly clear that IP telephony unified messaging requires voice processing cards: Will the DSP capacity on the voice processing card still be needed? Can load balancing create a very large virtual unified messaging system? What exactly is the hardware configuration of an IP telephony unified messaging server, and how does it fit into an IP network?

- How does the user create and control surrogates that answer calls for him? How do these H.323 surrogates fit into directory services? How do the conventional voice mail menus fit into this New World? These are issues that will be ironed out in further development of H.323 software, and in new services like Active Directory.

As telephony server companies improve and mature their products in successive generations, and as directory services are applied to solving some of these issues, unified messaging will be able to do all the things it should be able to do, and it will diverge significantly from its voice mail roots. This will be one way in which IP telephony will be able to create a perception of higher value. For example, multimedia messaging has the potential to make messaging far more productive than conventional voice mail, while reducing the frustration callers face when their call is answered by voice mail. In order to be attractive to the end user, IP telephony has to be better, not just technically interesting and different from conventional telephony.

Legal and Tariff Issues

Telephone service, despite the breakup of monopolies and the privatization of government-owned authorities, remains an area of entrenched incumbents and government intervention. Pricing that supports government's desire to subsidize one group at the expense of another, easy access by law-enforcement to people's supposedly private communication, and opaque business practices that entrench the biggest companies in their markets are all under attack from IP telephony. When the people get to buy cheap access to a global network, and there is no control over the content of the bits traversing that network, or their destination, the old ways are on the way out.

Incumbents vs. IP Telephony

Local telephone monopolies still exist, along with a regulatory framework that makes the relationship of local and long-distance providers predictable and stable, if not always to everyone's liking. With Internet telephony, phone calls become nearly free. Is it because IP telephony technology is so far superior to the existing telephone networks? No. Conventional telephone networks were built and operated by regulated monopolies that bought their privilege by accepting regulation calling for subsides, and taxes unique to the voice communications industry. Bypassing the telephone network means bypassing, for example, the points at which the long distance companies hand over your phone calls to the local phone companies and pay quite dearly for the local exchange companies to carry the last leg of the call. Circumvent this and you have annoyed the "Baby Bells," the local phone monopolies, and stepped around the taxman, too.

It is very unlikely that anything can be done about the advent of Internet telephony, except to reduce the cost of accessing local telephone networks and the rate of taxation on phone calls. The access charges that long distance carriers pay to local carriers are set at an arbitrary level, since there isn't a free market in local access. Now, that arbitrary level will have to go down.

Gateway Providers and Billing

If you can use IP telephony, why would you ever get a phone bill again? The reason is that you will probably want to call people on their conventional telephones. Otherwise IP telephony is a pretty lonely pursuit. You can build this gateway yourself, if you have a telephony server with gateway hardware in it. But even in this case there are good reasons to pay for outside gateway services. Internet-to-PSTN gateways can be near the far end of your call, and hence less expensive to use than your own gateway to the PSTN. Using third-party gateways means you can optimize the extent to which you use IP telephony in reaching numbers on the PSTN.

Security, Privacy, and IP Telephony

When used in conjunction with IP telephony, public key cryptography (described in Chapter 9) can create an unbreakable seal that can be opened only at the destination of your call. Standards for using encryption with IP telephony are only now emerging, but you should be aware of some issues in cryptography to make an intelligent choice. Cryptography that isn't really secure is worse than not using it at all. Using breakable encryption is simply calling attention to the fact that your communications are sensitive or commercially valuable without actually protecting them.

- Use strong cryptography with key lengths of 128 bits or more. With key lengths into the hundreds, you can be quite sure your communications are secure. If you are communicating internationally, you may have to buy separate, but compatible implementations of the same cryptographic technique in the U.S. and overseas, or buy a system developed outside the U.S. because of export restrictions on cryptography.

- Use cryptographic software where the source code for the product is easily available and has been reviewed by independent cryptography experts. Secret implementations of encryption technology can include "exploitable features"—intentional holes that intelligence and law enforcement can use to access your communications.

- Do not use, and do not buy products with *key escrow* systems. This is a particularly insidious form of big brotherism. In key escrow systems, intelligence and law enforcement agencies can access your communications without your knowledge because a supposedly independent authority holds a key to the encrypted material.

The Future of Internet Telephony

Once IP telephony is established as a normal means of distributing telephone service within an organization, and once computers become friendlier devices for communicating, demand for novel applications of IP telephony will emerge. This will happen in the form of questioning the limitations of telephony:

- Why shouldn't phone calls sound better? The high-quality speech coders IP telephony inherited from ISDN could be put to use making every phone call sound as good as an FM radio broadcast.

- Why should caller ID be the end-all of caller identification? Q.931 signaling can deliver rich information about calls. For example, your phone could tell you if a call is a fax call that should be deflected to the fax line, whether a call was deflected from some other address because that line was busy, or whether a call was part of a conference call.

The way to advance IP telephony is to take progressively more creative advantage of the information provided about calls. The programmability and flexibility of the PC combined with the rich information about calls provides a fertile basis for making IP telephony really deliver on the potential that ISDN had.

Should You Be Paying Attention?

The era of IP telephony is only now beginning. With only a handful of pioneering suppliers able to field fully sorted out systems, adopting IP telephony now can be an adventure. For some, such as businesses trying to go global early in their development, IP telephony can make intercontinental communications affordable and secure. For these, and some other segments of the market, there is enough justification to make the leap now. But nearly every business should be paying attention to IP telephony. The benefits of IP telephony are expanding, especially in the area of e-commerce. IP telephony will soon enough become synonymous with business telephony in e-commerce-oriented businesses. Here are some reasons to pay attention to IP telephony now:

- IP telephony means managing one network, not two. As a business grows and its phone systems grow big enough to require expert management, IP telephony enables the business to build and manage one network. The tools for managing data networks are less expensive, require less specialized knowledge, and have developed faster than tools for managing switched circuit voice telephony systems.

■ IP telephony means all your servers can now host interactive voice applications. More generally, it means that services available in your Intranet can be made available over the phone. Database access, for example, can be provided to your mobile employees on their cell phones, so they do not always need to carry a laptop and dial in with a modem.

■ IP telephony means enhanced security when used with encryption. You should not leave your business open to illegal snooping, especially if you do business outside of industrialized countries where the police and national intelligence agencies are generally well run. IP telephony and strong encryption make it possible to enforce the security of your communications even without the cooperation of the authorities.

■ IP telephony means a choice of local phone carriers for everyone with cable TV. With high-speed Internet access you will have enough bandwidth to make multiple, simultaneous, reliable, high-quality IP telephony calls through a cable modem or other high-speed access system.

■ IP telephony is the future of e-commerce blended with call centers. If you sell things over the phone or on the Web, you will have to blend the way you sell on the Web with the way you sell on the phone. Customers should be able to go from interacting with your Web page to interacting with a customer service representative without having to reenter all the data about the purchase they are trying to make. IP telephony enables this blending.

Right now, the global Public Switched Telephone Network is much larger, by most measures, than the Internet. The PSTN has hundreds of billions of dollars in switches, wire, and other equipment and infrastructure more than the Internet. Add the massive wavefront of cellular telephony sweeping over the parts of the globe where most people have not yet heard a dial tone, and you will find that, in absolute terms, the growth of the PSTN is far from over. The Internet, however, will be bigger than television, radio, the PSTN, and a good deal of the retail sales channel for any product short of haircuts and surgery. The Internet is perhaps one percent of its potential size in the foreseeable future. This is the most fundamental reason why IP telephony is the future of telephony.

Chapter 40

Classic Applications

The Internet has been around for more than 25 years, long before Netscape and Internet Explorer—or even Windows or the World Wide Web—were invented. This chapter describes how to use the Internet the old-fashioned way, by logging into a UNIX host computer as though you were using a terminal, and typing UNIX commands. Typing commands may be old-fashioned, but it's very efficient once you learn the commands, and text-only information downloads quickly from the Internet. This chapter also describes some other classic text-based Internet systems:

- **telnet**   Lets you log in to other computers over the Internet
- **finger**   Displays information about Internet host computers and individual Internet users
- **Gopher**   The predecessor to the Web

UNIX Shell Accounts

In the old days (that is, the 1980s), the most common way to use the Internet was to connect to an Internet host computer by using a *terminal*, a keyboard and screen with little computing ability of its own. If you didn't have a terminal, you could run a *terminal emulator* on your PC—a program that made your intelligent PC as dumb as a terminal. Once connected to the Internet host, you had to type commands that that host understood. Because most Internet host computers run the UNIX operating system, an Internet account that works like this is called a *UNIX shell account* (or *shell account*).

Some Internet accounts (PPP accounts, that is—the kind that let your PC or Mac run Netscape, Internet Explorer, and Eudora) also come with shell accounts. You use the PPP account 99.9 percent of the time, but you can take advantage of the shell account for tasks such as the following:

- **Changing your password**   Without a shell account, the only way to change your account password is to call your Internet provider and ask.
- **Deleting stray e-mail messages**   On occasion, e-mail messages can get stuck in your POP mailbox (see Chapter 5 for a description of a POP mailbox). You can use a UNIX e-mail program such as Pine (described in Chapter 6) to read and delete these messages.
- **Organizing Web site files**   If you run a Web site, you may be able to use telnet to connect to the Web server to rename files, delete unneeded files, fix file permissions, and do other administrative tasks (see Chapter 31).

To use a shell account, you need to learn at least a bit of UNIX. This section describes some UNIX basics. For more information, read *UNIX For Dummies*, 4th Edition (by John Levine and Margaret Levine Young, published by IDG Books Worldwide) or *UNIX in a Nutshell* (published by O'Reilly Associates).

Running a Terminal Emulator

To dial into a UNIX shell account from a PC or Mac, you use a terminal emulator. Luckily, a good one comes with Windows 95, Windows 98, and Windows NT: HyperTerminal. If you use a Mac, you can use MacTerminal. Windows 3.1 comes with Terminal. Other terminal-emulation programs are available on the Web (see Chapter 38).

All terminal-emulation programs work in the same way. After you load the program, you tell it to dial the phone to connect to your UNIX shell account. The program dials the phone and makes the connection. At this point, what appears in the terminal emulator's window reflects information that comes from the shell account, and the characters that you type are passed along over the phone to your shell account. This chapter shows HyperTerminal, which comes with Windows 95 and 98, in the examples, but other terminal programs work similarly.

Configuring HyperTerminal for Your Shell Account

To run HyperTerminal, choose Start | Programs | Accessories | Communications | HyperTerminal. From the C:\Program Files\Accessories\HyperTerminal window that appears, run the Hypertrm.exe icon. (That is, click or double-click the icon, depending on how Windows is configured.) You see the Connection Description dialog box (Figure 40-1).

When you see the Connection Description dialog box, follow these steps:

1. Type the name that you want to use for the connection, choose an icon, and then click OK. You see the Connect To dialog box, asking for information about how to dial the phone to connect to the computer.

Figure 40-1.   *Creating a new HyperTerminal connection*

2. Set the Connect Using box to the modem to use for the connection, and then choose the country, type the area code, and type the phone number to dial.

3. Click OK. You see the Connect window, shown in Figure 40-2.

4. To connect, click Dial. (If you don't want to connect right now, click Cancel. HyperTerminal saves your connection information.) HyperTerminal dials the phone. When HyperTerminal has established a connection with the remote computer, you see the HyperTerminal window (Figure 40-3).

5. Log in and use your shell account by typing UNIX commands (see the following sections in this chapter). You can use the scroll bar along the right side of the HyperTerminal window to see the backscroll buffer, which stores the last 500 lines of text that have scrolled up off the top of the terminal window.

6. When you are done using the remote computer, log out (see the section "Logging Out," later in this chapter). HyperTerminal disconnects, too. If you have trouble getting disconnected, tell HyperTerminal to hang up by choosing Call | Disconnect from the menu bar (or by clicking the Disconnect icon on the toolbar).

7. When you exit from HyperTerminal, it asks whether you want to save the session (connection) that you just created. Click Yes. (If you never plan to connect to this shell account again, click No to throw away the connection information that you previously typed.) HyperTerminal creates an icon for the connection in the C:\Program Files\Accessories\HyperTerminal window.

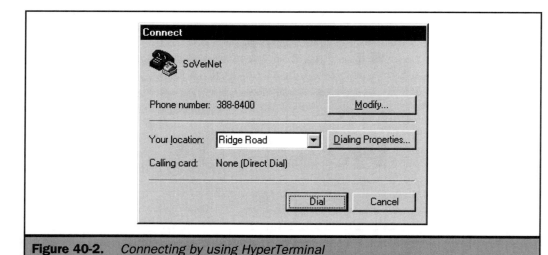

Figure 40-2. *Connecting by using HyperTerminal*

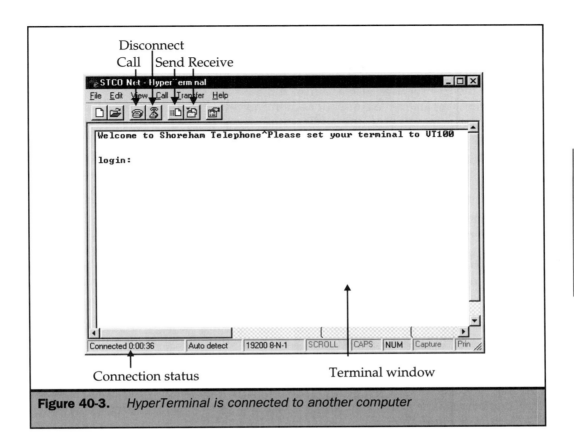

Figure 40-3. *HyperTerminal is connected to another computer*

Connecting with HyperTerminal

To connect to a computer for which you've already created a HyperTerminal connection, open the C:\Program Files\Accessories\HyperTerminal window. Then open the icon for the connection. HyperTerminal runs and displays the Connect window with information about the existing connection; click Dial to make the connection.

If you are already running HyperTerminal, to make a connection, choose File | Open (or click the Open icon on the toolbar) and choose the connection from the list. Then to connect, either click the Call icon on the toolbar or choose Call | Call.

When you are done using your shell account, log out (see the upcoming section, "Logging Out"); HyperTerminal should disconnect, too. If necessary, end the connection by choosing Call | Disconnect or by clicking the Disconnect icon on the toolbar.

For more information about HyperTerminal, see *Windows 98: The Complete Reference* (by John Levine and Margaret Levine Young, published by Osborne/McGraw-Hill).

Logging In, Typing Commands, and Logging Out

As with other Internet accounts, you must connect and log in before you get started. Unlike other Internet accounts, however, you type UNIX commands to run programs and to use Internet services such as e-mail and the Web. When you are done using your shell account, you log out to end your session and sever the connection.

Logging In

When you connect to your shell account, UNIX asks for your user name and password. Type each followed by pressing ENTER (or RETURN). UNIX is case-sensitive, so be sure to capitalize your user name and password correctly (user names are usually lowercase). If the system says that your password is no good, check that you spelled your user name correctly, too. Entering an incorrect user name or password three times in a row may cause the system to disconnect (to deter hackers).

Typing UNIX Commands

After you log in, you see a welcome message and the UNIX *shell prompt*, the symbol that means that UNIX is ready for you to type a command. The exact prompt varies from system to system, but it's frequently a dollar sign ($) or a percent sign (%). At the shell prompt, when you type a command and press ENTER, UNIX executes the command.

UNIX commands are single words, usually lowercase. They may be followed by additional information, which is separated from the command by a space. For example, you might type **ls -l** to run the **ls** command (which lists filenames, as explained later in this chapter) with the further specification that you want a detailed listing.

Here are some additional tips for typing UNIX commands:

- Capitalization matters to UNIX. Type commands as they appear here (or in whatever other UNIX book you refer to), usually all lowercase. If the instructions say to type *ls* and you type *LS*, you'll see an error message.

- If you make a mistake typing, press BACKSPACE, or try DELETE or CTRL+H. To cancel the entire command line before you press ENTER, press CTRL+U, or try CTRL+K. Misspelling a command usually results in a "command not found" error message.

- Don't type any extra spaces or punctuation. Separate commands from other information on the command line by a single space.

Logging Out

When you are done using the Internet, log out from your UNIX account. Type **exit** or **logout**, or press CTRL+D. The UNIX system logs you off and, if you are connected on a dial-up phone line, it hangs up the phone connection.

E-mail, the Web, and Usenet

To send and receive e-mail from your shell account, try typing **pine** to run the menu-based Pine e-mail program, which is described in Chapter 6. If Pine isn't installed on your system, type **elm** to run elm, which is described in *Unix For Dummies*. If neither program works, ask your system administrator which e-mail programs are available.

The most widely used Web browser for UNIX shell accounts is called *Lynx*: type **lynx** to run it. Lynx can't display pictures, play sounds, or show other glitzy special effects, but it works fine for text (see Chapter 21).

Many UNIX-based Usenet newsreaders exist. Try typing **trn**, **tin**, or **rn** to see what's installed on your system. See Chapter 14 for details on how to use UNIX-based newsreaders.

Other UNIX-based commands that you can type are **telnet** (to log in to another computer via the Internet, as described in "Logging in to Internet Hosts by Using Telnet," later in this chapter) and **finger** (as described in "Getting Information about People and Internet Hosts by Using Finger," also later in this chapter).

Working with Files on Your Shell Account

When you use a UNIX shell account, you can store files on the UNIX system in your *home directory*. UNIX systems have hierarchical (tree-structured) directories like Windows, DOS, and Mac systems. The directory name for your home directory is usually */usr/xxx* or */home/xxx* or *~/xxx*, where *xxx* is replaced by your user name. For example, if your user name were *elvis*, your home directory might be called */usr/elvis* or *~/elvis*.

One directory is the *current directory*, the directory where you are working. All commands refer to that directory unless you specify otherwise by including other information on the command line after the command. When you log in to your account, in the current directory is your home directory and you can give commands to move to other directories (as described in "Changing the Current Directory" later in this section).

> **Tip** *The UNIX commands for working with files and directories are a lot like DOS commands (this is no coincidence, since the first version of DOS was based partly on UNIX).*

Listing Your Files

To see a list of the files in the current directory, type **ls** and press ENTER. You see a listing like this one:

```
Mail            cheeselist      guruweb
Mailbox         fpc             internet101
Mailbox.lock    fpcweb          mail
News            greattapesweb   net101
```

The items—files and other directories that are contained in the current directory—are in alphabetical order down each column (UNIX feels that capital letters come before lowercase letters). To see more information about the items in the current directory, add the **-l** option to the ls command, like this:

```
ls -l
```

You get a more detailed listing like this one:

```
drwx------       2 margy  book       512 Feb  9  1998 Mail
-rw-------       1 margy  book    119487 Aug 31 21:35 Mailbox
-rw-rw-rw-  1 margy   book         0 Aug 20 14:55 Mailbox.lock
drwxr-xr-x  2 margy   book       512 Feb  9  1998 News
lrwxr-xr-x  1 margy   book        37 Aug 20 15:03 cheeselist ->
/usr/local/lib/smail/lists/cheeselist
-rw-r--r--       1 margy  book      1538 Jun  6 11:20 fpc
drwxrwxr-x 17 margy   guest     1024 Jul 13 12:53 fpcweb
drwxr-xr-x  5 margy   book      1536 Aug 12 15:32 greattapesweb
drwxrwxr-x 12 margy   book       512 Jul 15 23:02 guruweb
drwxrwxr-x  3 margy   book       512 Feb  9  1998 internet101
drwx------       2 margy  book       512 Feb  9  1998 mail
drwxr-xr-x  2 margy   book       512 Mar  3 14:28 net101
```

For each item, you see:

- **Permissions**   For example, *drwxrwxr-x*. If the first character is a *d*, the item is a directory; otherwise it is a file. The rest of the characters indicate who has permission to read, write, and execute the file. See the section "Displaying File Permissions" later in this chapter.

- **Owner**   For example, *margy*. Each file and directory has one individual owner, usually the person who created the file.

- **Group owner**   For example, *book*. Each file and directory is also owned by a group. See the section "Changing File Permissions" later in this chapter.

- **Size**   For example, 512. The file size is shown in bytes.

- **Date and time**   For example, *Mar 3 14:28*. The date and time this file was last modified.

- **File name**   For example, *net101*. File names are case-sensitive and cannot contain spaces.

Changing the Current Directory

To move to a directory (perhaps one you notice listed by the ls command), type **chdir** or **cd** followed by a space and the name of the directory to move to. For example, to move to the Mail directory, you'd type **cd Mail**. To move back to your home directory, type **chdir** or **cd** with no directory name. To find out the full name of the current directory, type **pwd** (which stands for *print working directory*).

Renaming, Copying, and Deleting Files

To rename a file in your home directory (or whatever the current directory is), type **mv** (short for *move*) followed by a space, the current file name, another space, and the new file name. For example, to rename *budget.new* as *budget.2000.jan*, you'd type **mv budget.new budget.1999.jan**.

If you want to make a copy of a file in a directory, use the cp (*copy*) command, specifying the name of the file you want to copy and the name to give the new file. For example, to copy *budget.2000.jan* as *budget.2000.feb*, you'd type **cp budget.2000.jan budget.2000.feb**.

If there is already a file with the name that you want to use for the copy, you may inadvertently delete the file by that name. Before copying, make sure that there is no file with the name you want to use for the copy.

To delete a file you never want to see again, use the rm (*remove*) command. Type **rm** followed by a space and the name of the file you want to delete. UNIX doesn't confirm the deletion; UNIX just does it, so watch out.

Once you delete a file, there is no way to get it back. Very few UNIX systems have recycle bins or other methods of retrieving deleted files.

To see what's in a file, you can use the **more** command. The **more** command works only for text files: if the file contains non-text information, you'll see garbage. To display a text file on the screen, type **more**, a space, and the file name. UNIX displays one screenful of information, then pauses. To see the next screenful, press SPACEBAR. To cancel the rest of the listing, press **q** (lowercase).

Displaying File Permissions

If you run a Web site (especially if you run it with other people), you may need to work with UNIX files permissions. *Permissions* are settings that control who can do what with each file or directory. Permissions come in three types:

- *Read permission* lets you look at the contents of a file or directory. Read permission for a file lets you use the UNIX more command to read text files. Read permission for a directory lets you list the contents of the directory using the **ls** command.

- *Write permission* lets you make changes to a file or directory. Although you can edit the file, you can't delete or rename it unless you also have write permission for the directory that contains the file. Write permission for a directory lets you create new files, delete files, and rename files in the directory.

- *Execute permission* lets you run the program contained in a file. If the file doesn't contain a program, execute permission is useless. Execute permission for directories lets you open files in the directory as well as letting you use the **cd** command to make the directory your current working directory.

Each file and directory belongs to a user and to a group. Each user belongs to one or more groups, too. To find out which groups you belong to, type the command **id**. You see something like this:

```
uid=112(margy) gid=10(users) groups=10(users), 20(staff), 30(LISTS)
```

The *uid* and *gid* are your user and group ID number and name, which you might need to tell your system administrator someday if you have a problem. Your user name is the same name you use to log in to your account. Your group is the one that the system administrator assigned you to when your account was created. Following that information is a list of the group names and numbers to which you belong. When you use the **ls -l** command for a detailed listing of files (shown in section "Listing Your Files" earlier in this chapter), you see the name of the user and the group that own each file, as well as the permissions.

The permissions shown by the **ls -l** command (the first item on each line of the listing) work like this:

- The first character is *d* if the item is a directory, and - (a dash) if it's a file.

- The next three characters show the read, write, and execute permissions for the user that owns the file. The first of the three characters is *r* if the owner has read permission and - otherwise, the second character is *w* if the owner has write permission and - otherwise, and the third character is *x* if the owner has execute permission and - otherwise.

- The next three characters show the read, write, and execute permissions for the people who belong to the group that owns the file.

- The last three characters show the read, write, and execute permissions for everyone else.

For example, the permissions *-rwxr-x--x* mean that the item is a file (not a directory), that the owner can read, write, and execute the file, that members of the group that owns the file can read and execute the file, but not write it, and that everyone else can only execute the file.

Changing File Permissions

If you own a file, you can change its permissions. For example, if you upload a Web page to your UNIX-based Web server and you want to let other members of your team edit the file, you may need to change the file's permissions.

To change a file's permissions, you use the **chmod** command, like this:

```
chmod permissions filename
```

Replace *filename* with the name of the file; replace *permissions* with code that specifies which permissions to change and what to change them to. Each code consists of three characters:

- u (user owner) , g (group), o (other, or everyone else), or a (all), to specify whose permissions to change
- + or - to add or remove a permission
- r (read), w (write), or x (execute) to specify which permission to change

For example, the command

```
chmod g+w index.html
```

gives members of the group that owns the file permission to write (edit) the file. If you own a file you can also change which group owns it. Type the command

```
chgrp groupname filename
```

Replace *groupname* with the name of the group that should own the file, and *filename* with the name of the file. (This command doesn't work on all versions of UNIX: if you get an error message, ask your system administrator or ISP to change the group.)

Hidden Files That Control Your Account

A number of *hidden files* (files that don't appear on a normal ls listing) control aspects of your UNIX account. Hidden files have file names that begin with a period (.). You can see them by typing **ls -a** or **ls -al**. The *a* says to list all files, including hidden files.

You may want to display or change the following hidden files:

- **.forward** tells your account to forward all mail to another account on the Internet. The file contains a single line, containing only one thing: the address to which to forward mail.

OTHER INTERNET TOPICS

- **.project** and **.plan** control what appears when others "finger" you at this account (see the section "Getting Information about People and Internet Hosts by Using Finger" later in this chapter.

- **.login**, **.profile**, **.cshrc** and other files control what happens when you first log in to your shell account. (Warning: don't change these without detailed knowledge of UNIX).

- **.mailrc**, **.pinerc**, and **.elm** control your e-mail settings, including those used by the Pine and Elm e-mail programs. These files are written by your e-mail programs, so don't edit them yourself.

To create or change one of these files, use a UNIX editor: Pico is the simplest to use. For example, to create a .forward file so that your mail will be forwarded automatically to another account, type **pico .forward**, type the address to which you want mail forwarded, press CTRL+O to save the file, and press CTRL+X to exit. (Pico displays a menu of commands at the bottom of the screen, by the way.)

If the UNIX system doesn't have Pico, you can tell UNIX to copy from your keyboard directly into the file. Type the following:

```
echo "address" > .forward
```

Replace *address* with the text that you want in the file (your forwarding address, if you are creating a .forward file). Replace ".forward" with a different file name if you want to create a different file. Be sure to type double quotes around the text. UNIX saves the text you typed in the file name you specified.

To check the contents of the file you just created, type **more .forward** and press ENTER, (replacing ".forward" with the name of the file you created). UNIX lists the contents of the file. If it doesn't look right, start over.

Transferring Files to and from Your UNIX Shell Account

While you are using the Internet from your shell account—reading e-mail, browsing the Web, or transferring files using FTP, you can save material in files in your home directory. But what if you want to get the files from your UNIX home directory to your own PC or Mac?

Several file transfer protocols exist for transferring files between UNIX systems and PCs or Macs, including Xmodem (regular or 1K), Kermit, Ymodem, Ymodem-G, and Zmodem. Most UNIX systems and terminal-emulation programs can send and receive files using many of these protocols. You must choose a protocol that both your terminal emulators can handle.

If you have a choice, use Zmodem to transfer files. Zmodem includes some error-checking and doesn't require you to give any command on the receiving computer.

OTHER INTERNET TOPICS

To transfer a file from your shell account to your PC or Mac, you give your terminal-emulation program a command to receive the file, and you type the UNIX command to send the file. Conversely, to transfer a file from your PC or Mac to your shell account, type the UNIX command to receive a file, then give your terminal emulator the command to send the file. Some file transfer protocols (like Zmodem) allow you to skip the step of telling the receiving computer to expect to receive a file.

Sending a File Using HyperTerminal

If you use HyperTerminal, follow these steps to send a file from your PC to your shell account:

1. Connect to your shell account. If applicable, move to the directory on the shell account in which you want to store the file.

2. Try sending the file using Zmodem, which HyperTerminal supports. Click the Send button on the toolbar or choose Transfer | Send File. You see the Send File dialog box, shown here:

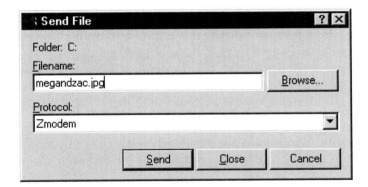

3. In the Filename box, type the name of the file you want to send, or click the Browse button to select the file.

4. Set the Protocol box to Zmodem.

5. Click the Send button. You see a window displaying the status of the file transfer (Figure 40-4). How much information the window displays depends on which file transfer protocol you use. You can click the Cancel button to stop the file transfer. Click the cps/bps button to control whether you see the transfer speed in characters per second (cps) or bits per second (bps). When the window disappears, file transfer is complete.

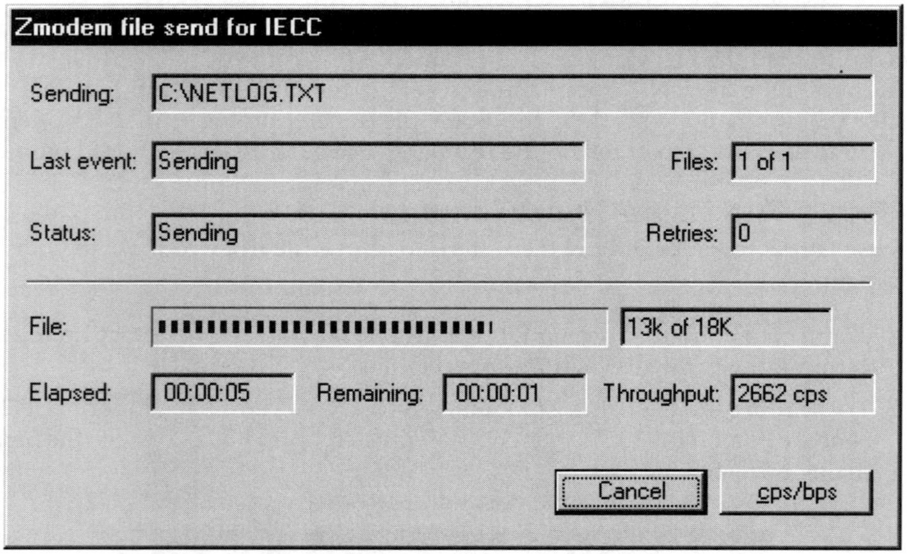

```
Zmodem file send for IECC

 Sending:   C:\NETLOG.TXT

 Last event:  Sending                      Files:  1 of 1

 Status:      Sending                      Retries:  0


 File:      ||||||||||||||||||||||||||||||||       13k of 18K

 Elapsed:   00:00:05    Remaining:  00:00:01    Throughput:  2662 cps


                              Cancel       cps/bps
```

Figure 40-4.   *HyperTerminal status while sending a file*

6. If the shell account can't receive files using Zmodem, try receiving via Xmodem. Type the command **rx** *filename* on the shell account, replacing *filename* with the name to give the file when it arrives in your shell account. Then repeat steps 2–5, choosing Xmodem as the protocol.

Receiving a File Using HyperTerminal

If you use HyperTerminal, follow these steps to transfer a file from your shell account to your PC:

1. Connect to your shell account. If applicable, move to the directory on your shell account in which the file is stored.

2. Try transferring the file using Zmodem: type the command **sz** *filename* on your shell account, replacing *filename* with the name of the file you want to transfer. If the sz command doesn't work, try Xmodem by typing **sx** *filename.*

3. If you are transferring using Zmodem, HyperTerminal detects that a file is arriving and begins receiving the file automatically (skip to step 8). Otherwise, click the Receive button on the HyperTerminal toolbar or choose Transfer | Receive File. You see the Receive File dialog box, shown next.

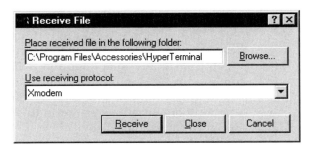

4. In the first box, type the path name of the folder in which you want to store the file, or click the Browse button to change the pathname.

5. Set the Use Receiving Protocol setting to the file transfer protocol you used in step 2, Xmodem.

6. Click the Receive button.

7. For some protocols, HyperTerminal may need additional information. For example, when using Xmodem, the sending computer doesn't include the filename with the file, so HyperTerminal asks you what to name the file it receives. Type the additional information, and then click OK.

8. HyperTerminal displays a window showing the progress of the file's transfer. You can click the Cancel button to stop the file transfer. Click the cps/bps button to control whether you see the transfer speed in characters per second (cps) or bits per second (bps). When the window disappears, the file transfer is complete.

Transferring Files Using FTP

Another way to transfer files between your PC or Mac and your UNIX shell account is by using FTP; see Part VI of this book.

Changing Your Password

You can change the password for your UNIX shell account any time you are connected. Type **passwd** and press ENTER. UNIX prompts you for your current password (to make sure that you are really authorized to change the password). Then UNIX asks you to type your new password twice. Because the password doesn't appear on-screen, typing it twice ensures that no typo occurred.

*Some versions of the **passwd** command require that your new password have at least seven characters, contain digits, or follow other rules.*

Logging in to Internet Hosts by Using Telnet

Telnet is an Internet service that allows you to log in to other computers over the Internet. In the early days of the Internet, many computers allowed anyone to "telnet in," log on, and use selected commands on the computer to find out public information. For example, libraries would allow the public to search the card files using commands via telnet. Now most organizations that want to offer public access do so via a Web site, and few offer public access via telnet.

However, telnet remains a useful Internet service. For example, if you maintain a Web site, a convenient way to clean up the files on the site is to telnet in to the Web server and use UNIX commands (described in the section "Working with Files on Your Shell Account" earlier in this chapter). Many people use telnet when they are out of town and need to check their e-mail: using any computer on the Internet, they can telnet in to their ISP's server and use a UNIX-based e-mail program to read their messages (see Chapter 6 for how to use Pine, a popular UNIX e-mail program).

To log in to a host computer using telnet, you first connect to the Internet using your regular account. Then you run a telnet program and tell it to connect to the host computer. The dialog with the host computer appears in the telnet window, and you log in to the host computer. When you are done, you disconnect from the host computer, usually by logging off. Then you exit from the telnet program, and (if you want) disconnect from the Internet.

Some host computers offer public access. When you telnet to a publicly accessible host, you see a message telling you how to log in, usually by typing a user name like *guest*. Most host computers allow only people with accounts to telnet in. Most ISPs and Web hosting services let their Internet account-holders connect using telnet. If you have an account, you type your user name and a password when the host computer prompts for them.

Windows 95 and 98 come with a telnet program, and HyperTerminal (described earlier in this chapter) also allows you to connect via telnet rather than dial-up. Other telnet programs are available over the Web (see Chapter 38), including telnet programs for Windows 3.1 and the Macintosh.

Telnetting by Using the Windows 98/95 Telnet Program

The telnet program that comes with Windows 98 and 95 is called Telnet.

Running the Windows 98/95 Telnet Program

To run the built-in Telnet program that comes with Windows 98 and 95:

1. Choose Start | Run, type **telnet**, and then click OK. You see the Telnet window, shown in Figure 40-5.

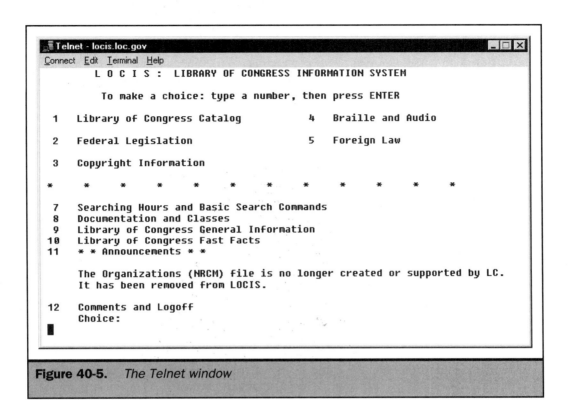

Figure 40-5.   *The Telnet window*

2. To connect to a host computer over the Internet, choose Connect | Remote System. You see the Connect dialog box, shown here:

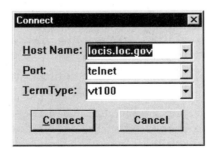

If you want to connect to a computer that you've connected to before, the host name may appear on the File menu; if so, choose the host name from the File menu and skip to step 7.

3. In the Host Name box, type the host name (host address) of the computer to which you want to connect. For example, the host name of the U.S. Library of Congress is **locis.loc.gov**. If you've connected to this host computer before, you can click the button at the right end of the Host Name box and choose the name from the drop-down list that appears.

4. Leave the Port box set to telnet. The other options connect to the host computer to use different Internet services, something that's useful only for network debugging.

5. Set the TermType box to the string of characters to send to the remote computer, if it asks what type of terminal you are using. Note that this setting does not control the type of terminal that Telnet emulates.

6. Click Connect. If your computer is not connected to the Internet, you see the Dial-Up Networking window, prompting you to connect; click the Connect button. Once you are online, Telnet connects to the host computer. The Telnet window contains the terminal window, showing the text that you receive from the host computer, and your replies (Figure 40-5).

7. Log in and use the host computer, typing the commands that the host computer requires. You can use the scroll bar at the right side of the window to see lines of text that have scrolled up off the top edge of the window.

8. When you are done using the host computer, log out by using the commands that it requires. Telnet disconnects, too. If you have trouble disconnecting, choose Connect | Disconnect to tell Telnet to hang up.

Configuring the Windows 98/95 Telnet Program

You can configure the Telnet window by choosing Terminal | Preferences. You see the Terminal Preferences dialog box, shown in Figure 40-6. You can control the following settings:

- **Local Echo**   This controls whether the Telnet program displays what you type, or whether it waits and displays the text that the host computer echoes back. This is turned off by default.

- **Appearance**   You can choose a blinking or block-style cursor, choose the font, and set the background color of the Telnet window.

- **Emulation**   You can control which terminal Telnet emulates (acts like). Telnet can emulate only two terminals: the DEC VT-100 and the DEC VT-52. (If the remote computer you want to use requires emulation of a different terminal, consider using the HyperTerminal program rather than Telnet.) If you choose to emulate a VT-100, you may also want to choose the VT100 Arrows options, so that the cursor motion keys send the same character sequences as would the same keys on a VT-100 terminal.

- **Buffer Size**   The Telnet program stores lines of text that have scrolled up off the top of the terminal window; you can choose how many lines are stored.

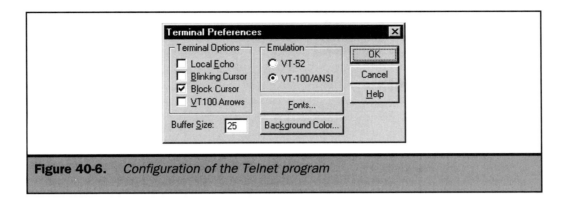

Figure 40-6. *Configuration of the Telnet program*

Other Windows 98/95 Telnet Commands

Here are other things that you can do with the Telnet program that comes with Windows 98/95:

■ The Telnet program doesn't handle file transfer (if you can telnet somewhere, you may be able to use FTP; see Chapter 36), but you can cut and paste by using the Windows Clipboard. In addition to Edit | Copy (for copying selected text to the Clipboard) and Edit | Paste (for sending the Clipboard contents to the remote computer as if you had typed it), you can also use Edit | Select All to select the entire contents of the terminal window, and Edit | Copy All to copy the entire contents of the window to the Clipboard.

■ You can capture the text that appears in the Telnet window by choosing Terminal | Start Logging. Telnet asks you for the folder and name of the log file in which to store the text. If the log file already exists, Telnet deletes its previous contents and replaces it with the log of this terminal session. To stop storing the terminal text, choose Terminal | Stop Logging.

 CTRL+C and CTRL+V don't work for cut and paste in Telnet. Choose Edit | Copy and Edit | Paste from the menu bar instead.

Telnetting with HyperTerminal

If you have Windows 98 or 95, you can use HyperTerminal for telnetting, too. You tell HyperTerminal to connect using TCP/IP (Winsock), along with the port number and host address of the computer to which you want to connect. The standard *port number* (a number that tells an Internet host computer whether you are connecting for e-mail, the Web, telnet, or another Internet service) is 23. The host address is the Internet host name of the computer you want to telnet in to; for example, the host address of the U.S. Library of Congress is **locis.loc.gov**.

To tell HyperTerminal to connect via telnet rather than dialing in, set the Connect Using box on the Connection Description dialog box to TCP/IP (Winsock), and then fill in the host address and port number.

Telnetting from UNIX

If you use a UNIX shell account, just type

```
telnet hostname
```

Replace *hostname* with the name of computer you want to log in to. Telnet connects you to the host system. In the process, it displays the *escape character*, the key combination that you press if you have trouble disconnecting from the host computer. Make a note of this character (it's frequently CTRL+ESC) in case you need it later.

Once you are connected to the host computer, the telnet program displays the text from the host computer on your screen and sends your keystrokes to the host computer. The host computer may ask when kind of terminal you are using (common terminal types include VT100, ANSI, and 3101). Accept the default if you are not sure. If you choose the wrong terminal type, the text on your screen may appear scrambled.

When you are done using the host computer, log out (usually by typing **logout** or **exit** or **bye**). The telnet program exits when the connection is broken. If the host computer doesn't want to let you log off (through confusion, not malevolence), type the escape character you noted when you connected. You should see this prompt:

```
telnet>
```

If this prompt doesn't appear within a few seconds, press ENTER. When you do see the prompt, type **quit** and press ENTER. The telnet program ends the connection and quits.

Getting Information About People and Internet Hosts by Using Finger

Finger was one of the early Internet services that allowed you to find out about computers or people on the Internet. If you "finger" the host name of the computer, you get information about that computer. If you finger an e-mail address, you see information about that person.

What Finger Reports

For example, if you finger the host computer iecc.com you might see the following:

```
[iecc.com]
Login     Name          Tty   Idle   Login Time    Office     Office Phone
margy     Margy L Y     co    7d     Aug 27 11:02  Tburg      1 802 555 1212
dave        David K     p0    3d     Aug 27 11:02  Tburg      1 802 555 1212
doug      Doug M        p1    3d     Aug 27 11:02  Tburg      1 802 555 1212
alison    Alison B      p2    3d     Aug 27 11:03  Tburg      1 802 555 1212
kathy     Kathy W       p2    3d     Aug 27 11:03  Tburg      1 802 555 1212
```

This listing includes general information about the computer or a list of the people who are using that computer right now, or both. The exact format of the information varies widely, depending on how the finger server program on that computer has been programmed to respond.

Fingering a user by his or her e-mail address might display:

```
[greattapes.com]
Login: margy                          Name: Margy Levine Young
Directory: /usr/home/margy            Shell: /bin/bash
Last login Mon Aug 31 21:46 (EDT) on ttyp7 from max1-15.shoreham.net
Project: Writing books, playing with kids, you name it!
Plan:
Set up the Great Tapes for Kids Web site at http://www.greattapes.com.
Write more computer books, like "Internet: The Complete Reference,"
Millennium Edition
```

Fingering from Windows or Macs

To get finger information, you need a finger program. If you use Eudora, the e-mail program described in Chapter 6, you can use its built-in finger program by choosing Tools | Directory Services (we've had mixed success, but it's worth a try). You can download finger programs for Windows and Macs from the Web; see Chapter 38.

Fingering from UNIX

If you use a UNIX shell account, or if you have telnetting into a UNIX host, run finger by typing the line shown next.

```
finger @hostname
```

or

```
finger username@hostname
```

Controlling What Finger Says About You

It's a good idea to finger your own e-mail address to find out what finger reports about you. If you don't like the "Plan" and "Project" parts of finger's report, you may be able to telnet in to your account and edit the .plan and .project files in your home directory (see the section "Hidden Files That Control Your Account" earlier in this chapter).

The Web's Predecessor: Gopher

Before there was the World Wide Web, there was Gopher. *Gopher* was (and still is) an Internet-based distributed system of information, like the Web. Unlike the Web, Gopher displays its information in the form of menus—lots and lots of menus. You choose items from menus until you find a file with information you want to see. Then Gopher displays the file, which may contain text or a few other formats.

When Gopher was first introduced, it was an exciting service for the Internet, because it made finding online information as easy as choosing items from menus. As *Gopherspace* (the collection of all Gopher menus) grew, finding information became harder, and a system called *Veronica* was developed to search Gopherspace for specific words or phrases.

Gopher has been almost entirely superceded by the Web, because Web pages can contain lots more information than menus can. However, some Gopher servers (programs than store and supply Gopher information on request) still exist.

To see Gopher menus, you can probably use your Web browser. Netscape and Internet Explorer both support Gopher, by using URLs that start with *gopher://* instead of *http://*. Figure 40-7 shows a Gopher menu as displayed by Netscape: the Gopher menu's URL appears in the Location box.

The icon to the left of each item on the menu tells you what kind of item it is. You see a folder icon for a directory, a piece-of-paper icon for a text file, a drawing icon for a graphics file, a computer icon for a computer into which you can telnet, and other icons for other types of files. If you click a directory item, you see that menu. If you click a text file item, you see the contents of that text file.

If you use a UNIX shell account, type **gopher** to see Gopher menus.

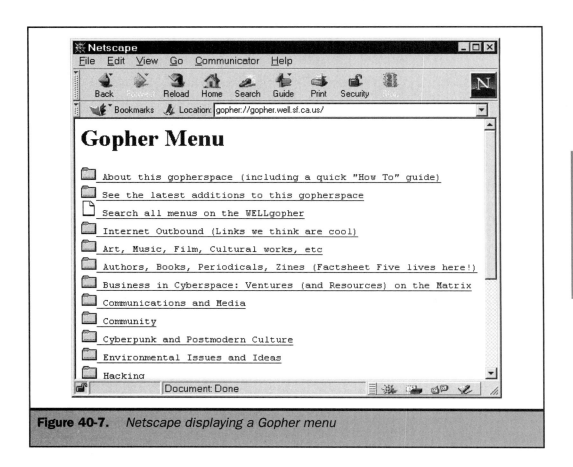

Figure 40-7.   *Netscape displaying a Gopher menu*

OTHER INTERNET TOPICS

To find Gopher menus, start at the University of Minnesota, where Gopher was developed, at **gopher://gopher.tc.umn.edu/**.

Index